ps 9-10

9/24 Chapter 4 read

10/20 pg 4

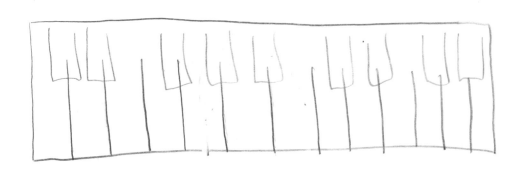

FCGDAEB
BEADGCF

Tonal Harmony

WITH AN INTRODUCTION TO TWENTIETH-CENTURY MUSIC

Seventh Edition

Tonal Harmony

WITH AN INTRODUCTION TO TWENTIETH-CENTURY MUSIC

Stefan Kostka
THE UNIVERSITY OF TEXAS AT AUSTIN

Dorothy Payne
THE UNIVERSITY OF SOUTH CAROLINA

Byron Almén
THE UNIVERSITY OF TEXAS AT AUSTIN

McGraw Hill

Connect
Learn
Succeed™

TONAL HARMONY WITH AN INTRODUCTION TO TWENTIETH-CENTURY MUSIC, SEVENTH EDITION

Published by McGraw-Hill, an imprint of The McGraw-Hill Companies, Inc., 1221 Avenue of the Americas, New York, NY 10020. Copyright © 2013, 2009, 2004. All rights reserved. Printed in the United States of America. No part of this publication may be reproduced or distributed in any form or by any means, or stored in a database or retrieval system, without the prior written consent of The McGraw-Hill Companies, Inc., including, but not limited to, in any network or other electronic storage or transmission, or broadcast for distance learning.

♻ This book is printed on recycled, acid-free paper containing 10% postconsumer waste.

3 4 5 6 7 8 9 0 QVS/QVS 1 0 9 8 7 6 5 4

ISBN: 978-0-07-802514-3
MHID: 0-07-802514-1

Vice President, General Manager: *Michael Ryan*
Managing Director: *William Glass*
Director: *Chris Freitag*
Director of Development: *Dawn Groundwater*
Content Developmental Editor: *Nadia Bidwell*
Content Project Manager: *Robin Reed*
Editorial Coordinator: *Jessica Holmes*
Copyeditor: *Barbara Hacha*
Interior Designer: *Margarite Reynolds*
Cover Designer: *Irene Morris Design*
Buyer: *Laura Fuller*
Media Project Manager: *Jennifer Barrick*
Composition: *10/12 Times Roman by Thompson Type*
Printing: *PMS 145, 45# New Era Matte, Quad/Graphics—Versailles*
Cover Image: © *Ocean photography/Veer*

Library of Congress Cataloging-in-Publication Data
Kostka, Stefan M.
   Tonal harmony : with an introduction to twentieth-century music / Stefan Kostka, Dorothy Payne, Byron Almén. — 7th ed.
      p. cm.
   Includes index.
   ISBN 978-0-07-802514-3 (hard copy : alk. paper) — ISBN 0-07-802514-1 (hard copy : alk. paper)
1. Harmony.   I. Payne, Dorothy.)   II. Almén, Byron, 1968–)   III. Title.
   MT50.K85 2013
   781.2'5—dc23
                                                                2012007911

The Internet addresses listed in the text were accurate at the time of publication. The inclusion of a website does not indicate an endorsement by the authors or McGraw-Hill, and McGraw-Hill does not guarantee the accuracy of the information presented at these sites.

www.mhhe.com

About the Authors

STEFAN KOSTKA

Holds degrees in music from the University of Colorado and the University of Texas and received his Ph.D. in music theory from the University of Wisconsin. He was a member of the faculty of the Eastman School of Music from 1969 to 1973. Since that time he has been on the faculty of the University of Texas at Austin. Dr. Kostka initiated courses in computer applications in music at both the Eastman School and the University of Texas. More recently he specialized in courses in atonal theory and contemporary styles and techniques, interests that led to a second book, *Materials and Techniques of Twentieth-Century Music.* Dr. Kostka is active in various professional organizations and is a past president of the Texas Society for Music Theory.

DOROTHY PAYNE

Held both bachelor's and master's degrees in piano performance and a Ph.D. in music theory, all from the Eastman School of Music. She was on the faculty of the University of South Carolina from 1994 until 1998. Former administrative positions include those of Dean at South Carolina, Director of the School of Music at the University of Arizona, and Music Department Head at the University of Connecticut. Prior faculty appointments were held at the University of Texas at Austin, the Eastman School of Music, and Pacific Lutheran University. Dorothy presented lectures and workshops on theory pedagogy at meetings of professional societies and served the National Association of Schools of Music as a visiting evaluator, member of the Accreditation Commission, and Secretary of the Executive Committee. Dorothy Payne passed away in 2010.

BYRON ALMÉN

Holds a bachelor's degree in music and physics from St. Olaf College, a master's degree in piano performance from Indiana University, and a Ph.D. in music theory from Indiana University. He has been a member of the faculty of the University of Texas at Austin since 1998. He is the author of *A Theory of Musical Narrative* and the coauthor, with Edward Pearsall, of *Approaches to Meaning in Music,* both published by Indiana University Press, along with various articles published in *Journal of Music Theory, Journal of Music Theory Pedagogy, Theory and Practice, Theoria,* and *Indiana Theory Review.* In addition to his continued performing activities as a pianist and organist, he is active in professional organizations in music and in semiotics. Dr. Almén teaches courses in the undergraduate harmony sequence, as well as courses in music theory pedagogy, the history of music theory, and score reading.

Preface

Tonal Harmony with an Introduction to Twentieth-Century Music is intended for a two-year course in music theory/harmony. It offers a clear and thorough introduction to the resources and practice of Western music from the seventeenth century to the present day. Its concise, one-volume format and flexible approach make the book usable in a broad range of theory curricula.

Approach

The text provides students with a comprehensive but accessible and highly practical set of tools for the understanding of music. Actual musical practice is emphasized more than rules or prohibitions. Principles are explained and illustrated, and exceptions are noted.

In its presentation of harmonic procedures, the text introduces students to the most common vocal and instrumental textures encountered in tonal music. Traditional four-part chorale settings are used to introduce many concepts, but three-part instrumental and vocal textures are also presented in illustrations and drill work, along with a variety of keyboard styles. To encourage the correlation of writing and performing skills, we have included musical examples in score and reduced-score formats as well as appendices on instrumental ranges and transpositions and lead-sheet symbols. Some of the assignments ask the student to write for small ensembles suitable for performance in class. Instructors may modify these assignments to make them most appropriate for their particular situations.

Pedagogical Features

The text employs a variety of techniques to clarify underlying voice leading, harmonic structure, and formal procedures. These include textural reductions, accompanying many of the examples, which highlight underlying voice leading. Our goal has been to elucidate tonal logic at the phrase and section level as well as from one chord to the next. Abundant musical illustrations, many with commentaries, serve as a springboard for class discussion and individual understanding.

The book provides an extensive series of review material. A large portion of the text is devoted to Self-Tests, consisting of student-graded drills in chord spelling, part writing, and analysis, with suggested answers given in Appendix D. The Self-Tests can be used for in-class drill and discussion, in preparation for the Workbook exercises, or for independent study. Periodic Checkpoints enable students to gauge their understanding of the preceding material. Chapter summaries highlight the key points of each chapter. A glossary of the bolded terms found throughout the text has been added to this edition.

Organization

Part One (Chapters 1–4) begins the text with a thorough but concise overview of the fundamentals of music, divided into one chapter each on pitch and rhythm. These chapters may be assigned in reverse order, if desired, except for the review questions in Chapter 2. Chapters 3 and 4 introduce the student to triads and seventh chords in various inversions and textures and places them in their tonal contexts.

Part Two (Chapters 5–12) opens with two chapters on the principles of voice leading, with practice limited to root position triads. Chapter 7 follows with a systematic discussion of normative harmonic progressions. Subsequent chapters deal with triads in inversion (Chapters 8 and 9), basic elements of musical form (Chapter 10), and nonchord tones (Chapters 11 and 12).

Part Three (Chapters 13–15) is devoted entirely to diatonic seventh chords, moving from the dominant seventh in root position and inversion (Chapter 13) through the supertonic and leading-tone sevenths (Chapter 14) to the remaining diatonic seventh chords (Chapter 15).

Part Four begins the study of chromaticism with secondary functions (Chapters 16–17) and modulation (Chapters 18–19), concluding in Chapter 20 with a discussion of larger musical forms. Chromaticism continues to be the main topic in Part Five (Chapters 21–25), which covers mode mixture, the Neapolitan, augmented sixth chords, enharmonicism, and other elements. The final chapter of this section concentrates upon harmony in the late nineteenth century.

Part Six (Chapters 26–28) provides a substantial introduction to twentieth-century music, beginning, in Chapter 26, with a survey of scales, chord structures, voice leading, and aspects of rhythm. Chapter 27 discusses the basics of atonal theory, including pitch-class sets, twelve-tone serialism, and total serialism. More recent developments, such as indeterminacy, minimalism, and electronic and computer music, are discussed in the final chapter.

Supplementary Materials

The following ancillary items can be used with the seventh edition of *Tonal Harmony*. Please consult your local McGraw-Hill representative for policies, prices, packaging options, and availability.

WORKBOOK

Each set of exercises in the Workbook (ISBN: 0-07-741017-3) is closely correlated with the corresponding chapter of the text and with a particular Self-Test within the chapter. Each set of Workbook exercises begins with problems similar to those found in the corresponding Self-Test, but the Workbook exercises also include problems that are too open-ended for the Self-Test format, as well as more creative types of compositional problems for those instructors who like to include this type of work.

RECORDINGS

The seventh edition is accompanied by recordings of virtually all the examples from music literature found in the text and the Workbook. A set of compact discs is available for the text (ISBN: 0-07-802514-2). The recordings that accompany the Workbook are now available as MP3 downloads from the Online Learning Center (www.mhhe.com/kostka7e),

DISC 1 : TRACK 5

17–2_A6.mp3

offering over 450 selections in all. All examples were recorded using the same instrumentations seen in the text and Workbook examples.

A listening icon, as shown left above, indicates that a piece from the text is contained on the CDs. Pieces in the Workbook that have accompanying MP3 recordings will be identified by their file name and a listening icon, as shown at left below.

INSTRUCTOR'S MANUAL

The Instructor's Manual (ISBN: 0-07-741015-7) follows the organization of the text and provides teaching notes, a key to "objective" exercises from the Workbook, sources from the literature for part-writing exercises and composition assignments, and chapter quizzes.

New to This Edition

All the chapters have undergone some revision, and the text and workbook contain 25 new examples from literature.

The most changed chapters are Chapters 21, 22, and 25. In Chapter 21 we have combined and shortened the material that in the sixth edition constituted Chapter 21 (Mode Mixture) and Chapter 22 (The Neapolitan Chord), omitting some of the more obscure Neapolitan examples. Chapters 23 and 24, which in the sixth edition discussed augmented sixth chords, have been shortened and combined to become Chapter 22 in the present edition, with less attention being given to nonstandard augmented sixth chords.

Chapter 25, "Tonal Harmony in the Late Nineteenth Century," which was previously the subject of Chapter 27, has been rewritten and reorganized. It now includes additional material on nineteenth-century uses of mediant relationships, progressions that move beyond traditional syntax but retain traditional chord types and smooth voice-leading motions, and an approach to late-Romantic music that seeks a balance between its destabilizing and systematic features.

The terminology in the discussion of serialism in Chapter 27 has been altered somewhat, adopting the "fixed zero" approach more in keeping with current practice.

An important addition to the text is the new Glossary, which contains several hundred key terms. Finally, four optional counterpoint units have been coordinated with the text. Students are directed to these units at appropriate points in the textbook, and they can access and download the counterpoint materials from the McGraw-Hill website.

Acknowledgments

Many colleagues and friends provided assistance and encouragement during the development of the first edition of this text, notably Professors Douglass Green, Jerry Grigadean, and Janet McGaughey. Reviewers of the manuscript contributed many helpful suggestions; our sincere thanks are extended to Judith Allen, University of Virginia; Michael Arenson, University of Delaware; B. Glenn Chandler, Central Connecticut State College; Herbert Colvin, Baylor University; Charles Fligel, Southern Illinois University; Roger Foltz, University of Nebraska, Omaha; Albert G. Huetteman, University of Massachusetts; William Hussey, University of Texas at Austin; Hanley Jackson, Kansas State University; Marvin Johnson, University of Alabama; Frank Lorince, West Virginia University;

William L. Maxson, Eastern Washington University; Leonard Ott, University of Missouri; John Pozdro, University of Kansas; Jeffrey L. Prater, Iowa State University; Russell Riepe, Southwest Texas State University; Wayne Scott, University of Colorado; Richard Soule, University of Nevada; James Stewart, Ohio University; William Toutant, California State University at Northridge; and John D. White, University of Florida.

We are also grateful to those who contributed to the development of the second edition: Richard Bass, University of Connecticut; James Bermighof, Baylor University; Richard Devore, Kent State University; Lora Gingerich, Ohio State University; Kent Kerman, University of Texas at Austin; James W. Krehbiel, Eastern Illinois University; Frank Lorince, West Virginia University (retired); Donald Para, Western Michigan University; Marian Petersen, University of Missouri at Kansas City; Donald Peterson, University of Tennessee; and John Pozdro, University of Kansas.

Contributors to the third edition included Shirley Bean, University of Missouri, Kansas City; Brian Berlin, University of Texas at Austin; Horace Boyer, University of Massachusetts; Polly Brecht, Middle Tennessee State University; John Buccheri, Northwestern University; Arthur Campbell, St. Olaf College; Lisa Derry, Western Michigan University; David Foley, Ball State University; Douglass Green, University of Texas at Austin; Andrew Grobengieser, University of Texas at Austin; Thom Hutcheson, Middle Tennessee State University; Robert Judd, California State University, Fresno; William Pelto, Ithaca College; H. Lee Riggins, Bowling Green State University; Lynne Rogers, University of Texas at Austin; and Judith Solomon, Texas Christian University.

Contributors to the fourth edition include Ron Albrecht, Simpson College; John Benoit, Simpson College; Claire Boge, Miami University; Lisa Derry, Albertson College of Idaho; Allen Feinstein, Northeastern University; Karl Korte, University of Texas at Austin; Jennifer Ottervick, University of South Carolina; Paul Paccione, Western Illinois University; William Pelto, Ithaca College; Timothy Smith, Northern Arizona University; William Schirmer, Jacksonville University; Bob Fleisher, Northern Illinois University; and Judith A. Solomon, Texas Christian University.

A number of graduate students also provided assistance in the preparation of the fifth edition, including Sarah Reichardt, Rob Deemer, and Danny Brod, all students at the University of Texas at Austin.

Special thanks are due to Reginald Bain, University of South Carolina, who served as editorial consultant for Chapter 28 and who created Appendices B and C.

Contributors to the sixth edition include Bob Fleischer, Northern Illinois University; and Marc Woodridge, Northwestern College.

Contributors to the seventh edition include Bruce Atwell, University of Wisconsin, Oshkosh; Ruth Rendleman, Montclair State University; Tobias Rush, University of Northern Colorado; Paul Seitz, University of Missouri; and Amy Williams, University of Pittsburgh. We are particularly grateful to Scott Schumann, University of Texas at Austin, for preparing the glossary.

Finally, we would express gratitude to Mary Robertson and Sarah Almén for their love and inspiration and to our colleagues and students for their continued encouragement.

Stefan Kostka

Dorothy Payne

Byron Almén

To the Student

Harmony in Western Music

One thing that distinguishes Western art music from many other kinds of music is its emphasis on harmony. In other words, just about any piece that you perform will involve more than one person playing or singing different notes at the same time or, in the case of a keyboard player, more than one finger pushing down keys. There are exceptions, of course, such as works for unaccompanied flute, violin, and so on, but even in such pieces an implied harmonic background is often still apparent to the ear.

In general, the music from cultures other than our own European-American one is concerned less with harmony than with other aspects of music. Complexities of rhythm or subtleties of melodic variation, for example, might serve as the focal point in a particular musical culture. Even in our own music, some compositions, such as those for nonpitched percussion instruments, may be said to have little or no harmonic content, but they are the exception.

If harmony is so important in our music, it might be a good idea if we agreed on a definition of it. What does the expression *sing in harmony* mean to you? It probably evokes impressions of something like a barbershop quartet, or a chorus, or maybe just two people singing a song—one singing the melody, the other one singing an accompanying line. Because harmony began historically with vocal music, this is a reasonable way to begin formulating a definition of harmony. In all of the examples above, our conception of harmony involves more than one person singing at once, and the *harmony* is the sound that the combined voices produce.

> **Harmony** is the sound that results when two or more pitches are performed simultaneously. It is the vertical aspect of music, produced by the combination of the components of the horizontal aspect.

Although this book deals with harmony and with chords, which are little samples taken out of the harmony, you should remember that musical lines (vocal or instrumental) produce the harmony, not the reverse.

Sing through the four parts in Example 1. The soprano and tenor lines are the most melodic. The actual melody being harmonized is in the soprano, whereas the tenor follows its contour for a while and then ends with an eighth-note figure of its own. The bass line is strong and independent but less melodic, whereas the alto part is probably the least distinctive of all. These four relatively independent lines combine to create harmony, with chords occurring at the rate of approximately one per beat.

Example 1   Bach, "Herzlich lieb hab' ich dich, o Herr"

soprano
alto

tenor
bass

The relationship between the vertical and horizontal aspects of music is a subtle one, however, and it has fluctuated ever since the beginnings of harmony (about the ninth century). At times the emphasis has been almost entirely on independent horizontal lines, with little attention paid to the resulting chords—a tendency easily seen in some twentieth-century music. At other times the independence of the lines has been weakened or is absent entirely. In Example 2, the only independent lines are the sustained bass note and the melody (highest notes). The other lines merely double the melody at various intervals, creating a very nontraditional succession of chords.

Example 2   Debussy, "La Cathédrale engloutie,"
from Preludes, Book I

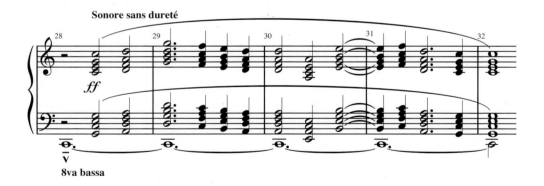

Tonal Harmony Defined

The kind of harmony that this book deals with primarily is usually called **tonal harmony.** The term refers to the harmonic style of music composed during the period from about 1650 to about 1900. This would include such composers as Purcell, Bach, Handel, Haydn, Mozart, Beethoven, Schubert, Schumann, Wagner, Brahms, Tchaikovsky, and all their contemporaries.

Much of today's popular music is based on tonal harmony, just as Bach's music was, which means that both types have a good deal in common. First, both make use of a **tonal**

center, a pitch class* that provides a center of gravity. Second, both types of music make use almost exclusively of major and minor scales. Third, both use chords that are tertian in structure. **Tertian** means "built of thirds," so a tertian chord might be C–E–G, a nontertian one C–F–B. Fourth, and very important, is that the chords built on the various scale degrees relate to one another and to the tonal center in fairly complex ways. Because each chord tends to have more or less standard roles, or functions, within a key, this characteristic is sometimes referred to as **functional harmony.** The details of these relationships between chords will be discussed more fully in the text; but to get an idea of what harmonic function is all about, play the chord of Example 3 on the piano.[†]

Example 3

Play it several times. Arpeggiate it up and down. The "function" of this chord is clear, isn't it? Somehow, you know a lot about this chord without having to read a book about it. Play it again, and listen to where the chord "wants" to go. Then play Example 4, which will seem to follow Example 3 perfectly. This is an example of what is meant by the relationships between chords in tonal harmony and why we sometimes use the term functional harmony.

Example 4

Tonal harmony is not limited to the period 1650–1900. It began evolving long before 1650, and it is still around today. Turn on your radio, go to a club, listen to the canned music in the supermarket—it's almost all tonal harmony. Then why do we put the demise of tonal harmony at 1900? Because from about that time, most composers of "serious," or "legitimate," or "concert" music have been more interested in nontonal harmony than in tonal harmony. This does not mean that tonal harmony ceased to exist in the real world or in music of artistic merit. Also, it is important to realize that not all music with a tonal center makes use of functional harmony—especially a good deal of the music composed since 1900—music by composers such as Bartók and Hindemith, for example.

---

* Pitch class: Notes an octave apart or enharmonically equivalent belong to the same pitch class (all C's, B♯'s and D♭♭'s, for example). There are twelve pitch classes in all.

† If you cannot arrange to be at a piano while reading this book, try to play through the examples just before or right after reading a particular section or chapter. Reading about music without hearing it is not only dull, it's uninformative.

From our discussion we can formulate this definition of tonal harmony:

Tonal harmony *refers to music with a tonal center, based on major and/or minor scales, and using tertian chords that are related to one another and to the tonal center in various ways.*

Using This Text

The information in this text is organized in the traditional chapter format, but there are several additional features of which you should be aware.

SELF-TESTS

All chapters contain one or more such sections. These Self-Tests contain questions and drill material for use in independent study or classroom discussion. Suggested answers to all Self-Test problems appear in Appendix D. In many cases more than one correct answer is possible, but only one answer will be given in Appendix D. If you are in doubt about the correctness of your answer, ask your instructor.

EXERCISES

After each Self-Test section, we refer to a group of Exercises to be found in the Workbook. Most of the Workbook Exercises will be similar to those in the equivalent Self-Test, so refer to the Self-Test if you have questions about how to complete the Exercises. However, the Workbook will also often contain more creative compositional problems than appeared in the Self-Test, as it would be impossible to suggest "answers" to such problems if they were used as Self-Tests.

CHECKPOINTS

You will frequently encounter Checkpoint sections. These are intended to jog your memory and to help you review what you have just read. No answers are given to Checkpoint questions.

RECORDINGS

A set of compact discs is available that accompanies this text (ISBN: 0-07-741013-0). The recordings for the Workbook are now available as MP3 downloads from the Online Learning Center (www.mhhe.com/kostka7e). They contain recordings of virtually every example from music literature found in the text and in the Workbook, performed using the same instrumentation seen in the examples. You will find that you learn more successfully and enjoy learning even more if you take advantage of these recordings.

WEB-BASED RESOURCES

The website that accompanies *Tonal Harmony* can be found at *www.mhhe.com/kostka7e*. The exercises, drills, and additional reading mentioned in the Variation boxes located throughout the text can be found at the website.

Contents

Part Two
Diatonic Triads 66

Chapter One
Elements of Pitch

The Keyboard and Octave Registers

Pitch in music refers to the highness or lowness of a sound. Pitches are named by using the first seven letters of the alphabet: A, B, C, D, E, F, and G. We will approach the notation of pitch by relating this pitch alphabet to the piano keyboard, using Cs as an example. The C nearest the middle of the keyboard is called middle C, or C4. Higher Cs (moving toward the right on the keyboard) are named C5, C6, and so on. Lower Cs (moving toward the left) are named C3, C2, and C1. Notes below C1 are followed by a 0, as in B0. All the Cs on the piano are labeled in Example 1-1.

Example 1-1

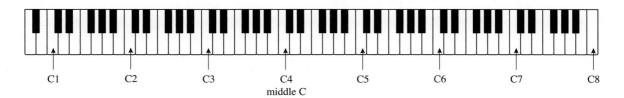

From any C up to or down to the next C is called an **octave.** All the pitches from one C up to, but not including, the next C are said to be in the same **octave register.** As Example 1-2 illustrates, the white key above C4 is named D4 because it is in the same octave register, while the white key below C4 is named B3.

Example 1-2

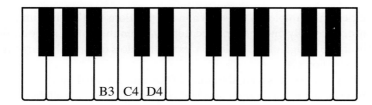

Notation on the Staff

Our system of musical notation is similar to a graph in which time is indicated on the X axis and pitch is shown on the Y axis. In Example 1-3, R occurs before S in time and is higher than S in pitch.

Example 1-3

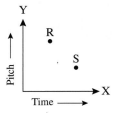

A **staff** is used in music to indicate the precise pitch desired. A staff consists of five lines and four spaces, but it may be extended indefinitely through the use of **ledger lines** (Ex. 1-4).

Example 1-4

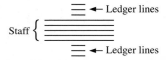

A **clef** must appear at the beginning of the staff in order to indicate which pitches are to be associated with which lines and spaces. The three clefs commonly used today are shown in Example 1-5, and the position of C4 in each is illustrated. Notice that the C clef appears in either of two positions.

Example 1-5

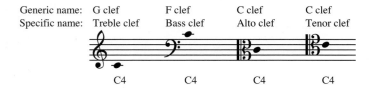

| Generic name: | G clef | F clef | C clef | C clef |
| Specific name: | Treble clef | Bass clef | Alto clef | Tenor clef |

| | C4 | C4 | C4 | C4 |

The clefs in Example 1-5 are shown in the positions that are in common use today, but you may occasionally find them placed differently on the staff in some editions. Wherever they appear, the design of the G clef circles G4, the dots of the F clef surround F3, and the C clef is centered on C4.

The **grand staff** is a combination of two staves joined by a brace, with the top and bottom staves using treble and bass clefs, respectively. Various pitches are notated and labeled on the grand staff in Example 1-6. Pay special attention to the way in which the ledger lines are used on the grand staff. For instance, the notes C4 and A3 appear twice in Example 1-6, once in relation to the top staff and once in relation to the bottom staff.

Example 1-6

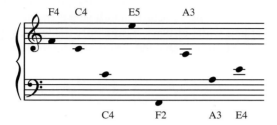

Self-Test 1-1

(Answers begin on page 552.)

A. Name the pitches in the blanks provided, using the correct octave register designations.

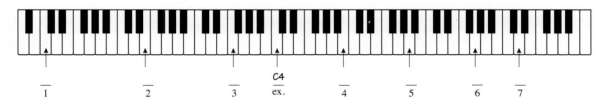

B. Notate the indicated pitches on the staff in the correct octave.

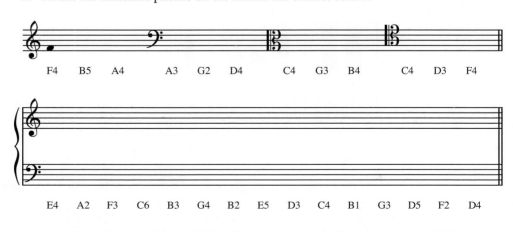

Exercise 1-1 See Workbook.

The Major Scale

In this chapter you will learn about major and minor scales, the scales that form the basis of tonal music. However, there are many other kinds of scales, some of which are covered in Chapter 26.

The **major scale** is a specific pattern of small steps (called half steps) and larger ones (called whole steps) encompassing an octave. A **half step** is the distance from a key on the piano to the very next key, white or black. Using only the white keys on the piano keyboard, there are two half steps in each octave, indicated by the letter "h" in Example 1-7.

Example 1-7

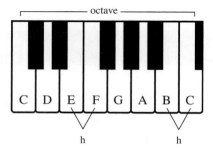

A **whole step** skips the very next key and goes instead to the following one. Using only the white keys on the piano keyboard, there are five whole steps in each octave, indicated by the letter "w" in Example 1-8.

Example 1-8

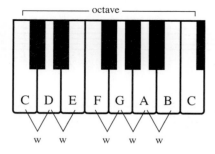

The major-scale pattern of whole and half steps is the same as that found on the white keys from any C up to the next C. In the next diagram, the numbers with carets above them ($\hat{1}$, $\hat{2}$, etc.) are scale degree numbers for the C major scale.*

---

*   Throughout this book we will refer to major scales with uppercase letters—for example, A major or A—and minor scales with lowercase letters—for example a minor or a.

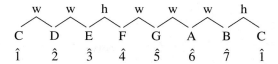

You can see from this diagram that half steps in the major scale occur only between scale degrees $\hat{3}$ and $\hat{4}$ and $\hat{7}$ and $\hat{1}$. Notice also that the major scale can be thought of as two identical, four-note patterns separated by a whole step. These four-note patterns are called **tetrachords.**

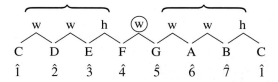

If we examine the steps on the white keys of a G-to-G octave, as in Example 1-9, we do not find the same pattern of whole and half steps that occurred in the C-to-C octave. To play a G major scale, we would need to skip the F key and play the black key that is between F and G. We will label that key with an **accidental,** a symbol that raises or lowers a pitch by a half or whole step. All the possible accidentals are listed in the following table.

Symbol	Name	Effect
✕	Double sharp	Raise a whole step
♯	Sharp	Raise a half step
♮	Natural	Cancel a previous accidental
♭	Flat	Lower a half step
♭♭	Double flat	Lower a whole step

Example 1-9

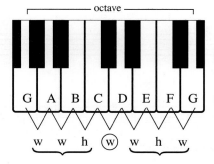

We can make our G scale conform to the major-scale pattern by adding one accidental, in this case a sharp.

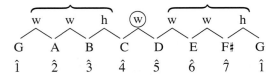

It is important to understand that major and minor scales always use all the letter names of the musical alphabet. It would not be correct to substitute a G♭ for the F♯ in a G major scale. The scale is written on the staff in Example 1-10.

Example 1-10

Notice that when we write or say the names of notes and accidentals, we put the accidental last (as in F♯ or F sharp), but in staff notation the accidental always *precedes* the note that it modifies (as in Ex. 1-10).

The Major Key Signatures

One way to learn the major scales is by means of the pattern of whole and half steps discussed in the previous section. Another is by memorizing the key signatures associated with the various scales. The term **key** is used in music to identify the first degree of a scale. For instance, the key of G major refers to the major scale that begins on G. A **key signature** is a pattern of sharps or flats that appears at the beginning of a staff and indicates that certain notes are to be consistently raised or lowered. There are seven key signatures using sharps. In each case, the name of the major key can be found by going up a half step from the last sharp (Ex. 1-11).

Example 1-11

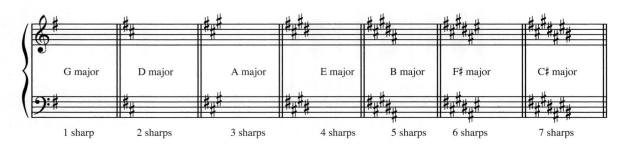

There are also seven key signatures using flats. Except for the key of F major, the name of the major key is the same as the name of the next-to-last flat (Ex. 1-12).

Example 1-12

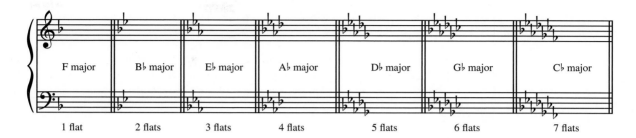

F major	B♭ major	E♭ major	A♭ major	D♭ major	G♭ major	C♭ major
1 flat	2 flats	3 flats	4 flats	5 flats	6 flats	7 flats

You may have noticed that there are three pairs of major keys that would sound exactly the same—that is, they would be played on the very same keys of the piano keyboard.

B major   =   C♭ major

F♯ major   =   G♭ major

C♯ major   =   D♭ major

Notes that have the same pitch but that are spelled differently, like E and F♭, are said to be **enharmonic.** Keys can be enharmonic as well, such as the three pairs of keys shown above. If two major keys are not enharmonic, then they are transpositions of each other. To **transpose** means to write or play music in some key other than the original.

The key signatures in Examples 1-11 and 1-12 must be memorized—not only the number of accidentals involved but also their order and placement on the staff. Notice that the pattern of placing the sharps on the staff changes at the fifth sharp for both the treble and the bass clefs. Try saying aloud the order of accidentals for sharps (FCGDAEB) and for flats (BEADGCF) until you feel confident with them.

Key signatures are written in much the same way using the alto and tenor clefs as they are for treble and bass. The only exception is the placement of sharps in the tenor clef, as you can see in Example 1-13.

Example 1-13

Some people find it easier to memorize key signatures if they visualize a **circle of fifths,** which is a diagram somewhat like the face of a clock. Reading clockwise around the circle of fifths on the following page, you will see that each new key begins on $\hat{5}$ (the fifth scale degree) of the previous key. If you go counterclockwise, each new key begins on $\hat{4}$ of the previous one.

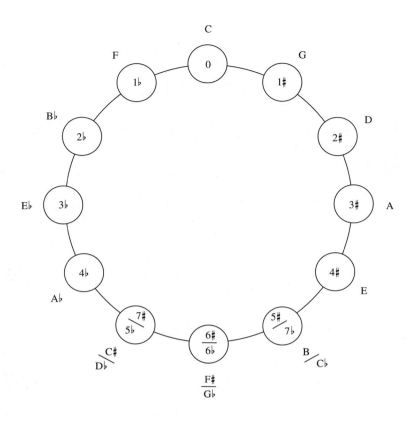

CHECKPOINT

1. Does G3 lie below or above middle C?

2. How is a double sharp notated?

3. Half steps in the major scale occur between scale degrees _____ and _____ as well as between scale degrees _____ and _____.

4. The major scale consists of two identical four-note patterns called _____.

5. What relationship can you see between the order of sharps and the order of flats?

6. Name the 15 major keys.

Self-Test 1-2

(Answers begin on page 553.)

A. Notate the specified scales using accidentals, *not* key signatures. Show the placement of whole and half steps, as in the example.

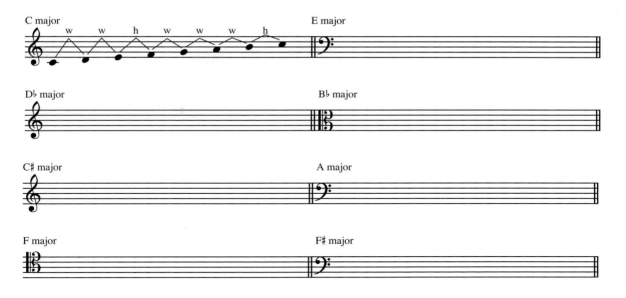

B. Identify these major key signatures.

<u>C</u> major	___ major	___ major	___ major	___ major	___ major	___ major	___ major
ex.	**1**	**2**	**3**	**4**	**5**	**6**	**7**

C. Notate the specified key signatures.

A major   Db major   F# major   Bb major   B major   Cb major   D major   C major

D. Fill in the blanks.

Key signature	Name of key	Key signature	Name of key
1. Three flats	___ major	8. _____	Bb major
2. Seven sharps	___ major	9. One sharp	___ major
3. _____	D major	10. Five flats	___ major
4. One flat	___ major	11. _____	F# major
5. _____	Ab major	12. _____	Cb major
6. _____	B major	13. Four sharps	___ major
7. Six flats	___ major	14. _____	A major

E. Fill in the blanks, using the example as a model.

	Major key	Key signature	Scale degree	Is this note
Ex.	C	0♯/0♭	$\hat{3}$	E
1.			$\hat{2}$	F
2.	D♭		$\hat{5}$	
3.	G			F♯
4.	B		$\hat{3}$	
5.	A♭			F
6.		7♭		F♭

Exercise 1-2 See Workbook.

Minor Scales

Musicians traditionally practice and memorize three minor-scale formations, although these are a simplification of how minor keys actually work, as we will see in Chapter 4. One of these is the **natural minor scale.** You can see from the following illustration that the natural minor scale is like a major scale with lowered $\hat{3}$, $\hat{6}$, and $\hat{7}$.

C major	C	D	E	F	G	A	B	C
Scale degree	$\hat{1}$	$\hat{2}$	$\hat{3}$	$\hat{4}$	$\hat{5}$	$\hat{6}$	$\hat{7}$	$\hat{1}$
c natural minor	C	D	E♭	F	G	A♭	B♭	C

Another minor scale type is the **harmonic minor scale,** which can be thought of as natural minor with a raised $\hat{7}$ or as major with lowered $\hat{3}$ and $\hat{6}$.

C major	C	D	E	F	G	A	B	C
Scale degree	$\hat{1}$	$\hat{2}$	$\hat{3}$	$\hat{4}$	$\hat{5}$	$\hat{6}$	$\hat{7}$	$\hat{1}$
c harmonic minor	C	D	E♭	F	G	A♭	B	C

The third type of minor scale is the **melodic minor scale,** which has an ascending form and a descending form. The ascending form, shown next, is like natural minor with a raised $\hat{6}$ and $\hat{7}$ or as major with lowered $\hat{3}$.

C major	C	D	E	F	G	A	B	C
Scale degree	$\hat{1}$	$\hat{2}$	$\hat{3}$	$\hat{4}$	$\hat{5}$	$\hat{6}$	$\hat{7}$	$\hat{1}$
c ascending melodic minor	C	D	E♭	F	G	A	B	C

The descending form of the melodic minor scale is the same as the natural minor scale.

The three minor scale types are summarized in Example 1-14. The scale degrees that differ from the major are circled. Notice the arrows used in connection with the melodic minor scale in order to distinguish the ascending $\hat{6}$ and $\hat{7}$ from the descending $\hat{6}$ and $\hat{7}$. Also note that scale degrees $\hat{1}$ through $\hat{5}$ are identical in all three forms of the minor scale. This pattern of w–h–w–w is known as the **minor pentachord.**

Example 1-14

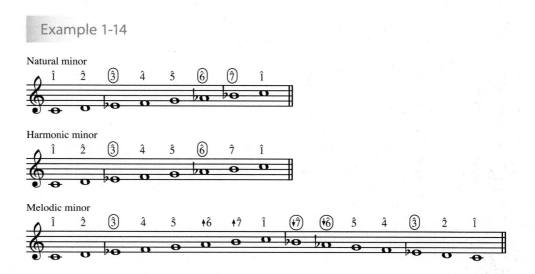

Natural minor

Harmonic minor

Melodic minor

Minor Key Signatures

Minor key signatures conform to the natural minor scale, no matter which minor scale type is actually in use. Looking back at Example 1-14, you can see that the natural minor scale on C requires three accidentals: B♭, E♭, and A♭. The key signature of c minor, then, is the same as the key signature of E♭ major; c minor and E♭ major are said to be **relatives** because they share the same key signature. The relative major of any minor key starts on $\hat{3}$ of the minor scale, and the relative minor of any major key begins on $\hat{6}$ of the major scale. If a major scale and a minor scale share the same $\hat{1}$, as do C major and c minor, for example, they are said to be **parallel keys.** We would say that C major is the parallel major of c minor.

The circle of fifths is a convenient way to display the names of the minor keys and their relative majors, as well as their key signatures. In the following diagram, the names of the minor keys (in lowercase, as usual) are inside the diagram.

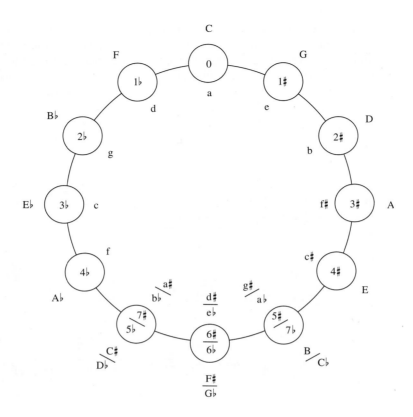

You may find it easier to learn the minor scales in terms of their relative majors, as in the preceding circle-of-fifths diagram, instead of in terms of their parallel majors, which is how minor scales were introduced on page 10. This will be most helpful regarding the keys of g♯, d♯, and a♯, which have no parallel major forms. If you do use the relative major approach, remember that the key signature for any minor scale conforms to the *natural minor* scale and that accidentals must be used to spell the other forms. Specifically, you have to raise $\hat{7}$ of the natural minor scale to produce the harmonic minor scale and raise $\hat{6}$ and $\hat{7}$ of the natural minor scale to get the ascending form of the melodic minor scale. Example 1-15 illustrates the spellings for the related keys of F major and d minor.

Example 1-15

F major scale

Relative minor, natural form

Harmonic minor raises $\hat{7}$

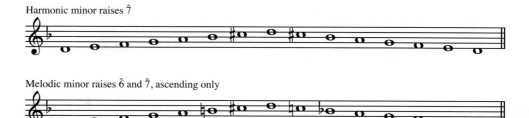

Melodic minor raises $\hat{6}$ and $\hat{7}$, ascending only

One final hint: a quick way to find any minor key signature other than g♯, d♯, or a♯ is to begin with the key signature of the *parallel* major and to add three flats and/or subtract three sharps. Examples:

Major key		Minor key	
B♭	2 flats	b♭	5 flats
E	4 sharps	e	1 sharp
D	2 sharps	d	1 flat

It is very important to practice faithfully all the major and minor scales on an instrument until they become memorized patterns. An intellectual understanding of scales cannot substitute for the secure tactile and aural familiarity that will result from those hours of practice.

Self-Test 1-3

(Answers begin on page 554.)

A. Notate the specified scales using accidentals, *not* key signatures. The melodic minor should be written both ascending and descending.

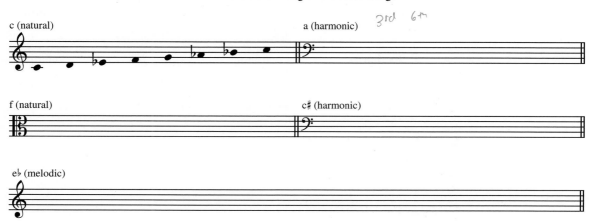

bb (natural)

g# (harmonic)

f# (melodic)

B. Identify these minor key signatures.

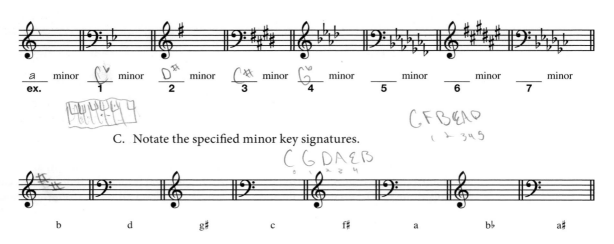

_a_ minor	C minor	D# minor	C# minor	G minor	_____ minor	_____ minor	_____ minor
ex.	**1**	**2**	**3**	**4**	**5**	**6**	**7**

C F B E A D
1 2 3 4 5

C. Notate the specified minor key signatures.

C G D A E B
0 1 2 3 4

| b | d | g# | c | f# | a | bb | a# |

D. Fill in the blanks.

	Key signature	Name of key	Key signature	Name of key
1.	F flat	d minor	8. Two flats	_____ minor
2.	Six flats	C# minor	9. _____	f minor
3.	Four sharps	_____ minor	10. _____	b minor
4.	_____	f# minor	11. Three flats	_____ minor
5.	Six sharps	_____ minor	12. _____	ab minor
6.	_____	bb major	13. One sharp	_____ minor
7.	_____	a# major	14. Five sharps	_____ minor

Exercise 1-3 See Workbook.

Scale Degree Names

Musicians in conversation or in writing often refer to scale degrees by a set of traditional names rather than by numbers. The names are shown in Example 1-16. Notice that there are two names for $\hat{7}$ in minor, depending on whether or not it is raised.

Example 1-16

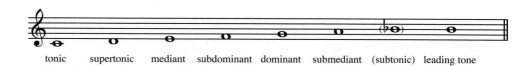

tonic   supertonic   mediant   subdominant   dominant   submediant   (subtonic)   leading tone

The origin of some of these names is illustrated in Example 1-17. Notice that the mediant lies halfway between the tonic and the dominant, while the submediant lies halfway between the tonic and the subdominant.

Example 1-17

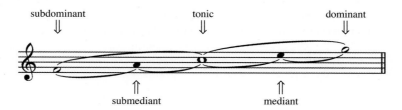

subdominant   tonic   dominant

submediant   mediant

CHECKPOINT

Now is the time to start learning the scale degree names, if you do not know them already. Here are a couple of exercises that will help.

1. Translate these numbers aloud to scale degree names as fast as possible. Repeat as often as necessary until speed is attained.

   $\hat{1}$ $\hat{2}$ $\hat{3}$ $\hat{4}$ $\hat{5}$ $\hat{6}$ $\hat{7}$ $\hat{1}$ $\hat{7}$ $\hat{6}$ $\hat{5}$ $\hat{4}$ $\hat{3}$ $\hat{2}$ $\hat{1}$

   $\hat{3}$ $\hat{5}$ $\hat{7}$ $\hat{6}$ $\hat{4}$ $\hat{2}$ $\hat{1}$ $\hat{6}$ $\hat{3}$ $\hat{7}$ $\hat{2}$ $\hat{5}$ $\hat{4}$ $\hat{3}$ $\hat{1}$

   $\hat{5}$ $\hat{2}$ $\hat{7}$ $\hat{4}$ $\hat{6}$ $\hat{3}$ $\hat{1}$ $\hat{2}$ $\hat{7}$ $\hat{5}$ $\hat{6}$ $\hat{4}$ $\hat{1}$ $\hat{3}$ $\hat{2}$

2. Call out or sing the scale degree names contained in each example that that follows.

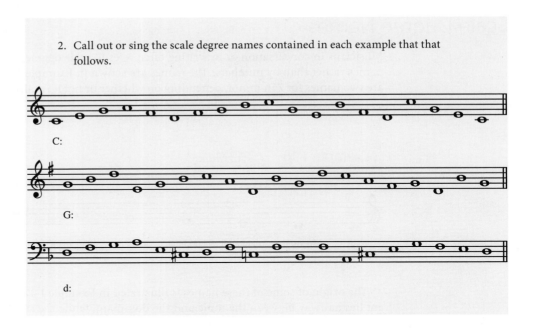

C:

G:

d:

Intervals

An **interval** is the measurement of the distance in pitch between two notes. A **harmonic interval** results when the notes are performed at the same time, whereas a **melodic interval** occurs when the notes are played successively (Ex. 1-18). The method of measuring intervals is the same for both harmonic and melodic intervals.

Example 1-18

Harmonic intervals   Melodic intervals

There are two parts to any interval name: the numerical name and the modifier that precedes the numerical name. As Example 1-19 illustrates, the numerical name is a measurement of how far apart the notes are vertically on the staff, regardless of what accidentals are involved.

Example 1-19

1   2   3   3   3   3   4   (etc.)

In talking about intervals, we use the terms **unison** instead of 1, and **octave** (8ve) instead of 8. We also say 2nd instead of "two," 3rd instead of "three," and so on. Intervals smaller than an 8ve are called **simple intervals,** whereas larger intervals (including the 8ve) are called **compound intervals.**

It is important to notice in Example 1-19 that the harmonic interval of a 2nd is notated with the top note offset a little to the right of the bottom note. Accidentals are offset in the same way for harmonic intervals of a 2nd, 3rd, or 4th, if both notes require an accidental.

Self-Test 1-4

(Answers begin on page 555.)

Provide the numerical names of the intervals by using the numbers 1 through 8.

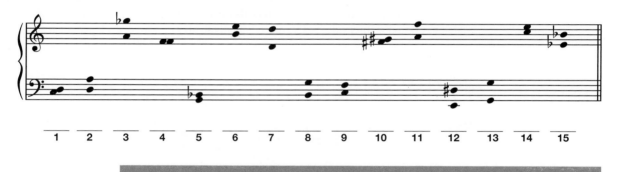

Exercise 1-4 See Workbook.

Perfect, Major, and Minor Intervals

One way to begin learning the modifiers for intervals is by relating them to the intervals contained in the major scale, specifically the intervals from 1̂ up to the other scale degrees. This method can then be applied in any context, whether or not the major scale is actually being used.

The term **perfect** (abbreviated P) is a modifier used only in connection with unisons, 4ths, 5ths, 8ves, and their compounds (11ths, and so on). As Example 1-20 illustrates, a P1, P4, P5, and P8 can all be constructed by using 1̂ in the major scale as the *bottom* note.

Example 1-20

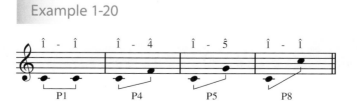

If we want to spell one of these intervals above E♭, for example, we need only to think of scale steps Î, 4̂, and 5̂ of the E♭ major scale. If the bottom note does not commonly serve as Î of a major scale (such as D♯), remove the accidental temporarily, spell the interval, and then apply the accidental to both notes (Ex. 1-21).

Example 1-21

The modifiers **major** and **minor** (abbreviated as M and m) are used only in connection with 2nds, 3rds, 6ths, and 7ths. The intervals formed by Î–2̂, Î–3̂, Î–6̂, and Î–7̂ in the major scale are all major intervals, as Example 1-22 illustrates.

Example 1-22

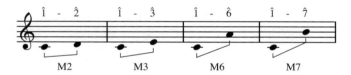

If a major interval is made a half step smaller without altering its numerical name, it becomes a minor interval (Ex. 1-23). Notice that you can make an interval smaller by lowering the top note or raising the bottom note.

Example 1-23

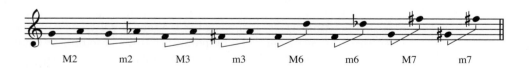

Self-Test 1-5

(Answers begin on page 555.)

A. All the intervals that follow are unisons, 4ths, 5ths, or 8ves. Put "P" in the space provided *only* if the interval is a perfect interval.

___ 5	___ 4	___ 1	___ 5	___ 8	___ 4	___ 5	___ 4	___ 5	___ 8
1	**2**	**3**	**4**	**5**	**6**	**7**	**8**	**9**	**10**

B. All the intervals that follow are 2nds, 3rds, 6ths, or 7ths. Write "M" or "m" in each space, as appropriate.

___ 3	___ 6	___ 7	___ 2	___ 6	___ 2	___ 3	___ 7	___ 6	___ 2
1	**2**	**3**	**4**	**5**	**6**	**7**	**8**	**9**	**10**

C. Notate the specified intervals above the given notes.

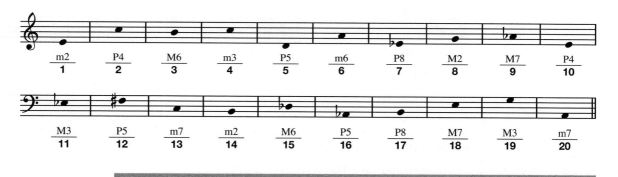

m2	P4	M6	m3	P5	m6	P8	M2	M7	P4
1	**2**	**3**	**4**	**5**	**6**	**7**	**8**	**9**	**10**

M3	P5	m7	m2	M6	P5	P8	M7	M3	m7
11	**12**	**13**	**14**	**15**	**16**	**17**	**18**	**19**	**20**

Exercise 1-5 See Workbook.

Augmented and Diminished Intervals

If a perfect or a major interval is made a half step larger without changing the numerical name, the interval becomes **augmented** (abbreviated +). If a perfect or a minor interval is made a half step smaller without changing its numerical name, it becomes **diminished** (abbreviated °). These relationships are summarized as follows:

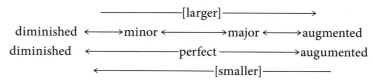

There is no such thing as a diminished unison. Doubly augmented and doubly diminished intervals are possible, but they seldom occur. **Tritone** is a term used for the +4 or its enharmonic equivalent, the °5.

Inversion of Intervals

Descending intervals, especially large ones, are often easier to spell and identify through the use of **interval inversion.** We invert an interval by putting the bottom pitch above the top one or the reverse; for example, the interval D-A inverts to A-D. When we invert an interval, the new numerical name is always different from the old one. The new numerical name can be calculated by subtracting the old numerical name from 9.

Constant value of 9	9	9	9	9	9	9
Minus old numeric name	−2	−3	−4	−5	−6	−7
Equals new numeric name	7	6	5	4	3	2

You can see that an inverted 2nd becomes a 7th, a 3rd becomes a 6th, and so on (Ex. 1-24).

Example 1-24

The modifier also changes when an interval is inverted, with the exception of perfect intervals.

Old modifier	m	M	P	+	°
New modifer	M	m	P	°	+

As an example of the usefulness of inversion, suppose you wanted to know what note lies a m6 below G3. Invert the m6 down to a M3 up, as in Example 1-25, transpose the B3 down an 8ve, and you find that the answer is B2.

Example 1-25

m6↓ = ?   M3↑ = B3   m6↓ = B2

Fluency with intervals, as with scales, is necessary for any serious musician and will provide a solid foundation for your further study. As you did with scales, you will benefit from finding out how various intervals sound and feel on a musical instrument.

One exercise you can do (you can think of others) is to write out the notes of the chromatic scale in random order. Include each black key twice—once as a sharped note and once as a flatted note. Then play some interval above and below each note. Work for speed, using your ear to correct yourself.

Consonant and Dissonant Harmonic Intervals

In tonal music, some harmonic intervals are considered to be consonant, whereas others are considered to be dissonant. The terms **consonant** and **dissonant** can be defined roughly as meaning pleasing to the ear and not pleasing to the ear, respectively, but these are very dependent on context. Some of the most exciting moments in tonal music involve dissonance, which is certainly not displeasing in that context, but the dissonances resolve eventually to the consonances that give them meaning. As you can imagine, this is a complex subject, and it is one with which much of this book is concerned.

For now it will suffice to say that major and minor 3rds and 6ths and perfect 5ths and 8ves are consonant. All other harmonic intervals, including all augmented and diminished intervals, are dissonant. An exception is the P4, which is considered dissonant in tonal music only when it occurs above the lowest voice (also called the **bass,** in both vocal and instrumental music).

CHECKPOINT

1. What is the term for an interval in which the notes are played in succession instead of simultaneously?

2. Is there such a thing as a m5? A P6?

3. A perfect interval made a half step smaller without changing its numerical name becomes _____.

4. A °5 inverted becomes a _____.

5. Intervals that are relatively displeasing to the ear are classified as _____.

Self-Test 1-6

(Answers begin on page 555.)

A. Most of the following intervals are either augmented or diminished. Label each interval.

| 1 | 2 | 3 | 4 | 5 | 6 | 7 | 8 | 9 | 10 |

B. Label what each interval becomes when it is inverted.

1. P4 becomes _____   5. °5 becomes _____

2. M7 becomes _____   6. m2 becomes _____

3. +2 becomes _____   7. m6 becomes _____

4. M3 becomes _____   8. +6 becomes _____

C. Notate the specified interval *below* the given note. (You may find it helpful to invert the interval first in some cases.)

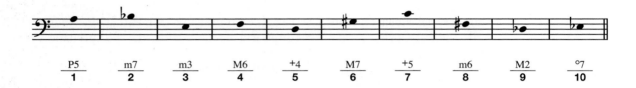

P5	m7	m3	M6	+4	M7	+5	m6	M2	°7
1	2	3	4	5	6	7	8	9	10

D. Label each interval in this melody (from Wagner's *Götterdämmerung*). Interval 8 is from the A5 down to the D♯5.

E. Beneath each of the following harmonic intervals, indicate whether it is consonant ("c"), dissonant ("d"), or dissonant only if the bass has the bottom note of the interval ("d bass").

	1. m7	2. P1	3. P8	4. °7	5. m6
c	_____	_____	_____	_____	_____
d	_____	_____	_____	_____	_____
d bass	_____	_____	_____	_____	_____

	6. M2	7. P5	8. M3	9. +2	10. P4
c	_____	_____	_____	_____	_____
d	_____	_____	_____	_____	_____
d bass	_____	_____	_____	_____	_____

Exercise 1-6 See Workbook.

Summary

Pitch in music refers to the highness or lowness of a sound. Particular pitches are named by using the **musical alphabet,** consisting of the letters A through G, at which point the alphabet starts over. From one letter up or down to its next occurrence is called an **octave,** whereas the space from any C up to the next B is called an **octave register.** Octave registers are numbered, with the lowest C on the **piano keyboard** designated as C1. The C nearest the middle of the piano keyboard is called **middle C,** or C4.

Pitches are notated on the **staff,** an arrangement of five lines and four spaces that can be extended through the use of **ledger lines.** A staff always begins with one of several **clefs,** which determine exactly what pitch is represented by each line or space. A **grand staff** consists of two staves joined by a brace, with a treble clef on the top staff and a bass clef on the bottom.

The **major scale** consists of two identical tetrachords that have a particular arrangement of **whole steps** and **half steps.** Most major scales also have a **parallel minor** scale that begins on the same note but that lowers scale degrees $\hat{3}$, $\hat{6}$, and $\hat{7}$ by a half step. This form of the minor is called the **natural minor scale.** The **harmonic minor scale** lowers only scale degrees $\hat{3}$ and $\hat{6}$ of its parallel major, whereas the **melodic minor scale** lowers scale degree $\hat{3}$ when ascending and scale degrees $\hat{3}$, $\hat{6}$, and $\hat{7}$ when descending.

Every scale has an associated **key signature,** consisting of zero to seven sharps or flats arranged in a particular way on the staff. There are 15 key signatures in all, with one major and one minor scale associated with each. Major and minor keys that share the same key signature are said to be **relative keys,** whereas those that share the same starting note are called **parallel keys.** The notes of a scale are all assigned **scale degree names,** which vary only slightly between major and minor. **Enharmonic** notes or keys sound the same but are spelled differently. To **transpose** music means to play it in another key.

The difference between any two pitches is called an **interval.** A **harmonic interval** separates pitches that are sounded simultaneously, whereas a **melodic interval** separates pitches that are sounded in succession. Intervals are defined by means of a numerical name and a modifier that precedes it. These modifiers include the terms **perfect, major, minor, augmented,** and **diminished.** To **invert** an interval, put the lower note above the upper one (or the reverse). The numerical name and modifier of an inverted interval can be predicted using the method explained in this chapter.

Consonant intervals include major and minor 3rds and 6ths, the P5, and the P8. The P4 is usually consonant, unless it occurs above the lowest voice.

Variations

For additional review and practice, please see Chapter 1 on our website at
www.mhhe.com/kostka7e.

Chapter Two
Elements of Rhythm

Rhythm

This chapter concerns the time aspect of music—how sounds are notated so that they will occur at a predictable moment and in a predetermined pattern. **Rhythm** is a general term used to refer to the time aspect of music, as contrasted with the pitch aspect.

Durational Symbols

Durations are notated by using symbols that are organized so that each symbol is twice the duration of the next shorter symbol and half the duration of the next longer symbol. The following table lists a number of these symbols.

Value	Note	Rest
Breve	𝄺 = 𝅝 + 𝅝	= +
Whole	𝅝 = 𝅗𝅥 + 𝅗𝅥	= +
Half	𝅗𝅥 = 𝅘𝅥 + 𝅘𝅥	= +
Quarter	𝅘𝅥 = 𝅘𝅥𝅮 + 𝅘𝅥𝅮	= +
Eighth	𝅘𝅥𝅮 = 𝅘𝅥𝅯 + 𝅘𝅥𝅯	= +
Sixteenth	𝅘𝅥𝅯 = 𝅘𝅥𝅰 + 𝅘𝅥𝅰	= +

The same series could be continued to thirty-seconds, sixty-fourths, and so on. Durations other than these must be indicated through the use of ties, dots, or other symbols. A **tie** is a curved line that connects two notes of the same pitch, creating a new duration that is equal to their sum. A **dot** following a symbol always adds to the duration one-half the value of the note, rest, or dot that precedes it, for example [𝅘𝅥. = 𝅘𝅥 𝅘𝅥𝅮] and [𝅘𝅥.. = 𝅘𝅥 𝅘𝅥𝅮 𝅘𝅥𝅯]. When notated on the staff, a dot is never placed on a staff line. If the notehead itself is on a staff line, the dot is put to the right of the note but in the space *above* it.

Beat and Tempo

The **beat** is the basic pulse of a musical passage. To determine the beat of a passage you are listening to, tap your foot to the music, or try to imagine the way a conductor would conduct the passage—the conductor's arm movement. The resulting steady pulse is called the beat, and the rate at which the beats occur is called the **tempo.**

A composer commonly specifies the tempo of a passage by one of two methods—sometimes by both. The first method uses words, often in Italian, to describe the tempo—words such as adagio, moderato, and allegro.

The second method is more exact because it shows precisely how many beats are to occur in the space of one minute. For example, if the desired tempo would result in 72 quarter notes in one minute, the tempo indication would be ♩ = 72 or M.M. ♩ = 72. The M.M. stands for Maelzel's metronome, after Johann Maelzel, who widely promoted the device during the early nineteenth century.

Meter

Beats tend to be grouped into patterns that are consistent throughout a passage; the pattern of beats is called the **meter.** Groups of two, three, and four beats are the most common, although other meters occur. Incidentally, a group of four beats could often also be interpreted as two groups of two beats each and vice versa. In any case, the groups of beats are called **measures** (abbreviated m. or mm.), and in notation the end of a measure is always indicated by a vertical line through the staff called a **bar line.** (A bar line also cancels any accidentals that appeared in the measure.) The words **duple, triple,** and **quadruple** are used to refer to the number of beats in each measure, as in **duple meter, triple meter,** and **quadruple meter.** These terms are summarized in the following table, along with the pattern of stresses usually found in each meter (referred to as **metric accent**).

Grouping	Meter type	Metric accent pattern
Two-beat measure	Duple	Strong-weak
Three-beat measure	Triple	Strong-weak-weak
Four-beat measure	Quadruple	Strong-weak-less strong-weak

As you might imagine, most marches are in duple meter because people have two feet, whereas contemporary popular music tends to be in duple or quadruple meter. Waltzes are always in triple meter, as are a number of traditional songs, such as "Amazing Grace" and "Scarborough Fair."

The meter of many passages is clear and easily identified, but in other cases the meter might be ambiguous. For example, sing "Take Me Out to the Ball Game" quite slowly while you tap you foot or conduct, then decide on the meter type. Now sing it again, but very fast. The first time you probably felt the meter was triple, but at a faster tempo you should have identified the meter as duple (or quadruple). Between those extreme tempos are more moderate tempos, which two listeners might interpret in different ways—one hearing a faster triple meter, the other a slower duple meter. Both listeners would be correct because identifying meter in a case such as this is a matter of interpretation rather than of right and wrong.

We use the term **hypermeter** to refer to a regular grouping of measures that is analogous to meter. Sing through "Amazing Grace," which is in triple meter, and notice how the measures form groups of four, creating a quadruple hypermeter.

Self-Test 2-1

(Answers begin on page 556.)

A. Show how many notes or rests of the shorter duration would be required to equal the longer duration.

ex. ♩ × __2__ = 𝅝

1. ♪ × ____ = ♩   9. ♪ × ____ = 𝅗𝅥♪

2. ♩ × ____ = 𝅝   10. 𝅘𝅥𝅰 × ____ = ♪.

3. ♪ × ____ = ♩.   11. 𝄿· × ____ = 𝄼·

4. 𝅘𝅥𝅯 × ____ = 𝅗𝅥   12. 𝄼 × ____ = 𝄻

5. 𝄿 × ____ = 𝄼   13. 𝄾 × ____ = 𝄼

6. 𝄿 × ____ = 𝄿·   14. 𝅗𝅥 × ____ = 𝄻

7. 𝄾 × ____ = 𝄼   15. ♪. × ____ = ♩.

8. 𝅘𝅥𝅰 × ____ = ♩..   16. ♪ × ____ = 𝅝·

B. Sing aloud each of the songs listed below. Then identify the meter type of each, using the terms *duple*, *triple*, and *quadruple*.

1. "Silent Night" (slow tempo) _____

2. "Jingle Bells" _____

3. "America the Beautiful" _____

4. "Seventy-Six Trombones" _____

5. "Home on the Range" _____

C. Scale review. Given the key and the scale degree, supply the note name. Assume the *melodic minor* form for each minor key.

ex. f♯	4̂	__B__		8. B♭	4̂	____
1. D♭:	6̂	____		9. c:	↓6̂	____
2. f:	3̂	____		10. e:	4̂	____
3. A:	5̂	____		11. A♭:	7̂	____
4. B:	3̂	____		12. F♯	2̂	____
5. g:	↑6̂	____		13. b♭:	5̂	____
6. c♯:	↓7̂	____		14. E:	6̂	____
7. E♭:	5̂	____		15. d:	↑7̂	____

Exercise 2-1 See Workbook.

Division of the Beat

In most musical passages, we hear durations that are shorter than the beat. We call these shorter durations **divisions of the beat.** Beats generally divide either into two equal parts, called **simple beat,** or into three equal parts, called **compound beat.** Be careful not to confuse beat type, which refers to how the **beat** divides (simple or compound), with meter type, which refers to how the **measure** divides (duple, triple, or quadruple). The common beat and meter types can be combined with each other in six possible ways.

	METER		
BEAT	**Duple**	**Triple**	**Quadruple**
Simple	Simple duple	Simple triple	Simple quadruple
Compound	Compound duple	Compound triple	Compound quadruple

For example, sing "Take Me Out to the Ball Game" quickly in duple meter, as you did in the discussion of meter on p. 25. You can hear that the beats divide into thirds, so this is an example of compound duple. Do the same with "I Don't Know How to Love Him" (from *Jesus Christ Superstar*) or "Around Her Neck She Wore a Yellow Ribbon," and you will find that both are simple duple (or simple quadruple).

CHECKPOINT

1. How many 16th notes are in a half note?
2. Two dots following a quarter note add what durations to it?
3. What is the term that refers to the number of beats in a measure?
4. What term refers to the ways in which the beats divide?

Self-Test 2-2

(Answers begin on page 556.)

Sing aloud each of the following songs. Then identify the beat and meter types of each, using terms such as *simple duple* and so on.

1. "Auld Lang Syne" _____ _____
2. "Pop Goes the Weasel" _____ _____
3. "Silent Night" _____ _____
4. "Jingle Bells" _____ _____
5. "Seventy-Six Trombones" _____

Simple Time Signatures

A **time signature** is a symbol that tells the performer how many beats will occur in each measure, what note value will represent the beat, and whether the beat is simple or compound. A time signature for a simple beat has 2, 3, or 4 as the top number. The top number indicates the number of beats in the measure; the bottom number indicates the beat note (2 = 𝅗𝅥, 4 = ♩, 8 = ♪, and so on). Some typical simple time signatures are listed in the following table. Notice that time signatures are not written as fractions—there should be no line between the numbers.

Time signature	Beats per measure	Beat note	Division of the beat
$\frac{2}{4}$	2	♩	♫
$\frac{2}{2}$ or ¢	2	𝅗𝅥	♩ ♩
$\frac{3}{16}$	3	♬	(sixteenths)
$\frac{3}{4}$	3	♩	♫
$\frac{4}{8}$	4	♪	♫
$\frac{4}{4}$ or 𝄴	4	♩	♫

Example 2-1 illustrates how some of the songs we have been considering might be notated. The beat values were chosen arbitrarily. "Jingle Bells," for example, could also be notated correctly in $\frac{2}{2}$ or $\frac{2}{8}$ or any other simple duple time signature.

Example 2-1

"Jingle Bells"

"America the Beautiful"

"Home on the Range"

Self-Test 2-3

(Answers begin on page 557.)

A. Fill in the blanks in the following table.

	Beat and meter type	Beat note	Division of the beat	Time signature
1.	Simple duple	♩		
2.				$\frac{3}{8}$
3.			♪ ♪	2
4.	Simple quadruple	𝅝	♬	
5.	Simple triple	♪		

B. Renotate the excerpts from Example 2-1 using the specified time signatures.
1. $\frac{2}{8}$ "Jingle Bells"
2. $\frac{4}{2}$ "America the Beautiful"
3. $\frac{3}{4}$ "Home on the Range"

Exercise 2-2 See Workbook.

Compound Time Signatures

If the beat divides into three equal parts, as in a compound beat, the note value representing the beat will be a dotted value, as shown next.

Beat note	Division of the beat
𝅗𝅥.	♩ ♩ ♩
♩.	♪ ♪ ♪
♪.	♬
♪.	𝅘𝅥𝅰 𝅘𝅥𝅰 𝅘𝅥𝅰

Dotted values present a problem where time signatures are concerned. For example, if there are two beats per measure, and the beat note is ♩., what would the time signature be? $\frac{2}{4½}$? $\frac{2}{4+8}$? $\frac{2}{8+8+8}$? There is no easy solution, and the method that survives today is the source of much confusion concerning compound beat. Simply stated, a compound time signature informs the musician of the *number of divisions* of the beat contained in a measure and what the *division duration* is. This means that the top number of a compound time signature will be 6, 9, or 12 because two beats times three divisions equals six, three beats times three divisions equals nine, and four beats times three divisions equals twelve. As a result, you must *divide the top number of a compound time signature by three* to find out how many beats will occur in each measure. Some examples are given in the following table.

Time signature	Beats per measure	Beat note	Division of the beat
$\frac{6}{8}$	2	♩.	♫♪
$\frac{6}{4}$	2	♩.	♩ ♩ ♩
$\frac{9}{16}$	3	♪.	♫♫
$\frac{9}{8}$	3	♩.	♫♪
$\frac{12}{8}$	4	♩.	♫♪
$\frac{12}{4}$	4	♩.	♩ ♩ ♩

Example 2-2 illustrates some familiar tunes that use compound beat. As before, the choice of the actual beat note is an arbitrary one.

Example 2-2

"Take Me Out to the Ball Game"

"Down in the Valley"

"Pop Goes the Weasel"

You can see from this discussion that compound time signatures do *not* follow the rule, so often learned by the student musician, that "the top number tells how many beats are in a measure, and the bottom number tells what note gets the beat." Of course, there are some pieces in $\frac{6}{8}$, for example, that really do have six beats to the measure, but such a piece is not really in compound duple. A measure of $\frac{6}{8}$ performed in six does not sound like compound duple; instead, it sounds like two measures of simple triple, or $\frac{3}{8}$. In true compound duple, the listener will hear two compound beats to the measure, not six simple beats. In the same way, a slow work notated in $\frac{2}{4}$ might be conducted in four, which would seem to the listener to be simple quadruple. In both cases, the usual division value has become the beat value.

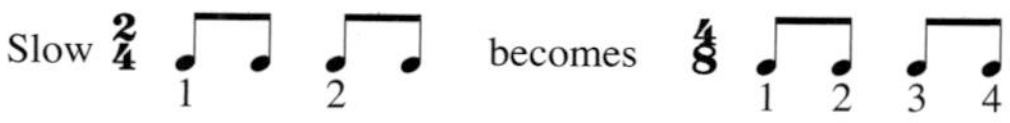

Slow $\frac{6}{8}$ ♩♩♩ ♩♩♩ becomes $\frac{3}{8}$ ♩♩♩ | ♩♩♩
1 2   1 2 3   1 2 3

Slow $\frac{2}{4}$ ♩♩ ♩♩ becomes $\frac{4}{8}$ ♩♩ ♩♩
1   2   1 2 3 4

The reverse also occurs—that is, the usual beat value sometimes becomes the actual division value. For example, a fast waltz or scherzo is almost always notated as simple triple, usually as $\frac{3}{4}$. But the aural effect is of one beat per measure, for which we might use the term **compound single.** If you didn't know the metric convention of such pieces, you would probably assume when hearing them that they were in compound duple because the measures tend to group into hypermetric pairs.

CHECKPOINT

1. What three numbers are found on the top of simple time signatures?
2. What three numbers are found on the top of compound time signatures?
3. If the top number of a compound time signature is **9,** how many beats will be in the measure?

Self-Test 2-4

(Answers begin on page 557.)

A. Fill in the blanks.

	Beat and meter type	Beat note	Division of the beat	Time signature
1.	Compound duple	 ♩.		
2.				$\frac{9}{4}$
3.		 ♩.		6
4.	Compound quadruple	 ♪.	 ♫♫	
5.			 ♫♫	9

(handwritten: PULSE above "Beat note"; PULSE above "Time signature")

B. Renotate the excerpts from Example 2-2 using the specified time signatures.

1. $\frac{6}{4}$ "Take Me Out to the Ball Game"
2. $\frac{9}{8}$ "Down in the Valley"
3. $\frac{6}{16}$ "Pop Goes the Weasel"

Exercise 2-3 See Workbook.

Time Signatures Summarized

There are two types of beat, simple and compound, and three common meters, duple, triple, and quadruple, which can be combined in a total of six ways. For each of these six combinations there is a number that will always appear as the *top* part of the time signature.

	METER TYPE		
BEAT TYPE	**Duple**	**Triple**	**Quadruple**
Simple	2 x	3 x	4 x
Compound	6 x	9 x	12 x

A listener can usually recognize the beat and meter types of a passage without seeing the music. Therefore, you can usually say what the top number of the time signature is (except that duple and quadruple are often indistinguishable). However, to know what the bottom number of the time signature is, you have to look at the music because any number representing a note value can be used for any meter.

Time signature	Simple beat duration	Compound beat duration
x 1	o	𝄺.
x 2	𝅗𝅥	o.
x 4	𝅘𝅥	𝅘𝅥.
x 8	𝅘𝅥𝅮	𝅘𝅥𝅮.
x 16	𝅘𝅥𝅯	𝅘𝅥𝅯.

Remember that the bottom number of a time signature (the leftmost column in the preceding table) stands for the *beat* value in a *simple* time signature and the *division* value in a *compound* time signature.

More on Durational Symbols

When rhythms are notated, it is customary to use rests, beams, ties, and dots in such a way that the metric accents and the individual beats are emphasized rather than obscured. Several incorrect and correct examples are notated in the following table.

Of course, it is correct to notate rhythms so as to obscure the metric accent when that is the desired result. **Syncopations** (rhythmic figures that stress normally weak beats or divisions) are frequently notated in that way, as shown next.

More involved figures, such as the following, are especially common in twentieth-century music.

A **tuplet** refers to the division of an *undotted value* into some number of equal parts other than two, four, eight, and so on or the division of a *dotted value* into some number of equal parts other than three, six, twelve, and so on, as you can see in the following table.

Of all the possibilities, the superimposition of triplets on a simple beat is the most common. The note value used for a tuplet is determined by the next longer available note value. For example, a third of a quarter note is longer than a sixteenth note but shorter than an eighth note, so the eighth note is chosen to represent it.

When a single-stem note is notated on the staff, the stem should go up if the note is below the middle line and down if the note is above the middle line. A note on the middle line theoretically can have its stem point in either direction, but most professional copyists consistently put a downward stem on notes that occur on the middle line (Ex. 2-3).

Example 2-3

Beams are used to connect durations shorter than a quarter note when the durations occur within the same beat. Not all professional copyists follow the same rules for determining the stem direction of beamed notes. Our preference is to decide the direction of the stems on the basis of the note that is farthest from the middle line. That is, if the note that is farthest from the middle line is below it, all the stems that are to be beamed together will point upward (Ex. 2-4).

Example 2-4

Self-Test 2-5

(Answers begin on page 558.)

A. Fill in the blanks.

Beat and meter type	Beat note	Division of the beat	Time signature
1.			$\frac{4}{4}$
2. Compound triple	𝅗𝅥.		
3.			$\frac{2}{8}$
4. Compound duple		♩ ♩ ♩	
5.		♩ ♩	3
6.		♬ ♬	12

B. Each measure below is incomplete. Add one or more rests to the end of each to complete the measure.

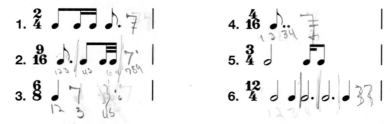

C. Provide the best time signature for each exercise. In some cases more than one correct answer might be possible.

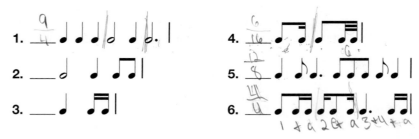

D. Each passage that follows is notated so that placement of the beats is obscured in some fashion. Without changing the way the music will sound, rewrite each one to clarify the beat placement. This may involve breaking some of the long notes into tied shorter notes or rebeaming groups of notes.

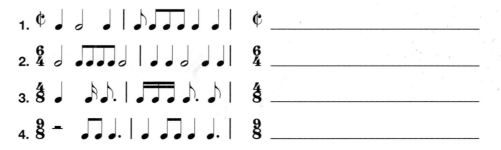

E. Add stems as required.

1. Each duration is a quarter note.

2. Each duration is an eighth note. Beam them in groups of three.

F. Listen to a recording of the beginning of each of the five movements of Beethoven's Symphony no. 6, op. 68, and identify the beat and meter types of each. Then name three time signatures that *could* have been used to notate the movement.

Movement	Beat type	Meter type	Possible time signatures
I	_____	_____	_____
II	_____	_____	_____
III	_____	_____	_____
IV	_____	_____	_____
V	_____	_____	_____

G. Scale review. Given the scale degree, the note, and whether the key is major or minor, supply the name of the key. Assume melodic minor for all minor key examples.

ex. ↑6̂ is C♯ in __e__ minor

1. 4̂ is B♭ in ____ minor
2. 3̂ is B in ____ major
3. ↑7̂ is B♯ in ____ minor
4. 6̂ is F♯ in ____ major
5. 4̂ is E♭ in ____ major
6. 5̂ is G in ____ minor
7. 6̂ is B in ____ major

8. 5̂ is B♭ in ____ major
9. ↑6̂ is G♯ in ____ minor
10. 5̂ is C in ____ major
11. 3̂ is B♭ in ____ minor
12. ↓7̂ is E in ____ minor
13. 7̂ is D♯ in ____ major
14. 2̂ is B♭ in ____ major

H. Interval review. Notate the specified interval above the given note.

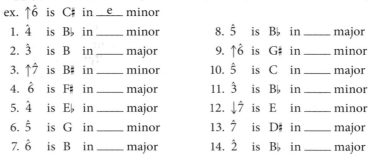

I. Interval review. Notate the specified interval below the given note.

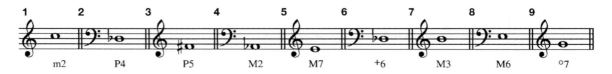

Exercise 2-4 See Workbook.

Summary

Rhythm refers to the time aspect of music, as contrasted with the pitch aspect. The relative duration of a musical sound is specified by a **durational symbol,** such as a whole note, half note, and so on. One or more **dots** may follow a durational symbol, each one adding to the duration one-half the value of the note or dot that precedes it; a **tie** connects two notes, creating a value equal to their sum. Most durational symbols use **stems,** and there are conventions of notation regarding the direction of the stems. **Beams** are often used to group together (but not to tie) durations shorter than a quarter note.

The basic pulse of a musical passage is called the **beat,** and the **tempo** is the rate at which the beats occur. The general tempo may be indicated by one of many terms in English or other languages, or it may be specified more exactly by a **metronome** marking.

Beats usually group into patterns of two, three, or four beats, referred to as **duple, triple,** and **quadruple meters,** respectively. Associated with each meter is its own pattern of **metric accents.** Beats in any meter usually divide into two equal parts (**simple beat**) or three equal parts (**compound beat**), giving rise to such terms as "triple simple" and "duple compound." A **tuplet** is used when a beat divides in a way that is contrary to the prevailing division of the beat. **Hypermeter** is the expression of a metric pattern at a higher level, as in groups of measures.

A **time signature** is a symbol that tells the performer the beat and meter types and what note value will represent the beat. A listener can identify the beat and meter types, but not the note value that represents the beat, just by listening to the music. The beat values for simple time signatures are always undotted notes, whereas those for compound time signatures are always dotted notes.

Variations

For additional review and practice, please see Chapter 2 on our website at
www.mhhe.com/kostka7e.

Chapter Three
Introduction to Triads and Seventh Chords

Introduction

In this chapter we begin working with chords, the basic vocabulary of tonal harmony. We will not be concerned at this stage with how chords are used compositionally or even what kinds of chords occur in the major and minor modes, although we will encounter these topics soon enough. First we have to learn how to spell the more common chord types and how to recognize them in various contexts.

Triads

In "To the Student" (pp. xi–xiv), we explained that tonal harmony makes use of **tertian** (built of 3rds) chords. The fundamental tertian sonority is the **triad,** a three-note chord consisting of a 5th divided into two superimposed 3rds. There are four possible ways to combine major and minor 3rds to produce a tertian triad.

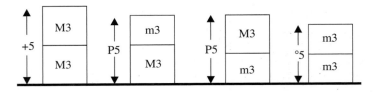

The names and abbreviations for these four triad types are given in Example 3-1.

Example 3-1

| augmented | major | minor | diminished |
| (+) | (M) | (m) | (°) |

Play these triads at the piano and compare the way they sound. You might be able to guess from listening to them that in tonal music the major and minor triads are found the most often, the augmented the least often. There are also names (in addition to note names) for the members of a triad (Ex. 3-2).

Example 3-2

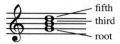

              — fifth
              — third
              — root

Study the preceding diagram and examples very carefully before going on.

CHECKPOINT

1. Which triad types contain a m3 as the bottom interval? As the top interval?
2. Which triad types contain a M3 as the top interval? As the bottom interval?
3. Which triad types contain a P5 between the root and the 5th? a °5? a +5?

Self-Test 3-1

(Answers begin on page 559.)

A. Spell the triad, given the root and the type. Major triads are indicated by an uppercase letter (G), minor by an uppercase letter followed by the letter "m" (Gm), augmented by a "+" (G+), and diminished by a "°" (G°).

1. B♭m _____   7. A _____
2. E _____   8. Dm _____
3. G° _____   9. G♭ _____
4. F° _____   10. B _____
5. Cm _____   11. A♭m _____
6. D+ _____   12. C♯m _____

B. Notate the triad, given the root and type.

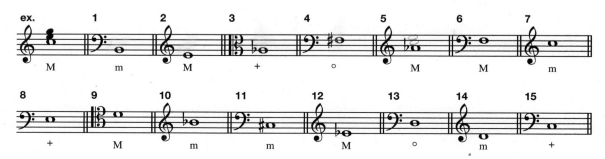

ex. M   1. m   2. M   3. +   4. °   5. M   6. M   7. m

8. +   9. M   10. m   11. m   12. M   13. °   14. m   15. +

C. Fill in the blanks.

	ex.	1.	2.	3.	4.	5.	6.	7.	8.	9.	10.
Fifth	F	___	___	___	D♯	___	___	___	___	G♯	B
Third	D	A	G♭	___	___	___	F♯	C♯	___	___	___
Root	B♭	___	___	B	___	C♭	___	___	F	___	___
Type	M	+	m	m	+	M	°	M	°	m	M

D. Given the chord quality and one member of the triad, notate the remainder of the triad, with the root as the lowest tone.

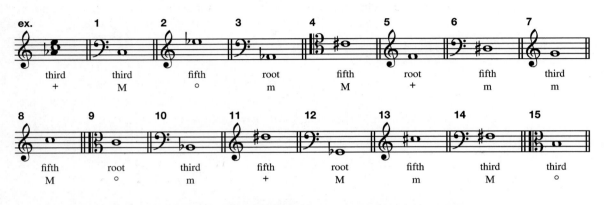

ex.	1	2	3	4	5	6	7
third	third	fifth	root	fifth	root	fifth	third
+	M	°	m	M	+	m	m

8	9	10	11	12	13	14	15
fifth	root	third	fifth	root	fifth	third	third
M	°	m	+	M	m	M	°

Exercise 3-1 See Workbook.

Seventh Chords

If we extend a tertian triad by adding another 3rd on top of the 5th of the triad, the result is a four-note chord. Because the interval between this added note and the root is some kind of 7th (major, minor, or diminished), chords of this sort are called **seventh chords.**

Because it would be possible to use more than one kind of 7th with each triad type, there are many more seventh-chord types than triad types. However, tonal harmony commonly makes use of only five seventh-chord types (Ex. 3-3). Below each chord in Example 3-3 you will find the commonly used name for each chord and the symbol used as an abbreviation. Be sure to play Example 3-3 to familiarize yourself with the sound of these chords.

Example 3-3

Type of chord:	major seventh	major-minor seventh	minor seventh
Symbol:	M7	Mm7	m7
Construction:	major triad	major triad	minor triad
	major 7th	minor 7th	minor 7th

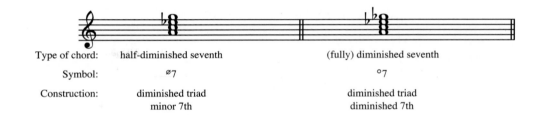

Type of chord:	half-diminished seventh	(fully) diminished seventh
Symbol:	⌀7	°7
Construction:	diminished triad	diminished triad
	minor 7th	diminished 7th

Quite soon we will begin composition exercises using triads. Although seventh chords will not be used in composition exercises for some time, you will nevertheless begin to become familiar with them from an analytical standpoint through examples and analysis assignments.

CHECKPOINT

1. Which seventh-chord types have a diminished triad on the bottom?
2. Which ones have a M3 between the 5th and the 7th of the chord?
3. Which ones have a m3 between the 3rd and the 5th of the chord?
4. Which ones contain at least one P5? Which contain two?
5. Which one consists entirely of a stack of minor thirds?

Self-Test 3-2

(Answers begin on page 560.)

A. Identify the type of each seventh chord, using the abbreviations given in Example 3-3 (M7, Mm7, m7, ⌀7, °7).

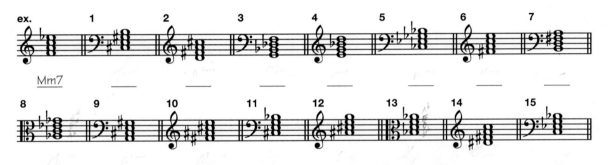

B. Notate the seventh chord, given the root and type.

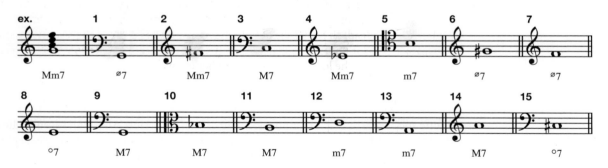

C. Given the seventh chord quality and one member of the chord, notate the rest of the chord.

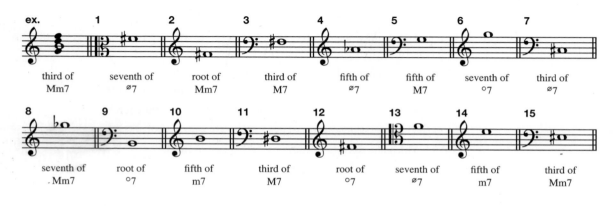

Exercise 3-2 See Workbook.

This would be an appropriate point at which to begin work on Counterpoint Unit 1, which can be found at www.mhhe.com/kostka7e.

Inversions of Chords

Up to now, we have been notating all chords with the root as the lowest tone. However, in a musical context, any part of a chord might appear as the lowest tone. The three possible **bass positions** of the triad are illustrated in Example 3-4.

Example 3-4

The bass position that we have been using, with the root as the lowest tone (or "in the bass"), is called **root position.** You might assume that "third position" would be the term for a chord with the 3rd as the lowest tone, but musical terminology is fraught with inconsistencies. Instead, this position is called **first inversion.** Reasonably enough, **second inversion** is used for chords with the 5th in the bass. The term **inversion** is used here to mean the transfer of the lowest note to any higher octave.

Example 3-5

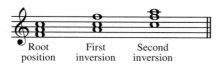

The inversion of seventh chords works just like the inversion of triads, except that three inversions (four bass positions) are possible (Ex. 3-7).

All the chords in Example 3-6 are F major triads in first inversion. Notice that the upper notes of the chord can be spaced in any way without altering the bass position. Also, any of the notes can be duplicated (or **doubled**) in different octaves.

Example 3-6

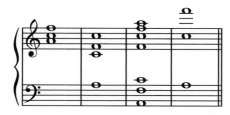

(All are in first inversion)

The inversion of seventh chords works just like the inversion of triads, except that three inversions (four bass positions) are possible (Ex. 3-7).

Example 3-7

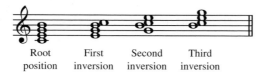

It is important to understand that the inversion of a triad or seventh chord is determined only by what member of the chord is in the *bass;* any chord members may appear in the soprano or in the other voices without changing the inversion.

Inversion Symbols and Figured Bass

In analyzing music we often use numbers to indicate the bass positions of chords. Instead of using 1 for first inversion, 2 for second inversion, and so on, we use numbers derived from the Baroque system called **figured bass** or **thoroughbass.** During the Baroque period (approximately 1600–1750), the keyboard player in an ensemble read from a part consisting only of a bass line and some symbols indicating the chord to be played above each bass note.

In the Baroque system, the symbols consisted basically of numbers representing intervals above the bass to be formed by the members of the chord, but the notes could actually be played in any octave above the bass. The system dealt only with intervals, not with roots of chords, because the theory of chord roots had not been devised when figured bass was first developed.

The following table illustrates the figured-bass symbols for root position and inverted triads and seventh chords for a G major triad and a G Mm 7.

Sonority desired							
Complete figured bass symbol	5 3	6 3	6 4	7 5 3	6 5 3	6 4 3	6 4 2
Symbol most often used		6	6 4	7	6 5	4 3	4 2
How to find the root	Bass note	6th above bass	4th above bass	Bass note	6th above bass	4th above bass	2nd above bass

The Baroque keyboardist reading a figured bass followed the key signature unless told to do otherwise. So a root position triad, for example, might be major, minor, or diminished, depending upon the key signature. If the Baroque composer wanted to direct the keyboard player to raise or lower a note, several methods could be used, including the following three.

1. An accidental next to an arabic numeral in the figured bass could be used to raise or lower a note.

2. An accidental by itself always referred to the 3rd above the bass and could be used to alter that note.

3. A slash or plus sign in connection with an arabic numeral meant to raise that note.

Another symbol that you will occasionally encounter is a horizontal line, usually short, meaning to keep the same note or chord. For instance, $\frac{5}{3}\frac{6}{\_}$ over a bass note means to use the same bass note for a root position triad followed by one in first inversion.

Example 3-8 illustrates a portion of an actual figured bass part from the Baroque period, along with a possible **realization** that would have been improvised by the keyboardist. Some keyboard players may have added embellishments not shown in this realization. Bach included the numeral 5 at several places to remind the player to play a root position triad.

Example 3-8   Bach, *Easter Oratorio*, II

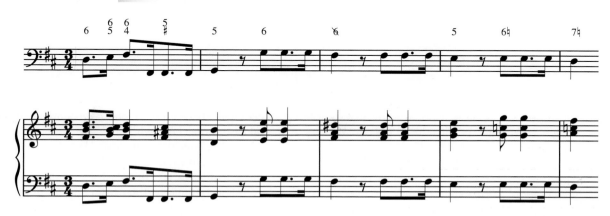

The realization of figured basses is still considered to be an effective way to learn certain aspects of tonal composition, and we will occasionally use exercises of this kind in the text.

A few figured-bass symbols have been adopted for use in harmonic analysis. We call these **bass-position symbols** to distinguish them from figured bass, which is not the same thing. Bass-position symbols are usually used with a roman numeral (as in I⁶ or V⁶₅) as part of a harmonic analysis. (Roman-numeral analysis is explained in the next chapter.) Notice that when a seventh chord is inverted, the 7 is replaced by the appropriate bass-position symbol.

Bass position	Triad symbol	Seventh chord symbol
Root position	(none)	7
~~Root position~~ 1ˢᵗ Inversion	6	$\frac{6}{5}$
Second inversion	$\frac{6}{4}$	$\frac{4}{3}$
Third inversion	(none)	$\frac{4}{2}$ (or 2)

Lead-Sheet Symbols

There are some intriguing parallels and contrasts between the figured-bass system of the seventeenth and eighteenth centuries and the lead-sheet symbols (sometimes called pop symbols) developed for use with jazz and other types of popular music in the twentieth and twenty-first centuries. Both facilitated the notation process and served to provide sufficient information to allow the performer to improvise within certain bounds. However, whereas the figured-bass system provided the bass line with symbols indicating the chords that were to be constructed *above* it, lead-sheet symbols appear along with a melody and indicate the chords that are to be constructed *below*.

Example 3-9 illustrates some **lead-sheet symbols** for the nine chord types that we have studied so far, along with some commonly used alternatives. Other chords and alternate symbols can be found in Appendix B in the back of this book.

Example 3-9

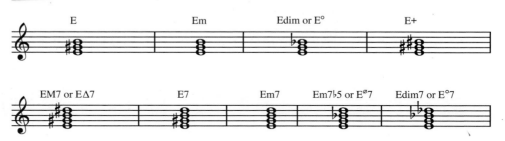

The list of symbols in Example 3-9 is incomplete because there are some chords that will be introduced in later chapters. A special case is the chord with an added sixth, as in C6, which calls for a triad with an added note a M6 above the root. Also, lead-sheet symbols will occasionally specify a particular bass note, as in C/G, which calls for a C major triad over a G in the bass—a triad in second inversion. This is called slash-chord notation. Finally, you may discover that lead-sheet symbols frequently differ from one edition to the next because editors and arrangers routinely make substitutions, simplifying or complicating the harmony as they see fit.

The top staff of Example 3-10 is from the beginning of a typical American "standard" ballad, and it uses five of the chord types seen in Example 3-9. The bottom staff shows the chords in close position, but they would be voiced differently by a jazz pianist. Notice that the ♭ in F♯m7♭5 does not literally mean to flat the fifth of the chord, but to lower it a half step—in this case from C♯ to C♮.

DISC 1 : TRACK 1

Example 3-10   Kosma, "Autumn Leaves"

Lead-sheet symbols can be a very helpful first step toward a harmonic analysis, and we will occasionally give you practice with them in self-tests and exercises.

Self-Test 3-3

(Answers begin on page 561.)

A. Identify the root and type of each chord, and show the correct bass-position symbol (Bps).

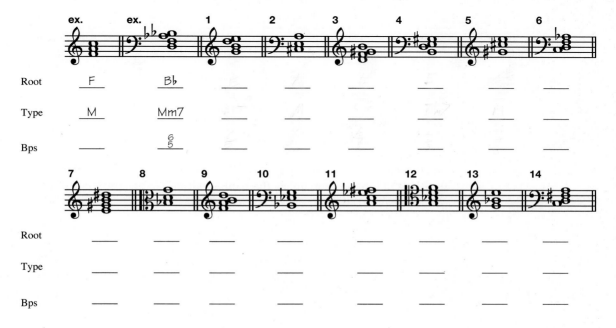

	ex.	ex.	1	2	3	4	5	6
Root	F	B♭	___	___	___	___	___	___
Type	M	Mm7	___	___	___	___	___	___
Bps	___	$\frac{6}{5}$	___	___	___	___	___	___

	7	8	9	10	11	12	13	14
Root	___	___	___	___	___	___	___	___
Type	___	___	___	___	___	___	___	___
Bps	___	___	___	___	___	___	___	___

B. The bottom staff of this recitative is played on bassoon and keyboard, the keyboard player (the "continuo") realizing the figured bass. Fill in each blank below the bass line with the lead-sheet symbol of the chord to be played at that point, using slash-chord notation for inverted chords, as in the example. Remember that a numeral 5 by itself is simply a reminder to use a root position triad.

Bach, *Easter Oratorio,* II

DISC 1 : TRACK 2

lebt,   und un-ser   Herz,   so erst in   Trau-rig-keit zer-flos-sen und ge -   schwebt, ver-gisst den Schmerz   und

sinnt auf   Freu -   den-lie - der;   denn un-ser   Hei - land   le - bet   wie - der.

C. Notate on the bottom staff the chords indicated by the lead-sheet symbols. Notate all chords in root position unless the symbol calls for an inversion. A 6 after a chord symbol means to add a note a M6 above the root.

Hendricks and Adderley, "Sermonette"

I   heard   me   a   Ser - mon - ette,____   have   you   heard   it   yet___

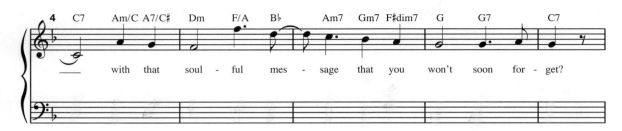

____   with   that   soul - ful   mes - sage   that   you   won't   soon   for - get?

Exercise 3-3 See Workbook.

Recognizing Chords in Various Textures

Some students, especially those without much keyboard experience, find it difficult at first to analyze a chord that is distributed over two or more staves, as in Example 3-11.

Example 3-11

Example 3-12

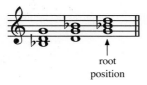

root
position

One procedure to follow with the chord is to make an inventory of all the **pitch classes*** found in the chord (B♭, G, and D) and to notate the chord with each pitch class in turn as the lowest note. The other notes should be put as close to the bottom note as possible. The version that consists only of stacked 3rds is in root position. We can see from Example 3-12 that the chord in Example 3-11 is a g minor triad in first inversion.

The chord in Example 3-13 contains the pitch classes E, A, C♯, and G, allowing four bass positions.

Example 3-13

Example 3-14 tells us that the chord in Example 3-13 is an A major-minor seventh chord in second inversion.

---

* The term *pitch class* is used to group together all pitches that have an identical sound or that are identical except for the octave or octaves that separate them. For example, all B♯s, Cs and D♭♭s belong to the same pitch class, no matter what octave they are found in.

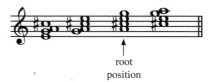

Example 3-14

root
position

You might already be able to carry out this process in your head, which will speed things up considerably. If not, you will learn to do so with practice.

CHECKPOINT

1. What is the symbol for the first inversion of a triad? Of a seventh chord?
2. Explain $\frac{4}{2}$, $\frac{6}{4}$, and $\frac{4}{3}$.
3. Which bass position for which chord type requires no symbol?

Self-Test 3-4

(Answers begin on page 562.)

A. Label each chord with an appropriate lead-sheet symbol in the space above the chord. Use slash-chord notation for inverted chords. All of the notes in each exercise belong to the same chord.

B. Provide the root, type, and bass-position symbol (Bps) for each chord in the following excerpt. Each chord is numbered. Put your analysis of the chords in the blanks below each excerpt.

1. Fischer, *Blumen-Strauss*

DISC 1 : TRACK 3

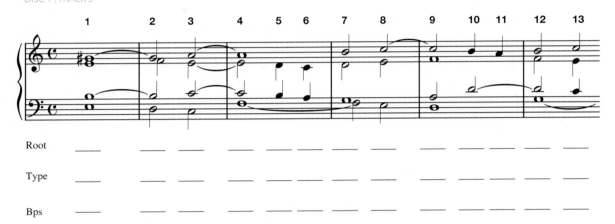

Root ____ ____ ____ ____ ____ ____ ____ ____ ____ ____ ____ ____ ____

Type ____ ____ ____ ____ ____ ____ ____ ____ ____ ____ ____ ____ ____

Bps ____ ____ ____ ____ ____ ____ ____ ____ ____ ____ ____ ____ ____

DISC 1 : TRACK 3

2. Byrd, *Psalm LIV*

The *8* under the treble clef on the tenor staff (third staff from the top) means that the notes are to be sung an 8ve lower than written.

Root ____ ____ ____ ____ ____ ____ ____

Type ____ ____ ____ ____ ____ ____ ____

Bps ____ ____ ____ ____ ____ ____ ____

DISC 1 : TRACK 3

3. Schumann, *Wiegenliedchen*, op. 124, no. 6
   (Note: Chord 14 is missing an A.)

Root

Type

Bps

C. Time signature review. Fill in the blanks.

	Beat and meter type	Beat note	Division of the beat	Time signature
1.	Compound duple		♫♫♫	
2.				$\frac{2}{2}$
3.			♫♫	4
4.		♩.		12

Exercise 3-4 See Workbook.

Summary

The fundamental sonority of tonal harmony is the **triad,** a three-note chord consisting of a 5th divided into two superimposed 3rds. The bottom note of the 5th is the **root,** and the top note is the **5th.** The note that divides the 5th is the **3rd.** There are four triad types: **major, minor, diminished,** and **augmented.**

A **seventh chord** may be thought of as a triad with another 3rd added above the 5th of the triad. The added note is a 7th above the root. Although many seventh chord types are possible, only five occur with any frequency in tonal harmony:

major seventh chord (M7): major triad with a M7 above the root

major-minor seventh chord (Mm7): major triad with a m7 above the root

minor seventh chord (m7): minor triad with a m7 above the root

half-diminished seventh chord ($^{\varnothing}$7): diminished triad with a m7 above the root

diminished seventh chord ($^{\circ}$7): diminished triad with a $^{\circ}$7 above the root

Root position is the term for a chord with the root notated as the lowest tone. Any other arrangement is called an **inversion.** A chord with the 3rd as the lowest tone is in **first inversion,** whereas one with the 5th as the lowest tone is in **second inversion.** A seventh chord with the 7th as the lowest tone is in **third inversion.** There are symbols for most of the various bass positions:

Bass position	Triad symbol	Seventh-chord symbol	Bass note
Root position	none	7	root
First inversion	6	$\frac{6}{5}$	third
Second inversion	$\frac{6}{4}$	$\frac{4}{3}$	fifth
Third inversion	n/a	$\frac{4}{2}$	seventh

Inversion symbols are derived from **figured bass,** a method of abbreviated notation used in the Baroque era. **Lead-sheet symbols** are used in jazz and most popular music to indicate chords to be played under a given melody. Both figured-bass symbols and lead-sheet (pop) symbols will be used occasionally throughout much of this text.

Variations

OLC

For additional review and practice, please see Chapter 3 on our website at **www.mhhe.com/kostka7e.**

Chapter Four
Diatonic Chords in Major and Minor Keys

Introduction

Now that we have presented the four triad types and the five common seventh-chord types, we can begin to look at how they are used in tonal music, which is really what most of this book is about. Most chords in tonal music are made up only of notes from the scale on which the passage is based. That is, if a passage is in G major, most of the chords contain only notes found in the G major scale. Chords of this kind are called **diatonic** chords. All other chords—those using notes not in the scale—are called **altered** or **chromatic** chords. We will get to them later. At this point we are not going to worry about how you might *compose* music using diatonic chords, although that will come up soon. For now, we are going to concentrate on spelling and recognizing diatonic chords in various keys.

Diatonic Triads in Major

Triads may be constructed using any degree of the major scale as the root. (You might need to review scale degree names, which were introduced on p. 15, because they will be used more frequently from this point on.) Diatonic triads, as we have mentioned, will consist only of notes belonging to the scale. To distinguish the triads built on the various scale degrees from the scale degrees themselves, we use roman numerals instead of arabic numerals (for example, V instead of $\hat{5}$). The triad type is indicated by the form of the roman numeral.

Triad type	Roman numeral	Example
Major	Uppercase	V
Minor	Lowercase	vi
Diminished	Lowercase with a °	vii°
Augmented	Uppercase with a +	III+

Taking C major as an example, we can discover the types of diatonic triads that occur on each degree of the major scale.

Example 4-1

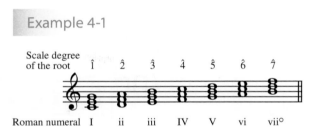

Scale degree of the root $\hat{1}$ $\hat{2}$ $\hat{3}$ $\hat{4}$ $\hat{5}$ $\hat{6}$ $\hat{7}$

Roman numeral   I   ii   iii   IV   V   vi   vii°

You should memorize the following table.

DIATONIC TRIAD TYPES IN MAJOR

Major	I, IV, and V
Minor	ii, iii, and vi
Diminished	vii°
Augmented	none

The Minor Scale

Before we can begin talking about diatonic chords in minor, we have to return to the subject of the minor scale. Because instrumentalists are taught to practice natural, harmonic, and melodic minor scales, we sometimes assume that the tonal composer had three independent minor scale forms from which to choose, but this is not at all how the minor mode works in tonal music.

We can make the following generalization about the three minor scales: there is, in a sense, one minor scale that has two scale steps, $\hat{6}$ and $\hat{7}$, that are variable. That is, there are two versions of $\hat{6}$ and $\hat{7}$, and both versions will usually appear in a piece in the minor mode. All the notes in Example 4-2 are diatonic to e minor. Notice the use of $\uparrow\hat{6}$ and $\uparrow\hat{7}$ to mean raised $\hat{6}$ and $\hat{7}$ and $\downarrow\hat{6}$ and $\downarrow\hat{7}$ to mean unaltered $\hat{6}$ and $\hat{7}$.

Example 4-2

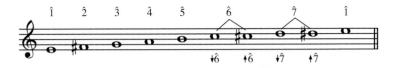

$\hat{1}$ $\hat{2}$ $\hat{3}$ $\hat{4}$ $\hat{5}$ $\hat{6}$ $\hat{7}$ $\hat{1}$

$\downarrow\hat{6}$ $\uparrow\hat{6}$ $\downarrow\hat{7}$ $\uparrow\hat{7}$

How do composers decide which version of $\hat{6}$ and $\hat{7}$ to use? Melodically, the most graceful thing for $\uparrow\hat{6}$ and $\uparrow\hat{7}$ to do is to ascend by step, whereas $\downarrow\hat{6}$ and $\downarrow\hat{7}$ tend naturally to descend by step; these tendencies conform to the melodic minor scale. Example 4-3 provides a good illustration of the use of the minor scale. If you look closely at Bach's treatment of $\hat{6}$ and $\hat{7}$ (circled notes), you will see that all the motion is stepwise, with two exceptions. The first leap involving $\hat{6}$ or $\hat{7}$ is from the G♭4 in m. 2. Here the eventual goal is F, not A, so the $\downarrow\hat{6}$ form is used. The other leap occurs in the bass in m. 4. Here the goal of the line is B♭, not G♭, so the $\uparrow\hat{7}$ form is used.

Example 4-3   Bach, *Well-Tempered Clavier*, Book II, Prelude 22

If a $\hat{6}$ or $\hat{7}$ is left by leap instead of by step, there will generally be an *eventual* stepwise goal for that scale degree, and the $\hat{6}$ and $\hat{7}$ will probably be raised or left unaltered according to the direction of that goal, as in Example 4-3. In the next excerpt, Example 4-4, the A♭4 in m. 1 ($\downarrow\hat{6}$) is left by leap to the C5, but the eventual stepwise goal of the A♭4 is the G4 in the next measure, so the descending form of the melodic minor is used. Still, the use of the melodic minor is just a guideline, not a rule. It is not difficult to find passages in minor where $\uparrow\hat{6}$ and $\uparrow\hat{7}$ lead downward, as in m. 3.

Example 4-4   Bach, *Well-Tempered Clavier*, Book I, Fugue 2

And, in some cases, $\downarrow\hat{6}$ and $\downarrow\hat{7}$ lead upward (Ex. 4-5).

Example 4-5   Bach, *Well-Tempered Clavier*, Book I, Prelude 10

In other instances, $\uparrow\hat{7}$ and $\downarrow\hat{6}$ appear next to each other, forming a harmonic minor scale (Ex. 4-6).

Example 4-6   Beethoven, Piano Sonata op. 2, no. 2, III, Trio

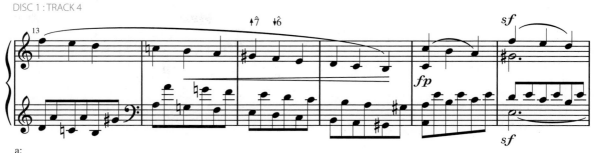

The reasons for such exceptions to the typical tendencies of $\hat{6}$ and $\hat{7}$ are usually harmonic. As we shall see soon, most of the underlying harmonies in minor conform to the harmonic minor scale.

CHECKPOINT

1. What is the term for chords that contain no notes outside of the scale? What about chords that do contain such notes?
2. Individual lines in tonal music tend to conform most closely to which of the three traditional minor scales?
3. Name the five common seventh-chord types.

Diatonic Triads in Minor

The construction of triads is somewhat more involved in the minor mode than in major. Because $\hat{6}$ and $\hat{7}$ are variable, and because nearly all triads contain $\hat{6}$ or $\hat{7}$, more diatonic triads are possible in minor. Nonetheless, there are seven triads in minor (one for each scale degree) that occur more frequently than the others, and these are the ones we will use in our exercises for now. The roman numerals of the more common diatonic triads are circled in Example 4-7.

Example 4-7

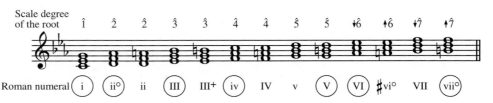

Notice that the *roots* of the triads circled in Example 4-7 all belong to the *harmonic* minor scale. In fact, all the notes of the circled triads belong to the harmonic minor scale, with the exception of the 5th of the III chord. Following is the table of minor-key triads, which you should also memorize.

COMMON DIATONIC TRIADS IN MINOR

Major	III, V, and VI
Minor	i and iv
Diminished	ii° and vii°
Augmented	none

CHECKPOINT

1. In a major key, which triads are minor?
2. In a minor key, which triads are major?
3. The triads on which two scale degrees are the same type in both major and minor?
4. Which of the four triad types occurs least often in tonal music?

Self-Test 4-1

(Answers begin on page 563.)

A. Given the key and the triad, supply the roman numeral *below* the staff. Be sure your roman numeral is of the correct type (correct case and so on), and include bass-position symbols (^{6} or $^6_4$) where needed. Finally, provide an appropriate lead-sheet symbol *above* the staff, using slash-chord notation where appropriate.

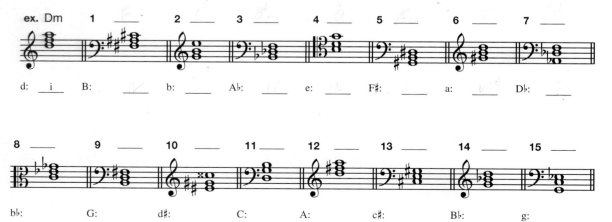

B. In the following exercises you are given the name of a key and a scale degree number. *Without using key signatures,* notate the triad on that scale degree in root position and provide the roman numeral. In minor keys be sure to use the triad types circled in Example 4-7.

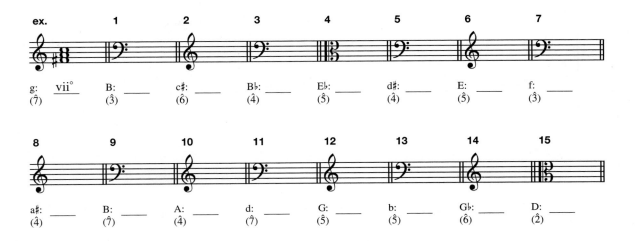

C. Analysis. Write roman numerals in the spaces provided, making sure each roman numeral is of the correct type and includes a bass-position symbol if needed. The tenor line sounds an octave lower than notated.

Brahms, *Ach lieber Herre Jesu Christ*

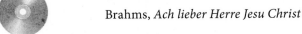

DISC 1 : TRACK 5

D. Fill in the blanks, using the example as a model.

	Key	This chord	Has this bass note
Ex.	C	V^6	B
1.	___	$ii^{\circ 6}$	G
2.	A	IV^6_4	___
3.	f	$vii^{\circ 6}$	___
4.	___	I^6_4	F
5.	e	V^6_4	___
6.	B	V^6	___

Exercise 4-1 See Workbook.

Diatonic Seventh Chords in Major

In the next chapter we will begin simple composition exercises using triads, but seventh chords will not be used compositionally until later. Nevertheless, we will continue to work with seventh chords in spelling exercises and in analysis to build a solid foundation for those later chapters.

The chords on each scale degree in major can include a 7th above the root. The roman-numeral system for seventh chords is similar to that for triads, as you will see in the following table.

Seventh-chord type	Roman numeral	Example
Major seventh	Uppercase with M7	I^{M7}
Major-minor seventh	Uppercase with a 7	V^7
Minor seventh	Lowercase with a 7	vi^7
Half-diminished seventh	Lowercase with ⌀7	$ii^{\varnothing 7}$
Diminished seventh	Lowercase with °7	$vii^{\circ 7}$

Four of the five seventh-chord types occur as diatonic seventh chords in major keys.

Example 4-8

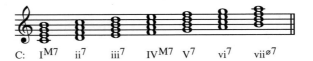

C: I^M7   ii^7   iii^7   IV^M7   V^7   vi^7   vii^ø7

You should learn the following table, which summarizes major-key seventh chords.

DIATONIC SEVENTH CHORDS IN MAJOR

M7	I^M7 and IV^M7
Mm7	V^7
m7	ii^7, iii^7, and vi^7
ø7	vii^ø7
°7	none

Diatonic Seventh Chords in Minor

Because of the variability of $\hat{6}$ and $\hat{7}$, there are 16 possible diatonic seventh chords in minor. Example 4-9 shows only the most commonly used seventh chords on each scale degree. Most of the others will be discussed in later chapters. Notice that most of the notes in Example 4-9 belong to the harmonic minor scale.

Example 4-9

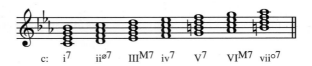

c: i^7   ii^ø7   III^M7   iv^7   V^7   VI^M7   vii°^7

Here is the last chord table to learn.

COMMON DIATONIC SEVENTH CHORDS IN MINOR

M7	III^M7 and VI^M7
Mm7	V^7
m7	i^7 and iv^7
ø7	ii^ø7
°7	vii°^7

Remember that the bass-position symbols for inverted seventh chords are $^6_5$, $^4_3$, and $^4_2$. This means that the V^7 in first inversion is symbolized as V^6_5, *not* as V^7_6. Also, remember that the symbol for a minor seventh chord does not include a lowercase "m." For instance, use ii^7, not ii^{m7}.

✓ CHECKPOINT

1. Most of the five common seventh-chord types appear diatonically in both major and minor. Which one type does not?

2. Does the m7 chord occur on more scale steps in minor than in major?

3. The seventh chords on most scale steps are different qualities in major and minor. Which scale step is the exception to this?

Self-Test 4-2

(Answers begin on page 564.)

A. Given the key and the seventh chord, supply the roman numeral *below* the staff. Be sure your roman numeral is of the correct type, and include bass-position symbols where needed. Finally, provide an appropriate lead-sheet symbol *above* the staff.

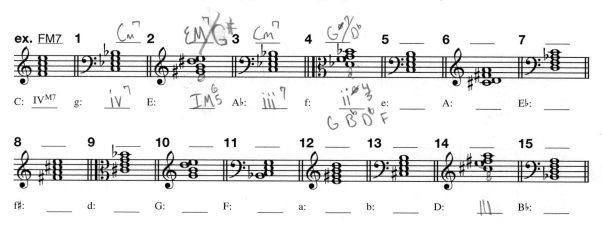

B. In the exercises that follow, you are given the name of a key and a scale degree number. *Without using key signatures,* notate the seventh chord on that scale degree in root position and provide the roman numeral. In minor keys be sure to use the chord types shown in Example 4-9.

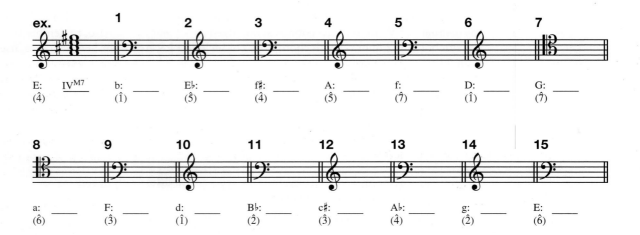

C. Analysis. Put roman numerals in the spaces provided, making sure each roman numeral is of the correct type and includes a bass-position symbol if needed.

1. Bach, *Nun lob', mein' Seel', den Herren*

DISC 1 : TRACK 5

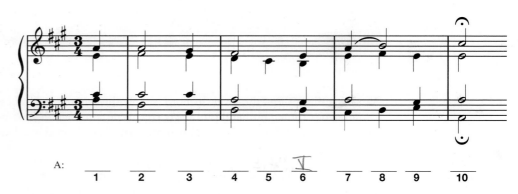

2. Schumann, Chorale op. 68, no. 4

D G B E

DISC 1 : TRACK 5

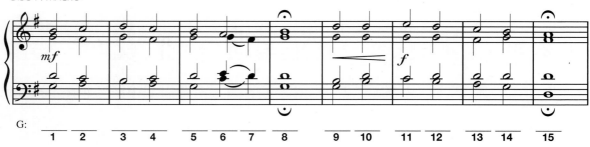

Exercise 4-2 See Workbook.

Summary

Minor scale usage in tonal music is not really based on the natural, harmonic, and melodic minor scales, the three traditional minor scale forms presented in Chapter 1. In actual practice, scale steps $\hat{6}$ and $\hat{7}$ are variable. Although ascending and descending lines usually follow the conventions of the melodic minor scale, this is by no means always true. Both melodic and harmonic considerations must be taken into account.

We analyze the triads and seventh chords used in tonal music by means of *roman numerals* indicating the scale degree that is the root of the chord and the quality, or sound, of the chord. Although the issue of the minor scale is somewhat complicated, we can say that as a rule the following triad types are found on the various degrees of the major and minor scales:

Major	I	ii	iii	IV	V	vi	vii°
Minor	i	ii°	III	iv	V	VI	vii°

Similarly, we can generalize about the types of seventh chords:

Major	I^{M7}	ii^7	iii^7	IV^{M7}	V^7	vi^7	$vii^{ø7}$
Minor	i^7	$ii^{ø7}$	III^{M7}	iv^7	V^7	VI^{M7}	$vii^{°7}$

The roots of the triads and seventh chords in the minor mode portions of these tables all conform to the harmonic minor scale, but this is not necessarily true of the other notes in each chord.

In this chapter we have been concerned only with how diatonic triads and seventh chords are spelled in tonal music. The more interesting and more complex topic of how they actually function in relation to each other will be the subject of later chapters.

Variations

For additional review and practice, please see Chapter 4 on our website at **www.mhhe.com/kostka7e.**

Chapter Five
Principles of Voice Leading

Introduction

The compositional process, being a creative one, is not entirely understood. It is reasonable to assume that a composer thinks of several aspects more or less simultaneously—melody, harmony, rhythm, and so on. Naturally, a complete analysis of a composition must take all these factors into account. For the most part, however, this text concentrates on questions relating to the harmonic aspect of tonal music because it is this aspect that most clearly delineates tonal music from other types.

We could say that the basic vocabulary of tonal harmony consists of triads and seventh chords and that its grammar involves the ways in which these chords are selected (**harmonic progression**) and connected (**voice leading**). In this chapter and the next we will concentrate on some of the basics of the voice-leading aspect: How does a composer write out a given succession of chords for some combination of performers? How does he or she decide in which direction each vocal or instrumental line should go?

Voice leading (or **part writing**) may be defined as the ways in which chords are produced by the motions of individual musical lines. A closely related term is **counterpoint**, which refers to the combining of relatively independent musical lines. Naturally, the style of voice leading will depend on the composer, the musical effect desired, and the performing medium (for example, it is easier to play a large melodic interval on the piano than it is to sing it). However, there are certain voice-leading norms that most tonal composers follow most of the time, and our study will concentrate on these norms.

The Melodic Line

Our beginning exercises will make use of short and simple melodies in vocal style in order to avoid, for now, the complications involved with more ornate vocal and instrumental melodies. The following procedures should be followed for Chapters 5 through 9.

1. **Rhythm.** Keep the rhythm simple, with most durations being equal to or longer than the duration of the beat. The final note should occur on a strong beat.

2. **Harmony.** Every melody note should belong to the chord that is to harmonize it.

3. **Contour.** The melody should be primarily **conjunct** (stepwise). The shape of the melody should be interesting but clear and simple, with a single **focal point,** the highest note of the melody.

Example 5-1a is a good example of the points discussed so far. Example 5-1b is not as good because it has an uninteresting contour. Example 5-1c, although more interesting, lacks a single focal point and contains one incorrectly harmonized tone (E5).

Example 5-1

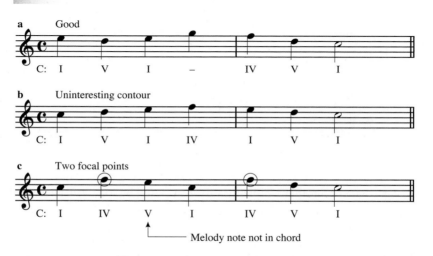

4. **Leaps.**
   a. Avoid augmented intervals, 7ths, and intervals larger than a P8. Diminished intervals may be used if the melody changes direction by step immediately after the interval.
   b. A melodic interval larger than a P4 is usually best approached and left in the direction *opposite* to the leap.
   c. When smaller leaps are used consecutively in the same direction, they should outline a triad.

5. **Tendency tones.** In tonal music $\hat{7}$ has a strong tendency to move up to $\hat{1}$. An exception to this is the scalewise line descending from $\hat{1}$: $\hat{1}$–$\hat{7}$–$\hat{6}$–$\hat{5}$. The only other tendency tone that needs to be considered is $\hat{4}$, which often moves down to $\hat{3}$, but not with the regularity with which $\hat{7}$ goes to $\hat{1}$.

Example 5-2a illustrates a good melody in the restricted style with which we are beginning. Example 5-2b, on the other hand, breaks all of rule 4 as well as rule 5.

Example 5-2

The melodic style we have outlined in the previous pages is admittedly a very restricted one, but it is a good place to start. Melodies such as these can be found in hymn tunes, for instance, as in the next two examples. In Example 5-3 we show part of one such melody along with Handel's harmonization.

Example 5-3   Melody from the *Gross Kirchen Gesangbuch* (1596)

Part of another simple melody, composed by Johann Crüger and harmonized by K. H. Graun, is seen in Example 5-4.

Example 5-4   Crüger, *Herzliebster Jesu, was hast du*

Even a more elaborate melody has a simpler background that may resemble the style of melodies we have been talking about. Example 5-5a illustrates the framework behind the original in Example 5-5b. Because Example 5-5b is an elaboration, it contains notes that do not belong to the underlying chords.

DISC 1 : TRACK 6

Example 5-5   Bach, French Suite no. 3, Gigue

i   V   i   V   i   ii°   V   i

Self-Test 5-1

(Answers begin on page 565.)

A. Criticize each melody in terms of the rules for simple melodies discussed under "The Melodic Line" on pages 66–68.

1

G: I   V   I   IV   V   I   IV   V   I

2

B♭:   I   –   V   I   IV   V   I   V   I

3

d: i   iv   V   i   iv   V   i   –   iv   V   i

B. Compose simple melodies that will conform to the given progressions. Slashes represent bar lines, and every chord except the last takes one beat.

1. D: I   V   I   /   IV   I   I   /   vi   ii   V   /   I   //
2. e: i   iv   i   i   /   V   V   i   i   /   iv   V   i   //
3. F: I   V   vi   IV   /   I   IV   ii   V   /   I   //

Exercise 5-1   See Workbook.

Notating Chords

A **musical score** is a tool used by a composer, conductor, or analyst. A score shows all the parts of an ensemble arranged one above the other, enabling the experienced reader to "hear" what the composition will sound like. In a **full score** all or most of the parts are notated on their own individual staves. Any musician should be able both to read and to prepare a full score, and some of your theory exercises should be done in full score. However, a **reduced score,** notated at concert pitch on as few staves as possible, might be more practical for daily theory exercises. Your choice of full or reduced score will depend partly on the sort of musical texture that the exercise will use. That is, if you are composing for four parts in chorale style, two staves will probably suffice. On the other hand, four active and independent instrumental lines might require four staves.

When you are notating more than one part on a single staff, be sure that the stems of the top part always point up and those of the bottom point down, even if the parts have crossed. Example 5-6 illustrates some common notational errors. The score in this case is the familiar SATB (Soprano, Alto, Tenor, Bass) reduced score.

Example 5-6

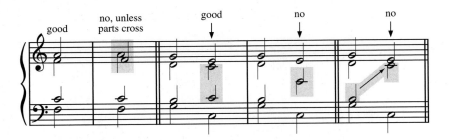

Voicing a Single Triad

After you have settled on the combination of instruments and voices for which you are writing and have selected the opening chord, the next consideration is **voicing:** how the chord is to be distributed or spaced. The way in which a chord is spaced has a great deal of influence on its aural effect. To convince yourself of this, play Example 5-7 at the piano. Each chord in the example contains five parts and covers the same range, but the aural effects are quite different. An even wider variety of effects could be obtained by playing Example 5-7 on various combinations of instruments. Although each of these spacings might be appropriate under certain circumstances, the spacing in Example 5-7e is the least commonly used because of its "muddy" effect.

Example 5-7

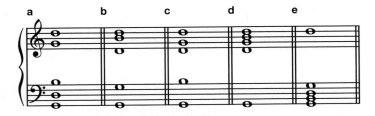

Because so much attention has been paid to four-part textures by authors of harmony texts, a terminology concerning the voicing of chords in four-part textures has been developed:

Close structure: less than an octave between soprano and tenor

Open structure: an octave or more between soprano and tenor

Example 5-8 illustrates these spacings in traditional hymn style.

DISC 1 : TRACK 6

Example 5-8 "Old One Hundredth" (Protestant hymn)

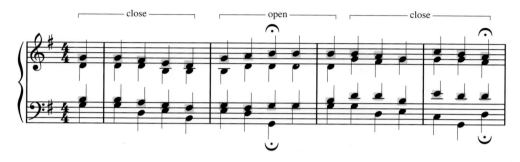

In your beginning part-writing exercises, it would be advisable for you to follow two simple conventions concerning spacing.

1. *Crossed voices.* Do not allow any part to cross above the soprano or below the bass because the essential soprano/bass counterpoint might become unclear (see Example 5-9). The alto and tenor lines may cross briefly if there is a musical reason to do so (see Example 5-10).

Example 5-9

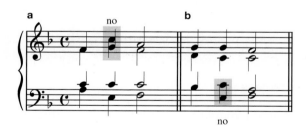

DISC 1 : TRACK 6

Example 5-10 Bach, *Gott, der du selber bist das Licht*

2. *Spacing.* When writing for three or more parts, avoid overly spacious sonorities by keeping adjacent upper parts (excluding the bass) within an octave of each other. For example, in a four-part texture there should be no more than an octave between soprano and alto (Example 5-11a) or between alto and tenor (Example 5-11b), although there might be more than an octave between tenor and bass (Example 5-11c).

Example 5-11

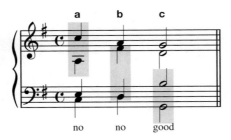

After you have gained some experience in composing, you may begin to experiment with exceptions to these conventions.

When you are composing for vocal ensembles, use the ranges given in Example 5-12.

Example 5-12

Self-Test 5-2

(Answers begin on page 566.)

DISC 1 : TRACK 7

A. Analyze the excerpt from a Bach chorale that follows, using roman numerals and bass position symbols. Then show beneath each roman numeral the structure of the chord by writing "O" or "C" for open or close structure. The note in parentheses in m. 3 is not part of the chord and should be ignored for the purpose of harmonic analysis.

Bach, *Wo soll ich fliehen hin*

g: ___ ___ ___ ___ ___ ___ ___ ___

B. Review the two conventions concerning spacing on pages 71–72. Then point out in the following example any places where those conventions are not followed.

C. Fill in the circled missing inner voice(s) to complete each root position triad, being sure that each note of the triad is represented. Follow the spacing conventions and stay within the range of each vocal part.

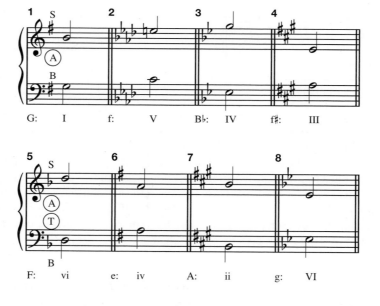

Exercise 5-2 See Workbook.

Parallel Motion

As we shall see, in tonal music it is important to consider the relationships between any voice in the texture and every other voice in the texture. When music progresses from one chord to the next, there are five possible relationships between any two voices (or parts). These are illustrated in Example 5-13.

Example 5-13

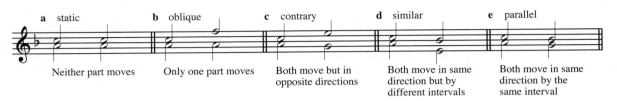

When the texture contains more than two voices, there will be more "pairs" of voices to look at. In a three-part texture, for instance, there are three pairs, as shown in Example 5-14.

Example 5-14

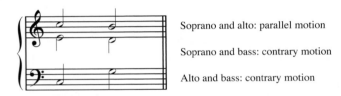

Soprano and alto: parallel motion

Soprano and bass: contrary motion

Alto and bass: contrary motion

In a four-part texture there are six such pairs, which can seem a little daunting at first, but you will soon be expert at seeing them.

One of the basic goals of voice leading in tonal music is to maintain the relative independence of the individual parts. Because of this, voices moving together in parallel motion must be given special attention. Look at Example 5-15, and you will see that it consists of three versions of the i-V-i progression in the key of b. Each version uses the same chords, and each version contains parallel voice leading (indicated by the diagonal lines in the example). However, only one version, Example 5-15c, would be considered acceptable by a composer of tonal music.

Example 5-15

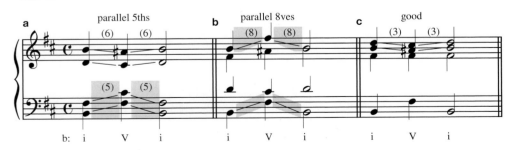

The reason that Examples 5-15a and 5-15b are unacceptable in the tonal style is that they contain parallel 5ths and 8ves. Although such parallels regained acceptance in the twentieth century, composers of tonal music generally followed the convention, dating from around 1450, of avoiding parallel 5ths and 8ves as well as their octave equivalents, such as 12ths and unisons. Note that this does *not* rule out the *duplication* of a line at the 8ve, which was common in orchestral writing (for example, see Ex. 7-7 on pages 98 and 99, in which the bass line is doubled at the 8ve between cellos and basses because the double basses sound a P8 lower than written). The reason for avoiding parallel 5ths and 8ves has to do with the nature of counterpoint. The P8 and P5 are the most stable of intervals, and to link two voices through parallel motion at such intervals interferes with their independence much more than would parallel motion at 3rds or 6ths. We can deduce a rule of parallel motion:

Objectionable parallels result when two parts that are separated by a P5 or a P8, or by their octave equivalents, move to new pitch classes that are separated by the same interval.

If you apply this rule to the three parts of Example 5-16, you will find that all of them are acceptable. In Example 5-16a the soprano and tenor do not move to new pitch classes, whereas in Example 5-16b the 5ths do not occur between the same pair of voices. Finally, the parallel 4ths in Example 5-16c are allowed, even though a P4 is the inversion of a P5. (Incidentally, remember that the unison is the octave equivalent of the P8, so parallel unisons should also be avoided.)

Example 5-16

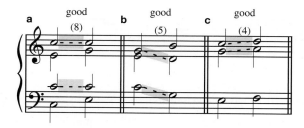

Contrary 5ths and 8ves (also called consecutive 5ths and 8ves by contrary motion) were also generally avoided, at least in vocal music. This means that the composer usually did not "correct" parallels (Ex. 5-17a) by moving one of the parts up or down an octave (Ex. 5-17b).

Example 5-17

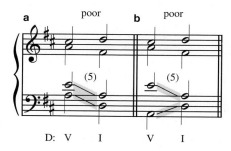

However, contrary octaves are occasionally found at cadences in instrumental music and especially in vocal writing, when both melody and bass outline $\hat{5}$–$\hat{1}$. You will see that this occurs in Example 5-18, below the arrow, but the listener probably understands that A4 and G4 are the basic notes of the melody in mm. 7–8, whereas the D4 is only a quick arpeggiation. Notice also in Example 5-18 that some of the notes are in parentheses. In many of the examples in this book, notes that do not belong to the chord are put in parentheses. Nonchord tones will be discussed in more detail in Chapters 11 and 12.

Example 5-18   Haydn, String Quartet op. 64, no. 4, II

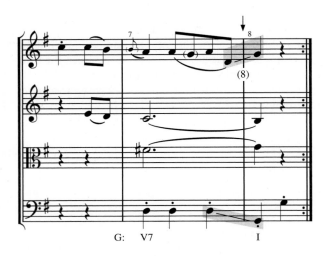

Unequal 5ths result when a P5 is followed by a °5, or the reverse, in the same two voices.

Apparently, some tonal composers avoided unequal 5ths involving the bass, and others used P5-°5 but not °5-P5, yet neither of these restrictions holds true for tonal music in general. For the purposes of our part-writing exercises, we will consider unequal 5ths acceptable *unless* they involve a °5-P5 between the bass and another voice. Several sets of unequal 5ths are illustrated in Example 5-19, with all but the last being acceptable.

Example 5-19

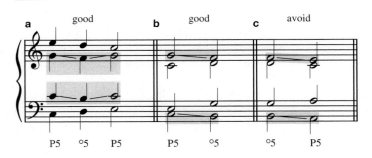

Direct (or hidden) 5th or 8ve results when the outer parts move in the same direction into a P5 or P8, with a leap in the soprano part (with a leap *or* a step in the bass).

The aural result is similar to parallel 5ths and 8ves. In Examples 5-20a and 5-20b the interval of a P5 or P8 between the outer voices is approached from the same direction with a leap in the soprano. In Example 5-20c the 5th involves the bass and alto, not the bass and soprano, whereas in Example 5-20d the soprano moves by step, not by leap. Both Examples 5-20c and 5-20d are correct.

Example 5-20

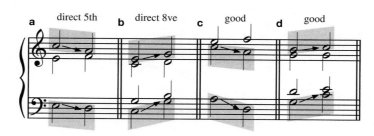

The avoidance of parallels of all types was somewhat less strictly maintained in instrumental than in vocal music. In piano writing, for instance, accompaniment figures frequently outlined 5ths or 8ves, as in Example 5-21.

DISC 1 : TRACK 8

Example 5-21   Mozart, Piano Sonata K. 284, III

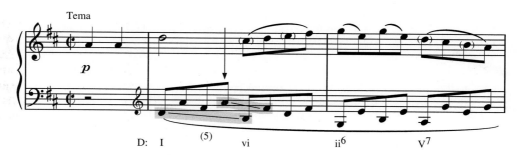

In most cases, such instances of parallels are confined to those textures and instrumental lines in which they are not obvious to the ear. When you attempt to compose music in the tonal style, you should use parallel 5ths and 8ves very sparingly, if at all, and in such a way that the listener's attention will not be drawn to them. Parallels involving both of the outer parts are especially rare and should be avoided. The few instances of such parallels, such as in Example 5-22, do not contradict the general validity of the rule. Possibly Beethoven was trying to evoke a rustic, unsophisticated atmosphere through the use of the parallels—the example is, after all, from the beginning of the *Pastoral* Symphony.

Example 5-22   Beethoven, Symphony no. 6, op. 68, I

CHECKPOINT

1. What do we mean by the focal point of a melody?
2. What scale degree is the strongest tendency tone in tonal music?
3. In a four-voice texture, adjacent upper parts should be kept within what interval?
4. Under what circumstances are unequal 5ths unacceptable?
5. What are direct octaves?

Self-Test 5-3

(Answers begin on page 567.)

A. First, put lead-sheet symbols in the blanks above this example. Then analyze the motion between each of the pairs of voices and fill in the blanks using this system:

st = static   o = oblique   c = contrary   s = similar   p = parallel

1. Bass/Soprano ___ ___ ___
2. Bass/Alto ___ ___ ___
3. Bass/Tenor ___ ___ ___
4. Tenor/Soprano ___ ___ ___
5. Tenor/Alto ___ ___ ___
6. Alto/Soprano ___ ___ ___

B. Label the chords in the following excerpt with roman numerals. Then label any examples of parallelism (objectionable or otherwise) that you can find.

Bach, *Ermuntre dich, mein schwacher Geist*

DISC 1 : TRACK 9

C. Find and label the following errors in this example:
1. Parallel 8ves
2. Parallel 5ths
3. Direct 5th
4. Contrary 5ths
5. Spacing error (review pp. 71–72)

D. Find and label the following errors in this example:
1. Parallel 8ves
2. Parallel 5ths
3. Direct 8ve
4. Contrary octaves
5. Unacceptable unequal 5ths
6. Spacing error

Exercise 5-3   See Workbook.

Summary

Chords in tonal music are produced by the motions of individual musical lines, and the manipulation of these lines is called **voice leading** or **part writing.** A closely related term is **counterpoint,** which refers to the combining of relatively independent musical lines.

In your first exercises, you will use melodies that are relatively short and simple and that conform to the suggestions given on pp. 66–67, and you will usually notate your exercises in **reduced score** rather than in **full score.** When two parts are notated on a staff, the stems of the top part always point up, and those of the bottom point down.

Spacing is an important consideration in voicing chords. In four-part textures, the space between the soprano and tenor parts categorizes a chord to be in **close structure** or **open structure.** Other suggestions regarding spacing are given on pp. 71–72.

Parallel 5ths and 8ves are avoided in most contexts in tonal music because they undermine the relative independence of the individual parts. Also generally avoided are **contrary 5ths and 8ves** and, in certain circumstances, **unequal 5ths** and **direct 5ths and 8ves.** See pp. 73–78 for details.

Variations

For additional review and practice, please see Chapter 5 on our website at **www.mhhe.com/kostka7e.**

Chapter Six

Root Position
Part Writing

Introduction

We will begin our first efforts at tonal composition by exploring the relatively restricted environment of root position triads. Inverted triads, introduced in Chapters 8 and 9, will allow us to write more melodic bass lines, but for now we will have to accept the somewhat rigid contour of a root position bass. The inner voices, however, should be treated as melodies, even if they are seldom as interesting as the soprano line. It is especially important to observe even in the inner voices the rules concerning leaps that you learned in the previous chapter (see rule 4, p. 67).

Although you learned quite a bit about seventh chords in Chapters 3 and 4, we will not begin using them compositionally until Chapter 13. However, seventh chords *will* appear frequently in musical examples and Self-Test analysis problems, as well as in exercises in the workbook, so you will have the opportunity to become better acquainted with them before we launch into their special voice-leading requirements.

We can reduce to four the number of different intervals that can separate the roots of any two chords. This is because a 2nd and a 7th, for example, are the same in this context because the part writing of the upper voices is the same whether the bass moves by a 2nd or by a 7th. The four combinations, then, are the following:

2nd apart (same as a 7th apart)

3rd apart (same as a 6th apart)

4th apart (same as a 5th apart)

same roots—a repeated chord

As we deal with these four combinations (which will be taken up in reverse order from the preceding list), the conventions followed in writing for three and four parts are presented. These conventions are not rules, but instead are tested recipes for successful part writing of chord progressions in root position, and you do not need to scan the texture for parallels or other problems when you follow them. Situations will occur when the melody or some other factor makes it impossible to follow the conventions, but this is relatively uncommon.

A major issue in part writing in the tonal style concerns which notes of a chord are doubled or even tripled. When we refer to a note being doubled or tripled, we mean that two or three of the parts are given that pitch class, although not necessarily in the same octave. For example, look at the Bach excerpt in Part B of Self-Test 5–3 (p. 79). The root of the first chord, G, is tripled in the alto, tenor, and bass. The root of the second chord, C, is doubled in the soprano and bass.

Root Position Part Writing with Repeated Roots

FOUR-PART TEXTURES

1. All members of the triad are usually present. The final I chord is sometimes incomplete, consisting of a 3rd and a tripled root.
2. The root is usually doubled. The leading tone ($\hat{7}$) is almost never doubled because it is such a strong tendency tone (review p. 67).

THREE-PART TEXTURES

1. The 5th of the triad is often omitted. The final I chord may consist only of a tripled root.
2. An incomplete triad will usually have the root doubled. The leading tone ($\hat{7}$) is almost never doubled.

When a root position triad is repeated, the upper voices may be arpeggiated freely, as long as the spacing conventions are followed (review discussion of voicing a single triad, pp. 70–71). The bass may arpeggiate an octave. Example 6-1 illustrates appropriate part writing for repeated roots.

Example 6-1

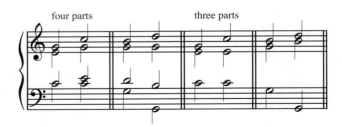

Self-Test 6-1 Using repeated roots

(Answers begin on page 568.)

Test your understanding of the preceding section by filling in the inner voice or voices in the second chord of each pair. The key is C major throughout.

three parts

Exercise 6-1 See Workbook.

Root Position Part Writing with Roots a 4th (5th) Apart

As you will learn in the next chapter, one of the most fundamental root movements in tonal music is that of the descending P5 (or ascending P4). The part-writing principles involved in this root movement are identical to those concerned with the ascending P5 (or descending P4). Other principles that must always be kept in mind are those concerning spacing, parallelism, and the resolution of $\hat{7}$ to $\hat{1}$ when $\hat{7}$ occurs in the melody.

FOUR-PART TEXTURES

1. **Common tone and stepwise.** One method for writing this root relationship in four parts is to keep in the same voice the tone that is common to both chords, while the remaining two upper parts move by step in the same direction. The stepwise motion will be ascending for root movement of a P5 down (Ex. 6-2a) and descending for root movement of a P5 up (Ex. 6-2b). The purpose of the ties here and in subsequent examples is only to point out the common tones and not to imply that they must be tied.

Example 6-2

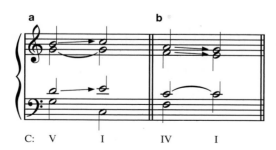

2. **Similar motion by 2nd or 3rd.** A second method moves all three upper parts in the same direction, with no leap larger than a 3rd. The motion will be descending for a root movement of a P5 down (or a P4 up) and ascending for a root movement of a P5 up (or P4 down). Notice that the leading tone in Example 6-3c does not resolve to $\hat{1}$ but instead leaps down to $\hat{5}$. This is perfectly acceptable if it occurs in an inner voice, as it does here.

Example 6-3

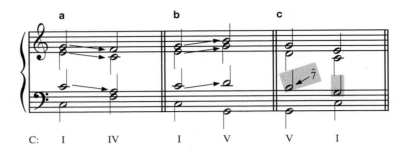

C: I   IV   I   V   V   I

3. **Tertian leap, common tone, stepwise.** A third method, although not as smooth as the first two, is useful for changing between close and open structures. As in the first method, we keep in the same voice the tone that is common to both chords, but the voice that has the 3rd in the first chord leaps to provide the 3rd in the second chord. The remaining voice moves by step. Notice that the leading tone in Example 6-4c does not resolve to $\hat{1}$ but instead leaps up to $\hat{3}$. As with Example 6-3c, this is perfectly acceptable if it occurs in an inner voice.

Example 6-4

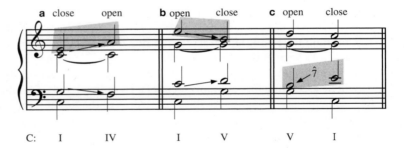

C: I   IV   I   V   V   I

THREE-PART TEXTURES

The more flexible nature of three-part writing makes it impossible to distill a few conventional methods, as was done for four-part textures. Remember that each chord must contain at least a root and 3rd, and observe conventions concerning spacing and parallelism (Ex. 6-5). Aim for smooth voice leading instead of complete chords.

Example 6-5

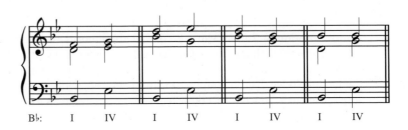

B♭:   I   IV   I   IV   I   IV   I   IV

Self-Test 6-2 Using roots a 4th (5th) apart

(Answers begin on page 568.)

A. Add alto and tenor parts to each of the following exercises. Each progression involves roots a P5 (P4) apart. Use one of the three methods outlined on pages 83–84 in each case, and state which you have used (1, 2, or 3).

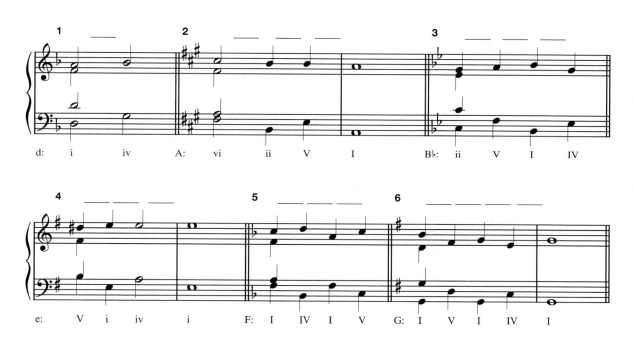

B. Add an alto part to each example. Be careful to observe conventions concerning spacing, parallels, and doubling. Each triad should include at least a root and a 3rd.

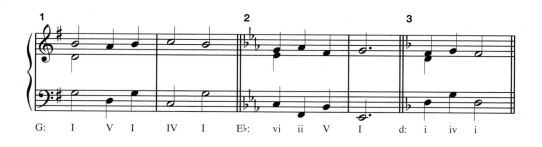

Exercise 6-2 See Workbook.

Root Position Part Writing with Roots a 3rd (6th) Apart

The voice leading that involves root position triads a 3rd or 6th apart is usually quite smooth because the two triads will always have two pitch classes in common.

FOUR-PART TEXTURES

Two common tones and stepwise. Assuming that the first of the two root position triads has a doubled root, only one of the upper voices will need to move. The two upper voices that have tones in common with the second chord remain stationary, whereas the remaining voice moves by step. The stepwise motion will be upward for roots a descending 3rd apart (Ex. 6-6a) and downward for roots an ascending 3rd apart (Ex. 6-6b).

Example 6-6

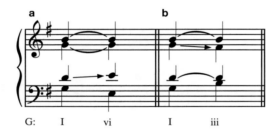

THREE-PART TEXTURES

Commonly encountered part-writing situations are more diverse in three-part textures. Some possibilities are illustrated in Example 6-7. Especially tricky is the ascending root movement. In that case, you should not omit the 5th of the second chord because the listener might assume that the music has progressed only from a root position triad to an inverted form of the same triad (compare Ex. 6-7c and d with Ex. 6-7e and f).

Example 6-7

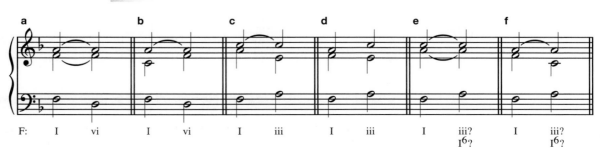

(Answers begin on page 569.)

A. Add alto and tenor parts to each exercise. Use the smoothest voice leading in each case. For roots a 4th (5th) apart, state which method you have used.

Bb: vi   IV   ii   V   f#: i   VI   iv   i   G: I   iii   vi   ii   V   –   I

B. Add an alto part to each exercise. Be careful to observe the conventions concerning parallels, spacing, and doubling.

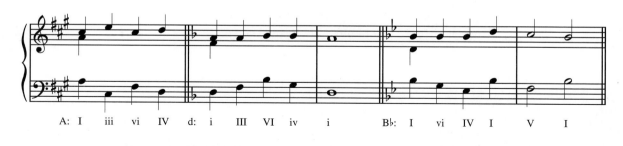

A: I   iii   vi   IV   d: i   III   VI   iv   i   Bb: I   vi   IV   I   V   I

Exercise 6-3 See Workbook.

Root Position Part Writing with Roots a 2nd (7th) Apart

Two triads with roots a 2nd (or 7th) apart have *no* pitch classes in common, so every part must move from the first chord to the second. In this discussion we will assume that the bass moves by 2nd rather than by 7th.

FOUR-PART TEXTURES

Contrary to the bass. If the root is doubled in the first chord, as is usually the case, the voice leading is usually quite simple: If the bass moves up by step, the upper voices move down to the nearest chord tone (Ex. 6-8a), whereas if the bass moves down by step, the upper voices move up to the nearest chord tone (Ex. 6-8b).

Example 6-8

The progression V–vi (or V–VI) is known as the **deceptive progression,** for reasons that will become clear in the next chapter. In terms of voice leading, deceptive progressions present some special problems. In most cases the leading tone ($\hat{7}$) moves parallel with the bass, resolving up to tonic ($\hat{1}$), whereas the other two voices move down, contrary to the bass, to the next available chord tones. This results in a doubled 3rd in the vi (or VI) chord, as in Example 6-9a and b. In the major mode, if the leading tone is in an inner voice, it may move down by step to $\hat{6}$, as in Example 6-9c, because the lack of resolution is not so apparent to the ear. This is not acceptable in the minor mode, however, because of the awkward interval of a +2 that results, as in Example 6-9d.

Example 6-9

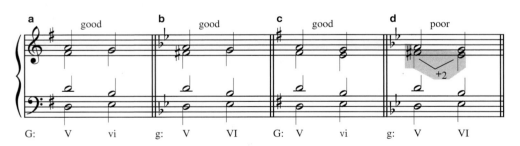

The voice leading away from a triad with a doubled 3rd must be handled carefully because the conventions discussed in this chapter all assume doubled roots.

Example 6-10 provides two examples of the deceptive progression, one in B♭ and one in g. In the first one, the V–vi progression in B♭, the leading tone is in an inner voice (the alto), and Bach avoids resolving it to tonic (as in Ex. 6-9c). Remember that this is *only* practicable when in major mode with the leading tone in an inner voice. In the V–VI progression, where the key has shifted to g, Bach resolves the leading tone to tonic, resulting in a doubled 3rd in the VI chord (as in Ex. 6-9b).

Example 6-10   Bach, *Herr Christ, der ein'ge Gott's-Sohn*

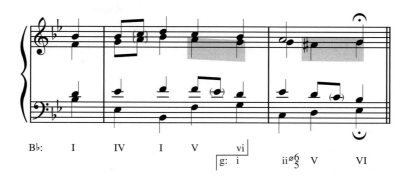

THREE-PART TEXTURES

The smoothest voice leading will find a complete triad followed by a triad with two roots and a 3rd (Ex. 6-11a and b) or a triad consisting of two roots and a 3rd followed by a complete triad (Ex. 6-11c and d). In other words, with roots a 2nd apart, the sequence will usually be complete to incomplete or incomplete to complete. Remember to resolve $\hat{7}$ to $\hat{1}$ in the V–vi progression—with the possible exception of cases in which $\hat{7}$ is in the inner voice in a major key.

Example 6-11

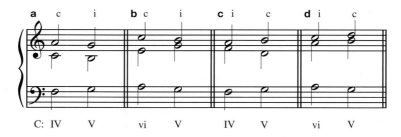

CHECKPOINT

1. How many pitch classes are shared between triads with roots a 2nd apart? A 3rd apart? A 4th or 5th apart?

2. Describe the three methods of connecting triads with roots a 4th or 5th apart.

3. What is usually doubled in the second chord of a V–vi (or V–VI) progression? What is the possible exception to this?

Self-Test 6-4 Using all root relationships

(Answers begin on page 569.)

A. Complete each progression. Make two versions of each: one for three parts (adding an alto) and one for four parts (adding alto and tenor). In the four-part versions, state which method you have used for any progression by 4th or 5th.

G: I   vi   IV   d: i   iv   V   A: I   vi   ii   e: i   V   VI   B♭:   iii   vi   V

B. Fill in alto and tenor parts in these two exercises. For roots a 4th (5th) apart, state which method you have used.

1

E♭:   I   vi   V   I   IV   I   IV   V   —   I

2

b: V   i   VI   iv   V   VI   iv   V   —   i
        *

C. Name the keys and analyze the chords specified by these figured basses. Then compose a good melody line for each. Finally, fill in alto and tenor parts to make a four-part texture.

---

*   The given soprano here and elsewhere might make it impossible to follow the conventions. Watch out for parallels and spacing, and double the root in most cases.

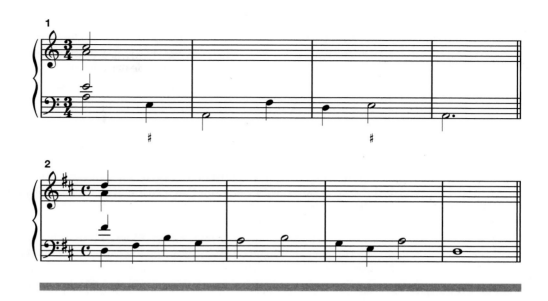

Exercise 6-4 See Workbook.

Instrumental Ranges and Transpositions

Many of the exercises suggest that you compose examples for combinations of instruments in your class, and your instructor may make additional assignments that also call for instrumental combinations. To carry out these assignments successfully, you will need to understand the ranges and transpositions of the various instruments.

Appendix A provides suggested ranges for many of the instruments for which you may want to write. A "written range" is given next to the "sounding range" for each instrument in Appendix A. This is necessary because, strange as it might seem at first, players of certain instruments of the band and orchestra do not read music at concert pitch. This means that the notes that they read in their parts produce pitches that are higher or lower than the notes that have the same names on the piano.

The reasons that we have transposing instruments are somewhat complicated, but we will try to explain two of them here as examples. The French horn was originally a valveless instrument that could play only the notes of the **harmonic series.** A harmonic series with C2 as a fundamental is illustrated in Example 6-12. The filled-in noteheads represent pitches that are quite out of tune in comparison to the modern equal-tempered system.

Example 6-12

To play in different keys, the horn player had to insert the proper **crook,** a piece of tubing of a precisely calculated length. A longer crook lowered the instrument's **fundamental** and, correspondingly, its harmonic series, whereas a shorter crook did the reverse. No matter what crook was used, it was the custom to write for the horn as if it were in the key of C so that the C fundamental and its familiar harmonic series would remain unchanged. This practice was retained even after valves were introduced and the horn settled into its modern F fundamental.

Perhaps an easier example to understand is the saxophone family, which consists of eight different instruments, each of which has a different sounding range (only two of the saxophones are included in Appendix A). To make it easier for players to "double"—to switch from one saxophone to the other—saxophone music is written as if all saxophones had the same range, with the result that a written G4, for example, is fingered the same way on every saxophone.

Naturally, a musician has to understand transpositions thoroughly to compose, arrange, conduct, or read instrumental music. To write music that you have composed or arranged from concert pitch for a transposing instrument, follow the instructions under "written range" in Appendix A. To write music from a transposing instrument into concert pitch, you have to reverse the process. Example 6-13 illustrates this. Notice that key signatures are transposed as well.

Example 6-13

If you don't have Appendix A or a similar guide handy, remember that a transposing instrument "sees a C but sounds its key." This means that a horn player who sees a C will sound an F because the French horn is pitched in F. To go from concert pitch to the transposed part, remember that "to hear its key, you must write a C."

One procedure to use when writing for an ensemble is this:

1. Notate the sounding ranges of the performers at the top of your page of manuscript paper.

2. Compose the exercise in the form of a reduced score on as few staves as practicable. Keep an eye on the ranges.

3. Provide enough copies for the ensemble so that players will not have to huddle around a single stand. Instrumental parts should be copied onto separate sheets using correct transpositions.

Self-Test 6-5

(Answers begin on page 571.)

A. Notate the chords below for the specified instruments. Each chord is written at concert pitch, so transpose as needed for the performers. Note that the instruments are listed in **score order,** the order used in Appendix A, which is not always the same as order by pitch. You do not need to use key signatures, but *use the correct clef for each instrument.*

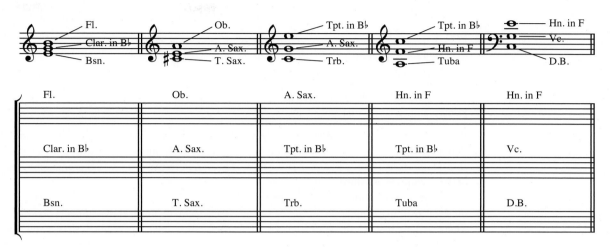

B. Here is a short chord progression to use in these exercises:

F: I   vi   ii   V   I

1. Make an arrangement for two alto saxophones and one tenor saxophone. Copy out the parts, using correct transpositions.

2. Make a four-part arrangement for SATB chorus.

C. Write a version of the following excerpt on a grand staff by transposing the parts to concert pitch. Play your version on the piano and analyze the harmonies if you can (there are some nonchord tones, so be sure to listen carefully).

Exercise 6-5 See Workbook.

Summary

The possible relationships between the roots of any two triads can be reduced to four. Part-writing conventions involving all four relationships are discussed in terms of both three- and four-part textures on the pages indicated next.

Repeated roots, p. 82.

Roots a 4th (or 5th) apart, pp. 83–84.

Roots a 3rd (or 6th) apart, pp. 86–87.

Roots a 2nd (or 7th) apart, pp. 87–89.

Whereas the 5th of the triad is frequently omitted in three-part textures, this is seldom found in four-part textures, with the exception of the final I chord. In most cases, when a member of the chord is *doubled*, the doubled tone is the root. However, in the V–vi (or V–VI) progression, the 3rd of the vi chord is usually doubled.

You will need to understand instrumental transpositions if you want to write instrumental music or read instrumental scores. For various reasons, many musical instruments do not sound where written; instead, the music must be transposed, either *from* concert pitch so that you can notate the part or *to* concert pitch so that you can understand the score. Appendix A provides ranges and transpositions for a number of different instruments.

This would be an appropriate point at which to begin work on Counterpoint Unit 2, which may be found at www.mhhe.com/kostka7e.

Chapter Seven
Harmonic Progression and the Sequence

Introduction

Tonal harmony developed slowly out of the great polyphonic* modal tradition of the Renaissance period (from around 1430 to about 1600). That Renaissance tradition depended in turn on the "rules" of counterpoint that had begun to be developed in the late Middle Ages. The application of those rules resulted in certain recurring and recognizable combinations of chords, and out of that the norms of tonal harmony gradually coalesced, norms that form the heart of this chapter. Let us be clear: Tonal harmony was not "invented"; it developed from counterpoint. Yet harmony can be, and frequently is, taught as a separate subject from counterpoint in colleges and universities. Nevertheless, supplementing this text are four online counterpoint units, two of which have already been referenced (in Chapters 3 and 6), and completing them will certainly enhance your understanding of tonal music.

Before you can begin to compose convincing tonal music or to learn anything from harmonic analyses, you must learn which chord successions are typical of tonal harmony and which ones are not. Why is it that some chord successions seem to "progress," to move forward toward a goal, whereas others tend to wander, to leave our expectations unfulfilled? Compare the two progressions in Example 7-1. The first was composed following the principles that will be discussed in this chapter, but the chords for the second were selected randomly. Although the random example has a certain freshness to it, there is no doubt that the first one sounds more typical of tonal harmony. This chapter will explore this phenomenon, but first we must turn to a topic that concerns melody as well as harmony.

Example 7-1

G: I   V⁶   I   vii°⁶ I⁶   IV   ii   V⁷   I

G: IV   vi   V   IV   ii   vi   IV   vii°⁶   ii

---

* Music with multiple voice parts, in contrast to monophonic, single-part music.

Sequences and the Circle of Fifths

One of the important means of achieving unity in tonal music is through the use of a **sequence,** a pattern that is repeated immediately in the same voice but that begins on a different pitch class. A **tonal sequence** will keep the pattern in a single key, which means that modifiers of the intervals (major, minor, and so on) will probably change, as in Example 7-2a. A **real sequence,** as in Example 7-2b, transposes the pattern to a new key. Real sequences (also known as modulating sequences) will be discussed in more detail in a later chapter.

Example 7-2

It is important to understand the difference between sequence, which occurs in a single voice, and **imitation,** which occurs between two or more voices. In Example 7-3 the first violin (top staff) plays an exact transposition of the melody first heard in the second violin (bottom staff), but this is an example of **real imitation,** not a real sequence, because the repetition of the pattern occurs in a different voice.

DISC 1 : TRACK 11

Example 7-3   Bach, "Double" Concerto, II (solo violins only)

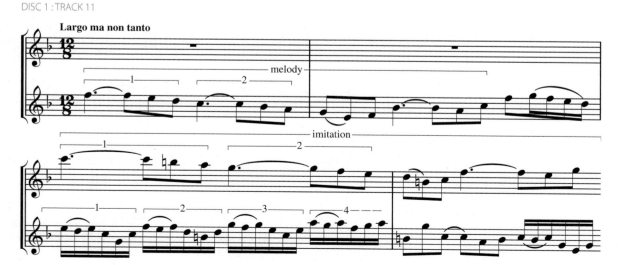

However, in addition to imitation, there are also sequences in Example 7-3. There is a sequence in m. 1 (the ♩ ♪ ♩ ♩ pattern) that is imitated by the first violin in m. 3. Another sequence occurs in the second violin in m. 3 (the ♪♪♪♪♪ pattern), but notice that the interval of a 4th in the first occurrence of the pattern becomes a 3rd in the second and third occurrences. A sequence such as this, where the repetitions of the pattern are neither tonal nor real, is called a **modified sequence**.

We will return to the subject of the sequence later in the chapter. For now, we will concentrate on only one sequential pattern: the **circle-of-fifths progression,** which consists of a series of roots related by descending 5ths (and/or ascending 4ths). Although most of the 5ths (and 4ths) will be perfect, if a diatonic circle-of-fifths progression goes on long enough in root position, a °5 (or +4) will appear (Ex. 7-4).

Example 7-4

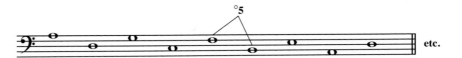

The bass line in Example 7-4 can be seen in the next example, where there is also a melodic sequence in the first violin. (The bass notes within the sequence have the root of the chord in each case.)

DISC 1 : TRACK 11

Example 7-5   Vivaldi, Concerto Grosso op. 3, no. 11, I (soloists only)

Although the chords in Example 7-5 are all in root position, if some or all of them were inverted, the progression would still contain a circle-of-fifths *harmonic* sequence.

Sequential progressions involving the circle of fifths are frequently found in twentieth-century popular music and jazz (see Ex. 7-6). Notice that both Example 7-5 and Example 7-6 include a °5 (or +4) in their root movements, which is not at all uncommon in circle-of-fifths progressions. In Example 7-5 the °5 occurs between the chords on F and B, and in Example 7-6 it occurs between the chords on B♭ and E.

Example 7-6   Richie, "Hello"

The root progression of a 5th down (or 4th up) is the most basic progression in tonal harmony, whether or not it occurs in the context of a sequence. The circle-of-fifths progression offers a useful memory aid in learning harmonic function, and we will organize most of the chapter around it. We will begin with the strongest of all root movements by a descending 5th, the V—I progression. (The following discussion applies equally to progressions in major and minor modes, except as noted.)

The I and V Chords

The ultimate harmonic goal of any tonal piece is the tonic triad, and this triad is often also the goal of many of the formal subdivisions of a composition. The tonic triad is most often preceded by a V (or V^7) chord, and it would be safe to say that $V^{(7)}$ and I together are the most essential elements of a tonal work. It is not difficult to find examples in which the harmony for several measures consists only of I and V chords, as in Example 7-7, which Mozart composed at the age of fifteen. (Notice in the analysis that we do not repeat the roman numeral when only the inversion changes, as with the V^6_5 in m. 32 and the i^6 in m. 33. This is an acceptable method of abbreviation.)

Example 7-7   Mozart, Symphony K. 114, III

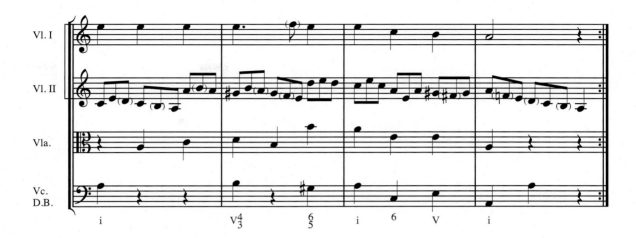

It would be difficult to exaggerate the importance of the I–V–I progression at all levels of musical structure, from the phrase on up. However, not all dominant chords have the same significance, and the same could be said of tonic chords. Often the domain of a chord will be expanded through the use of one or more subsidiary chords, a process known as **prolongation.** In Example 7-7 (preceding) the first four measures (mm. 27–30) contain a large I–V progression. The opening tonic is prolonged through the first three measures with the help of the relatively weak V^6_5 that occurs in the second measure. The second four measures (mm. 31–34) also begin with a prolongation of the tonic, this time by means of the V^6_5, V^4_3, and i^6 chords. The important dominant chord here is the root position V at the end of m. 33. We could diagram the deeper harmonic structure of the example as the following:

$$i \quad | \quad V^6_5 \quad | \quad i \quad | \quad V \quad | \quad i \quad | \quad V^4_3 \quad ^6_5 \quad | \quad i \quad ^6 \quad V \quad | \quad i \quad \|$$

$$i \text{ ----------------------------- } V \quad | \quad i \text{ ------------------------------- } V \quad \quad i \quad \|$$

The II Chord

If we extend our circle-of-fifths progression backward one step from the V chord, we have the following progression:

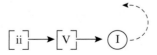

This diagram illustrates the normal function of ii, as an important **pre-dominant** chord, to progress to V and of V to progress to I. The dotted line after the I indicates that if the piece continues, the I chord might be followed by anything.

Many phrases contain only a I–ii–V–I progression. Example 7-8 shows a typical soprano/bass framework for such a progression.

Example 7-8

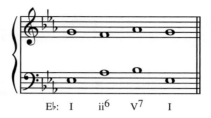

Eb: I   ii⁶   V⁷   I

Play Example 7-8 and then compare it with Beethoven's version of this progression in Example 7-9. Here Beethoven uses a ii_5^6 instead of a ii^6.

DISC 1 : TRACK 12

Example 7-9   Beethoven, Minuet

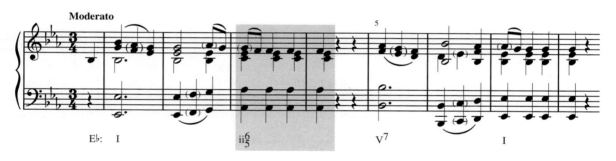

Eb: I   ii$_5^6$ V⁷   I

The VI Chord

One more step in the circle of fifths brings us to the vi chord.

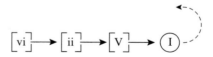

Put in root position, this progression illustrates an ostinato (repeated) bass pattern often found in popular tunes. Play Example 7-10 and see whether it sounds familiar.

Example 7-10

F: I   vi   ii   V

The same progression, but in minor, is seen in Example 7-11. As we will demonstrate in a later section, chord functions in minor are almost identical to those in major. (The key signature here is correct. Verdi uses accidentals to create the minor mode.)

Example 7-11   Verdi, *La forza del destino,* act II (piano-vocal score)

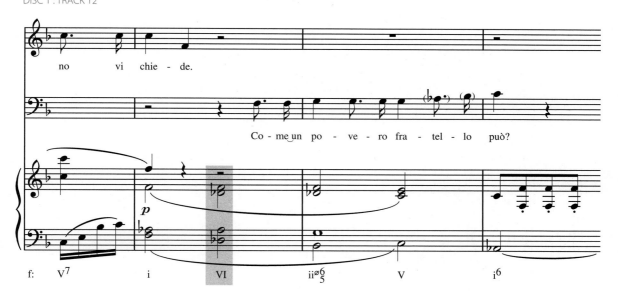

The III Chord

Another 5th backward brings us to the iii chord, far removed from the tonic triad.

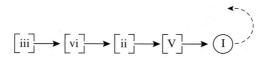

Beginning theory students often assume that the iii chord is frequently encountered and that they should be sure to include at least one iii chord in each exercise they write. This is not at all the case, at least not in the major mode. When $\hat{3}$ is found in a major-mode bass line, the chord above it is almost always a I^6 rather than a iii. The iii chord does occur occasionally, of course. When it follows the natural descending 5ths progression, it will go to vi, as in Example 7-12. The III chord in minor is used more frequently and is discussed further on p. 105.

Example 7-12   Bach, *O Ewigkeit, du Donnerwort*

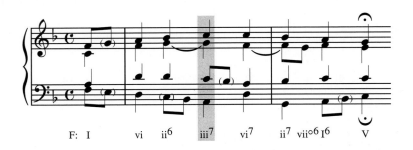

F: I   vi   ii^6 iii^7 vi^7 ii^7 vii°^{6} I^6 V

Also, the iii chord is useful for harmonizing a $\hat{1}$–$\hat{7}$–$\hat{6}$ soprano line, as in Example 7-13, although $\hat{7}$ is usually harmonized by V or vii° in other contexts.

Example 7-13

D: I   iii   IV   I^6

The VII Chord

Continuing the circle of fifths backward from iii brings us to vii°. Although the vii°–iii progression does occur in sequential passages, the vii° usually acts instead as a substitute for V. In fact, vii° and V are so closely related that moving from one to the other is not considered to be a "progression" at all. This is because they share the dominant function, which is to define the tonality by resolving to the tonic triad. Therefore, the customary goal of the vii° (except in circle-of-fifths sequences) is not iii or III, but instead is the tonic triad.

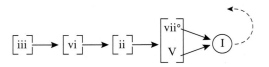

If vii° and V are used next to each other, V will usually follow the vii° because the V is the stronger sound.

The most common use of vii° is to prolong a tonic triad by appearing in first inversion between two positions of the tonic triad: I–vii°^{6}–I^6 or I^6–vii°^{6}–I. Sometimes that progression involves a **voice exchange** between the bass and some upper voice in which one voice line outlines Î–Ẑ–Ȝ and the other mirrors it with Ȝ–Ẑ–Î. This occurs in Example 7-14 between the bass and soprano voices. (You have seen this famous melody before in Example 5-4 on p. 68.)

Example 7-14   Graun, *Herzliebster Jesu, was hast du verbrochen*

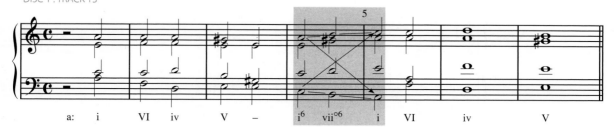

The vii°⁶ is also useful in harmonizing a 6̂–7̂–1̂ soprano line. Compare Examples 7-13 and 7-15.

Example 7-15

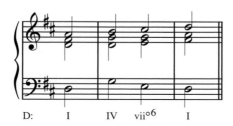

The IV Chord

Still missing from our chord diagram is the IV chord, which lies a P5 *below* the tonic. Most often, IV has a pre-dominant function, moving directly to V or vii°, or it may prolong the pre-dominant area by moving first to ii or ii⁶. In a very different role, IV may proceed to a I chord, sometimes called a **plagal** progression. These common uses of the IV are summarized in the following chord diagram:

In Example 7-16 the IV appears in a plagal progression. (The I_4^6 in the last measure indicates that the notes of the tonic triad are present at that point. However, the bracket with the V under it means that everything within the bracket *functions* as V. The I_4^6 is actually a kind of embellishment called a **cadential six-four,** which will be explained further in Chapter 9.)

Example 7-16   Haydn, Piano Sonata no. 35, II

Later on in the same sonata in which Example 7-16 appears, IV is used in its pre-dominant function (Ex. 7-17).

Example 7-17   Haydn, Piano Sonata no. 35, III

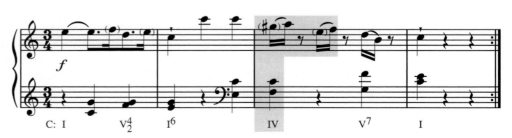

The V_2^4 in the first measure helps prolong the tonic area, which occupies the first two measures. The root position V^7 that precedes the final tonic is a much stronger chord.

Common Exceptions

The chord diagram on page 103 includes all the diatonic triads and gives a reasonably accurate picture of the chord progressions most often found in tonal music. However, to make our chart of chord functions more complete, we must include two commonly encountered exceptions to the norms discussed so far.

1. V–vi (the deceptive progression, introduced on p. 88)
2. iii–IV (see Ex. 7-13)

These additions are included in the following diagram, which may be considered complete for the *normative* harmonic functions in major keys. Remember that the dotted line after the I chord means that any chord may follow it. Likewise, when vi substitutes temporarily for I in a deceptive progression, it might be followed by any chord. To see some examples of this, turn ahead to Examples 8-5 (p. 117) and 8-20 (p. 126), where vi is followed by V^6 and I^6, respectively.

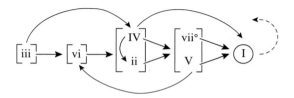

Differences in the Minor Mode

Most chords function the same way in minor as in major. However, the mediant triad, so seldom found in the major mode, is a common feature of the minor mode: it represents the relative major key, and minor-mode music has a decided tendency to drift in that direction.

In addition, the variability of $\hat{6}$ and $\hat{7}$ will occasionally produce chords of different quality and function. The most important of these are the following:

1. The subtonic VII, sounding like the V in the key of the relative major—that is, a V of III.
2. The minor v, usually v^6, after which the $\downarrow\hat{7}$ will move to $\downarrow\hat{6}$, usually as part of a iv^6 chord. The minor v chord does not have a dominant function.

The first of these possibilities is included in the following chord diagram.

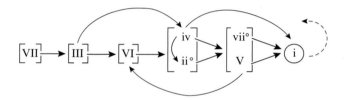

The second possibility, v^6–iv^6, is illustrated in Example 7-18. Here the v^6 is clearly a **passing chord** that connects the tonic chord to the pre-dominant iv^6.

Example 7-18   Bach, *"Als vierzig Tag' nach Ostern"*

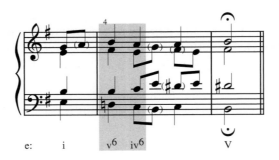

Other chord qualities produced by the variable $\hat{6}$ and $\hat{7}$ will be encountered later:

Progressions Involving Seventh Chords

We will not be using seventh chords in part-writing or composition exercises for a while, but they will occur in examples and in analysis exercises. You will see that in almost every case, seventh chords function in the same way as triads; for example, both V and V7 tend to be followed by the I chord (or sometimes by the vi chord). The only exception is the tonic seventh chord (I^{M7} or i^{7}), which loses its stability as a harmonic goal. In most cases a tonic seventh is followed by a subdominant chord, although other possibilities will be discussed in Chapter 15.

More about Harmonic Sequences

We have concentrated in this chapter on the crucial circle-of-fifths sequence, but other harmonic sequences do occur, and we will discuss a few of them here. Before doing that, though, here are a few things to remember about sequences:

1. The sequential pattern may result in unusual doublings, root position diminished chords, and unusual leaps, but these are acceptable in a sequence.

2. Chords may not function in a sequence in their usual ways—that is, according to the chord diagrams on p. 105. If you want, you can indicate this by putting the roman numerals in parentheses or by using lead-sheet symbols instead.

3. Inversions do not affect a harmonic sequence. For example, vi–ii–V–I and vi–ii⁶–V–I are both circle-of-fifths harmonic sequences.

4. Sequences may begin and end at any point in the pattern.

For review, Example 7-19a begins with a root position circle-of-fifths sequence. Much less common is the reverse, seen in 7-19b, but it does occur. In 7-19c the pattern is a 3rd down followed by a 4th up. This is often found with the second chord of the pattern in first inversion, as in 7-19d (sometimes called a 5-6 sequence because a $\frac{5}{3}$ chord is followed by a $\frac{6}{3}$ chord). In 7-19e a 4th down is followed by a step up, and the same pattern, with the second chord inverted, is seen in 7-19f.

Example 7-19

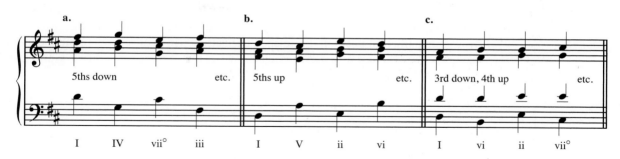

The sequence shown in Example 7-19e forms the background of the Pachelbel Canon (Ex. 7-20).

DISC 1 : TRACK 14

Example 7-20   Pachelbel, Canon in D

We have not exhausted the subject of sequences, and you will encounter others elsewhere in this book as well as in the music that you play, listen to, and study.

CHECKPOINT

1. What is the difference between a tonal sequence and a real sequence?

2. Does a circle-of-fifths sequence use descending fifths or ascending fifths?

3. What are three conventional uses of the IV chord?

Harmonizing a Simple Melody

Because we have so far discussed part writing only of root position chords, any melody harmonization exercises will have to be restricted to root position. For the best results, avoid using any root position diminished triads (this will be discussed in more detail in the next chapter). Your first step should be to select the chords for the very beginning and for the last two or three chords, as in Example 7-21.

Example 7-21

Next, write out the possibilities for each remaining chord, remembering that every melody note can serve as the root, third, or fifth of a triad, as in Example 7-22. Notice that we have not included the vii° chord as a possibility because we want to avoid root position diminished triads.

Example 7-22

The next step is to compose the rest of the bass line. The challenge here is to try to create a good harmonic progression while avoiding creating parallel or direct 5ths and 8ves with the melody. For example, parallel fifths would result if we began the third measure with a I–vi progression. After you are satisfied with both the bass line and the progression, the final step is to add one or two inner voices, following as much as possible the conventions that you learned in Chapter 6. A possible harmonization is given in Example 7-23.

Example 7-23

D: I   V   vi   IV   V   I   I   I   IV   ii   V   I

Conclusion

The last two chord diagrams on page 105 are somewhat complex, but both are based on the circle-of-fifths progression. Keep this in mind while you are learning them. At the same time, be aware that Bach and Beethoven did *not* make use of diagrams such as these. They lived and breathed the tonal harmonic style and had no need for the information the diagrams contain. Instead, the diagrams represent norms of harmonic practice observed by theorists over the years in the works of a large number of tonal composers. They do not represent rules; they are just guidelines for your use in analyzing and composing tonal music.

Self-Test 7-1

(Answers begin on page 572.)

A. Complete each harmonic fragment to conform with the major-mode diagram presented on p. 105. The chord in the blank should be different from those on either side of it. In most cases there is more than one correct answer.

    1. I __?__ vi   (____ or ____)   4. I __?__ IV   (____ or ____)

    2. IV __?__ V   (____ or ____)   5. vi __?__ V   (____ or ____)

    3. V __?__ IV   (____ or ____)   6. vii° __?__ V   (____)

B. Bracket any portions of these progressions that do not conform to the complete major and minor chord diagrams (p. 105).

    1. I   V   ii   vii°   I

    2. i   iv   i   VII   i   V   i

    3. I   IV   iii   vi   ii   V   I

    4. I   IV   ii   V   vi   ii   V   I

C. Analysis. Label all chords with roman numerals and bass-position symbols. Bracket any successions of roman numerals that do not agree with the complete major and minor chord diagrams.

DISC 1 : TRACK 15

1. Bach, *O Herre Gott, dein göttlich Wort*

In addition to roman numerals, provide lead-sheet symbols above the top staff.

DISC 1 : TRACK 15

2. Vivaldi, Cello Sonata in G Minor, Sarabande*

In addition to labeling the chords, bracket any melodic sequences (including modified sequences) in the cello part. Nonchord tones in the solo part have not been put in parentheses, but the harmonic analysis can be done by concentrating on the accompaniment. The key is g minor despite what appears to be an incorrect key signature. Key signatures had not yet become standardized when this work was composed.

*   Unfigured bass realization by S. Kostka.

3. Play through Example 3-10 (p. 46), supplying the chords in your left hand as well as you can. Then fill in blanks below with roman numerals in the key of e minor. Finally, bracket the longest circle-of-fifths sequence that you can find.

    1   2   3   4   5   6   7

D. Analyze the chords specified by these figured basses and add inner voices to make a four-part texture. Bracket all circle-of-fifths progressions, even those that contain only two chords. Before beginning, review the part writing for deceptive progression on pp. 87–89.

E. Analyze this figured bass, then add a good soprano line and inner voices. Bracket all circle-of-fifths progressions.

F. Harmonize the melodies below by using root position major or minor (not diminished) triads in an acceptable progression. Try to give the bass a good contour while avoiding parallel and direct 5ths and 8ves with the melody. Be sure to include analysis. Finally, add one or two inner parts to make a version for SAB three-part chorus or SATB four-part chorus, as indicated.

1. SAB

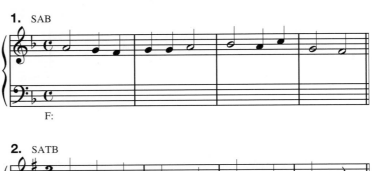

F:

2. SATB

e:

3. SATB

E♭:

4. SATB

d:

5. SAB

A:

G. Add an alto part (only) to mm. 1 to 2. Then compose a good soprano line for mm. 3 to 4 and fill in an alto part.

Bb: I   iii   IV   V   vi   ii   V   I   iii   vi   IV   ii   V   I

H. Review. Label the chords with roman numerals and bass-position symbols (where needed).

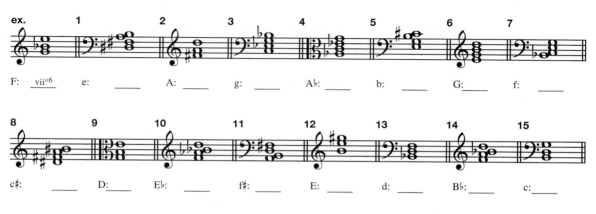

Exercise 7-1 See Workbook.

Summary

The contrapuntal music of the Renaissance period led gradually to what we today call tonal harmony. In the course of that development, certain combinations of chords came about more often than others, creating the normative harmonic progressions with which much of this chapter is concerned. Many—but by no means all—of those normative progressions involve a root movement of a descending 5th or ascending 4th.

A **sequence** is a pattern that is repeated immediately in the same voice but beginning on a different pitch class. A **diatonic sequence** keeps the pattern within a single key, whereas a **real**, or **modulating, sequence** transposes the pattern to a different key.

A sequential pattern may be melodic, harmonic, or both. A harmonic sequence that is very important in tonal music is the **circle-of-fifths sequence,** which consists of a series of root movements down a 5th (and/or up a 4th). The most important circle-of-fifths progression is the V–I (or V–i) progression, but the circle-of-fifths progression also forms the basis of the diagrams given on page 105 illustrating normative harmonic progressions in major and minor modes.

Chapter Eight
Triads in First Inversion

Introduction

Listen to the following short phrase, paying special attention to the bass line.

Example 8-1

D: I   V   7   I   ii   V⁷   I

It's not bad, but it could be improved. The melody line is fine, having both shape and direction, but the bass seems too repetitive and too rigid. Compare Example 8-1 with Example 8-2.

Example 8-2   Haydn, Piano Sonata no. 33, III

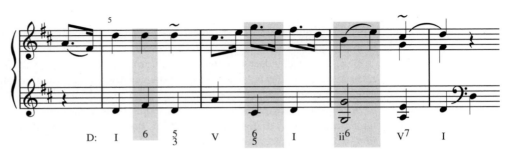

D: I   6 5 3   V   6 5   I   ii⁶   V⁷   I

Now the bass line is improved through the use of inverted chords (indicated by high-lighted notes in the example). Although the harmony is the same, the inverted chords have created a bass line with a more interesting contour and with more variety. The tonic area is prolonged by the V and V_5^6 in the second measure of the example, expanding what is basically a I—ii—V—I progression.

Most phrases of tonal music contain at least one inverted chord, and the inversions usually serve the purposes that we have just demonstrated. We are not saying that a phrase without inverted chords is poorly composed—it just depends on what effect the composer is after.

Bass Arpeggiation

One way in which first inversion triads often originate is through bass arpeggiation. If you look back at the first measure of Example 8-2, you will see that D4 is the primary bass note in the measure. The F♯4 serves the dual purpose of providing the 3rd of the chord and of giving the bass some variety. A similar situation is found in the first two beats of the second measure. When you analyze a bass arpeggiation such as these, you should identify the arpeggiations only with arabic numerals (as in Ex. 8-2) or omit symbols altogether (as in Ex. 8-3).

Accompaniment figures in keyboard music often involve faster arpeggiations. Two examples by Haydn are shown next (Ex. 8-3 and 8-4). In both, the real bass line is the one shown in the textural reduction. The other pitches played by the left hand should be considered as inner voices that are simply filling in the chords. They are not part of the bass line, so we would not consider these notes to be creating inversions at all.

Example 8-3   Haydn, Piano Sonata no. 43, I

Textural reduction

Example 8-4   Haydn, Piano Sonata no. 45, I

Textural reductions such as those of Examples 8-3 and 8-4 appear throughout this text. Their purpose is to simplify the texture and make the voice leading easier to understand. Notice that in the reduction of Example 8-4, the E♭5 in m. 20 has been transposed up one octave from the original. The octave transposition helps clarify the essentially conjunct (stepwise) nature of the melodic line.

Substituted First Inversion Triads

There are three main reasons why triads are used in first inversion.

1. To improve the contour of the bass line.
2. To provide a greater variety of pitches in the bass line.
3. To lessen the weight of V and I chords that do not serve as the goals of harmonic motion.

Instances of the third type can be seen in Examples 8-3 and 8-4, where V^6 and V$^6_5$ prolong the tonic. In Example 8-5 the V^6 allows the stepwise motion of the bass line to continue and also lessens the effect of this interior V–I progression. The I^6 in the second measure provides variety and allows the bass to imitate the soprano figure from the previous beat (A–B♭–C). The second line of roman numerals beneath the example indicates that the tonic area is prolonged for $1\frac{1}{2}$ measures.

Example 8-5 Bach, *Schmücke dich, o liebe Seele*

The diminished triad was used almost exclusively in first inversion throughout much of the tonal era. Earlier composers had considered a sonority to be acceptable only if all the intervals above the *bass* were consonant, and, as the diagram illustrates, a dissonant °5 or +4 occurs above the bass of a diminished triad unless it is in first inversion.

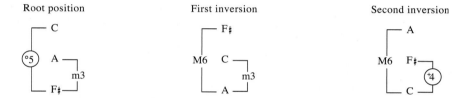

Tonal composers, although perhaps being unaware of the historical background, accepted for a time the tradition of using the diminished triad only in first inversion.

One first inversion triad that should *not* be freely substituted for the root position is vi⁶ (or VI⁶). A good rule to remember is that V in root position should not be followed by vi⁶. The reason for this can best be understood by playing Example 8-6 and comparing the effect of the V–vi and V–vi⁶ progressions. The V–vi sounds fine—a good example of a deceptive progression—but the vi⁶ sounds like a mistake.

Example 8-6

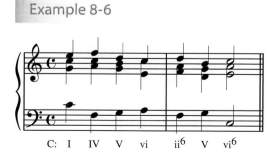

One correct use of the vi⁶ chord is between a root position I and a root position ii, as in Example 8-7a, where it prolongs the tonic harmony. (This is sometimes called 5-6 technique because the vi⁶ avoids parallel 5ths between the I and ii chords.) The vi⁶ will also occur occasionally as part of a sequential pattern, as in Example 8-7b.

Example 8-7

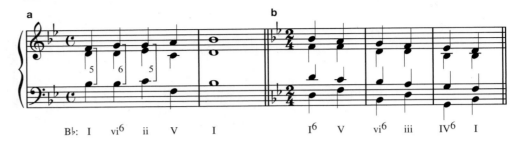

Bb: I   vi⁶   ii   V   I   I⁶   V   vi⁶   iii   IV⁶   I

Inversions in Lead Sheets

When playing from a lead sheet, the bass player in a jazz group tends to emphasize the roots of chords on the strong beats or where the chord begins, unless there is a reason to do otherwise. One reason would be if the lead sheet uses **slash chords,** such as C/E, which calls for a C major triad in first inversion. Often slash-chord notation is used to create a stepwise bass line, as in the second half of Example 8-8. The essential bass line (not part of the lead sheet) is shown in the staff below the melody, but a bass player would probably play other pitches while still emphasizing the notes shown.

Example 8-8   Loewe, "Wouldn't It Be Loverly"

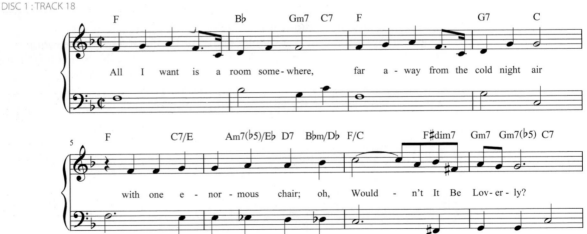

F   Bb   Gm7   C7   F   G7   C

All I want is a room some-where,   far a-way from the cold night air

F   C7/E   Am7(b5)/Eb D7   Bbm/Db F/C   F#dim7   Gm7 Gm7(b5) C7

with one e-nor-mous   chair; oh,   Would—n't It Be Lov-er-ly?

Parallel Sixth Chords

Most passages use a reasonable balance of root position and first inversion triads, but there are many passages in which this is not true. Some styles call for a preponderance of root position chords. On the other hand, a whole series of parallel first inversion triads (or **sixth chords,** from figured-bass symbols) is often found, especially in sequences. Chords used in parallel motion in this way generally do not function in the usual fashion. Instead, they serve as passing chords, connecting some chord at the beginning of the passage to some chord at the end of it. In Example 8-9 the parallel motion connects the root position I chord in m. 4 with another root position I chord in m. 7. The roman numerals in the sixth-chord passage are in parentheses to show that the chords are not functioning in their usual manner.

Example 8-9   Haydn, Symphony no. 104, I

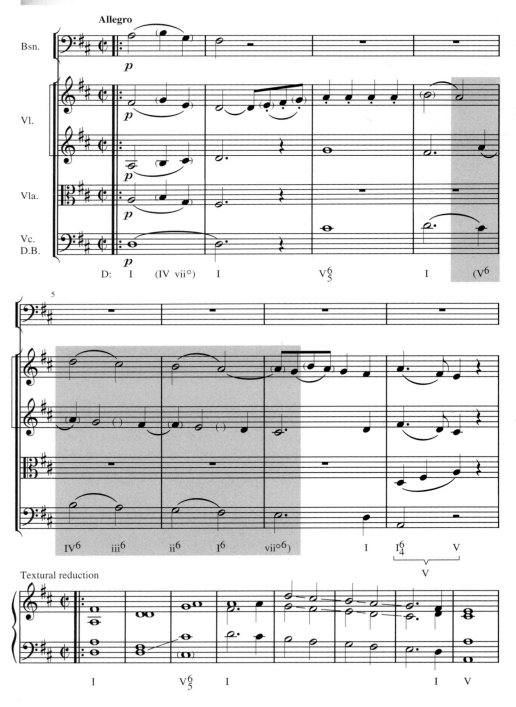

Textural reduction

In the textural reduction of Example 8-9 the line in mm. 2–3 connecting D3 to C♯4 shows that a simplified version of the bass line would have stepwise motion here (m2 down) instead of the leap. Notice also the parallel 5ths in the reduction of mm. 5–7. Haydn disguised the 5ths in the original through the use of nonchord tones. The usual technique used to avoid parallel 5ths in a sixth-chord passage is to put the root of each chord in the melody, thus producing acceptable parallel 4ths instead of objectionable parallel 5ths (Example 8-10a). In a four-voice texture, at least one voice will have to use leaps to avoid parallels, as in Example 8-10b.

Example 8-10

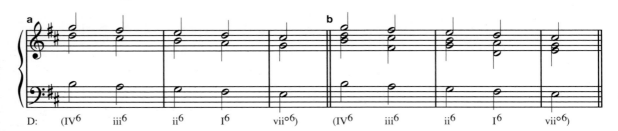

D: (IV⁶   iii⁶   ii⁶   I⁶   vii°⁶)   (IV⁶   iii⁶   ii⁶   I⁶   vii°⁶)

CHECKPOINT

1. What are the three uses of first inversion triads discussed in this chapter?
2. What type of triad (major, minor, or diminished) is usually used in first inversion rather than in root position?
3. How are inversions indicated in lead sheet symbols?

Part Writing First Inversion Triads

Composition exercises using triads in first inversion as well as in root position are much more satisfying musically than are exercises restricted to root position only. Previous suggestions concerning spacing and voice leading still apply, of course, and should be considered together with those that follow.

FOUR-PART TEXTURES

Inverted triads are nearly always complete in four-part textures. Because there are four voices and only three chord members, one of the members will have to be doubled. The following suggestions should prove helpful.

1. In a contrapuntal texture—that is, in a texture consisting of relatively independent melodic lines—the doubling to use is the one that results from the best voice leading.
2. In a homophonic texture—that is, one that is primarily chordal or consists of a melody with chordal accompaniment—the doubling selected should be the one that provides the desired sonority.
3. In any texture, it is usually best not to double the leading tone.

The first of these suggestions probably needs no further explanation. Concerning the second suggestion, you should play Example 8-11, listening carefully to the different sonorities produced. If possible, you should also hear the example sung and performed by several combinations of instruments. The four parts of the example are presented in what is generally considered the order of preference on the part of composers of tonal music. However, this ordering is *not* to be interpreted as a rule. The quality of the sonority is affected as much by spacing as it is by doubling, as you will discover by comparing the last two chords in Example 8-11.

Example 8-11

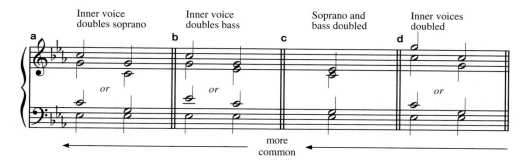

A doubled leading tone usually results in or implies parallel 8ves because of the strong tendency of $\hat{7}$ to resolve to $\hat{1}$. If you play Example 8-12a through c, you will probably agree that Example 8-12c produces the most pleasing effect. Example 8-12a is obviously incorrect because of the parallel 8ves. However, Example 8-12b, which avoids the parallels, still produces an unpleasant effect, probably because the parallels are still implied by the doubled leading tone.

Example 8-12

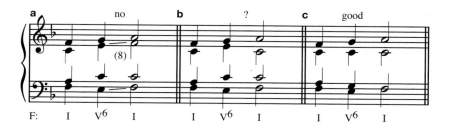

THREE-PART TEXTURES

Inverted triads are usually complete in three-part writing. Although incomplete inverted triads do occur, they are not used with the same frequency as incomplete root position triads. If a member of the triad is omitted, it will almost always be the 5th. The omitted member obviously cannot be the 3rd because that is the bass note. If the root is omitted, the resulting sonority might be heard *not* as an inverted triad but as a root position triad, as in Example 8-13. However, there are cases in which such lack of clarity is not a problem, as in Example 8-13, where IV and ii^6 have the same pre-dominant function.

Example 8-13

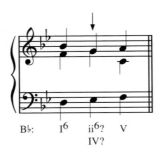

Bb: I⁶   ii⁶?   V
              IV?

Example 8-14 is from a composition for TTB (Tenor, Tenor, Bass) chorus. The tenor parts sound an octave lower than written. There are two incomplete I⁶ chords in this excerpt. In the first of these the 5th is omitted, as we would expect. In the second incomplete I⁶, however, the root is omitted, but the listener recognizes the sonority as representing a I⁶ because it follows a V chord. Notice also that the IV at the beginning of m. 46 could also be analyzed as a ii⁶, as in Example 8-13. Since IV and ii⁶ have the same pre–dominant function in this context, either analysis is correct. All the other inverted triads in the excerpt are complete.

Example 8-14   Schubert, *Bardengesang*

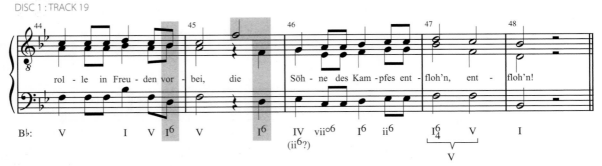

rol - le in Freu - den vor - bei,   die   Söh - ne des Kam - pfes ent - floh'n,   ent -   floh'n!

Bb: V   I V I⁶ V   I⁶   IV vii°⁶ I⁶ ii⁶   I⁶₄ V   I
                                   (ii⁶?)   V

Soprano-Bass Counterpoint

Now that we will be using triads in first inversion, the bass lines of your exercises can be much more interesting and musically satisfying than they were when you had only root position triads available. This bring us back to the subject of **counterpoint,** which was mentioned briefly on page 66, where it was defined as "the combining of relatively independent musical lines." We will now consider the idea of counterpoint a little more closely.

The words *relatively independent* are crucial to the understanding of counterpoint. The word *relatively* has to do with the style of the music in which the counterpoint is found. In tonal music, contrapuntal relationships are governed by certain voice-leading conventions (restrictions against parallel fifths, and so on) and by conventions of harmonic progression. It would be unthinkable in tonal music, for example, for two lines to be in different keys. The word *independent,* in our definition of counterpoint, means that each line in a contrapuntal texture will ideally have its own unique contour and rhythm. Of these, the more important is contour. Let's begin with a counterexample. The opening of Haydn's Symphony no. 8, shown in Example 8-15, is pleasing and effective, but it is not contrapuntal because the lines have identical contours and rhythms and move in parallel motion throughout.

DISC 1 : TRACK 20

Example 8-15   Haydn, Symphony no. 8, I (violins only)

The instruments in Example 8-16 also have identical rhythms and contours, but they are offset by one measure, creating a contrapuntal form known as a **canon.** You no doubt have sung **rounds,** such as "Row, Row, Row Your Boat," which are canons that are perpetual—there is no notated ending for the ensemble, as there is for Haydn's canon (not shown). Canons and rounds make use of a special type of counterpoint called **imitative counterpoint.** Most of the counterpoint discussed in this section is not imitative or is only incidentally imitative.

DISC 1 : TRACK 20

Example 8-16   Haydn, String Quartet op. 76, no. 2, III

In Example 8-17, Bach gives the soprano and bass different contours, although they have identical rhythms, so this is an example of counterpoint as well. Under the music, we show the relationships between the two lines as **p, s,** or **c,** for parallel, similar, or contrary (review p. 74). Notice that the prevailing relationships between the voices are contrary or similar.

Example 8-17   Bach, *Ermuntre dich, mein schwacher Geist*
(outer voices only)

Counterpoint, like that in the previous example, in which the two parts move with identical rhythms, is called 1:1 (one-to-one), or first species, counterpoint. In another harmonization of the same melody, shown in Example 8-18, Bach allows a little more rhythmic variety between the voices. Notice that he also uses a different time signature here. Oblique motion is indicated by **o.**

Example 8-18   Bach, *Ermuntre dich, mein schwacher Geist*
(outer voices only)

It is often instructive to simplify a texture by removing repetitions and embellishments to reveal the simpler underlying counterpoint. This is the approach frequently taken in the reductive examples in this text. For instance, the reduction following Example 8-19 shows that the music begins with a step down and back up in the soprano and a step up and back down in the bass—figures that are known as **neighbor motions.** This is followed in the melody by a leap to $\hat{5}$ in the soprano and a stepwise descent to $\hat{7}$, against which the bass unfolds a somewhat more complicated counterpoint.

Example 8-19   Beethoven, Rondo op. 51, no. 1

So, where in tonal music are we apt to encounter counterpoint? The music of the Baroque period (roughly 1600–1750) is known for contrapuntal textures. Although not all Baroque music is contrapuntal, much of it is, and it is not unusual in Baroque music for all the voices in a contrapuntal texture to have that relative independence that we have been talking about. This is also true in tonal music after the Baroque when the composer is working within one of the traditionally contrapuntal forms, such as the canon, discussed earlier. Another example is the **fugue,** a piece in which each voice states a short theme (the **subject**) in turn, after which it is tossed about among the voices, fragmented, and developed. However, in most tonal music *after* 1750, the greatest contrapuntal interest is found between the outer voices (the soprano and bass lines). This is true not just of vocal music but of tonal music in general. The inner voice or voices in tonal music are frequently "filler" for the most part. In the previous Beethoven example, the inner voice comes to the fore only in m. 3, where it continues the eighth-note arpeggiations begun by the bass at the beginning of the measure.

When you are composing your harmony exercises, whether from scratch or with a given bass or soprano line, you should first try to create a good soprano/bass counterpoint, and only after that is accomplished should you fill in the inner parts. The melodies should be simple, like the ones you learned to write in Chapter 5. The bass line should also be effective, although bass lines tend to be more disjunct than soprano lines, especially at cadences, and the bass should move contrary to the soprano whenever practicable. Later, when you have learned more about adding embellishments, the results will be more musical if the basic contrapuntal framework between the soprano and bass is a good one.

As a final illustration, listen to Example 8-20 and the reduction that follows it. You can see that the counterpoint between the outer parts is quite simple. In fact, the reduction could easily be further simplified so that the top line would consist of $\hat{5}$ $\hat{1}$ $\hat{2}$ $\hat{3}$ in the first four measures and $\hat{5}$ $\hat{1}$ $\hat{2}$ $\hat{1}$ in the last four. The counterpoint is very effective, however; notice that there is *no* parallel motion between the two parts. Mozart took this contrapuntal framework and embellished the top line to create a pleasing and interesting melody.

Example 8-20   Mozart, Quintet for Horn and Strings, K. 407

Textural reduction

Self-Test 8-1

(Answers begin on page 575.)

A. Analysis.

1. Bracket the longest series of complete parallel sixth chords you can find in this excerpt. Do not attempt a roman numeral analysis. Does the voice leading in the sixth-chord passage resemble more closely Example 8-9 or Example 8-10?

Mozart, Piano Sonata K. 279, III

2. Label all chords with roman numerals. Then classify the doubling in each inverted triad according to the methods shown in Example 8-11.

Bach, *Jesu, meiner Seelen Wonne*

DISC 1 : TRACK 23

3. Label all chords with roman numerals. Write out the contour of the bass line in quarter-note heads (without rhythm). Can you find part or all of the bass line hidden in the melody?

Beethoven, Piano Sonata op. 2, no. 1, I

DISC 1 : TRACK 23

B. The following excerpt is from Mozart's *Eine kleine Nachtmusik*. Supply the missing tenor line (viola part in the original) and then compare your result with Mozart's (in Appendix D).

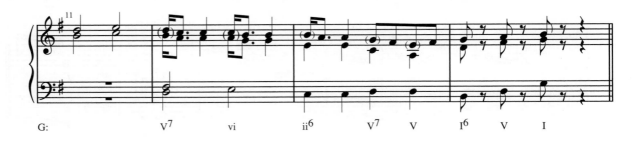

C. Supply alto and tenor lines for the following excerpts.

D. Using the first six problems from Part C, add an alto line to each to create a three-part texture.

E. Analyze the chords specified by these figured basses and then add alto and tenor parts.

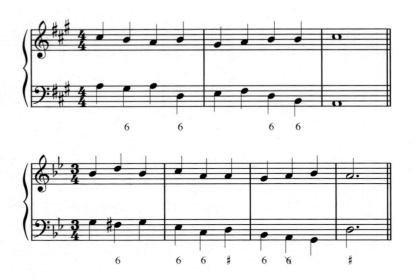

F. The following excerpt is from the Gavotte from Bach's French Suite no. 5. Supply the missing alto line (only) and then compare your result with Bach's original three-part version (Appendix D). Because this is written for a keyboard instrument, you do not need to worry about the range of the alto part, but the right hand should be able to reach both the melody and the alto part.

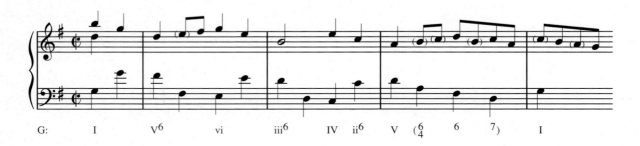

G. Analyze the chords implied by the following soprano and bass lines, remembering to use only triads in root position and first inversion. Then add alto and tenor parts to make a four-part texture.

H. The following example is reduced from Beethoven's Piano Sonata op. 79, III. Analyze the implied harmonies (more than one good solution is possible) and add two inner parts, one on each staff.

I. Continue your solution to Part H with a second four-measure segment, similar to the first.

J. In what ways are Parts F and H similar? What example in Chapter 7 most resembles Parts F and H?

Exercise 8-1 See Workbook.

Summary

Triads in first inversion are not at all unusual in tonal music. They are commonly used to improve the contour of the bass line, to provide a greater variety of pitches in the bass line, or to lessen the weight of V and I chords that do not serve as the goals of harmonic motion. They also come about more incidentally through an arpeggiated bass, and they are sometimes used in a series of parallel chords in first inversion (called *parallel sixth chords*).

Inverted triads in four-part textures are usually complete, with no tones omitted. In three-part textures, if a tone is omitted, it is usually the 5th of the chord. If a tone is to be doubled, any tone but the leading tone will do. In four parts, the most common doublings are soprano or bass with alto or tenor.

Counterpoint is an important element of music throughout the tonal era. Some pieces, such as canons and fugues, feature counterpoint throughout and in all the voices, but in much tonal music the counterpoint is borne mostly by the outer voices (soprano and bass lines).

Variations

To read more about counterpoint, please see Chapter 8 on our website at **www.mhhe.com/kostka7e.**

Chapter Nine

Triads in Second Inversion

Introduction

It would be logical to assume that second inversion triads are used in tonal music in the same ways as first inversion triads: as bass arpeggiations and as substitutes for the root position. However, this is only partly true. Although both first and second inversion triads are created through bass arpeggiations, second inversion triads are *not* used as substitutes for the root position. The reason is that the second inversion of a triad is considered to be a much less stable sonority than either of the other two bass positions. For centuries before the development of tonal harmony, the interval of a P4 had been considered a dissonance if the *lowest voice* in the texture was sounding the bottom pitch of the P4. Although each of the sonorities in Example 9-1 contains a P4 (or a P4 plus a P8), the first two are considered to be consonant because the interval of a P4 does not involve the lowest voice (review the discussion of the diminished triad in first inversion on p. 117). The other two sonorities are dissonant in the tonal style, although our twenty-first-century ears might not easily hear the dissonance.

Example 9-1

Notice that diminished and augmented $^6_4$ triads would also contain dissonant intervals above the bass—an +4 and a °4, respectively.

Because the composers of the tonal era recognized the instability of the $^6_4$ (six-four) chord (the only position in which there is a 4th above the bass), the chord is not used as a substitute for the more stable root position or first inversion sonorities. It is used in bass arpeggiations as well as in several other contexts to be described next. In fact, if you use a six-four chord that is *not* representative of one of the categories discussed next, it would probably be considered an incorrect usage in this style.

Bass Arpeggiation and the Melodic Bass

As with triads in first inversion, six-four chords may come about through a **bass arpeggiation** involving a root position triad, a first inversion triad, or both (Ex. 9-2).

DISC 1 : TRACK 24

Example 9-2   Mendelssohn, Symphony no. 4, op. 90, I

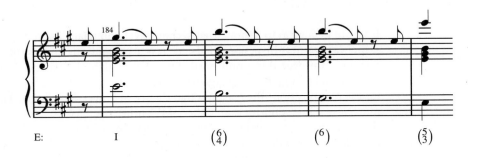

Your analysis of the "real" bass note will depend on the context, taking into account such factors as metric placement, duration, and register. The figures in parentheses in Example 9-2 are often omitted when analyzing a passage employing an arpeggiated bass.

Another somewhat incidental way in which six-four chords can be formed is through a melodic bass. If the bass part has an important melodic line instead of fulfilling its usual supporting role, any number of inverted chords may result. Because a melodic bass is no longer the harmonic foundation of the texture, inversions should not be indicated in such a passage. For example, the bass melody in Example 9-3 is accompanied only by repeated As and Cs, implying the tonic harmony in F major. It would not be correct to analyze the excerpt as beginning with a I$^6_4$.

DISC 1 : TRACK 24

Example 9-3   Beethoven, String Quartet op. 59, no. 1, I

The Cadential Six-Four

Besides its appearance in a bass arpeggiation or a melodic bass, the six-four chord tends to be used in three stereotyped contexts. If you compare the two halves of Example 9-4, you can see that they have much in common. Both begin with a tonic triad and end with a V–I progression. In Example 9-4b, however, the movement from ii^6 to V is momentarily delayed by a I$^6_4$ in a *metrically stronger position*. This is a very typical illustration of the **cadential six-four,** the most familiar of all six-four uses. Notice that the I$^6_4$ resolves to a *root position* V chord. Other resolutions of the cadential six-four will be introduced in Chapters 13 and 17.

Example 9-4

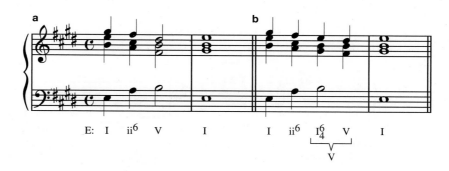

It is important at this point to emphasize that the cadential I$^6_4$ does *not* represent a tonic triad, even though it contains all the notes of a tonic triad. The progression in both parts of Example 9-4 is I–ii–V–I, and it would be incorrect to think of Example 9-4b as representing a I–ii–I–V–I progression. This has led to much debate over the years as to what symbols to use to represent the cadential six-four. The approach used in this text puts the V below the I$^6_4$–V to show that the pair of chords together have a dominant function. Your instructor may prefer that you use a different method, such as V$^{6\text{-}5}_{4\text{-}3}$.

The voice leading in the upper parts into and away from the cadential I$^6_4$ is usually smooth, as in Example 9-4b, and the resolution of the I$^6_4$ to V (or V^7) usually sees scale degrees $\hat{1}$ and $\hat{3}$ moving down by step to $\hat{7}$ and $\hat{2}$, respectively. The cadential I$^6_4$ occurs either on a stronger beat than the V, as in Example 9-4b, or on a stronger *portion* of the beat, as in Example 9-5. The textural reduction shows that Scarlatti's three-voice texture is actually derived from four voices.

Example 9-5 Scarlatti, Sonata L. 489

Textural reduction

However, in triple meter, if the V chord occurs on the third beat of a measure, the I_4^6 will frequently appear on the normally weak second beat, as in Example 9-6. (This is also a four-voice texture. The arpeggiations disguise parallel octaves from the I^6 to the ii^6.)

Example 9-6 Scarlatti, Sonata L. 363

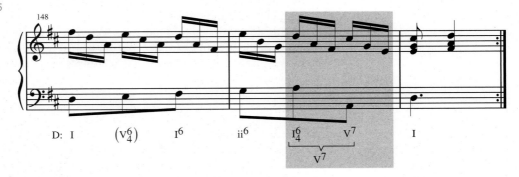

The most dramatic demonstration of the delaying character of the cadential I_4^6 is found at the cadenza of many solo concertos. In such cases, the orchestra stops on a I_4^6, after which the soloist performs the cadenza. No matter what the length of the cadenza, it eventually reaches V and, simultaneously with the return of the orchestra, resolves to I. In a cadenza played by a single-line instrument, the V chord at the end of the cadenza will often be represented by a single tone or a trill, as in Example 9-7.

Example 9-7   Mozart, Violin Concerto K. 271a, III

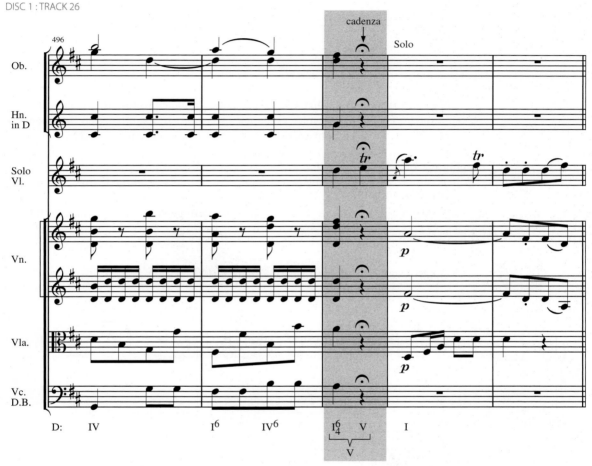

The Passing Six-Four

Second inversion triads are frequently encountered harmonizing the middle note of a three-note scalar figure in the bass, a usage that is called a **passing** six-four chord. The figure may be ascending or descending. Although any triad may be used as a passing six-four chord, those in Example 9-8 are the most common and are found in both major and minor modes. The passing six-four usually falls on a *weak* beat and typically features smooth voice leading, as in Example 9-8. As with the cadential six-four, some theorists prefer not to assign a roman numeral to passing six-fours because of their weak harmonic function. In this text we will indicate this weak function by putting such roman numerals in parentheses.

Example 9-8

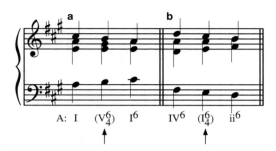

A: I   (V$_4^6$)   I^6 IV^6 (I$_4^6$)   ii^6

Notice in Example 9-8a that a voice exchange (review pp. 102–103) occurs between the soprano and bass lines. A voice exchange also occurs in Example 9-8b (between bass and tenor), but more prominent are the parallel sixths between soprano and bass. Both of these soprano/bass patterns—voice exchange and parallel sixths—are commonly found in passing six-four chords.

Example 9-9 contains both a passing I$_4^6$ (m. 25) and a cadential I$_4^6$ (m. 27) in a three-part texture. The first inversion chords in mm. 24–26 are all substituted first inversions. Notice that the melody in mm. 24–27 is an embellished stepwise descent from A5 to B4.

Example 9-9   Mozart, Piano Sonata K. 309, III

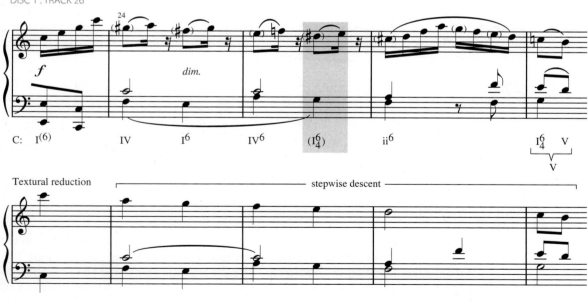

C: I$^{(6)}$ IV   I^6 IV^6 (I$_4^6$)   ii^6 I$_4^6$ V

Textural reduction   ———— stepwise descent ————

Longer stepwise motions in the bass often use passing six-four chords, as in Example 9-10. The textural reduction shows that the melody is also essentially stepwise and moves for several measures in parallel 6ths with the bass.

Example 9-10   Mozart, Symphony no. 40, K. 550, IV (piano score)

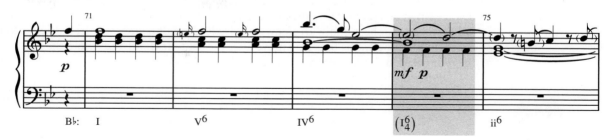

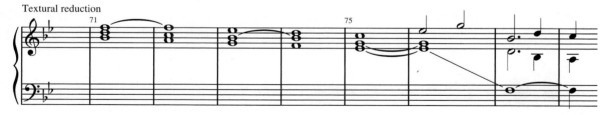

The Pedal Six-Four

One way of elaborating a static root position triad is to move the 3rd and 5th of the triad up by step and then back down by step to their original positions. The sonority that results is a six-four chord (Ex. 9-11).

Example 9-11

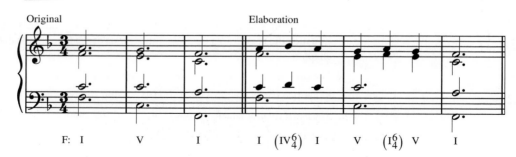

Because this elaboration is similar to a pedal point (discussed in Chapter 12), it is called a **pedal six-four** (some theorists call it an embellishing or stationary six-four). The roman numeral beneath a pedal six-four is put in parentheses to indicate its weak harmonic function.

Pedal six-four chords usually work exactly like those in Example 9-11. That is, they involve either a I–(IV$^6_4$)–I progression or a V–(I$^6_4$)–V progression, with the six-four chord falling on a weak beat and with stepwise voice leading into and away from the six-four chord. Exceptionally, the bass may move after the six-four chord and before the return of the root position triad, as in Example 9-12.

DISC 1 : TRACK 27

Example 9-12   Mozart, String Quartet K. 465, I

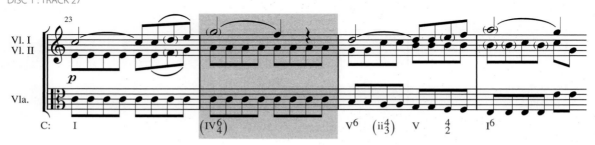

As with other types of six-four chords, pedal six-fours are occasionally seen in lead-sheet notation. Example 9-13 contains a clear instance of a pedal six-four in a I–(IV$^6_4$)–I progression.

DISC 1 : TRACK 28

Example 9-13   Webber, "Don't Cry for Me, Argentina"

CHECKPOINT

1. Two ways in which six-four chords are produced is through bass arpeggiation and by a melodic bass. Name the three other kinds of six-four chords discussed in this chapter.

2. The cadential six-four chord precedes what root position triad?

3. What two triads are most often used as passing six-four chords?

4. The pedal six-four usually involves one of two progressions. What are they?

Part Writing for Second Inversion Triads

In a four-part texture, the bass (5th of the chord) should be doubled. Exceptions to this are rarely encountered in tonal music. The other voices generally move as smoothly as possible—often by step—both into and out of the six-four chord. In a three-part texture, it is generally best to have all members of the triad present (Ex. 9-14a), but sometimes the root or 3rd is omitted, in which case the 5th is doubled (Exs. 9-14b and 9-14c).

Example 9-14

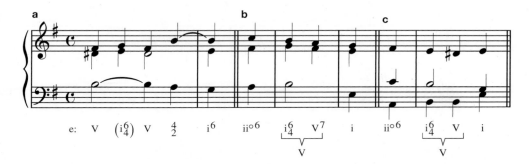

Self-Test 9-1

(Answers begin on page 579.)

A. Analysis. In addition to the specific instructions for each example, label each six-four chord by type.

    1. Label the chords with roman numerals. Be sure to include the F♯5 at the beginning of m. 69 and m. 70 as a chord member.

    Mozart, Piano Sonata K. 333, III

DISC 1 : TRACK 29

2. Label the chords with roman numerals. Remember to label the type of any six-four chords you find.

Handel, Suite no. 5 in E Major, "Air"

3. Label the chords with roman numerals, and label any six-four chords.

Mozart, Piano Sonata K. 311, II

Andante con espressione

B. Fill in one or two inner parts, as specified. Identify any six-four chords by type.

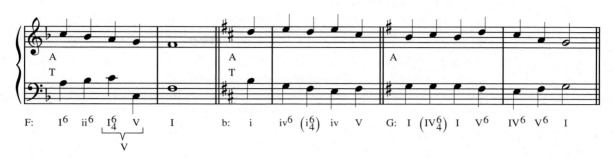

C. Realize these figured basses for three or four voices, as specified. Notice the frequent
    use of $\frac{5}{3}$ (or the equivalent, such as $\frac{5}{\sharp}$) to indicate a root position triad following an
    inverted chord. Analyze with roman numerals and label six-four types.

Exercise 9-1 See Workbook.

Summary

Six-four chords may come about incidentally through bass arpeggiation, or they may occur if the
melody is in the bass. However, in other contexts, triads in second inversion are treated in special
ways in tonal music because the six-four chord is considered dissonant in this style.

   The **cadential six-four chord** is a tonic six-four that delays the arrival of the V chord that follows
it. It depends totally on the V chord for its meaning, and it should not be thought of as a substitute

for a tonic triad in root position or first inversion. The cadential six-four occurs in a metrically stronger position than the V chord that it delays.

A **passing six-four chord** harmonizes the middle note of a three-note scalar figure in the bass. The most common passing six-four chords are the V_4^6 and the I_4^6 chords, and they tend to fall on a weak beat.

A **pedal six-four chord** elaborates the root position chord that precedes it and usually follows it as well. Most pedal six-four chords are I_4^6 or IV_4^6 chords.

The voice leading into and out of a six-four chord is usually as smooth as possible, with stepwise motion prevailing. In a four-voice texture, the bass (5th of the chord) is almost always doubled.

Chapter Ten
Cadences, Phrases, Periods, and Sentences

Musical Form

Understanding tonal harmony requires more than the knowledge of how each chord tends to function harmonically in a progression and how the voice leading might bring the chord into being. We must also give some consideration to musical **form,** the ways in which a composition is shaped to create a meaningful musical experience for the listener.

A thorough study of lengthy compositions is beyond the scope of this text. However, it will be helpful for you to learn something of the harmonic basis of the smaller building blocks that combine to produce larger forms, several of which are introduced in Chapter 20.

Cadences

Although the ultimate harmonic goal of a tonal composition is the final tonic triad, there will also be many interior harmonic goals found within the piece, some of them tonic triads and some of them not. These interior goals might be reached at a fairly regular rate (often every four measures), or sometimes their appearances might not form a pattern at all. We use the term **cadence** to mean a harmonic goal, specifically the chords used at the goal. There are several types of cadences commonly found in tonal music. Some cadences sound more or less conclusive, or final, whereas others leave us off balance, feeling a need for the music to continue.

Locating the cadences in a composition is easier to do than it is to explain. Remember that what you are listening for is a goal, so there will often be a slowing down through the use of longer note values, but even a piece that never slows down (a "perpetuum mobile") will contain cadences. As you listen to the examples in this chapter, you will realize that you are already aurally familiar with tonal cadences and that finding them is not a complicated process.

There is a standard terminology used for classifying the various kinds of cadences, and the terms apply to both major and minor keys. One very important type of cadence consists of a tonic triad preceded by some form of V or vii°. This kind of cadence is called an **authentic cadence** (which is an unfortunate term because it implies that all the others are less than authentic). The **perfect authentic cadence** (abbreviated PAC) consists of a V–I (or V^7–I) progression, with both the V and I in root position and $\hat{1}$ in the melody over the I chord (Ex. 10-1). The PAC is the most final sounding of all cadences. Most tonal compositions end with a PAC, but such cadences might also be found elsewhere in a piece.

Example 10-1   Bach, *Well-Tempered Clavier,* Book II, Prelude 10

e: V   i (PAC)

An **imperfect authentic cadence** (IAC) is usually defined simply as any authentic cadence that is not a PAC. However, it is useful to identify several subcategories, as follows:

1. *Root position IAC:* Like a PAC, but $\hat{3}$ or $\hat{5}$ is in the melody over the I chord (Ex. 10-2).

Example 10-2   Bach, *Well-Tempered Clavier,* Book II, Prelude 12

A♭:   V   I   (IAC)

2. *Inverted IAC:* $V^{(7)}$–I, but with either or both of the chords inverted (Ex. 10-3).

Example 10-3   Schumann, *Nachtlied,* op. 96, no. 1

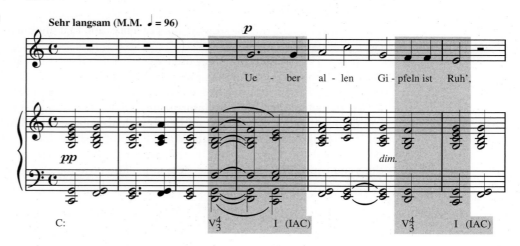

Sehr langsam (M.M. ♩ = 96)

Ue - ber   al - len   Gi - pfeln ist   Ruh',

C: V^4_3 I (IAC) V^4_3 I (IAC)

3. *Leading-tone IAC:* Some form of vii°–I, the vii° substituting for a V chord (Ex. 10-4).

DISC 1 : TRACK 31

Example 10-4   Bach, *Befiehl du deine Wege*

C: vii°⁶   I (IAC)

The root position IAC is certainly the most final sounding of the three IAC types, and you might find some compositions that end with such a cadence. The other types are limited almost exclusively to less important interior cadences.

Remember that not every V–I progression constitutes an authentic cadence. Only when the I chord seems to serve as the goal of a longer passage—usually at least a few measures—would we term a V–I progression a cadence. This same distinction also applies to the other types of cadences.

A **deceptive cadence** (DC) results when the ear expects a V–I authentic cadence but hears V–? instead. The ? is usually a submediant triad, as in Example 10-5, but others are possible. A DC produces a very unstable feeling and would never be used to end a tonal work. Remember that V–vi involves special part-writing problems. Review Example 6-9 (p. 88).

DISC 1 : TRACK 32

Example 10-5   Haydn, Piano Sonata no. 4, II

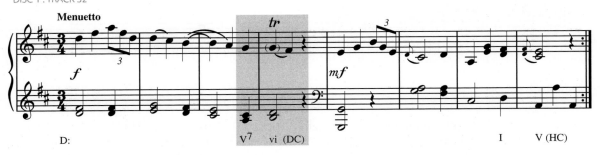

D: V⁷   vi (DC)   I   V (HC)

A deceptive progression is often used not to really *end* a phrase but to *extend* it a few measures until it reaches the true cadence.

The **half cadence** (HC) is a very common type of unstable or "progressive" cadence. The HC ends with a V chord, which can be preceded by any other chord (Ex. 10-6).

Example 10-6   Haydn, Piano Sonata no. 44, II

The **Phrygian half cadence** (Ex. 10-7) is a special name given to the iv⁶–V HC in minor. The name refers to a cadence found in the period of modal polyphony (before 1600), but it does not imply that the music is actually in the Phrygian mode.* Notice, incidentally, that Example 10-7 contains a deceptive progression (V⁷–VI) but not a deceptive *cadence* because the goal of the passage is the V in m. 4, not the VI in m. 3.

Example 10-7   Schumann, "Folk Song," op. 68, no. 9

A **plagal cadence** (PC) typically involves a IV–I progression. Although plagal cadences are usually final sounding, they are not as important in tonal music as the authentic cadence. In fact, a plagal cadence is usually added on as a kind of tag following a PAC. A familiar example of this is the "Amen" sung at the end of hymns, as in Example 10-8.

---

*   Modal polyphony used a number of scalar patterns seldom employed by tonal composers. One of these was the Phrygian mode, which used a scale pattern the same as E to E with no accidentals.

Example 10-8 Dykes, "Holy, Holy, Holy!"

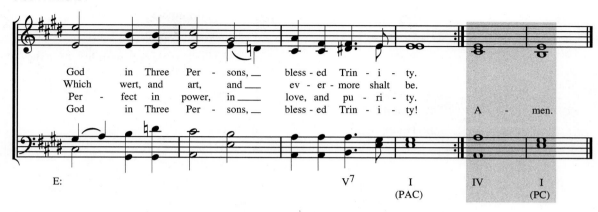

The preceding definitions of cadence types are standard, for the most part, and they will apply to most cadences found in tonal music. Exceptions will be found, however, in which case the more general definitions listed in the following table should be applied.

Cadence type	First chord	Second chord
Authentic	Contains leading tone	Tonic
Plagal	Does not contain leading tone	Tonic
Deceptive	Contains leading tone	Not tonic
Half	Does not contain leading tone	Not tonic

A still more general but useful method of classifying cadences puts them into two groups: **conclusive** (authentic and plagal) and **progressive** (deceptive and half).

Cadences and Harmonic Rhythm

As a very general rule, the last chord of a cadence usually falls on a stronger beat than the chord that precedes it. This assumes that the rate at which the chords change—the harmonic rhythm—is faster than one chord per measure. The following rhythmic examples illustrate this using authentic cadences; possible cadential I_4^6 chords are shown in parentheses.

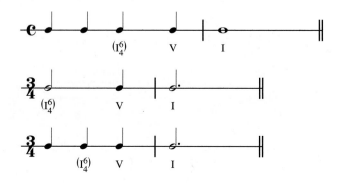

CHECKPOINT

Match the cadence-type abbreviations with the definitions and examples.

Cadence types	*Definitions and examples*
1. PAC	a. V–I, both in root position, with $\hat{3}$ or $\hat{5}$ in the melody over the I chord
2. Root position IAC	b. IV–I
3. Inverted IAC	c. ?–V
4. Leading tone IAC	d. V–vi
5. PC	e. vii°⁶–I
6. HC	f. V–I⁶
7. Phrygian HC	g. V–I, both in root position, with $\hat{1}$ in the melody over the I chord
8. DC	h. iv⁶–V in minor

Motives and Phrases

A **motive** is the smallest identifiable musical idea. A motive can consist of a pitch pattern, a rhythmic pattern, or both, as you can see next.

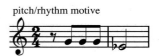

Of the two aspects of a pitch/rhythm motive, rhythm is probably the stronger and more easily identified when it reappears later in a composition. It is best to use motive to refer only to those musical ideas that are "developed" (worked out or used in different ways) in a composition.

A **phrase** is a relatively independent musical idea terminated by a cadence. A **subphrase** is a distinct portion of a phrase, but it is not a phrase either because it is not terminated by a cadence or because it seems too short to be relatively independent. Essentially, a subphrase is a melodic event, whereas a phrase is a harmonic event. Phrases are usually labeled with lowercase letters (a, b, c, and so on), as in Example 10-9.

Example 10-9   Beethoven, Symphony no. 6, op. 68, I

As you might guess from the definition of *phrase*, there is a good deal of subjectivity involved in identifying phrases. What sounds like a phrase to one listener might be a subphrase to another listener. The first four measures of Example 7-9 (p. 100) seem to meet the requirement for relative independence, but the I–ii$^6_5$ progression in those measures does not provide a cadence. Mm. 1–8 of the same example meets both requirements, however, so this is an eight-measure phrase ending with an IAC. Nor can the issue be decided only by finding cadences, because subphrases frequently end with progressions that could be cadences. For instance, the first two measures of Example 10-10 end with a V^7–I progression over the barline, but most would agree that this span of music is too inconsequential to be called relatively independent. Also, phrases are often extended by means of a deceptive progression followed by an authentic cadence, or they might be extended by repetition of the cadence, as in phrase a of Example 10-10 (mm. 1–6). The final phrase of this minuet, phrase a′, returns phrase a with an added repetition of the first subphrase, creating an eight-measure phrase. Phrases b and c also contain repetitions of their opening subphrases, but with some variation in each case.

DISC 1 : TRACK 35

Example 10-10   Haydn, Piano Sonata no. 15, II

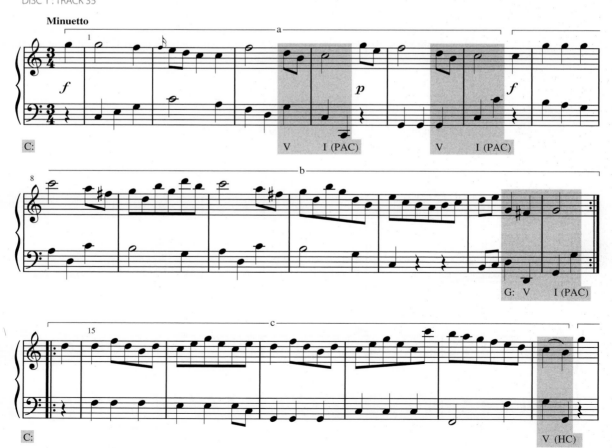

The last note of one phrase sometimes serves as the first note of the next one, a process referred to as **elision.** An even more extreme overlap can be seen by looking back at Example 10-3, in which the cadence in the fourth measure of the introduction serves also as the first measure of the first phrase of the song.

Mozart: *An die Freude*

All the concepts we have presented so far in this chapter are well illustrated in Example 10-11. This deceptively simple song was composed by Mozart when he was eleven years old. The singer doubles the right hand of the piano part throughout, and a nice effect is obtained in performance if the left hand of the piano part is doubled by a cello or a bassoon.

DISC 1 : TRACK 35

Example 10-11   Mozart, *An die Freude*, K. 53

Cadences occur regularly every four measures in this song, each cadence marking the end of a phrase. Because the texture contains only two lines, the chords are necessarily incomplete, but the implied harmonies at the cadences are clear enough and have been labeled for you. The cadences illustrate all the types discussed in this chapter, with the exception of the PC.

Notice that two cadences occur in the key of the dominant (C), and one occurs in the key of the supertonic (g). Because we do not lose track aurally of the key of F as we listen to the song, it would be appropriate to refer to mm. 13 to 24 as embellishments of V and ii rather than as a true change of tonal center. All the cadences are listed in the following table:

Measure	Cadence type	Key
4	DC	F
8	Root position IAC	F
12	HC	F
16	DC	C
20	PAC	C
24	Inverted IAC	g
28	HC	F
32	Leading-tone IAC	F
36	DC	F
40	PAC	F

Many of the phrases in this song can be heard as consisting of two subphrases. For instance, mm. 1–2 and mm. 3–4 are two segments that combine to make the first phrase. Although most people would agree that the mm. 1–2 segment is too short to be a phrase, the distinction is not always clear, and it is perfectly possible for two informed musicians to disagree about this and other examples.

An die Freude also contains motives, of course. Two of the most important are primarily rhythmic: ♩. ♫ and ♩♩♩♩. The grace note in m. 22 is performed as an eighth note on beat 1, so m. 22 is an instance of the second motive.

Period Forms

Certain patterns for organizing phrases or groups of phrases are so effective that they are found over and over again in music literature. One such pattern is the larger structural unit called the **period**. A period typically consists of two phrases in an antecedent-consequent (or question-answer) relationship, that relationship being established by means of a stronger cadence at the end of the second phrase. The most commonly encountered patterns are the following:

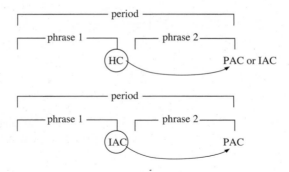

Notice that by definition the phrase endings in a period must be different. If both phrases are identical, the result is not a period but a **repeated phrase.** Repetition is important in tonal music, but it does not contribute to the growth of a musical form.

We use the term **parallel period** if both phrases *begin* with similar or identical material, even if that material is embellished. Example 10-12 illustrates a parallel period. (You might hear two-measure phrases in this excerpt instead of the four-measure phrases we have analyzed. If so, this would be a parallel *double* period, which is discussed later in this chapter.)

Example 10-12   Schubert, *Am Meer*

A formal diagram of Example 10-12 would show the parallel relationship between the phrases by labeling them a and a′ (pronounced "a prime").

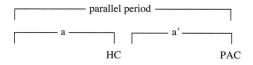

Sometimes the parallel relationship between the phrases is not so obvious. In Example 10-13, the melody of the second phrase begins like the first, but it is a third lower. Sequential relationships like this one are similar enough to be labeled a parallel period. The antecedent-consequent relationship here is established by the IAC in mm. 3 to 4 (V_3^4–I with $\hat{3}$ in the melody over the I chord) and the PAC in mm. 7–8.

DISC 1 : TRACK 36

Example 10-13   Gershwin, "I Loves You Porgy"

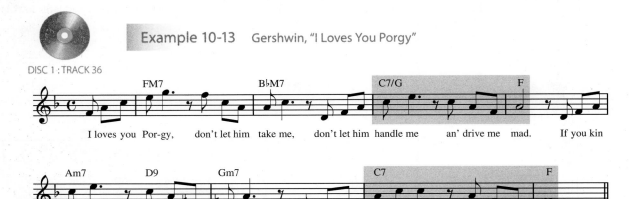

A period in which the phrase beginnings are not similar is called a **contrasting period.** Example 10-14 illustrates a contrasting period.

DISC 1 : TRACK 37

Example 10-14   Beethoven, Violin Sonata op. 12, no. 1, III

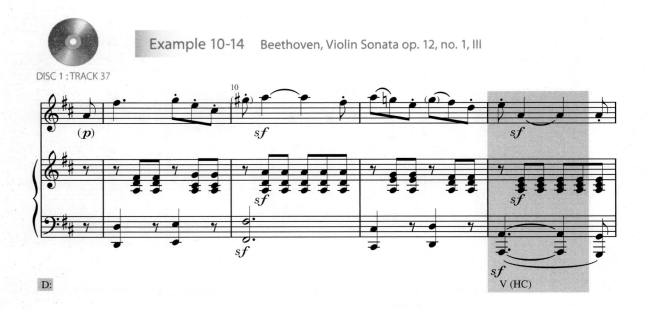

A common way of expanding a two-phrase period is by repeating the antecedent phrase (as in *aab*) or the consequent phrase (*abb*). It is also possible to repeat both (*aabb*), which is not the same as a repeated period (*abab*).

A genuine **three-phrase period,**[*] however, has three different phrases—two antecedents and a consequent or one antecedent and two consequents, as determined by the cadences. In Example 10-15 there are two antecedents because the first two phrases end with half cadences.

DISC 1 : TRACK 37

Example 10-15   Mozart, *The Marriage of Figaro*, K. 492, "Voi, che sapete"

CHERUBINO

Voi,   che   sa - pe - te   che   co - sa è a - mor,

B♭:   V (HC)

[*]   Some writers use the term *phrase group* for what we call a three-phrase period.

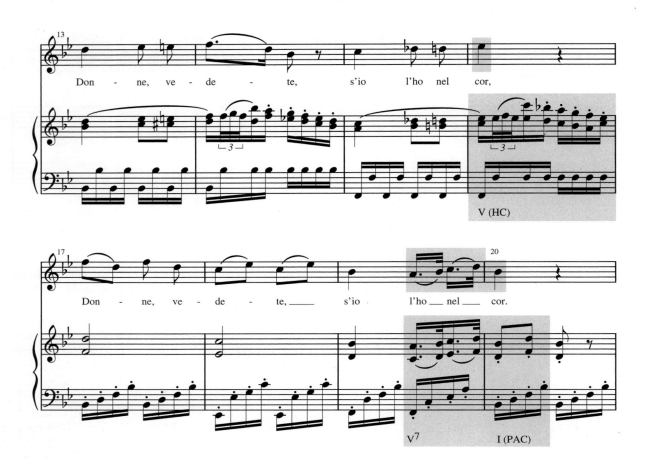

A **double period** consists typically of four phrases in two pairs, the cadence at the end of the second pair being stronger than the cadence at the end of the first pair.

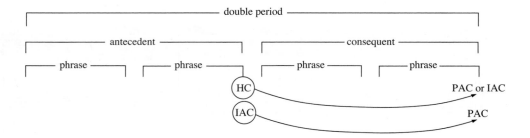

There are several things that should be pointed out about this diagram. First, notice that this structure is much like a period, with the only difference being that each half consists here of a pair of phrases instead of one phrase. Also notice that the first two phrases will probably not form a period according to our original definition, so a double period does not usually consist of two periods. Finally, notice that a **repeated period** is not the same as a double period because a double period requires contrasting cadences.

Double periods are called parallel or contrasting according to whether the melodic material that begins the two halves of the double period is similar. Example 10-16 illustrates a parallel double period, and its structure is outlined in the following diagram.

Example 10-16   Beethoven, Piano Sonata op. 26, I

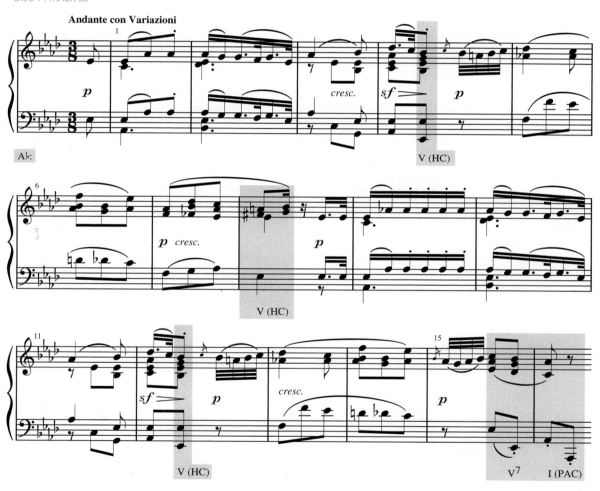

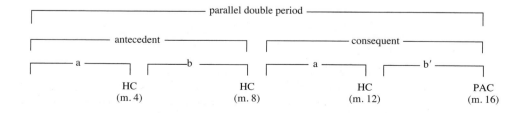

Because the first and third phrases have the same cadence, the third phrase in the diagram is labeled a, not a′, even though the original a is somewhat ornamented when it returns as the third phrase.

Often several phrases will seem to belong together structurally while clearly not constituting a period or double period—typically when the final cadence is not the strongest one. This is especially common in transitional passages that connect more significant thematic areas. The term **phrase group** is used for such situations. Before assigning this term, however, study the music (especially the cadences) closely to see whether a passage might be analyzed as a variant of some period form.

The Sentence

As we have seen, the most important distinguishing feature of the period is the weak-strong cadence pattern formed by the endings of its two halves. It is possible to employ musical features other than cadence patterns to create larger structural units. One such unit, the **sentence,** is characterized by the immediate repetition or variation of a musical idea followed by a motion toward a cadence. Unlike the period, a sentence is typically, though not always, a single phrase in length. The formal diagram of a sentence is shown next (the idea and its variant are indicated as x and x′).

Example 10-17 illustrates a sentence. An initial idea in mm. 7–8 is immediately followed by a variation of that idea in mm. 9–10 that is motivically similar but features a different harmonization. The final six measures (mm. 11–16) drive to an emphatic HC and feature a stepwise sixteenth-note motive first found in the left hand in mm. 8 and 10.

Example 10-17   Mozart Piano Sonata K. 311, I

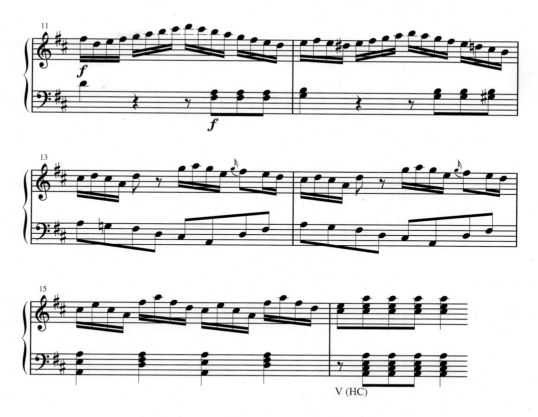

V (HC)

The relationship between the initial idea and its variant can take many forms. The variant may be an exact or ornamented repetition of the initial idea (Ex. 10-18). Or it may use the same harmony, but transpose the melody to different chord tones. It may contrast two harmonies (I and V, for example) or two parts of a complete progression (Ex. 10-17; for example, I–V, V–I or I–ii^6, V–I), or it may form a sequential progression (Ex. 10-19).

Example 10-18 Mozart Piano Sonata K 279, I

The second half of the sentence is less strictly defined. It may be shorter than the first part of the sentence (Ex. 10-20), or it may be longer (like Ex. 10-18). It may continue to use motives from the initial idea (like the stepwise sixteenth-note motive in Ex. 10-17), or it may introduce new material (Ex. 10-18). In most cases, this material provides a sense of increased drive or momentum toward the final cadence.

Because the length of the initial idea may vary in size, the sentence itself can be of different lengths. Mm. 1–4 of Example 10-19 feature a four-measure sentence that begins with two one-measure ideas. The same is true of mm. 5–8.

Example 10-19 Beethoven, Piano Sonata op. 49, no. 1, II

Toward the other end of the spectrum is the 14-measure sentence shown in Example 10-20, in which the initial ideas are each four measures long. Because of the length of this passage, it might be easier to hear this sentence as containing two phrases, with x and x′ as the first phrase and the remaining material as the second phrase.

Example 10-20 Haydn, String Quartet op. 77, no. 1, I

For an interesting twist, look back at Example 10-19 for a moment and notice the weak-strong cadence pattern formed by its phrases. This cadence pattern would allow us to treat the two sentences as the antecedent phrase and consequent phrase of a parallel period. There are many examples in music of passages like this, where one formal type appears inside another.

When you are listening to—and analyzing—a group of phrases for the first time, it is useful to think about certain musical features that can enable you to distinguish between different kinds of forms. The following clues, when considered in combination, can serve as effective points of orientation:

1. *Look for the location of repetitions—exact or varied—of the initial measures.* If a repetition occurs somewhere in the middle of the passage, a parallel period (or some kind of repeated form) is a likely possibility. If it occurs immediately after the initial measures, a sentence (or a sentence nested inside a larger period) is possible. Note also that repetitions in parallel periods are typically exact or very similar, whereas repetitions in sentences may be exact or quite varied.

2. *Look for the location and number of very strong cadences* (unambiguous PACs, HCs, or root position IACs). Periods tend to feature at least two of these (four or more in the case of some double periods), but sentences often contain only one—at or near the end.

3. *Look at the order and pattern of cadences.* If the cadence pattern repeats itself (such as HC-PAC-HC-PAC), a repeated period or sentence is likely. If there is a single strong cadence, a sentence is likely. If there are many strong cadences, a double period is possible; we would want to look for repetition of the initial measures to find the beginning of the consequent phrase.

Self-Test 10-1

(Answers begin on page 580.)

A. Identify the cadence type for each example that follows. For each IAC, provide a modifier: root position, inverted, or leading tone.

B. Identify the form of each of the following examples:
1. Mozart, Piano Sonata K. 279, III, mm. 23–32 (p. 127).
2. Example 18-5 (p. 294)
3. Beethoven, Piano Sonata op. 2, no. 1, I, mm. 1–8 (p. 128).
4. Schubert, *Aufenthalt,* mm. 111–118 (p. 227).
5. Example 20-7: Mozart, Piano Sonata K. 331, I, mm. 1–8 (p. 325).
6. Schumann, *Album Leaf,* op. 99, no. 1, mm. 9–16 (p. 344).

C. Analysis. The cadence chords have been analyzed for you in each example.
1. Make a diagram of this excerpt similar to the diagrams used in the text. Include labels for phrases or initial ideas (a, b, and so on, or x and x'), cadence types and measures numbers, and the form of the excerpt.

DISC 1 : TRACK 41

Beethoven, Piano Sonata op. 10, no. 3, III

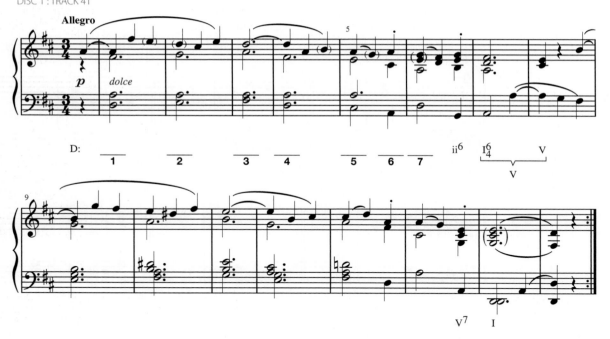

2. Diagram the form of this excerpt as above. Then diagram mm. 1–8 by itself and do the same for mm. 9–16. Which example in the chapter does the entire excerpt resemble formally?

Mozart, Piano Sonata K. 284, II

DISC 1 : TRACK 41

3. There is certainly more than one way to interpret this famous theme. Most writers seem to prefer the three-phrase analysis shown here, the third phrase being an unusually long one (mm. 9–17). What would the form of the theme have been if it had ended in m. 8? Is there any way to hear the entire theme as an expansion of that form? Diagram the theme to illustrate your interpretation.

Beethoven, Piano Sonata op. 13, III

4. Diagram this excerpt. See if you can find an example of contrary 8ves (review pp. 75–76) between the melody and bass.

Chopin, Mazurka op. 33, no. 2

D. Review. Notate the chords in the keys and bass positions indicated.

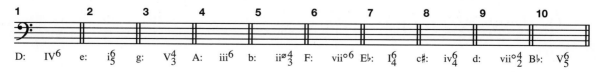

Exercise 10-1 See Workbook.

Summary

Musical **form** concerns the ways in which a composition is shaped to create a meaningful experience for the listener.

The term **cadence** can refer to a harmonic goal or the chords that are used at a harmonic goal. Cadence types in tonal music include the following:

authentic: some form of V or vii° followed by I or I^6

perfect authentic (PAC): root position V or V^7 followed by a root position I with $\hat{1}$ in the soprano over the I chord

imperfect authentic (IAC): any authentic cadence that is not a PAC

deceptive (DC): V followed by some chord other than I, usually vi

half (HC): a cadence that ends on V

Phrygian half (HC): iv^6–V in minor

plagal (PC): IV–I

A **motive** is the smallest identifiable musical idea. A **phrase** is a relatively independent musical idea terminated by a cadence. A phrase is usually constructed of two or more distinct portions called **subphrases.**

Two phrases can be combined to form a **period** if they seem to go together as a musical unit and if the second phrase ends with a more conclusive cadence than the first. **Double periods** are just like periods, except that each half of the structure consists of two phrases rather than just one. Both periods and double periods may be either parallel or contrasting, according to whether the two halves begin with similar melodic material. A **repeated phrase** or **repeated period** does not produce a new kind of formal unit and should not be confused with a period or double period. A **phrase group** is a group of phrases that seem to belong together without forming a period or double period.

A **sentence** is a musical unit consisting of an initial musical idea, a repetition or variation of that idea, and a subsequent passage that moves to a cadence. Sentences are typically organized as a single phrase (of variable length), although long sentences may contain more than one phrase.

This would be an appropriate point at which to begin work on Counterpoint Unit 3, which may be found at www.mhhe.com/kostka7e.

Chapter Eleven
Nonchord Tones 1

Introduction

Many of the examples in the preceding chapters contain notes that do not belong to the chord as analyzed. In many of those examples these notes have been put in parentheses to emphasize the embellishing quality of such nonchord tones, in contrast to chord tones, which are structurally more important. However, to understand tonal music we have to understand nonchord tones because most passages of tonal music contain at least a few of them.

A **nonchord tone** (abbreviated NCT) is a tone, either diatonic or chromatic, that is not a member of the chord. The tone might be an NCT throughout its duration, or, if the harmony changes before the tone does, the tone might be an NCT for only a portion of its duration.

Obviously, you have to analyze the chords before you can begin labeling NCTs, but the process is nearly simultaneous. In multipart music, recognizing the chords and the NCTs is often quite simple, as in Example 11-1.

DISC 1 : TRACK 43

Example 11-1   Schubert, *An Emma*, op. 58, no. 2

Other textures and compositional techniques may make the separation of chords from NCTs more problematic. This will be discussed in greater detail at the conclusion of Chapter 12.

Classification of Nonchord Tones

One way of classifying NCTs is according to the ways in which they are approached and left.* The following table presents the basic definitions of the various types along with abbreviations. Those in the top half of the table will be discussed in detail in this chapter. The others are discussed in Chapter 12.

NCT name (and abbreviation)	Approached by	Left by
Passing tone (p)	Step	Step in same direction
Neighboring tone (n)	Step	Step in opposite direction
Suspension (s)	Same tone	Step down
Retardation (r)	Same tone	Step up
Appoggiatura (app)	Leap	Step
Escape tone (e)	Step	Leap in opposite direction
Neighbor group (n.gr)	(see p. 187)	
Anticipation (ant)	Step or leap	Same tone (or leap)
Pedal point (ped)	(see pp. 190–191)	

Example 11-2 provides illustrations of each of the NCT types in a three-part texture.

Example 11-2

Other terms used in the description of NCTs include **accented/unaccented, diatonic/chromatic, ascending/descending,** and **upper/lower.** These terms will be brought up in connection with the appropriate NCTs. The remainder of this chapter is devoted to a more detailed discussion of the NCT types that involve only stepwise motion: passing tones, neighboring tones, suspensions, and retardations.

---

* NCT terminology is not standardized, and your instructor may prefer that you use different labels and definitions. However, the definitions given here are widely used.

Passing Tones

The **passing tone** is used to fill in the space between two other tones. The two other tones may belong either to the same or to different chords, or they might be NCTs themselves. Usually the space between them is a 3rd, either up or down, and the passing tone is given whatever scale degree lies in between. In Example 11-1 the B♭4 in m. 3 is used to fill in the space between A4 and C5; similarly, the A4 in m. 5 fills in the gap between G4 and B♭4. The B♭4 and the A4, then, are passing tones or, more specifically, *unaccented, diatonic, ascending passing tones.* You might think that this terminology is too detailed to be really useful, and you would be right. Most of the time we would refer to the B♭4 and the A4 as passing tones and let it go at that. However, a good musician, although perhaps not consciously using all the modifiers employed above, will still be aware of the possibilities and their influence on the musical effect.

Occasionally a passing tone fills the space between two notes that are only a M2 apart. Look at Example 11-3, from the "Jupiter" Symphony. The G♯5 in m. 56 is a passing tone, but the two tones that it connects, G5 and A5, are only a M2 apart. The G♯5, then, is a chromatic passing tone, as is the A♯3 in the bass line in m. 58.

Still referring to Example 11-3, look at the first violin part in m. 59. The tones G5 and D5, which are a P4 apart, are connected by two passing tones, F♯5 and E5. In m. 61 several passing tones appear in the first violin part. Technically, the A4, the D5, and the F♯5 are chord tones, and the others are passing tones. In a functional sense, however, *all* the tones after the A4 serve as passing tones filling in the m7 between A4 and G5, connecting the half cadence in m. 61 to the beginning of the next phrase. (See the textural reduction that follows the example.)

Finally, notice that the A♯3 in the second violin part in m. 58 is a chromatic passing tone, as analyzed. Two lines are being played simultaneously by the second violins.

DISC 1 : TRACK 43

Example 11-3   Mozart, Symphony no. 41 ("Jupiter"), K. 551, I

Textural reduction

Neighboring Tones

The **neighboring tone** is used to embellish a single tone, which is heard both before and after the neighbor. It may appear above the tone (upper neighbor) or below it (lower neighbor), and it may be diatonic or chromatic. Example 11-1 contains a neighboring tone in the melody in m. 6; this is an *accented, diatonic upper neighbor.* The neighbors in Example 11-4 are also accented because they fall on stronger metrical positions than the notes they resolve to. The upper neighbors (the As and the D) are *diatonic,* whereas the lower neighbors (the F♯ and the B) are *chromatic.* (The vii°⁴₃ in Example 11-4 is fully diminished instead of half-diminished because it is a "borrowed" chord, to be discussed more fully in Chapter 21.)

Example 11-4   Schumann, Scherzo op. 32

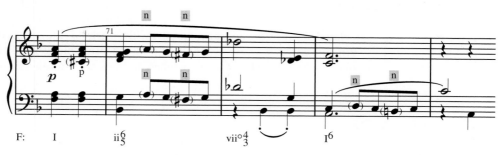

We can only speculate about Schumann's reason for using the chromatic form of the lower neighboring tone here because diatonic neighbors would have been possible. A chromatic neighbor lends more tonal color to a passage, and it tends to draw more attention to the pitch that it is embellishing. A chromatic lower neighbor, like those in Example 11-4, acts as a leading tone to the tone it ornaments. As an experiment, try playing Example 11-4 four ways: (1) all diatonic neighbors, (2) chromatic upper neighbors, (3) chromatic lower neighbors, and (4) all chromatic neighbors. Compare the results.

Suspensions and Retardations

The **suspension** holds on to, or suspends, a chord tone after other parts have moved on to the next chord. Although the suspension may not seem more important than any other type of NCT, considerably more study has been devoted to it. Part of the reason for this is that the suspension is the primary source of dissonance on the *accented* beat in much tonal and pretonal music. Suspensions almost always fall on accented beats or accented portions of beats.

A special terminology has developed concerning the suspension. The **preparation** is the tone preceding the suspension, and it is the same pitch as the suspension. The **suspension** itself may or may not be tied to its preparation. The **resolution** is the tone following the suspension and lying a 2nd below it. The preparation and resolution are almost always chord tones (Ex. 11-5), although the preparation is sometimes an NCT.

Example 11-5

Suspension terminology also provides a means of categorizing suspensions according to the harmonic intervals created by the suspended tone and the resolution. For instance, in Example 11-5, the harmonic interval above the bass created by the suspension is a 7th and that created by the resolution is a 6th, so the entire figure is referred to as a 7–6 suspension.

Example 11-6 summarizes the common suspensions. Notice that the second number is larger than the first only in the 2–3 suspension, a type sometimes referred to as a **bass suspension.** In textures involving more than two parts, the vertical intervals are calculated between the *bass* and the suspended part. If the bass itself is suspended, the interval is calculated between the bass and the part with which it is most dissonant (generally a 2nd or 9th above in a 2–3 suspension). With the exception of the 9–8 suspension, the note of resolution should *not* be present anywhere in the texture when a suspension occurs.

Example 11-6

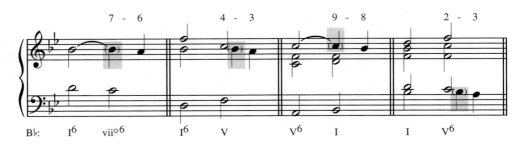

The names of most suspensions remain constant, even if compound intervals are involved. For instance, even if the 4–3 is actually an 11–10, as in Example 11-6, it is still referred to as a 4–3. The exception to this is the 9–8. It is always called a 9–8 suspension unless it does *not* involve a compound interval, in which case it is labeled a 2–1 suspension. The reason for this inconsistency is that the 2–1 suspension is found much less frequently than the 9–8, so it is appropriate that they have different labels.

When a suspension occurs in one of the upper voices, the bass will sometimes move on to another chord tone at the same time as the suspension resolves. This device is referred to as a **suspension with change of bass.** In such a case, a 7–6 suspension, for example, might become a 7–3 suspension because of the movement of the bass. It is also possible to move the upper part of the dissonance as the bass resolves in a 2–3 suspension, creating a 2–6 suspension (Ex. 11-7).

Example 11-7

Although most suspensions are dissonant, consonant suspensions do occur. Example 11-8 contains a suspension in the second measure, even though no dissonance is present. It would *not* be correct to analyze Example 11-8 as vii°$^6_5$—vi^6—I.

Example 11-8

6 - 5

C: vii°$^6_5$ I

Suspensions are very often embellished. That is, other tones, some of them chord tones and some not, may appear after the suspended tone but before the true resolution. In Example 11-9 an embellished 7–6 suspension occurs at the beginning of the second measure. In other words, the G5 is a suspension that resolves to F5, but three ornamenting tones are heard before the F5 is reached. A similar figure appears at the beginning of the next measure, but here the 7th is a chord tone, part of the G^7 chord. In this case, the F5 is a chord tone that is *treated* as a suspension. Such **suspension figures,** in which the suspension is actually a chord tone, are quite common. Notice also in this example the use of the minor v^6 as a passing chord between i and iv^6.

DISC 1 : TRACK 44

Example 11-9   Bach, French Suite no. 2, Sarabande

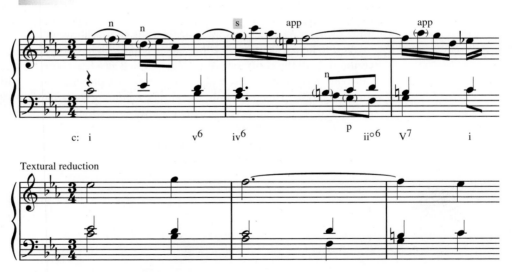

Textural reduction

When the resolution of one suspension serves as the preparation for another, the resulting figure is called a **chain of suspensions.**

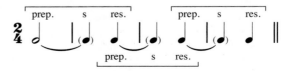

Example 11-9 contains a chain of suspensions: the G5 is suspended, resolving to F5, which in turn is suspended (although not as an NCT), resolving to E♭5. A chain of 7–6 suspensions can be seen in mm. 5–7 of Example 8-9 (p. 119).

Much of what has been said about the suspension applies also to the **retardation,** which is simply a suspension with an upward resolution. Retardations may occur anywhere in a passage, but they are especially common at cadences in Classical style, where they appear in combination with suspensions. As in Example 11-10, the retardation in this context usually involves $\hat{7}$ resolving up to $\hat{1}$.

Example 11-10

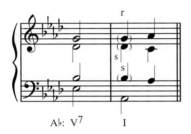

A♭: V⁷   I

Notice in this example that the I chord begins as soon as the tonic note is reached in the bass. It would be incorrect to analyze the first beat of the second measure as a vii° or V⁷ over a pedal point A♭. As you will see in Chapter 12, a pedal point starts out as a chord tone and only later becomes dissonant against the chords above it.

As if to help us summarize the suspension, Bach has provided us with a chorale phrase containing all the common suspensions as well as a less common one. To help you get the most out of Example 11-11, lead-sheet symbols are provided along with the functional harmonic analysis. This is because the phrase *modulates* (changes key) from a to C and back again, and we have not yet presented the ways in which modulations are analyzed. After you understand the chords, follow each voice part through, looking at the NCTs and following the discussion below the example. Finally, play through Example 11-11 and listen to the effect of the suspensions.

Example 11-11   Bach, *Danket dem Herren, denn Er ist sehr freundlich*

a: i   V⁶   i   V⁶   I   6   V⁽⁷⁾   a: i   V
                    C: vi   vi

Soprano
No NCTs

Alto

m. 1   The B4 is a 9–8 suspension. Its resolution, A4, becomes a 7–6 suspension on the next beat. Therefore, this is a chain of suspensions.

Tenor

m. 2   The D4 eighth note is a 9–8 suspension. The suspension is ornamented by the two sixteenth notes that follow it, one of them being a chord tone that anticipates the resolution, the other being a lower neighbor. Notice that by the time the "real" resolution arrives (beat 2), the bass has moved to another chord tone, so this is a 9–6 change of bass suspension.

The B3 on beat 4 is an example of a relatively unusual suspension, the 2–1.

m. 3   The quarter note A3 is a 4–3 suspension. The suspension is ornamented with an augmentation of the figure used to ornament the suspended D4 in m. 2.

Bass

m. 1   The empty parentheses on beat 2 remind us that the A3 is still sounding but is no longer part of the chord. This is an example of a 2–3 suspension.

m. 2   The NCTs in this measure are unaccented, ascending passing tones.

Now examine Example 11-12, and play through it slowly. It sounds like a theory exercise, doesn't it, instead of "real" music? But in fact this is a simplified version of Example 11-11, which certainly is real music. The only thing we have done is to take out the embellishments and to avoid the large leap in the bass in m. 1. The point here is that you should try from now on to make any part-writing exercise into music by adding some embellishments. A word of caution, though: You should work at a keyboard because what looks fine on paper may have a disappointing and unmusical effect when you hear it.

Example 11-12

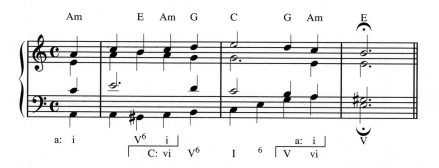

Embellishing a Simple Texture

One way to compose in the tonal style is to begin with a simple texture that has an interesting soprano/bass counterpoint and then embellish it. Two common types of NCT embellishments are the neighbor and the passing tone. Another type of embellishment, although it is not an NCT, is arpeggiation, which we have encountered before. Arpeggiations can be used in any part to create motion or a more interesting line.

Adding neighbors, passing tones, and arpeggiations to the texture is not difficult, but you must be careful not to create objectionable parallels in the process. Example 11-13a illustrates a simple texture without parallels. Example 11-13b shows the same music embellished, but each embellishment has created objectionable parallels. Although parallels created by passing and neighboring tones may occasionally be found in tonal music, you should try to avoid them for now.

Example 11-13

Adding suspensions to the texture does not usually create parallels, but it is still somewhat tricky at first. You may find the following suggestions helpful.

1. Find a step down in the bass. Is the harmonic interval between the bass and some upper voice over the second bass note a 3rd (or 10th)? If so, the 2–3 suspension will work.

2. Find in one of the upper voices a step down. Is the harmonic interval between the second note and the bass a 3rd, 6th, or 8ve? If so, the 4–3, 7–6, or 9–8 suspension, respectively, will work. Exception: Do not use the 4–3 or 7–6 if the resolution of the suspension would already be present in another voice. The aural result is very disappointing.

Following is a simple two-voice example (Ex. 11-14). Possible locations for suspensions are shown with an X. The second part of Example 11-14 is an embellished version containing all the embellishments discussed so far.

Example 11-14

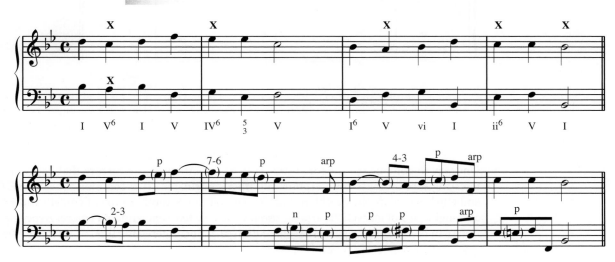

CHECKPOINT

1. A suspension is an NCT that is approached by _____ and left by
   _____ .

2. A neighboring tone is an NCT that is approached by _____ and left by
   _____ .

3. A retardation is an NCT that is approached by _____ and left by
   _____ .

4. A passing tone is an NCT that is approached by _____ and left by
   _____ .

5. What are some other terms that are sometimes used to describe NCTs? (Review p. 172.)

6. Provide the arabic numerals that are used to label the four common types of suspensions.

Figured-Bass and Lead-Sheet Symbols

With the exception of suspensions, NCTs are generally not indicated in a figured bass or in lead-sheet symbols. Most suspensions in figured basses are shown by the use of symbols identical or similar to the numbers we use to name suspension types. Some of the customary figured-bass symbols are given in the following table.

Suspension	Symbols
9–8	9 8
7–6	7 6 or $\frac{7}{3}\frac{6}{-}$
4–3	4 3 or 4 ♯
2–3	$\frac{5}{2}$ under first bass note, 6 under the next

Change of bass suspensions can be recognized by such combinations as "7 3" or "9 6" appearing over a moving bass.

In lead-sheet symbols, a sound that is related to the traditional 4–3 suspension is indicated by "sus" appended to the symbol, as in C7sus, which calls for a chord containing C, F, G, and B♭. The "suspension" may or may not have been prepared in the previous chord, and it will not necessarily resolve in the traditional sense. If the "suspension" does resolve, this could occur within the same chord, as in C7sus C7, or it may resolve in the next chord like a change of bass suspension, as in C7sus FM7. Often, as in Example 11-15, there is no resolution of the 4th at all, and instead it is carried into the next chord. Remember that the G6 symbol calls for a triad with an added note a M6 above the root. (The piano accompaniment in the example is provided for illustration only and does not necessarily reflect the way a jazz pianist would play this excerpt.)

DISC 1 : TRACK 45

Example 11-15   Hampton and Kynard, "Red Top"

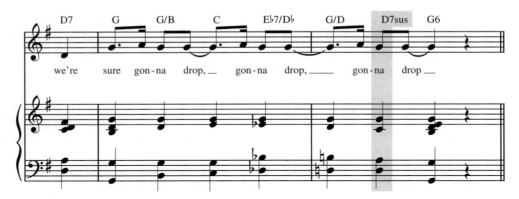

Self-Test 11-1

(Answers begin on page 582.)

A. Analysis.

   1. Go back to Example 7-9 (p. 100), which shows NCTs in parentheses, and identify
the type of each NCT in the blanks below. Always show the interval classification
(7–6 and so on) when analyzing suspensions.

Measure	Treble	Bass
1	___	
2	___	___
3	___	
5	___	
6	___	___
7	___	

   2. Do the same with Example 10-4 (p. 147).

Soprano: ___

Alto: ___   ___

Tenor: ___   ___   ___

3. Analyze chords and NCTs in this excerpt. Then make a reduction by
   (1) removing all NCTs, (2) using longer note values or ties for repeated notes,
   and (3) transposing parts by a P8 when necessary to make the lines smoother.
   Study the simplified texture. Do any voice-leading problems appear to have
   been covered up by the embellishments?

Bach, Schmücke dich, o liebe Seele

DISC 1 : TRACK 46

B. After reviewing the discussion of embellishment (pp. 179–181), decide what *one*
   suspension would be best in each of the following excerpts. Then renotate with the
   suspension and at least one other embellishment. Remember to put parentheses
   around NCTs and to label NCTs and arpeggiations.

C. The following example is a simplified excerpt from a Bach chorale harmonization. Analyze the chords using roman numerals and activate the texture with embellishments of various kinds. Although many correct solutions are possible, it will be interesting to compare yours with Bach's, which can be found in Appendix D.

Exercise 11-1   See Workbook.

Summary

A **nonchord tone** (NCT) is a tone, either diatonic or chromatic, that is not a member of the chord. In addition to the usual nomenclature for NCTs, a number of adjectives may be used to describe the context of a particular NCT. These include the following:

Accented	Diatonic	Ascending	Upper
Unaccented	Chromatic	Descending	Lower

A **passing tone** is an NCT that fills in the space between two other tones by moving stepwise between them. A **neighboring tone** is an NCT that embellishes a single tone by moving stepwise away from and then back to the tone.

A **suspension** is an NCT that delays a stepwise descent in a line. A suspension involves three phases: preparation, suspension, and resolution. Suspensions that occur in a voice other than the bass are classified by the intervals between the bass and the suspension and between the bass and the resolution. Most suspensions above the bass are 9–8, 7–6, or 4–3 suspensions. The only common bass suspension is the 2–3 suspension, in which the bass at the point of suspension forms the interval of a 2nd (or 9th) with some upper voice.

A **retardation** is similar to a suspension, but it delays a stepwise ascent and resolves upward.

This would be an appropriate point at which to begin work on Counterpoint Unit 4, which may be found at www.mhhe.com/kostka7e.

Chapter Twelve
Nonchord Tones 2

Appoggiaturas

All the NCTs discussed so far are approached and left by step or by common tone. In most tonal music, most NCTs will be of the types already discussed. NCTs involving leaps (appoggiaturas, escape tones, neighbor groups, and some anticipations) are not rare, however, and they tend to be more obvious to the listener.

   As a very general rule, **appoggiaturas** (also called incomplete neighbors) are accented, approached by ascending leap, and left by descending step. The Tchaikovsky theme in Example 12-1 (notice the transposition) contains two appoggiaturas that fit this description. The first, A4, might also be heard as a 4–3 suspension from the previous measure.

Example 12-1   Tchaikovsky, Symphony no. 5, op. 64, II

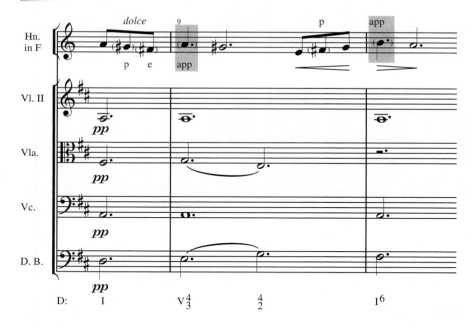

All appoggiaturas are approached by leap and left by step, but the sequence is not always ascending leap followed by descending step. In fact, Example 11-9 (p. 177) has already provided us with an example of an unaccented appoggiatura approached from above (the E5 in m. 2). Notice that it is also chromatic. Probably the only other generalization that could be made concerning appoggiaturas is that the appoggiatura is more typical of the nineteenth century than the eighteenth. As an illustration, consider Example 12-2. Four of the five NCTs in the melody are appoggiaturas, and two of the four last longer than a beat (the dotted quarter). It is largely this aspect—though in combination with others (slow harmonic rhythm, disjunct melody, homophonic texture, wide range, and so on)—that gives this phrase its Romantic flavor.

DISC 1 : TRACK 47

Example 12-2   Chopin, Nocturne op. 27, no. 2

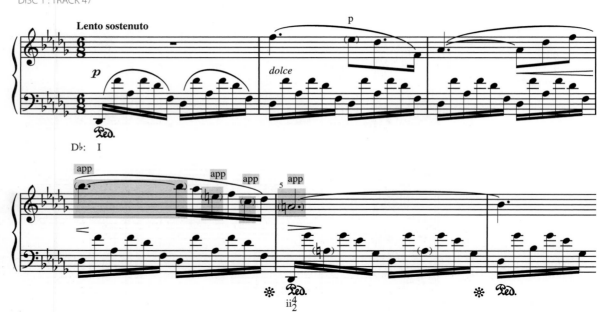

The reduction of Example 12-2 shows that when we move from the surface of the piece to a more background level, our interpretation of the longer appoggiaturas changes considerably. Issues of this sort are discussed further toward the end of this chapter.

Escape Tones

The contour of the **escape tone** (also called an incomplete neighbor) is the reverse of that of the appoggiatura because the escape tone is approached by step and left by leap in the opposite direction. Escape tones are usually shorter than a beat, unaccented, and diatonic. They are often used in sequence to ornament a scalar line, as in mm. 59–60 of Example 11-3 (pp. 173–174). Notice in Example 11-3 that although escape tone *figures* ornament the line D5–C5–B4, actual escape tones occur only two times.

The escape tone is also frequently used at cadences to ornament the scale degree progression $\hat{2}$–$\hat{1}$. An instance of this can be seen in Example 12-3.

DISC 1 : TRACK 48

Example 12-3   Haydn, Piano Sonata no. 35, I

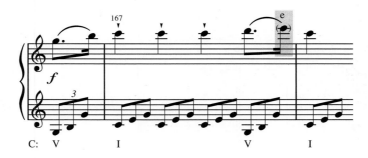

All the escape tones cited in this section have been short, unaccented, and diatonic; these are all usually characteristic of the escape tone in tonal music.

The Neighbor Group

A common method of embellishing a single tone involves a combination of two NCTs in succession, the first being an escape tone, the second an appoggiatura. The figure is referred to as a **neighbor group** (also called a cambiata or "changing tones"). As Example 12-4 illustrates, the neighbor group bears a resemblance to a neighboring tone figure.

Example 12-4

Anticipations

An **anticipation,** as the name implies, anticipates a chord that has not yet been reached. This NCT moves, by step or by leap, to some pitch that is contained in the anticipated chord but that is not present in the chord that precedes it. For example, if the triad F/A/C were to proceed to the triad B♭/D/F, you could use either the note B♭ or the note D to anticipate the B♭/D/F chord while the F/A/C chord is still sounding. The note F could not be used as an anticipation because it is common to both chords. Of the two notes B♭ and D, the B♭ is probably the better choice. In Example 12-5a the anticipated B♭4 forms a satisfying dissonance with the other pitches and is clearly an NCT, but in Example 12-5b the D5 forms no true dissonance with any other pitch.

Example 12-5

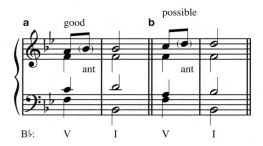

An anticipation very much like the one in Example 12-5a appears in Example 12-6. Notice that this excerpt ends with a major tonic triad. In the Baroque period it was not at all uncommon to end a phrase or a composition in the minor mode in this way. This device, known as the *Picardy third,* is discussed further in Chapter 21.

DISC 1 : TRACK 48

Example 12-6   Bach, *Well-Tempered Clavier,* Book II, Fugue 22

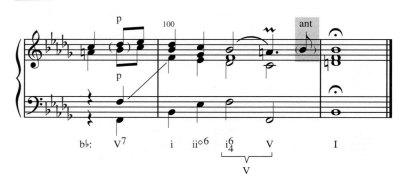

Most anticipations are approached by step, but the approach by leap is not rare. In Example 12-7 there are three anticipation *figures,* each approached by leap and left by common tone, but only one figure, that in the bass, is an NCT. The others are chord tones.

Example 12-7   Schumann, "Little Morning Wanderer," op. 68, no. 17

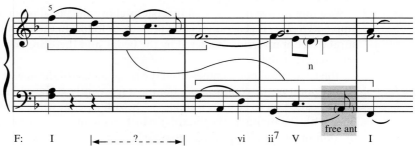

The least commonly encountered variety of NCT is the anticipation approached and *left* by leap. This is sometimes referred to as a **free anticipation.** Example 12-8 is an excerpt from Mozart, in which the bass anticipates the tonic triad before the dominant chord has resolved, allowing the bass in mm. 7 to 9 to imitate the soprano in mm. 5 to 7.

Example 12-8   Mozart, Piano Sonata K. 332, I

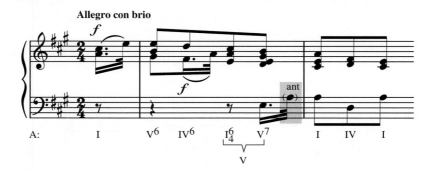

The Pedal Point

The pedal point has been saved for last in the discussion of NCTs because it is really in a class by itself. The **pedal point** is a compositional device that begins as a chord tone, then becomes an NCT as the harmonies around it change, and finally ends up as a chord tone when the harmony is once more in agreement with it. The other kinds of NCTs that we have discussed are clearly decorative and are always dependent on the harmony for their meaning. However, the pedal point often has such tonal strength that the harmonies seem to be embellishing the pedal point rather than the other way around. This sounds more complicated than it is. Look at Example 12-9, which shows the ending of a fugue by Bach.

Example 12-9   Bach, *Allein Gott in der Höh' sei Ehr*

In one sense, the piece ends on beat 1 of m. 88 with the IAC. What follows that cadence is a short codetta, with the tonic note sustained in the bass beneath a IV–vii°–I progression in the upper voices. The chords above the tonic pedal are analyzed, but in a very real sense the pedal overpowers the upper parts and represents the tonic harmony. Incidentally, the relatively weak inverted IAC is used to end this work because the bass line is presenting the melody on which the piece is based.

You might have noticed that inversions above the pedal point are not indicated in Example 12-9. This is generally a good practice to follow in the analysis of such passages. The aural effect of inversion is altered by the pedal, and there are no conventional symbols to represent this alteration.

The term pedal point comes from the frequent use of the device in organ compositions. At any point in the composition, but most frequently at the end of the work, the organist will be called on to sustain a single pitch with a pedal while continuing to play moving lines with the manuals (keyboards). Most frequently the sustained pitch is the tonic or the dominant, and the passage often includes the triad whose root is a P4 above the pedal point (hence the term "pedal six-four chord"). Therefore, if the tonic pitch is the pedal, the IV chord will often be used above it (as in Ex. 12-9), and if the dominant pitch is the pedal, the I chord will often be used above it.

Pedal points occasionally occur in parts other than the bass, in which case they are referred to as **inverted pedal points.** Another possibility is for the pedal point to contain more than one pitch class (**double pedal point** and so on), as in Example 12-10. Although most pedal points are sustained, rearticulated pedal points, as in Example 12-10, are not uncommon.

Example 12-10   Schumann, "Reaper's Song," op. 68, no. 18

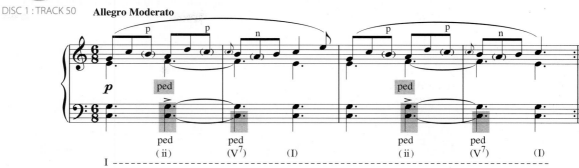

A pedal point may also contain rests, as in Example 12-11. Although this is similar to the double pedal point in Example 12-10, here only the lowest pitch, the A2, is an NCT.

Example 12-11   Prout, Flute Sonata op. 17, III

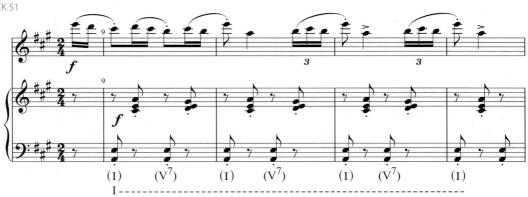

There is one situation in which what might appear to be a pedal point or an anticipation really is not. In authentic cadences, the notes of the V or V^7 chord sometimes recur over the tonic pitch in the bass, as in Example 10-14 on pp. 156–157. Here, and in similar situations, it is better to analyze the upper notes as suspensions and retardations, rather than analyzing the bass note as a pedal point or as an anticipation.

Special Problems in the Analysis of Nonchord Tones

In this section we discuss three excerpts that demonstrate special problems that you might encounter from time to time in analyzing NCTs in tonal music. First, the actual label that you assign to a tone may change as you reduce the passage. Such possibilities were mentioned in connection with Examples 12-1 and 12-2. For variety, we will do a reverse textural reduction of a similar passage. Example 12-12 shows two versions of a portion of a melody in E♭, the first melody being diatonic, the second incorporating a series of chromatic and diatonic passing tones.

Example 12-12

If we embellish each tone of Example 12-12b, we create the melody found in Example 12-13.

DISC 1 : TRACK 51

Example 12-13   Schubert, Impromptu op. 90, no. 2

The labeling of the NCTs in Example 12-13 is problematic. For example, the first E♮4 in m. 3 is, on the surface, a neighboring tone (E♭4–E♮4–D♯4). However, Example 12-12b showed that the E♮4 is not a neighbor but a passing tone (E♭4–E♮4–F4), as are the F, F♯, and G that follow. The best solution is to label these notes as passing tones (as in Example 12-12) and the others as neighbors.

Example 12-14 is our second problematic excerpt. It is very unlikely that you would be able to determine the harmonic background of this excerpt just from looking at it, and it involves too many advanced harmonic concepts to allow detailed discussion of the harmonies at this time. However, if you play it slowly, you will discover that the right hand lags further and further behind the left.* The cadence on f♯ in the right hand comes three eighth notes later than the cadence on f♯ in the left, and the cadences on A are four eighth notes apart. Both cadences are identified in the example.

---

*   Reminiscent of Erroll Garner's jazz piano style.

Example 12-14   Brahms, *Variations on a Theme by Schumann,*
op. 9, var. 2

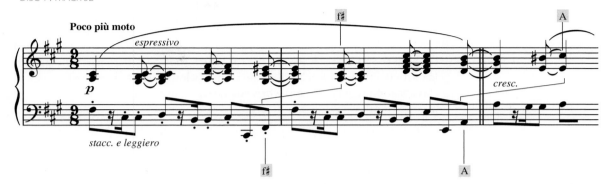

When the two staves are "correctly" aligned, it becomes apparent that the texture contains no NCTs at all (except, perhaps, for the B♯4). Example 12-15 brings the right hand into alignment with the left. Play through both examples slowly and compare them.

Example 12-15

Conventional NCT terminology is inadequate to explain a passage such as this. Instead, it is better to use an approach such as the one we have demonstrated.

Finally, we consider the problem of implied harmonies and the analysis of unaccompanied melodies. As a general rule, NCT analyses based on melodies alone are arbitrary and uninformative. Nevertheless, the experienced musician can sometimes recognize the NCTs in an unaccompanied melodic line solely on the basis of implied harmonies. Example 12-16 shows one interpretation (others are possible) of the harmonies implied by a Bach fugue subject. The textural reduction shows that the melody is an elaboration of a simple stepwise line.

Example 12-16   Bach, *Well-Tempered Clavier,* Book II, Fugue 14

Textural reduction

Self-Test 12-1

(Answers begin on page 584.)

A. Analysis.

1. Go back to Self-Test 8-1, Part F (p. 130), which shows NCTs in parentheses, and
    identify the type of each NCT in the blanks below. Always show the interval
    classification (7-6 and so on) when you analyze suspensions.

    m. 1   _____

    m. 3   _____   _____   _____

    m. 4   _____   _____

2. Analyze the NCTs in Example 9-9 (p. 138).

    m. 24   _____   _____

    m. 25   _____   _____

    m. 26   _____   _____   _____

3. Analyze the NCTs in Example 9-10 (p. 139).

    m. 72   _____   _____   m. 76   _____   _____

    m. 74   _____   _____   m. 77   (melody)   _____

    m. 75   _____   _____   _____   (alto)   _____

4. Label the chords and NCTs in this excerpt. Then make a simplified version without
    NCTs. Comment on the simplified version. Analyze two chords in m. 11, beat 3.

    Bach, *Ermuntre dich, mein schwacher Geist*

DISC 1 : TRACK 53

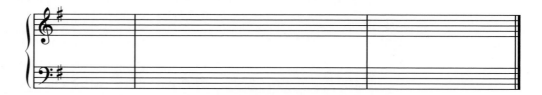

5. The two excerpts that follow are from a theme and variations by Mozart. The first
    excerpt is from the end of the theme, whereas the second excerpt is from the end
    of the first variation. Analyze the harmonies (they are identical in the theme and
    the variation) and label all NCTs.

Mozart, Piano Sonata K. 284, III, Theme and Variation I

6. NCTs in jazz and popular melodies tend to be used in ways that are not typical of music of earlier centuries. In analyzing the NCTs in this excerpt, be on the lookout for enharmonic spellings. "E♭6" calls for an E♭ major triad with an added note a M6 above the root.

Carmichael, "Skylark"

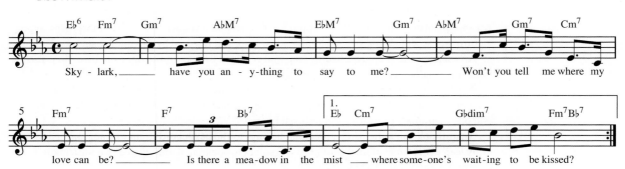

B. The following example is for three-part chorus. Analyze the chords using roman numerals. Then add the specified NCTs at the points indicated. Show the interval classification of each suspension.

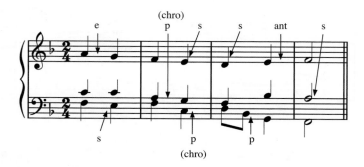

C. The excerpt below is a reduction of Mozart's Piano Sonata K. 330, III, mm. 1–8. Use it as a framework for elaboration, employing arpeggiations and NCTs as you see fit. It is also possible to thicken the texture occasionally, if you want.

Exercise 12-1 See Workbook.

Summary

An **appoggiatura** is an NCT that is approached by leap and resolved by step. In most cases, appoggiaturas are accented, approached by ascending leap, and resolved by descending step.

An **escape tone** is approached by step and resolved by leap in the opposite direction. Escape tones are usually unaccented and diatonic.

A **neighbor group** embellishes a single pitch by sounding its upper and lower neighbors in succession (in either order). The first neighbor is approached by step and left by leap, whereas the second one is approached by leap and resolved by step.

An **anticipation** anticipates a tone that belongs to the next chord. It may be approached by step or by leap. An anticipation almost always resolves to the tone it anticipated. An anticipation that resolves by leap is called a **free anticipation.**

A **pedal point** is a stationary pitch that begins as a chord tone, then becomes an NCT as the harmonies change, and finally ends up as a chord tone again. Pedal points usually occur in the bass, but they occasionally occur in other parts as well.

The analysis of chords and NCTs must always be carried out simultaneously. Although most NCTs are clearly recognizable as embellishments of the basic harmony, ambiguous cases will be encountered occasionally.

Variations

To read more about levels of harmony, please see Chapter 12 on our website at **www.mhhe.com/kostka7e.**

Chapter Thirteen
The V⁷ Chord

Introduction

Diatonic seventh chords were introduced quite early in this text, in Chapter 4. Subsequent examples and exercises have included the analysis of many seventh chords, but we have not dealt with the details of how composers have used seventh chords in tonal music. The use of seventh chords is the subject of the next several chapters.

Before reading further, review the material on seventh chords on pages 61–63. In those sections you learned, among other things, that the five most common seventh-chord qualities are the major seventh, major-minor seventh, minor seventh, half-diminished seventh, and (fully) diminished seventh chords. Of these types, the major-minor seventh is by far the most frequently encountered. It is generally built on $\hat{5}$, with the result that the terms **dominant seventh** and major-minor seventh are used more or less interchangeably.

Dominant seventh chords are almost always major-minor sevenths—that is, when spelled in root position, they contain a major triad plus the pitch a m7 above the root. In major keys a seventh chord built on $\hat{5}$ will be automatically a major-minor seventh chord. But in minor keys it is necessary to raise $\hat{7}$ (the leading tone, not the seventh of the chord) to obtain the major-minor seventh quality. The seventh chord built on $\hat{5}$ without the raised $\hat{7}$ (v7 instead of V7) is seldom used. It serves only as a passing chord, not as a true dominant, because it lacks the tonic-defining leading tone essential for a chord with a dominant function. When it does occur, it is the result of a descending line: $\hat{1}$–$\hat{7}\downarrow$–$\hat{6}\downarrow$.

Example 13-1

Often the 7th of a chord occupies only a portion of the chord's duration, as in Example 13-2. In that case, the chord may be labeled either as a 7th chord or as a triad with an NCT; either analysis is correct. To label Example 13-2 as containing both a V and a V^7 is unnecessary.

Example 13-2

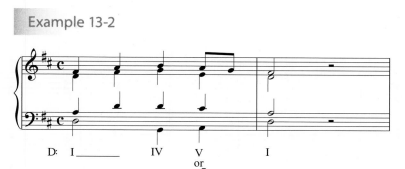

General Voice-Leading Considerations

The essential concept in the handling of *any* seventh chord involves the treatment of the 7th of the chord: *the 7th almost always resolves down by step.* We are naturally suspicious of generalizations, as we should be, but the downward resolution of the 7th as a general principle is extremely important. The 7th originated in music as a downward-resolving suspension or descending passing tone, and the downward resolution came to be the only one acceptable to the musical ear. To compare a 7th resolving down with one resolving up, listen to Example 13-3. The difference may or may not seem startling to you, but tonal music contains very few instances of the second resolution.

Example 13-3

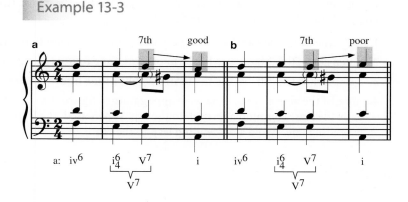

When you are working with the V^7, you must also consider the leading tone: *When it is an outer part, the leading tone almost always resolves up by step,* as in Example 13-4a. To convince yourself of the reason for this, play Example 13-4b and notice the disappointing effect of the cadence.

Example 13-4

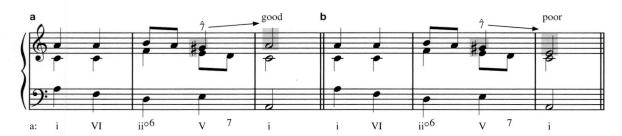

When you apply these two principles, remember not to confuse the 7th of the chord with the seventh scale degree. We will summarize what we have presented so far in this chapter.

1. The V^7 chord is a major-minor seventh chord.
2. The 7th of the chord ($\hat{4}$) resolves down to $\hat{3}$.
3. The 3rd of the chord ($\hat{7}$) resolves up to $\hat{1}$, especially when it is in an outer part.

The Approach to the 7th

We have seen that the resolution of the 7th of the V^7 (or of any seventh chord) is usually down by step. The way in which the 7th is approached should also be considered in any detailed analysis because different approaches have different musical effects. One way of doing this is to classify the contour of the voice that has the chord 7th using NCT terminology. If the chord tone preceding the 7th is

1. the same pitch class as the 7th, we use the term **suspension figure** (Ex. 13-5a);
2. a step above the 7th, we use the term **passing tone figure** (Ex. 13-5b);
3. a step below the 7th, we use the term **neighbor tone figure** (Ex. 13-5c);
4. none of the above, we use the term **appoggiatura figure** (Ex. 13-5d). This is historically the least common approach to the 7th. When used, the leap is almost always an ascending one. Avoid a descending leap to the 7th.

Example 13-5

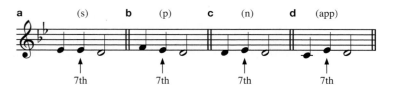

The contours defined above are put into context in Example 13-6. In the example, the 7th of the V^7 is given to the soprano for purposes of illustration. In practice, of course, the 7th may occur in any voice.

Example 13-6

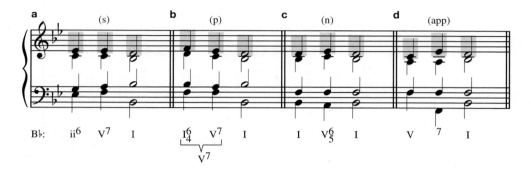

The V⁷ in Root Position

The resolution of the dominant seventh in root position to the tonic in root position is more difficult than that of any other combination. To master this technique, however, you need only to remember two principles.

1. The 7th ($\hat{4}$) must resolve *down* by step to $\hat{3}$.

2. The 3rd of the chord ($\hat{7}$), when in the *top* part, must resolve *up* by step to $\hat{1}$.

Another way of looking at these principles is in terms of the resolution of the tritone: the +4 tends to resolve outward to a 6th (Ex. 13-7a), the °5 inward to a 3rd (Ex. 13-7b). If we follow these principles, we find that the tonic triad is incomplete—it has no 5th.

Example 13-7

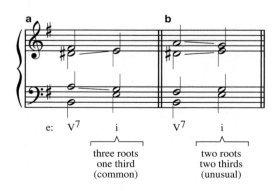

The resolution of V^7 to an incomplete triad is not an "error" to be avoided and is, in fact, a very common occurrence, especially at final cadences. In Example 13-8 the leading tone, even though it is not in the top voice, resolves up by step, resulting in an incomplete tonic triad.

Example 13-8   Schubert, String Quartet ("Death and the Maiden"), op. post., I

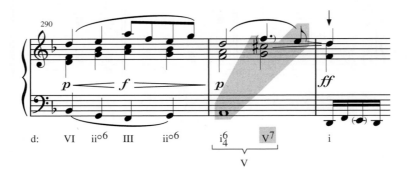

If you want to resolve the root position V^7 in four parts to a complete tonic triad, either of these methods will work:

1. Use an incomplete V^7, omitting the 5th (or, much less commonly, the 3rd) and doubling the root.
2. Use a complete V^7, but put the leading tone (3rd of the V^7) in an *inner* part and "frustrate" its natural resolution by taking it down a M3 to the 5th of the tonic triad.

The first solution works because the incomplete V^7 is a perfectly usable sonority. The second method, which is the more common, succeeds by tucking away the leading tone in an inner voice, where its lack of resolution is not so apparent to the listener. Both options are summarized in Example 13-9.

Example 13-9

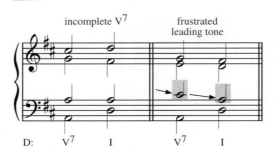

Illustrations of these two procedures from the literature are seen in the next two examples. In the first (Ex. 13-10) an incomplete V^7 (5th omitted) is used.

Example 13-10 Bach, *Nun ruhen alle Wälder*

In the second (Ex. 13-11) Beethoven uses a complete V^7 but frustrates the leading tone.

Example 13-11 Beethoven, String Quartet op. 18, no. 1, IV

You may have discovered by now that there *is* a way to resolve a complete V^7 in four parts to a complete tonic triad while still resolving both the leading tone and the 7th of the chord: if the 5th of the V^7 leaps to the 5th of the tonic triad, the complete tonic triad is obtained, but at the expense of parallel 5ths. This resolution is illustrated in Example 13-12.

Example 13-12

In instrumental music, this solution is occasionally found when the 5ths are taken by contrary motion, as in Example 13-13. Notice how the rests in the lower parts and the continued activity in the first violin distract the listener's attention from the 5ths.

DISC 1 : TRACK 56

Example 13-13   Haydn, String Quartet op. 76, no. 1, III (piano score)

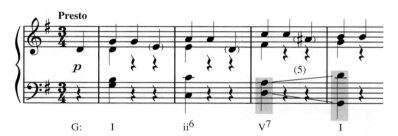

However, the use of contrary 5ths or an upward resolution of the 7th (see mm. 17–18 of Beethoven's Piano Sonata op. 14, no. 2, second movement) to achieve a complete tonic triad is certainly the exception, and these devices should be avoided in beginning exercises.

The V⁷ in Three Parts

The V⁷ in a three-part texture will have to appear with one of the chord tones missing, unless one part articulates two pitches. Obviously, neither root nor 7th can be omitted without losing the flavor of the seventh chord. Of the two remaining members, the 5th is more commonly omitted, but examples with the 3rd omitted are not rare (Ex. 13-14).

Example 13-14

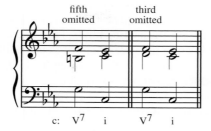

fifth omitted   third omitted

c: V⁷   i   V⁷   i

Example 13-15 illustrates the V^7 with omitted 5th.

Example 13-15   Bach, Sinfonia no. 9

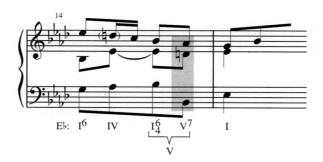

Eb: I⁶   IV   I⁶₄   V⁷   I
                    V

A V^7 with the 3rd omitted can be seen in Example 13-16.

Example 13-16   Mozart, Piano Sonata K. 570, III

Bb: I⁶   ii⁶   I⁶₄   V⁷   I
                          V

Other Resolutions of the V^7

The V^7 in root position often moves deceptively to the submediant triad, as illustrated in Example 13-17. The voice leading in this progression is just like that of the V–vi (or V–VI) progression discussed on pp. 88–89: The leading tone ($\hat{7}$) resolves up by step to tonic, and the other upper voices move down to the nearest chord tone, resulting in a doubled 3rd in the vi (or VI) chord. The only exception to this is when the leading tone is in an inner voice in the *major mode,* in which case it may move down by step to $\hat{6}$ instead, as in Example 13-17c.

Notice that in the four-voice versions the V^7 chord is always *complete;* an incomplete V^7 chord does not work well in a deceptive progression in four parts. Also notice that in almost every case it is only the bass that "deceives." That is, all the other voices move as they normally would in an authentic cadence.

Example 13-17

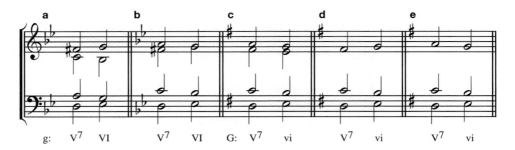

To summarize part writing the V^7–vi (VI) progression:

1. The bass (root) moves up by step to $\hat{6}$, the root of the vi (or VI) chord.
2. The leading tone ($\hat{7}$) resolves up by step to tonic ($\hat{1}$).
   a. Exception: If the leading tone is in an *inner voice* in the *major mode,* it may move down by step to $\hat{6}$.
3. The other voices move down by step.

The only diatonic triads that commonly follow the V^7 chord are the root position tonic and submediant triads. There are some altered chords that can embellish the deceptive progression, and we will see these in later chapters, but for now you should probably restrict your exercises to V^7–I(i) and V^7–vi(VI). The V^7–I^6 (i^6) resolution, seen in Example 13-18, is *not* a good choice because of the sound of the implied parallel 8ves.

Example 13-18

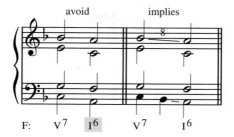

avoid   implies

F: V⁷   I⁶   V⁷   I⁶

CHECKPOINT

1. In the resolution of any seventh chord, the 7th of the chord almost always moves (up/down) by (step/leap).

2. In the resolution of a V⁷ chord, the 3rd of the chord ($\hat{7}$) usually moves (up/down) by (step/leap). This principle is sometimes not followed when the 3rd of the chord is in an (inner/outer) part, in which case it may leap down to $\hat{5}$.

3. If a member of the V⁷ is to be omitted, it is usually the (3rd/5th).

4. If a member of the V⁷ is to be doubled, it is usually the _____ .

5. If the principles listed in questions 1 and 2 are followed in a four-part texture, an incomplete V⁷ chord will lead to (a complete/an incomplete) I chord.

6. Describe two good methods for attaining a complete I chord in a V⁷–I progression in four parts.

7. Two good resolutions of the V⁷ chord are V⁷– _____ and V⁷– _____ .

Self-Test 13-1

(Answers begin on page 586.)

A. The note given in each case is the root, 3rd, 5th, or 7th of a V⁷ chord. Notate the chord in root position and name the major key in which it would be the V⁷.

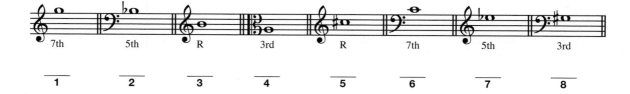

7th   5th   R   3rd   R   7th   5th   3rd

1   2   3   4   5   6   7   8

B. Go back to Self-Test 11-1, A.3, on page 183. Study carefully the V^7 chords in mm. 1, 2, and 5 and comment on the voice leading. (Note: You may have analyzed the A♭3 in m. 1 as a passing tone, but it could also be considered a 7th.)

C. Resolve each chord below to a root position I. (Note: *c* means complete chord, *i* means incomplete chord.)

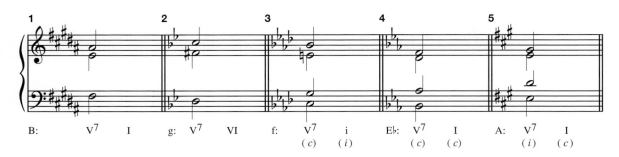

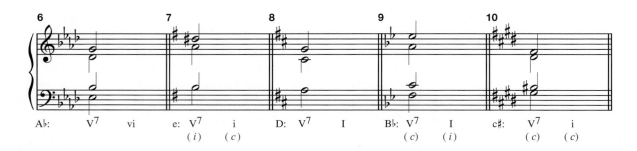

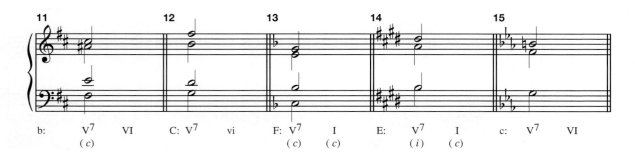

D. Notate the key signature and the V^7 chord, then resolve it.

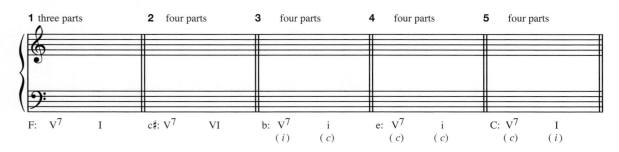

E. Analyze the chords specified by this figured bass using lead-sheet symbols and roman numerals. Then make two harmonizations, one for SAB chorus and one for SATB chorus.

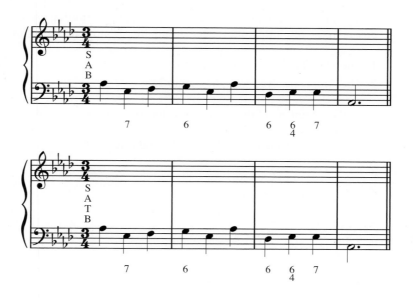

F. Analyze the harmonies implied by these soprano/bass frameworks. Then make four-part versions with embellishments and at least one root position V^7.

Exercise 13-1 See Workbook.

The Inverted V^7 Chord

The inversions of the V^7 chord are actually easier to handle than the root position V^7. However, no inversion of the V^7 should be considered to be a possible substitution for the root position V^7 at an important cadence. The voice-leading principles followed by composers in the resolution of inverted dominant sevenths are the following:

1. The 3rd ($\hat{7}$) resolves up by step to $\hat{1}$.
2. The 7th ($\hat{4}$) resolves down by step to $\hat{3}$.

The other members of the V^7 have greater freedom, but they generally move by step ($\hat{2}$–$\hat{1}$) or are retained ($\hat{5}$–$\hat{5}$).

You will recall that the symbols used to indicate inverted seventh chords are the following:

$^6_5$	3rd in the bass
$^4_3$	5th in the bass
$^4_2$ (or 2)	7th in the bass

The V$^6_5$ Chord

Example 13-19 illustrates the basic voice leading in the resolution of the V$^6_5$.

Example 13-19

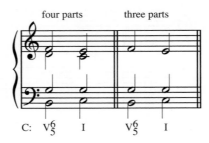

four parts   three parts

C: V$^6_5$ I   V$^6_5$ I

In practice, the V$^6_5$ is often used in a relatively weak position in the phrase. Example 13-20 is typical, with the V$^6_5$ prolonging the tonic area by harmonizing an F5 that is essentially a harmonized passing tone in the melody. The root position V that ends the passage has a much stronger effect than the V$^6_5$. The circled roman numerals draw attention to the main I–V progression.

Example 13-20   Mozart, Piano Sonata K. 309, III

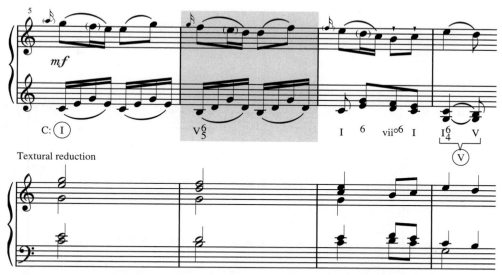

Textural reduction

The V$^4_3$ Chord

The V$^4_3$ is often used in a fashion similar to that of the passing V$^6_4$: to harmonize $\hat{2}$ in a $\hat{1}$–$\hat{2}$–$\hat{3}$ or $\hat{3}$–$\hat{2}$–$\hat{1}$ bass line. The V$^4_3$ is seldom used in three-part textures, the V$^6_4$ or vii°^{6} being used instead. Example 13-21 summarizes the treatment of the V$^4_3$ in four parts.

In Example 13-21c, the 7th of the V$^4_3$ moves *up* to $\hat{5}$, one of the few situations in which composers frustrated the normal resolution of the 7th, probably to create the parallel 10ths. The unequal 5ths seen between the soprano and alto in Example 13-21c are also acceptable.

Example 13-21

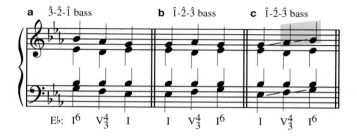

Example 13-22 contains a I–V$^4_3$–I^6 progression with an ascending 7th (in the Horn and Violin I). The V$^6_5$ and the V$^4_3$ both prolong the tonic area in what is really an embellished I–ii^6–V progression.

Example 13-22   Mozart, Horn Concerto no. 3, K. 447, II

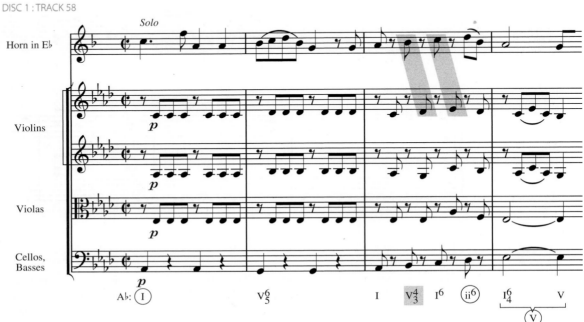

The V$^4_2$ Chord

Because of the downward resolution of the 7th, the V$^4_2$ is almost always followed by a I^6. The V$^4_2$ is often preceded by a I^6 (Ex. 13-23a) or by some form of IV or ii chord (Ex. 13-23b), but it may also be preceded by a passing I$^6_4$ or a cadential I$^6_4$ chord (Ex. 13-23c).

Example 13-23

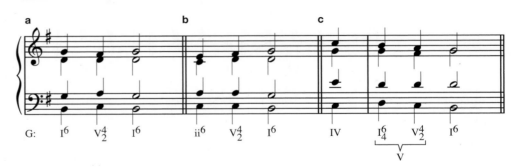

A less conventional but certainly effective treatment of the upper voices is seen in Example 13-24, in which the 5th of the V$^4_2$ leaps to the 5th of the I^6 chord.

DISC 1 : TRACK 58

Example 13-24   Beethoven, Piano Sonata op. 13, II

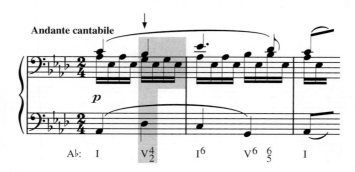

Ab: I   V$^4_2$ I^6 V^6 $^6_5$ I

Self-Test 13-2

(Answers begin on page 589.)

A. Notate the specified chords. Use accidentals instead of key signatures.

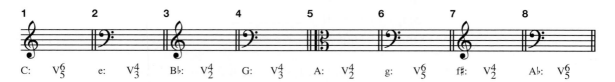

C: V$^6_5$ e: V$^4_3$ Bb: V$^4_2$ G: V$^4_3$ A: V$^4_2$ g: V$^6_5$ f#: V$^4_2$ Ab: V$^6_5$

B. Comment on the resolution of the leading tone and both the approach to and the resolution of the 7th in the following examples.
   1. Self-Test 4-2, C.1, p. 64 (V$^4_2$).
   2. Self-Test 4-2, C.2, p. 64 (V$^4_3$).
   3. Example 7-17, p. 104 (V$^4_2$).

C. Resolve each chord to a tonic triad (except as indicated). Analyze both chords.

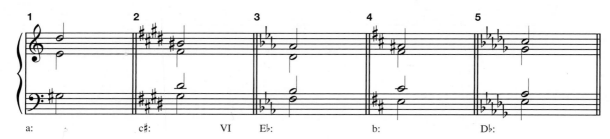

a: c#:   VI   Eb: b: Db:

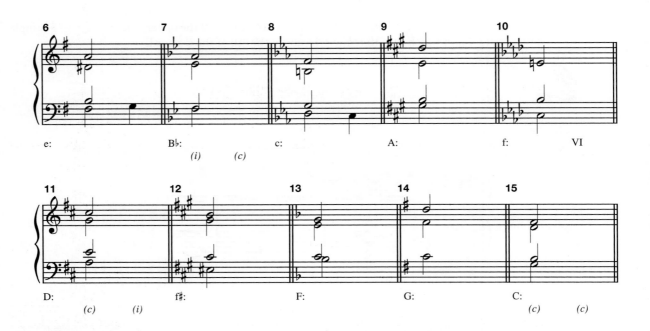

D. Review the section on the approach to the 7th on pp. 200–201. Then classify the approach to the 7th in each of the following examples.

1. Example 13-10 (p. 203) _____

2. Example 13-11 (p. 203) _____

3. Example 13-20 (p. 211) _____

4. Example 13-22 (p. 212) _____

5. Example 13-24 (p. 213) _____

E. Notate, introduce, and resolve the specified chords. Each chord 7th is to be approached as a suspension, a neighbor, a passing tone, or an appoggiatura, as indicated. Include key signatures, lead-sheet symbols, and roman numerals.

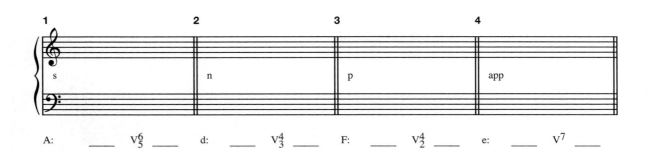

F. Show with lead-sheet symbols and roman numerals the chords that this figured bass calls for. Then complete the realization in four voices.

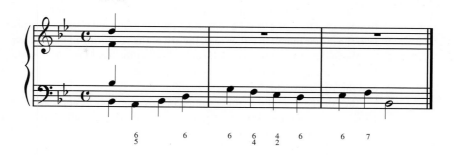

G. Review. Identify the following keys. If the chord occurs diatonically in both major and minor, name both keys.

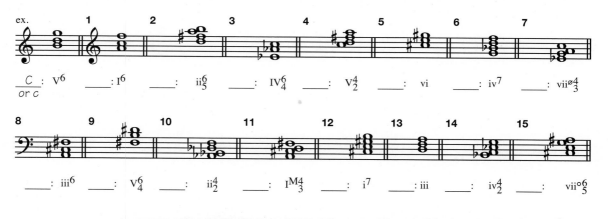

Exercise 13-2 See Workbook.

Summary

The V^7 is a major-minor 7th chord in both major and minor modes. This means that the leading tone must be raised in the V^7 chord in the minor mode.

Two fundamental voice leadings should be followed when the V^7 chord is used. First, the 7th of the chord ($\hat{4}$, not $\hat{7}$) should resolve down by step in the next chord (usually I or vi). The only common exception to this is the V$_3^4$–I^6 progression, where the 7th may move up by step to $\hat{5}$. Second, when it is in an outer part, the leading tone almost always resolves up by step.

The root position V^7 usually moves to I or vi. When a V^7 in a four-voice texture resolves to I, the I chord is frequently incomplete, with a tripled root and a 3rd. To arrive at a complete I chord, either the V^7 must be incomplete itself (no 5th, with the root doubled) or the leading tone of the V^7 must be in an inner voice so that it may leap down to the 5th of the I chord. When a V^7 in a four-voice texture resolves to vi, the leading tone must resolve to tonic if it is in the soprano voice or if the music is in the minor mode. In either case, the 3rd of the vi chord will be doubled.

The inverted V^7 is easy to use if you remember the basic principles outlined previously concerning the leading tone and the 7th of the V^7. In general, the V^6_5 resolves to I, the V^4_3 resolves to I or I^6, and the V^4_2 resolves to I^6.

The 7th of a V^7 chord in root position or inversion may be approached by means of a suspension figure, a passing tone figure, a neighbor tone figure, or an appoggiatura figure. Avoid approaching the 7th by a descending leap.

Chapter Fourteen
The II^7 and VII^7 Chords

Introduction

Any diatonic triad may appear with a 7th added, but the various diatonic seventh chords do not occur with equal frequency in tonal music. In fact, most seventh chords used are dominant sevenths, appearing either as the V^7 or as a secondary V^7 (to be discussed in Chapter 16). In the major mode, by far the most common diatonic seventh chord other than the V^7 is the ii^7. A ranking by frequency of the seventh chords in major would be approximately that shown next.

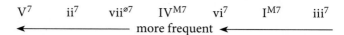

$$V^7 \qquad ii^7 \qquad vii^{ø7} \qquad IV^{M7} \qquad vi^7 \qquad I^{M7} \qquad iii^7$$
$$\longleftarrow \text{\quad more frequent \quad} \longleftarrow$$

Because of the larger number of possible seventh chords in the minor mode (see p. 62) a corresponding diagram for minor would be difficult to produce. The leading-tone seventh is more frequently found in minor than in major, but the supertonic seventh is still the more common of the two in minor. At any rate, a diagram showing the order of frequency of seventh chords in minor would not differ radically from that shown for major. In this chapter and the next, each of the diatonic seventh chords is illustrated and discussed briefly. This chapter covers only the supertonic and leading-tone seventh chords, the remainder being discussed in Chapter 15.

You will not find the voice-leading principles to be difficult. Actually, Chapter 13 presented the most formidable part-writing problems to be found in tonal harmony. Because the principles are not difficult, there are not separate sections dealing with the handling of each chord in three and four voices. Instead, the following principles apply throughout:

1. The 7th of the chord almost always resolves down by step.
2. The 7th of the chord may be approached in various ways (review pp. 200–201). Especially common is the suspension figure, although the passing tone figure also works well. Neighbor and appoggiatura figures are less common.
3. Incomplete chords must contain at least the root and the 7th.
4. Doubled tones should not be the chord 7th or the leading tone.

The II⁷ Chord

By far the most common of nondominant diatonic seventh chords, supertonic sevenths may be found in most compositions of the tonal era. In major the ii⁷ is a minor seventh chord (Ex. 14-1a), whereas in minor keys the iiø7 is half-diminished (Ex. 14-1b).

Example 14-1

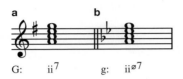

G: ii⁷   g: iiø⁷

Like the supertonic triad, the supertonic seventh typically moves to V. The root position V may be delayed by the appearance of a cadential I⁶₄ chord, or the V may be represented by a vii°⁶ (see Ex. 14-2 for some typical resolutions).

Example 14-2

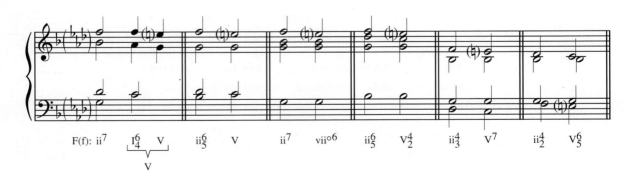

F(f): ii⁷   I⁶₄ V   ii⁶₅ V   ii⁷   vii°⁶   ii⁶₅ V⁴₂   ii⁴₃ V⁷   ii⁴₂ V⁶₅
                 └──┬──┘
                    V

Examples of all the cases seen in the previous example, as well as of others, are not difficult to find, but the first inversion of the ii⁷ is the most common bass position. A ii⁶₅–V⁷ progression in a three-part texture is illustrated in Example 14-3. Notice the suspension figure that prepares the 7th of the ii⁶₅ (the C4).

Example 14-3   Mozart, Symphony no. 41, K. 551, IV

A ii$^4_2$ chord appears in Example 14-4 with the 7th (the F3) approached as a passing tone. The reduction clarifies the stepwise nature of the outer parts of the accompaniment. Notice that the voice attempts to escape the downward motion in mm. 16 to 17 for the climax of the song, but it soon rejoins the descent.

Example 14-4   Clara Wieck Schumann, *Beim Abschied*

A much less typical use of the supertonic seventh chord is as a substitute for a IV chord in a plagal cadence. In such cases, the ii⁷ is usually in first inversion, where its close resemblance to the IV is most obvious. In Example 14-5, which may be somewhat difficult to follow because of the clefs, Dvořák appears to close the phrase with a ii°⅚–i plagal cadence. The cello is carrying the melody. The textural reduction makes the voice leading clearer and points out that most of the phrase is sequential.

DISC 1 : TRACK 60

Example 14-5 Dvořák, Symphony no. 9, op. 95 ("From the New World"), I

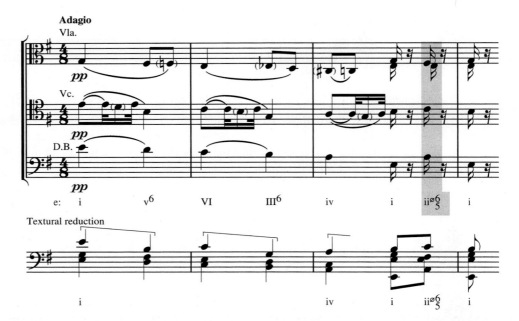

Perhaps a better explanation of the ii°⅚ in the preceding example is that it is a iv^add6, a iv chord with an added 6th (the F♯3). This is especially convincing in that it accounts for the E3, which is otherwise an unresolved 7th in the ii°⁷ chord.

The VII⁷ Chord in Major

The leading-tone seventh in major is a half-diminished seventh chord,* possessing, as does the vii° triad, a dominant function. It normally resolves directly to the tonic, but it may first move to the V⁷ simply by taking 6̂ (the 7th of the chord) down one step. Typical resolutions to tonic in four parts are demonstrated in Example 14-6. The third inversion, which is quite rare, is not shown, nor is vii°⅚–I, which would contain parallel 5ths.

---

* The fully diminished vii°⁷ in major is discussed in Chapter 21.

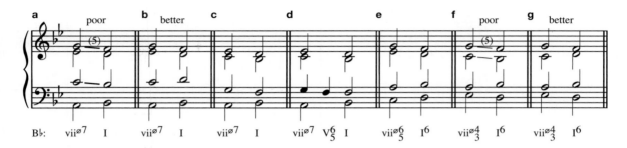

Example 14-6

Notice that both the vii°⁷ and the vii°⁴₃ resolutions must be handled carefully to avoid parallel 5ths (see Ex. 14-6a and f). This can be done by doubling the 3rd of the I chord (Ex. 14-6b and g) or by revoicing the leading-tone chord so that parallel 4ths replace the parallel 5ths (Ex. 14-6c). The rare example from the literature of such parallels, as in Example 14-7, does not invalidate the principle.

DISC 1 : TRACK 60

Example 14-7   Haydn, Symphony no. 94, IV

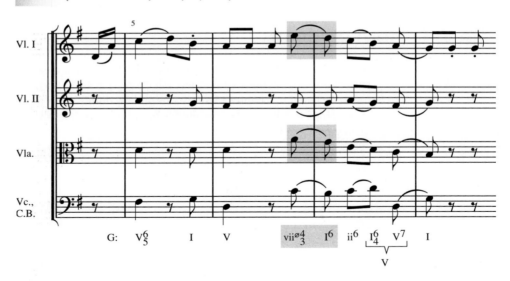

A less common resolution of the vii°⁴₃ is to a root position I chord, shown in Example 14-8 (from a composition for two four-part choruses). The vii°⁴₃ that resolves to I is typically brought about, as it is here, by a IV chord that is left by parallel 3rds or 6ths outlining $\hat{1}$–$\hat{2}$–$\hat{3}$ in one voice and $\hat{6}$–$\hat{7}$–$\hat{1}$ in another (the two alto lines). The result is an interesting combination of both plagal and authentic cadences. Compare the vii°⁴₃–I cadence and the ii°⁶₅–i (or iv^add6–i) cadence discussed in connection with Example 14-5.

Example 14-8   Brahms, *Unsere Vater hofften auf dich*, op. 109, no. 1

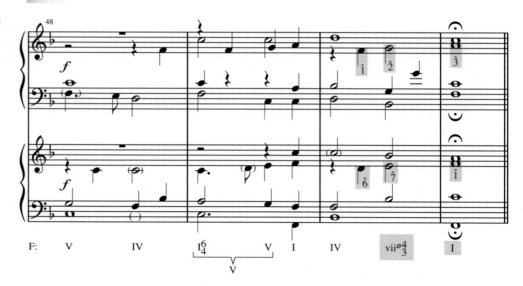

Otherwise, the vii°⁷ poses no new problems. It should be remembered, however, that the vii°⁷ in major is much less common than the other chords with dominant functions—V, V⁷, and vii°⁽⁶⁾.

The VII⁷ Chord in Minor

In the minor mode, the leading-tone seventh (Ex. 14-9a) appears as a fully diminished seventh chord (vii°⁷). The subtonic seventh chord (Ex. 14-9b) generally is used in sequences, to be discussed in Chapter 15, or as a secondary dominant seventh (V⁷ of III), a usage that is explained in Chapter 16. The vii°⁷ is found more frequently and is discussed in the following paragraphs.

Example 14-9

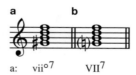

The vii°⁷, whether in root position or inverted, has a dominant function and tends to resolve to tonic. As with the vii⁷, the vii°⁷ may move first to the V⁷ simply by moving the 7th of the chord down to $\hat{5}$. The resolution of vii°⁷ to i, however, requires more discussion.

The vii°⁷ contains two tritones. The tendency of the tritone is to resolve inward by step when spelled as a °5 and outward by step when spelled as a +4. If these tendencies are followed in four parts, as in Example 14-10, the tonic triad will have a doubled 3rd.

Example 14-10

e:

Composers have not always cared to follow these tendencies, often taking $\hat{2}$ down to $\hat{1}$ instead of moving it up to $\hat{3}$ (compare Ex. 14-11a and b). In certain voicings, this can result in unequal 5ths (Ex. 14-11c).

Example 14-11

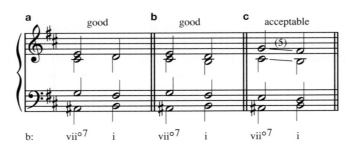

b: vii°⁷   i   vii°⁷   i   vii°⁷   i

The unequal 5ths, although acceptable, are often disguised through the use of NCTs, as in the root position vii°⁷–i progression in Example 14-12.

Example 14-12   Bach, Passacaglia in C Minor

Textural reduction

The members of the vii°⁷ usually move in the same ways when the chord is inverted as they do when it is in root position, and our discussion of the optionally doubled 3rd still applies (for example, see the i⁶ chord in Ex. 14-12). The vii°$_5^6$ (Ex. 14-13a) usually is followed by i⁶ because resolution to the root position tonic creates unequal 5ths involving the bass (review p. 76). The vii°$_3^4$ (Ex. 14-13b) moves smoothly to the i⁶; occasionally found is vii°$_3^4$–i, which is similar to the vii°$_3^4$–I cadence discussed in connection with Example 14-8. The vii°$_2^4$ (Ex. 14-13c) is generally followed by V⁷ or by a cadential or passing i$_4^6$.

Example 14-13

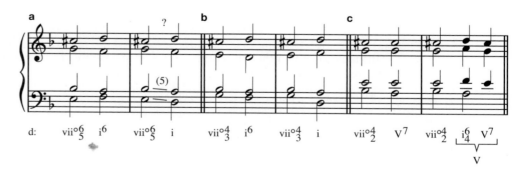

A vii°$^4_3$ in chorale texture is shown in Example 14-14, where it resolves to a i^6 with a doubled 3rd. An alternative analysis would eliminate two of the chords that occur in the same measure with the vii°$^4_3$—the ii$^{ø6}_5$ and the ii^{ø7}—by regarding the A4s as suspensions. This approach is shown beneath the example in parentheses. It would not be equally good to analyze the G♯4s as lower neighbors, thereby eliminating the vii°$^4_3$ and the vii°^{6}, because that analysis results in an unconvincing progression: ii$^{ø6}_5$–i^6–ii^{ø7}–i.

DISC 1 : TRACK 61

Example 14-14 Bach, *Als Jesus Christus in der Nacht*

a: VI   ii$^{ø6}_5$ vii°$^4_3$ i^6 ii^{ø7} vii°^{6} i   ii$^{ø6}_5$ V   (7)   I
                (vii°$^4_3$ i^6 vii°^{6} i)

CHECKPOINT

1. The most frequently used diatonic seventh chord is the V^7. Which one ranks second in frequency?

2. What tones of a seventh chord should not be omitted?

3. The 7th of a diatonic seventh chord resolves (up/down) by (step/leap).

4. Which types of seventh chords are found on $\hat{2}$ and $\hat{7}$ in major and minor? Which forms in minor are the most common?

5. The ii^7 tends to be followed by _____ , the vii°^{7} by _____ .

6. Which chord discussed in this chapter contains two tritones?

7. The natural tendency of the +4 is to resolve (inward/outward) by step, whereas the °5 resolves (inward/outward) by step.

8. Try to recall the implications of the preceding question in connection with the vii°^{7} chord.

Self-Test 14-1

(Answers begin on page 591.)

A. Notate the following chords. Use accidentals, not key signatures.

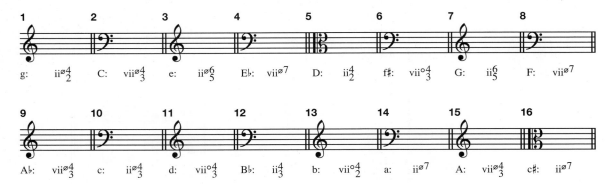

g: ii⁰⁴₂   C: vii⁰⁴₃   e: ii⁰⁶₅   E♭: vii⁰⁷   D: ii⁴₂   f♯: vii°⁴₃   G: ii⁰⁶₅   F: vii⁰⁷

A♭: vii⁰⁴₃   c: ii⁰⁴₃   d: vii°⁴₃   B♭: ii⁴₃   b: vii°⁴₂   a: ii⁰⁷   A: vii⁰⁴₃   c♯: ii⁰⁷

B. Analyze the following chords. Be sure your symbols indicate chord quality and inversion.

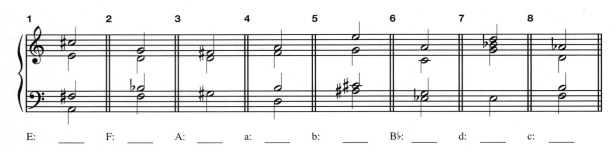

E: ____   F: ____   A: ____   a: ____   b: ____   B♭: ____   d: ____   c: ____

C. Analyze the chords and NCTs in the following excerpts. Whenever you encounter a ii⁷ (ii⁰⁷) or vii⁰⁷ (vii°⁷) chord, discuss the voice leading into and out of the chord.

1. Each numbered blank indicates where a chord is to be analyzed. In many cases it would be equally valid to analyze the "chords" as NCTs.

    Bach, *Gib dich zufrieden und sei stille*

DISC 1 : TRACK 62

1   2   3   4   5   6   7   8   9   10   11   12   13

2. Again, the chords are numbered. Also, the "real" bass notes of chords 1 to 3 are circled.

Mozart, Piano Sonata K. 284, III, Variation 5

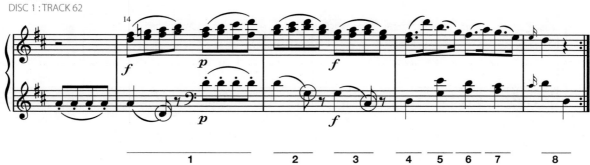

3. Trace the predominant rhythmic idea in this excerpt.

Schubert, "Aufenthalt"

4. The melody notes on beat 2 of each odd-numbered measure are NCTs. Try to make a reduction that would show the simple model of which this excerpt is an elaboration. What is the meaning of the asterisks in mm. 9 and 15?

Chopin, Mazurka op. 33, no. 3

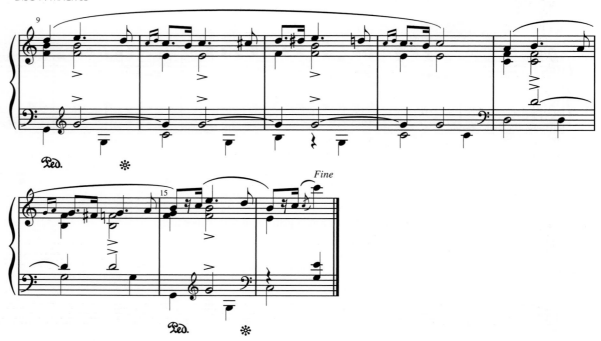

D. Notate, introduce, and resolve the specified chords. Each chord 7th is to be approached as a suspension, as a neighbor, or as a passing tone, as specified. Include key signatures, lead-sheet symbols, and roman numerals.

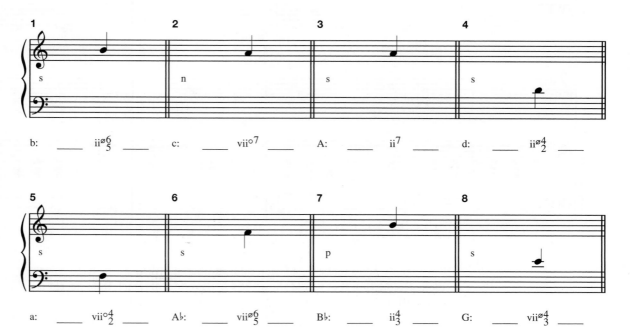

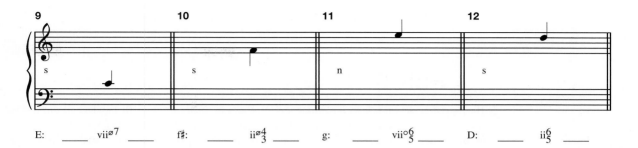

E: _____ viiø7 _____   f♯: _____ iiø$^4_3$ _____   g: _____ vii°$^6_5$ _____   D: _____ ii$^6_5$ _____

E. Analyze the chords called for by this figured bass, analyzing in D major throughout. Then add two upper treble-clef parts conforming to those chords. Note: This trio would actually be performed by four musicians: two violinists, someone playing the bass line (probably a cellist), and a keyboard player realizing the figured bass. (The numerals 3 and 5 call for root position triads.)

Corelli, Trio Sonata op. 3, no. 2, II

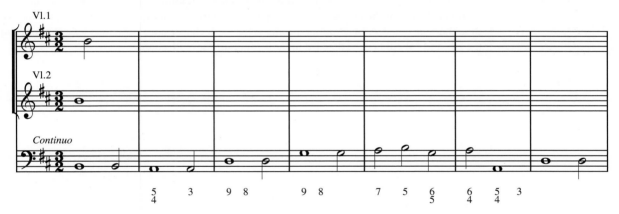

F. Harmonize these chorale phrases for four-part chorus.

1. Include a vii°7 and a iiø$^6_5$.

2. Include a ii⁷ (on the first half of beat 3 in m. 1).

Exercise 14-1 See Workbook.

Summary

The *supertonic seventh chord* is a minor seventh chord in the major mode (ii^7) and a half-diminished seventh chord in the minor mode (ii^{ø7}). Like the supertonic triad, it is usually followed by a V chord (or by a V delayed by a I$^6_4$). A less common usage finds the supertonic seventh, usually in first inversion, substituting for IV (or iv) in a plagal cadence.

The *leading-tone seventh chord* is a half-diminished seventh chord in the major mode (vii^{ø7}) and a fully diminished seventh chord in the minor mode (vii^{o7}). Like the leading-tone triad, it is usually followed by a I chord, but it may move first to a V^7 in root position or inversion simply by resolving the 7th down by step. The voice leading is usually stepwise in all voices as the leading-tone seventh chord resolves, although one occasionally encounters a vii$^{o4}_3$ (or vii$^{ø4}_3$) resolving to a root position tonic triad, which involves a leap of a 4th or 5th in the bass.

The most crucial aspect of part-writing supertonic and leading-tone seventh chords is the resolution of the 7th of the chord down by step in the following chord, and for that reason, the 7th should not be doubled. In addition, incomplete seventh chords must contain at least the root and the 7th, and $\hat{7}$ should not be doubled in the leading-tone seventh chord.

Chapter Fifteen
Other Diatonic Seventh Chords

Introduction

The most commonly encountered diatonic seventh chords are those that we have covered in the previous two chapters: those seventh chords built on $\hat{5}$, $\hat{2}$, and $\hat{7}$. Diatonic seventh chords built on the remaining four scale degrees are much less commonly used in traditional tonal music, but they certainly are used on occasion. One context in which they are relatively common is in circle-of-fifths sequences, a subject that we will revisit at the end of this chapter.

The IV^7 Chord

The diatonic subdominant seventh chord is found in the forms shown in Example 15-1.

Example 15-1

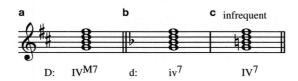

$$\text{D:}\quad \text{IV}^{M7} \qquad \text{d:}\quad \text{iv}^7 \qquad \text{IV}^7$$

Like the subdominant triad, the subdominant seventh moves to V (or vii°^{6}), often passing through some form of the ii chord on the way. The resolution to ii^7 (possibly inverted) is especially easy to handle because only the 7th needs to move. This is illustrated in Example 15-2.

Example 15-2

$$\text{e:}\quad \text{iv}^7 \quad \text{ii}^{\emptyset{6\atop5}} \quad \text{iv}^{6\atop5} \quad \text{ii}^{\emptyset{4\atop3}}$$

When iv^7 moves directly to V, parallel 5ths may result if the 7th of the chord is placed above the 3rd (Ex. 15-3a). This can be corrected through the use of a cadential six-four (Ex. 15-3b) or by doubling the 5th of the V chord (Ex. 15-3c). The solutions illustrated in Example 15-3d and e, although less commonly used, are also acceptable. Bach's solution in Example 14-12 (p. 224) closely resembles Example 15-3a, but the parallel 5ths are avoided (or disguised) by the alto continuing on to F4 before the soprano resolves to D5.

Example 15-3

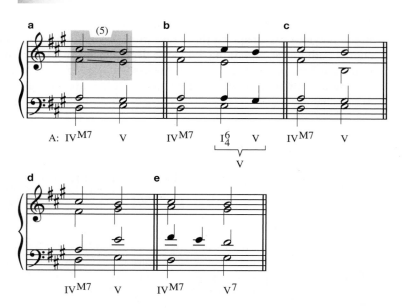

Otherwise, the voice leading to and from the root position or inverted subdominant seventh is smooth and offers no new problems. A iv^7 in a three-part texture is seen in Example 15-4, which features a circle-of-fifths sequence using seventh chords. Notice that mm. 200 to 201 sound as if they are in $\frac{2}{4}$ rather than in $\frac{3}{4}$. This metric device, which is known as *hemiola*, has been in use for many centuries and is still used today. (The vii°^{7}/V shown beneath m. 202 is discussed in Chapter 17.)

DISC 1 : TRACK 64

Example 15-4   Mozart, Piano Sonata K. 332, I

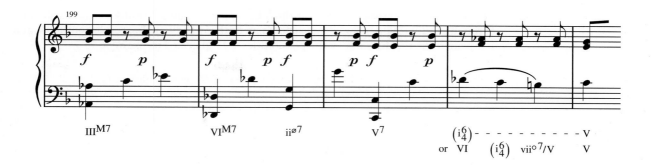

$$\text{III}^{M7} \quad \text{VI}^{M7} \quad \text{ii}^{ø7} \quad \text{V}^7$$

$$\left(\text{i}^6_4\right) \text{-------- V}$$
$$\text{or VI} \quad \left(\text{i}^6_4\right) \quad \text{vii}^{\circ 7}/\text{V} \quad \text{V}$$

The subdominant seventh in minor with a raised $\hat{6}$ (see Ex. 15-1) is a major-minor seventh chord, but it does not have a dominant function. Instead, it results from ascending motion toward the leading tone ($\uparrow\hat{6}$–$\uparrow\hat{7}$–$\hat{1}$), as in the Bach example shown next (Ex. 15-5). This phrase is especially interesting in that it contains subdominant chords using both $\uparrow\hat{6}$ and $\downarrow\hat{6}$ as well as a V⁶ (using $\uparrow\hat{7}$) and a v⁶ (using $\downarrow\hat{7}$). Notice also the Phrygian cadence (review p. 148).

DISC 1 : TRACK 64

Example 15-5 Bach, *Als vierzig Tag' nach Ostern*

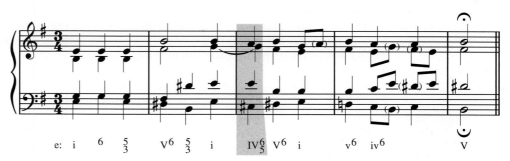

$$\text{e:} \quad \text{i} \quad 6 \quad \overset{5}{3} \quad \text{V}^6 \quad \overset{5}{3} \quad \text{i} \quad \text{IV}^6_5 \quad \text{V}^6 \quad \text{i} \quad \text{v}^6 \quad \text{iv}^6 \quad \text{V}$$

The VI⁷ Chord

The submediant seventh is found in three forms (Ex. 15-6).

Example 15-6

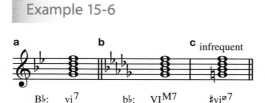

$$\text{B}\flat\text{:} \quad \text{vi}^7 \qquad \text{b}\flat\text{:} \quad \text{VI}^{M7} \quad \sharp\text{vi}^{ø7}$$

Like their parent triads, the vi^7 and the VI^{M7} typically move toward V, usually passing through subdominant or supertonic chords, or both, on the way. The resolutions to IV and ii are not difficult, and some of the possibilities are illustrated in Example 15-7.

Example 15-7

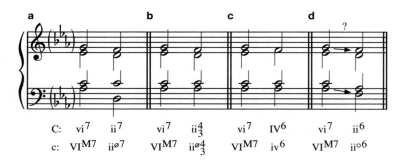

Example 15-4 on page 232 contains a typical VI^{M7} in three voices in a circle-of-fifths progression. Notice the stepwise or common-tone voice leading in the upper voices. However, in freer textures, especially in piano music, composers sometimes paid less attention to voice-leading conventions. In Example 15-8 parallel 5ths are seen in the vi^7–ii^7 progression. Notice also the unresolved 7th in the cadence.

DISC 1 : TRACK 65

Example 15-8   Chopin, Ballade op. 38

In minor, when the root of the submediant seventh moves up by step to ↑$\hat{7}$, the $\hat{6}$ must be raised to avoid the interval of a $^+2$. The chord that results when $\hat{6}$ is raised is a half-diminished seventh: ♯vi^{ø7}. The origin of this chord is illustrated in Example 15-9.

Example 15-9

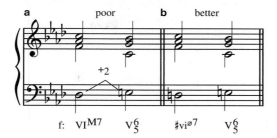

The ♯vi⁰⁷ usually serves as a passing chord between two chords of dominant function (V or vii°). It moves most smoothly to the otherwise unusual root position vii°, as in Example 15-10, where we put the ♯vi⁰⁷ in parentheses to indicate the chord's passing function. The ♯vi⁰⁷ can move directly to V^6_5 instead of vii° if $\hat{1}$ leaps to $\hat{5}$ (as in Ex. 15-9b).

DISC 1 : TRACK 65

Example 15-10   Bach, *Warum betrübst du dich, mein Herz*

The I⁷ Chord

The tonic seventh chord in its diatonic form is a M⁷ chord in a major key (Ex. 15-11a) and a m⁷ chord in a minor key (Ex. 15-11b). The minor-major seventh chord in minor (Ex. 15-11c), although possible, is quite rare in the tonal tradition, although it is used freely in jazz.

Example 15-11

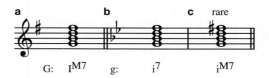

Adding a 7th to the tonic triad obviously deprives it of tonal stability. Rather than being a harmonic goal or resting place, in traditional tonal music the tonic seventh is an active chord that demands resolution. It tends to move to a IV or sometimes to a ii or vi, any of which might also contain a 7th. The chord of resolution must be one that contains $\hat{6}$ so that the chord 7th ($\hat{7}$) can resolve down to it. Some possibilities are illustrated in Example 15-12.

Example 15-12

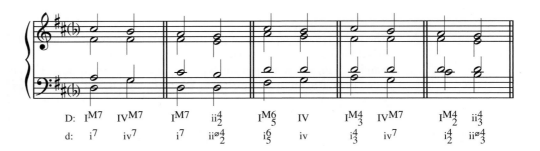

Although the tonic seventh is by no means a frequently encountered sonority, it can be very effective when handled well. Two examples by Robert Schumann and his wife, Clara, appear next, with the 7th approached as a passing tone in each case. In both cases the chord 7th could be analyzed as an NCT, as is frequently the case with seventh chords. The decision to analyze a tone as a 7th will be influenced by such factors as its relative duration (Ex. 15-13) or its suspension into the next chord (Ex. 15-14). The textural reduction of Example 15-13 shows that the chord 7ths resolve down by step, even in this fairly free texture (see the bracketed notes). In the roman numeral analysis "V$^4_3$/V" represents a secondary dominant, which will be discussed in Chapter 16.

Example 15-13   Schumann, "Mignon," op. 68, no. 35

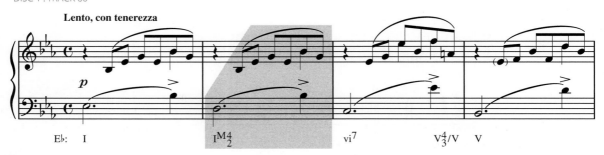

Textural reduction

The analysis below Example 15-14 emphasizes the basic I–ii–V–I progression.

Example 15-14   Clara Wieck Schumann, "Romance," op. 5, no. 3

DISC 1 : TRACK 66

The III⁷ Chord

The diatonic mediant seventh chord takes the forms illustrated in Example 15-15. These chords occur most often in sequences of seventh chords.

Example 15-15

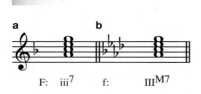

F: iii⁷   f: III^M7

A typical instance of such a sequence is seen in Example 15-16. The iii⁷ usually progresses to a VI⁽⁷⁾, as here, but it may also be followed by a IV chord. The music shown is played by the string orchestra, whereas the soloists have a somewhat embellished version. A keyboard player would have improvised a realization of the figured bass.

Example 15-16   Corelli, Concerto Grosso op. 6, no. 3, V

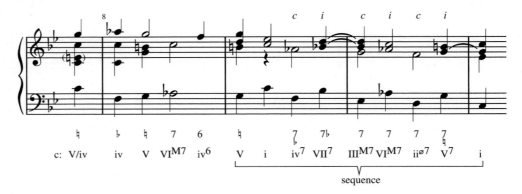

CHECKPOINT

1. The subdominant seventh chord often passes through some form of the _____ chord on its way to V.

2. What condition creates the IV^7 chord (not the iv^7 chord) and the $\#vi^{\varnothing7}$ chord in minor?

3. How does the addition of a seventh change the usual function of the tonic triad?

Seventh Chords and the Circle-of-Fifths Sequence

As we explained in Chapter 7, the usual harmonic functions of most diatonic chords are closely related to the circle-of-fifths sequence. It is not surprising, then, that this is one of the most commonly used sequential patterns, and it can be found in various kinds of twentieth-century popular music as well (as in Example 3-10, on p. 46, which contains a iv^7–VII^7–III^{M7}–VI^{M7}–$ii^{\varnothing7}$–V^7–i progression). If the chords used in a circle-of-fifths sequence are seventh chords, certain voice-leading conventions are almost always followed.

1. If the seventh chords are in root position in a four-part texture, *complete* chords will alternate with *incomplete* chords (5th omitted), as in Example 15-17a. (Compare to Example 15-16.)

2. If the seventh chords are inverted in a four-part texture, either $^6_5$ chords will alternate with $^4_2$ chords (Ex. 15-17b) or $^4_3$ chords will alternate with root position chords (Ex. 15-17c).

Notice that, with the exception of the bass line in Example 15-17a, every voice either *stays the same* (indicated by the dotted ties) or *moves down by step.*

Example 15-17

In three-part textures, a circle-of-fifths sequence will usually be in root position. A root position circle-of-fifths sequence in a three-part texture was illustrated in Example 15-4 (pp. 232–233). The relevant part of that example is shown in reduction in Example 15-18, every chord omitting the 5th.

Example 15-18

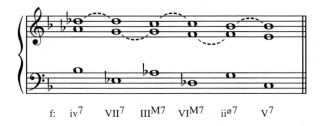

Notice that the previously stated principle about four-part textures holds true here as well: Except for the bass in a root position sequence, from one chord to the next, all parts either stay the same or move down by step.

Self-Test 15-1

(Answers begin on page 596.)

A. Notate the following chords. Use accidentals, not key signatures.

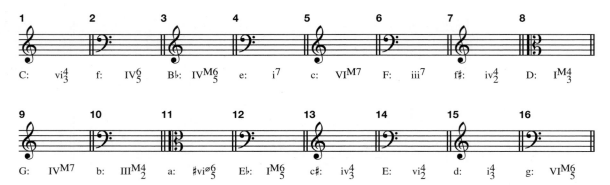

B. Analyze the following chords. Be sure your symbols indicate chord quality and inversion.

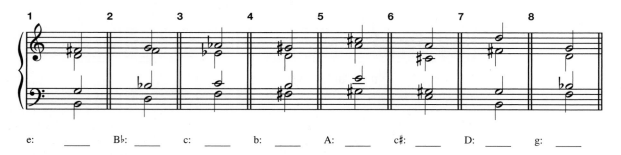

C. Analyze chords and NCTs in the excerpts that follow. Comment on the voice leading involving any of the chords discussed in this chapter.

1. Analyze two chords on beat 3 of the first measure.

Bach, *Warum sollt' ich mich denn grämen*

DISC 1 : TRACK 67

G:

2. A _____ progression occupies most of this excerpt. The seventh chords in this three-part texture each lack a _____ . If you were to add a fourth voice beginning on F4, how would it proceed? (Do not label NCTs in this exercise.)

Mozart, Rondo K. 494

3. In addition to analyzing the chords in this excerpt, label the NCTs.

Schumann, "Spring Song," op. 68, no. 15

4. Following is the harmonic progression from the first 16 measures of Richard Rodgers' "My Favorite Things" from *The Sound of Music*. Continue the realization of the lead-sheet symbols, using a five-part texture and providing roman numerals as shown. Use smooth voice leading and be sure to resolve all chord 7ths.

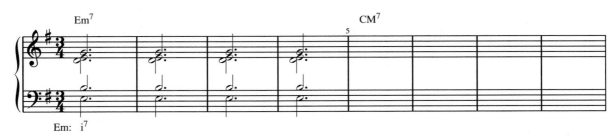

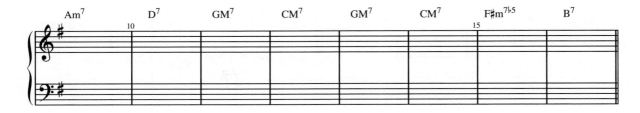

D. Notate, introduce, and resolve the specified chords. Each chord 7th is to be approached as a suspension, as a neighbor, or as a passing tone, as indicated. Include key signatures, lead-sheet symbols without slash symbols, and roman numerals.

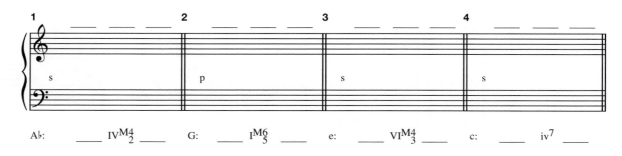

Ab: ___ IV$^{M4}_{2}$ ___   G: ___ I$^{M6}_{5}$ ___   e: ___ VI$^{M4}_{3}$ ___   c: ___ iv^7 ___

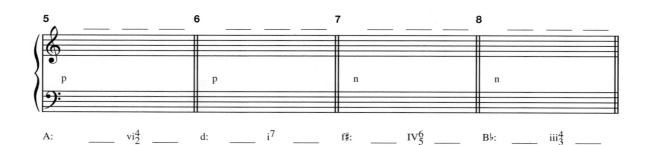

A: ___ vi$^4_2$ ___   d: ___ i^7 ___   f#: ___ IV$^6_5$ ___   Bb: ___ iii$^4_3$ ___

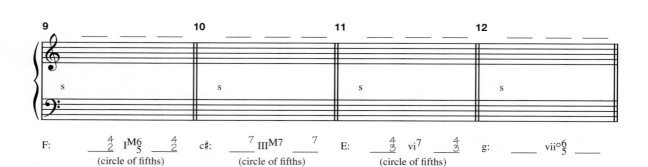

F: __$^4_2$__ I$^{M6}_{5}$ __$^4_2$__   c#: __^{7}__ III^{M7} __^{7}__   E: __$^4_3$__ vi^7 __$^4_3$__   g: ___ vii$^{o6}_{5}$ ___
(circle of fifths)   (circle of fifths)   (circle of fifths)

E. Add a top voice to create a three-part texture.

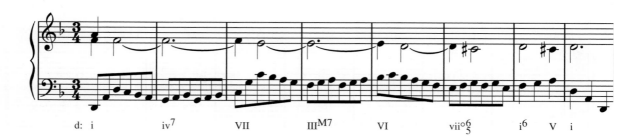

d: i   iv^7 VII   III^{M7} VI   vii$^{o6}_{5}$ i^6 V   i

F. Analyze the chords specified by each figured bass and make a harmonization for four-part chorus.

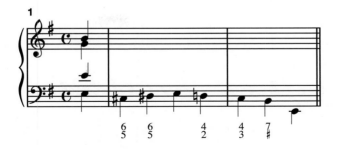

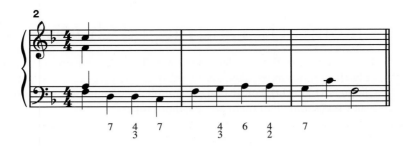

Exercise 15-1 See Workbook.

Summary

Some 17 different seventh chords have been discussed in this chapter and the preceding one. Rather than trying to memorize the typical resolutions of these chords, we suggest that you simply remember and apply these principles:

1. The function of a triad is not changed by the addition of a 7th. Because, for example, iv tends to progress to ii° or V, you may assume that iv⁷ has these same tendencies. Exception: The tonic becomes an active chord instead of a stable harmonic goal.

2. Smooth approach to the 7th of the chord is a feature of many, but not all, passages employing diatonic seventh chords.

3. Chord 7ths almost always resolve down by step. It follows, therefore, that the chord of resolution must contain the note to which the 7th will resolve. The resolution is sometimes delayed, as in iv⁷-i$^6_4$-V, or, in rare cases, simply not employed.

4. In minor, the movement of the individual lines usually conforms to the melodic minor scale. Because of this, more seventh-chord types are possible in minor than in major.

5. In a circle-of-fifths progression of root position seventh chords in four parts, incomplete and complete chords must be used in alternation.

Chapter Sixteen
Secondary Functions 1

Chromaticism and Altered Chords

The term **chromaticism** refers to the use of pitches foreign to the key of the passage. The only chromaticism we have discussed so far involves chromatic nonchord tones (review Chapters 11 and 12). For instance, Example 16-1 contains several notes not found in the B♭ major scale, and all of them are nonchord tones.

Example 16-1   Haydn, String Quartet op. 64, no. 3, I

Some people use the term **nonessential chromaticism** to describe the use of chromatically altered tones as NCTs. **Essential chromaticism** refers to the use of tones from outside the scale as members of chords. Such chords are called **altered chords**.

Secondary Functions and Tonization

By far the most common sort of altered chord in tonal music is the **secondary function.** A chord whose function belongs more closely to a key other than the main key of the passage is called a secondary function. Listen to Example 16-2, paying special attention to the ending. Although the two-part texture means that incomplete chords will have to be used, it is clear that the F♯4 in m. 7 is not an NCT. In fact, the last two chords are D and G, and they sound like V–I in the key of G.

DISC 1 : TRACK 68

Example 16-2   Haydn, Symphony no. 94, II

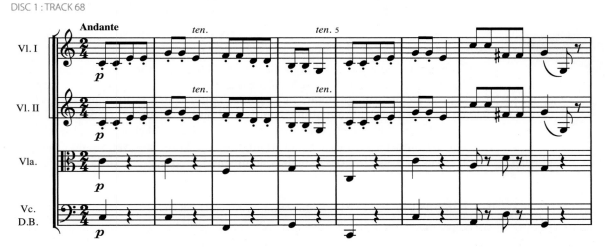

If our ears were to lose track of the original tonic at this point, or if the music were to continue in the key of G, employing F♯s and centering on G, we would analyze this as a change of key (a modulation). However, because we still hear the G chord as a V, and because the next phrase is a repeat of the first one, we label the G chord as V and call the D chord a *V of V* (the symbol is V/V). We say that the D chord has **tonized** the G chord, giving it special emphasis, but that a change of tonic has not taken place.

Most secondary functions are either secondary dominants (*V of* and *V⁷ of*) or secondary leading-tone chords (*vii° of, vii°⁷ of,* and *vii°⁷ of*).

Secondary Dominant Chords

Because tonic triads are always major or minor, it makes sense that only major and minor triads can be tonized by secondary dominants. This means that you would not expect to find V/ii° in minor or V/vii° in either major or minor. All other diatonic chords (other than I, of course) may be tonized by secondary V or V7 chords. Example 16-3 illustrates the possibilities in F major. Notice that most of the accidentals create a leading tone to the root of the chord being tonized.

Example 16-3   Secondary dominants in F major

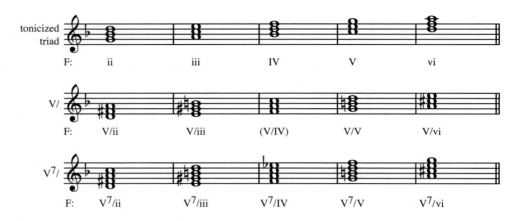

Only one of these chords, V/IV, is identical to a diatonic chord in F. Because V/IV sounds like I, composers most often use V⁷/IV instead of V/IV to make the secondary function clear.

The secondary dominants in d minor are illustrated in Example 16-4. Here three chords are identical to diatonic chords in d minor. The V/III (= VII) and the V⁷/III (= VII⁷) are both usable, even though they are not altered chords, because VII and VII⁷ usually function as dominants of III anyway. The V/VI, however, would usually be analyzed as III instead of as a secondary dominant.

Example 16-4   Secondary dominants in D minor

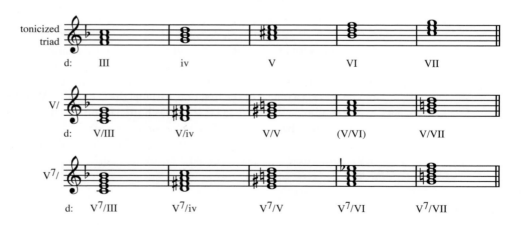

The major or minor triad that is tonicized by a secondary dominant may occur with its 7th, or the tonicized chord may itself be altered to become a secondary dominant. This means, for example, that any of the following progressions might be encountered in C major.

V⁷/ii–ii	V⁷/ii–ii⁷	V⁷/ii–V/V	V⁷/ii–V⁷/V
C: A7–Dm	A7–Dm7	A7–D	A7–D7

Spelling Secondary Dominants

There are three steps involved in spelling a secondary dominant.

1. Find the root of the chord that is to be tonicized.

2. Go up a P5.

3. Using that note as the root, spell a major triad (for V of) or a major-minor seventh chord (for V^7 of).

For example, to spell a V/vi in E♭, the steps are the following (Ex. 16-5).

1. The root of vi in E♭ is C.

2. A P5 above C is G.

3. A major triad on G is G–B♮–D.

Example 16-5

E♭: vi   P5↑   V/vi

Or, to spell a V^7/V in b minor (Ex. 16-6),

1. The root of V in b is F♯.

2. A P5 above F♯ is C♯.

3. A Mm^7 on C♯ is C♯–E♯–G♯–B.

Example 16-6

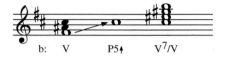

b: V   P5↑ V^7/V

Recognizing Secondary Dominants

If you encounter an altered chord in a passage, there is a good chance that it will be a secondary dominant. These steps will work in most cases.

1. Is the altered chord a major triad or major-minor seventh chord? If not, it is not a secondary dominant.

2. Find the note a P5 below the root of the altered chord.

3. Would a major or minor triad built on that note be a diatonic triad in this key? If so, the altered chord is a secondary dominant.

You may find that beginning an analysis with lead-sheet symbols will help you to identify secondary dominants as well as other altered chords.

CHECKPOINT

1. What is the definition of a secondary function?

2. Most secondary functions are either secondary dominants (*V of* and *V⁷ of*) or
_____ .

3. Why is a V/IV in major less convincing than a V⁷/IV?

4. The root of a secondary dominant is how far above the root of the chord being tonicized?

5. In a major key, which triad(s) cannot be tonicized by a secondary dominant? What about minor keys?

Self-Test 16-1

(Answers begin on page 599.)

A. Review how to spell secondary dominants (p. 247). Then notate these secondary dominants in the specified inversions. Include key signatures and lead-sheet symbols without slash symbols.

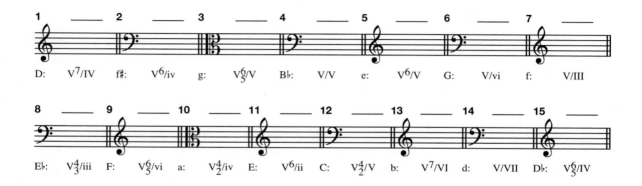

1 ____ D: V⁷/IV   2 ____ f♯: V⁶/iv   3 ____ g: V⁶₅/V   4 ____ B♭: V/V   5 ____ e: V⁶/V   6 ____ G: V/vi   7 ____ f: V/III

8 ____ E♭: V⁴₃/iii   9 ____ F: V⁶₅/vi   10 ____ a: V⁴₂/iv   11 ____ E: V⁶/ii   12 ____ C: V⁴₂/V   13 ____ b: V⁷/VI   14 ____ d: V/VII   15 ____ D♭: V⁶₅/IV

B. Review how to recognize secondary dominants (pp. 247–248). Then label with a roman numeral any chord that might be a secondary dominant according to the steps outlined previously. Label all others with an X.

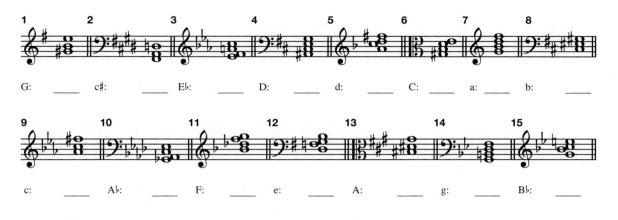

G: _____   c#: _____   Eb: _____   D: _____   d: _____   C: _____   a: _____   b: _____

c: _____   Ab: _____   F: _____   e: _____   A: _____   g: _____   Bb: _____

Exercise 16-1 See Workbook.

Secondary Dominants in Context

Secondary dominants generally resolve just as primary dominants do. That is, a V_5^6/V in C will resolve the same way as V_5^6 would in the key of G (Ex. 16-7a). The only exception is that sometimes the chord of resolution contains a 7th. In that case, the leading tone may need to slide down a half step to become the 7th of the chord of resolution (Ex. 16-7b). Notice that complete seventh chords in root position alternate with incomplete ones in Example 16-7c. This part-writing principle should be familiar to you from the discussion of circle-of-fifths sequences in Chapter 15 (pp. 238–239). The *arrow notation* shown on the second line of the analysis is an acceptable method of abbreviation.

Example 16-7

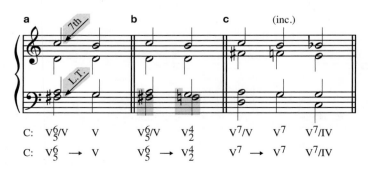

The V⁷/V is the most frequently encountered secondary dominant. In Example 16-8 the V is delayed by a cadential six-four. This is not an irregular resolution of the V⁷/V because, as we know, the I_4^6–V together stands for V.

Example 16-8   Schumann, "Noveletten," op. 21, no. 1

Textural reduction

In our preceding discussion of Example 16-7b, we pointed out that the leading tone of the secondary dominant will sometimes move down by half step if the chord that follows contains a 7th. This is illustrated by the F♯ to F♮ in the bass of Example 16-9.

Example 16-9   Chopin, Mazurka op. 68, no. 1

The common deceptive progression V$^{(7)}$–vi is often given added impetus by inserting a dominant of vi between the V and the vi, as in Example 16-10.

DISC 1 : TRACK 70

Example 16-10   Schumann, "Eintritt," op. 82, no. 1

B♭: I   V   I   IV   V^7 V^6/vi vi   IV   ii^7 V^7 I

The only deceptive progression that we have discussed up to this point is the progression from V or V^7 to vi (or VI), but there are other kinds of deceptive progressions that we will encounter through the next several chapters. (Remember that a deceptive progression is not necessarily a deceptive cadence.) In general, a deceptive progression is the result anytime that a dominant chord is followed by something other than a tonic triad, as in the V$^6_5$–V$^4_2$/IV progression in Example 16-11. Notice also the stepwise bass line.

DISC 1 : TRACK 70

Example 16-11   Tchaikovsky, Piano Trio op. 50, II

E: I^6 V$^4_3$ I   V$^6_5$ V$^4_2$/IV   IV^6 (I$^6_4$) ii$^6_5$ I^6 ii^7

A much less smooth introduction to a V^7/IV is shown in Example 16-12. Here we see the ending of a phrase that concludes with a deceptive cadence (m. 24). All parts then immediately leap to C♮, which is ♭$\hat{7}$, to state the three-note motive that began the piece. This example also illustrates the V^6/ii.

Example 16-12   Haydn, String Quartet op. 20, no. 4, I

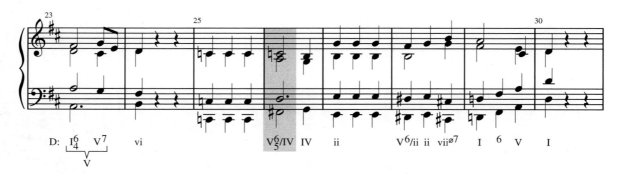

Examples of dominants of iii in major are not frequently encountered because the iii it-self is the least often used diatonic triad. However, the III in minor, which represents the relative major key, is very often tonicized by VII or VII^7, which should be labeled as V/III or V^7/III. Listen to Example 16-13, and hear the brief shift to B♭ in the second measure. Notice also the root position vii°, not all that unusual after a IV$^6_5$ because of the smooth voice leading it allows.

Example 16-13   Bach, *Jesu, du mein liebstes Leben*

Secondary dominants abound in jazz and popular music, as do many other kinds of chro-maticism. The harmonically simple but effective film theme in Example 16-14 reaches a half cadence in mm. 7 to 8 with a V^7/V–V progression. The V chord in the last measure includes a 4-3 suspension. Notice the stepwise descent in the bass in mm. 1 to 5 (C–B–A–G–F), specified by the lead-sheet symbols and including a passing I$^6_4$ chord.

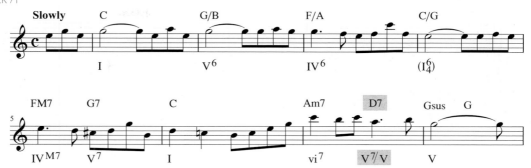

Example 16-14   Bacalov, "Il Postino"

Self-Test 16-2

(Answers begin on page 600.)

A. Analysis

1. This excerpt is from a set of variations on a tune that we know as "Twinkle, Twinkle, Little Star." Label the chords and the NCTs, and number the suspensions (as in 7-6). Draw an arrow to any consonant suspensions that you find.

Vogler, Variations on *"Ah! vous dirai-je, Maman"*

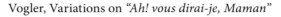

2. Analyze with roman numerals. Find the sequence and enclose it in brackets. Although the voice leading is conventional throughout most of this excerpt, parallel 5ths do occur. Find them. Be sure to play this example so that you can appreciate the effect of the last four measures.

Schumann, *Papillons,* op. 2, no. 12

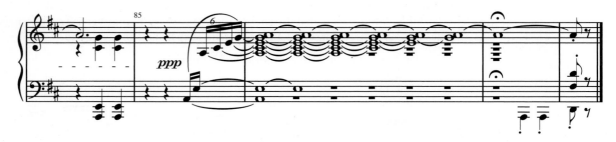

3. Label the chords and NCTs.

Schubert, Symphony in B♭, II

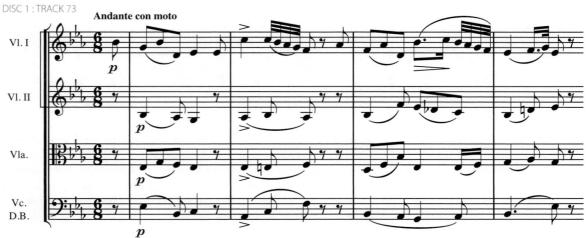

4. Analyze chords and NCTs. To what extent is this example sequential? If you play the first half of m. 1 as a chord, you will discover that there are seven different parts in the texture. To what extent are some of these voices doubling another voice at the octave? Except for this doubling, are there any parallel 8ves to be found?

Schumann, Romanze, op. 28, no. 1

DISC 1 : TRACK 74

5. Analyze chords and NCTs. To what extent is this example sequential?

Mozart, Violin Sonata K. 481, II

6. This passage, from the beginning of Verdi's *Requiem,* is a beautiful example of *a cappella* writing. It features two circle-of-fifths progressions that employ secondary dominants. Label all chords and NCTs. (The ii°$^4_3$ in m. 53 is an example of mode mixture, the subject of Chapter 21.)

Verdi, *Messa da Requiem,* "Requiem aeternam"

DISC 1 : TRACK 74

7. This excerpt is the introduction to a piece for chorus and piano. Label chords and NCTs.

Schumann, *Beim Abschied zu singen,* op. 84

B. For each of the following problems, first analyze the given chord. Next, find a smooth way to lead into the chord. Although there are many possibilities, it will often work to use a chord whose root is a P5 above the root of the secondary dominant. Experiment with other relationships also. Then resolve each chord properly, taking special care with the leading tone and the 7th resolutions. Analyze all chords with roman numerals and lead-sheet symbols without slash symbols.

C. Below each note list the secondary V and V⁷ chords that could harmonize that note.
You might find it helpful to refer to the examples on page 246.

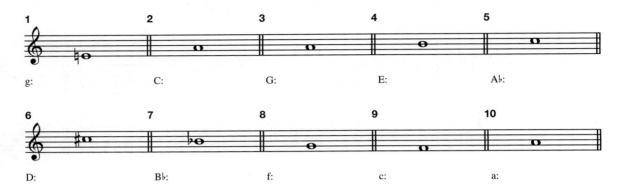

D. Provide roman numerals to show how the first note could be harmonized as a
secondary dominant. The second note should be harmonized by the tonicized triad.

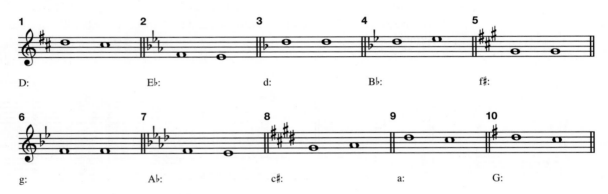

E. Following is the first phrase of "America" (or "God Save the Queen"), along with lead-sheet symbols. Put roman numerals below the staff and complete the four-part harmonization. Be careful with the voice leading around m. 4, which can be tricky. Where is the hemiola in this excerpt? (Review p. 232.)

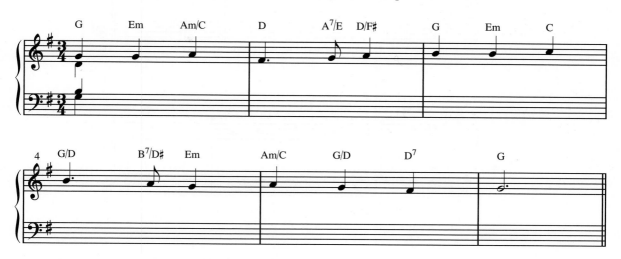

F. Harmonize each chorale phrase for SATB chorus. Include one or more secondary dominants in each phrase and activate the texture with some NCTs. Note that the key of the phrase does not always agree with the key signature.

3

e:

4

e:

G. Analyze the harmonies specified by each figured bass and make a setting for SATB chorus.

1

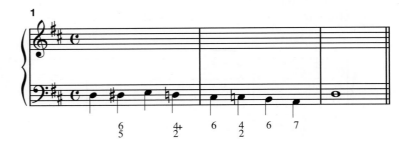

2

Exercise 16-2 See Workbook.

Summary

Chromaticism refers to the use of pitches that are not diatonic in the key of the passage. Chords that employ chromaticism are called **altered chords,** and the most commonly encountered altered chord in tonal music is the **secondary function.** A secondary function is a chord whose function belongs more closely to a key other than the main key of the passage. Most secondary functions are either secondary dominants (*V of* and *V⁷ of*) or secondary leading-tone chords (*vii° of, viiᵒ⁷ of,* and *vii°⁷ of*).

Secondary dominants can tonicize only major or minor triads or major or minor triads with a 7th. This means that the vii° chord, for example, cannot be tonicized by a secondary dominant.

To spell a secondary dominant, go up a P5 from the root of the chord to be tonicized and spell a major triad (for V of) or a major-minor seventh chord (for V⁷ of). To determine whether an altered chord that you encounter in analysis might be a secondary dominant, see whether it is a major triad or a major-minor seventh chord with a root that is a P5 above a scale degree that usually carries a major or minor triad in that key. If so, the altered chord is a secondary dominant.

Secondary dominants resolve just as primary dominants do, except that the chord of resolution frequently contains a 7th. In that case, the leading tone of the secondary dominant moves down by half step if necessary to become the 7th of the chord of resolution.

The V⁷/V is the most frequently encountered secondary dominant. Two variations on the deceptive progression that employ secondary dominants are V⁽⁷⁾–V⁷/vi–vi and V⁽⁷⁾–V⁷/IV. The V⁽⁷⁾/iii in major is seldom used, but the V⁽⁷⁾/III in the minor mode is quite common.

Variations

For additional review and practice, please see Chapter 16 on our website at **www.mhhe.com/kostka7e.**

Chapter Seventeen
Secondary Functions 2

Secondary Leading-Tone Chords

The $V^{(7)}$ and $vii^{\circ(7)}$ chords have similar functions in tonal music (review pp. 102–103), the main difference being that $V^{(7)}$, which contains a P5 above the root, sounds like a more substantial sonority. The same generalizations hold true for secondary functions, which means that any chord that can be tonicized by a $V^{(7)}$ can also be tonicized by a $vii^{\circ(7)}$.

One small complication arises when a leading-tone seventh chord (in contrast to a leading-tone *triad*) is used as a secondary function. Should the resulting chord be a $vii^{\circ7}/$ or a $vii^{\varnothing7}/$? Almost all examples follow these principles:

1. If the triad to be tonicized is minor, use $vii^{\circ7}/$.
2. If the triad to be tonicized is major, use either $vii^{\varnothing7}/$ or $vii^{\circ7}/$, although the fully diminished version appears to be used more often.

Examples 17-1 and 17-2 list all the secondary leading-tone chords in major and minor. Although all these chords are theoretically possible, leading-tone chords of ii, IV, V, and vi in major and of iv and V in minor are more common than the others. One chord, the $vii^{\circ}/$ III in minor, is identical to a diatonic triad (ii°), and the $vii^{\varnothing7}/$III is identical to a diatonic seventh chord ($ii^{\varnothing7}$). The functions of these chords can be made clear only by the context. You might also notice that there is no $vii^{\varnothing7}/V$ in the minor mode, even though the V chord is major. This is an exception to rule 2 above, and the reason for it is that the dominant *key* is minor, even though the dominant triad is major.

Example 17-1   *Secondary leading-tone chords in G major*

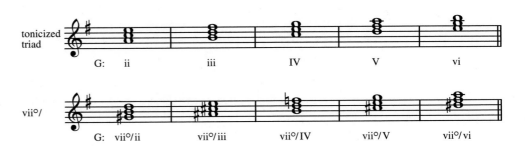

tonicized triad					
G:	ii	iii	IV	V	vi

$vii^{\circ}/$					
G:	vii°/ii	vii°/iii	vii°/IV	vii°/V	vii°/vi

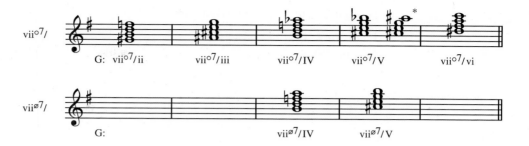

Example 17-2   *Secondary leading-tone chords in E minor*

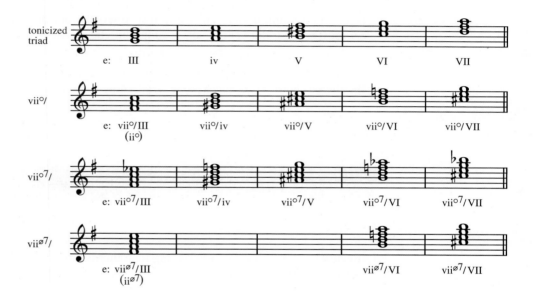

Spelling Secondary Leading-Tone Chords

The procedure for spelling secondary leading-tone chords is not difficult and can be summarized as follows:

1. Find the root of the chord that is to be tonicized.

2. Go down a m2.

3. Using that note as the root, spell a diminished triad (for vii° of), a diminished seventh chord (for vii°⁷ of), or a half-diminished seventh chord (for viiø⁷ of).

---

*   This spelling is sometimes used if the next chord is I$^6_4$.

For example, to spell a vii°⁷/vi in E♭,

1. The root of vi in E♭ is C.
2. A m2 below C is B.
3. A diminished seventh chord on B is B–D–F–A♭.

Recognizing Secondary Leading-Tone Chords

If you find an altered chord in a passage and it is not a V⁽⁷⁾/, there is a good chance it will be a secondary leading-tone chord. These steps will work in most cases:

1. Is the chord a diminished triad, a diminished seventh, or a half-diminished seventh chord? If not, it is not a secondary leading-tone chord.
2. Find the note a m2 above the root of the altered chord.
3. Would a major or minor triad built on that note be a diatonic triad in this key? If so, the altered chord is probably a secondary leading-tone chord.

Self-Test 17-1

(Answers begin on page 607.)

A. Review how to spell secondary leading-tone chords (pp. 263–264). Then notate these secondary leading-tone chords in the specified inversion. Include key signatures.

B. Label any chord that could be a secondary leading-tone chord according to the steps outlined on page 264. Label all others with an X.

C: _____   F: _____   f: _____   A: _____   c: _____   Eb: _____   b: _____

D: _____   Bb: _____   g: _____   Ab: _____   Bb: _____   a: _____   G: _____   E: _____

Exercise 17-1 See Workbook.

Secondary Leading-Tone Chords in Context

Secondary leading-tone chords resolve in the same way as do primary leading-tone chords—leading tone up, 7th down—but be careful not to double $\hat{7}$ in resolving a vii°⁷/V or a viiø⁷/V. Smooth voice leading is usually, but not always, a feature of the progressions. A few examples will give you the idea.

In Example 17-3, Schubert intensifies the motion toward the first cadence by means of a viiø⁷/V. As with the V/V, the motion to a I$_4^6$ is not considered an irregular resolution because the I$_4^6$ only delays the V chord. We noted on page 250 that the V$^{(7)}$–vi deceptive progression is often embellished by inserting a V$^{(7)}$/vi between the V and the vi. Just as common in this context is the vii°⁷/vi, as in the second phrase of Example 17-3.

Example 17-3   Schubert, *An die Musik,* op. 88, no. 4

In Example 17-4 we encounter still another variant of the deceptive progression. Here the cadential I_4^6 in m. 2 is followed not by a V but by a vii°^{7}/vi.

Example 17-4   Schumann, *Herberge,* op. 82, no. 6

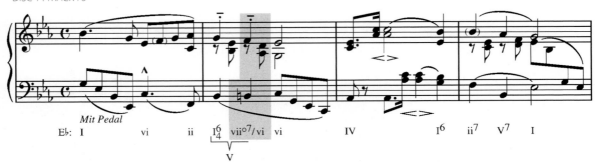

A vii°$^4_3$/iv and a vii°$^4_2$ of V both appear in Example 17-5. There is a cadential six-four in m. 67, but there is not a real modulation to F♯ here. You can prove this for yourself by playing through the example. You will almost certainly hear the last chord as V, not I. Notice the long bracket at the end of Example 17-5. This is a convenient abbreviation that can be used for longer tonicizations.

DISC 1 : TRACK 76

Example 17-5   Schumann, *Die feindlichen Brüder*, op. 49, no. 2

Example 17-6 is interesting in several respects. Notice that the V$^6_5$/V in m. 41 is followed not by a V, as expected, but by a V$^4_3$/IV (we have chosen the A in m. 43 as the bass of the V$^4_3$/IV). This and other unexpected resolutions of secondary functions will be discussed more fully later in this chapter. The V$^4_3$/IV itself resolves normally, as do the vii°$^4_3$/ii and the vii°$^6_5$/ii, except for some liberties taken with the viola part.

Example 17-6   Beethoven, Symphony no. 2, op. 36, I

Sequences Involving Secondary Functions

Sequential patterns often use secondary functions. One that is especially common is the circle-of-fifths sequence, but with one or more secondary functions (V/ or vii°/) substituting for diatonic chords. Following is a short circle-of-fifths sequence, with possible substitutions shown for the first three chords.

Diatonic circle of fifths in C	$Em^7(iii^7)$	–	$Am^7(vi^7)$	–	$Dm^7(ii^7)$	–	$G^7(V^7)$–$C(I)$
V^7/substitutes	$E^7(V^7/vi)$	–	$A^7(V^7/ii)$	–	$D^7(V^7/V)$		
$vii°^7$/substitutes	$G\sharp°^7(vii°^7/vi)$	–	$C\sharp°^7(vii°^7/ii)$	–	$F\sharp°^7(vii°^7/V)$		

By choosing one chord from each of the first three columns in the preceding chart, we can make up some variations on the circle-of-fifths progression.

Diatonic version	Em^7	–	Am^7	–	Dm^7	–	G^7	–	C
Variation	E^7	–	Am^7	–	D^7	–	G^7	–	C
Variation	E^7	–	$C\sharp°^7$	–	Dm^7	–	G^7	–	C
Variation	$G\sharp°^7$	–	A^7	–	$F\sharp°^7$	–	G^7	–	C

An instance of substitutions of this sort is seen in Example 17-7. There is a circle-of-fifths progression in mm. 2 to 5 that is essentially a VI–ii°–V–i progression, with two °7 chord substitutions.

Diatonic circle of fifths in e	C(VI)	–	$F\sharp°$ (ii°)	–	B (V)	–	Em (i)
$vii°^7$/substitutes			$A\sharp°^7$		$D\sharp°^7$		
			$(vii°^7/V)$		$(vii°^7)$		

Example 17-7   Beethoven, Piano Sonata op. 14, no. 1, II

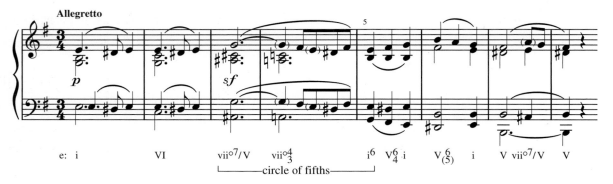

When a series of major-minor seventh chords is used in a circle-of-fifths sequence, certain voice-leading problems come up. For one thing, each leading tone will resolve down by chromatic half step to become the 7th of the next major-minor seventh chord. Also, as you might recall from page 238, if the chords are in root position in a four-part texture, incomplete seventh chords must alternate with complete seventh chords. These points are illustrated in Example 17-8.

Example 17-8

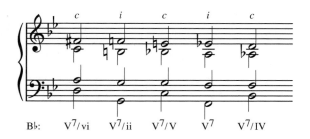

The voice leading in Example 17-8 is the precise voice leading Mozart uses in the first two measures of Example 17-9. However, he goes a step "too far," to an E♭^{7} in m. 58, implying a resolution to A♭. A change of key from B♭ to A♭ would be quite unexpected here. For five measures Mozart prolongs the suspense, until the E♭ in the bass is finally bent up to E♮, creating a vii°^{7}/V in B♭. This leads back to a PAC in B♭. Notice also the A♭ $^6_4$ chords (pedal six-fours) that occur in mm. 58 to 61, adding to the listener's anticipation of A♭ as the goal. In studying this example, remember that the basses on the bottom staff sound an octave lower than written. *Be sure to listen to this example.*

Example 17-9   Mozart, Symphony no. 40, K. 550, I

Bb: ii^6 V^7/vi V^7/ii V^7/V V^7 V^7/IV V^7/Ab- - - - - - - - - - - - - - - -

└——— circle of fifths ———┘

Deceptive Resolutions of Secondary Functions

Some resolutions of secondary functions that appear to be irregular or deceptive are really not. For instance, you probably realize that the resolution of the vii°⁽⁷⁾/V in Example 17-10a is perfectly normal because the cadential I_4^6 stands for the V that it is delaying. But what about Example 17-10b, where what appears to be a vii°⁶₅/iii also resolves to a V delayed by a cadential I_4^6? Here it is important to recognize that the vii°⁷/V is spelled enharmonically, even though it is theoretically "incorrect." It is not uncommon to find this respelling in major keys when the V is delayed by a I_4^6.

Example 17-10

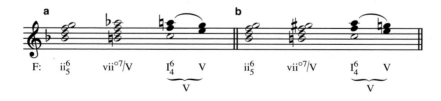

However, deceptive resolutions of secondary functions certainly do occur. Especially common is the resolution of a V⁷/ up to the vi (or VI) of the chord that was being tonicized. For instance, in the key of F:

Chords   A⁷   B♭

Analysis   V⁷/vi   VI/vi

A beautiful example of this progression occurs near the end of one of Schumann's songs (Ex. 17-11), as does the "misspelled" vii°⁷/V shown in Example 17-10b.

DISC 1 : TRACK 78

Example 17-11   Schumann, *Auf dem Rhein,* op. 51, no. 4

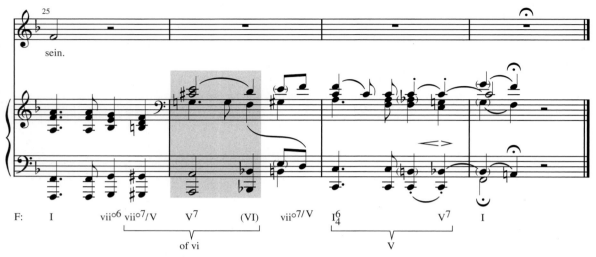

Another kind of deceptive resolution was seen in Example 17-6, in which a V^6_5/V was followed by a V^4_3/IV. One of the reasons this progression "works" here is that it features smooth voice leading, summarized in Example 17-12a. Even smoother is the connection between any two Mm7 chords a m3 apart (Ex. 17-12b and c) or, surprisingly, a tritone apart (Ex. 17-12d) because all such pairs of Mm7 chords share two pitch classes. In the example, the common tones are tied. Notice that the remaining voices move by half step in contrary motion. Play through the example and notice how surprisingly convincing these progressions sound.

Example 17-12

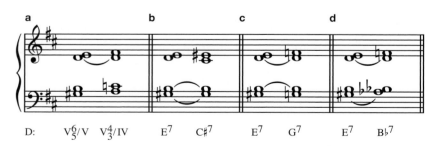

In Example 17-13 there is a root movement down a m3 from the V^4_2/IV (F^7) to the V^7/ii ($D7$). Notice that the composer (who was Felix Mendelssohn's sister) retains the common tones A and C in the accompaniment in the same registers and moves the outer voices chromatically in contrary motion.

Example 17-13 Fanny Mendelssohn Hensel, *Von dir, mein Lieb, ich scheiden muss*

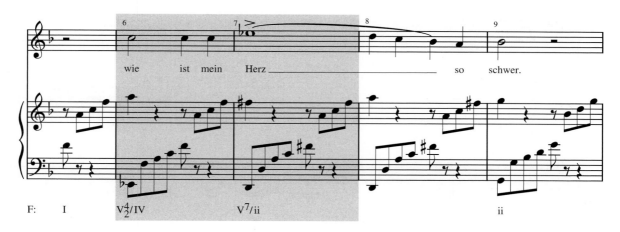

Other Secondary Functions

We have discussed secondary dominants, secondary leading-tone chords, and, in the preceding section, secondary submediants. Other secondary functions do occur, but less commonly. We tend to hear a change of key when we encounter several chords that are drawing our attention away from the original tonic. However, a short progression of chords will generally not be enough to accomplish a change of key, and it is in such passages that other secondary functions occasionally occur.

Listen to Example 17-14. Although one could argue in favor of a quick change of key to C in mm. 69 to 70, it is unlikely that we would really lose track of G as the tonal center so quickly. In this case, IV⁶/IV would seem to be a better analysis than IV⁶ in the key of C.

Example 17-14   Mozart, Piano Sonata K. 545, II

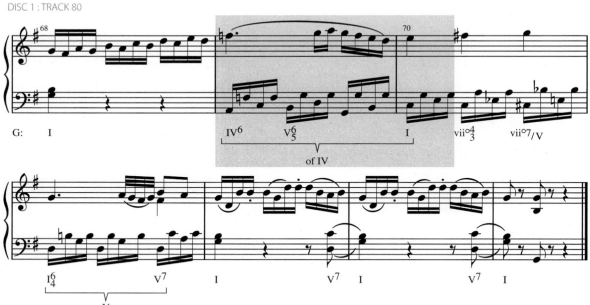

Example 17-15 is considerably more complicated, but it is worth the effort. You might want to begin by playing through the textural reduction that follows the example. The basic outline of the progression is I–V–I–iii–ii–V–I, but the iii and ii chords are elaborated by ii–V–i progressions of their own. Underlying all of this is an unusually long circle-of-fifths progression that involves the root of every chord in the excerpt except the first: A–D–G♯–C♯–F♯–B–E–A–D. Despite the harmonic complexity, the passage flows seamlessly, part of a famous theme that surely must be listened to, if you don't know it already.

Finally, notice that although the chords that are the point of this discussion—the ii°⁷/iii and the ii°⁷/ii—are spelled the same as a vii°⁷/V and a vii°⁷/IV, respectively, we can tell from the context that they are secondary ii°⁷ chords, not secondary vii°⁷ chords.

Example 17-15   Tchaikovsky, Symphony no. 5, op. 64, II
(Instruments sound where written)

Self-Test 17-2

(Answers begin on page 607.)

A. Analysis

1. Label chords and NCTs.

   Bach, *Warum betrübst du dich, mein Herz*

2. Label chords and NCTs. Review pages 271–272, then find two circle-of-fifths progressions that contain more than three chords. Remember that a leading-tone chord may substitute for a chord in the circle of fifths.

   Haydn, Piano Sonata no. 43, Minuetto I

3. First review the discussion of Example 17-10, then label the chords in this excerpt. Some of the chords and NCTs have been labeled for you.

Spohr, Salonstück, op. 145, no. 3

4. Label chords and NCTs. Analyze the chords in m. 47 in two ways: once in the key of F, once in some key hinted at in m. 46.

Mozart, Piano Sonata K. 333, I

5. Label chords and NCTs. Explain why this excerpt is not a period. Do not include the grace notes in your analysis.

Mozart, Violin Sonata K. 379, I

6. Label the chords with roman numerals, but do not label NCTs. Analyze the chords from the middle of m. 88 to the middle of m. 90 in some key other than B♭. Bracket the longest circle-of-fifths progression you can find.

Mozart, Bassoon Concerto K. 191, I

B. For each of these problems, first analyze and resolve the given chord, being especially careful with the 7th chord and the leading tone. Then find a smooth way to lead into the given chord. Analyze all chords with roman numerals and lead-sheet symbols.

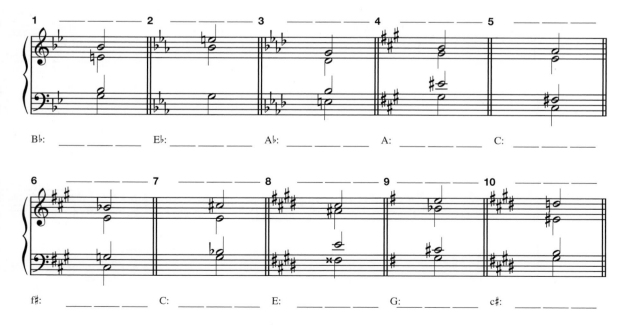

C. Harmonize each of these chorale phrases for SATB chorus. Include at least one
    secondary leading-tone chord or incorporate some other aspect discussed in this
    chapter in each harmonization.

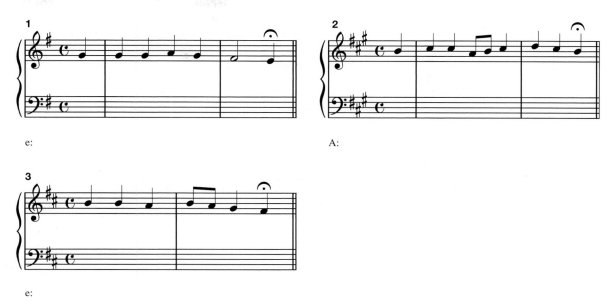

e: A:

e:

D. Analyze the harmonies specified by each figured bass, then make an arrangement of
    each for SATB chorus.

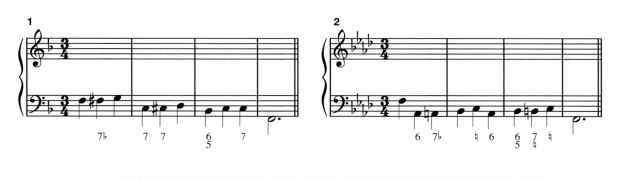

Exercise 17-2 See Workbook.

Summary

Any chord that can be tonicized by a secondary dominant can also be tonicized by a secondary leading-tone chord. The vii°/ and vii°7/ chords may be used to tonicize major or minor triads, but the vii°7/ may tonicize only major triads. However, a major chord that is never tonicized by vii°7/ is the V chord in minor.

To spell a secondary leading-tone chord, go down a m2 from the root of the chord that is to be tonicized and spell a diminished triad (for vii° of), a diminished seventh chord (for vii°7 of), or a half-diminished seventh chord (for vii°7 of). To determine whether an altered chord that you encounter in analysis might be a secondary leading-tone chord, see whether it is a diminished triad, a diminished seventh chord, or a half-diminished seventh chord with a root that is a m2 below a scale degree that usually carries a major or minor triad in that key. If so, the altered chord is probably a secondary leading-tone chord.

Secondary dominant or secondary leading-tone chords are frequently substituted for diatonic chords in circle-of-fifths sequences. A substituted secondary dominant will have the same root as the diatonic chord for which it substitutes, whereas a substituted secondary leading-tone chord will have a root a M3 higher.

The vii°7/vi is used in two more variants of the deceptive progression: V7–vii°7/vi–vi and I$^6_4$–vii°7/vi–vi. In addition, secondary dominants may themselves resolve deceptively, usually to the vi (or VI) of the chord being tonicized. Secondary functions other than V, vii°, and vi also occur occasionally.

Chapter Eighteen
Modulations Using Diatonic Common Chords

Modulation and Change of Key

Almost all compositions from the tonal era begin and end in the same key. Sometimes the *mode* will be changed, usually from minor to major, but the *keynote* (tonic note) remains the same. A piece that begins in c minor and ends in C major is still in C. Even multimovement works begin and end in the same key if the movements are intended to be performed together as a unit. (An interesting exception to this is the song cycle.) The principle also holds for each individual movement of a multimovement work (sonatas, symphonies, song cycles, and so on), although the interior movements will often be in different keys. We will use the term **change of key** for such situations, as in "There is a change of key from C major in the first movement to F major in the second movement."

Modulation is another matter. A modulation is a shift of tonal center that takes place *within* an individual movement. Although a tonal work or movement begins and ends in the same key, other tonalities generally will be hinted at, referred to, or even strongly established. The longer the work, the more time is likely to be devoted to tonalities other than the tonic and the more keys are likely to be touched on.

The tonal structure of a composition is closely related to its overall form. For example, a Classical piano sonata might have the following tonal structure. The crooked arrows represent modulations, and roman numerals represent other keys in relation to the tonic.

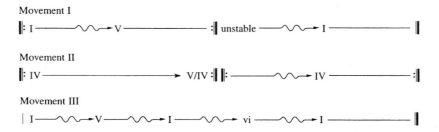

Modulation and Tonicization

The line between modulation and tonicization (using secondary functions—V/V and so on) is not clearly defined in tonal music, nor is it meant to be. One listener might find that a very short passage tonicizing a new tonality is enough to make a convincing modulation.

For instance, you might have heard some of the excerpts in Chapters 16 and 17 as modulations, whereas other listeners might not have. The single most important factor in convincing the listener of a modulation is time, although other elements, such as a cadential I_4^6–V or V/V in the new key, contribute as well. Listen to Example 18-1. At the end of the excerpt, do you hear C or A as tonic? You could analyze this passage as **tonicizing** C or as **modulating** to C major. The difference in the analyses would not be an important one. There is no right or wrong here—there are just the interpretations of different listeners.

DISC 1 : TRACK 85

Example 18-1   Beethoven, Symphony no. 7, op. 92, II

It seems clear, however, that composers have always hoped the sophisticated listener (surely a minority of the audience) would manage to follow the modulations aurally. If not, many important effects would be lost. For example, if a composer has brought back a tune in another key when we had expected it to return in tonic, the composer expects us to be surprised. Otherwise, why bother? The fact that such effects might be lost on many listeners should not keep us from trying to appreciate what the composer is doing.

Key Relationships

Two keys that sound the same but that are spelled differently are called **enharmonically equivalent keys.** C♯ major and D♭ major are enharmonically equivalent. If a composer for some reason respells C♯ as D♭, no modulation has occurred because the keynote is unchanged.

If a major key and a minor key have the same tonic tone, they are called **parallel keys.** The parallel minor of C major is c minor. Because parallel keys share the same tonic, we do not use the term modulation when talking about movement from one key to its parallel. The term **change of mode,** or **mode mixture,** is used instead. (Mode mixture is discussed in more detail in Chapter 21.)

If a major key and a minor key share the same key signature, they are called **relative keys.** The relative minor of C major is a minor. The term modulation is appropriate here because movement from one tonic to another is involved. Modulations between relative keys are common, especially from minor to relative major.

Most modulations in tonal music are between **closely related keys.** Two keys are said to be closely related if there is a difference of no more than one sharp or flat in their key signatures. Because this definition applies to both major and minor keys, it includes the relative major or minor key, where there is no difference at all in the key signatures. Here are the keys closely related to C major and c minor:

Starting Key: C major			Starting Key: c minor		
1♯	G	e	2♭	g	B♭
0♯, 0♭	Ⓒ	a	3♭	ⓒ	E♭
1♭	F	d	4♭	f	A♭

Another way to find the keys closely related to some starting key is to take the keys represented by the tonic, subdominant, and dominant triads and their relatives. In minor use the *natural minor scale* in determining the closely related keys.

Starting Key: C major			Starting Key: c minor		
Dominant	G	e	Dominant	g	B♭
Tonic	Ⓒ	a	Tonic	ⓒ	E♭
Subdominant	F	d	Subdominant	f	A♭

Still another method is to take the keys represented by the diatonic major and minor triads (only) of the home key. Again, use natural minor for the minor keys. The diatonic major and minor triads are also those that can be tonicized by secondary dominant or secondary leading-tone chords.

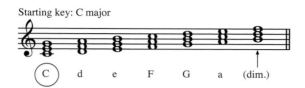

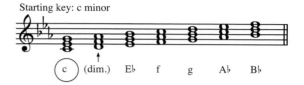

If you compare the preceding three methods, you will see that each approach yields the same result. There are always five keys closely related to the starting key. Use whichever method seems easiest to you.

All key relationships that are not enharmonic, parallel, relative, or closely related are called **foreign relationships,** and such pairs of keys are said to be **distantly related.** Some relationships are more foreign than others. Often we describe foreign key relationships in terms of simpler relationships used in the composition. Thus, a modulation from C major to D major might be described as a modulation to the dominant of the dominant; one from C major to E♭ major might be called a modulation to the relative major of the parallel minor.

CHECKPOINT

1. Is movement from E major to e minor a modulation? Explain. If not, what is it called? What about a♯ minor to b♭ minor?

2. Compare and contrast *modulation* and *change of key.*

3. Name the five kinds of key relationships.

4. Describe three ways to find the five keys closely related to some starting key.

Self-Test 18-1

(Answers begin on page 612.)

A. Name the relative key in each case.

1. D _____   2. b♭ _____   3. f♯ _____   4. C♭ _____   5. F _____

6. d♯ _____   7. E _____   8. f _____   9. E♭ _____   10. g♯ _____

B. Name all the closely related keys to the given key. Be sure to use uppercase for major, lowercase for minor.

1. B♭: _____   _____   _____   _____   _____

2. D♭: _____   _____   _____   _____   _____

3. c: _____   _____   _____   _____   _____

4. a♯: _____   _____   _____   _____   _____

5. c♯: _____   _____   _____   _____   _____

6. A: _____   _____   _____   _____   _____

C. Name the relationship in each case (enharmonically equivalent, parallel, relative and closely related, closely related, or foreign).

1. G/f _____   6. C♭/G♭ _____

2. B/E _____   7. d/D _____

3. a♯/b♭ _____   8. E♭/D♭ _____

4. c/A♭ _____   9. B♭/g _____

5. f♯/A _____   10. c♯/F♯ _____

Exercise 18-1 See Workbook.

Common-Chord Modulation

Most modulations are made smoother by using one or more chords that are common to both keys as an intersection between them. The **common chord** (or chords) serves as a hinge or pivot linking the two tonalities. In the following diagram, the shaded rectangle represents the common chord (also called a pivot chord) in a modulation from B♭ to F.

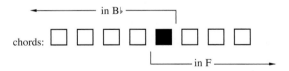

Whereas any pair of closely related keys will have at least one diatonic triad in common, this is not always the case with foreign key relationships. Modulation to a foreign key often requires the use of an altered chord as a common chord; techniques for such modulations are presented in Chapter 19.

To discover the potential common chords between two keys, consider the diatonic triads found in the first key to see whether they also occur in the second key. For example, there are four triads in common between B♭ and F.

First key, B♭	I	ii	iii	IV	V	vi	vii°
Triads in B♭	B♭	Cm	Dm	E♭	F	Gm	A°
Triads in F	B♭	C	Dm	E°	F	Gm	Am
Second key, F	IV	V	vi	vii°	I	· ii	iii

In minor keys, we usually consider the chord types commonly found on each scale degree: i, ii°, III, iv, V, VI, vii° (less frequently, other chords that occur in minor, such as IV and v, are used as common chords). This yields two common chords between B♭ major and c minor.

First key, B♭	I	ii	iii	IV	V	vi	vii°
Triads in B♭	B♭	Cm	Dm	E♭	F	Gm	A°
Triads in c	B°	Cm	D°	E♭	Fm	G	A♭
Second key, c	vii°	i	ii°	III	iv	V	VI

Example 18-2 illustrates a modulation from B♭ major to c minor, using the ii in B♭ as the common chord. Notice the symbol used to show the common-chord modulation. The roman numerals following the modulation are put right below the staff, even though they are in the new key.

Example 18-2

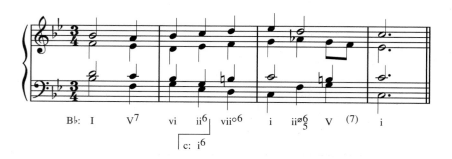

B♭: I   V⁷   vi   ii⁶ vii°⁶   i   ii∅⁶₅   V   (7)   i

c: i⁶

When you are composing a modulation, you will find that the V or vii° in either key is often the least successful choice as common chord. As Example 18-3a illustrates, such a modulation can sound too abrupt. The modulation will be smoother if the V–I progression in the new key is delayed by several chords, especially through the use of a deceptive progression, a cadential six-four, or both, as in Example 18-3b.

Example 18-3

a

G: I   V⁶₅   I   IV   I   G: I   V⁶₅   I   IV   vi   ii⁶   I⁶₄   V⁷   I

F: V   F: V   V

The goal-directed melody in Example 18-3b also contributes to making this modulation to a foreign key convincing and successful.

Analyzing Common-Chord Modulation

In analyzing modulations, the procedure to follow is this:

1. Listen to the passage carefully.

2. Find the **point of modulation,** that is, the first chord that seems to be functioning more naturally in the second key than in the first one. (This step is open to differing interpretations, but often this chord contains an accidental not found in the first key or is a tonic six-four chord (I_4^6 or i_4^6) in the second key.)

3. Back up one chord from the one you identified in step 2. If there is a diatonic common chord, it should be in this position.

In Example 18-4 the F♯° chord in the middle of m. 5 serves as a vii°6 in G but only as a secondary leading-tone chord in C, so it functions more naturally in G than in C. This is the chord that signals the modulation. Backing up one chord to the beginning of the measure brings us to the common chord, C (I = IV).

DISC 1 : TRACK 85

Example 18-4   Mozart, Viennese Sonatina no. 6, II

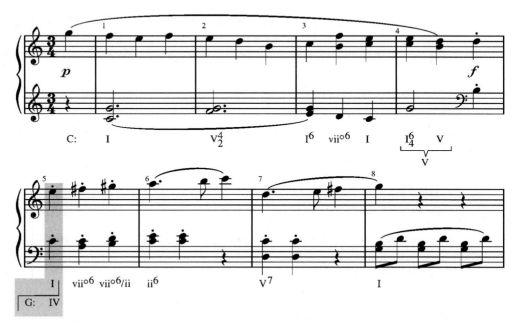

Example 18-4 is "recomposed" in Example 18-5 to illustrate the fact that *the common chord itself does not signal the modulation* but just smooths it out. In Example 18-5 the C chord is followed not by a modulation to G but by a cadence in C.

Example 18-5

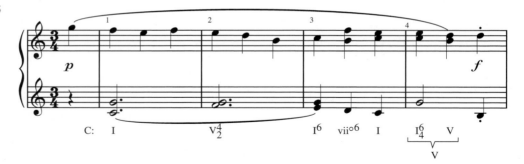

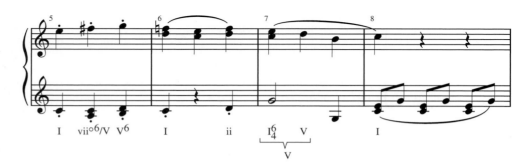

The most common modulation in major keys is I–V, as in Example 18-4. In minor keys, modulations to III or to v are the most frequently encountered. Example 18-6 illustrates a i-III modulation. The C7 chord (B♭ is the implied bass note) functions more naturally in F than in d and is preceded by the common chord.

Example 18-6   Tchaikovsky, Mazurka op. 39, no. 10

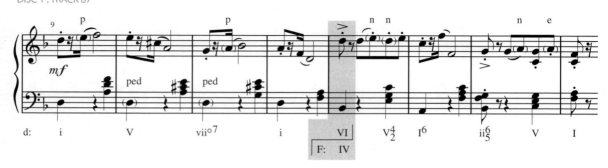

Incidentally, you might hear some of the examples and exercises in this chapter as tonicizations instead of true modulations. Analyze them as modulations anyway for practice in locating common chords.

Although I–V and i–III are the most frequently encountered modulations, all other closely related modulations do occur. In Example 18-7, the tonality moves briefly from I to iii. Notice that there is no change of key signature here. Indeed, the key signature of the main tonality is usually maintained throughout the work, no matter how many modulations occur.

Example 18-7   Dvořák, String Quartet op. 51, IV

E♭: ii   V⁷   I   V⁷/IV   ii⁶   V⁷   I

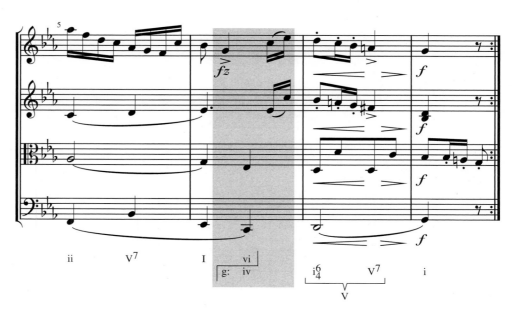

ii   V⁷   I   vi
            g: iv

i⁶₄   V⁷   i
   V

Self-Test 18-2

(Answers begin on page 613.)

A. Analysis.

    1. This excerpt begins and ends in e, with a modulation to the relative major in between. Label chords and NCTs, showing the common chords as demonstrated in this chapter.

       Bach, *Keinen hat Gott verlassen*

DISC 1 : TRACK 88

    2. Label chords and NCTs. Why is it unlikely that Bach was thinking of the sonority on the last eighth of m. 7 as a seventh chord?

       Bach, *Jesu, Jesu, du bist mein*

DISC 1 : TRACK 88

3. This song firmly establishes e minor at the beginning and then briefly modulates to a foreign key. Label chords and NCTs. (It would be a good idea to begin by playing the piano accompaniment slowly and then adding lead-sheet symbols.)

Schubert, *Auf dem Flusse,* op. 89, no. 7

4. Label chords and NCTs. Remember this is an excerpt; don't be fooled by the key signature.

Schubert, *Am Feierabend,* op. 25, no. 5

fal - len;   und das   lie - be Mäd - chen sagt___   al - len   ei - ne gu - te Nacht,

5. Label chords but not NCTs. Find the longest circle-of-fifths harmonic progression in the excerpt. To what extent does that progression generate a sequence in the melody and bass lines?

Schumann, *Freisinn*, op. 25, no. 2

Lasst mich nur___ auf mei-nem Sat - tel

gel - ten!   Bleibt in

eu - ren Hüt-ten, eu-ren Zel - ten! Und ich rei - te froh in al - le

Fer - ne, ü - ber mei - ner Mü-tze nur die Ster - ne.

B. Fill in the name of the new key on the second line of each exercise.

1. B♭: I   V   I   ii⁶   V   vi⌐
                          └____ : ii   V$_3^4$ I   V⁷   I

2. f♯: i   V   VI   iv⁶⌐
                     └____: ii⁶   V   vi   IV   V   I

3. d: i   V$_5^6$/iv   iv   V$_2^4$ i⁶⌐
                               └____: iv⁶   (i$_4^6$)   ii°$_5^6$ V$_2^4$ i⁶   vii°⁶   i

4. A: I   V   vi   ii⁶   vii°⁶⌐
                           └____: ii°⁶   ⌐i$_4^6$ V⌐   i
                                        └___V___┘

5. E♭: I   V$_3^4$ I⁶   IV⌐
                      └____: I   vii°⁶   I⁶   V$_2^4$ I⁶   ii⁶   V   I

C. List the diatonic triads that could serve as common chords between each pair of keys.
In minor keys, assume the usual chord qualities: i, ii°, III, iv, V, VI, vii°.

Example: First key: C: I   iii   V   vi
             Triads: C   Em   G   Am
             Second key: G: IV   vi   I   ii

1. First key, A♭:
   Triads:
   Second key, D♭:

2. First key, c:
   Triads:
   Second key, f:

3. First key, a:
   Triads:
   Second key, F:

4. First key, G:
   Triads:
   Second key, D:

5. First key, c♯:
   Triads:
   Second key, E:

6. First key, D:
   Triads:
   Second key, f♯:

D. Make choral settings of part B, progressions 1 (SATB) and 2 (SAB). Activate the texture with NCTs and/or arpeggiations. Arrange the metric structure so that the last chord comes on a strong beat.

E. Harmonize the following chorale tune for SATB chorus. The first phrase should modulate to V; the second should return to I.

F. Analyze the chords specified by this figured bass, then make an arrangement for SATB chorus.

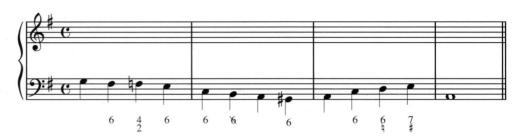

Exercise 18-2 See Workbook.

Summary

A modulation is a shift of tonal center that takes place within an individual movement. A tonicization is like a short modulation, and listeners frequently will disagree as to whether a particular passage really modulates.

Enharmonically equivalent keys sound the same but are spelled differently. If major and minor keys have the same tonic note, they are called **parallel keys.** A **change of mode,** but not a modulation, occurs when music moves between two parallel keys. If two major and minor keys share the same key signature, they are called **relative keys.** Two keys are said to be **closely related** if their key signatures differ by no more than one accidental. All key relationships that are not enharmonic, parallel, relative, or closely related are called **foreign relationships,** and such pairs of keys are said to be **distantly related.**

Common-chord modulations use one or more chords that are diatonic to both keys as a kind of hinge or pivot linking the two tonalities. Whereas any two closely related keys will have at least one diatonic triad in common (and therefore available as a common chord), this will not necessarily be true of two distantly related keys.

To discover the potential common chords between two keys, list the diatonic triads found in the first key to see whether they also occur in the second key. To analyze a common-chord modulation, find the first chord that functions more convincingly in the second key than in the first, then back up one chord. If there is a diatonic common chord between the two keys, this should be where it is found.

Chapter Nineteen
Some Other Modulatory Techniques

Altered Chords as Common Chords

In Chapter 18 we discussed modulations using chords that are diatonic in both keys as common chords. Although diatonic common-chord modulation is probably the most frequently used modulatory technique, there are many others. This chapter will present a few of them.

In Chapter 18 we listed a three-step procedure for the analysis of modulations. These steps bear repeating here:

1. Listen to the passage carefully.
2. Find the first chord that seems to be more directly related to the second key than to the first one (the point of modulation).
3. Back up one chord. If there is a diatonic common chord, it should be in this position.

The phrase "if there is a diatonic common chord" might have suggested to you that altered chords may sometimes be used as common chords. For example, consider the following modulation:

Key of G: $\longrightarrow$
$\qquad$ ... D^7 $\quad$ G $\quad$ Am $\quad$ A^7 $\quad$ D ...
$\qquad\qquad\qquad$ Key of D: $\longrightarrow$

Here the first chord that is more directly related to D than to G is the A^7 (V^7 in D). However, the Am triad that precedes it cannot serve as a common chord because it makes no sense in the context of D major. Instead, the A^7 is itself the common chord, functioning as V^7/V in G. This modulation is illustrated in Example 19-1.

DISC 1 : TRACK 91

Example 19-1   Beethoven, Piano Sonata op. 14, no. 2, I

Secondary $V^{(7)}$ and $vii°^{(7)}$ chords can be used as common chords. The chord might be a secondary function in the first key, in the second key, or in both keys. Sometimes the secondary function coincides with the point of modulation, as in Example 19-1, whereas at other times the secondary function precedes it.

A number of other altered chords, to be discussed in Chapter 21, frequently serve as the common chord in a modulation, as examples in that chapter will illustrate. An additional common-chord technique involving enharmonic reinterpretation of the common chord is the principal topic of Chapter 23.

Sequential Modulation

It is not uncommon for a modulation to come about through the use of a sequence. This is a simple device: the composer merely states something at one pitch level and then states it again immediately at another pitch level. However, the modulating sequence, instead of being diatonic, tonicizes a different pitch. Often a common chord could be analyzed in such a modulation, but the sequence is equally important in establishing the new tonal center.

Example 19-2 is a clear instance of a sequential modulation. The first phrase, in C major, is transposed with little change up to d minor to create the second phrase. Sequences up by step are very frequently encountered. Notice that the d:i could also have functioned as C:ii, so this modulation is both sequential and by common chord.

Example 19-2   Schubert, Five Piano Pieces, D. 459, no. 3

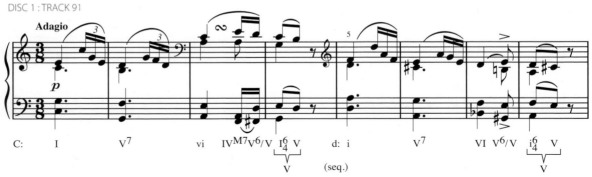

Whereas the sequential motion in Example 19-2 is up by step, that in Example 19-3 is down by step, from C major to B♭ major. (Some would analyze these measures as G: IV–V$^4_2$–I^6 followed by the same progression in F.)

Example 19-3   Beethoven, Piano Sonata op. 53, I

Keep in mind that many modulations are of short duration and might more properly be called tonicizations. Both Examples 19-2 and 19-3 return to the first key immediately after the sequence.

Another common pattern for sequential modulation is the circle of fifths. The circle-of-fifths sequences we have studied so far have been diatonic (such as vi–ii–V–I), with occasional secondary functions thrown in. However, the circle-of-fifths progression can also be used to get from one key to another with a sequential progression such as C–C7–F–F7–B♭–B♭7, etc. In Example 19-4, on the other hand, Schubert begins with a sequence of ascending minor thirds through the keys of C, E♭, and G♭, then breaks it off with a circle-of-fifths progression (G♭/F♯–Bm), only to leap back into C, the opening tonality of the passage.

DISC 1 : TRACK 93

Example 19-4   Schubert, Piano Sonata D. 850, III

Modulation by Common Tone

In some modulations, the hinge between the two keys is not a common chord but a common tone. Unlike the common-chord modulation, where the progression usually makes the modulation smooth and undramatic, common-tone modulations often announce themselves clearly to the listener by isolating the common tone. This is the case in Example 19-5, where the note F♯ joins the keys of b minor and D major.

Example 19-5   Mozart, Fantasia K. 475

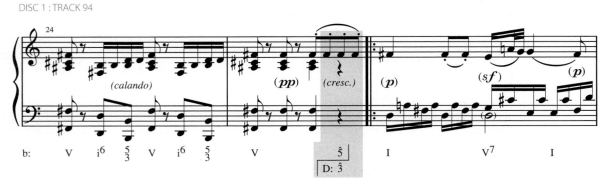

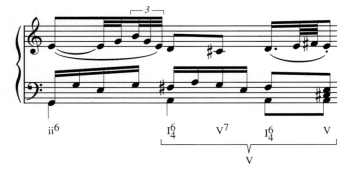

Even more dramatic is Example 19-6, which occurs at the end of the slow introduction to Beethoven's Symphony no. 4. Here an A links a pianissimo V in d minor with a fortissimo V^7 in B♭ major.

Example 19-6   Beethoven, Symphony no. 4, op. 60, I

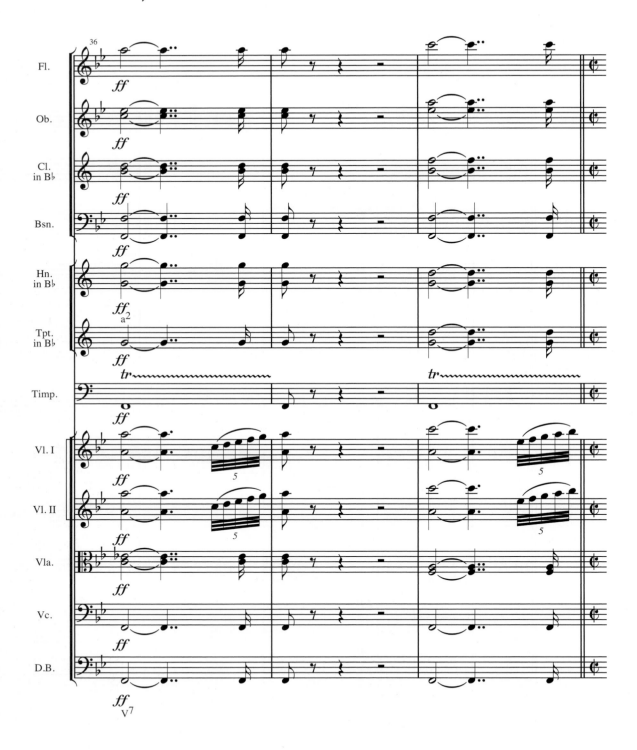

I

The two chords linked by the common tone in a common-tone modulation usually exhibit a **chromatic mediant relationship,** which has the following characteristics:

1. The roots of the chords are a m3 or M3 apart. Sometimes the interval of the m3 or M3 is spelled enharmonically as a $^+$2 or °4.

2. They are either both major triads or both minor triads (or, in the case of seventh chords, the triad portions of the chords are both major or both minor).

Some examples of chromatic mediant relationships are illustrated in Example 19-7, with the common tones shown as whole notes.

Example 19-7

The chromatic mediant relationships that were used by Mozart and Beethoven in Examples 19-5 and 19-6 are shown in Example 19-8.

Example 19-8

In both the Mozart and the Beethoven examples, the two keys involved were closely related. However, the chromatic mediant relationship used in common-tone modulations makes it easy to modulate to foreign keys as well. In Example 19-9 Brahms begins a movement from a symphony with a melody that emphasizes E, C, and G—the notes of a C major triad. The listener might expect the music to continue in C major, but in the fourth measure the note E is isolated, after which it becomes the tonic of E major. C major and E major are in a chromatic mediant relationship to each other.

Example 19-9   Brahms, Symphony no. 4, op. 98, II
(piano arrangement)

Monophonic Modulation

Sometimes a modulation is carried out by a single vocal or instrumental line. This is done by introducing and emphasizing the tones that are found in the second key but not in the first. Although harmonies are more or less clearly implied in a monophonic modulation, it is often best just to label the keys, as we have done in Example 19-10. Here the modulation is signaled by the F♯ and E♭ in m. 23.

DISC 1 : TRACK 96

Example 19-10   Bach, Partita no. 2 for Solo Violin, "Gigue"

Direct Modulation

Sometimes **direct modulations** occur without any attempt to smooth them over through the use of common chords, common tones, or sequences. Such modulations most frequently occur between phrases, so this kind of direct modulation is often called a **phrase modulation.** A typical example from a chorale appears in Example 19-11.

Example 19-11   Bach, *Für Freuden, lasst uns springen*

g: V
   Bb: I

Most phrase modulations could also be analyzed as common-chord or common-tone modulations or both, as is the case here: the I in Bb could be analyzed as a III in g minor, whereas the D4 in the tenor provides a common tone between the V in g minor and the I in Bb major. Such analyses are not incorrect, but we prefer the term *phrase modulation* because it more accurately reflects the way we hear this excerpt—as one phrase ending in g minor and another beginning in Bb major, with little effort being made to bridge the gap.

Some direct modulations occur *within* the phrase. However, this kind of modulation is not frequently encountered, and you should try to eliminate all the other possibilities for explaining the modulation before labeling it a direct modulation.

Example 19-12 shows a textural reduction of the kind of difficult modulatory passage that you might occasionally encounter. Play through the example slowly (you will definitely need to hear it), observing the analysis below the example.

Example 19-12   Mozart, Fantasia K. 475, mm. 6–16 (simplified)

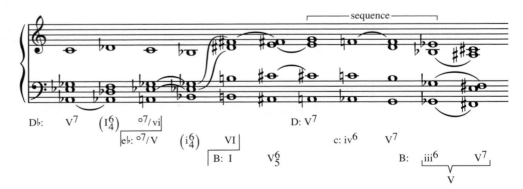

The first two tonicizations (these are too short to be called modulations), Db → eb and eb → B, are achieved by common chords. Next, a short sequence hints at D major (or minor) and c minor. The key of B then emerges as the goal of the passage. In a larger sense, the sequence connects the V_5^6 in B to the root position V^7 in B, which makes the sequence somewhat less important harmonically than the rest of the passage. The fleeting tonicizations of D and c would be considered direct because no other reasonable explanation is available. (The iii⁶ serves the same function as a cadential I_4^6.)

CHECKPOINT

1. What do we call a modulation that is carried out by a single vocal or instrumental line?

2. What kind of modulation involves transposing a pattern up or down to a new key?

3. What is the term for a modulation in which a single tone joins the two keys?

4. Name the other two types of modulation discussed in this chapter.

Self-Test 19-1

(Answers begin on page 618.)

A. Analysis

1. Analyze chords and NCTs. In addition, label the approach to the 7th of each seventh chord (review pp. 200–201).

Bach, *Die Nacht ist kommen*

DISC 1 : TRACK 98

2. This excerpt begins in D♭ major and ends in A major. Are these two keys in a chromatic mediant relationship? Listen to the excerpt carefully to determine the modulatory technique employed. Label all chords and NCTs.

Schubert, *Im Gegenwartigen Vergangenes*, D. 710

DISC 1 : TRACK 98

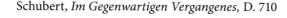

hin - ten _ an, _____ be - buscht und _ trau - lich steigt _ der Fel - sen in ____ die Hö - he.

3. In this excerpt, mm. 10 to 12 and 17 to 19 are all in the same key. Label the chords in those measures with roman numerals. Label the chords in mm. 13 to 16 with roman numerals in another key. Listen to mm. 11 to 14. How is the second key achieved? The return to the first key comes with the last chord in m. 16. What would be the best way to describe this kind of modulation?

Schubert, *Der Wegweiser,* op. 89, no. 20

DISC 1 : TRACK 99

mir ver - steck-te __ Ste - ge durch ver - schnei-te __Fel - sen - höhn, _ durch _ Fel - sen - höhn?

Now try to make a reduction of the voice and bass parts of the excerpt above, using one note in each part per chord.

4. Name the two keys established in this excerpt. How is the modulation accomplished? What is the relationship between the two keys?

Mozart, Symphony no. 41, K. 551, I

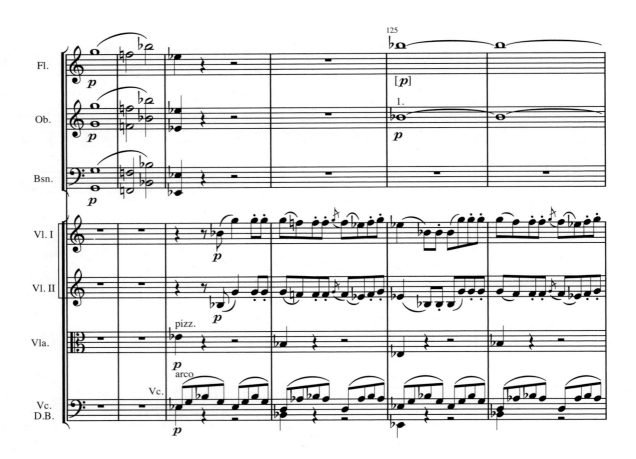

B. Analyze the harmonies implied by the following soprano-bass framework. Then add alto and tenor parts. Identify the modulatory technique used.

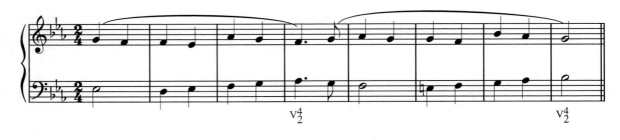

Exercise 19-1   See Workbook.

Summary

Although diatonic common-chord modulations are the type most frequently encountered, other kinds of modulation do exist. For example, a chord that is an **altered chord** in one or both keys may serve as the common chord. The only altered chords we have studied so far are secondary functions, but we will study others in later chapters. Another possibility is the **sequential modulation,** in which the transposition of a pattern causes the change of tonal center. In a **modulation by common tone,** a single tone serves as the common element between the two keys. The chords joined by the common tone usually exhibit a **chromatic mediant** relationship. A single unharmonized line establishes the new tonal center in a **monophonic modulation.** A modulation that uses no common chords or common tones is a **direct modulation.** Because most direct modulations occur between phrases, this kind of modulation is often called a **phrase modulation.**

Chapter Twenty
Larger Forms

Formal Terminology

In Chapter 10 you learned the terminology of period forms—such terms as **phrase, contrasting period,** and **parallel double period.** These terms are widely used and have generally accepted meanings. The terms we introduce in this chapter are also widely used, but in some cases writers on musical form disagree on some important aspects of their meanings. In addition, some writers recognize and name subcategories and modifications of the formal types discussed in this chapter. Although our approach attempts to find a common ground among the various systems, you should be aware that any book on musical form that you might read will disagree with our definitions to some extent, and your instructor might prefer to use a different approach.

Binary Forms

The word binary has to do with the concept of twoness. You are probably familiar with binary arithmetic, in which only two digits are used. In music a **binary form** is one that consists of two approximately equivalent sections, although they may be of unequal length. "Approximately equivalent" means that we would not use the term *binary* for a piece just because it has an introduction; the introduction is obviously not equivalent to the main body of the work.

Periods and double periods are binary forms, but we do not usually use the term *binary* for them, either, because a term such as **parallel period** is more informative. However, in Example 20-1 we see a familiar tune whose four phrases do not add up to a double period.

Example 20-1   "Greensleeves"

A diagram of the phrase structure reveals two parallel periods.

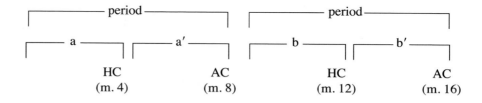

Although the structure is not a double period (because of the two authentic cadences), it is a binary form. Furthermore, "Greensleeves" is in **sectional** binary form because the first part ends with tonic harmony. If the first part of a binary form ends with something *other* than a tonic triad in the *main key* of the form, it is called a **continuous** binary form. The distinction between sectional and continuous forms is an important one, involving tonal independence in the first case and large-scale tonal drive in the second.

The two parts of the binary form in Example 20-2 are quite unequal in length, the second being twice as long as the first. The first half ends with a PAC in a minor, but because the main key of the piece is not a minor but d minor, this is an example of a continuous binary form.

DISC 2 : TRACK 1

Example 20-2   Bach, French Suite no. 1, Minuet I

a: PAC

F: HC

F: PAC

d: HC

d: PAC

Notice in this example that the second section is constructed largely from the two main motives of the first section. However, there is no area of contrast followed by a clearly stated return of the opening material, so the example is not in ABA form. Instead, like most binary examples, it lies somewhere between AA′ and AB, the second section containing elements of both contrast and continuation. This is also true of "Greensleeves" (Ex. 20-1), where the endings of phrases 3 and 4 are identical to the endings of phrases 1 and 2.

The Bach example (Ex. 20-2) repeats each of the two sections exactly. Repetition does not usually change our formal analysis. This minuet is a continuous binary form whether both, one, or no repeats are taken. However, movements or themes that consist of two repeated sections are so commonly encountered that a special term, **two-reprise,** is often used for them. To be thorough, then, we would say that Example 20-2 is a two-reprise continuous binary form. Incidentally, composers sometimes write out the repeats instead of using repeat signs, but we would still use the term *two-reprise.* Schumann and Chopin were especially fond of writing out repeats.

Notice in "Greensleeves" that the two parts of the binary form are of equal length (8+8), whereas in the Bach the second part is much longer (8+16). Some writers use the terms **balanced binary** and **unbalanced binary** for these situations.

Ternary Forms

The idea of statement-contrast-return, symbolized as ABA, is an important one in musical form. The ABA, or **ternary form,** is capable of providing the structure for anything from a short theme to a lengthy movement of a sonata or symphony. The B section of a ternary form can provide contrast with the A sections by using different melodic material, texture, tonality, or some combination of these.

The minuet from an early Haydn keyboard sonata is shown in Example 20-3, where we have labeled the cadences at the end of each section. Notice that this example is a two-reprise structure, that part one ends on the dominant (m. 8), and that all of part 1 returns (mm. 17–24), with an adjustment of the cadence to allow an ending on the tonic triad. Therefore, this minuet is an example of two-reprise continuous ternary form.

DISC 2 : TRACK 2

Example 20-3   Haydn, Piano Sonata no. 11, III, Minuet

In short ternary forms the B section often is clearly based on the A material. This was true of the Haydn minuet throughout the B part, but especially in the first few measures. Example 20-4 is the trio that continues the movement begun in Example 20-3. Again there is a two-reprise structure, but here the A section ends with an authentic cadence in e, the main key of the trio. The B part (mm. 11–19) is based on the A material, but some of the figures are inverted (compare mm. 1–2 with mm. 11–12), and it is in the key of the relative major. The return of A at m. 20 is quite obvious to the listener, although this A section is slightly longer than the original and considerably varied and even includes some of the inverted figures from B. The form is two-reprise sectional ternary.

DISC 2 : TRACK 3

Example 20-4   Haydn, Piano Sonata no. 11, III, Trio

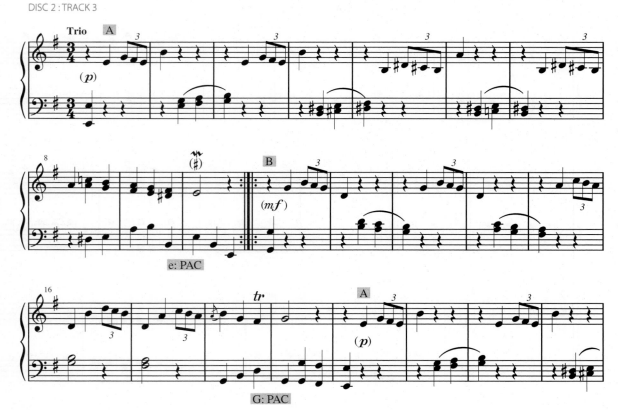

As with most minuets and trios, Haydn's minuet (Ex. 20-3) is played both before and after the trio (Ex. 20-4), so that the entire movement is itself a sectional ternary form.

At first glance, Example 20-5 might appear to be a five-part form:

‖:   A   :‖   B   A′   B   A′

However, on closer inspection we see that Schumann has written out only the second repeat of a two-reprise continuous ternary form.

‖:   A   :‖‖:   B   A′   :‖

DISC 2 : TRACK 4

Example 20-5   Schumann, "Melody," op. 68, no. 1

A great number of twentieth-century popular songs, especially those composed before the advent of rock music, adhered to a sectional ternary pattern that we will call the American popular ballad form. It consists of an eight-bar period that is repeated with a different text, followed by an eight-measure "bridge" that is often in another key and a return to the opening period. The following diagram summarizes this form:

Music:	A	A	B	A
Text:	1	2	3	4
Measures:	1–8	9–16	17–24	25–32

Hundreds of songs ("The Lady Is a Tramp," "Moonlight in Vermont," and so on) follow this same general format.

Rounded Binary Forms

Frequently, the last part of what appears to be a ternary form returns only half of the first A section.

A   B   ½A

The term that some writers use for this form is **rounded binary.** Often the phrase structure of a sectional rounded binary example will be

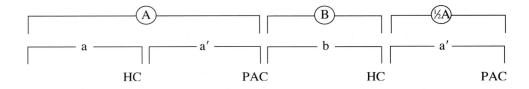

This is the form of many traditional tunes, such as "Oh, Susannah" (Ex. 20-6).

Example 20-6   Foster, "Oh! Susannah"

Example 20-7 is the theme from a set of variations. This is an example of a two-reprise sectional rounded binary form. Its form differs from "Oh! Susannah" only in that the return of the a′ phrase is extended by two measures.

DISC 2 : TRACK 5

Example 20-7   Mozart, Piano Sonata K. 331, I

The 12-Bar Blues

The **12-bar blues** is an important form in jazz, rock, and related styles. It consists of three four-bar phrases, sometimes in an *aab* pattern ("You Ain't Nothin' but a Hound Dog") and sometimes in an *abc* pattern ("Rock Around the Clock"). If the blues has a text (there are many purely instrumental blues compositions), the text may also be either *aab* or *abc*.

The most basic harmonic pattern for the 12-bar blues is the following:

Phrase 1 | I | I | I | I |
Phrase 2 | IV | IV | I | I |
Phrase 3 | V | IV | I | I |

Although this pattern is always perceptible in a blues, there are a great many variants, and few blues heard today will follow this simple pattern exactly. In Example 20-8 only the second phrase follows the model. The first phrase is embellished with augmented dominants and ends with a V^7/IV to lead smoothly into the second phrase. The final phrase uses V^7 and IV^9 instead of the triad forms and ends with I–IV^7–I. Notice also the mixture of major and minor modes (through the use of G♮, G♭, and F♯, a common blues feature.

DISC 2 : TRACK 6

Example 20-8   Wyche and Watts, "Alright, Okay, You Win"

CHECKPOINT

1. What is the difference between sectional binary and continuous binary?
2. What is the difference between rounded binary and ternary?
3. What does the term *two-reprise* mean?
4. What is the basic harmonic outline of the 12-bar blues?

Other Forms with Ternary Design

Binary and ternary forms, especially the latter, provide the structure for many pieces and movements from multimovement works. The typical minuet and trio (see the discussion of Examples 20-3 and 20-4) is sectional ternary because the minuet is played both before and after the trio.

A	B	A
Minuet	Trio	Minuet

The minuet itself is generally a two-reprise ternary or a two-reprise rounded binary, as is the trio.

Slow movements are also often in ternary form, an example being the second movement from Brahms's Symphony no. 1. It makes use of **transitions,** which are passages that connect different themes or tonal centers, and a **coda,** which is a special concluding section.

Section:	A	trans.	B	trans.	A	coda
Tonality	E	mod.	c♯	mod.	E	E
	(I)		(vi)		(I)	(I)
Measures:	1–27	28–38	39–57	57–66	67–100	101–128

Sonata Form

Many other musical forms are beyond the scope of this text, but two of the more important forms will be discussed briefly.

Sonata form (or sonata-allegro form) is usually found as the first movement of a sonata, string quartet, symphony, or similar work, although other movements may also be in sonata form. Early examples of sonata form resemble two-reprise continuous ternary form. However, the three sections are greatly expanded to include themes or groups of themes interspersed with transitional or developmental material. Although every movement in sonata form displays its material in unique ways, a normative version of the form is given next.

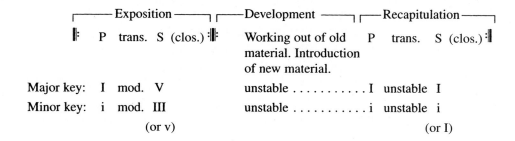

Several points can be made about the sonata as summarized in this diagram.

1. Instead of ABA, we use the labels exposition, development, and recapitulation for the three large sections of the sonata form. These labels tell us something about the thematic and tonal function of each section.

    a. The **exposition** presents the important themes as well as the tonal conflict between the two most important keys in the movement.

    b. The **development** has a more variable organization: it may develop motives from the exposition's themes, feature sequential activity, or (occasionally) introduce a new theme. It also develops the tonal conflict, touching upon several, usually more distant, keys before preparing for the return of the home key.

    c. The **recapitulation** replays the movement's important themes, usually in the same order, but the modulation to the secondary key is removed. In other words, the themes that were originally in the secondary key are now found in the home key. This resolves the tonal conflict set up in the exposition.

2. The roman numerals in this diagram do not refer to single chords. Instead, they represent the key of each section and show their relationship to the tonic key of the movement—the **home key.** So, in most sonatas where the home key uses the major mode, the most important **secondary key** is V, the key of the dominant. In minor-mode sonatas, the secondary key is typically III, the key of the relative major.

3. P and S stand for the **primary theme** (P theme, main theme, first theme) and **secondary theme** (S theme, subordinate theme, second theme) groups. These theme groups appear in both the exposition and recapitulation, separated by a more unstable transitional passage. Each may contain one or more themes, which are frequently constructed as periods, sentences, or binary/ternary forms. Notice that in the exposition these two areas are presented in different keys, but they both appear in the tonic key in the recapitulation. Like the exposition, development, and recapitulation themselves, these theme groups have unique characteristic functions.

    a. **Primary themes** establish the home key with at least one cadence (usually a PAC or HC) in that key. They frequently sound more vital, grand, or ceremonial than the secondary themes, although lyrical primary themes can also be found.

    b. The **transition,** a passage between P and S, destabilizes the home key, typically through restless musical material and a HC in either the home key or the secondary key. Thus, the transition may or may not modulate. Modulating transitions (and some nonmodulating transitions) are typically rewritten in the recapitulation to become nonmodulating.

    c. **Secondary themes** set up the tonal contrast in the exposition by establishing the secondary key, confirming it with a PAC in that key. In the recapitulation, secondary themes reconfirm the home key in the same manner after the destabilizing transition. Secondary themes frequently have a lyrical or gentle character.

    d. Expositions and recapitulations often end with a **closing section** that further confirms the prevailing key with simple sequential and cadential gestures.

4. The repeats are seen less often in nineteenth-century music than in eighteenth-century music, although lengthy introductions and codas are more commonly found. The number of themes presented in the two key areas also tends to be larger in the later music.

These points are further discussed and illustrated in the following sonata movement:

Example 20-9   Mozart, Piano Sonata K. 309, I*

Let us look at Example 20-9 in more detail to see how the sonata form is realized. The exposition (mm. 1–58) initiates the tonal conflict between the home key and secondary key, in this case C major and G major, respectively.

The primary theme (mm. 1–21) has an unusual structure and interestingly varied ideas. The first (mm. 1–8) and second phrases (mm. 8–21) both begin with a grand, two-measure arpeggiated gesture (mm. 1–2 and 8–9) that gives way to a more extended and lyrical passage. The second phrase takes longer to reach its final cadential goal (m. 21), lingering briefly on ii^6 and IV^6 before moving through additional material to the PAC. The length of the second phrase has the added effect of providing extra emphasis for the home key.

The transition section (mm. 21–32) in this example—a sentence with an extra repetition of the initial idea (mm. 25–26)—is of the modulating type and leads to a HC in G major in m. 32 that sets up the secondary theme. This modulation is rather subtle: the leading-tone F♯ of the new key actually appears first as a chromatic passing tone in m. 21 (along with D♯). When it reappears over a G chord in m. 23, we are at first uncertain whether this note is a chromatic embellishment in C major or a diatonic member of a new G major scale. Indeed, we are only really certain that we have modulated when the dominant of the new key appears as the goal of the HC in m. 32. Notice also that the first chord of the transition overlaps with the final cadential chord of the primary theme in m. 21; this elision (review p. 152) is a common feature of transitions.

After the restless, agitated character of the transition, the secondary theme (mm. 33–53) begins in a calmer vein. In fact, the languid two-measure lead-in (mm. 33–34) suggests a theme that is in no hurry to begin. Like the preceding transition, this theme is a sentence, but the longer, four-measure initial ideas (mm. 35–38 and 39–42) give the secondary theme a more expansive feeling. Notice also how long the theme takes to reach the PAC in m. 54; the repeated cadential progressions and harmonic detours in mm. 43–54 are typical of secondary theme groups, which require time to erase the listener's impression of the home key in favor of the new secondary key.

Following the cadence, a brief closing section continues the work of confirming the new key with a repeated idea that clearly outlines the diatonic relationships of the G major scale.

With the tonal and thematic conflict having been established in the exposition, the development (mm. 59–93) intensifies the notion of "conflict" by employing musical procedures that suggest instability and turmoil: frequent modulations and sequential passages, with few strong cadences or clear thematic units. It begins with the motive used to open the piece, but places it in the minor mode. Instead of confirming a single key, however, this motive initiates the first of several modulating sequences or near-sequences: mm. 59–66, which modulates from g minor to d minor, is followed by a shortened restatement in mm. 67–72 that does the same thing a fourth lower (from d minor to a minor).

Subsequent sequences get shorter and shorter as the drive to the cadence intensifies. A two-measure unit in mm. 73–74 is repeated down a whole step in mm. 75–76. The final measure of this unit is then repeated twice more in different keys (mm. 77, 78) before leading into the PAC in m. 82.

The use of a PAC in a development section is fairly rare because it contradicts the prevailing impression of instability. A HC in the home key, setting up the return of the opening themes in the recapitulation, would have been more typical. However, Mozart appears to be setting up a brief deception with this unusual cadence. Mm. 82–85 feature the return of the closing material from the end of the exposition, leading us to expect the beginning of the next section—the recapitulation. We do indeed hear the opening motive in m. 86—but in the wrong key and mode! This situation, in which the apparent arrival of the recapitulation turns out to be in the wrong tonal location, is called a **false recapitulation** (some would call it a false start). Mozart then restores the dominant of the real home key, C major, in m. 90 in preparation for the recapitulation.

The typical recapitulation returns the themes from the exposition in the same order: primary theme, transition, secondary theme, and closing section. However, those passages that featured the secondary key now appear in the home key. When we look at a recapitulation, then, we are especially interested in the differences between the recapitulation and the exposition. Apart from removing or adjusting the modulation in the transition, changes might be made for the sake of adding variety, confirming the home key more strongly, or developing themes that were ignored in the development.

In Example 20-9, the recapitulation (mm. 94–155) returns the exposition themes in the expected, original order. However, each theme has been changed in some manner. For example, the second phrase of the primary theme is now in the minor mode, while the material from mm. 12–14 has been removed and replaced with a new cadential passage (mm. 105–109); the theme gets back on track by m. 110. This excursion to c minor breaks up the tonal "sameness" of the recapitulation and reminds us of earlier passages where this material was found in minor: the beginning of the development and the false recapitulation.

Because the exposition's transition modulated from C major to G major, the recapitulation's transition (mm. 116–126) is adjusted to remove that modulation. The material after the sentence's initial ideas (mm. 122–126), though using similar motives, keeps the passage entirely within C major. As a result, the HC in m. 126 involves the dominant of the home key rather than that of the secondary key. This allows the secondary theme to begin in the home key.

Apart from its being in the home key, the secondary theme (mm. 127–148) is relatively unchanged from the exposition. The initial idea of this sentence (mm. 129–132) is slightly varied and has the melody in the left hand instead of the right, but otherwise proceeds as in the exposition.

The closing section also remains close to the version in the exposition. However, the last measure is replaced by four measures (mm. 152–155) that bring back the opening motive and further confirm the home key with repeated V–I harmonic motions. Ending with the opening motive is a typical strategy that nicely rounds off the movement.

Rondo Form

Rondo form is characterized by a refrain theme that alternates with contrasting thematic passages. The notion of a formal return puts it in the same category with ternary forms, including the sonata, but the larger number of returns is unique to the rondo. It is found most frequently as the final movement of a sonata, string quartet, or symphony, although slow movements are also sometimes in rondo form. There are four common types.

Five-part rondo (classic rondo)	A I	B V (or i or vi)		A I	C x	A I	
Five-part rondo (variant)	A I	B V (or i or vi)		A I	B ?	A I	
Seven-part rondo	A I	B V	A I	C x	A I	B I	A I
Sonata-rondo	A I	B V	A I	C (dev.) x	A I	B I	A I

The x in the preceding diagram symbolizes some key other than I or V; the ? means that a number of common possibilities exist. Rondos can also employ the minor mode. In such cases, the relative major (III) often substitutes for V.

Example 20-10 illustrates a typical five-part rondo; here the A section is a continuous binary theme. The B and C sections modulate to vi and IV, respectively, while the final A return is more extensively treated, functioning like a lengthy coda (a characteristic typical of rondos of all types).

Example 20-10   Beethoven, Piano Sonata op. 79, III*

* You can listen to a recording of this movement by going to the McGraw-Hill website: www.mhhe.com/kostka7e.

The **sonata-rondo** is distinguished from the seven-part rondo by the development of earlier material in the C section. Further, the B section of *any* rondo may function like the transition and secondary theme of a sonata exposition—modulating to a secondary key and then establishing that key with a clearly stated theme. When this is applied to a sonata-rondo, that form resembles a sonata with an "extra" return of the primary theme (A) after the exposition and another after the recapitulation.

Self-Test 20-1

(Answers begin on page 620.)

A. Sing "America" ("My Country, 'Tis of Thee"), then diagram its phrase structure. Include measure numbers and cadence types in your diagram. What is the form?

B. Diagram the following piece down to the phrase level and name the form. Assume there is a HC in m. 12, although there are other ways to hear this. Also, complete the following exercises:

1. Explain the G♮4's in mm. 1 and 2.

2. If there were a modulation at the end of the first section (most people hear it as a tonicization), where would the common chord be?

3. Can you relate mm. 9 to 12 to anything in mm. 1 to 4?

4. Find a 9–8 suspension with change of bass.

5. Find contrary octaves.

    Beethoven, Bagatelle op. 119, no. 4

DISC 2 : TRACK 7

C. Diagram this trio down to the phrase level and name the form. Assume that the phrases are four measures long. Also, complete these exercises.

1. The violas double what part (until m. 39)?

2. Explain the C♯5 in m. 36.

3. Find parallel 5ths between the outer voices.

Mozart, Symphony K. 97, III

D. Diagram this piece down to the phrase level and name the form. Assume that all phrases are four measures in length, except for an eight-measure phrase in mm. 9 to 16. Also, complete these exercises.

1. Discuss the choice of keys (tonicizations) in this piece.

2. Label the chords in mm. 17 to 24. Assume that the modulation back to f♯ is a phrase modulation.

3. Find a disguised set of parallel 5ths in the same measures.

4. What about this piece is reminiscent of two-reprise form?

Schumann, Album Leaf op. 99, no. 1

Exercise 20-1 See Workbook.

Summary

The term **binary form** is applied to a movement or portion of a movement that consists of two main sections (except that periods and double periods are not usually referred to as binary forms). If the first section of a binary form ends on the tonic triad in the main key of the form, it is **sectional binary;** if the first section ends with any other chord, it is **continuous binary.** Most binary forms could be symbolized as AA′, with the A′ section containing elements of both continuation and contrast.

Music that is in **ternary form** is in three parts, with the middle section providing contrast through the use of different melodic material, texture, tonality, or some combination of these, and the third part returning all or most of the first. Ternary form is symbolized as ABA and may be sectional or continuous, depending on whether or not the first A section ends with the tonic triad in the main key of the form.

Rounded binary form refers to music in which the opening A section returns after contrasting material but in a considerably abbreviated form, as in A, B, ½A. In many instances the choice between rounded binary and ternary is difficult to make. Like binary and ternary forms, rounded binary forms may be sectional or continuous.

Many binary, ternary, and rounded binary forms are also **two-reprise** forms, meaning that they consist of two repeated sections. The first repeated section is always the first A section, whereas the second repeated section is the rest of the form. The repeats are sometimes written out, perhaps with ornamentation or changes in register. Also, the main sections of a binary, ternary, or rounded binary form may be connected by **transitions,** and the form may end with a special concluding section called a **coda.**

The American popular ballad form is a 32-bar AABA ternary design. The 12-bar blues form consists of three phrases with a basic harmonic structure that is in most cases elaborated on in any particular blues composition.

Sonata form contains three large formal units. The **exposition** presents a succession of characteristic themes and establishes a tonal conflict between an initial **home key** and a contrasting **secondary key.** The **development** is more variously organized, but often features motivic development of the exposition's themes, sequential activity, and the exploration of more distant keys. The **recapitulation** restates the exposition's themes, transposing the secondary-key material into the home key. Many sonatas also contain a concluding **coda** section.

Sonata expositions generally contain 1) a **primary theme** or themes that establish and confirm the home key, 2) a **transition** that destabilizes the home key, 3) a **secondary theme** or themes that establish the secondary key, and, frequently, 4) a **closing section** that further confirms the secondary key.

A second formal type, the **rondo,** is characterized by a refrain theme that alternates with contrasting thematic passages. The different variants of this form, such as the five-part rondo and seven-part rondo, differ with respect to the number of refrain returns and contrasting passages. The **sonata-rondo** combines its characteristic use of refrain returns with the developmental characteristics and tonal conflict of the sonata.

Variations

To read more about forms, please see Chapter 20 on our website at **www.mhhe.com/kostka7e.**

Chapter Twenty-One
Mode Mixture
and the Neapolitan

Introduction

In this chapter we introduce a number of chords that are used to provide color to a musical passage. Most of them do this by injecting elements of the minor mode into a passage in major, and they do this through the use of ♭$\hat{6}$, ♭$\hat{3}$, and even ♭$\hat{7}$. This process is called **mode mixture,** and the resulting chords are called **borrowed chords.** Mode mixture occurs in the minor mode, too, but to a much lesser extent. We also discuss the **Neapolitan chord,** a major triad used chiefly in the minor mode and which uses ♭$\hat{2}$ as its root.

Borrowed Chords in Minor

Some writers feel that the use of raised $\hat{6}$ and $\hat{7}$ in minor is an example of mode mixture. According to that view, every V, for example, is borrowed from major, which makes mode mixture in minor a very common occurrence. Our approach is that scale degrees $\hat{6}$ and $\hat{7}$ each have two versions (review pp. 55–57), which means that the raised $\hat{3}$ is the only scale degree that can be borrowed in a minor key.

As it happens, there is a chord frequently borrowed from major that contains the raised $\hat{3}$, and that chord is the major tonic triad itself. The raised $\hat{3}$ in the tonic triad is called the **Picardy third,** and it was used to end most compositions in minor from the early 1500s until around 1750. A typical use of the Picardy third is seen in Example 21-1. Notice that the uppercase roman numeral I is enough to indicate the mode mixture. It is not necessary to add any explanatory note in the analysis. The voice leading in this example is worth examining, especially the descending tenor line and the alto part, which actually contains two lines. The textural reduction shows a simplification of the texture.

Example 21-1   Bach, *Helft mir Gottes Güte preisen*

b: i   V   VI   i⁶   ii°⁶₅   V⁷   V⁷/iv   (iv⁶₄)   I

Textural reduction

The idea of the Picardy third is sometimes used on a very large scale. For example, Beethoven's Symphony no. 5 begins in c minor, but the main key of the last movement is C major.

Borrowed Chords in Major: The Use of ♭6̂

The most frequently encountered examples of mode mixture in the major mode involve chords that employ ♭6̂. The "♭6̂" here refers to the lowered sixth scale degree. The accidental to be used in the music might be a ♮, a ♭, or a ♭♭, depending on the key signature, but we will refer to the lowered sixth scale degree as ♭6̂ in any case. Borrowing ♭6̂ from the parallel minor creates four borrowed chords that are frequently used in major: vii°⁷, ii°, ii;ø⁷, and iv. Example 21-2 illustrates these in the key of A major. Notice that the roman numerals are identical to those used in minor.

Example 21-2

A: vii°⁷   ii°   ii;ø⁷   iv

The vii°⁷ is actually a more useful chord than the viiᵒ⁷ because parallel 5ths are never a problem in approaching or resolving it. The vii°⁷ chord is one of the primary motivic elements in Example 21-3, where it is accented each time it occurs. Although the ♭$\hat{6}$, F♭, is in an inner voice, it forms the beginning of an important line begun in the first phrase and completed in the second: F♭–E♭–D♭ | F♭–E♭–D♭–C. Notice also the nice effect created by the unusual V–ii–V in m. 15.

Example 21-3   Chopin, Mazurka op. 17, no. 3

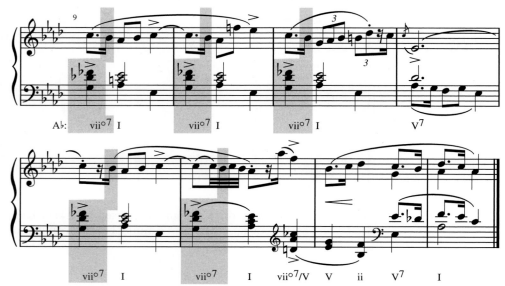

Incidentally, you will recall that either viiᵒ⁷/ or vii°⁷/ may be used to tonicize a major triad (review p. 262). We can now understand that the use of vii°⁷ to tonicize a major triad is an example of mode mixture. The vii°⁷/V in Example 21-3 illustrates this, the C♭ being the ♭$\hat{6}$ "borrowed" from E♭ minor.

Frequently, the vii°⁷ does not resolve directly to I but is followed instead by V⁷. Only one voice needs to move to accomplish this, as Example 21-4 illustrates.

Example 21-4

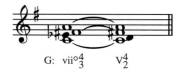

The borrowed iv is frequently used in first inversion as part of a stepwise descending bass line, as in Example 21-5. The imitation between soprano and tenor in mm. 4 to 5 and the soaring tenor line in mm. 5 to 6 are among the many points to appreciate in this beautiful phrase.

Example 21-5   Bach, *Herzliebster Jesu, was hast du*

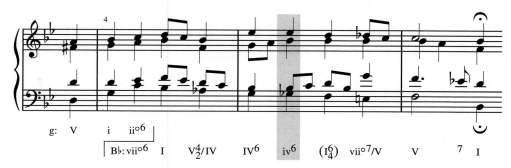

g: V   i   ii°6

B♭: vii°6   I   V$\frac{4}{2}$/IV   IV6   iv6   (I$^6_4$)   vii°7/V   V   7   I

The borrowed ii°7 is probably used more often than the borrowed ii° because of the added direction provided by the 7th. Example 21-6 is typical.

Example 21-6   Clara Schumann, Piano Trio op. 17, IV

D: I   ii$^{ø4}_2$ V$^6_5$ I   ii$^{ø4}_2$ V$^6_5$

In general, $\flat\hat{6}$ in vii°⁷, iv, or ii°⁽ø⁷⁾ moves down by half step to $\hat{5}$. It is often also approached by step, either from $\natural\hat{6}$ or from $\hat{5}$.

Other Borrowed Chords in Major

The most frequently encountered examples of mode mixture in major are those chords that "borrow" only $\flat\hat{6}$: ii°, ii°⁷, iv, and vii°⁷. The next most common examples of mode mixture make use of $\flat\hat{3}$: i, $\flat$VI, and iv⁷. Least common are those that use $\flat\hat{7}$: $\flat$III and $\flat$VII. All of these chords are shown in Example 21-7. Notice that the symbols for the borrowed submediant and mediant triads are preceded by a flat to show that the root is lowered. Use the flat in your analysis regardless of the actual accidental found in the notation, which might be a natural, a flat, or a double flat, depending on the key.

Example 21-7

If you have seen the film *2001: A Space Odyssey* (1968), you are already familiar with a famous instance of a minor tonic from the film's score, which makes use of Richard Strauss's

Also sprach Zarathustra (1896). In that work, the major tonic struggles dramatically to prevail over its minor version, with which it alternates. However, although vii°⁷, iv, and ii°⁽ø⁷⁾ are often found alone in major-mode passages, the minor tonic triad occurs more often in longer passages in the parallel minor. In Example 21-8 the minor mode takes over in m. 31, and major is not reestablished until the arrival of the D♮ in m. 36. Notice that because B♭ is the tonal center throughout, this is *not* a modulation. This example also illustrates the ♭VI, preceded here by its secondary dominant. The ♭VI is sometimes used with dramatic effect in deceptive cadences: V–♭VI. The V$^{+6}_{5}$/IV in Example 21-8 is an augmented dominant, which is discussed in Chapter 24.

DISC 2 : TRACK 12

Example 21-8   Haydn, String Quartet op. 9, no. 2, I

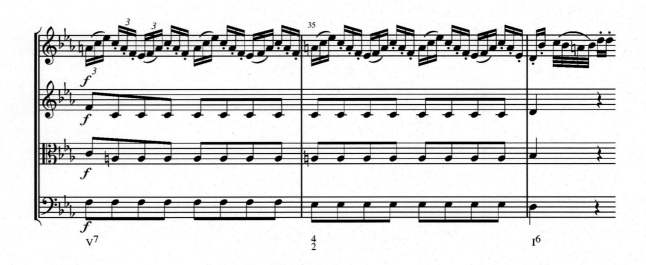

The ♭VII and ♭III chords are by no means commonly encountered. The ♭VII, when it occurs, frequently functions as a V/♭III, just as the same chord does in the minor mode. In Example 21-9 the ♭III is preceded by its secondary dominant and followed by a borrowed vii°^{7}. The sonorities in mm. 26 to 27 with C and C♯ in the bass are passing chords that connect the V^7 to the V$^6_5$ (see the textual reduction). These chords do not require roman numerals.

DISC 2 : TRACK 12

Example 21-9 Schumann, *Ein Jüngling liebt ein Mädchen,*
op. 48, no. 11

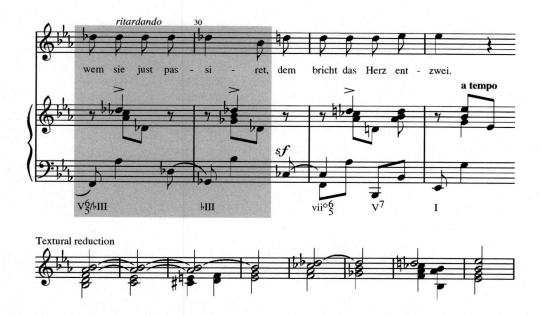

Textural reduction

CHECKPOINT

1. What is the name for the raised $\hat{3}$ in the tonic triad in the minor mode?

2. Show the chord symbols for the borrowed chords in major discussed in this chapter.

3. How does $\flat\hat{6}$ most often proceed: up by step, down by step, or down by leap?

4. Which borrowed chords are minor triads?

The Neapolitan Chord

Although the I–V–I progression is the basic organizing force in tonal harmony, much of the foreground harmonic interest in a tonal passage may be provided by the ways in which the dominant is approached. One of the more colorful chords that can be used to precede the dominant is the Neapolitan.

The **Neapolitan chord** derives its name from an important group of eighteenth-century opera composers who were associated with the city of Naples. Although the composers of the "Neapolitan school" frequently used this chord in their music, they did not originate it but inherited it from earlier composers. Nevertheless, the term *Neapolitan* has survived, and we will make use of it and its abbreviation, N (the symbol ♭II is an acceptable alternative). Simply stated, the Neapolitan triad is a *major triad* constructed on the *lowered second scale degree*. One accidental is required to spell the Neapolitan in a minor key and two in a major key, as is illustrated in Example 21-10.

Example 21-10

d: N   D: N

The Neapolitan is usually found in the minor mode and in first inversion. In fact, the first inversion is so typical that the Neapolitan triad is often referred to as the **Neapolitan sixth chord.** It has a pre-dominant function, much like a diatonic ii^6 (or ii°^{6}) chord, going eventually to V, but its aural effect is strikingly different. Example 21-11 illustrates several contexts in which the N^6 is commonly found. At the piano, establish the key of e minor and play through the example to become familiar with the distinctive sound of the N^6.

Example 21-11

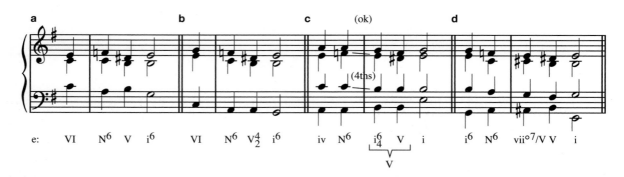

Example 21-11 illustrates several characteristics of the N^6.

1. When a tone is doubled, it is usually the 3rd of the N^6.

2. The N^6 moves to V (or i$_4^6$–V), but vii°^{7}/V may appear between the N^6 and the V. The N^6 would usually not be followed by iv or ii°.

3. The ♭$\hat{2}$ (the root of the N^6) moves down, especially when it appears in the melody. Its goal is the leading tone, which lies at the unusual interval of a °3 below ♭$\hat{2}$ (see the

soprano line in Ex. 21-11a and b). However, the °3 is filled in by the tonic pitch when the N⁶ moves first to i$^6_4$ or vii°⁷/V (Ex. 21-11c and d).

4. When the N⁶ moves to i$^6_4$, as in Example 21-11c, parallel 4ths should be used to avoid parallel 5ths. Parallel 5ths would be created in Example 21-11c by transposing the alto line an octave lower.

5. The N⁶, like the unaltered ii°⁶, is usually preceded by VI, iv, or i.

Example 21-12 illustrates the N⁶ in a three-part texture. Notice the leap in the tenor voice from A3 to E4 to provide the 3rd for the i$^6_4$ chord. The textural reduction brings out the stepwise ascent in the bass from Î up to 5̂.

Example 21-12   Haydn, Piano Sonata no. 36, I

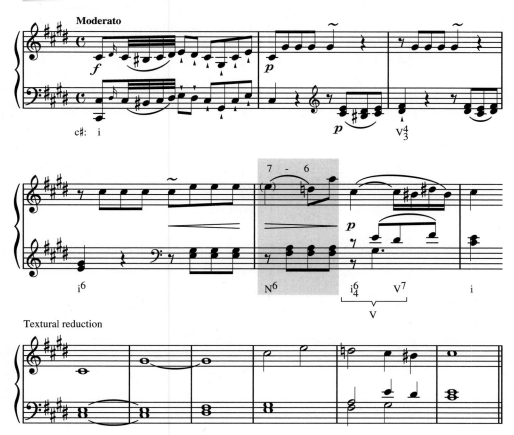

In Example 21-13 the Neapolitan appears in a more complicated keyboard texture. (The clarinet is in B♭, sounding a M2 lower than written.) The ♭2̂ in m. 8 appears in both hands; the G♭ in the right hand moves down to E♮, as expected, but the G♭ in the left hand moves up chromatically to G. Notice how the melodic G♭ in m. 4 foreshadoes the N⁶ to come. Also noteworthy is the unusual root-position minor dominant triad in m. 11, resulting from the descending melodic minor scale.

Example 21-13   Brahms, Clarinet Sonata op. 120, no. 1, I

The N⁶ chord occurs occasionally in popular music as well. Example 21-14, a theme from a film score, ends with a circle-of-fifths progression: iv(7)–VII⁷–III⁽ᴹ⁷⁾–VI–N⁶–V⁷–i. The Neapolitan is indicated by the "F/A" symbol, which specifies an F major triad with A in the bass.

Example 21-14   Rota, "Godfather II"

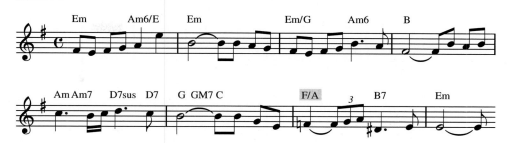

The Neapolitan is usually employed in first inversion in the minor mode. However, several other contexts for the Neapolitan might be encountered.

1. The Neapolitan may appear in root position (N) or, rarely, in second inversion (N_4^6). In both cases, the bass will probably be doubled in a four-part texture.

2. The Neapolitan may occur in the major mode.

3. The Neapolitan may be tonicized. This can take the form of a single chord (such as V^7/N), or it might be a genuine modulation to the key of the Neapolitan. In some cases VI (or ♭VI) may function as V/N.

The following examples illustrate these uses of the Neapolitan.

Both a V^7/N and a root position Neapolitan occur in Example 21-15. Notice the tritone leap in the bass between the N and V chords. The textural reduction clarifies the sequence in mm. 13-16.

Example 21-15   Chopin, Mazurka op. 7, no. 2

In Example 21-16 Verdi uses the N in a major key (and in root position). However, he does prepare for the N by using mode mixture in the previous two measures. (Only the main chords are analyzed in the first five measures.)

DISC 2 : TRACK 15

Example 21-16   Verdi, Il *Trovatore,* act I, no. 5

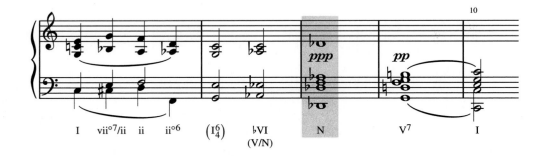

An earlier excerpt from popular music, Example 7-6 (p. 98), also used a root position N, this time in a long circle-of-fifths progression: iv–VII–III–VI–N–V–i. (Compare that progression to the one in Example 21-14, discussed earlier.)

CHECKPOINT

1. Name four chords that commonly follow a N^6 chord.
2. What is usually doubled in a N^6 chord?
3. Does the $\flat\hat{2}$ in a N^6 tend to move up or down?
4. Name several less common uses of the Neapolitan chord.

Modulations Involving Mode Mixture and the Neapolitan

Borrowed chords and the Neapolitan may be used as common chords in modulation, a procedure that may facilitate a modulation to a foreign key. If a passage in major slips into the parallel minor, all the keys that are closely related to the parallel minor come within easy reach. For example, as the chart below demonstrates, mixture in the key of F gives us access to five foreign keys: A♭, c, E♭, b♭, and D♭.

a — C
d — F → mixture → f — A♭
g — B♭   c — E♭
                 b♭ — D♭

Schubert uses mode mixture in Example 21-17 to move to the relative major of the parallel minor: F → (f) → A♭.

DISC 2 : TRACK 15

Example 21-17   Schubert, *Originaltanze*, op. 9, no. 33

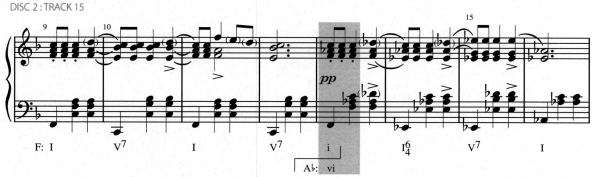

A Neapolitan chord is used as the common chord in Example 21-18. The excerpt begins in A and ends in a♭ (although neither key signature agrees with that analysis). The I⁶ chord in A before the double bar is enharmonically the same as a B♭♭ major triad, which is the Neapolitan in a♭. It then moves normally to i⁶₄–V in a♭.

Example 21-18   Schubert, Moment Musical, op. 94, no. 6

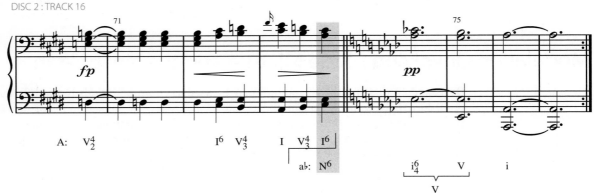

Mode mixture in the new key is often employed as a signal to the listener that a modulation is taking place. In Example 21-19 a modulation from f to E♭ occurs. In m. 5 Beethoven uses an f minor chord, which is the common chord linking the two keys. The $f^{ø7}$ chord that follows announces the modulation to the listener because this chord is a very unlikely one in the key of f. (The Ger⁺⁶ chord in m. 3 is discussed in Chapter 22.)

Example 21-19   Beethoven, Horn Sonata, op. 17, II

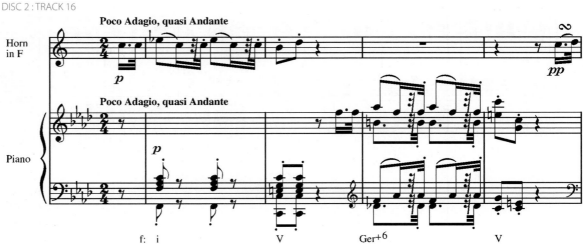

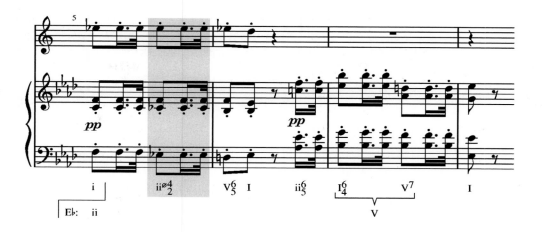

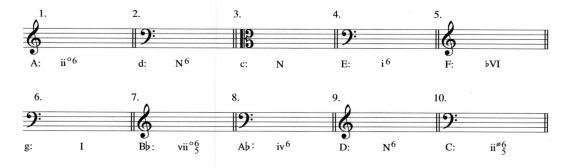

Self-Test 21-1

(Answers begin on page 622.)

A. Notate the following chords in the specified inversions. Include key signatures.

1.	2.	3.	4.	5.
A: ii°⁶	d: N⁶	c: N	E: i⁶	F: ♭VI

6.	7.	8.	9.	10.
g: I	B♭: vii°⁶₅	A♭: iv⁶	D: N⁶	C: ii°⁶₅

B. Label the chords with lead-sheet symbols (including slash notation) and roman numerals (including bass-position symbols).

f♯: _____   A: _____   A♭: _____   B♭: _____   D: _____

C. Analysis.

　　1. This is the end of a Cole Porter song that begins in C minor and ends in C major. These final eight measures are the C major portion, although the composer provides several reminders of the minor mode. Label the chords with roman numerals and circle any melody notes that recall C minor.

　　Porter, "My Heart Belongs to Daddy"

DISC 2 : TRACK 17

　　2. a. Label the chords.
　　　　b. Identify any six-four chords by type.
　　　　c. Name the form of the excerpt.

　　Mozart, Piano Trio K. 542, III

DISC 2 : TRACK 18

3. Label the chords, circling the roman numerals of any borrowed chords. Discuss any diminished seventh chords that occur in terms of the resolution of their tritones. Review p. 223.

Schubert, Symphony in B♭, I

DISC 2 : TRACK 19

4. This excerpt from a well-known Mozart sonata begins in a minor and ends in F, with the first chord in m. 41 serving as the common chord. Label all the chords.

Mozart, Piano Sonata K. 545, I

5. Label the chords, circling the roman numerals of any borrowed chords. Which part is doubling the violas in mm. 47 to 51? The horn in D sounds a m7 lower than written.

Haydn, Symphony no. 73, I

A:

6. The piece from which this example is drawn was originally intended to be the slow movement of Beethoven's famous "Waldstein Sonata," op. 53. Instead, it is known popularly today as the "Andante favori." (a) Analyze in the key of F throughout. NCTs in the melody have been put in parentheses. (b) How would you categorize the last NCT? (c) Where is there a pedal point?

Beethoven, Andante WoO 57.*

7. In this remarkable excerpt, Beethoven manages to modulate from a♭ minor to D major, a tritone away. Explain how he accomplishes this. (It is not necessary to label every chord in the excerpt.)

Beethoven, Piano Sonata op. 26, III

* WoO stands for "without opus," meaning a work to which Beethoven did not assign an opus number.

D. For each exercise provide the key signature and notate the missing chords, using correct voice-leading procedures

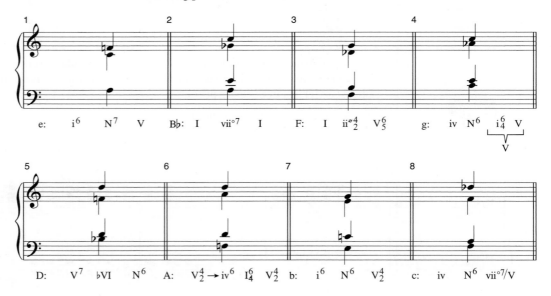

E. Analyze the chords implied by the soprano-bass frameworks, and supply alto and tenor parts.

1. Include a Neapolitan chord.

2. Include a ii^{ø6}₅.

F. Analyze the chords specified by this figured bass, then make an arrangement for SATB chorus.

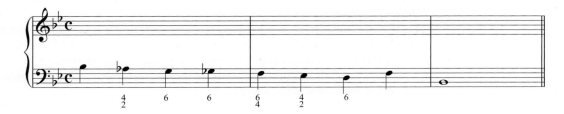

G. Make a setting of the following progression in d minor for three-part chorus. Then make another setting in b minor for four-part chorus. Arrange the rhythm and meter so that the final chord comes on a strong beat.

i   V^6 V$^4_2$/iv   iv^6 V   V$^4_2$/N   N^6 V$^4_2$ i^6 vii^{o6} i   V

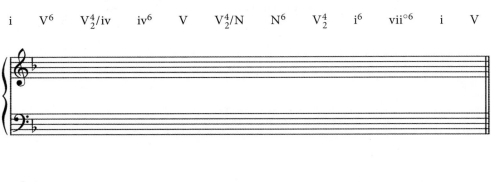

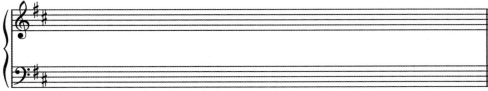

Exercise 21-1 See Workbook.

Summary

The term **mode mixture** refers to the use of tones from one mode in a passage that is predominantly in the other mode. The only case in which a chord is "borrowed" from the major mode for use in minor is the **Picardy third,** a major tonic triad that was used to end most minor mode compositions in the early tonal era.

Borrowing from minor into the parallel major, on the other hand, is more common and involves a large number of chords. Several of these come about through the use of $\flat\hat{6}$. These include vii°7, ii°, ii⌀7, and iv. Other borrowed chords require the use of $\flat\hat{3}$ and even $\flat\hat{7}$. These chords include the i, $\flat$VI, iv7, $\flat$III, and $\flat$VII chords, and of these the i and the $\flat$VI are the most commonly encountered.

The Neapolitan chord (symbolized as N) is a major triad constructed on the lowered second scale degree. The Neapolitan chord occurs most often in the minor mode and typically appears in first inversion, so it is often called the Neapolitan sixth chord. Like the diatonic supertonic triad, the N6 progresses to V, sometimes passing through i$^6_4$ or vii°7/V, or both, on the way. In four parts, the 3rd of the N6 is doubled and—in the resolution of the N6—the $\flat\hat{2}$ moves down to the nearest chord tone. Although the Neapolitan chord is characteristically found in the minor mode and in first inversion, it also occurs in the major mode and in other bass positions.

Borrowed chords and the Neapolitan can serve as the common chord in modulations, often facilitating the movement to a foreign key.

Variations

For additional review and practice, please see Chapter 21 on our website at **www.mhhe.com/kostka7e.**

Chapter Twenty-Two
Augmented Sixth Chords

The Interval of the Augmented Sixth

One way to emphasize a tone is to approach it by a half step, either from above or from below. In Examples 22-1a and b the dominant in g minor is approached by half steps. Approaching the dominant by half steps from above *and* below at the same time makes for an even stronger approach to the dominant, which is illustrated in Example 22-1c. You will notice that the two approaching tones form a vertical interval of an **augmented 6th.** This method of approaching the dominant distinguishes a whole category of pre-dominant chords called **augmented sixth chords.**

The characteristic elements of most augmented sixth chords are those illustrated in Example 22-1c.

1. The chord being approached is the V chord.
2. The minor-mode $\hat{6}$ (chromatically lowered if in a major key) appears in the bass.
3. The $\sharp\hat{4}$ is in an upper part.

The interval of an $^+6$ formed by these pitches is enharmonically equivalent to a m7, but the difference between the effect of the $^+6$ and that of the m7 is easily detected by the ear. The m7 tends to resolve as in Example 22-2a, the $^+6$ as in Example 22-2b. Play both parts of Example 22-2 and notice the contrast in the effect of these two intervals.

Example 22-2

In a two-part texture the augmented sixth chord appears as in Examples 22-1c and 22-2b. The analytical symbol to be used is simply $^+6$. Notice that the numeral is an arabic $^+6$ and not a roman $+VI$.

The interval of the $^+6$ usually resolves outward by half step, following the tendencies of the tones to lead to the dominant. Less commonly, the top pitch of the $^+6$ may descend chromatically to produce the 7th of a V^7. This generally occurs only in $^+6$ chords that have three or more pitch classes (discussed below), with the top pitch of the $^+6$ interval in an inner part.

For the reasons mentioned above, the $^+6$ chord is among the strongest of all predominant chords, and it generally moves directly to V (or i_4^6–V). It is frequently used just after a modulation to make it clear to the listener that a modulation has, in fact, occurred. Like the N^6, the $^+6$ originated in the minor mode, but it was soon found to be equally useful in major keys. When used in major keys, it is often preceded by mode mixture.

The Italian Augmented Sixth Chord

In most cases $^+6$ chords contain more than two pitch classes. When a third pitch class is included, it is usually the tonic pitch, which lies a M3 above the bass note. This combination of tones is referred to as an **Italian augmented sixth chord** (It^{+6}), which is illustrated in Example 22-3. This geographical term, like the others we will be using, has no historical authenticity—it is simply a convenient and traditional label.

Example 22-3

The It^{+6}, like any other $^+6$ chord, resolves to V or I_4^6–V. In a four-part texture the tonic pitch is doubled. Typical resolutions are shown in Example 22-4.

Example 22-4

Example 22-5 includes an illustration of the It^{+6} in a three-part texture. Most of the excerpt consists of parallel 6ths (soprano and bass) surrounding a tonic pedal (alto). Notice that the bass reaches $\hat{5}$ four times, with different harmony in each case.

DISC 2 : TRACK 21

Example 22-5   Mozart, *The Magic Flute*, K. 620, Overture
(piano reduction)

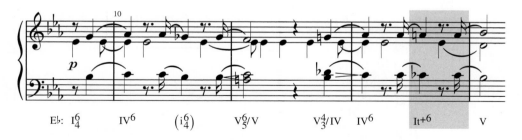

The French Augmented Sixth Chord

There are two common $^{+6}$ chords that contain four pitch classes, and both of them may be thought of as It^{+6} chords with one pitch added. If the added tone is $\hat{2}$, the sonority is referred to as a **French augmented sixth chord** (Fr^{+6}), which is shown in Example 22-6. Be sure to label a French $^{+6}$ chord as Fr^{+6} and not F^6, which is a lead-sheet symbol.

Example 22-6

The Fr^{+6} works best in four-part or free textures. Typical resolutions are illustrated in Example 22-7.

Example 22-7

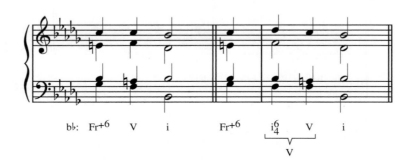

$\flat\flat$:   Fr^{+6} V   i   Fr^{+6} i$^6_4$ V   i

              V

In Example 22-8 a three-part sequence tonicizing i, VI, and iv leads to a half cadence that is preceded by a Fr^{+6}. The smooth voice leading into and out of the Fr^{+6} is typical. Notice also the different functions of the two i$^6_4$ chords, the first passing between a iv and a ii$^{\varnothing4}_3$ the second delaying the V chord.

Example 22-8   Schumann, *Albumblätter*, op. 124, no. 12, Burla

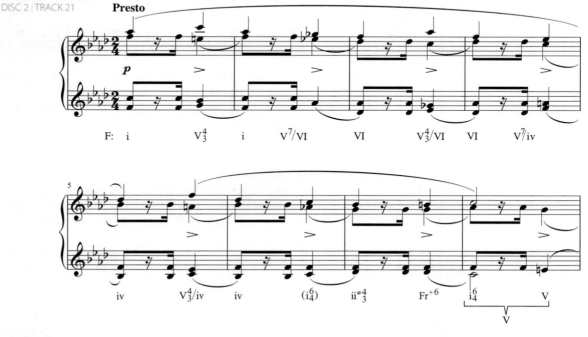

Presto

F: i   V$^4_3$ i   V^7/VI   VI   V$^4_3$/VI   VI   V^7/iv

iv   V$^4_3$/iv   iv   (i$^6_4$)   ii$^{\varnothing4}_3$ Fr^{+6} i$^6_4$ V

                   V

The Fr^{+6} occurs occasionally in popular music and jazz as well. The symbol used calls for a Mm7 chord with a lowered 5th. For instance, the Fr^{+6} in Example 22-8 above would appear as a G7($\flat$5). In the key of d, a Fr^{+6} would be symbolized as B$\flat$7($\flat$5), as in Example 22-9.

Example 22-9   Miller, "Bernie's Tune"

The German Augmented Sixth Chord

The other common $^+6$ chord that contains four pitch classes is the **German augmented sixth chord** (Ger^{+6}, not G6). It may be thought of as an It^{+6} with the addition of a minor-mode $\hat{3}$ (chromatically lowered if in a major key). The Ger^{+6} is shown in Example 22-10.

Example 22-10

As with any $^+6$ chord, the usual resolutions of the Ger^{+6} are to V and to i$^6_4$–V. When the Ger^{+6} moves directly to V, parallel 5ths are apt to result, as in Example 22-11. Because the ear is distracted by the resolution of the interval of the $^+6$, the parallels are not so objectionable here, and they may occasionally be encountered.

Example 22-11   Mozart, String Quartet K. 173, II

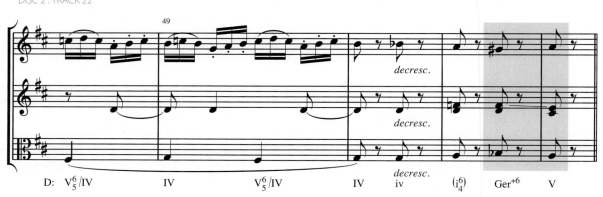

However, composers usually manage either to hide the parallels through anticipations or suspensions or to avoid them through the use of leaps or arpeggiations. In Example 22-12 Mozart first avoids the 5ths by leaping the E♭4 to B3 (a °4) and then, in the second Ger^{+6}, by arpeggiating the B♭3 to G3 before the resolution, turning the Ger^{+6} into an It^{+6}. (Notice that Examples 22-11 and 22-12 are both drawn from the same work.)

Example 22-12   Mozart, String Quartet K. 173, I

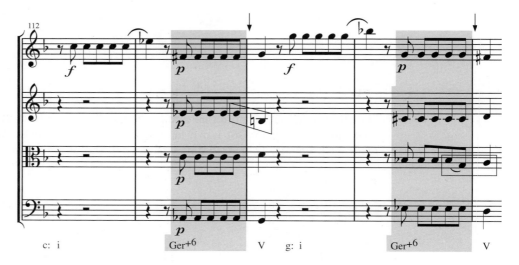

A simpler resolution to the problem of the parallels is to delay the V through the use of a cadential six-four, as in Example 22-13.

Example 22-13

You might have noticed that the last Ger^{+6} in Example 22-13 is spelled differently from the others, although it sounds the same (A♯ = B♭). This is a fairly common enharmonic spelling of the Ger^{+6}, used in the major mode only, when the Ger^{+6} is going to I$^6_4$. The reason for its use is more for the eye than for the ear: A♯ to B♮ looks more reasonable than B♭ to B♮ because we usually expect raised notes to ascend and lowered ones to descend. Notice that this involves ♭3̂ vs. ♯2̂, just as in the enharmonically spelled vii°^{7}/V in major (see Example 17-10 on p. 275).

Enharmonic spellings are also involved when we compare the Ger^{+6} with the V^7/N. The listener can tell the Ger^{+6} from a dominant seventh chord only by its resolution, a feature that can lead to some interesting modulations (to be discussed in Chapter 23). For example, the Ger^{+6} in m. 33 of Example 22-14 sounds like a V^7/N (a D♭^{7}), especially because it is preceded by a N^6. The resolution to V^7 is needed before its function is clear to us. Notice also that the ♯$\hat{4}$ (B♮3) moves down chromatically to ♮$\hat{4}$ (B♭3) to provide the 7th of the V^7 chord.

Example 22-14   Beethoven, String Quartet op. 18, no. 1, II

DISC 2 : TRACK 23

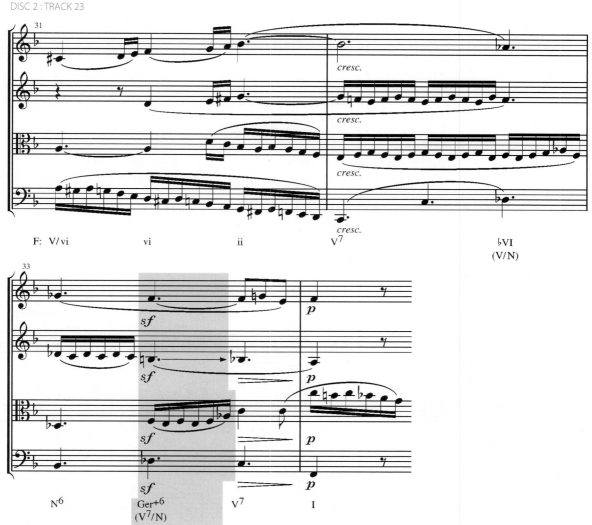

Ger^{+6} chords are encountered frequently in lead-sheet symbols, where they are indicated as a Mm7 chord on the minor sixth scale degree, as in C: A♭7–G7, which represents C: Ger^{+6}–V^7. Jazz theory explains the A♭7 as a tritone substitution; that is, the A♭7 is a substitute for a D7 (V7/V) chord. Their roots are a tritone apart, *and* the two chords share a tritone: C–G♭ in the A♭7 and C–F♯ in the D7.

CHECKPOINT

1. The $^+6$ in an augmented sixth chord results from a combination of what two scale degrees?

2. To create an It^{+6} chord, what scale degree do you add to the $^+6$?

3. What scale degree do you add to an It^{+6} chord to form a Fr^{+6} chord?

4. What scale degree do you add to an It^{+6} chord to form a Ger^{+6} chord?

Other Uses of Conventional Augmented Sixth Chords

The conventional $^+6$ chord, as described in this chapter, usually functions as the final element of a series of chords leading to a dominant or cadential six-four chord. However, a number of other contexts might be encountered, even with what would be considered conventional $^+6$ chords. A few examples will give you an idea.

The $^+6$ may be used as a neighbor chord, as in V–$^+6$–V, which is in some ways a weaker function than its use as a pre-dominant chord. An instance of this was seen in Example 21-19 on p. 360.

Less commonly, another chord, usually some form of V/V or vii°/V, comes between the $^+6$ and V chords, as in Example 22-15, where vii°7 substitutes for V.

DISC 2 : TRACK 24

Example 22-15   Mozart, Rondo K. 494

Measures 110 to 112 of Example 22-15 contain an interesting variant on the circle-of-fifths patterns that were discussed in Chapter 15 (review pp. 238–239). Example 22-16a shows a much simpler model, whereas Example 22-16b elaborates that model slightly. Finally, compare Example 22-16b with mm. 110 to 112 in Example 22-15.

Example 22-16

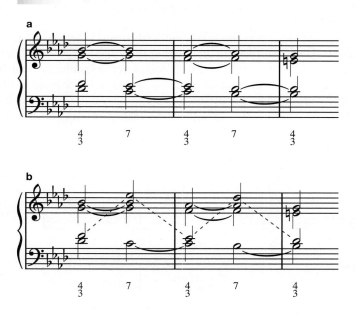

In Example 22-17 the Ger^{+6} resolves normally to a I$^6_4$ chord, but it turns out to be a passing six-four instead of the expected cadential six-four. Notice also the contrary motion in mm. 11 to 12 between the melody and the bass.

DISC 2 : TRACK 24

Example 22-17   Fanny Mendelssohn Hensel, *Auf der Wanderung*

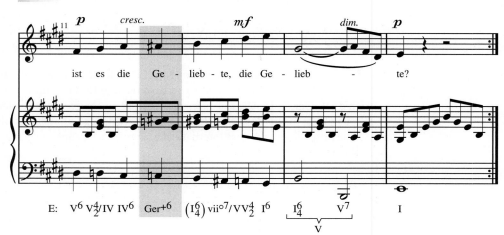

Other Bass Positions

We have not yet discussed what pitch serves as the root of an augmented sixth chord. The reason for this is that the augmented sixth chord is a linear sonority that has *no root.* One can arrange the notes of a Fr^{+6} to resemble an altered V^7/V, and the It^{+6} and Ger^{+6} sonorities can be likened to altered iv^7 chords. Indeed, some theorists prefer to use modified roman numerals as a convenient way to represent augmented sixth chords. Still, these chords are rootless; they have only a most common bass position, that position having the (♭)$\hat{6}$ in the bass.

Although the minor mode $\hat{6}$ usually constitutes the bass of an $^{+6}$ chord, other bass positions do occur, especially in music of the Romantic period. Generally, the voice leading will be identical or similar to that found in the standard resolutions discussed earlier in this chapter, but the interval of the $^{+6}$ will often be inverted to become a $°3$. The most common of the various possibilities is that with $\sharp\hat{4}$ in the bass, as in Example 22-18. Notice also the enharmonic spelling of the Ger^{+6}, substituting C♯ for D♭.

Example 22-18   Brahms, *Ruf zur Maria,* op. 22, no. 5

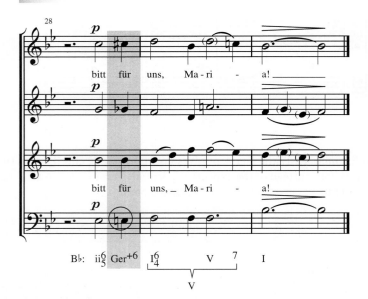

A progression very similar to the one in Example 22-18 is seen in an excerpt from a jazz tune in Example 11-15 (p. 182). If you turn back to that example, you will see that it ends with a IV–Ger^{+6}–I$^6_4$–V^7–I progression with $\sharp\hat{4}$ in the bass of the Ger^{+6} chord. The lead-sheet symbol in this case is E♭7/D♭, the D♭ functioning enharmonically as a C♯.

The only other bass position that occurs with any frequency is that with the tonic pitch in the bass, as in Example 22-19.

Example 22-19   Brahms, Symphony no. 1, op. 68, II (piano reduction)

Because $^+6$ chords have no root and therefore technically cannot be inverted, it is not necessary to show the bass position of the chord in the analytical symbol. Just use It^{+6}, or whatever is appropriate, regardless of the bass position.

Resolutions to Other Scale Degrees

The crucial interval in any augmented sixth chord is, of course, the interval of the $^+6$ itself. Because that interval usually embellishes $\hat{5}$, we could have used symbols like Ger$^{+6}/\hat{5}$, but it is understood that "$/\hat{5}$" is implied when we write "Ger^{+6}." However, especially in the Romantic period, the $^+6$ is sometimes applied to scale degrees other than $\hat{5}$, and in those cases we make this clear by using the method shown in Example 22-20.

Example 22-20

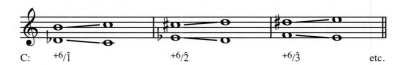

To spell or recognize the various $^+6$ types in these contexts, you will have to be familiar with the intervallic structure of the three kinds of augmented sixth chord. In Example 22-21, $^+6$ chords embellishing $\hat{1}$ are formed by transposing the intervals from the more familiar $^+6/\hat{5}$ spellings.

Example 22-21

The Ger^{+6}/$\hat{1}$–I cadence in Example 22-22 comes at the very end of a song, following a more conventional V$^4_3$–I cadence a few measures earlier.

DISC 2 : TRACK 26

Example 22-22   Chausson, *Sérénade italienne*, op. 2, no. 5

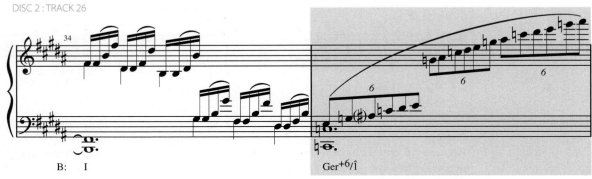

Often when an augmented sixth chord resolves to something other than V, the chord that it resolves to is a secondary dominant. In that case, it is probably better to show the analysis in relationship to the chord being tonicized. For example, the chord in m. 44 of Example 22-23 could be analyzed as an It^{+6}/$\hat{6}$, but it is better understood as part of a tonicization of F minor (ii).

DISC 2 : TRACK 26

Example 22-23   Mozart, Piano Sonata K. 457, I

Self-Test 22-1

(Answers begin on page 625.)

A. Label each chord, using inversion symbols where appropriate.

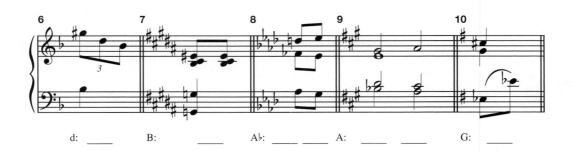

B. Notate each chord in close position. Augmented sixth chords should be in their customary bass position ($\flat$6 in the bass). Include key signatures.

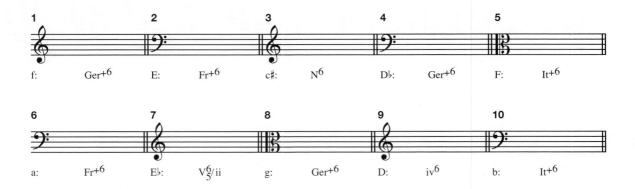

C.

1. Provide roman numerals along with bass-position symbols where appropriate. Place them above the lead-sheet symbols.

Evans and Mann, "No Moon at All"

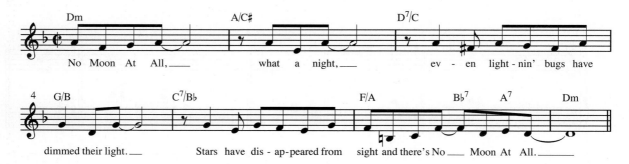

No Moon At All,____ what a night,____ ev - en light - nin' bugs have

dimmed their light. ___ Stars have dis - ap-peared from sight and there's No ___ Moon At All._____

2. In this and in each of the following excerpts, label the chords and discuss the details of the resolution of each $^{+}6$ chord. Do $\sharp 4$ and $\flat 6$ follow their expected resolutions to $\hat{5}$? How are parallel fifths avoided in the Ger^{+6} resolution(s)?

Clara Wieck Schumann, Polonaise op. 6, no. 6

3. This excerpt modulates.

Haydn, String Quartet op. 64, no. 2, III

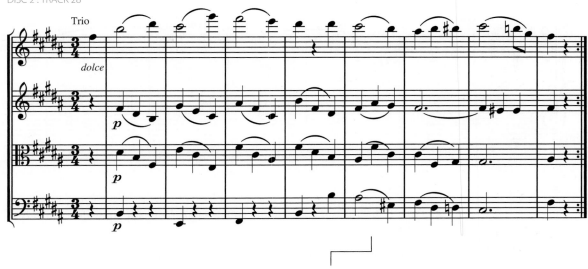

4. This is the ending of one of Schumann's better-known songs. What national anthem is hinted at in the vocal part? Notice also the contrast between the diatonic setting of the text and the more chromatic codetta that ends the song. Label chords and NCTs.

Schumann, "Die beiden Grenadiere," op. 49, no. 1

Schwer-ter __ klir - ren und bli - tzen; dann steig' ich ge-waff - net her - vor ans dem Grab, den

G:

Kai - ser, den Kai - ser zu schü - tzen!"

DISC 2 : TRACK 29

5. Find in this excerpt two chords that are enharmonically equivalent but very different in function.

Reinecke, Flute Concerto op. 283, I

6. Label all chords and find an example of a chromatic passing tone.

   Haydn, String Quartet op. 20, no. 5, I

7. Label the chords in this short excerpt.

   Brahms, String Quartet op. 51, no. 2, III

e:

8. Label all the chords in this excerpt, which is not as straightforward as it looks because of the sparse texture. Try playing it slowly on the piano and supplying "missing" notes. See if you can find melodic intervals of a +2 and a °4. What is the form of this excerpt?

   Benda, Sonatina no. 23

Andante un poco allegretto

D. Supply the missing voices for each of the following fragments. All but exercise 5 are four-part textures.

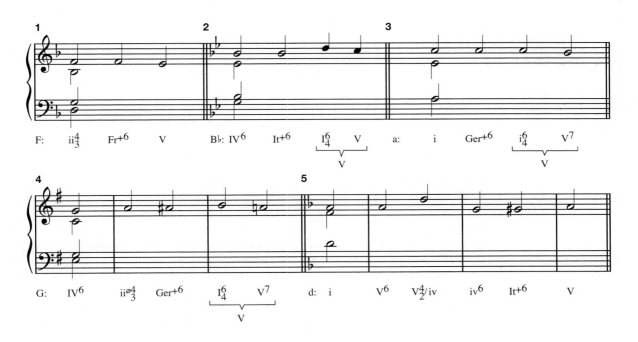

E. Analyze the harmonies implied by this soprano-bass framework and try to include a Fr^{+6} and an example of mode mixture in your harmonization. Then complete the piano texture by filling in two inner parts in the treble-clef staff, following good voice-leading procedures.

F. Analyze the chords specified by this figured bass, then make an arrangement for SATB chorus.

Exercise 22-1   See Workbook.

Summary

The class of chords known as augmented sixth chords get their name from the interval of an augmented 6th. The $^{+}6$ is typically formed between the minor sixth scale degree ($\flat\hat{6}$ if in major) in the bass voice and $\sharp\hat{4}$ in some upper voice. The interval of a $^{+}6$ expands to an octave on $\hat{5}$ harmonized by V or I$^{6}_{4}$–V.

In textures of three or more voices, the tonic scale degree usually appears along with $\flat\hat{6}$ and $\sharp\hat{4}$, and this combination of intervals is called an **Italian augmented sixth chord.** The other two conventional augmented sixth chords add a fourth tone to the Italian augmented sixth chord: the **French augmented sixth chord** adds a second scale degree, whereas the **German augmented sixth chord** adds $\hat{3}$ from the minor mode (in major either $\flat\hat{3}$ or $\sharp\hat{2}$.)

Augmented sixth chords typically progress to V, although the V chord may be delayed by a tonic $^{6}_{4}$ chord. The tonic $^{6}_{4}$ chord is especially useful in avoiding parallel 5ths in the resolution of the Ger$^{+}6$ chord, although the 5ths might also be avoided or hidden by other means.

Exceptional uses of conventional augmented sixth chords are occasionally encountered. A few of these are discussed on pp. 380–382.

Variations

For additional review and practice, please see Chapter 22 on our website at **www.mhhe.com/kostka7e.**

Chapter Twenty-Three
Enharmonic Spellings and Enharmonic Modulations

Enharmonic Spellings

Enharmonic spellings are used by composers for a variety of reasons. One reason is to indicate clearly the direction in which a pitch will move. For example, consider the vii°⁷/V in Example 23-1a. When the vii°⁷/V moves to the cadential I$^6_4$, there is nowhere for the A♭ to go but up to A♮. This motion looks a little more sensible when the A♭ is spelled as G♯, as it is in Example 23-1b, but the aural result with any fixed-pitch instrument is the same. This new spelling changes the chord visually from a b°⁷ to a g♯°⁷, but it does not change its sound or its function or the analysis. Of course, when the vii°⁷/V moves directly to V, as in Example 23-1c, the A♭ spelling poses no problem because the seventh resolves immediately downward to the G.

Example 23-1

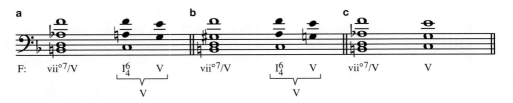

If you turn back to an earlier excerpt (Ex. 17-11 on p. 276), you will see on the last beat of m. 26 an illustration of the enharmonically spelled vii°⁷/V, voiced exactly as in Example 23-1b. Very similar to the enharmonically spelled vii°⁷/V is the enharmonically spelled Ger⁺⁶ chord (review Ex. 22-13 on p. 376). Notice that both involve the respelled ♭3̂/♯2̂ preceding a I$^6_4$ in the major mode.

Another reason for enharmonic spellings is the desire on the part of the composer to make things easier for the performer. This is presumably the case in Example 23-2, which tonicizes F♭, the ♭VI of A♭. In the ♭VI portion Mendelssohn notates the second violin and viola enharmonically in the key of E, presumably to make their tremolos easier to read.

Example 23-2   Mendelssohn, String Quartet op. 80, IV

Instead of enharmonically spelling only some of the parts, as Mendelssohn did in the preceding example, composers usually respell the key entirely. In Schubert's String Trio there is a modulation from B♭ to G♭ (♭VI), which then changes by mode mixture into g♭ minor. To avoid this awkward key (the key signature would contain nine flats!), Schubert quite reasonably notates it in f♯ minor. The harmonic skeleton of this passage is shown in Example 23-3.

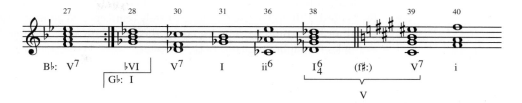

Example 23-3   Schubert, String Trio D. 581, I (textural reduction)

Examples of enharmonically spelled keys abound in nineteenth-century music. One of Schubert's impromptus contains a passage with the following tonal structure: E♭–e♭–c♭, the last being spelled as b minor. The e♭–c♭ portion of that passage is given in Example 23-4.

Example 23-4   Schubert, Impromptu op. 90, no. 2

DISC 2 : TRACK 31

Composers will often—but not always—change the key signature in situations such as this. Otherwise, they will use whatever accidentals are required. This is the case with the Self-Test 21-1, part C7 (pp. 367–368), where Beethoven used accidentals to notate passages in b minor and D major, even though the key signature contains seven flats. However it is notated, the enharmonically spelled key is an example of enharmonic spelling for convenience; the listener is entirely unaware of the enharmonic spelling, and no special analytical symbols are required. Enharmonic spelling for convenience is *not* the same as enharmonic modulation, which is a much more interesting topic and which is the subject of the rest of this chapter.

Enharmonic Reinterpretation

The enharmonic spelling discussed so far in this chapter is intended primarily for the eye, not the ear. However, four sonorities used in tonal music can be reinterpreted enharmonically *in a different key* (not in enharmonic keys, like G♭ and F♯), and the listener can hear this reinterpretation when these chords resolve.

One such sonority is the major-minor seventh, which can serve either as a V^7 or as a Ger^{+6} (Ex. 23-5a). Another is the diminished seventh chord, where any tone can serve as the leading tone (Ex. 23-5b). The other two possibilities are the augmented triad and the Fr^{+6} chord, although these chords are rarely reinterpreted enharmonically. Parallel major or minor keys could be substituted for the keys shown in Example 23-5 and in similar examples throughout the rest of this chapter.

Example 23-5

a

D♭: V^7 =   c: Ger^{+6}

b

a: vii$^{\circ 7}$ =   f♯:   vii$^{\circ 6}_5$ =   e♭:   vii$^{\circ 4}_3$ =   c: vii$^{\circ 4}_2$

The implications of all this are that when the listener hears a major-minor seventh or diminished seventh sonority, certain expectations will probably arise (such as, "This chord will resolve as a V^7 in D♭"), only to be pleasantly thwarted on occasion by an equally logical enharmonic reinterpretation (such as, in this case, a Ger^{+6} in c). This process, which is often reserved for especially dramatic spots in a composition, is known as **enharmonic modulation.**

CHECKPOINT

1. Contrast enharmonic spelling for convenience and enharmonic modulation.
2. Make up a key scheme starting with B♭ that might result in enharmonic spelling for the convenience of the performer.
3. What four sonorities can be reinterpreted enharmonically so that they occur in different keys?
4. Which two of these four sonorities are commonly used for enharmonic modulations in tonal music?

Enharmonic Modulations Using the Major-Minor Seventh Sonority

The term **enharmonic modulation** is used to refer to a modulation in which the common chord is reinterpreted enharmonically to fit into the second key. The actual spelling of the chord is not important—it might be spelled as it would appear in the first key, or in the second key, or even in both if it occurs more than once. What is important is that the common chord can be *heard* as a sensible chord in both keys.

The person listening to Example 23-6 probably expects the fourth chord to resolve as a V^7/IV in G, as it does in the top staff. However, the possibility exists that it may be enharmonically reinterpreted as a Ger^{+6} in B, as seen on the bottom staff. This reinterpretation results in an enharmonic modulation from G to B. Play Example 23-6 several times, comparing the effect of the two resolutions of the major-minor seventh sonority.

Example 23-6

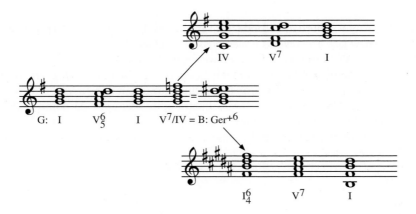

Now compare Example 23-6 with Example 23-7. The last chord in m. 41 of Example 23-7 sounds like a G^7 chord. Because the tonality at this point is G, the listener probably expects the next measure to begin with a C chord (IV in G). Instead, the G^7 is treated and spelled as a Ger^{+6} in B major. Notice that we have not analyzed the first chord in m. 41 as the common chord (G: I = B: ♭VI). This is because it is the cadential six-four chord in m. 42, not the $V^7/IV = Ger^{+6}$, that tells us that a modulation is taking place. Remember to always look for the common chord by backing up one chord from the chord that signals the modulation.

Example 23-7   Schubert, "Der Neugierige," op. 25, no. 6

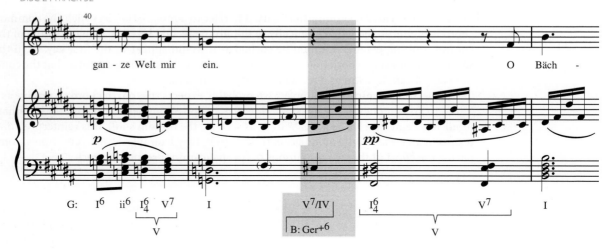

Any V^7 chord or secondary V^7 in the first key can be reinterpreted as a Ger^{+6} chord in the new key. The reverse is also possible—a Ger^{+6} in the first key can become a V^7 or secondary V^7 in the second key. However, in the majority of cases the common chord is a Ger^{+6} in the second key, presumably because of its more dramatic effect. Also, the major-minor seventh chord in the first key seems most often to be a V^7/IV. This common relationship, V^7/IV becoming Ger^{+6}, was illustrated in Examples 23-6 and 23-7. It would also be possible to use an It^{+6} as the enharmonic equivalent of an incomplete V^7, but this is not often encountered, perhaps because of doubling problems.

Enharmonic Modulations Using the Diminished Seventh Chord

Surprisingly, the diminished seventh chord is not used as frequently as the major-minor seventh chord in enharmonic modulations, even though any diminished seventh chord can lead in four directions, compared to the two possible with the major-minor seventh (see Ex. 23-5). The top staff of Example 23-8 shows four resolutions of the same diminished seventh sonority. The bottom staff is similar, except that the diminished seventh chord in each case is followed by a V^7 before the resolution to tonic. Both methods—$vii°^7$–I and $vii°^7$–V^7–I—are used in enharmonic modulations. You should play through Example 23-8 to familiarize yourself with the sound of these resolutions.

Example 23-8

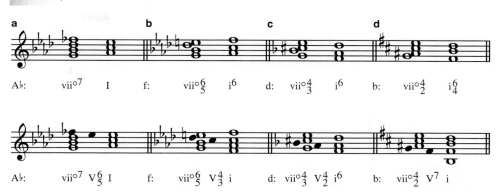

Ab: vii°7 I f: vii°$_5^6$ i6 d: vii°$_3^4$ i6 b: vii°$_2^4$ i$_4^6$

Ab: vii°7 V$_5^6$ I f: vii°$_5^6$ V$_3^4$ i d: vii°$_3^4$ V$_2^4$ i6 b: vii°$_2^4$ V7 i

Example 23-9 is from the end of the exposition from a sonata-form movement by Haydn. The movement begins in f minor and modulates to Ab, the relative major. Because the composer is going to repeat the entire exposition, he must modulate back to f minor before the repeat. Haydn prepares for the modulation in mm. 46 to 47 by using a G°7 chord (vii°7 in Ab), just as in the top staff of Example 23-8a. In the first ending, however, he uses the same sonority, respelled as vii°$_5^6$ in f, and resolves it as in the bottom staff of Example 23-8b, bringing us back to f minor for the repeat. Here it is the C4 in the second violin that signals the modulation by turning the diminished seventh chord into a V$_3^4$ in f, so the common chord is the one that precedes the V$_3^4$.

DISC 2 : TRACK 32

Example 23-9   Haydn, String Quartet op. 20, no. 5, I

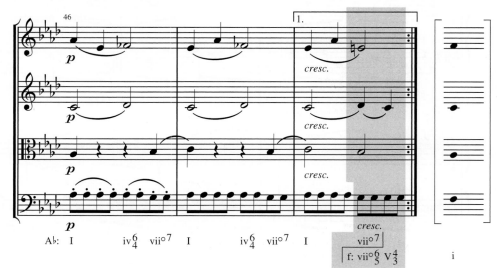

Ab: I   iv$_4^6$ vii°7 I   iv$_4^6$ vii°7 I   vii°7   i

f: vii°$_5^6$ V$_3^4$

Example 23-10 begins and ends in A major. A C#°7 chord appears in m. 140, but the listener probably hears it as an A#°7, which is a vii°6/5/ii in A major (vii°7/IV would be another possibility). However, Beethoven treats this chord as a vii°4/2 in F, the c# in the bass really acting like a d♭. This is similar to the bottom staff of Example 23-8d. When this same chord recurs in m. 145, it *sounds* like a vii°7/vi in F because it follows V and seems to imply a V–vii°7/vi–vi deceptive progression. Instead, it is treated (and notated) as an A#°7, a vii°6/5/ii in A major.

DISC 2 : TRACK 33

Example 23-10   Beethoven, Piano Sonata op. 2, no. 2, IV

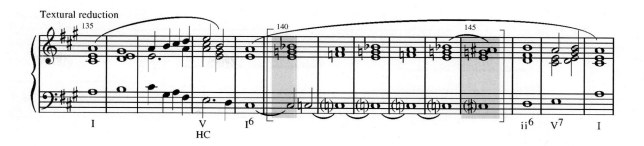

The textural reduction that appears after Example 23-10 is worth studying. Play it and listen to it, paying special attention to the bass line. You will find that mm. 140 to 145 constitute a harmonic digression, keeping the C♯ in m. 139 from reaching its goal, D, until m. 146. The entire example is a parallel period. The first phrase is four measures long, ending with a half cadence in m. 138. The second phrase begins like the first (thus the parallel structure), but it is expanded from four to ten measures by the tonicization of ♭VI in mm. 140 to 145. This expansion is indicated by the brackets in the reduction.

Other Examples of Enharmonicism

Major-minor seventh chords and diminished seventh chords are sometimes used enharmonically at a more local level. In Example 23-11 there is a brief tonicization of a♭ (the minor Neapolitan!) in mm. 160 to 161, but it is much too brief to be a modulation. Measure 162 sounds like the same chord that was used in m. 160—a V^7 of a♭—but here it functions as a Ger^{+6} in G. The extremely unusual minor Neapolitan comes about through a harmonic sequence: G7–c–E♭7–a♭.*

Example 23-11   Schubert, Impromptu op. 90, no. 3

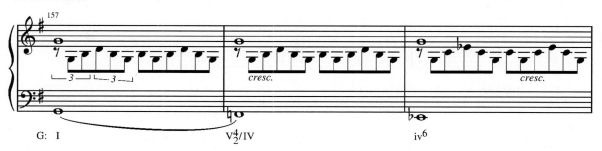

* The original version of this impromptu is in G♭ instead of G, which means that it tonicizes a♭♭! Schubert was considerate, however, and wrote the key of a♭♭ enharmonically as g.

Self-Test 23-1

(Answers begin on page 628.)

A. Analyze the given chord. Then show any possible enharmonic reinterpretation(s) of that chord, keeping the same key signature. Each enharmonic reinterpretation should involve a new key, not just an enharmonically equivalent key (such as g♯ and a♭).

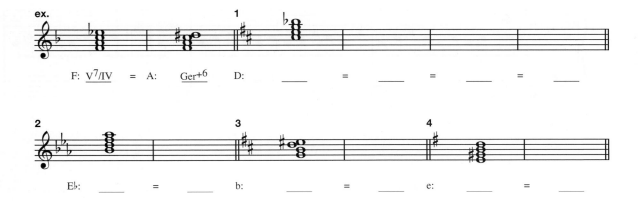

B. Each of the following short examples contains an enharmonic modulation. Analyze each example *after* playing it slowly at the piano and listening for the point of modulation. Do not try to analyze these examples without hearing them.

1

2

3

C. Analysis. Be sure to play as much of each excerpt at the piano as you can, simplifying the texture as necessary.

1. This excerpt begins in G♭ and ends in b♭ minor, although B♭ major is the eventual goal. Label all the chords. Can you relate the F–G♭–F figure in the last measure to anything that has happened earlier? That is, does it remind you of any other figure heard in this excerpt?

Beethoven, "Adelaide," op. 46

A - bend - lüft - chen im zar - ten Lau - be flü - stern,   Sil - ber-

glöck - chen des Mais im Gra - se säu - seln,   Wel - len rau-schen   und Nach - ti - gal - len

flö - ten,   und Nach - ti - gal - len flö - ten: V - - - - - - - -

2. Look back at the Schubert excerpt in Self-Test 19-1, part A2 (pp. 313–314). Is this an enharmonic modulation? Explain your answer.

3. This excerpt begins in B♭ and modulates to f♯. Before you try to analyze the modulation, play the excerpt slowly as block chords, listening carefully as you play.

Schubert, Piano Sonata D. 960, I

DISC 2 : TRACK 35

4. This excerpt begins in D♭ and ends in c minor. Label all the chords.

Beethoven, Piano Sonata op. 10, no. 1, III

5. This passage begins in C and ends in E, although the eventual goal is the key of A. Label all chords in this excerpt.

Schubert, String Quartet op. 125, no. 2, II

6. This excerpt is from a passage returning to the A theme of a seven-part rondo form. The excerpt begins in C and ends in c♯/C♯, although it soon moves to E for the return of the theme. Label the chords, including the enharmonic modulation.

Beethoven, Piano Sonata op. 90, II

DISC 2 : TRACK 36

Exercise 23-1 See Workbook.

Summary

Enharmonic spellings are sometimes used when a composer wants to make the direction of a line more apparent to the performer—as in D–D♯–E as opposed to D–E♭–E♮—or when a composer simply wants to make something easier to read—by notating a passage in E instead of F♭, for example. These sorts of enharmonic spellings come about for the performer's convenience, but they are inaudible to the listener. **Enharmonic reinterpretations,** on the other hand, are audible because they reinterpret a chord in a new key as part of a modulation. Enharmonic modulations almost always use either a major-minor seventh chord or a diminished seventh chord as the common chord. The major-minor seventh chord will be heard as a German augmented sixth chord in one key and a V^7 (or secondary V^7) in the other. The diminished seventh chord used as a common chord will be a $vii^{\circ7}$ (or secondary $vii^{\circ7}$) in both keys, but different pitch classes will serve as roots in the two keys.

Variations

For additional review and practice, please see Chapter 23 on our website at **www.mhhe.com/kostka7e.**

Chapter Twenty-Four

Further Elements of the Harmonic Vocabulary

Introduction

Tonal harmony, on the surface a simple and natural musical phenomenon, is really a very complex and variable set of relationships. Many people have devoted years to the study of tonal harmony and to the almost limitless number of musical structures for which it has provided the foundation. It surely represents one of the highest achievements of Western art and intellect.

Because the subject is so complex, we have been concerned throughout this text with those harmonic events in tonal music that could be thought of as the basic vocabulary of the system—those events that occur with a relatively high degree of frequency. This chapter deals with a few details that are perhaps less fundamental but that, nevertheless, deserve attention. However, even with this chapter we will not completely exhaust the harmonic vocabulary. The variations in detail and exceptions to the norms found in tonal music are too numerous to codify; in fact, it is doubtful that they ever will be codified. This complexity is one of the really fascinating aspects of tonal music, an aspect you can look forward to exploring in your further study of the literature.

The Dominant with a Substituted 6th

You may be familiar with the concept of added-note chords, such as the triad with an added 6th. Such chords were not really a standard part of the vocabulary of Western music before impressionism, but they were recognized as a possibility long before that time. For example, Jean Philippe Rameau (1683–1764), an influential French theorist and composer, considered the first chord in Example 24-1 to be a IV chord with an added 6th. Although you might prefer to label it as a ii^6_5, that approach does not explain the unresolved 7th (B♭3). Whichever analysis you choose, the cadence is plagal (review p. 149).

Example 24-1

B♭: IVadd6   I
    (ii⁶₅)

Although triads with added 6ths are not characteristic of most tonal music, the dominant chord in root position with a *substituted 6th* is not uncommon, especially in the nineteenth century. In this case, the 6th above the root is substituted for the 5th, which does not appear. If you play the three cadences in Example 24-2, you will find that they have a similar effect. The first one is a familiar form of the perfect authentic cadence. Example 24-2b incorporates an escape tone that embellishes the 5th of the V chord. In Example 24-2c the A4 appears in place of the 5th—it is a substituted 6th (V$_{6th}^{subs}$). You might have noticed that the V$_{6th}^{subs}$ contains the same scale degrees as those found in a iii⁶ chord, but the function is clearly dominant. To analyze the cadence in Example 24-2c as iii⁶–I would certainly be an error.

Example 24-2

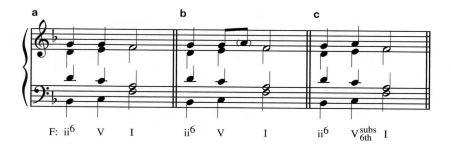

F: ii⁶   V   I   ii⁶   V   I   ii⁶   V$_{6th}^{subs}$ I

Example 24-3 contains an illustration of the V$_{6th}^{subs}$. Notice that the E5, the pitch that would have been the 5th of the V chord, appears immediately before the F#5. The V$_{6th}^{subs}$ is usually prepared in this manner, which leads some theorists to analyze the V$_{6th}^{subs}$ as a V chord with a nonstandard escape tone. Either approach is acceptable.

Example 24-3   Haydn, Symphony no. 101, IV

Example 24-4 is strikingly similar to the previous example, but it is in the minor mode. Notice again the preparation of the 6th.

Example 24-4   Schumann, "Folk Song," op. 68, no. 9

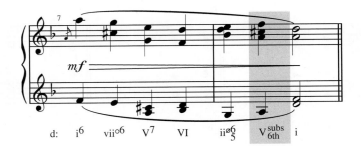

The substituted 6th may appear in connection with the dominant triad in root position, as in the preceding examples, or with the V^7 in root position, as in Example 24-5a. The 7th of the chord is always placed *below* the added 6th, as in Example 24-5a, not above it, as in Example 24-5b. Play both versions, and notice the disagreeable effect of the second one.

Example 24-5

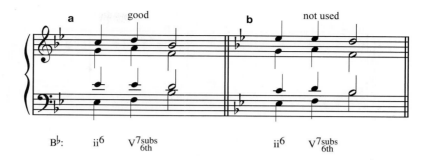

Example 24-6 illustrates the $V^{7\text{subs}}_{6\text{th}}$ in practice. If you are a jazz musician, you might be tempted to label the $V^{7\text{subs}}_{6\text{th}}$ as a V^{13}. We do not consider this to be a true 13th chord, however, because it lacks so many chord members (5th, 9th, and 11th).

DISC 2 : TRACK 38

Example 24-6   Schumann, *Humoresque,* op. 20

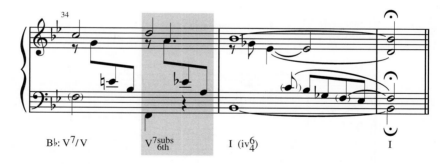

When you resolve a V or V^7 with a substituted 6th, *the 6th should leap down to tonic* (as in $\hat{3}$ to $\hat{1}$); the 6th never acts as an anticipation (as in $\hat{3}$ to $\hat{3}$).

The Dominant with a Raised 5th

When the 5th of a V or V^7 is chromatically raised, the sonority that results is either an augmented triad (V^+) or an augmented minor-seventh chord (V^{+7}). This alteration is useful in the major mode because the raised 5th creates a leading tone to the 3rd of the tonic triad. The leading-tone effect would not be present if the tonic triad were minor, and for this reason the **augmented dominant** is not found resolving to a minor triad. These concepts are illustrated in Example 24-7. Remember that the "+" in V^{+7} refers to the triad, not to the 7th.

Example 24-7

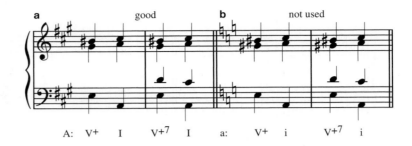

Notice that the V^{+7} may contain the interval of an $^+6$, depending on the voicing (between the soprano and tenor in Ex. 24-7a). Try not to confuse this altered dominant, whether in root position or inversion, with more conventional $^+6$ chords.

Most instances of V^+ and V^{+7} find the augmented dominant preceded by its diatonic form, which means that the $\sharp\hat{2}$ could also be analyzed as a chromatic passing tone. The C$\sharp$5 in Example 24-8 is a chromatic passing tone, but at the same time it creates a V^{+7} for a duration of four eighth notes.

DISC 2 : TRACK 38

Example 24-8   Beethoven, Symphony no. 9, op. 125, III (strings)

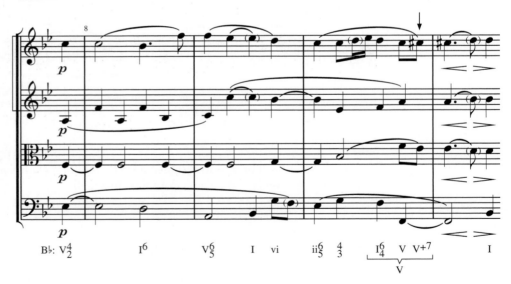

The V^+ and V^{+7} in the major mode are enharmonic with the V^{subs}_{6th} and V^{7subs}_{6th} in the minor mode, as Example 24-9 illustrates. The resolutions are quite different, however: the raised 5th of the V^+ moves *up* by half step to $\hat{3}$ (Ex. 24-9a), whereas the substituted 6th of the V^{subs}_{6th} leaps *down* to $\hat{1}$ (Ex. 24-9b).

Example 24-9

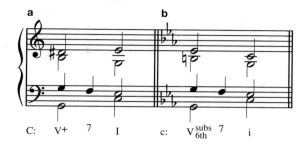

Example 24-10 begins with a V chord in the key of C♯, and the chord eventually resolves to a I, enharmonically spelled as D♭. In the second measure of the example, the E4 would appear to create a V^{7subs}_{6th}, but if you play the example, you will hear that the E4 is really a D×4, and the chord is a $G♯^{+7}$ (compare Ex. 24-9a). Chopin used this enharmonic spelling for the convenience of the performer, who would rather read G♯–E–F♯ in the soprano than G♯–D×–F♯. The textural reduction simplifies the situation by putting the notation entirely in D♭.

Example 24-10   Chopin, Nocturne op. 48, no. 2

Textural reduction

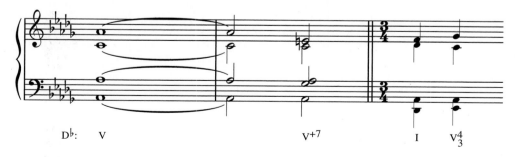

Secondary dominants may also appear in augmented form. Most common are the V^{+}/IV and the V^{+7}/IV, as in Example 24-11.

Example 24-11   Haydn, String Quartet op. 9, no. 2, I

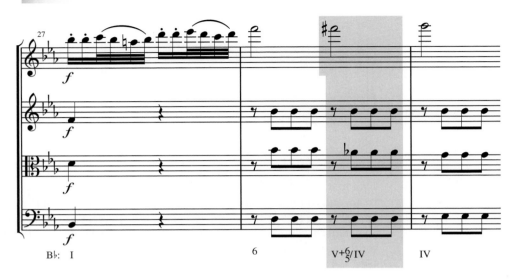

$$\text{B}\flat: \quad \text{I} \qquad\qquad\qquad 6 \qquad\qquad \text{V}^{+\frac{6}{5}}/\text{IV} \qquad \text{IV}$$

Remember not to confuse V^{+7} with augmented 6th chords. In Example 24-12 the $V^{+\frac{4}{2}}/IV$ has an $^+6$ between the outer parts ($G\natural$–$E\sharp$), so in a sense it *is* a kind of augmented sixth chord, but the better analysis is the one shown.

Example 24-12   Schubert, String Quartet op. 29, IV

$$\text{A}: \text{V}^{6}_{5} \qquad\quad \text{V}^{4}_{2}/\text{IV} \quad \text{IV}^{6} \quad \text{IV} \qquad \text{V}^{6}_{5}/\text{IV} \quad \text{IV} \; \text{V}^{+\frac{4}{2}}/\text{IV} \; \text{IV}^{6}$$

Ninth, Eleventh, and Thirteenth Chords

Just as superimposed 3rds produce triads and seventh chords, continuation of that process yields ninth, eleventh, and thirteenth chords (which is not to say that this is the manner in which these sonorities evolved historically). These chords are shown in Example 24-13.

Example 24-13

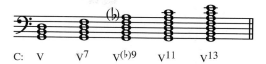

Interesting as these chords may be, the triad and the seventh chord were really the standard fare of music in the eighteenth and nineteenth centuries. True elevenths and thirteenths are rare before impressionism, which began in the late nineteenth century. Ninths occur throughout the tonal era, but the 9th of the chord often can be analyzed as an NCT and usually disappears before the chord resolves. The most common way to dispense with the 9th is to resolve it down a step to double the root of the chord. This is what happens in Example 24-14, where the minor-mode 9th, F♭5, moves down by step to E♭5, the root of the V^7. As is frequently the case with ninth chords, the 9th of the $V^{♭9}$ could also be analyzed as an NCT. (The flat in $V^{♭9}$ indicates a minor 9th above the root, not a literal flat.)

Example 24-14   Beethoven, Piano Sonata op. 2, no. 1, I

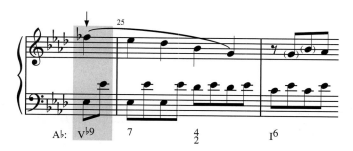

Another possibility, illustrated in Example 24-15, is to arpeggiate from the 9th of the chord down to the 7th or to some other chord member.

Example 24-15   Beethoven, String Quartet op. 59, no. 2, III
(piano reduction)

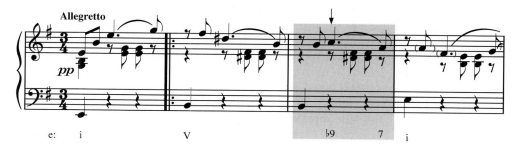

Certainly, examples may be found of ninth chords that maintain the quality of a ninth chord right up to the resolution, at which point the 9th resolves down by step, just as a 7th does. This is illustrated in Example 24-16, where the 9th, F, resolves to E in the next chord.

Example 24-16   Schumann, "Leides Ahnung," op. 124, no. 2

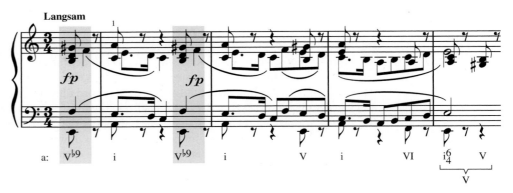

All the examples of ninth chords cited so far have been dominant ninths. Although dominant ninths are the most commonly encountered, other ninth chords do occur. Example 24-17 contains a clear instance of a iv⁹.

Example 24-17   Schumann, *Scheherazade*, op. 68, no. 32

The symbols used in the analysis of ninth chords are not standardized. The easiest approach is to let the roman numeral reflect the triad type, with the 9 or ♭9 appended to it. Inversions of ninth chords are not as common as inversions of triads and seventh chords. Moreover, the figured-bass symbols for inversions of ninth chords are too cumbersome to be practicable. A useful, if unscientific, solution is to give in parentheses the figures used for inversions of seventh chords: $V^9(^6_5)$ and so on. This will not work in the case of a ninth chord in fourth inversion, but the fourth inversion is very uncommon. Using that approach, mm. 2 and 4 of Example 24-18 would be labeled as $V^9(^4_3)$ chords. Franck interrupts the dominant sonority in m. 6, giving us, instead of the expected $V^9(^4_3)$, a ii chord (which contains three of the five notes of a V^9).

Example 24-18   Franck, Violin Sonata, I

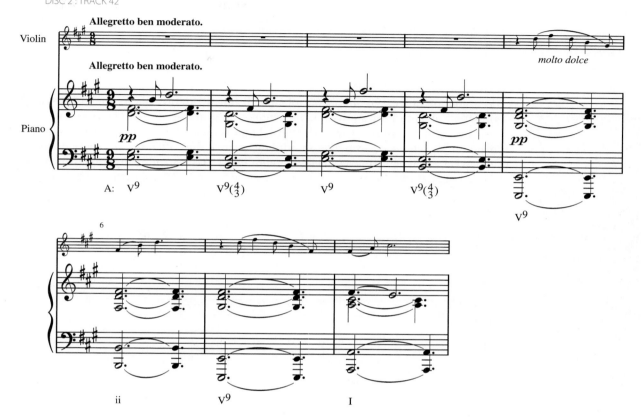

The Common-Tone Diminished Seventh Chord

Most diminished seventh chords function as leading-tone sevenths of tonic or of some other chord within the tonality. Although the enharmonic potential of the diminished seventh chord is occasionally exploited in enharmonic modulation, the resolution of the chord generally clarifies its function.

However, there is a diminished seventh chord usage that does not conform to the usual pattern. In this case, the diminished seventh chord progresses to a major triad or dominant seventh chord, the *root* of which is the *same* as one of the notes of the °7 chord. In Example 24-19, G5, the 7th of the A#°7, is retained to become the root of the next chord. It is obvious that the a#°7 is not a leading-tone 7th of the G6 or the G6/5. We refer to a diminished seventh chord used in this way as a **common-tone diminished seventh** (ct°7). Remember that the tone in common is the root of the major triad or dominant seventh chord. The ct°7 chord may be spelled in any manner, the only criterion being that one of the notes be the same as the root of the embellished chord. Usually, though, they are spelled as in Example 24-19, with the common tone being the 7th of the chord.

Example 24-19

a#°7   G6   a#°7   G6/5

The function of a ct°7 is simply one of embellishment, and we put its analytical symbol in parentheses to indicate its weak harmonic function. A ct°7 can be used to embellish any triad or dominant seventh chord, but it is most often found progressing to I in major or V(7) in major (examples in minor are rare). Most often the ct°7 has a distinctly nonessential flavor, acting as a neighbor chord (Exs. 24-20a and b) or as a passing chord (Ex. 24-20c). Notice the smooth voice leading in all the parts. Because the ct°7 has no theoretical root, no inversions should be indicated when labeling ct°7 chords.

Example 24-20

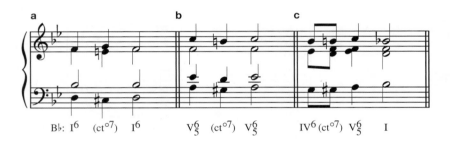

Bb: I6   (ct°7)   I6   V6/5   (ct°7)   V6/5   IV6 (ct°7) V6/5   I

Example 24-21 illustrates the ct°7–I progression interpolated between a pedal IV6/4 and its resolution back to I. The textural reduction of the accompaniment shows that the only significant harmonic event here is the presentation of the tonic triad. The V4/3 consists only of neighbor tones on a weak beat, whereas the IV6/4 and ct°7 in combination form a double neighbor group figure in the inner voices.

DISC 2 : TRACK 43

Example 24-21   Mozart, Piano Sonata K. 545, II

Andante

G: I   V4/3   I   (IV6/4)   (ct°7)   I

Textural reduction

Whereas ct°⁷ chords are usually complete, incomplete versions are sometimes encountered, as in Example 24-22, where the ct°⁷ chord is missing an A.

DISC 2 : TRACK 43

Example 24-22 Clara Wieck Schumann, Concert Variations, op. 8, var. 2

The ct°⁷ chords in Example 24-23 embellish a dominant chord. Although ct°⁷ chords are clearly ornamental, their flavor is crucial to this passage and to the waltz that follows.

Example 24-23   Tchaikovsky, *Nutcracker Suite,* "Waltz of the Flowers" (piano arrangement)

Another prominent ct°⁷ embellishing V is seen in Example 24-24. The eight-measure introduction to this famous Sousa march is essentially a long dominant harmony.

Example 24-24   Sousa, "Semper Fidelis"

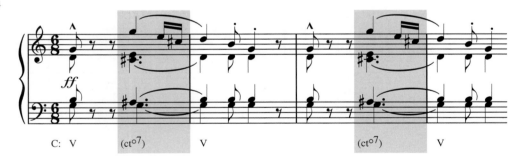

The ct°⁷ that embellishes I is usually spelled as a ♯ii°⁷ and that which embellishes V as a ♯vi°⁷, as in Example 24-20. However, enharmonic spellings are frequently found. In Example 24-25, Brahms spells the ct°⁷ embellishing I as a ♯iv°⁷ to clarify the F–A♭–F arpeggiation in the melody (instead of F–G♯–F). One feature of the theme that begins in Example 24-25 is extensive use of mode mixture, and the A♭ introduces this technique more clearly than G♯ would have. This marvelous theme should be studied in its entirety (mm. 1–15), using a recording and a full score. You will discover not only mode mixture but also additional ct°⁷ chords, other altered chords, and polymeter (the aural effect of two or more different meters occurring at the same time). Motivic relationships are also of interest. For example, compare the melody in mm. 1 to 3 with the bass in mm. 3 to 5. Incidentally, the inner voices of this example have been included only to clarify the harmonies—they do not indicate Brahms's actual voice leading, which is too complicated for a piano reduction.

Example 24-25   Brahms, Symphony no. 3, op. 90, I (simplified texture)

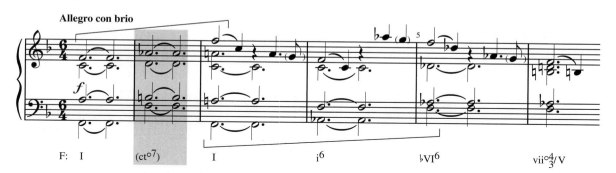

Lead-sheet symbols sometimes call for ct°⁷ chords. Just look for a diminished seventh chord that seems to resolve incorrectly, and see whether it shares a tone with the root of the chord just before or (more often) just after it. In Example 24-26, the E^{dim7} shares a tone with the root of the B♭ chord that follows it.

Example 24-26   Parker, "Thriving from a Riff"

It is easy to confuse the vii°⁷/V with the ct°⁷ that embellishes the tonic, because they are enharmonically equivalent and both are sometimes spelled enharmonically (review Chapter 23, p. 391). This is especially clear in Example 24-25, where the ct°⁷ is spelled as a vii°⁴₃/V (B°⁷). You should have no trouble if you keep the following in mind:

Chord following the °7 chord:	Should be analyzed as:
I or I⁶	ct°⁷
V or I⁶₄	vii°⁷/V

In Example 24-27 Schumann spells the chord on the second beat of m. 15 as a D#°7, a ct°7 of I, but its resolution to I_4^6–V^9 requires an analysis as a vii°7/V. The texture of this example is quite complex and features imitation between the soprano and alto parts.

DISC 2 : TRACK 46

Example 24-27   Schumann, "Lento espressivo," op. 68, no. 21

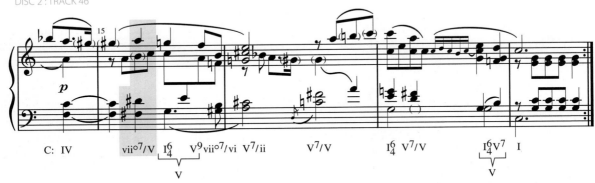

Common-tone diminished seventh chords are sometimes used to embellish secondary dominants as well as the usual I and V chords. The climactic point in the passage in Example 24-28 is the A°7 chord in mm. 65 to 66, which is a ct°7 of the very short I6 chord in m. 67 or of the V^7/ii that is the main harmony in that measure, or both.

DISC 2 : TRACK 46

Example 24-28   Joplin, "Fig Leaf Rag"

In Example 24-29 a ct°⁷ chord is used enharmonically as part of a tonicization of the Neapolitan. When we first hear the diminished seventh chord in m. 12, we probably hear it as vii°⁷/vi and expect a vi to follow as a deceptive resolution of the preceding V⁷. Instead, it functions as a ct°⁷ of the V⁷/N that follows it. Notice also the unusual Ger⁺⁶ chord in m. 15.

DISC 2 : TRACK 47

Example 24-29   Fanny Mendelssohn Hensel, *Beharre*

CHECKPOINT

1. Is the V_{6th}^{subs} the same as a triad with an added sixth?

2. In the resolution of a V_{6th}^{subs}, how does the 6th resolve?

3. In a V_{6th}^{7subs}, is the 7th put above the 6th, or is it the reverse?

4. How does the raised 5th of a V⁺ or a V⁺⁷ resolve?

5. In the progression V♭⁹–i, how does the 9th resolve?

6. What two chords are most likely to be embellished by a ct°⁷ chord?

7. What member of those chords (root, third, and so on) will be shared with the ct°⁷?

8. The ct°⁷ that embellishes _____ is usually spelled as a ♯ii°⁷, whereas the one that embellishes _____ is usually spelled as a ♯vi°⁷.

Self-Test 24-1

(Answers begin on page 630.)

A. In each exercise that follows, analyze the given chord. Then notate the specified chord in such a way that it leads smoothly into the given chord with acceptable voice leading. Some of the problems use a five-part texture for simpler voice leading.

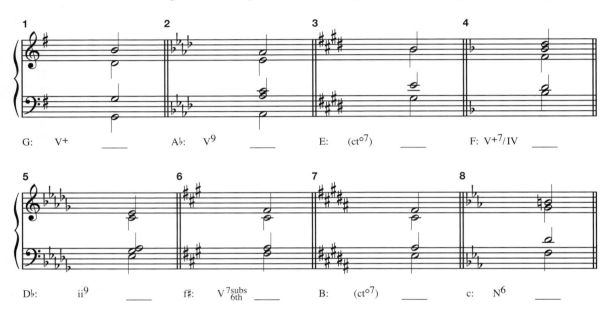

1. G: V+   ____
2. A♭:   V9   ____
3. E: (ct°7)   ____
4. F: V+7/IV   ____
5. D♭:   ii9   ____
6. f♯:   V7subs 6th   ____
7. B: (ct°7)   ____
8. c: N6   ____

B. Analysis. Throughout this section, highlight (using arrows and so on) any occurrences of the chords discussed in this chapter.

   1. Label the chords in this excerpt. Pedal points occur in mm. 44 and 52.

     Schumann, "Das Schifflein," op. 146, no. 5

DISC 2 : TRACK 48

2. This excerpt is in E throughout. What bass notes are implied in the second half of m. 90 and m. 94? The chord in mm. 96 to 97 appears to be unrelated to the chord in m. 98. Can you think of a better explanation? Label all chords.

Schumann, "Aus alten Märchen," op. 48, no. 15

DISC 2 : TRACK 48

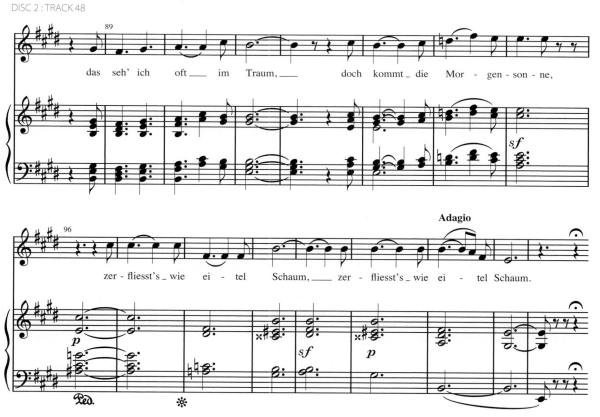

3. Provide a roman-numeral analysis of this excerpt, including two analyses of the first chord in m. 13. Where is the longest circle-of-fifths sequence in this passage? (Review p. 271.) And where is there a progression involving a chromatic mediant relationship?

Silver, "The Preacher"

DISC 2 : TRACK 49

4. This passage begins in A and ends in C. Label the chords with roman numerals, including the common-chord modulation.

Beethoven, Symphony no. 7, op. 92, II (piano reduction by Liszt)

DISC 2 : TRACK 49

5. This example is from Schumann's *Kinderszenen* (*Scenes of Childhood*) which comprises 13 short pieces. Although it could be analyzed entirely in F, your analysis should somehow reflect the strong tonicizations of C, g, and d. How can the reharmonization heard in the last three measures be related to the rest of the piece? Label chords and NCTs throughout, except for measures that are exactly the same as earlier measures. What is the best name for the form of this piece?

Schumann, "Träumerei," op. 15, no. 7

DISC 2 : TRACK 50

6. We have provided an analysis of the first few measures of this excerpt. It would be possible to analyze a modulation to E in the last few measures, but analyze secondary functions in the key of A instead.

DISC 2 : TRACK 51

Spohr, Salonstück, op. 145, no. 3

Exercise 24-1   See Workbook.

Summary

The **dominant with a substituted sixth** is a V or V^7 chord in which the 6th above the root ($\hat{3}$) is used *instead* of the 5th of the chord ($\hat{2}$). The 6th is usually approached by ascending step and left by descending leap: $\hat{2}$–$\hat{3}$–$\hat{1}$.

Augmented dominants (V^+ and V^{+7}) occur in the major mode. The raised 5th ($\sharp\hat{2}$) leads to the 3rd of the I chord. Secondary dominants may also be augmented.

Although **ninth, eleventh, and thirteenth chords** are theoretically possible, only the ninth chord appears with any frequency before the twentieth century. Most often the 9th of the chord disappears before the chord resolves. Otherwise, the 9th resolves down by step.

The **common-tone diminished seventh chord** has a tone in common with the root of the chord it embellishes, but be careful not to analyze the vii°7/V as a ct°7 of a cadential I^6_4. The common-tone diminished seventh chord typically embellishes either a I chord (in which case it will usually be spelled as $\sharp$ii°7) or a V chord (usually spelled as a $\sharp$vi°7). Enharmonic spellings do occur.

Chapter Twenty-Five

Tonal Harmony in the Late Nineteenth Century

Introduction

In Chapter 7, we presented a pair of diagrams—one each for the major and minor modes—that describes the most common diatonic harmonic progressions. Subsequent chapters introduced various chromatic elements—secondary, borrowed, Neapolitan, augmented-sixth, altered dominant, and common-tone diminished seventh chords—that expand this basic diatonic framework.

These chromatic elements, though appearing to create an unruly mass of exceptions and complications to the harmonic system, can in many cases be understood as the result of a single tendency: *intensifying the sense of resolution* from one chord to another *by narrowing the distance between pitches* in a given line. For example, the ii-V progression can be intensified by using the secondary dominant chord V/V, either as a substitute for ii (as in V/V-V) or as a "passing" chord (ii-V/V-V). The appearance of $\sharp\hat{4}$ in place of, or in addition to, $\hat{4}$ creates a stronger bond between the two chords resembling that of a leading tone moving to tonic. Likewise, replacing IV-I with iv-I or IV-iv-I *via* mode mixture results in bringing $\hat{6}$ closer to $\hat{5}$ through the addition or substitution of $\flat\hat{6}$.

However, these kinds of chromatic progressions—those that reinforce and enrich more basic diatonic progressions—are not the only ways that chromaticism can be employed. In growing degrees throughout the nineteenth century, composers experimented with contrapuntal and harmonic devices that gave more weight to the full spectrum of chromatic pitches, instead of drawing primarily from the diatonic collection. This created different effects in different pieces, such as the following:

1. Exploring harmonic models other than the circle-of-fifths, such as chromatic mediant chains and an increased number of chromatic sequence types.

2. Giving greater emphasis to chromatic pitches through longer durations, strong metric and registral placement, greater dynamic intensity, etc., thus blurring the sense of which harmonies are essential and which are inessential.

3. Moving rapidly from one temporary key or tonality to another.

4. Making use, within a single piece, of multiple modulatory paths available through the enharmonic reinterpretation of dominant sevenths, augmented sixths, diminished sevenths, and augmented triads (see Chapter 23) and new kinds of chromatic progressions.

5. Avoiding strong, key-affirming dominant-to-tonic cadences for long spans of time.

---

* For further reading related to concepts discussed in this chapter, see Richard Cohn, "Maximally Smooth Cycles, Hexatonic Systems, and the Analysis of Late-Romantic Triadic Progressions," *Music Analysis* 13/1 (March, 1996), 9–40; Cohn, "Neo-Riemannian Operations, Parsimonious Trichords, and Their "Tonnetz" Representations," *Journal of Music Theory* 41/1 (Spring, 1997), 1–66; David Kopp, *Chromatic Transformations in Nineteenth-Century Music* (Cambridge: Cambridge University Press, 2002); and Dmitri Tymoczko, *A Geometry of Music: Harmony and Counterpoint in the Extended Common Practice* (Oxford: Oxford University Press, 2011).

6. Loosening the requirement of dissonances or tendency tones to be prepared and resolved—and employing chords for their sonorous, "coloristic" qualities rather than in their traditional functional roles.

7. Withholding the establishment of a clear tonal center.

This is an important consideration when looking at the significant amount of highly chromatic music written in the late nineteenth and early twentieth century by composers as varied as Franz Liszt, Richard Wagner, Johannes Brahms, Hugo Wolf, Max Reger, Gustav Mahler, and Richard Strauss, among others. This music appears to resist easy comprehension, especially in light of what we have learned up until now—the effects listed above, some of which we will discuss below, appear to lead to greater complexity and even incoherence. However, this is balanced by new kinds of order and systematic thinking involving 1) *an emphasis on conjunct, linear motion and smooth voice leading between chords* combined with 2) a willingness to explore *the entire collection of chromatic pitches* in addition to the functional chromaticism that depends on diatonic resolution—in other words, to break away from the model presented in Chapter 7.

This difference of approach can be seen in Example 25-1a, a reduction of the opening measures of Richard Strauss's *Metamorphosen*.*

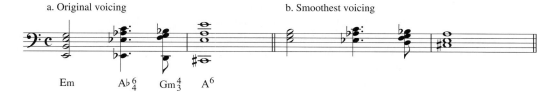

Example 25-1   R. Strauss, *Metamorphosen* for 23 Solo Strings, op. 142 (piano reduction)

a. Original voicing   b. Smoothest voicing

There is no diatonic key or collection into which all four of these chords will fit; in fact, several keys are suggested, depending on what chords we emphasize (such as e minor, for the opening chord, A major or minor for the first and last chords, and d minor for the final two chords). It would also not be quite accurate to try to understand this as a modulating passage. For one thing, we would have to propose a new key for almost every chord, and we don't feel secure enough about the place of any chord in a particular key to place it with certainty—key determination is based in part on the local context. It appears, then, that it would be inappropriate to try to understand this passage using our traditional harmonic model—we will substitute lead-sheet and bass-position symbols for Roman numerals in labeling chords whenever this situation applies throughout the chapter.

So what principles might we appeal to instead? Strauss certainly could have written this passage so as to establish a single key. See Example 25-2 for several possible, but boring, alternatives.

---

* Also analyzed in Daniel Harrison, *Harmonic Function in Chromatic Music* (Chicago: University of Chicago Press, 1994), 132–34.

Example 25-2   Single-key rewritings of the opening motive

The benefit to Strauss of using the more multifaceted version is that he can try out several different continuations to the passage to bring out the connections with each provisional key. Indeed, Strauss evokes his title at various points throughout the piece by showing how this little opening idea can metamorphose into different keys.

But apart from using the same multifaceted idea to explore multiple compositional pathways (an important late-nineteenth-century strategy), this piece holds together in another important way. Consider Example 25-1b: Here, the opening passage has been rewritten to show the smoothest possible voice-leading relationships between each chord tone. Strauss did not choose this version, likely because he wanted to highlight the upward-thrusting motive G3-C4-B♭3-E4 in its original voicing (Example 25-1a). However, the fact that these chords have the *potential* to move very smoothly means in part that we as listeners have little problem hearing them as belonging together. This is reinforced by Strauss, in that he retains the bass line of the smoothest voicing, in which only a single half step separates the adjacent voices. This line would not have been possible in a single key, which leads to another important conclusion: by considering chords that can contain any chromatic pitch, new and previously impossible harmonic and contrapuntal combinations become possible.

This is an important principle in analyzing many examples of highly chromatic music. Composers often weakened the pull of diatonic pitches, but *did not weaken the cohesive appeal of linear motion*. As the relationship between harmony and key became more complex, the role of linearity—of conjunct motion, of smooth voice leading between chords—tended to play a stronger unifying role.

More About Mediants

One interesting way that composers found to move beyond circle-of-fifths relationships was to explore chords with other kinds of close relationships. If we emphasize smooth voice leading (and/or common tones) and are not concerned about moving outside a single diatonic collection, mediant relationships turn out to be useful in this respect.

In Chapter 6, we learned that diatonic triads with roots a third apart contained two common tones, while the other voice could move by step (see Example 6-6 on p. 86). One useful way that theorists have determined the degree of closeness between chords is to add together the voice-leading distances between all the voices in the chord. For these diatonic mediants, the **total voice-leading distance** moved by all three voices—excluding the bass, which often contains the doubled roots—only amounts to either one or two half steps. In fact, we found in Chapter 6 that this motion between a major and minor triad (or the reverse) with roots a third apart creates the smoothest voice leading between any two diatonic triads.

In Chapter 19, when discussing common-tone modulations, we described another kind of progression between chords whose roots are a third apart: the chromatic mediant relationship (see Examples 19-5 through 19-9, especially Example 19-7 on p. 310). In this case, the chords do not belong to the same diatonic collection. Recall that these pairs of chords can have roots a m3 or M3 apart and are either both major triads or both minor triads. If we connect them as smoothly as possible, the total voice-leading distance is still about as small as between the diatonic mediants—two half steps for chords a M3 apart and three for those a m3 apart, and there will still be one common tone. In fact, the voice leading for triads with roots a M3 apart is the smoothest of any triads of the same type (major to major, minor to minor), and m3-related triads are not much more distant. (By contrast, the smoothest version of a progression like IV-V has a total voice-leading distance of six half steps—with or without parallels—whereas ii-V has four half steps.)

Example 25-3 summarizes all the various mediant relationships from C major and C minor, featuring the smoothest possible voice leading between each pair of chords. The root relationship and total voice-leading distance between each pair is indicated below the score.

Example 25-3   Summary of mediant relationships

a. From C major

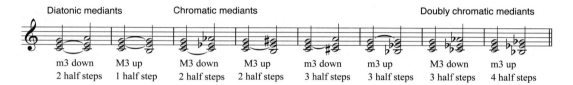

b. From C minor

You can see from this example that the diatonic and chromatic mediants account for six of the eight possible ways to connect a major or minor triad with another major or minor triad where the roots are related by third. The remaining possibility—the **doubly chromatic mediant relationship**—connects chords less strongly than those of the chromatic mediants. Like the diatonic mediants, these chords are of *opposite* mode and have roots a m3 or M3 apart, but unlike the other mediant types, they share *no* common tones—although the total voice-leading motion between chords is still only three or four half steps. Examples of such a relationship would be C to a♭ and c to A.

The move from an A♭ major to an e minor triad in mm. 1–2 of Examples 25-4 are in a doubly chromatic mediant relationship because the roots A♭ and E are enharmonically a M3 apart and the two triads share no pitch classes. Because the chords in this passage do not seem to function in a traditional sense in any key, we will simply indicate their roots and sonority types. The listener would not be likely to guess that these chords will lead to an authentic cadence in f♯ minor.

Example 25-4   Puccini, *Tosca*, act II

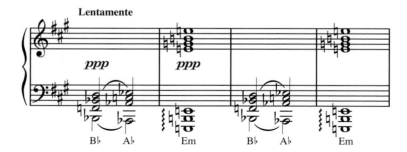

None of the chromatic mediant progressions fit easily into a diatonic context. And yet their potentially smooth voice-leading connection allows chromatic mediants to sound related in a different way. There are several ways to accomplish this. One way is simply to modulate *via* third-related chords, as in Chapter 19. For example, in Example 19-5, the chromatic mediant progression F♯-D (M3 down) connects the dominant of b minor to the new tonic D major of the next phrase *via* common-tone modulation. In Example 19-6, the chromatic mediant progression A7-F7 (M3 down) connects the respective dominants of d minor and B♭ major. In both cases, the tonic chords of each key are diatonic mediants (b and D in Example 19-5; d and B♭ in Example 19-6), so it would not have been necessary for Mozart and Beethoven to use a chromatic mediant relationship. By using one or both dominants, however, they achieve a much more startling expressive effect.

Such relationships between keys have been around since the eighteenth century and can be found with some frequency in the music of Beethoven, Schubert, and Chopin. As the nineteenth century progressed, however, composers increasingly used chromatic mediant relationships in other, more destabilizing ways. Because they do not rely on circle-of-fifths relationships (and hence on our model from Chapter 7), they can be employed 1) to temporarily blur the sense of a prevailing key, 2) to move from one transient tonality to another, or—more globally—3) to undermine the role of the circle of fifths as the primary factor in generating tonality.

Mediant Chains and Other Combinations

If the same chromatic mediant relationship is repeated multiple times, it will eventually return to the same chord from which it started. This is because a stack of M3s (or a stack of m3s) divides the octave into equal parts.

Example 25-5 illustrates the four possible chains of chromatic mediants that divide the octave equally. The four versions differ with respect to whether major or minor triads are used, and whether the roots are related by M3 or m3. They can also be read from right to left resulting in chains of *descending* thirds.

In the examples, the half-note chords are chromatic-mediant related. The intervening quarter notes illustrate how these chromatic-mediant progressions can be broken into two steps: a change to the parallel mode plus a diatonic mediant (or vice versa). Composers have used each of these progressions, although the chromatic-mediant-only versions (without the intervening chords) are more common. Ties show common tones that carry over from the strong-beat chords.

Example 25-5   Chain of Chromatic Mediants

a. Major triads with roots a M3 apart

C   (Em)   E   (G♯m = A♭m)   A♭   (Cm)   C

b. Minor triads with roots a M3 apart

Cm   (C)   Em   (E)   G♯m = A♭m   (A♭)   Cm

c. Major triads with roots a m3 apart

C   (Cm)   E♭   (E♭m) G♭ = F♯   (F♯m)   A   (Am)   C

d. Minor triads with roots a m3 apart

Cm   (E♭)   E♭m   (G♭ = F♯)   F♯m   (A)   Am   (C)   Cm

The versions with major triads (Example 25-5a and c) are more common that those with minor triads (b and d).

Likewise, the M3-related versions (a and b) are more common than the m3-related versions (c and d), possibly because they feature a smaller total voice-leading distance and are, therefore, smoother.

Example 25-6 illustrates a complete chain of descending M3-related triads (corresponding to Example 25-5a in reverse) in context. Here, the gentle, undulating eighth-note motive is propelled from the G-major tonic to E♭ major, B major, and back to G major again. Observe that the descending progression is balanced by a registral ascent.

Example 25-6   Schubert, Piano Sonata in G major, D 894, IV

A smoother version of the m3 chain can be obtained by using major-minor seventh chords instead of triads (see Example 25-7). The chromatic mediant relationships apply to the triads to which sevenths have been added. This seventh-chord version creates two common tones (instead of one) and a total voice-leading distance of only two half steps (excluding the doubled roots). Interestingly, this progression also illustrates that the motion from a Mm7 to a similar chord a tritone away is potentially quite smooth as well. For example, a C^7-$F\sharp^7$ progression contains two common tones (E and B♭/A♯), with the other two voices moving by half step (C-C♯ and G-F♯).

Example 25-7   Major-minor sevenths with roots a m3 apart

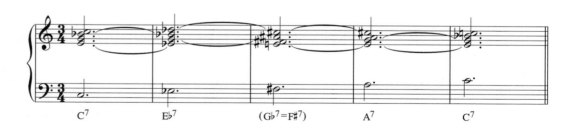

Example 25-8, a reduction of the opening theme from the finale of Gustav Mahler's Symphony no. 9, illustrates incomplete versions of both the M3 and m3 chromatic mediant chains (chromatic-mediant related chords are shown in bold type).

Example 25-8   Mahler, *Symphony no. 9,* IV (piano reduction)

In m. 3, Mahler presents a chromatically altered version of the diatonic "4th down, 2nd up" sequence (see Example 7-19e and 7-20 on p. 107: the so-called "Pachelbel Canon" or "deceptive" sequence) in which the expected vi chord is replaced by ♭VI in beat 3. Observe for now that I and ♭VI, the beginning and the end of the deceptive progression, possess a chromatic mediant relationship, although the "deceptive progression" explanation serves us better here. The rest of the sequence proceeds normally and leads to a perfect authentic cadence at the end of m. 4.

Another modified sequence appears in mm. 4–6, where the succession I-V-IV⁶-vi-iii appears to be standing in for the "5ths up" sequence I-V-ii-vi-iii (see Example 7-19b). Notice that iii appears to stand in for the typical dominant chord V, progressing directly to I in m. 7. This is another frequent late-Romantic effect: because the iii and V chord share two common tones ($\hat{5}$ and $\hat{7}$), we are able to hear the iii chord as a **third substitute** for V, much in the way that IV and ii can substitute for one another as chords leading to V, or vi can substitute for I in the deceptive progression.

The near-sequences allow Mahler to sneak in a much more extreme departure from the diatonic collection in mm. 7–9. Measure 7 begins as though it were a repetition of the near-"deceptive" sequence in m. 3. This time, however, ♭VI gets reinterpreted as I in AM, beginning a descending M3 chromatic mediant chain that extends from D♭ to A(=B♭♭) to F in mm. 7–8. Each chord in the chain is followed by its own dominant, creating a version of the "deceptive" sequence that wanders from the tonic key.

Mahler could have continued this for one more step by moving from F to C and then back to the original tonic D♭, and this appears to be happening when F moves to C in m. 8, b. 3. However, he postpones the return of this tonic—and increases our disorientation—by changing the function of the F-C progression from tonic-dominant to subdominant-tonic. Now we have to migrate away from C major to get to D♭ major—a tricky half step away.

Mahler accomplishes this through yet another incomplete chromatic mediant chain in mm. 8–9, this time using minor 3rds instead of major 3rds. C moves to A (down a m3) and then to a ninth chord on F♯ (down another m3). At this point, we find ourselves back in the home key—F♯ is equivalent to G♭, the subdominant harmony of D♭ major—so the complete chain of m3-related triads is not needed. A second PAC follows in mm 9–11 to complete the theme.

In this short excerpt, what begins as a brief chromatic intensification of the home key (the modified sequences) turns into an excursion to remote keys, an excursion made smooth and orderly by a pair of chromatic mediant chains that lead eventually back to the home key.

Counterpoint and Voice Leading

Although we will treat various elements of the late Romantic style separately, you will notice that in some cases they become inseparable. Excessive melodic chromaticism unavoidably affects harmonic motion; unusual harmonic progressions inevitably affect the motion of individual melodic lines.

We have seen that, understood harmonically, the late Romantic style features a predilection for 1) preserving smooth voice leading and 2) using familiar chord types while 3) exploring new possibilities for harmonic progression outside the traditional diatonic system. The mediant relationships discussed in the previous section represent one possible—but by no means the only—solution to this set of conditions.

We can also explain these new harmonic directions in contrapuntal terms, however. Because primary and supporting voices tend to be chromatically inflected, and because they often pursue goals and paths that are independent of one another, the harmonies that result from them—and, hence, a clear sense of functional harmonic progression—can become blurred.

The F$^{\sharp 6}_{5}$ chord in Example 25-8, m. 5, beat 2 is a simple example of this interrelationship between chromatic harmony and contrapuntal chromaticism. This chord connects two chords (V and IV⁶) that fit reasonably well within the traditional diatonic system as part of a modified sequence. This contrapuntal chord, however, does not do so: It would not make sense to call this a iii°⁶₅ chord, for example, because it doesn't function like a iii chord would be expected to function. Furthermore, the C♭ in this chord lies outside the D♭ major scale. We could call it an example of "mode mixture," but we have not really explained its function by doing this. Most examples of mixture are substitutes for more familiar diatonic chords, and here a iii⁶₅ chord would be no more enlightening.

It is easiest to understand this chord as serving to connect two melodic gaps in the voice leading from V to IV⁶: the first filling E♭ and G♭ diatonically and the second filling C and B♭ chromatically, as shown in Example 25-9. The resulting chord might be called a **simultaneity**—a chord for which a traditional roman numeral label would be meaningless. But just because this chord seems to result from the coincidental activity of melodic lines (or, in this case, from the layering of important musical motives), it is important to note that Mahler chose a chord that sounds like a traditional chord type—the half-diminished seventh. Had this chord been, for example, a cluster of m2s instead, it would have stood out in a way that Mahler might have found inappropriate at this moment. In other words, using traditional chord types in nontraditional ways guarantees that the overall sound of the passage will be coherent.

Example 25-9 Connecting melodic gaps between two diatonic harmonies

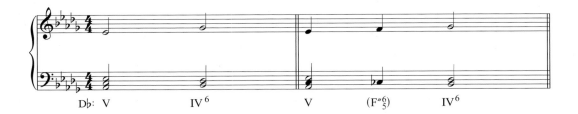

Richard Wagner, a prolific author as well as composer, is generally considered to have been one of the most influential figures in the late Romantic era, particularly with respect to the intricacy of his contrapuntal chromaticism and his exploration of progressions and modulations that result from using the entire chromatic collection.

The Prelude to *Tristan und Isolde,* shown in Example 25-10, illustrates how chromatic melodic lines can appear to obscure, or even misrepresent, vertical harmonies.

DISC 2 : TRACK 54

Example 25-10 Wagner, *Tristan und Isolde,* Prelude (piano reduction)

The sonority found on the first beat of m. 2 suggests a F$^{\varnothing7}$ chord (enharmonically spelled). Yet before this chord is allowed to function in any traditional way, the G♯ resolves to A, creating an apparent Fr^{+6} chord that seems to suggest the key of A. The ultimate conclusion of the phrase in m. 3 confirms the tonal center of A by means of its dominant. Although we anticipate a resolution to tonic, we are uncertain whether to expect a major or a minor chord.

The voice leading in this example is worthy of mention. First, the bass line in mm. 2–3 echoes the alto in m. 1. Second, the soprano line in mm. 2–3 represents an *exact mirror* of the alto line in mm. 1–3. Finally, there is a voice exchange (see p. 103) between the soprano and tenor voices: G♯ moves to B in the soprano line, and B moves to G♯ in the tenor line. We will shortly return to this last point.

The Prelude then continues as follows (Example 25-11).

Example 25-11   Wagner, *Tristan und Isolde,* Prelude (piano reduction)

Although the opening leap of B to G♯ appears to confirm A as the tonal center, it serves instead as the link in a sequential passage that leads first to a half cadence in the key of C, and finally to a pair of half cadences in E. These mediant-related keys—A, C, and E—will later serve as important tonal regions in the rest of the prelude.

The searching, unstable effect of these first eleven measures, then, arises from several features: 1) the contrapuntal relationships are quite dense—there's a lot going on; 2) the independent motion of the various voices creates harmonic ambiguities—we're not always sure what is, and what is not, a chord; 3) the use of dominant harmonies in several different keys creates uncertainty about our true harmonic goal—or even whether it is appropriate to ask about a "true" harmonic goal; and 4) the denial of a tonic resolution—an effect that characterizes much of the entire opera and many late-Romantic works—generates an overwhelming sense of longing and forward momentum.

However, there are also aspects of this passage that work in the other direction—toward order and coherence. First, despite the fact that F^{ø7} and E^7 (mm. 2–3) suggest different keys, they still preserve the traditional harmonic syntax: a half-diminished ("supertonic-like") chord progresses to a dominant seventh chord.

Second, if we remove the voice exchange in mm. 2–3, allowing the G♯ and B to resolve as common tones, we are left with a very smooth voice-leading motion between chords: the total voice-leading distance is only two half steps (D♯ to D and F to E) between the two chords. As a result, the instability of the harmonic motion is balanced by a relatively traditional use of counterpoint—smooth motion between individual voices. Although Wagner chose to move the soprano voice by third, apparently to display the important ascending chromatic idea, the possibility of a smooth voice-leading connection between the two chords still creates a strong link between them. In fact, throughout the Prelude, Wagner experiments with close connections between other half-diminished and dominant-seventh chords, as if exploring the potential of the chromatic environment.

This kind of exploration is rather common in the late-nineteenth century. It turns out that, due to the particular kinds of chords that are used by traditional harmony (triads, seventh chords, etc.), it is possible to connect almost any chords of almost any types together *relatively* smoothly as long as we allow any inversion of the chords to be used, don't limit ourselves to the diatonic collection, and are not restricted by traditional preparations and resolutions of dissonances. The resulting progressions often juxtapose chords not traditionally found together. For nondoubled chords with the same number of pitches, this process is fairly easy.

1. Write the first chord in close structure.
2. Find the inversion of the second chord in close structure that creates the smallest total voice-leading distance between the voices of the first and second chords.
3. If you change the spacing of the first chord, keep the voice-leading pairs from step 2 intact.

For example, suppose we want to connect a Bm^7 chord to an F^7 chord as smoothly as possible. We would first write out Bm^7 in close position in any inversion we preferred, then find the inversion of F^7 in close structure that best connects with this chord, as given in Example 25-12c. If we add up the number of half steps needed to connect the four possibilities, the progression Bm^7-F$^4_3$ is clearly the smoothest with three half steps (and a common-tone A). If we wanted to, we could invert these chords, as long as we preserve the voice pairs A-A, F♯-F, D-E♭, and B-C. We could also reverse the progression (F$^4_3$-Bm^7) without changing the three half-step total distance between the voices.

Example 25-12   Connecting Bm^7 and F^7 chords

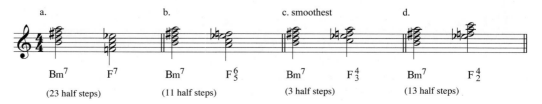

a.   b.   c. smoothest   d.

Bm^7 F^7 Bm^7 F$^6_5$ Bm^7 F$^4_3$ Bm^7 F$^4_2$

(23 half steps)   (11 half steps)   (3 half steps)   (13 half steps)

Late-Romantic composers frequently made use of such voice-leading motions in their compositions. Even if they chose to use less-smooth connections between the same chords—for example, to allow for a motive with large intervals to be used—an awareness of the smoothest voice leading can be useful in deciding how to connect the remaining voices and how to avoid doublings.*

When we are working with chords of different sizes, this process is slightly more difficult. In this case, assume that one voice in the smaller chord will be doubled. If you begin with the larger chord, and experiment with the various inversions of the smaller chord, it will usually be clear which two notes in the larger chord should merge into a doubled note of the smaller chord. (The opening gesture of *Metamorphosen,* shown in Example 25-1, can easily be constructed using this approach through the smoothest version shown in the second half of the example.)

Sequences and Other Systematic Procedures

Sequences also played an important part in the music of many late-Romantic composers, especially as a way to modulate from one tonal region to another. The following example by Rimsky-Korsakov, who was an enormous influence both on later Russian composers and on the craft of orchestration, reveals procedures in which chromatic sequences serve to legitimize nontraditional harmonic relationships.

Example 25-13   Rimsky-Korsakov, *Scheherezade* (piano reduction)

---

*   See also Tymoczko, *A Geometry of Music,* pp. 144–49.

G   A

This passage, found near the beginning of the work, establishes the key of E major. The excerpt quoted here opens with C♯ major harmony, suggesting V/ii. The sequence that begins in m. 13 (the third measure of the excerpt), moves through a series of tonicizations—each a whole step higher than the last—from C♯ up to A, ultimately leading to a half cadence on B in m. 24. Example 25-14 shows a textural reduction of the first four chords—the three-chord model and the first chord of the next sequential group—showing the basic voice leading.

Example 25-14   Rimsky-Korsakov, *Scheherezade* (textural reduction)

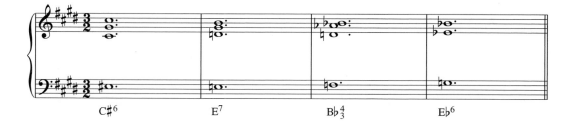

C♯⁶   E⁷   B♭⁴₃   E♭⁶

Looking back at Examples 25-7, we can see that the first three chords of Rimsky-Korsakov's progression are chromatic-mediant related (by m3). Rimsky-Korsakov is exploiting the close voice-leading connection between dominant seventh chords a m3 or tritone apart to make the nontraditional harmonic progression—and the whole-step tonicizations

C#-E♭-F-G-A—more convincing. The first and second chords in the sequential model would have been even more smoothly connected if the first chord had contained a seventh, but the first chord needs to be a triad because it serves as both the beginning of the model and as a temporary harmonic goal. For example, E♭^{6} both begins the next sequential group (transposed up a step) and resolves the preceding B♭$^4_3$.

A number of nineteenth-century composers were also drawn to the possibility of harmonizing a *non-functional* chromatic bass line using familiar chord types. One such harmonization, called the **omnibus,** is shown in Example 25-15.

Example 25-15   Omnibus

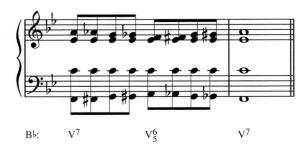

B♭:   V^7 V$^6_5$ V^7

Like the *Tristan und Isolde* excerpt, the omnibus progression features voice exchange—in this case between the bass and soprano, with the root and the third of the V^7 chord trading places *via* chromatic stepwise lines. Although it would be possible to analyze each of the chords between V^7 and V$^6_5$ as tonicizations of c minor (Ger^{+6}-i$^6_4$-Ger^{+6} in that key), the rapid tempo at which such passages are normally performed will more likely suggest extended V^7 harmony with chromatic passing tones in the bass and soprano.

An example of this basic omnibus progression can be found in the Sonata in A minor by Schubert, where it occurs as part of the transition leading to the second theme in C major (see Example 25-16).

DISC 2 : TRACK 55

Example 25-16   Schubert, Piano Sonata in A minor, D 845, I

By shifting between pairs of voices moving in contrary motion, it is possible to extend this progression to harmonize longer chromatic ascents or descents. Example 25-17 illustrates one version of this extended omnibus harmonization of a descending chromatic bass; it cycles through the first three chords of 25-15 (^{7}, $^4_2$, m) in reverse order (m, $^4_2$, ^{7}) in a systematic manner.

Example 25-17   Extended Omnibus

Notice that each upper voice in turn moves in contrary motion to the bass before repeating the process. Notice also that each minor triad bears a chromatic mediant relationship to the minor triads before and after it. This extended omnibus progression is useful for modulating quickly and smoothly to these m3-related keys.

An example of an omnibus progression being used to modulate from G major to D♭ major is found in Example 25-18. This excerpt begins in E♭ major with a root-position tonic chord. The addition of a C♯ creates a German-sixth sonority that leads to G major (I$^6_4$) in m. 12. In the following measure, the omnibus progression begins—with the bass-soprano pair B-D expanding outward by half step until it arrives on a D♭ sonority in m. 16, clearly suggesting D♭ as the new tonic.

Example 25-18   R. Strauss, *"Allerseelen,"* op. 10, no. 8

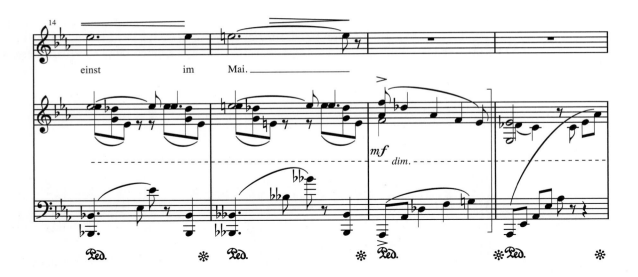

einst   im   Mai.

The preceding examples and techniques indicate some of the many ways that nineteenth-century composers systematically explored the chromatic collection. They may often be effectively combined; for example, Chopin's well-known Prelude in C minor contains a stepwise harmonization of a bass line that descends chromatically from Î down to Ŝ; the resulting progression is a fascinating hybrid of nontraditional harmonic progression—created by moving only one or two chord tones at a time—and the traditional Baroque "chaconne" bass. Many other possibilities exist, and you should feel free to design your own such techniques in your compositions.

Self-Test 25-1

(Answers begin on page 633.)

A. Total voice-leading distance. You are given several paris of chords. For each pair:

  1. Label the chords using lead-sheet and bass-position symbols (ex.: F#°$_3^4$).

  2. Indicate the distance between roots by interval (ex: m3). Use the simplest enharmonic interval.

  3. Calculate the total voice-leading distance between each pair of chords in half steps.

Chord: ____ ____ ____ ____ ____ ____ ____ ____ ____ ____ ____ ____

Root int.: ____   ____   ____   ____   ____   ____

Total dist.: ____   ____   ____   ____   ____   ____

Which chord pair(s) above are in a chromatic mediant relationship?

_____

Which chord pair(s) above are in a doubly chromatic mediant relationship?

_____

B. Mediant relationship of triads. You are given a triad built on F. Show all triads, above and below, that illustrate the following:

1. Chromatic mediant relationship (one common tone with one chromatic alteration)

2. Double chromatic relationship (no common tones, two chromatic alterations)

C. Play through and/or listen to this excerpt from Brahms's Rhapsody op. 79, no. 1 and answer the following questions.

1. What key is being suggested in the first phrase of the excerpt? _____

2. Locate an augmented sixth in the composition. _____

3. There are four modulations in this example. (Treat m. 158 as a temporary change of mode instead of a modulation.) Identify the keys involved, the measures where these modulations take place, and the type of modulation used in each case (review Chapters 18, 19, and 25). _____

_____

_____

4. How would you describe the overall pattern of these modulations? _____

_____

5. How would you explain the chord in m. 151, beat 3? _____

_____

6. How would you explain the chord in m. 162, beats 3–4? _____

_____

Brahms, *Rhapsody* op. 79, no. 1

D. Harmonic and melodic procedures. The Prelude by Scriabin, though brief, illustrates some interesting departures from tradition. Play through the piece and answer the following questions:

1. What is the overall key of the piece? _____

2. In what way does the opening melody obscure this key? _____
_____
_____

3. Show roman-numeral analysis for mm. 4 to 6. _____ /
_____ / _____

4. Mm. 7 to 8 contain two somewhat deceptive progressions. Where do these occur?
_____ and _____

5. Locate an augmented sixth chord in the composition. _____

6. What is unusual about the end of the piece? _____
_____
_____

DISC 2 : TRACK 57

Scriabin, Prelude op. 16, no. 4

E. Given the following pairs of chords, notate the inversion of the second chord that connects most smoothly with the first chord as given. Indicate the total voice-leading distance in the space provided. Ignore traditional resolutions (leading tones, sevenths, etc.). There may be more than one right answer.

dist. _____   _____   _____   _____   _____   _____   _____   _____

F. Chromatic sequence. Analyze the following chromatic sequences, then continue each as indicated.

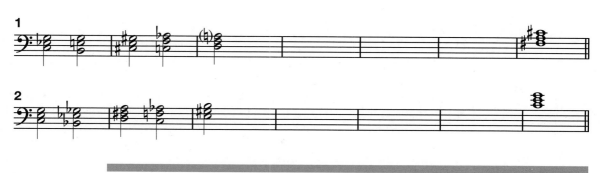

Exercise 25-1 See Workbook.

Summary

It is possible to identify a number of trends that arose during the last decades of the nineteenth century and the first decades of the twentieth century. In general, we can describe this as a time in which there was significant interest in exploring the entire collection of chromatic pitches and tonal regions, even as certain other features—such as an emphasis on smooth connection between harmonies and the use of traditional chord types—were often retained. Consequently, there was a resurgence of interest in contrapuntal manipulation, particularly as a means of obscuring harmonic rhythm and tonality or developing new kinds of chromatic chord successions. Mediant relationships of all kinds were particularly suitable for this treatment, due to their potential for smooth voice-leading connection; composers also experimented with using chains of mediant progressions to exploit its symmetrical division of the octave and to move away from traditional, circle-of-fifths harmonic logic. Chromatic sequences, omnibus progressions, and other systematic techniques proved to be useful in creating relationships between seemingly disparate musical elements, embellishing otherwise conventional relationships, or, in some cases, as a means of prolonging a single tonality. Composers began to lead toward less-traditional key associations and harmonic progressions. The means for establishing a key became more varied as dominant-tonic cadences became less frequent and chords were employed for their coloristic qualities rather than for their established functional roles. Pieces were often not as tightly controlled by a single key as an organizing force. All of these trends represent significant—but not complete—departures from earlier tonal practices.

Chapter Twenty-Six
Materials and Techniques

Introduction

As the traditional tonal system was being stretched to its limits, composers became increasingly aware of the growing need for alternative means of musical organization and for a vocabulary that would adequately deal with new methods and concepts. Basic elements that seemed to lend themselves to significant modification included scale, chord structure, harmonic succession, rhythm and meter, and overall musical texture. The early experiments that took place seemed to lead along two somewhat different paths: one, an extension of the principles of ultrachromaticism; the other, a reaction against chromatic excess. The former path may be seen to have culminated in the development of the twelve-tone system, whereas the latter caused many composers to investigate the pre-tonal era, along with folk music, as a source of materials. Increasingly, many of today's musicians are turning to non-Western musics as a source of fresh ideas.

Throughout the unfolding of the twentieth century, we can see each of these paths branching off in various directions, creating a vast array of musical styles, philosophies, and practices. In some instances, one may observe the inexorable overlapping of seemingly disparate patterns of musical thought. In others, particularly the realm of jazz, pop, film, and commercial music, we note a continued reliance on principles of tonality. Worthy of note is the relative speed with which this expansion has taken place, especially in comparison with the time span from c. 1650 to 1900, sometimes referred to as the common-practice period, during which Western music composition was based on the principles of tonal harmony.

The richness and diversity of today's musical experience present problems for any musician attempting to synthesize, codify, or define the prevailing trends in twentieth-century music, even from the vantage point of a new millennium. The next three chapters will provide an overview, not only of certain historically significant events that ultimately brought about today's cultural environment, but also of twentieth-century materials, techniques, and practice. In this way it may serve as a reference for continued study and analysis.

Impressionism

The term **impressionism** was first applied to a style of painting that sprang up in France in the late nineteenth century, and is most often associated with the work of Claude Monet (1840–1926) and his contemporaries. The primary aim of the artist was that of evoking a certain mood or atmosphere, using light and color in nontraditional ways. This concept was reflected in music by a turning away from more orderly formal procedures of the late eighteenth and early nineteenth centuries and a fascination with *color,* as expressed through harmony, instrumentation, and the use of rhythm.

Claude Debussy (1862–1918) is considered by many to have made some of the most significant contributions to the evolution of early-twentieth-century musical thinking. His compositional style reveals departures from previous practices that, though easily accessible to the tonally oriented ear, clearly defy traditional tonal expectations. Most noteworthy among these departures are his innovative use of new scale materials and chord structures, features that will be illustrated in the following example and subsequent illustrations.

You will notice the clear suggestion of G♭ major in Example 26-1.

Example 26-1   Debussy, "La Fille aux cheveux de lin," from *Preludes,* Book I

But notice, too, the nontraditional procedures he employs.

1. The opening two measures outline an E♭m7 chord, whose function is far from obvious.

2. The first cadence (mm. 2–3) is plagal and thus avoids functional use of the leading tone.

3. The progression beginning in m. 5, with its predominance of mediant relationships, serves to render the G♭ tone center still more elusive.

In general, some of the most revealing aspects of early twentieth-century music may be discovered through an examination of the treatment of tonality. The analyst should ask the following questions: Does the piece seem to have a tone center (or centers)? If so, how is it accomplished? If not, how is it avoided? The answers to these questions will do a great deal to shed light on a composer's style and musical inclinations.

Scale Materials

THE DIATONIC MODES

One reaction to the chromatic saturation of the late nineteenth century was a renewed interest in the **diatonic modes.** The simplest way to represent each of the modes is by using the tones of the C major scale, but with a tone other than C serving as the tone center for each mode. The seven modes of C major are shown in Example 26-2.

Example 26-2

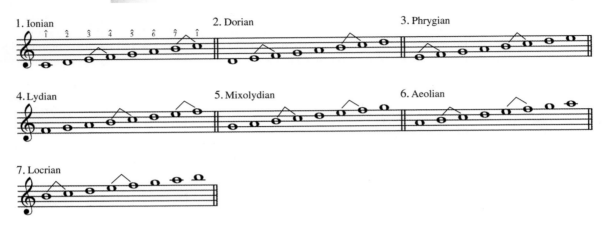

These seven modes can be transposed to any of the 12 major keys. As you will see in Examples 26-3 and 26-4, modal scales can be notated either using a referential major key signature or by adding accidentals. The diatonic modes are commonly identified by tone center and mode name. For example, the modes in Example 26-2 are referred to as 1. C-Ionian, 2. D-Dorian, 3. E-Phrygian, 4. F-Lydian, 5. G-Mixolydian, 6. A-Aeolian, and 7. B-Locrian. Like the major and minor scale formations discussed in Chapter 1, each mode has a distinctive arrangement of whole steps and half steps. In Example 26-2, the half steps have been marked. Note how the location of the half steps with respect to the mode's tone center is different for each mode.

If we compare the modes directly to major and minor scales (Ex. 26-3), we find that the Ionian and Aeolian modes are identical to the major and natural minor scales, respectively, and that the remaining modes (except Locrian) may be likened either to a major scale or to a natural minor scale with one alteration. In this regard, compare the Locrian and Phrygian modes. This method of identification has the advantage of providing an aural description that is clearly related to familiar scales.

Example 26-3

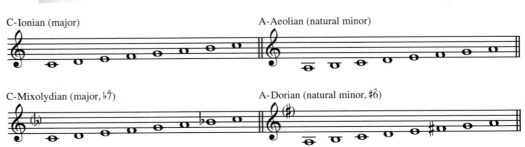

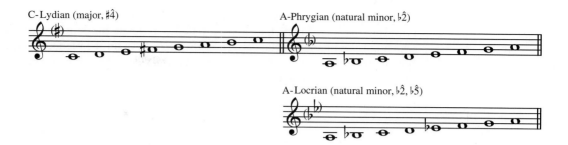

The Locrian mode, which requires two accidentals compared to natural minor, lacks a true dominant chord. Although it is rarely encountered in the music of Debussy and other French impressionist composers, it is commonly employed by jazz performers as a basic structure for improvisation.

The modes may also be arranged as shown next, in decreasing relative order of "brightness," that is, according to the number of major or augmented intervals above the mode's tone center. To facilitate comparison, each mode in Example 26-4 is built on C.

Example 26-4

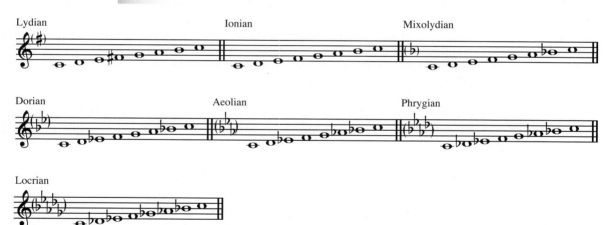

PENTATONIC SCALES

Five-note scales have played a significant role in music, particularly non-Western music, for centuries. The term *pentatonic* literally denotes any five-note scale. Example 26-5 shows three **pentatonic scales** that are encountered in the literature.

Example 26-5

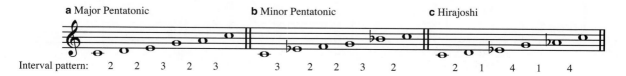

All three pitch collections may be viewed as subsets of a diatonic scale. You will notice, however, that there are no half steps or tritones in the **major pentatonic scale** (Ex. 26-5a), which may be likened to the pattern of the black keys on the piano. By means of reiteration, metric accent, and so forth, any one of its tones may be made to serve as a tone center. The five modes based on C major pentatonic are shown in Example 26-6.

Example 26-6

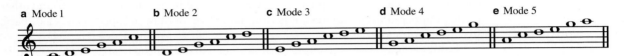

The effect of the major pentatonic scale is likely to be harmonically static, particularly if its use is prolonged. For this reason a composer will seldom use the scale as the basis for a composition of any length. Also shown in Example 26-5 are the **minor pentatonic scale** (Ex. 26-5b) and **Hirajoshi scale** (Ex. 26-5c). Notice that the minor pentatonic scale is equivalent to Mode 5 of the major pentatonic scale (Ex. 26-6e). This may be determined by comparing the interval patterns of the two scales. The interval pattern of a scale lists its adjacent intervals in left-to-right order using semitones as shown in Example 26-5.

If you refer back to Example 26-1, you will notice that with the exception of the passing F in m. 3, the melody of the first six measures is based entirely on the **black-key pentatonic scale.** A somewhat more sophisticated use may be observed in Example 26-7.

Example 26-7   Debussy, "Nuages," from *Nocturnes* (piano reduction)

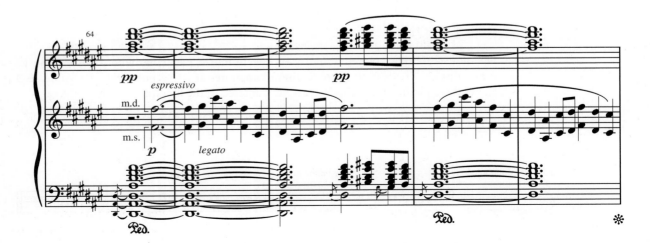

The pentatonic melody in mm. 64 to 70 centers around F♯ and is harmonized by a minor triad built on D♯ and a major triad built on G♯. To the traditional ear, this might possibly suggest ii–V in C♯ major or perhaps i–IV in a D♯-Dorian mode. At no point in the passage, however, is either C♯ or D♯ permitted to function decisively as a tone center.

SYNTHETIC SCALES

The pitch collections we have discussed so far bear a clear resemblance to scales or fragments of scales associated with the diatonic system. Composers have also, however, made extensive use of **synthetic scales.** The available variety of synthetic scales is limited only by the composer's imagination. Three collections that are interesting because of their symmetrical structure are shown in Example 26-8.

Example 26-8

One of the most prominent of these, the **whole-tone scale** (Ex. 26-8a), composed entirely of adjacent major 2nds, was a favorite of Debussy's. This scale is derived from the juxtaposition of two augmented triads at the interval of a whole step and is used by Debussy in his piano prelude "Voiles," the closing section of which appears in Example 26-9. Note that this prelude is composed in ABA structure. The A sections are based on the whole-tone scale, whereas the B section is based exclusively on the black-key pentatonic scale. Note the use of enharmonically equivalent spellings, such as G♯ and A♭ in mm. 58–59, and the pedal B♭ in mm. 58–61 that serves as a unifying element throughout the A and B sections of the prelude.

DISC 2 : TRACK 59

Example 26-9   Debussy, "Voiles," from *Preludes*, Book I

Like the major pentatonic scale, the whole-tone scale possesses several structural limitations because it contains basically only three intervals: the major 2nd, the major 3rd, and the tritone (along with their inversions). Its symmetry and its total lack of perfect intervals (and hence of major and minor triads) bestows on it an elusive, tonally ambiguous quality that has proved attractive to many composers. The augmented triad is, in fact, the only tertian triad possible within this pitch collection.

The vertical sonorities that may result from whole-tone simultaneities are often referred to as **whole-tone chords.** Some whole-tone chords have traditional tonal implications. For example, an incomplete dominant seventh chord (fifth omitted) and a Fr^{+6} chord may be derived from the whole-tone collection.

Like the whole-tone scale, the **octatonic scale** is derived from the juxtaposition of two traditional tonal sonorities. As shown by the brackets in Example 26-8b, it is derived from two diminished seventh chords at the interval of a half step (or whole step).

Its interval pattern may be viewed as a repeated series of half-whole or whole-half successions. Notice that whether we begin on C (C–D♭–E♭–E–F♯–G–A–B♭) or D♭ (D♭–E♭–E–F♯–G–A–B♭–C) the same collection of eight tones results. In addition to the two diminished seventh chords, a variety of other tonal sonorities may be derived from its tones, including three of the four traditional triad types. Using lead-sheet symbols to describe triads built on a root C, we find Cdim, Cm, and C. We may also find the following seventh chords built on C: Cdim7, Cm7, Cm7♭5, and C7. Due to the symmetrical nature of this scale, any sonority found among its tones will be reproduced three, six, and nine semitones higher. For example, in addition to the Cdim, Cm, and C triads found in Example 26-8b, we also find the following triads: E♭dim, E♭m, E♭, F♯dim, F♯m, F♯, Adim, Am, and A. This scale, frequently employed by composers from the Russian Five, was also of interest to Scriabin, Stravinsky, Bartók, Debussy, Messiaen, and countless jazz composers.

The **hexatonic scale** is a six-note collection derived from the juxtaposition of two augmented triads at the interval of a half step. Shown in Example 26-8c, the vertical sonorities that may be derived from it show some resemblance to the whole-tone chords discussed earlier, yet the half step interval creates a number of additional melodic and harmonic possibilities, including major and minor triads. Its interval pattern may be viewed as a repeated series of half-step/minor third or minor third/half-step successions.

A scale that Debussy particularly favored is the **Lydian-Mixolydian scale,** or ♯4̂/♭7̂ scale. The seven modes of the Lydian-Mixolydian scale are shown in Example 26-10. This hybrid scale may well have resulted from the juxtaposition of two major-minor seventh chords with roots a whole step apart, as indicated by the brackets in Example 26-10a.

Example 26-10

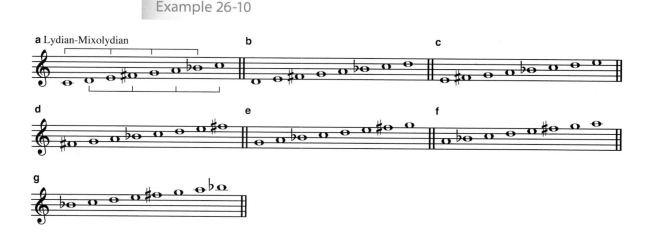

You will notice, given the presence of both B♭ and F♯, that it would be impossible to realize this scalar pattern using only the white keys of the piano. Just as each of the diatonic modes possesses unique color characteristics, the scale discussed previously may be made to sound quite different when different scale tones are allowed to serve as tone centers. For example, beginning on D will result in a major scale with a ♭6̂ and ♭7̂ (Ex. 26-10b). Likewise, beginning on A will yield a Phrygian-Dorian pattern, a natural minor scale with a ♭2̂ and ♯6̂ (Ex. 26-10f). When G is used, an ascending melodic minor scale is created (Ex. 26-10e).

When we start this scale on the note B♭, the resulting pattern begins with five notes in whole-tone relationship to one another (Ex. 26-10g).

Example 26-11 provides an interesting and highly contrapuntal illustration of this scale as it occurs in Stravinsky's ballet *Petrouchka*. Although the piano reduction used here does not permit us to view individual lines, it nonetheless demonstrates the density of the passage. Using C, the lowest pitch, as a reference point, we discover the excerpt to be based on a ♯$\hat{4}$/♭$\hat{7}$ scale (C–D–E–F♯–G–A–B♭); yet at no point is the ear permitted to accept C as a tone center.

Example 26-11   Stravinsky, "Danse Russe," from *Petrouchka* (piano reduction)

The opening four measures of Example 26-12 make use of all 12 members of the chromatic scale.

Example 26-12   Kennan, Prelude no. 1

Although the pedal F in the left hand is obviously an important referential point, the simultaneities formed by the moving chromatic lines do not seem to confirm F as a tonal center. Such chromatic saturation becomes increasingly commonplace as the twentieth century progresses, and eventually leads to the development of dodecaphonic music, music composed using the twelve-tone method, which will be discussed in the next chapter.

Self-Test 26-1

(Answers begin on page 635.)

A. Scale characteristics.

1. Which three of the diatonic modes are essentially major in quality?

_____ , _____ , and _____

2. Which two of the seven diatonic modes begin with a minor second?

_____ and _____

3. Name two six-note symmetrical scales and the derivation of each.

_____ and _____

Derivation: _____

4. What scale is created by the juxtaposition of two major-minor seventh chords whose roots are one whole step apart?

_____

5. What traditional seventh chord type forms the basis for derivation of the octatonic scale? _____

6. Three of the four traditional triad types may be derived from the octatonic scale. They are _____ , _____ , and _____

7. When compared with the diatonic scale, what two intervals are missing from the major pentatonic scale?

_____ and _____

B. Add the appropriate accidentals to create the type of scale asked for.

C. Scale transposition.

1. Taking the major pentatonic pattern C–D–E–G–A as a model, transpose the collection so that it will begin, respectively, on each of the pitches indicated.

2. Which of the preceding three transposed patterns represents the black-key pentatonic collection? _____

3. Notate whole-tone scales starting on each of the following pitches (remembering that it is permissible to mix sharps and flats).

4. Using a key signature (rather than appropriate accidentals), notate the following modal scales in the clef indicated.

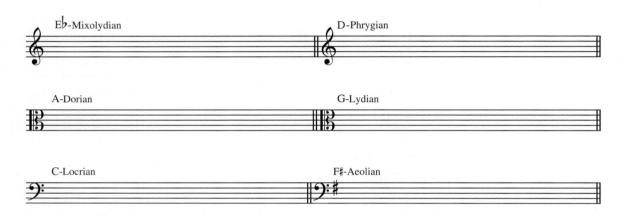

E♭-Mixolydian

D-Phrygian

A-Dorian

G-Lydian

C-Locrian

F♯-Aeolian

D. Identify the scale that forms the basis of each of the following melodies:

Exercise 26-1   See Workbook.

Chord Structures

EXTENDED TERTIAN HARMONY

You will recall the discussion in Chapter 24 regarding the occasional use of ninth chords in tonal music. In most cases, these sonorities represent dominant function, with the ninth often treated as a nonchord tone and resolving down by step. Functional dominant ninth chords, although far less common than dominant seventh chords, may be found in the music of such composers as Schumann, Chopin, and Beethoven. Eleventh and thirteenth chords, on the other hand, were rarely encountered prior to the twentieth century. For that reason, the increased use of ninth, eleventh, and thirteenth chords on the part of some twentieth-century composers represents an obvious extension of the post-Romantic tradition of tertian harmony. These chords may occur in both functional and nonfunctional settings.

Example 26-13, by Ravel, illustrates a coloristic use of **extended tertian sonorities,** or tall chords, in the sense that traditional rules of resolution fail to apply. Notice the clear sense of root movement in mm. 1 to 2 (indicated in the analysis) as well as the meticulous attention to voice leading. The texture of the succeeding measures (mm. 3–5) continues to employ tall sonorities, created through the scalewise motion of the bass line. The effect of this passage is to prolong the sense of C as a tone center until the music slips unobtrusively into G in mm. 6–7 of the excerpt, by returning to a functional bass line.

DISC 2 : TRACK 60

Example 26-13   Ravel, "Rigaudon," from *Le Tombeau de Couperin*

As has been noted in Chapter 24, extended tertian sonorities are created through the stacking of major and minor 3rds. Frequently, a composer may choose to omit those chord members that create dissonance, such as the chord 5th (for example), which creates a dissonance when heard against the chord 11th. Chord members that are found in the lower part of a harmonic series (see pp. 91–92) with the root as a fundamental are also frequently omitted. Depending on the context, such omissions may tend to alter the listener's perception of the basic chord structure. Play the three chords of Example 26-14.

Example 26-14

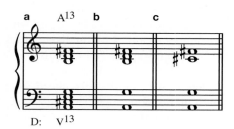

Example 26-14a is clearly a thirteenth chord. If we interpret the root A as being a dominant, we can see that all pitches of the D major scale are being sounded. The omission of the 3rd and 5th of the chord, as shown in Example 26-14b, does little to alter our perception of the sonority, because both are prominent members of the root A2's harmonic series. In Example 26-14c, however, when we systematically displace the 3rd by an octave and omit the 5th, 9th, and 11th, we might interpret the sonority as a $V^{7\text{subs}}_{6\text{th}}$ (a chord introduced in Chapter 24), or we might hear the F♯ as a nonchord tone. The "correct" interpretation is obviously dependent to a large extent on the voice leading of the example, as well as the context in which the chord occurs.

The lead-sheet symbols associated with common triads, seventh chords, and the added sixth chord (as in C6) were introduced in Chapter 3. Chapter 11 added the "sus" symbol (as in C7sus). Lead-sheet symbols can also be used to identify the ninth, eleventh, and thirteenth chords introduced in Chapter 24. Appendix B, "Lead-Sheet Symbols," lists chords commonly encountered in jazz, popular, and twentieth-century classical music. Take a moment to familiarize yourself with this appendix because we will be using these symbols in the pages that follow.

POLYHARMONY

A **polychord** consists of two or more chords from different harmonic areas, sounded simultaneously. The components of a polychord are called **chordal units.** A variety of polychords may be built from superimposed triads, seventh chords, and other tertian sonorities. As shown in Example 26-15, lead-sheet symbols can be used to identify the chordal units of polychords, which may be separated either by a "_" (when written vertically) or by a "/" symbol (when written horizontally).

Example 26-15

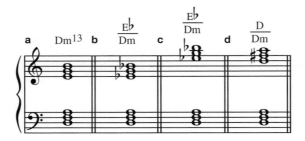

In Example 26-15a the diatonic relationship of the pitches might well suggest a thirteenth chord. Example 26-15b might still be perceived as a Dm chord with upper extensions, but the chromatic inflection of the upper triad is far more likely to suggest two independent triads (Dm and E♭) with their roots a m9 apart. This effect is greatly enhanced by the octave displacement and chordal spacing shown in Example 26-15c. The sonority occurring in Example 26-15d is often referred to as a **split-third chord,** because it represents both major and minor qualities built on the same root. Although it might seem reasonable to refer here to a "major/minor" chord, the similarity of this term to that used for the major-minor seventh chord could be somewhat confusing.

Now play Example 26-16, which is polychordal.

Example 26-16

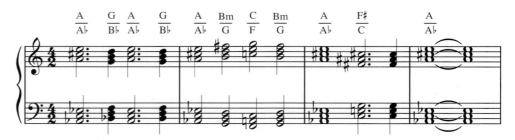

Notice the contrary motion in the voice leading and sharp dissonance created by (1) polychords whose chordal units have roots a half step or tritone apart and (2) polychords containing even a single contrasting chromatic inflection, such as G/B♭, in contrast to pairs of chords that may be found in the same key signature, such as C/F or Bm/G.

Example 26-17 is taken from *Four Sketches for Piano,* by Darius Milhaud, a prominent member of a group of French composers known as Les Six, whose members included, among others, Francis Poulenc and Arthur Honegger. The excerpt begins at m. 43 with a somewhat angular melody presented in widely spaced parallel minor thirds. The following two measures make use of a split-third chord (Fm against A♮ in the left hand) in a passage that remains tonally ambiguous. Although G major is implied in the following three measures, the shifting accidentals in the right hand strongly suggest B major (m. 46) followed by D major (m. 47), creating fleeting moments of dissonance that are typical of Milhaud's writing. Also worthy of mention are the careful voice leading and the use of parallel thirds and triads in the right hand part. We will see more extensive use of this technique later in this chapter.

Example 26-17   Milhaud, "Eglogue," *Four Sketches for Piano*

When two or more key centers are heard at the same time—which occurs considerably less frequently than polychordality—we may refer to **bitonality** or **polytonality.** For the listener to perceive a duality of tone center, it is necessary for the voice leading and melodic motion of each voice to be relatively independent. Bitonality is suggested in Example 26-18, in which we find two pentatonic lines presented in imitation.

Example 26-18   Bartók, "Playsong," *Mikrokosmos* no. 105

The overall aural impression is that of tonal ambiguity produced by imitative two-voice counterpoint. Finally, note the differing key signatures, a common feature of both bi-modal and bitonal passages. Although composers sometimes create meaningful sonorities from three or more chordal units, it is unlikely that three independent and simultaneous tone centers would be perceived by even the most astute listener.

CHORD/SCALE CONNECTIONS

Whereas in the tonal system the pitches of a tertian triad or seventh chord may be perceived as a discrete and identifiable unit, despite doubling, inversion, chord member omissions, and even the presence of nonchord tones, the aural effect of sonorities in twentieth-century composition is far more dependent on scale reference, doubling, spacing, and arrangement in general.

Example 26-19 shows five possible chords that can be derived from the tones of a major pentatonic scale built on F (F–G–A–C–D). As you play each of the five, you will probably hear in turn:

1. a major triad with added 6th and 9th
2. a stack of perfect 5ths
3. a 4th-rich sonority
4. an implied V^9 with suspension
5. a diatonic tone cluster (chord built from 2nds)

Example 26-19

Chord/scale connections also play a prominent role in jazz theory. *The Jazz Theory Book* by Mark Levine provides a comprehensive introduction to the subject.*

DISC 2 : TRACK 61

Example 26-20   Debussy, "La Cathédrale engloutie," from *Preludes*, Book I

Except for the moving bass line and C♯ in m. 7, the pitches used in Example 26-20 adhere strictly to a major pentatonic scale built on G (G–A–B–D–E).

Profondément calme (Dans une brume doucement sonore)

---

*   Mark Levine, *The Jazz Theory Book* (Petaluma, CA: Sher Music Co., 1995).

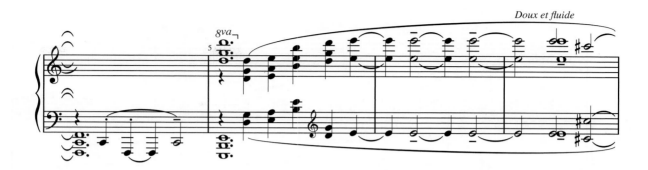

If we view the major pentatonic scale in terms of its derivation from stacked 5ths (G–D–A–E–B), this interdependence of scale and chords seems almost inevitable.

It may well have been the process of experimentation with connections between scale materials and chord structures that suggested to composers the possibility of experimenting with other intervals for constructing chords. As we will see in the next section, the P4 and its inversion, the P5, seem particularly well suited to avoiding any commitment to traditional tonal implications.

QUARTAL AND SECUNDAL HARMONY

A **quartal harmony** is a sonority derived from stacked 4ths, while a **quintal harmony** is a sonority derived from stacked 5ths. Although there is obviously a close relationship between chords built in 4ths and those constructed in 5ths, the aural effect can be quite different because of the inherent dissonance traditionally associated with the perfect fourth. A predominantly quartal harmony may be observed in Example 26-21.

Example 26-21   Hindemith, Flute Sonata, II

The opening measure is essentially derived from the following stacked 4th sonority: G♯–C♯–F♯–B, first heard in an inverted form. Notice, too, the voice leading, which ensures that the P4 sonority is prominently maintained in the right hand of the piano part up until m. 7. You will also perceive that the sense of B as tone center is supported by the bass line, which consists of a descending B-Dorian scale (B–A–G♯–F♯–E–D–C♯–B), as well as frequent reference to F♯ in the flute part and the right hand of the accompaniment.

The term **secundal harmony** is used to refer to a chordal sonority derived from 2nds. The use of 2nds as a method of chord construction also proved attractive to many composers. Example 26-22 illustrates the use of secundal harmony by Ross Lee Finney.

Example 26-22   Finney, from "Playing Tag," from *24 Piano Inventions*

Notice how, in addition to the accentuation and forward motion provided by the secundal chords, the fragmentary melody is based primarily on 2nds.

Any collection of three or more adjacent pitches in secundal relationship may correctly be referred to as a **tone cluster.** The term was coined by the American composer Henry Cowell, whose early experiments called for pianists to play certain passages with fists, palms, and, frequently, the entire forearm. Example 26-23, an excerpt from "The Tides of Manaunaun," illustrates this technique. The sonorities thus created by a simple folk-like melody and the tall tone clusters are powerful and richly programmatic. You will also notice the use of a bitonal key signature.

Example 26-23   Cowell, "The Tides of Manaunaun," from *Tales of Our Countryside*

The concept of **cluster chords,** especially when used in conjunction with the rich timbral palette of an orchestra or chamber group, has continued to prove extremely useful for composers in the latter half of the twentieth century and will be further explored in Chapter 28.

Other Concepts

PARALLELISM

You may have noticed by now that the treatment of texture plays a significant role in our perception of twentieth-century music. The instrumental timbre, the structure of the chords, the doublings, the vertical spacing, the melodic construction, and the method of movement from one musical event to another—all these aspects contribute significantly to our impression of the music as having a tonal center or not.

One of the earliest indications of a break with traditional procedures of harmonic progression was the use of parallelism in the voice motion. In some forms, of course, parallelism has been known before the twentieth century; you have already been exposed to parallel sixth chords in a tonal context, as illustrated in Example 26-24. Although not needed in this particular example, the lead-sheet symbols notated above the staff can prove extremely useful as a means of accurately and succinctly describing **nonfunctional** (and even marginally functional) **harmonic progressions.** Note that in this case, the slash symbol "/" in the lead-sheet symbols is used to indicate particular bass notes, not polychords.

Example 26-24

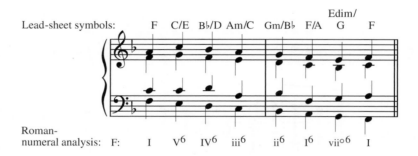

Even in this diatonic, triadic progression, the ear experiences at least a brief period of confusion in the space between the beginning and the ending tonic chords because of the sliding effect produced by parallel movement between the outer voices.

Even more disruptive to our tonal expectations is Debussy's use of parallel movement of inverted major-minor seventh chords, contrasted in the intervening measure with parallel movement of augmented triads (Ex. 26-25). The term **planing,** essentially synonymous with parallelism, is frequently used to describe this device when it occurs in twentieth-century music, usually as a means of obscuring any sense of functional progression. In an example such as this one, you will find lead-sheet analysis (shown above the staff) to be particularly useful in describing the chord succession in m. 61, as well as the alternation of D+ and E+ sonorities in m. 62 (an obvious reference to a whole-tone scale).

Example 26-25   Debussy, "Nuages," from *Nocturnes* (piano reduction)

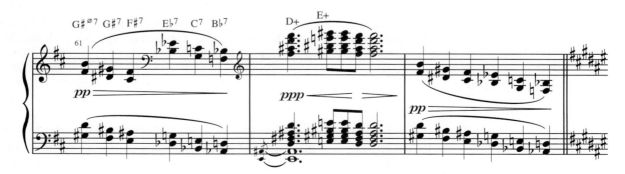

Following the first beat of m. 61, the melody outlines the pitches of a dominant ninth chord on A♭, enharmonically respelled for convenience. The parallelism observed in this example is referred to by some theorists as strict or **real planing,** because the construction of each sonority remains unchanged. Such a passage will inevitably require a substantial number of accidentals. This is because such consistent chord quality does not normally occur within a diatonic key; as a result, the feeling of a tone center will be unclear. In contrast, **diatonic planing** involves parallel movement of vertical sonorities whose quality is determined by the prevailing diatonic scale. Example 26-26 shows the use of diatonic planing to harmonize a chantlike melody.

DISC 2 : TRACK 62

Example 26-26   Debussy, "La Cathédrale engloutie," from *Preludes,* Book I

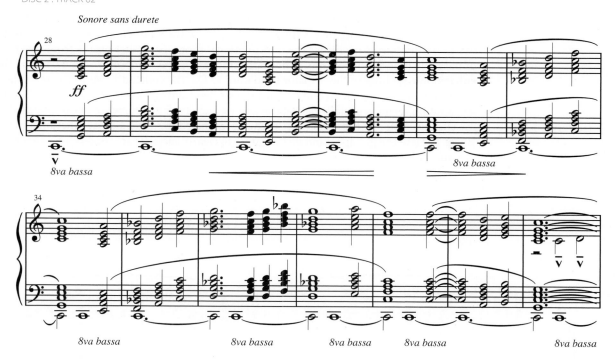

All of the voices move in parallel over a C pedal point. Notice the orchestrational doubling of the right hand by the left hand, often found in the music of French impressionist composers. The extended pedal on C and the rhythmic emphasis on C, E, and G all serve to maintain the sense of C as a tone center. You will notice, however, that B-flat is substituted for B-natural in the melody beginning in m. 33, suggesting a collectional shift from C-Ionian to C-Mixolydian. The C-Ionian collection returns in m. 39 with the reintroduction of the B-natural. Note that Debussy consciously avoids the melodic tritone, a device commonly employed in chant melodies.

We occasionally encounter **mixed planing,** parallel voice motion that can be explained neither by consistency of chord type nor by the limitations of a single scale. Such a passage is shown in Example 26-27.

Example 26-27   Debussy, "Fêtes," from *Nocturnes* (piano reduction)

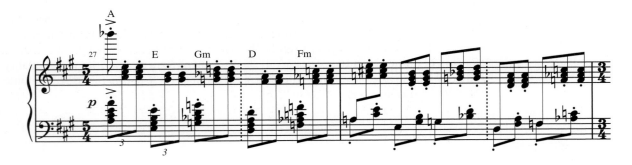

In this case, the composer's aim is harmonization of the descending chromatic line A–G♯–G–F♯–F. This descending line is further enhanced by the secondary line C♯–B–B♭–A–A♭, which harmonizes it in thirds. The nonfunctional progression that results from this type of parallelism is described above the staff using lead-sheet symbols. In m. 27, notice the enharmonic spelling of the A major triad's 3rd as D♭. The concluding A♭ in the secondary line might be considered an enharmonically spelled leading tone in the key of A. This interpretation seems especially plausible when we encounter a recurrence of this material in the closing section of the work (Ex. 26-28), harmonized to sound almost functional in the key of A. Here the juxtaposition of A♭ against B♭ clearly suggests an $^{+}6$, serving as a means of tonicization.

Example 26-28   Debussy, "Fêtes," from *Nocturnes* (piano reduction)

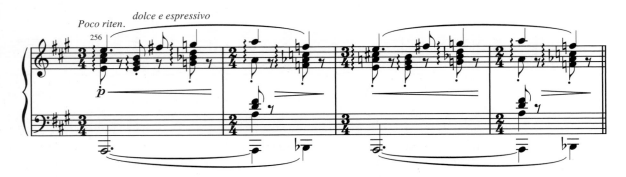

The principle of parallelism may also be applied to other structures, such as quintal and quartal chords, as well as to parallel voice leading of various intervals.

The second movement of Bartók's *Concerto for Orchestra* provides us with a virtual catalogue of planing techniques. The movement opens with a duet for bassoons moving in parallel minor sixths, as illustrated in Example 26-29.

Example 26-29   Bartók, *Concerto for Orchestra*, II (reduction)

This is followed by a passage featuring new melodic material for oboes (Ex. 26-30), moving in parallel thirds (primarily minor thirds, but with the occasional major third appearing).

Example 26-30   Bartók, *Concerto for Orchestra*, II (reduction)

Following a brief transition by the strings, the work continues with other pairs of instruments: clarinets at the m7, flutes at the P5, and trumpets playing in parallel major 2nds.

PANDIATONICISM

The term **pandiatonicism** refers to the attempt to equalize the seven tones of the diatonic scale so that no single pitch is heard as a tone center. A pandiatonic passage may often be identified by the presence of the following characteristics: (1) use of a key signature, (2) absence of accidentals, (3) free use of the seven (or fewer, in some cases) tones of the major scale associated with that key signature, and (4) the absence of functional harmonic movement.

Example 26-31, by Samuel Barber, clearly meets all of these requirements. It uses a key signature of G♭ major, has a marked absence of any accidentals, features the use of all seven tones of the G♭ major scale, and we get no sense of functional harmonic movement as we play or listen to this passage. Though there is some emphasis on G♭ (tonic) in the right hand and D♭ (dominant) in the left hand, the bass alternation of D♭ and E♭, the irregular division of the meter, and the use of nontertian sonorities all contribute to the seeming absence of tonal direction. In looking back at Example 26-13, we might also consider mm. 3 to 5 as a brief pandiatonic passage based on a C major collection.

Example 26-31   Barber, *Excursions*, op. 20, III

The term pandiatonicism is also used by some theorists to refer to the free use of collections, such as the minor scale formations that have essentially been derived from the diatonic scale. For instance, all the pitches in Example 26-32 belong to an ascending melodic minor scale on C (C–D–E♭–F–G–A–B).

Example 26-32   Bartók, "Subject and Reflection," *Mikrokosmos* no. 141

The passage results from the canonic mirroring of two outer voices. Note that the emphasis on D and A in the top voice tends to negate any clear sense of C as a tone center.

Another example of pandiatonicism is shown in Example 26-33. Although the passage is clearly based on an E♭ major collection, no member of that collection is allowed to serve as a tone center. Taken from Stravinsky's ballet *Petrouchka*, the reduction provided here gives some idea of the passage's textural and timbral variety. You may also notice the relationship of the time signature to the subdivisions implied by the various independent lines. The combining of multiple rhythmic streams in this manner will be discussed in the following section on rhythm and meter.

Example 26-33   Stravinsky, "The Masqueraders," from *Petrouchka* (reduction)

Self-Test 26-2

(Answers begin on page 637.)

A. Extended tertian, quartal/quintal, and secundal sonorities

Describe the structure of the chords shown below by providing the correct symbol: use the symbol "Q" for quartal/quintal chords, "S" for secundal chords, and lead-sheet symbols for tertian sonorities and polychords.

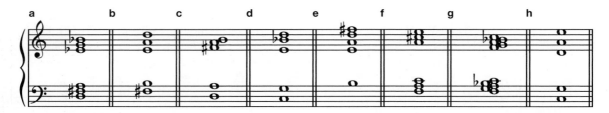

B. Other vertical sonorities

Identify the following sonorities as split-third, whole-tone, or cluster chords.

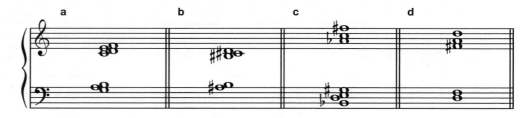

C. Analysis

1. Identify the scale on which the following composition is based.

    _____

2. What is the tonal center at the opening of the piece? _____

    In what measure does it change? _____ To what? _____

3. What technique is used for most of the accompaniment? _____

4. What is the most prominent melodic interval in this composition? _____

DISC 2 : TRACK 63

Payne, *Skipping*

D. Sequence construction

1. Harmonize the following phrase by continuing the parallel motion of dominant ninth chords in the spacing indicated.

2. Now provide a quartal harmonization, again continuing to use the chord structure provided for the first chord.

E. Composition (piano)

Using the following ostinato pattern for the left-hand part in each case, compose one or two brief phrases of music that demonstrate the following techniques:

Example 1: pandiatonicism

Example 2: secundal harmony/tone clusters

Example 3: bitonality

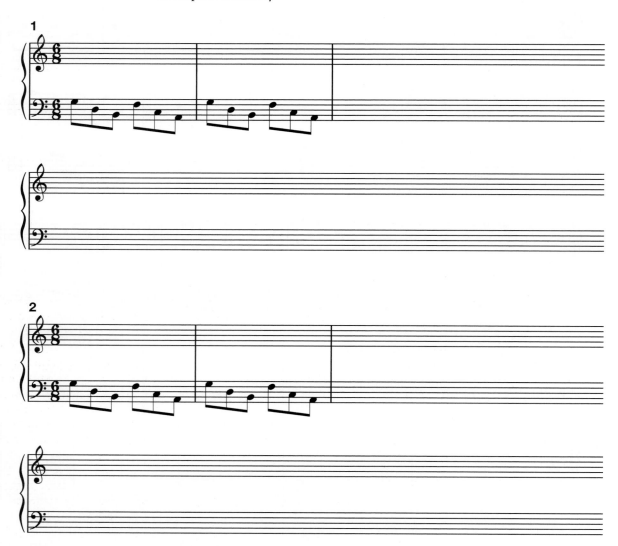

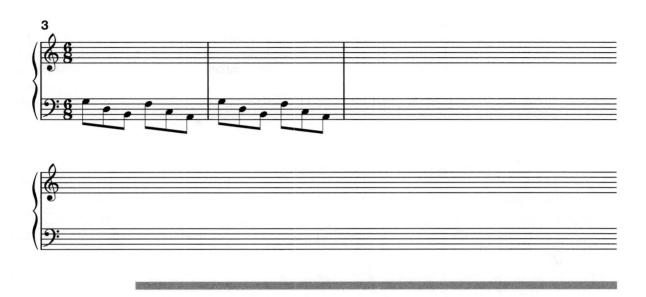

Exercise 26-2 See Workbook.

Rhythm and Meter

Because the study of pitch associations constitutes the primary bulwark of the traditional tonal system, it would seem reasonable that most attempts to establish alternative systems of organization would tend to concentrate on that area. Nonetheless, the mainstream of early twentieth-century composition saw significant innovations in the areas of rhythm and meter, procedures that impart a distinctive twentieth-century flavor to the music involved.

The basic elements of rhythm and meter were introduced in Chapter 2. To briefly summarize, rhythm refers to the time aspect of music. The basic pulse of a musical passage is called the beat, and tempo refers to the rate at which the beat occurs. In traditional meters, beats usually group into regular patterns of two, three, or four beats. Associated with each meter is its own pattern of metric accents, implied groupings based on recurring strong-weak alternation patterns. When a rhythmic figure stresses a normally weak beat, a syncopation is said to occur. Any time-value relationship can be expressed as a ratio, for example, 2:1, 3:1, 3:2, 4:1, 4:2, 4:3, and so forth. One of the most frequently encountered rhythmic devices is **hemiola,** an interaction between rhythm and meter that implies a 3:2 ratio.

In the previous section dealing with pandiatonicism, we saw examples of irregular rhythmic organization. The first occurred in Example 26-31 by Barber in which, despite a meter signature of ¢ (cut time), each measure was clearly subdivided into seven in the time of four (7:4) quarter-note beats. Example 26-33 by Stravinsky featured multiple instrumental lines, each operating with a slightly different temporal organization despite the meter signature of $\frac{5}{8}$. In this particular example, we hear no clear reference beat but rather a shimmering palette of sound.

Composers seemed primarily interested in escaping the established norm of traditional **symmetrical meters,** meters based on regular recurring pulses subdivided into groups of two or three. Various procedures have been employed in an effort to achieve this end, and the results are fascinating. Perhaps the most common of these is the use of an **asymmetrical meter,** such as $\frac{5}{4}$ or $\frac{7}{8}$, or a **composite meter** indicating recurring irregular subdivisions, such as $\frac{3+3+2}{8}$, which we encounter frequently in the music of Bartók. These are used to provide what we might describe as a "regular irregularity" in that the groupings in a $\frac{5}{4}$ piece are likely to occur consistently as either 2+3 or 3+2. Example 26-34 demonstrates some of these concepts.

Example 26-34   Adler, *Capriccio*

Notice how the 2+3 and 3+2 groupings alternate in the right hand mm. 1 to 7. The use of a **dotted bar line,** as shown in Example 26-27 and Example 26-39, is another way to indicate irregular subdivisions of the bar.

A composer may achieve rhythmic irregularity in other ways. Two common devices are the use of **mixed meter** and **displaced accent.** Mixed meter refers to the use of rapidly changing meter signatures as demonstrated in Example 26-34, mm. 8 to 11. Displaced accent is a technique whereby the composer intentionally violates the normal metric accent pattern implied by the meter, shifting the accent to a relatively weak beat as shown next:

Both procedures provide the listener with a sense of intense rhythmic activity coupled with constantly shifting metric accentuation. When the effect on the listener is a lack of any perceived meter created by unequal groupings of subdivisions being added together, the process is sometimes referred to as **additive rhythm.**

The terms **cross rhythm** and **polyrhythm** are used to denote the simultaneous presentation of two or more strikingly contrasted rhythmic streams, as illustrated in the following rhythmic reduction of m. 55 of Barber's *Excursions* (Ex. 26-31):

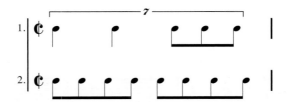

Notice the simultaneous presentation of 1. a rhythm based on a septuplet and 2. a rhythm based on a steady stream of eighth notes.

The term polyrhythm is sometimes confused with another term in common usage, **polymeter.** We use the former to denote the aural phenomenon of simultaneous rhythmic streams and the latter to refer to the notation of two or more meters at once. It is possible for a passage to be polyrhythmic and polymetric at the same time, as shown in Example 26-35.

Example 26-35   Stravinsky, "The Shrovetide Fair," from *Petrouchka*
                  (piano reduction)

Again, the effect of this passage on the listener may imply a total lack of a perceived meter. Instead, one is aware of a constant triplet background against which seemingly spontaneous bursts of rhythmic activity occur. You should keep in mind that *Petrouchka,* which we most often hear performed in the concert hall, was first composed as a ballet score. In this particular scene, the conflicting musical events represent specific contrasting actions taking place on the stage.

Music that lacks an aurally perceivable meter is called **ametric music.** Although Example 26-36 employs a traditional time signature, it does not seem to imply a regular series of recurring pulses and thus may be described as ametric.

Example 26-36   Varèse, *Density 21.5*

It should also be mentioned that the elimination of bar lines and time signatures is a notational device commonly associated with the creation of ametric music.

The term **tempo modulation** (also called **metric modulation**) is used to describe an immediate change in tempo created by equating a particular note value to another note value, a proportional note value, usually located in the next bar. A simple example of this procedure follows:

This procedure, which bears some resemblance to the common-chord modulation procedure discussed in Chapter 18, is associated with the music of Elliott Carter. An example from the second movement of Carter's Second String Quartet is shown in Example 26-37.

Example 26-37   Carter, String Quartet no. 2, II

In his book *The Technique of My Musical Language*, Olivier Messiaen used the term **added value** to describe a process by which rhythmic irregularity is created through the addition of a note value or rest to a rhythmic figure. The addition of a note value (indicated by a '+' in the following example) may be accomplished through the addition of a dot or tie, or through a change in note duration. For example, consider the following rhythm:

This figure might be transformed in any of the following ways, to mention but a few of what are almost limitless possibilities:

Example 26-38 shows the principles of added value in operation.

Example 26-38   Messiaen, "Dance of Fury for Seven Trumpets," from *Quartet for the End of Time*

Messiaen himself admitted to a fondness for the subtleties of Indian rhythms, and we see abundant evidence of this in his music. He particularly prized what he referred to in his book as "the charm of impossibilities," as represented by **nonretrogradable rhythms.** Nonretrogradable rhythms are the same whether played forward or backward. They are, in essence, rhythmic palindromes. For example, the following rhythm is nonretrogradable:

Note that the preceding rhythmic figure is symmetrical about the central quarter note value. Returning to Example 26-38, we see that the first bar, with the exception of the last quarter note value, provides an interesting example of a nonretrogradable rhythm in operation, the rhythmic figure:

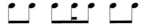

The **Fibonacci sequence,** an infinite sequence of numbers (for example: 1, 1, 2, 3, 5, 8, 13, 21, 34, 55, 89, etc.) in which each new number in the sequence is the sum of the previous two numbers, has been a source of rhythmic inspiration for many twentieth-century composers. The consecutive ratios implied by this sequence (for example: 3:2, 5:3, 8:5, 13:8, 21:13, etc.) approach the **golden ratio** (ca. 1.618:1). This proportion is found throughout nature and has been associated with proportional balance in art and architecture since its discovery by ancient Greek mathematicians. In the first movement of *Music for String Instruments, Percussion, and Celeste,* Bartók uses Fibonacci numbers to determine the measure in which important events begin. He also uses the golden ratio to determine where to place the climax of the work, a point approximately .618 of the way through the piece, as well as to determine the length of smaller formal divisions of the work. Bartók has also been known to use Fibonacci numbers to determine the number of notes in a phrase, as illustrated in the first two measures of Example 26-39.

Example 26-39   Bartók, *Music for String Instruments, Percussion, and Celeste,* I

The term **polytempo** is similar to polymeter in that it refers to the simultaneous use of two or more strikingly contrasted tempos. One of the earliest examples of this device, dating from the first decade of the twentieth century, may be found in *The Unanswered Question* by Charles Ives, shown in Example 26-40.

Example 26-40   Ives, *The Unanswered Question*

Over the course of this programmatic work for solo trumpet, four flutes, and offstage strings (also note the alternative scoring indicated by Ives), the trumpet intones its theme (mm. 48–49) seven times against the soft, sustained, slowing moving diatonic materials in the strings. Ives characterized the trumpet theme as symbolizing the "perennial question of existence" and the strings as symbolizing the "silence of the druids." The strings and rhythmically disconnected trumpet part are presented at a constant tempo of ♩ = 50. The flutes answer each statement of the trumpet's "question" with highly chromatic reinterpretations of the theme at increasing dynamic levels and tempos.

In the second half of the twentieth century, composers continued to expand the palette of available rhythmic resources. In a series of over 50 *Studies for Player Piano,* which the composer created by hand punching holes in player piano rolls, Conlon Nancarrow explored a wide variety of polytempo relations. The opening of Study No. 2a is shown in Example 26-41.

Example 26-41   Nancarrow, *Studies for Player Piano No. 2a*

Each voice in this two-voice texture is an **ostinato,** a musical pattern that is repeated many times in succession. Notated in ¾ time at a tempo of ♩ = 69, the top ostinato states a two-note pitch motive (A♭–D♭). The bottom ostinato, which is notated in ⅝ time at a tempo of ♪ = 115, simultaneously states a four-note pitch motive (F–G–B♭–D). The bottom ostinato uses a rhythmic procedure called **isorhythm,** a modern term for a rhythmic technique associated with Medieval motets and masses. In twentieth-century music, an isorhythm typically consists of a repeated rhythmic figure, called the **talea** (after Medieval theory) in combination with a repeated pitch sequence of a different length, called the **color.** In Example 26-41, the *talea* is

and the *color* is F–G–B♭–D. Notice that the isorhythmic process reaches its natural completion in m. 4. The proportion associated with the polytempo relation in Example 26-41 might be described as 6 against 5, or 6:5.

A number of Nancarrow's player piano studies are **tempo canons,** canons in which the individual voices are presented at different tempos. In Nancarrow's Study No. 32, for example, the tempo ratios between the four canonic voices are 5:6:7:8. The term **mechanical rhythm,** a rhythm that requires a machine for precise execution, is implicit in Nancarrow's music for the player piano. The rhythmic ideas that can be expressed by machines can reach breathtaking levels of complexity. For example, Nancarrow explores the irrational tempo relationships $\frac{\sqrt{2}}{2}$ (the square root of 2 over 2) in Study No. 33 and $\frac{e}{\pi}$ (the base of natural logarithms over the ratio of the diameter of a circle to its circumference) in Study No. 40.

Self-Test 26-3

(Answers begin on page 639.)

A. Rhythmic procedures

    Which of the rhythmic procedures mentioned in this chapter are illustrated by the following examples?

B. Nonretrogradable rhythms

    Which of the following rhythms are nonretrogradable?

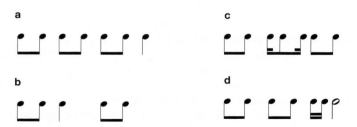

C. Analysis

In the excerpt that follows:

1. Which of the following is illustrated by this excerpt: asymmetric meter, composite meter, or mixed meter? _____

2. What term is used to describe the immediate and proportional tempo change that occurs in m. 469? _____

3. Where do you notice hemiola occurring? _____

4. Where do you notice displaced accent occurring? _____

Rogers, *Prodigal Child,* for saxophone quartet, (C score)

In the excerpt that follows:

5. What proportion can be used to describe the relationship between the two
   tempos? _____ : _____

6. Where is hemiola implied? _____

7. What rhythmic procedures contribute to the ametric effect of the excerpt?

   _____

   _____

   _____

Bain, *Illuminations,* for alto saxophone and piano

Note: Handing and key depression durations mm. 1-21 and in similar passages are for dramatic effect.

Exercise 26-3 See Workbook.

Summary

At the beginning of this chapter, we observed that at least two major and divergent compositional paths emerged from the post-Romantic era. One of these was based on the expansion and further development of certain elements of tonality, including scales, chords, principles of harmonic progression, texture, and use of folk music. Our examination of scale materials and chord structures thus far has been centered on those procedures that reflect the goals of composers in the more traditional stream.

The second path was a somewhat more revolutionary one that embraced and expanded the principle of chromatic saturation found in the music of composers such as Wagner, Mahler, Richard Strauss, and others, as a means of emancipating music from principles of tonality. In the next chapter, we will further explore these developments that brought about profound changes in attitudes and approaches to the craft of music composition.

Chapter Twenty-Seven
Post-Tonal Theory

Introduction

Much music of the post-Romantic period remained sufficiently tonal to yield, if imperfectly, to traditional methods of analysis. However, even as early as the first decade of the twentieth century, some composers were creating music that seems to resist any application of traditional harmonic theory. Post-tonal theory provides us with a systematic way to describe the underlying structure of this music. Although it is not within the scope of this brief chapter to provide a comprehensive overview of post-tonal theoretical techniques, we will introduce you to some basic aspects of atonal and twelve-tone theory, including the extension of the latter into the realm of total serialization.

Basic Atonal Theory

Listen to or play Example 27-1, the opening measures of a piece that was composed in 1909. Most analysts consider this to be one of Schoenberg's first **atonal** works, meaning a musical composition that avoids reference to a tonal center or centers. (Schoenberg, incidentally, despised the term and preferred pantonal instead.) It is possible to find references to tonal structures in this excerpt that are also found in tonal music, such as the implied G7 chord (fifth omitted) in the left hand m. 11, but these sonorities lose their tonal identities when placed in this atonal setting.

Example 27-1   Schoenberg, Three Piano Pieces, op. 11, no. 1

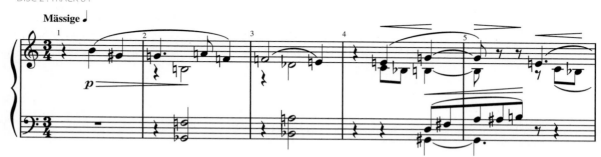

Theorists and composers who were faced with the task of analyzing music such as this found that many of their traditional analytical techniques did little to uncover the underlying structure of the music. A new vocabulary was especially critical if they were going to be able to describe in a systematic way the new pitch structures that composers were using. Although notable attempts were made in this regard by Paul Hindemith and Howard Hanson, the analytical technique that is in wide use today was first codified by Allen Forte in *The Structure of Atonal Music.** Forte's work has subsequently been refined and extended by many other theorists, including John Rahn, David Lewin, and Robert Morris. This type of analytical approach to atonal music is commonly known as **atonal theory** or **set theory.**

The first step in analyzing a piece of atonal music is to partition it into meaningful groups of related pitch classes called **pitch class sets** (abbreviated pc sets), a term introduced by composer and theorist Milton Babbitt. This process of **segmentation** takes into account various musical considerations. Groupings are based on relationships created by pitch, rhythm, phrasing, register, timbre, and so on. For instance, in Example 27-1 one might segment the opening three bars into the melodic pc set (B,G♯,G,A,F,E) and two harmonic pc sets (G♭,F,B) and (B♭,A,D♭), or alternatively choose to focus attention exclusively on the opening three-note melodic motive (B,G♯,G) after discovering that this particular pc set and its many related forms seem to serve as a unifying element in the passage and throughout the movement as a whole. Other valid segmentations are, of course, possible. As you can see from the preceding notation, pc sets are notated by listing their members. The set is enclosed within parentheses and each member is separated by a comma. It is important to understand that a set does not include doublings and is inherently unordered. Consequently, it may be notated in a variety of equivalent ways. Using letter name notation, the set (B,G♯,G) may be notated as (B,G♯,G), (G♯,G,B), (G,B,G♯), (G♯,B,G), and so forth. Sets may also be written using integer notation. Theorists have mapped the 12 pitch classes to a fixed series of integers 0–11 inclusive. The system based on C, called fixed-zero notation, is shown next:

Integers [C=0]	0	1	2	3	4	5	6	7	8	9	10	11
Letter names	C		D		E	F		G		A		B
	B♯	C♯		D♯		E♯	F♯		G♯		A♯	
		D♭		E♭	F♭		G♭		A♭		B♭	C♭

* Allen Forte, *The Structure of Atonal Music* (New Haven, Conn.: Yale University Press, 1973).

In fixed-zero notation, the **reference pc** is C (abbreviated [C=0]), so C=0, C♯/D♭=1, D=2, D♯/E♭=3, E=4, and so forth. Notice that the preceding chart does not take double-sharps or double-flats into account, but that would be easy to do. For example, C double-sharp and E double-flat would belong to the same pitch class (abbreviated pc) as D, pc 2. To demonstrate the process of converting between pc letter names and fixed-zero pc integers, let's compare the notation for four sets that occur in Example 27-1, mm. 1 to 3:

Letter name	Integer [C=0]
(B,G♯,G)	(11,8,7)
(G♭,F,B)	(6,5,11)
(B♭,A,D♭)	(10,9,1)
(D♭,E,F)	(1,4,5)

In common-practice music we could easily identify triads and seventh chords using names like major, minor, major seventh, minor seventh, and so on, because the music was based on a referential major or minor scale, and the available sonorities were so few in number. In atonal music, however, there frequently is no referential scale, and any combination of the 12 pitch classes is possible. Atonal theory offers a consistent method for naming these combinations. This type of descriptive power comes at the cost of some lengthy calculation. Fortunately, there is a relatively straightforward procedure you can use to identify a pc set. This procedure will be the main topic of the remainder of this section.

NORMAL FORM

Putting a pc set in **normal form** (also called **normal order**) means to arrange its members into an arbitrary ordering that is most compact. This is similar to what we do when we stack a triad in root position. You can often figure out the normal form of a pc set just by looking at it, but for most pc sets you will need to use the following procedure. For example, let's attempt to determine the normal form of the pc set (B,G♯,G). The first thing to do is to write out all possible *ascending orderings* within an octave, as shown in Example 27-2. There will always be as many ascending orderings as there are members in the pc set—in this case, three.

Example 27-2

Ascending orderings

d   Normal form

[G,G♯,B]

The *outside interval* is the interval between the first and last note of an ordering. Its size is usually indicated by the number of semitones spanned. Of the three possible ascending orderings shown in Example 27-2, Example 27-2a has the *smallest outside interval*, so the normal form of this pc set is [G,G♯,B]. We will use square brackets to designate the normal form of a pc set after the convention used by Joseph Straus in *Introduction to Post-Tonal Theory.** Example 27-2d shows the normal form of this pc set using staff notation. One major drawback of staff notation is that it indicates specific pitches rather than pitch classes. Nonetheless, the notation of a pc set on a musical staff is a useful representation, and we will continue to use it throughout the remainder of the chapter.

The normal form of the first five melodic notes in Example 27-1 would be [F,G,G♯,A,B], and the normal forms of the half-note chords in mm. 2 to 3 would be [F,G♭,B] and [A,B♭,D♭], respectively. It should be mentioned that any pc set can be notated in a variety of enharmonically equivalent ways. For example, [G,G♯,B] could also be spelled [G,A♭,B], [G,G♯,C♭], [G,A♭,C♭], and so on.

You will find that most pc sets cannot be put into normal form as quickly as the pc set shown in Example 27-2. For example, consider the pentachord (set of five pitch classes) that occurs three times in the left hand in mm. 4 to 8: (D,F♯,A,A♯,B). It is difficult to determine just by looking at this pc set which ascending ordering would be most compact. The five possible ascending orderings are shown in Example 27-3.

Example 27-3

[F♯,A,A♯,B,D]

Again, the outside interval of each ascending ordering is indicated in semitones. Of the five possible orderings shown in Example 27-3, Example 27-3b has the smallest outside interval, so the normal form of this pc set is [F♯,A,A♯,B,D].

In some pc sets, there will be a tie for the smallest outside interval. In that case, you will need to check the *next-most-outside interval,* the interval between the first and next-to-last notes. Example 27-4 shows the four possible ascending orderings of (B♭,A,D♭,F), a pc set that occurs in m. 3 of Example 27-1.

Example 27-4

[A,B♭,D♭,F]

* Joseph Straus, *Introduction to Post-Tonal Theory,* 3rd Edition (Upper Saddle River, NJ: Prentice Hall, 2005).

Notice that Examples 27-4c and 27-4d result in an outside interval tie. The tie is resolved by checking the next-most-outside interval. Example 27-4d has the smallest next-most-outside interval, so the normal form of this pc set is [A,B♭,D♭,F].

Pitch class sets like the one shown in Example 27-5, a pc set that first appears in mm. 4 to 5 of Example 27-1, result in a series of endless next-most-outside interval ties.

Example 27-5

[D,F♯,A♯]

In this case, you will need to use step 4 of the following procedure, which can be used to determine the normal form of any pc set:

Procedure to Determine the Normal Form of a PC Set

1. List the ascending orderings of the pc set. The number of ascending orderings is equal to the number of members in the set.

2. The ascending ordering with the smallest outside interval is the normal form.

3. If a tie results from the previous step, compare the next-most-outside intervals, the intervals between the first and second-to-last notes, first and third-to-last notes, etc. Select the ascending ordering with the smallest outside interval.

4. If there is still a tie after applying repeated applications of the previous step, select the ordering that begins with the smallest first pc integer.

Adapted from Straus's *Introduction to Post-Tonal Theory,* this general procedure was first suggested by John Rahn in *Basic Atonal Theory.** Applying step 4 in Example 27-5, we find that Example 27-5a begins with the least first pc integer, so the normal form is [2,6,10] or [D,F♯,A♯].

EQUIVALENCE RELATIONS AND MOD 12

Before we proceed further, it is important to understand that atonal theory invokes a number of equivalence relations. You are already familiar with a number of important equivalence relations. For example, octave equivalence allows you to say that "Happy Birthday" is the same song no matter what octave you sing it in. The concept of transpositional equivalence allows you to say that "Happy Birthday" is the same song no matter what key you sing it in. The theory of enharmonic equivalence was discussed in Chapter 23. Octave equivalence and enharmonic equivalence combine to create the 12 pitch classes. A pc clockface diagram, like the one shown in Example 27-6, may be used to explore pitch-class relations.

Example 27-6

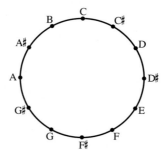

The diagram is similar to the circle-of-fifths diagram introduced in Chapter 1; however, this circle is partitioned into 12 equal semitones (increasing in the clockwise direction) rather than fifths. Each dot represents a pitch class, labeled above using sharps-only letter name notation. In Example 27-7, the same diagram is labeled using integer notation [C=0].

Example 27-7

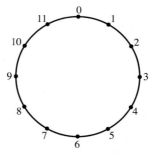

The diagram is useful because the clock and pitch-class systems are both modulo 12 systems (abbreviated mod 12). You are already familiar with mod 12 arithmetic. Suppose it's 10 a.m. and you're hungry, but you can't eat lunch until 1 p.m. You might ask, "How many hours until lunchtime?" The answer, of course, is 3 hours. In a mod 12 system, arithmetic results are mapped onto their mod 12 equivalents, integers between 0 and 11 inclusive. When traditional addition or subtraction yields a result outside of this range, add or subtract 12 repeatedly from the result until you obtain a number between 0 and 11 inclusive. Note that adding or subtracting 12 is equivalent to going up or down an octave, respectively. Here are some examples of mod 12 arithmetic: $11 + 2 = 1, 6 + 6 = 0, 10 - 12 = 10, 4 - 10 = 6, 3 + 2 = 5, 7 + 0 = 7, -1 + 2 = 1$, and so on.

TRANSPOSITION (T_n) AND INVERSION (T_nI)

The mathematical aspect of atonal theory begins to become apparent when we study transposition (T_n), one of the fundamental operations of atonal theory. To transpose a pc set, add the transposition number n to each member of the set in turn. For example, let's apply T_1

to [G,G♯,B], the opening three-note motive in Example 27-1. First, convert the set to integer notation, then add 1 (mod 12) to each set member in turn, as shown in Example 27-8a.

Example 27-8

a.

$$[7, \quad 8, \quad 11]$$
$$+ \quad 1 \quad 1 \quad 1$$
$$= \quad [8, \quad 9, \quad 0]$$

b.

$$[G, \quad G♯, \quad B]$$
$$+ \quad 1 \quad 1 \quad 1$$
$$[A♭, \quad A, \quad C]$$

Example 27-8b shows the same operation using letter name notation. Example 27-8a may also be written more compactly, as shown in Example 27-9:

Example 27-9

$$T_1[7,8,11] = [8,9,0]$$

We say that [8,9,0] is T_1 of [7,8,11] and that the two sets are equivalent under T_n. When we put sets into normal form it is easier to see when they are related by T_n. Notice that [8,9,0], or [G♯,A,C], appears in Example 27-1 in the right hand, m. 10.

Let's try another T_n operation on the set [G,G♯,B]:

$$T_2[7,8,11] = [9,10,1]$$

Again, we say that [9,10,1] is T_2 of [7,8,11] and that the two sets are equivalent under T_n. Notice that the set [9,10,1], or [A,B♭,D♭], appears in Example 27-1 as a chord in m. 3.

The other fundamental operation of atonal theory is inversion (T_nI). Inversion is a compound operation: pc inversion followed by T_n. In atonal theory, pc inversion is defined as subtraction from 12 mod 12. The twelve possible pc inversions are shown in Example 27-10 using integer notation.

Example 27-10

pc	0	1	2	3	4	5	6	7	8	9	10	11
12-pc:	0	11	10	9	8	7	6	5	4	3	2	1

To invert a set, apply pc inversion to each set member in turn, then apply T_n. For example, let's apply T_6I to [G,G♯,B], which may be written:

$$T_6I \, [7,8,11]$$

First, perform pc inversion on the set. That is, 7 inverts to 5, 8 inverts to 4, and 11 inverts to 1, subtracting each from 12 mod 12 (Ex. 27-10). This simplifies T_6I [7,8,11] to the following:

$$T_6 \, (5,4,1)$$

Notice that pc inversion knocks the original set out of normal form, so we use parentheses rather than square brackets from this point forward. Second, applying T_6 we get the following:

$$T_6 (5,4,1) = (11,10,7)$$

The normal form of (11,10,7) is [7,10,11], so we say that [7,10,11] is T_6I of [7,8,11] and that the two sets are equivalent under T_nI.

Let's try another T_nI operation on the set [G,G♯,B]:

$$T_{11}I [7,8,11]$$

Performing pc inversion on the set and applying T_{11} yields:

$$T_{11} (5,4,1) = (4,3,0)$$

The normal form of (4,3,0) is [0,3,4], so we say that [0,3,4] is $T_{11}I$ of [7,8,11] and that the two sets are equivalent under T_nI.

Finally, consider the set [D♭,E,F], or [1,4,5], which appears in Example 27-1 in the right hand, m. 3. Notice that T_0I [1,4,5] = (11,8,7), the opening three-note motive in Example 27-1.

SET CLASS AND PRIME FORM

One of the most important ways to classify a set is by its **cardinality** (*c*), the number of members it contains. For example, an interval has two members, a triad has three members, a seventh chord has four members, and so forth. Following the convention established in John Rahn's *Basic Atonal Theory*, we assign each cardinality type a name as shown in Example 27-11.

Example 27-11

c	Name	c	Name
0	empty set	12	aggregate
1	monad	11	undecachord
2	dyad	10	decachord
3	trichord	9	nonachord
4	tetrachord	8	octachord
5	pentachord	7	septachord
6	hexachord		

A **set class** is a family of pc sets related by T_n or T_nI. There will usually be 24 such members in a set class. The family of sets related to [G,G♯,B] by T_n or T_nI is shown in Example 27-12 using letter name (Ex. 27-12a) and integer (Ex. 27-12b) notation.

Example 27-12

a.

SET CLASS 3–3 (014)			
T_0	[G,G♯,B]	T_0I	[C♯,E,F]
T_1	[G♯,A,C]	T_1I	[D,F,F♯]
T_2	[A,A♯,C♯]	T_2I	[D♯,F♯,G]
T_3	[A♯,B,D]	T_3I	[E,G,G♯]
T_4	[B,C,D♯]	T_4I	[F,G♯,A]
T_5	[C,C♯,E]	T_5I	[F♯,A,A♯]
T_6	[C♯,D,F]	T_6I	[G,A♯,B]
T_7	[D,D♯,F♯]	T_7I	[G♯,B,C]
T_8	[D♯,E,G]	T_8I	[A,C,C♯]
T_9	[E,F,G♯]	T_9I	[A♯,C♯,D]
T_{10}	[F,F♯,A]	$T_{10}I$	[B,D,D♯]
T_{11}	[F♯,G,A♯]	$T_{11}I$	[C,D♯,E]

b.

SET CLASS 3–3 (014)			
T_0	[7,8,11]	T_0I	[1,4,5]
T_1	[8,9,0]	T_1I	[2,5,6]
T_2	[9,10,1]	T_2I	[3,6,7]
T_3	[10,11,2]	T_3I	[4,7,8]
T_4	[11,0,3]	T_4I	[5,8,9]
T_5	[0,1,4]	T_5I	[6,9,10]
T_6	[1,2,5]	T_6I	[7,10,11]
T_7	[2,3,6]	T_7I	[8,11,0]
T_8	[3,4,7]	T_8I	[9,0,1]
T_9	[4,5,8]	T_9I	[10,1,2]
T_{10}	[5,6,9]	$T_{10}I$	[11,2,3]
T_{11}	[6,7,10]	$T_{11}I$	[0,3,4]

It should be mentioned that **transpositionally symmetrical sets,** those that map onto themselves under T_n (at levels other than T_0), and **inversionally symmetrical sets,** those that map onto themselves under T_nI, have fewer than 24 distinct forms. The whole-tone scale, for example, belongs to a set class with only two distinct forms, whereas the octatonic and hexatonic scales belong to set classes that have three and four distinct forms, respectively.

The **prime form** of a pc set provides us with a convenient way to name a set class. Prime forms begin with 0 and are most packed to the left. Of the 24 normal forms listed in Example 27-12b, two begin with a 0: [0,1,4] and [0,3,4]. Of those two forms, [0,1,4] is most packed to the left. As noted earlier, we have adopted the set notation used by Joseph Straus in *Introduction to Post-Tonal Theory*. Straus notates prime forms using parentheses without intervening commas or spaces, so the prime form of [0,1,4] is (014). Straus also substitutes T for 10 and E for 11 in prime forms. An even more compact way to refer to a set class is to use its **Forte name.** Theorist Allen Forte assigned each prime form a compact name based on its cardinality and relative position within Appendix C, "Set Class List." This appendix is similar to the one that appears in Forte's *The Structure of Atonal Music.* Use Appendix C now to look up the Forte name associated with the prime form (014). Prime forms are listed in the second and sixth columns. Forte names are listed in the first and fifth columns. You will find that the Forte name associated with (014) is 3–3. In an analysis, a set class is usually referred to by its Forte name, prime form, or both, for example, 3–3 (014).

Straus's general procedure to determine the prime form of any pc set is given next, along with an example using the pc set (B,G♯,G).

Procedure to Determine the Prime Form of a PC Set

Step	Description	Example using (B,G♯,G)
1.	Determine the normal form of the set.	Normal form is: [7,8,11]
2.	Determine which T_n operation will transpose the set so that its first member is 0, and apply it to the set.	T_5 [7,8,11] = **[0,1,4]**
3.	Invert the set and repeat the previous two steps for the inverted set.	[7,8,11] inverted is: (5,4,1) Normal form is: [1,4,5] T_{11} [1,4,5] = **[0.3,4]**
4.	Compare the forms produced by steps 2 and 3. Select the form that is most compact to the left as the prime form.	Compare [0,1,4] and [0,3,4] Prime form is: (014)

We should mention here that the notation used in atonal theory varies depending on the theorist cited. For example, some theorists notate prime forms using square brackets with intervening commas. Using this style of notation, the prime form of 3–3 would be written as [0,1,4]. The main advantage of the Straus notation is that a pc set, its normal form, its prime form, and its set class membership can easily be distinguished from one another. Returning to the opening trichord of the Schoenberg excerpt (B,G♯,G), the chart below compares the various notational formats:

	PC Set	Normal Form	Prime Form	Set Class
Notation:	(B,G♯,G)	[G,G♯,B]	(014)	3–3 (014)

INTERVAL VECTOR

The third and seventh columns in Appendix C show the **interval vector** (also called **interval-class vector**) for each set class. From Appendix C, we find that the interval vector for 3–3 (014) is 101100. A full explanation of the interval vector is beyond the scope of this chapter. Let it suffice to say that it gives a rough approximation of the quality of a sonority by listing the number of occurrences of each **interval class** (ic). An interval class can be conveniently thought of as the shortest distance between two pitch classes. The six interval classes and their relation to the common tonal intervals (within the octave) are listed below:

Traditional tonal interval name:	m2, M7	M2, m7	m3, M6	M3, m6	P4, P5	A4/ d5
Interval class:	ic1	ic2	ic3	ic4	ic5	ic6

To demonstrate its significance, let's calculate the interval vector for the pc set (B,G♯,G). There are three intervals in this sonority—B–G♯ (ic3), G♯–G (ic1) and B–G (ic4) as summarized below:

As you can see, there is one occurrence each of ic3, ic1, and ic4. Notice that ic2, ic5, and ic6 are absent from this sonority. The interval vector is usually listed as a string of six numbers that indicate the number of occurrences of ic1, ic2, ic3, ic4, ic5, and ic6, respectively. Counting the number of occurrences, we again find that the interval vector of (B,G♯,G), which belongs to set class 3–3 (014) is 101100.

Although there is much more to atonal theory, you now have the vocabulary to identify some basic atonal sonorities. Do not expect to find that entire pieces are based on one or two set classes or basic cells, because such pieces are quite rare. You may find, however, that a few set classes do account for many or most of the notes in a given passage, or that subset or superset relations exist between the sets in a passage. In any case, atonal theory offers a precise way to describe sonorities in music in which traditional harmonic and intervallic relationships are absent.

Self-Test 27-1

(Answers begin on page 639.)

A. Mod 12 and pitch class. Reduce the following integers to an integer mod 12 (0 to 11 inclusive).

1.	15	5.	13
2.	18	6.	−1
3.	22	7.	−3
4.	12	8.	−7

B. Transposition (T_n) and inversion (T_nI). Transpose and invert the following pc sets given in integer notation.

1.	T_3 (6,5,2)	6.	T_5I (3,2,1)
2.	T_1 (9,11,4)	7.	T_9I (8,7,5)
3.	T_{11} (0,3,2)	8.	$T_{10}I$ (3,7,6)
4.	T_6 (6,8,10)	9.	T_7I (4,5,0)
5.	T_4 (0,4,8)	10.	T_2I (11,0,9)

C. The opening trichord

1. We saw in Example 27-1 that the notes in the right hand in m. 3 (F,D♭,E) are an inversion of the first three notes (B,G♯,G). This means they are members of the same set class. What is its prime form?

2. List some other occurrences of this set class in the excerpt. Try to make your segmentations musically defensible. Put your answers in normal form.

3. Which of those occurrences uses the same pitch classes as the opening three notes?

D. Other segmentations

1. There are four half-note trichords in mm. 1 to 11. Label them a through d and provide the normal form, prime form, and Forte name for each.

2. Provide the normal form, prime form, and Forte name for the three-note melodic figure that opens the melody in mm. 9 to 11.

3. What is the normal form, prime form, and Forte name of the melodic segment presented in mm. 1 to 2? Is this pc set inversionally symmetrical; that is, does it map onto itself under T_nI?

4. An expansion of the opening melody appears in mm. 9 to 10. What is the normal form, prime form, and Forte name of this pc set? Is it inversionally symmetrical?

5. What is the normal form, prime form, and Forte name of the recurring five-note figure in the tenor in mm. 4 to 8? Is it inversionally symmetrical?

6. Bonus question: The opening three measures of the melody can be partitioned into four trichords that are the same set classes as those used for the half-note chords. This can be done in such a way that each trichord is used only once and every note of the melody is used at least once. Try it. (This may not be of consequence analytically, but it's good practice and kind of fun.)

Exercise 27-1 See Workbook.

Twelve-Tone Serialism

The **twelve-tone method** is perhaps the most methodically revolutionary compositional technique of the twentieth century. The Vienna-born composer Arnold Schoenberg is generally credited with developing and codifying this method that he believed would more systematically facilitate the composition of large-scale forms. Having been profoundly influenced by the music of Wagner, Mahler, and Brahms, his earlier works embody many elements of the post-Romantic style. As we saw in the previous section on atonal theory, Schoenberg consciously sought to create a new harmonic language. Through the use of angular melodies, sudden and extreme contrast of dynamics and texture, and use of instruments and the voice in nontraditional ways, Schoenberg's music demonstrates a sharp departure from the compositional styles that we have studied thus far.

Even before Schoenberg had organized his ideas into an actual method of composition, certain procedures were operational in his music, such as the following:

1. Avoidance of the octave as either a melodic or harmonic interval.

2. Avoidance of traditional pitch collections, such as the diatonic scale, that might suggest major or minor triads and hence traditional harmonic function.

3. Use of wide-ranging and extremely disjunct melodies.

The preceding principles continued to hold true in much of Schoenberg's twelve-tone music as well as in the music of his students Alban Berg and Anton Webern. His system was designed to methodically equalize all 12 pitch classes by the following means:

1. A twelve-tone composition is to be based on a precompositional ordering of the 12 pitch classes that is determined by the composer. This ordering is called the **series** or **row**.

2. No pitch class may be used again until all other pitch classes have been sounded. There is one general exception to this restriction: a pitch class may be repeated. Repetitions may also occur within the context of common musical figures as trills, tremolos, and pedal points.

3. The series may, within the confines of the procedure, legitimately be used in *transposition, retrograde* (reversed order of the transposed form), *inversion* (mirroring of each interval), or *retrograde inversion* (reversed order of the inverted form), the four basic transformations at the foundation of the twelve-tone system.

A series may be transposed to 12 different levels, resulting in 12 different prime forms of the series. There are also 12 retrograde forms, 12 inversion forms, and 12 retrograde-inversion forms for a total of 48 possible series forms. We will use the symbol P_x to designate the 12 prime forms P_0 through P_{11}, where the subscript x or **transposition index** indicates the first pitch class of the series, with C = 0, C♯ = 1, etc. We will use the symbol R_x (R_0 through R_{11}) to indicate the retrograde forms, I_x (I_0 through I_{11}) to indicate the inversion forms, and RI_x (RI_0 through RI_{11}) to indicate the retrograde-inversion forms. Note that R_x forms are simply the P_x forms presented backward, and that RI_x forms are simply the I_x forms presented backward. It should also be noted that I_x forms are really the product of a compound transformation, inversion followed by transposition.

It is important to remember that the series is not necessarily restricted to a role as a "theme" or "melody" but is an organizational tool used by the composer to impose order over the entire composition. Before discussing more complex illustrations, let us examine a simple example titled "All Alone," which is taken from a set of twelve-tone piano pieces titled *24 Piano Inventions* by Ross Lee Finney. The series is shown in Example 27-13 using staff notation.

Example 27-13   Finney, Series from *24 Piano Inventions*

Order numbers: 1   2   3   4   5   6   7   8   9   10   11   12

Example 27-14 shows "All Alone" in its entirety. Notice that all 12 pitch classes are stated over the course of the first four bars in the order seen in Example 27-13. Because the first note of the prime form in Example 27-14 is A, or pc 9, we label the row as P_9.

The **order numbers** below the staff in Example 27-13 and on the score in Example 27-14 indicate the relative order position of each pitch class within a particular series form. The inclusion of series forms and order numbers on the score is a useful way to show what series form the composer is employing at any given point in a twelve-tone composition. In bar 4, Finney employs an overlap technique; that is, the D at the end of the fourth measure has two identities: one as the 12th note of P_9 and one as the 1st note of R_9. Notice, too, that the melody in mm. 1 to 8 is orchestrationally doubled at the octave (a device Schoenberg consciously avoided), that the second time P_9 is stated (mm. 8–12) it is presented as chords, and that the A in m. 8 is allowed to serve as a pedal throughout the remainder of the piece. Although this example illustrates only the most basic use of the twelve-tone technique, we can see the possibilities for creating a very expressive melody and for variety in texture.

Example 27-14   Finney, "All Alone," from *24 Piano Inventions*

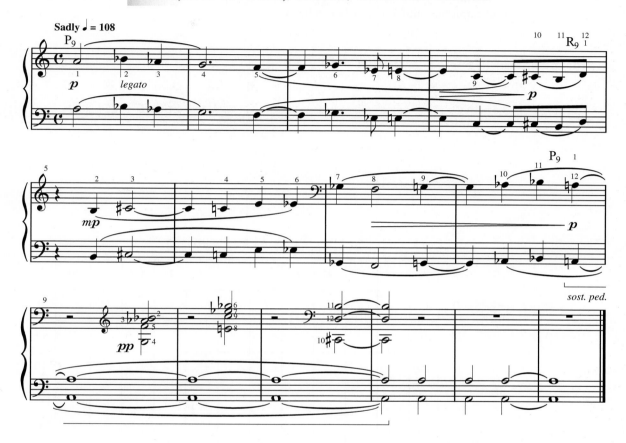

Now let us take a closer look at the 48 possible forms of the series. Example 27-15 shows the series from Symphony op. 21 by Anton Webern.

Example 27-15   Webern, Series from Symphony op. 21

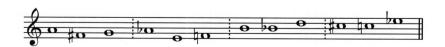

When you examine a twelve-tone composition, it is helpful to have immediate access to the 48 series forms. This is most conveniently obtained by use of a 12×12 matrix, illustrated in Example 27-16. P_9, the original form of the row, is listed across the top row of the matrix, and the inversion beginning with the same pc is listed down the first column. The I form can be calculated by inverting the intervals of the P form. For example, the 1st and 2nd notes of P_9, A–F♯ (down three semitones) inverts to A–C (up three semitones) in I_9. The 2nd and 3rd notes of P_9, F♯–G (up one semitone) inverts to C–B (down one semitone) in I_9. The 3rd and 4th notes of P_9, G–A♭ (up one semitone) inverts to B–B♭ (down one semitone), and so on, as shown below:

Order numbers:	1	2	3	4	5	6	7	8	9	10	11	12	
$P_9 \rightarrow$	A	F♯	G	A♭	E	F	B	B♭	D	C♯	C	E♭	$\leftarrow R_9$
$I_9 \rightarrow$	A	C	B	B♭	D	C♯	G	A♭	E	F	F♯	E♭	$\leftarrow RI_9$

Example 27-16

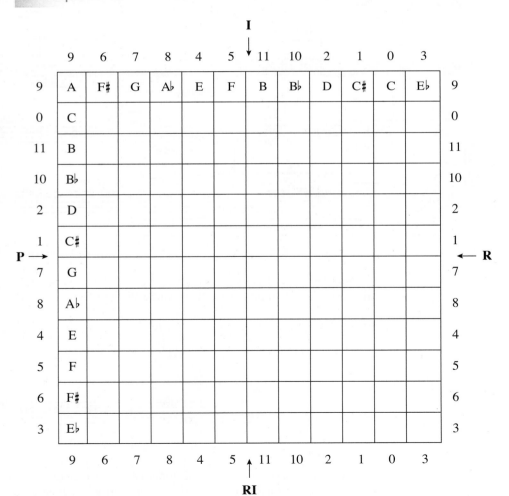

Index numbers are indicated on all sides of the matrix. Prime series forms may be read from the matrix in left-to-right order, whereas retrograde forms may be read from right to left. Inversion forms may be read in top-to-bottom order, whereas retrograde-inversion forms may be read from bottom to top. When correctly done, the note in the upper left corner of the matrix (A, in this case) will appear along the main diagonal of the matrix. Example 27-17 illustrates the completed matrix.

Example 27-17

	I_9	I_6	I_7	I_8	I_4	I_5	I_{11}	I_{10}	I_2	I_1	I_0	I_3	
P_9	A	F♯	G	A♭	E	F	B	B♭	D	C♯	C	E♭	R_9
P_0	C	A	B♭	B	G	A♭	D	C♯	F	E	E♭	F♯	R_0
P_{11}	B	A♭	A	B♭	F♯	G	C♯	C	E	E♭	D	F	R_{11}
P_{10}	B♭	G	A♭	A	F	F♯	C	B	E♭	D	C♯	E	R_{10}
P_2	D	B	C	C♯	A	B♭	E	E♭	G	F♯	F	A♭	R_2
P_1	C♯	B♭	B	C	A♭	A	E♭	D	F♯	F	E	G	R_1
P_7	G	E	F	F♯	D	E♭	A	A♭	C	B	B♭	C♯	R_7
P_8	A♭	F	F♯	G	E♭	E	B♭	A	C♯	C	B	D	R_8
P_4	E	C♯	D	E♭	B	C	F♯	F	A	A♭	G	B♭	R_4
P_5	F	D	E♭	E	C	C♯	G	F♯	B♭	A	A♭	B	R_5
P_6	F♯	E♭	E	F	C♯	D	A♭	G	B	B♭	A	C	R_6
P_3	E♭	C	C♯	D	B♭	B	F	E	A♭	G	F♯	A	R_3
	RI_9	RI_6	RI_7	RI_8	RI_4	RI_5	RI_{11}	RI_{10}	RI_2	RI_1	RI_0	RI_3	

We should mention here that the actual procedure for labeling series forms tends to vary somewhat, depending on the theorist cited. Some theorists, for example, use a moveable zero approach, labeling the first appearance of the row as P_0. In the writings of earlier twelve-tone theorists, we find the term original used in the place of prime. The inevitable confusion arising between the letter "o" (original) and the numeral "0" (zero) may have prompted the change in terminology. Other ways you may see theorists label a series form such as P_0 include P0, P^0, and P–0. Order numbers may sometimes be labeled using the numbers 0 through 11, rather than 1 through 12. The series itself may be referred to by a variety of terms including tone row, twelve-tone set, pitch set, and set. Intervallic spellings need not conform to the rules that apply to traditional tonal intervals unless a specific musical context demands such. In post-tonal theory, enharmonic equivalence may usually be assumed to be the rule.

The construction of the series from Webern's Symphony op. 21 (Ex. 27-15) is an interesting one from many standpoints. Each half of the series, or discrete hexachord, is made up of adjacent members of the chromatic scale [E,F,F♯,G,A♭,A] and [B♭,B,C,C♯,D,E♭]. Also note that the second hexachord is a transposed retrograde form of the first. On comparing P_9 with R_3 in the matrix shown in Example 27-17, we discover that they are identical. The same is true of P_0 and R_6, P_{11} and R_5, and so on. Likewise, for each I form, there is an identical RI form: I_9 and RI_3, I_6 and RI_0, etc. This built-in correlation between series forms will, of necessity, reduce the available series forms to 24 possibilities rather than the usual 48. Note also the symmetrical arrangement of the discrete trichords of the series, that is, the non-overlapping sets (A,F♯,G), (A♭,E,F), (B,B♭,D), and (C♯,C,E♭). These sets belong to set classes 3–2 (013), 3–3 (014), 3–3 (014), and 3–2 (013), respectively. Note, too, that the series begins and ends with 3–2 (013), whereas the middle trichords belong to set class 3–3 (014). The discrete tetrachords display a symmetry of their own, belonging to 4–1 (0123), 4–9 (0167), and 4–1 (0123), respectively. The intervallic arrangement of such a series guarantees that these melodic and harmonic cells will recur throughout the piece. Variety is achieved through the manipulation of other musical elements such as rhythm, phrasing, articulation, register, timbre, and so on.

Example 27-18 shows the theme of *Variationen,* the second and final movement of Symphony op. 21, with the instruments sounding as written. As you examine this excerpt with the matrix (Ex. 27-17), you will discover that the clarinet states I_5 (or RI_{11}), while the accompaniment in the harp and horns states I_{11} (or RI_5). Finally, note the palindromic symmetry of the clarinet part's rhythm. The rhythm is the same forward or backward, as are the dynamics and articulation groupings. This is also the case for the accompaniment. Just as we found symmetry in the set class membership of the discrete trichords and tetrachords, here we find symmetry in the rhythmic dimension of the music.

Example 27-18   Webern, Symphony op. 21, II

Certain series, such as the two shown in Example 27-19, have achieved a certain renown by virtue of their having formed the basis for well-known twelve-tone compositions.

Example 27-19

Berg, Series from Violin Concerto

Dallapiccola, Series from *Quaderno musicale di Annalibera*

These rows illustrate the care composers have taken to anticipate the melodic and harmonic possibilities of the series. The predominance of the 3rd in the Berg series, for example, plays an important role in bringing about an almost triadic texture within the body of the work. Also in the Berg row, notes 1, 3, 5, and 7 of the series (bracketed) represent the open strings of the violin, whereas the last four notes, which comprise a segment of a whole-tone scale, represent the opening pitches of "Es ist genug," the Bach chorale prominently featured in the last movement. The second example, from Dallapiccola's *Quaderno musicale di Annalibera,* illustrates an **all-interval series,** in which 11 different intervals make up the series.

Example 27-20 illustrates two processes, both of which occur with some frequency in Webern's music. The first is the atomization of the melodic line, a process known as **pointillism.** The second is the deliberate juxtaposition of minute melodic fragments of contrasting timbre and register; this compositional device, in which melody is in a sense created by the rapid shifting of tone colors, is referred to as **Klangfarbenmelodie,** or, literally, "sound color melody." The term was introduced by Arnold Schoenberg, and the technique is associated with the third movement of his composition *Five Pieces for Orchestra,* op. 16, which was originally published under the title *Farben* (colors). As you listen to a recording of this work, it may be helpful to try to listen for associations between timbres and rhythms rather than pitches.

Example 27-20   Webern, Concerto op. 24, II

This composition, like most compositions by Webern, lends itself to pc set analysis. Notice the consistent use of set classes 3–1 (012) and 3–3 (014) in Example 27-20, several instances of which are labeled on the score.

We should also mention here that the twelve-tone method, although conceived specifically as a systematic means for avoiding (or rather for providing alternatives to) tonality, has been adapted by later composers as an effective means for organizing more tonally oriented music. For example, examine the tonal orientation of the series from Berg's Violin Concerto (Ex. 27-19). The series may even be employed as a means of organizing a quasi-pandiatonic passage or involve more than 12 notes or even fewer than 12 notes. Stravinsky, for example, makes use of a 28-note series for the variations found in the second movement of his *Sonata for Two Pianos* and a 5-note series for *In Memoriam Dylan Thomas*.

Self-Test 27-2

(Answers begin on page 641.)

A. 12×12 matrix. The series given next forms the basis for Schoenberg's String Quartet no. 4, op. 37. Notate the I_2 form on the blank staff provided, then complete the 12×12 matrix using the guidelines found in this section. Label the series forms around the outside of the matrix, using the blanks provided.

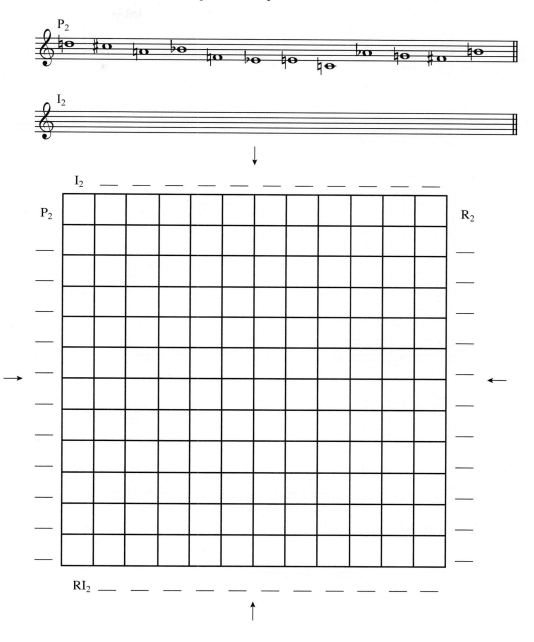

B. Using the series from Schoenberg's op. 37, for which you have just constructed a matrix, compose a brief twelve-tone piece using the structural design of "All Alone" by Ross Lee Finney (Ex. 27-14). Your piece should have three series form statements: (1) P_2, (2) a retrograde form of the series (or other series form from the possible 48), and (3) chords based on P_2. Keep in mind that the use of one or more recurring rhythmic motives will help lend unity and coherence to your composition. Label the row forms that you use.

Exercise 27-2 See Workbook.

Integral Serialism

Inevitably, as composers became fascinated with the concept of ordering pitches, there evolved a keen interest in ordering other musical parameters. This approach is referred to as **total serialization** or **integral serialism.** Two composers associated with the origins of this practice are Anton Webern, whose fascination with issues of order and symmetry we have already observed, and Olivier Messiaen, whose rhythmic etude *Mode de valeurs et d'intensités* exerted a profound influence on his students at the summer music course in Darmstadt, especially Pierre Boulez and Karlheinz Stockhausen. Example 27-21 shows Messiaen's *Mode de valeurs,* a work for solo piano written on three staves.

Example 27-21 Messiaen, *Mode de valeurs et d'intensités,* from *Quatre Etudes de rhythme*

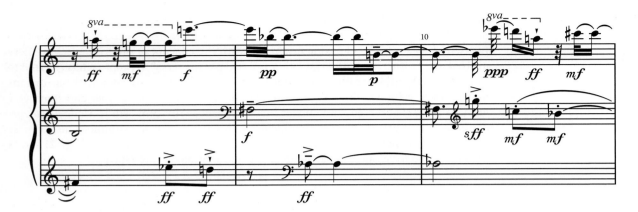

The pitch orderings in *Mode de valeurs* are not determined in a strictly serial manner. Messiaen explains on the introductory page of the score that he has employed a 36-pitch series consisting of three separate 12-note divisions, each of which is assigned to a specific register of the piano. Example 27-22 shows the three divisions.

Example 27-22   Messiaen, Series from *Mode de valeurs et d'intensités*

Register is to a certain extent controlled by the pitch series. For example, note how the three divisions overlap in terms of register and how the highest pitches are assigned shorter durations, whereas the lowest pitches are assigned longer durations. Messiaen also explains that he has employed seven dynamic levels ranging from *ppp* to *fff* and 12 modes of attack, as follows:

Thus no two appearances of the same pitch class will be identical.

American composer Milton Babbitt was evidently the first to explore the serialization of elements other than pitch in *Three Compositions for Piano,* a work composed in 1947. Unaware of Babbitt's experiments with total serialization, Pierre Boulez composed *Structures Ia* for two pianos in 1952. Example 27-23 shows the beginning of *Structures Ia.*

Example 27-23   Boulez, *Structures Ia*

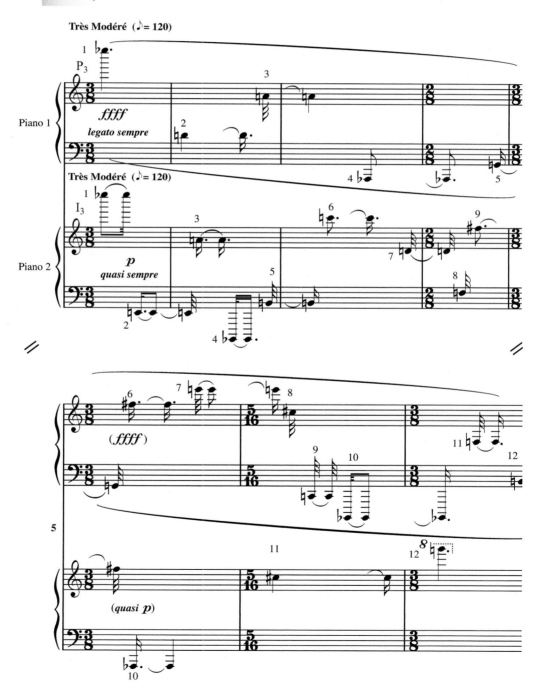

The pitch series for *Structures Ia* was adapted from the first division of Messiaen's *Mode de valeurs* series (Ex. 27-22). Boulez assigned a fixed order number, duration, dynamic level, and mode of attack to each member of the pitch series, as shown in Example 27-24.

Example 27-24   Boulez, Series from *Structures Ia*

Order Numbers	1	2	3	4	5	6	7	8	9	10	11	12
Pitch Series	E♭	D	A	A♭	G	F♯	E	C♯	C	B♭	F	B
Durations	♪	♪	♪.	♪	♪	♪.	♪..	♩	♩	♩	♩.	♩.
Dynamics	*pppp*	*ppp*	*pp*	*p*	*quasi p*	*mp*	*mf*	*quasi f*	*f*	*ff*	*fff*	*ffff*
Mode of Attack	>	⋛	.		normal	⌢	'	*sfz* ∧	⋗		⋅⁻	⌢

In Example 27-23, Piano I presents the P_3 form of the pitch series, and Piano II presents the I_3 form:

Piano I	E♭	D	A	A♭	G	F♯	E	C♯	C	B♭	F	B
Piano II	E♭	E	A	B♭	B	C	D	F	F♯	A♭	C♯	G

To identify the duration series employed in mm. 1 to 7, look up the fixed order number for each duration you encounter in the score using Example 27-24. You will find that Piano I and Piano II state the following duration series:

Piano I	12	11	9	10	3	6	7	1	2	8	4	5
Piano II	5	8	6	4	3	9	2	1	7	11	10	12

Mapping the fixed order numbers of the duration series back to pitch classes using Example 27-24, we find that Piano I's duration series is equivalent to RI_7 of the pitch series, and Piano II's duration series is equivalent to R_{11}.

Piano I	12	11	9	10	3	6	7	1	2	8	4	5
RI_7	B	F	C	B♭	A	F♯	E	E♭	D	C♯	A♭	G

Piano II	5	8	6	4	3	9	2	1	7	11	10	12
R_{11}	G	C♯	F♯	A♭	A	C	D	E♭	E	F	B♭	B

Self-Test 27-3

(Answers begin on page 642.)

A.

1. How does the process of total serialization differ from the original twelve-tone method?

_____

_____

2. Name two composers who experimented with this technique.

_____ and _____

Exercise 27-3 See Workbook.

Summary

Post-tonal theory provides analytical approaches that help us uncover the underlying structure of atonal music. Set theory offers a systematic way to describe the pitch structures of atonal music, providing us with a consistent method for naming any combination of the 12 pitch classes. Schoenberg's twelve-tone method was as influential as it was revolutionary. After World War II, nearly every composer felt the necessity of integrating serial principles into his or her compositional technique. Even composers like Copland and Stravinsky, who initially resisted its adoption, eventually succumbed to the lure of serialism. Webern's interest in issues of order and symmetry paved the way to total serialization, the ordering of musical parameters other than pitch, such as rhythm, dynamics, and articulation.

As you will see in the next chapter, there can be a striking similarity between two seemingly contradictory compositional processes—namely, the effort to achieve total control and the effort to abdicate control entirely through chance procedures. Both of these processes can achieve similar musical results, and sometimes reflect a composer's desire to be freed from making traditional compositional choices, thereby opening up the possibility for the discovery of new sounds and forms that are the result of these processes.

Chapter Twenty-Eight
New Directions

Introduction

In the previous two chapters, we have observed that the early twentieth century was characterized by a curious dichotomy: on the one hand, an extension of post-Romantic tendencies, and, on the other, a conscious (at times almost militant) attempt to establish a totally new musical language. Composers in both camps succeeded in developing distinctly new methods of expression that were clearly indigenous to their age. This early ambivalence has continued to manifest itself in the ongoing diversity of musical language.

In this chapter, we will discuss some other directions that composers have chosen to explore. The expansion of textural and instrumental resources has played an important role in the development of twentieth-century musical practice, as have compositional techniques involving chance and process procedures. The implications of technological developments for composers and performers are also important to consider. Although it is not within the scope of this brief chapter to discuss all the new methods of expression explored by contemporary composers, we will consider developments in these areas in the discussion that follows.

Explorations of Texture, Timbre, and Tuning

We have seen the increasingly important role played by texture in the evolution of twentieth-century musical thought. One reason for this lies in its capability to provide a convincing means of musical organization free from the traditional conventions of key and chord. Even in the relatively conservative textural style of Debussy we find an unusual preponderance of unaccompanied, angular melodies; figuration independent of functional considerations; and vertical sonorities used solely for the sake of color.

As composers turned their attention to further explorations of texture, changes occurred not only in the performance demands placed on players of traditional instruments but also in the structure and size of ensembles. The massive orchestral forces of works like Stravinsky's *Le Sacre du printemps* (1913) gave way to a renewed interest in chamber groups. Interest in nontraditional ensembles did a great deal to legitimize the concept of a smaller, more heterogeneous instrumental body. Schoenberg's *Pierrot lunaire* (1912), for reciter, flute/piccolo, violin/viola, clarinet/bass clarinet, violoncello, and piano is one important example. Stravinsky's *L'Histoire du soldat* (1918), for clarinet, bassoon, cornet, trombone, percussion, violin, and bass also became a model of innovative procedure that many composers chose to follow. An example of theater music, it includes a narrator and speaking roles for one or more characters along with specific directions for stage movement and dance.

Other methods of exploiting the coloristic properties of traditional instruments proved attractive to composers. We have already noted Henry Cowell's experimentation with tone clusters on the piano in *The Tides of Manaunaun* (1912). In *Aeolian Harp* (1923), Cowell calls for the pianist to silently depress the keys of the keyboard and then strum and pluck the strings in a manner inspired by the wind harp to which the title refers. In *The Banshee* (1925), Cowell again calls for the performer to play inside the instrument. Effects created by plucking the strings or drawing the finger or fingernail across the length of the string attempt to evoke the legendary figure of Irish folklore for which the piece is named. It should be mentioned that Charles Ives also made extensive use of tone clusters in his Sonata no. 2 for piano (subtitled *Concord, Massachusetts, 1840–60*) (1910–15), even calling for a 14¾-inch board to execute one of the clusters in the second movement.

John Cage, whose pioneering efforts in the area of indeterminacy will be discussed in the next section, began writing works in the 1930s for **prepared piano,** which involved the placement of various objects and/or materials (such as screws, bolts made of metal or rubber, plastic, felt, and coins) on the strings of the piano at precisely specified locations. The percussive nature of this music is immediately apparent in *Sonatas and Interludes* (1946–48) and in Cage's *Concerto* (1951) for prepared piano and chamber orchestra, which calls not only for extensive preparation of the piano strings but also for a large battery of percussion.

In the 1970s, George Crumb continued the tradition of coloristic exploration of the piano using extended instrumental techniques. In two works written for pianist David Burge, *Makrokosmos,* Volume I (1972) and Volume II (1973), for amplified piano, Crumb attempts to achieve a synthesis of conventional (keyboard) and unconventional (inside the piano) techniques. Subtitled *Twelve fantasy pieces after the Zodiac,* the works pay homage to Bartók's *Mikrokosmos* and Debussy's *Preludes.* Crumb's style of notation is highly personal and, at times, even picturesque in support of his extramusical ideas. Example 28-1 shows No. 8, "The Magic Circle of Infinity," from *Makrokosmos,* Volume I.

Example 28-1 Crumb, "The Magic Circle of Infinity," from *Makrokosmos*, Volume I

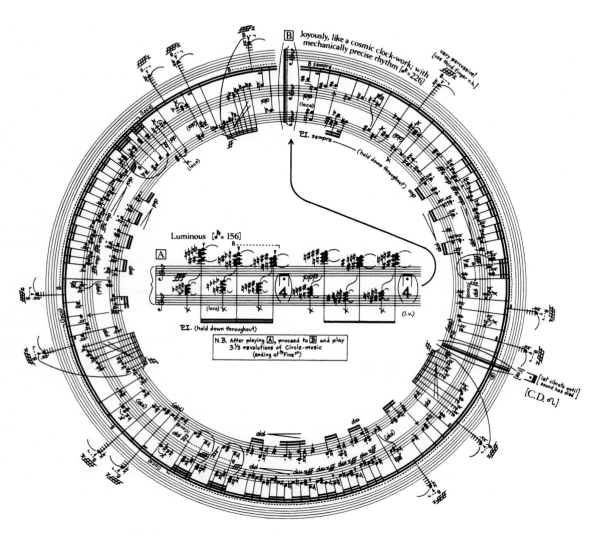

Makrokosmos calls for the performer to strum, pluck, and precisely execute harmonics on the strings inside the piano, as well as to chant, whistle, and whisper into the piano. It should be noted here that Crumb's interest in exploring all available timbral possibilities extends to other mediums. In *Black Angels* (1970) for electric string quartet, for example, he explores the string quartet in similar fashion, calling on the players to use a wide array of extended techniques, to play percussion instruments, and to chant rhythmically in various languages.

The role of percussion was greatly expanded in the twentieth century. One of the earliest landmarks in this field is Edgard Varèse's *Ionisation* (1931). This work calls for 13 musicians to play a total of 37 percussion instruments, including, in addition to the standard battery, anvils, sleigh bells, high and low siren, güiro, castanets, maracas, slapstick, cowbell, tam-tam, tubular chimes, glockenspiel, and piano. Another landmark from the 1930s is John Cage's *First Construction (in Metal)* (1939) for six percussionists, which calls for exotic instruments like thundersheets, brake drums, oxen bells, Japanese temple bells, Turkish cymbals, water gongs, and string piano, among others.

American composers, including Lou Harrison and Harry Partch, have experimented extensively with new percussive effects and music for percussion ensembles modeled on Eastern traditions, such as the Javanese *gamelan*. Partch, known primarily as the inventor of new percussion instruments like the diamond marimba, cloud-chamber bowls, cone gongs, and gourd tree, also experimented with unconventional tunings based on **just intonation,** a system of tuning in which the intervals are represented using whole-number ratios. His influential book *Genesis of a Music* (1949) presents a comprehensive history of tuning theory and documents his own tuning theories and aesthetics.

Threnody to the Victims of Hiroshima (1960) for string orchestra by Krzysztof Penderecki represents a striking departure from the conventional use of texture and sonority. The work's subtle alternation of blocks of sound, clusters, and quasi-imitative polyphonic strands is the primary determinant in the listener's perception of its form. Penderecki divides the orchestra into 52 individual parts, calling for a diverse palette of extended string techniques including *sul ponticello, sul tasto, col legno,* and *col legno battuto,* as well as more recent innovations like playing behind the bridge and playing the highest note possible. He also calls for the execution of microtonal pitch inflections based on the **quarter tone,** an interval that divides the octave into 24 equal parts. Example 28-2 shows a page from the score of this work.

Example 28-2   Penderecki, *Threnody to the Victims of Hiroshima*

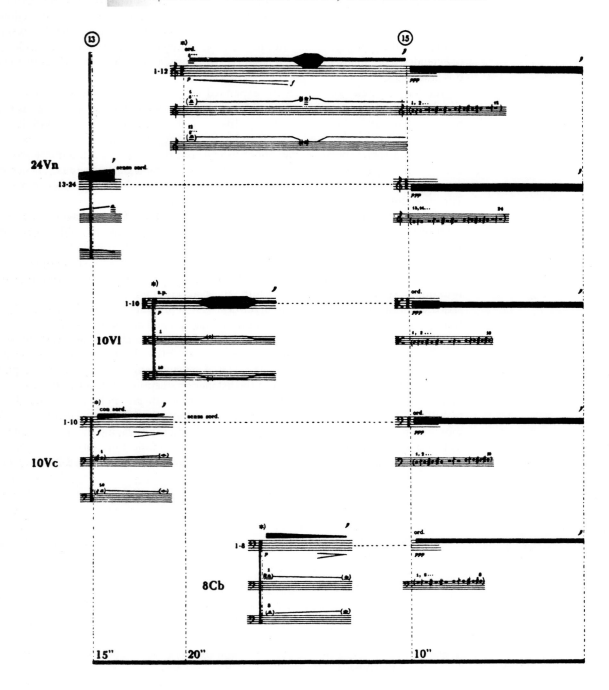

This score is an example of **graphic notation,** a notational style that uses nontraditional symbols to represent musical information. Notice the cluster bands at No. 13 that slowly expand and contract. Also notice the static quarter-tone cluster in the 24 violins beginning at No. 15 that is orchestrationally reinforced by similar cluster bands in the lower string parts. The score is also an example of **proportional notation,** a notational style indicating approximate durations through the spacing of events and timings, in this example, given in seconds on the time line at the bottom of the score.

The idea of creating compositions out of sound masses distinguished not by pitch but by timbre, rhythm, density, register, and so on, can be traced back to Ives, Cowell, and Varèse. Another composer widely recognized for his sound-mass compositions is György Ligeti. The complex, clusterlike surface of his early orchestral works, such as *Atmosphères* (1961), are derived from **micropolyphony,** a term used to describe the canonic relationships between the voices. It is interesting to note that Ligeti's music was brought to the attention of a much wider audience when a number of his works were prominently featured in Stanley Kubrick's 1968 film *2001: A Space Odyssey.* Ligeti's works for keyboard, especially *Volumina* (1962) for organ, *Continuum* (1968) for harpsichord, and his three books of *Etudes* for solo piano (1985–2001) are a compendium of contemporary innovations that continue to serve as a model for other composers.

The use of extended vocal techniques can be traced back to Schoenberg's use of *Sprechstimme* (speech-song), a cross between singing and dramatic declamation, in *Pierrot lunaire.* Works like Peter Maxwell Davies' *Eight Songs for a Mad King* (1969) and George Crumb's *Ancient Voices of Children* (1970) have continued this tradition of vocal experimentation. Many of the vocal works of Luciano Berio also bear the mark of the **new vocalism,** a term sometimes used to refer to the use of vocal techniques based on the talents of a particular performer. Berio's collaborations with Cathy Berberian produced a number of stunning works including *Circles* (1960) for female voice, harp, and two percussionists on a text by e. e. cummings.

The gradual incorporation of jazz and rock elements into the language of contemporary composers is worthy of note. The unique harmonic and rhythmic language of jazz, especially ragtime, inspired numerous composers to incorporate elements of jazz into their music after World War I. Examples include Stravinsky's *Ragtime* (1918), Darius Milhaud's *La création du monde* (1923), George Gershwin's *Rhapsody in Blue* (1924), and Aaron Copland's *Music for the Theatre* (1925). Stravinsky even composed a concerto for clarinet and jazz band titled *Ebony Concerto* (1945) at the request of clarinetist and bandleader Woody Herman. After World War II, composer Gunther Schuller led a movement called **third-stream** which blended elements of jazz and serious contemporary music. An interest in using jazz elements in opera that stretches back to Kurt Weill's *Three Penny Opera* (1928) and George Gershwin's *Porgy and Bess* (1935) continues in operas like John Eaton's *Tempest* (1985) and Anthony Davis's *X, The Life and Times of Malcolm X* (1986).

Rock represents a readily identifiable approach to instrumentation. The use of drum set, electric guitar, electric bass, synthesizers (to be discussed later), microphones, and live-sound reinforcement are all characteristics that have been brought into the contemporary concert hall. Michael Daugherty's music, which is often based on contemporary popular culture icons such as Elvis, Superman, and Liberace, is an obvious fusion of rock and classical avant-garde traditions. Scored for the same instrumentation as Stravinsky's *L'Histoire du soldat,* Daugherty's *Dead Elvis* (1993) features a bassoon soloist who dresses as an Elvis impersonator. The work might be described as a continuous series of variations on the plainchant melody *Dies irae* from the Roman Catholic Mass for the Dead set against a steady rock beat.

Indeterminacy

Indeterminacy or **aleatory** refers to music in which elements of a composition have intentionally been left undetermined by the composer. Although both terms are essentially twentieth-century additions to the vocabulary of music, the idea of chance in music is by no means new to the realities of musical notation and performance.

A famous eighteenth-century example of indeterminacy may be found in J. S. Bach's *Art of the Fugue* (1750), whose instrumentation is left unspecified by the composer. To a certain extent, the time-honored practice of jazz improvisation, especially as it pertains to the spontaneous music making of a soloist or group of live performers, may be considered to involve the element of chance. However, the term is usually reserved for music in which the composer consciously gives up control over aspects of the work's composition and/or performance.

The application of aleatory to music composition may manifest itself in one of two ways: (1) the compositional process itself may be indeterminate in one way or another, or (2) the overall plan of the piece may be precisely notated, with specific details left either to the performer or to chance.

The best-known, and perhaps the earliest, advocate of aleatory as a valid approach to music composition and performance was the American John Cage. In *Music of Changes* (1951) for solo piano, Cage used chance procedures derived from the *I Ching,* the ancient Chinese *Book of Changes,* to determine the work's pitches, durations, dynamics, and so forth, which were then notated in a conventional "fixed" score.

The piece with which Cage is perhaps most widely identified is *4′33″* (1952). The first performance took place at Woodstock, New York, on August 29, 1952, and featured David Tudor, a pianist and longtime professional associate of Cage. The published score of the piece consists of a single page indicating three movements, with the playing instruction "TACET" given for each movement. A performance note at the bottom of the page specifies that the work may last any length of time and is playable by any instrument or instrumental ensemble. The title of the work is derived from the total duration in minutes and seconds of its performance. Tudor marked the beginning of the movements by closing the keyboard lid; the opening of the keyboard lid signaled the end of each movement. For the duration of each movement (33″, 2′40″, and 1′20″, respectively), Tudor remained essentially motionless on stage. Michael Nyman, in his book *Experimental Music: Cage and Beyond,* describes the chief importance of the work this way:

> *4′33″* is a demonstration of the non-existence of silence, of the permanent presence of sounds around us, of the fact that they are worthy of attention, and that for Cage 'environmental sounds and noises are more useful aesthetically than the sounds produced by the world's musical cultures'. *4′33″* is not a negation of music but an affirmation of its omnipresence.*

Cage's *Imaginary Landscape No. 4* (1951) for 12 radios provides us with another example of the **experimental music** tradition that Cage helped to initiate. A model of precise

---

*   Michael Nyman, *Experimental Music: Cage and Beyond,* 2nd ed. (Cambridge: Cambridge University Press, 1999), p. 26.

notation, each pair of 24 performers is furnished with a radio and an individual part, on which is indicated tuning, volume, and tone control information. There is, in addition, a conductor equipped with a stopwatch. Obviously, despite the precision of the performance instructions, every performance will differ greatly from every other one, depending on geographic location and time of day. A performance in New York City, for example, will always be a totally different experience than one in Omaha, Nebraska (where the premiere performance took place).

The length to which Cage's disciples carried his original ideas can be seen in a group of pieces by Max Neuhaus, composed between 1966 and 1968. The set comprises six sound-oriented compositions, specifically designed for a situation other than that of the concert hall. The first of these, *Listen: Field Trips Thru Found Sound Environments,* specifies that the audience, who arrives expecting a concert or lecture, are to be put on a bus, have their hands stamped with the word "Listen," and then be driven through an existing sound environment. One such "performance," for example, took place in the Consolidated Edison Power Station at Fourteenth Street and Avenue D in New York City. *Drive-In Music,* the fifth piece in the group, is designed for people in automobiles. The original score consists of a street map of a small area in Buffalo, New York, designating the streets along which the listener is to drive. At various locations along the route, radio transmitters, which may be heard only through an AM radio, are mounted on telephone poles or trees. Their broadcast areas are designed to overlap, so that at any given time the listener is hearing a combination of signals. Because the actual "music" heard by the concertgoer is subject to such a multitude of fluctuations, brought about not only by the choice of sounds (which might range anywhere from noise to snippets of classical repertoire) but also by the weather, speed of travel, engine noise, and so on, we simply cannot conceptualize or describe the resulting musical effect without having experienced it.

Cage's pioneer efforts inspired a host of followers, and the result was an incredible diversity of experimentation. Composers associated with the experimental music tradition include Morton Feldman, Alvin Lucier, Gordon Mumma, Frederic Rzewski, LaMonte Young, and Christian Wolff, as well as Terry Riley, Steve Reich, and Philip Glass, whose music we will discuss in the next section.

Minimalism

The term **minimalism** refers to a style that seems to have evolved out of the music of John Cage and Morton Feldman and was later interpreted as a reaction to the seemingly arbitrary complexities of integral serialism. Minimalism is characterized by a return to tonal elements and diatonicism, as well as the use of restricted pitch materials, static harmony, and rhythmic elements inspired by Eastern music. The three American composers most closely identified with minimalism, Terry Riley, Steve Reich, and Philip Glass, all studied Eastern music. Rhythmic devices associated with Eastern music, such as repetition, ostinato, polyrhythm, organization around a steady pulse, phasing, and elements of indeterminacy, are also common.

Terry Riley's *In C* (1964) is one of the earliest examples of minimalism. The first 15 melodic figures of Riley's *In C* are shown in Example 28-3.

Example 28-3   Riley, *In C*, the first 15 of 53 figures

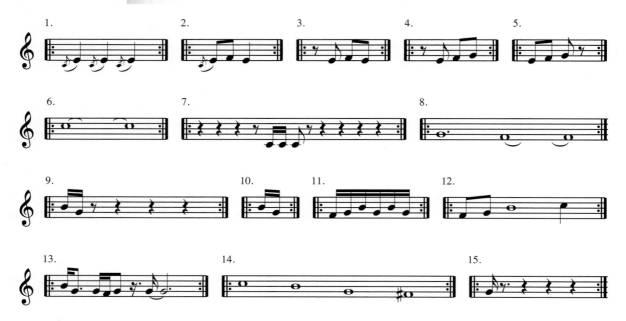

The 53 figures in the composition are to be played in order and in tempo by an ensemble that may consist of any number of players and any instrumental combination. Each player decides for himself or herself (1) when to enter and (2) whether, and how often, to repeat each figure. The music is organized around a steady pulse that is maintained by a pianist playing steady eighth notes on the top two Cs of a grand piano. Note the use of very limited pitch materials. Note, too, the static harmony that begins around C major and leads to a half cadence at figure 15. The aesthetic effect of a performance, which in some cases may extend beyond an hour, depends in large part on the audience's expectations and the performers' ability to establish a compelling counterpoint of shifting pitches, rhythms, and colors.

The concept of **phasing** may be seen as a process that is a logical extension of aleatoric procedures. The technique was first introduced by Steve Reich in his tape pieces (to be discussed later) *It's Gonna Rain* (1965) and *Come Out* (1966). *Come Out* is based on a recording of a victim of the 1964 Harlem riots explaining his injury. His recorded words, "I had to, like, open the bruise up and let some of the bruise blood come out to show them" are used as the source material for the work. Reich created a **tape loop** out of the phrase "come out to show them." The work begins with a unison presentation of two copies of the loop playing on two separate channels of a tape recorder. The second channel is allowed to slowly drift out of phase, with the first producing echo or reverberation effects, and ultimately, two, four and eight-voice canons. In "Music as a Gradual Process" (1968), taken from the collection of essays *Writings on Music,* Reich articulates his approach in such works, an approach now commonly referred to as **process music:**

I do not mean the process of composition, but rather pieces of music that are, literally, processes. The distinctive thing about musical processes is that they determine all the note-to-note (sound-to-sound) details and the overall form simultaneously. (Think of a round or infinite canon.) I am interested in perceptible processes. I want to be able to hear the process happening throughout the sounding music. To facilitate closely detailed listening a musical process should happen extremely gradually.

Performing and listening to a gradual musical process resembles: pulling back a swing, releasing it, and observing it gradually come to rest; turning over an hour glass and watching the sand slowly run through to the bottom; placing your feet in the sand by the ocean's edge and watching, feeling, and listening to the waves gradually bury them.*

Reich later applied this technique in an instrumental work, *Piano Phase* (1967). *Piano Phase* consists of 32 musical figures played by either two pianos or two marimbas, a type of indeterminacy in the specification of the instrumentation that is common in Reich's music. The first 12 figures of *Piano Phase* are given in Example 28-4.

Example 28-4   Reich, *Piano Phase*, the first 12 of 32 figures

piano phase

for two pianos
or two marimbas*

steve reich

---

* Steve Reich, *Writings on Music, 1965–2000* (Oxford: Oxford University Press, 2002), p. 34.

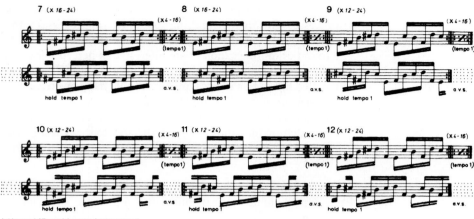

hold tempo 1 / Tempo 1 fortsetzen / tenir le tempo 1.

* The piece may be played an octave lower than written, when played on marimbas. / Wenn Marimbas verwendet werden, kann das Stück eine Oktave tiefer als notiert gespielt werden. / La pièce pourra être jouée à l'octave inférieure quand est exécutée par des marimbas.

a.v.s. = accelerando very slightly. / sehr geringfügiges accelerando. / très légèrement accelerando.

The directions for performance are given in Example 28-5.

Example 28-5   Reich, *Piano Phase,* directions for performance

Directions for Performance

Repeats

The number of repeats of each bar is not fixed but may vary more or less within the limits appearing at each bar. Generally speaking a number of repeats more than the minimum and less than the maximum should be aimed for. The point throughout, however, is not to count repeats, but to listen to the two voice relationship and as you hear it clearly and have absorbed it, move on to the next bar.

Duration

Although duration may obviously vary, experience has shown that it should be about 20 minutes.

Performance

The first performer starts at bar 1 and, after about 4 to 8 repeats, the second gradually fades in, in unison, at bar 2. After about 12 to 18 repeats getting into a comfortable and stable unison, the second performer gradually increases his or her tempo very slightly and begins to move very slowly ahead of the first until, after about 4 to 16 repeats, he or she is one sixteenth note ahead, as shown at bar 3. This relationship is then held steadily for about 16 to 24 repeats as outlined above. The dotted lines indicate this gradual movement of the second performer and the consequent shift of phase relation between both performers. This process of gradual phase shifting and then holding the new stable relationship is continued with the second pianist becoming an eighth (bar 4), a dotted eighth (bar 5), a quarter note (bar 6), etc. ahead of the first performer until he or she passes through all twelve relationships and returns to unison at bar 14. The second performer then gradually fades out and the first continues alone at bar 15. The first performer changes the basic pattern at bar 16 and the second performer gradually fades in with still another pattern at bar 17. The second performer again very slowly increases his or her tempo and slowly moves ahead and out of phase until he or she arrives one sixteenth note ahead as shown at bar 18. This relationship is then held steadily as before. After moving through all eight relationships in this way the second performer returns to his or her starting point at bar 25. The first performer then gradually fades out and the second performer continues alone at bar 26. The second performer changes the basic pattern at bar 27 and the first fades in, in unison, at bar 28. The second performer again slowly increases his or her tempo and moves ahead and out of phase as before until he or she returns to unison at bar 32. After several repeats in unison one performer nods his or her head on the downbeat and, after 4 repeats, both performers end together.

Rehearsal

When first rehearsing the piece it may be useful for the first performer to play bar 1 and keep on repeating it while the second performer tries to enter directly at bar 3 exactly one sixteenth note ahead *without trying to phase there*. After listening to this two voice relationship for a while the second performer should stop, join the first performer in unison and only then try to increase very slightly his or her tempo so that he or she gradually moves one sixteenth note ahead into bar 3. This approach of first jumping in directly to bar 3, 4, 5, etc., listening to it and only then trying to phase into it is based on the principle that *hearing* what it sounds like to be 1, 2 or more sixteenth notes ahead will then enable the performer to phase there without increasing tempo too much and passing into a further bar, or phasing ahead a bit and then sliding back to where one started. Several rehearsals spread over several weeks before performance will help produce smooth phase movements and the tendency to phase too quickly from one bar to the next will be overcome allowing performers to spend due time-the slower the better-in the gradual shifts of phase between bars.

Instruments

When two pianos are used they should be as identical as possible. The lids should both be open or removed. The pianos should be arranged as follows:

AUDIENCE

When two marimbas are used they should be as identical as possible. Soft rubber mallets are suggested. *The piece may be played an octave lower than written, when played on marimbas.* The marimbas may be moderately amplified by conventional microphones if the hall holds more than 200 people. The marimbas should be arranged as follows:

AUDIENCE

Reich has described the phasing technique he employed in his early works as a form of canon based on irrational numbers. The rich surface texture of *Piano Phase* is essentially the product of unforeseen **resultant patterns** that are created by the constantly shifting relationship between the two identical parts.

Philip Glass's opera trilogy *Einstein on the Beach* (1975), *Satyagraha* (1980), and *Akhnaten* (1984), and his film scores for *Koyaanisqatsi* (1982), *Kundun* (1997), and *Notes on a Scandal* (2006) are a testament to the popularity and staying power of minimalism. Glass, whose studies with the Indian sitarist Ravi Shankar in the 1960s deeply influenced his musical thinking, does not employ a phasing technique. Rather, the focus is on the repetition of a pattern that, after long durations, changes abruptly. This type of repetition allows the listener to focus on the complexity of the constantly changing rhythmic surface. One such pattern, from *Einstein on the Beach,* is shown in Example 28-6.

Example 28-6   Glass, *Einstein on the Beach,* act IV, scene 3

One of the principal themes of the opera, this pattern forms the basis of nearly all of the music for act IV, scene 3, the "Spaceship." Note its triadic basis, its 4+3+4+3+4 rhythmic structure, and the authentic cadence implied by the last two chords.

More recently, John Adams has introduced more traditional rhythmic procedures into his use of the minimalist technique. *Short Ride in a Fast Machine* was commissioned for the opening concert of the Great Woods Festival in Mansfield, Massachusetts, in 1986. It is a joyfully exuberant piece with a pervasive and infectious motor rhythm. Scored for full orchestra with the persistent presence of wood block, the work is occasionally suggestive of the earlier orchestral scores of Stravinsky. At the same time, the listener is aware of a new and contemporary language, one indigenous to the present day.

Electronic and Computer Music

Inevitably, with the mounting interest in textural and coloristic complexity, the possibilities for electronic sound generation began to be investigated more closely. One of the earliest examples of an electronic instrument is Thaddeus Cahill's **Telharmonium,** a large electronic keyboard instrument that used telephone network technology to transmit sounds. It was first demonstrated in public in 1906. The earliest instruments to have practical applications were developed in the 1920s and included the **Theremin** and the **Ondes Martenot.** Both instruments made use of an electronic oscillator (to be discussed later) as a tone generator. The Theremin enjoyed a period of renewed interest in 1945 when employed by composer Miklós Rózsa in his scores for the films *Lost Weekend* and *Spellbound.* Its characteristic vibrato, tremolo, and glissando are often associated with science fiction themes, as in Bernard Herrmann's use of two Theremins in his film score for *The Day the Earth Stood Still* (1951). The Ondes Martinot, which plays a very prominent role in Messiaen's *Turangalîla-symphonie* (1948), has been employed by a number of important composers, including Darius Milhaud, Edgard Varèse, and Pierre Boulez.

Toward the midpoint of the twentieth century, technical developments in tape-recorder technology resulted in the growing popularity of **tape music,** music that exists primarily in the medium of magnetic tape. In 1948 Pierre Schaeffer, a radio engineer and broadcaster, created a series of five etudes for broadcast over French radio. His first study, *Étude aux chemins de fer,* explored railroad sounds. The sounds were not modified, but were simply juxtaposed to create interesting musical structures. He called this approach **musique concrète** because he worked directly with the sounds, organizing them into musical structures without the use of traditional notation. His early works were created using phonograph equipment. Later works took advantage of the new capabilities of tape technology. Sounds were subjected to modifications that fall into five broad categories: (1) altered playback speed, (2) reversed tape direction, (3) cutting and splicing of tape, (4) creation of a tape loop, and (5) tape delay. Timbral manipulations that result from a combination of these transformations were also used.

Strictly speaking, the term **electronic music** originally referred to music that was generated synthetically by means of an **electronic oscillator,** an electronic circuit that uses an amplifier and filter to generate a repeating signal. Electronic circuits were designed to produce basic waveshapes such as the **sine wave,** a sound devoid of overtones or harmonics that is similar to the sound of a tuning fork or open flute. Other circuits were designed to generate more complex patterns of harmonics, including the **sawtooth wave** (a jagged, nasal tone that contains all harmonics) and the **square wave** (a clarinetlike tone that contains only odd-numbered harmonics).

The tones produced by oscillators can be precisely controlled in terms of the following parameters: (1) frequency, (2) amplitude, and (3) waveform. Waveforms that repeat a basic waveshape over time are called periodic waveforms. Our sensation of pitch is associated with this type of periodicity, among other factors, while our sensation of loudness is associated with amplitude. Frequency is related to the number of repetitions of the waveshape per second. For example, a sine wave that repeats its waveshape 440 times per second is said to have a frequency of 440 Hertz (abbreviated Hz.), the pitch A4, which is a standard for tuning in the United States in an audible frequency spectrum that spans ca. 20 Hz. to 20,000 Hz.

The **white noise generator,** whose essentially random waveshape produces a "hissing" sound consisting of frequency components that are equally distributed across the audible frequency spectrum, also played an important role in early electronic music. Finally, an **amplitude envelope** gives musical shape to an oscillator's static tone by imparting an attack, decay, sustain, and release phase to the tone's overall loudness profile. Further manipulation by means of amplifiers, mixers, filters, modulators, and reverberation units was also common.

Many of the most important early developments in electronic music composition took place toward the middle of the twentieth century at the Studio for Electronic Music of the West German Radio in Cologne, Germany. The composer Karlheinz Stockhausen brought the studio into prominence with electronic works such as *Gesang der Jünglinge* (1956) and *Kontakte* (1960). It attracted many prominent composers including Gottfried Michael König, Henri Pousseur and György Ligeti, among other composers who were intrigued by the new medium and its potential to implement the principles of total serialization.

The first published score of an electronic composition was Stockhausen's *Elektronische Studie II* (1954). The first page of the score is shown in Example 28-7.

Example 28-7   Stockhausen, *Studie II*, graphic score notation (opening)

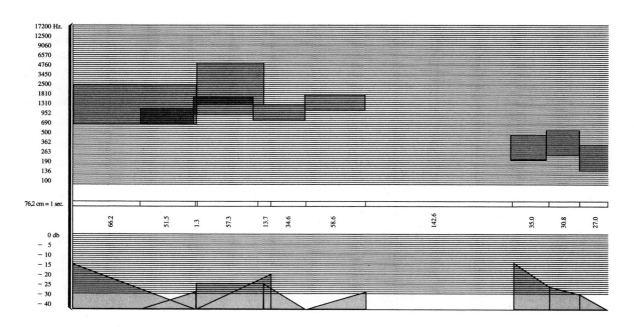

Its composition was based entirely on sine-wave tones that are grouped into structures called tone mixtures. The score is designed to provide all the data necessary to realize the work. Each tone mixture, consisting of five sine waves of equal amplitude whose frequencies were determined mathematically, is represented graphically as rectangles that span specific regions of the audio spectrum from 100 to 17,200 Hz. Heavier shading is used to indicate the overlap of mixtures. The amplitude envelope of each tone mixture is shown at the bottom of the score using triangular and rectangular shapes plotted against a decibel scale (−40 to 0 db). The duration of each mixture is indicated in the middle of the score in terms of tape length measured in centimeters (cm). The vertical strokes mark the beginnings and endings of tone-mixture events for a tape running at a speed of 76.2 cm/sec.

Composed at the Philips laboratories in Eindhoven, Netherlands, Edgard Varèse's *Poème électronique* was specifically created for performance in the Philips Pavilion, a building designed by the architect Le Corbusier for the 1958 Brussels World's Fair. Architect-composer Iannis Xenakis assisted Le Corbusier on the project. This spatially conceived composition for tape was projected over 425 loudspeakers that filled the curved space of the pavilion, sending continuous waves of sound over the visitors who passed through it. It combined projected images, moving colored lights, and sounds ranging from purely electronic to recorded voice, organ, bells, and percussion in a visual and sonic synthesis that evoked reactions ranging from wild enthusiasm to stark terror among its audience.

Working at the Studio di Fonologia Musicale in Milan, which he cofounded with Bruno Maderna in 1955, Luciano Berio created two highly influential works using traditional tape techniques: *Thema (Omaggio a Joyce)* (1958), which is based on recorded readings from James Joyce's *Ulysses*; and *Visage* (1961), a collage of emotional utterances and electronic sounds organized around a single intelligible Italian word: *paroles* (words). Both works feature the specialized vocal talents of soprano Cathy Berberian.

The splicing and mixing of tape to create a composition was a laborious task. The development of synthesizers allowed the composer to combine and sequence source signals more efficiently than traditional tape techniques. Invented in the 1950s by Harry Olsen and Hebert Belar, the RCA Synthesizer offered the composer control over the parameters of sound through punched paper rolls. In 1959, Milton Babbitt, Otto Luening, and Vladimir Ussachevsky received a grant from the Rockefeller Foundation to establish a permanent center for computer music at Columbia University. The second generation of the RCA Synthesizer, called the Mark II, was installed in the newly established Columbia-Princeton Electronic Music Center later that year. Milton Babbitt's interest in the principles of total serialization found expression in *Composition for Synthesizer* (1961) and other works created with the Mark II. Another important work that was executed, in part, on the Mark II using serial procedures is Charles Wuorinen's composition *Time's Encomium* (1969).

The inevitable loss of drama in concert hall performances of tape music spawned efforts to combine live performers and taped sound. Babbitt used the Mark II to compose two influential works for soprano and tape: *Vision and a Prayer* (1961), on a poem by Dylan Thomas, and *Philomel* (1964), on a poem by John Hollander. Luening and Ussachevsky also experimented with this form of interactivity. Champions of indeterminacy, such as John Cage, found that the theatrical possibilities of this combination were well suited to their musical philosophies. More recent composers especially well known for their work in this medium include Mario Davidovsky and Jacob Druckman. Davidovsky's *Synchronisms* (1963–92) for various solo instruments and tape, along with Druckman's series of compositions titled *Animus I-III* (1966–69), for tape and trombone, voice/percussion, and clarinet, respectively, have become part of the standard contemporary recital literature for these instruments. In some instances, the collaboration calls for the performer to play into a tape recorder. The sounds thus generated are electronically modified and played back, providing an interactive partnership. In other cases, prerecorded music by the solo instrument is combined on tape with electronic sounds. The final product may be the result of strict control on the part of the composer or may represent processes of indeterminacy.

The first two pages of Davidovsky's *Synchronisms No. 6* for piano and electronic sound are shown in Example 28-8.

Example 28-8   Davidovsky, *Synchronisms* no. 6

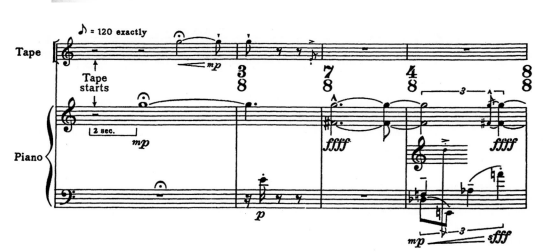

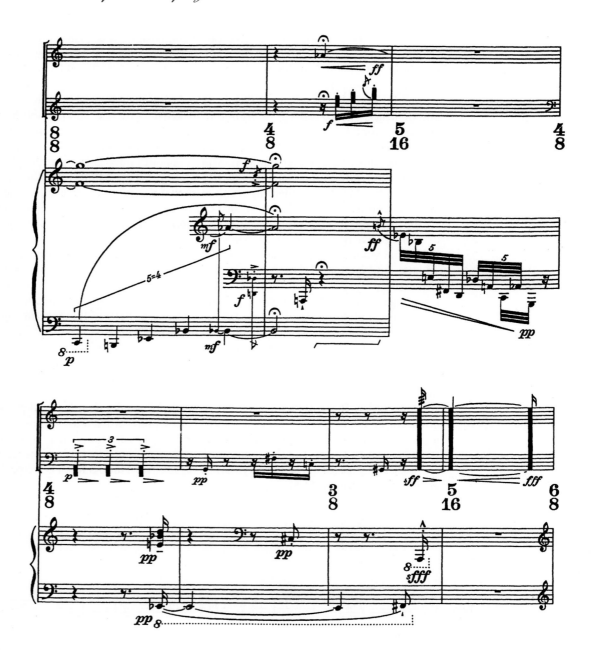

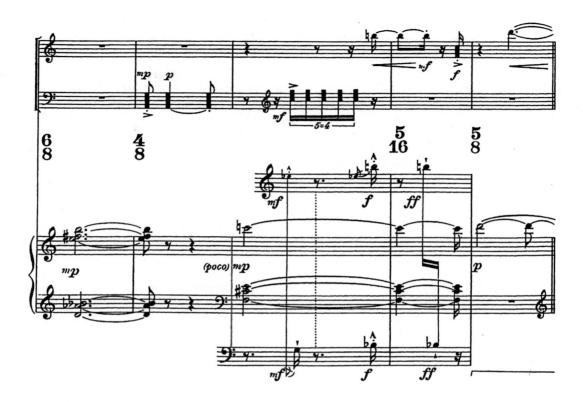

The work, which requires a tape playback unit of high professional quality, was premiered in 1970. In his introduction to the work, Davidovsky states, "the electronic sounds in many instances modulate the acoustical characteristics of the piano by affecting its decay and attack characteristics. The electronic segment should perhaps not be viewed as an independent polyphonic line, but rather as if it were inlaid into the piano part." Note the composer's tempo marking (♪ = 120 exactly), indicating the obvious need for precise coordination with the tape.

The introduction of modular analog **synthesizers** in the 1960s, marketed under trade names of Moog, Buchla, and ARP, offered a wide palette of new sounds. To create an "instrument," the composer connected the various voltage-controlled modules of the synthesizer using cables called patch cords. Wendy Carlos used the Moog synthesizer to create the popular album *Switched-on Bach* (1968), a set of electronic realizations of works by J. S. Bach. Morton Subotnick used the Buchla synthesizer to create a number of highly original works, including *Silver Apples of the Moon* (1967) and *The Wild Bull* (1968).

The introduction of digital synthesizers, such as the Yamaha DX series, and **samplers,** such as the Ensoniq Mirage, the Emulator II, and those designed by Ray Kurzweil, represented an important development in the evolution of electronic music. They became the mainstay of many popular music groups of the 1970s and 1980s, not only because of their variety of timbres but also because of their relative portability. Some synthesizers, like the highly influential Synclavier developed at Dartmouth College, offered both synthesis and sampling in a single system. The essential unit in a digital synthesizer is the digital oscillator. Released in 1983, the Yamaha DX-7 was one of the first commercially successful digital synthesizers. It was based on an FM synthesis technique discovered by John Chowning at Stanford in the late 1960s. Whereas an additive synthesis approach requires a dedicated oscillator for each harmonic of a musical tone, FM synthesis can produce realistic-sounding tones using a modulation technique that requires comparatively few oscillators. A sampler has the capability of recording, storing, editing and playing back audio information. The actual sampling involves the encoding of an analog signal by reading its wave form at precisely spaced intervals of time using a device called an **analog-to-digital converter.** For CD-quality audio, this is done 44,100 times per second. Once encoded as a series of discrete numbers, the audio data can be manipulated using modern editing software. A **digital-to-analog converter** converts the numbers back to a continuous voltage stream that drives a loudspeaker.

The introduction of **MIDI** (Musical Instrument Digital Interface) and personal computer technology in the 1980s started a trend toward miniaturization, reduced cost, and rapid adoption that continues today. MIDI was originally designed to allow the keyboard of one synthesizer to drive the tone generator of another and allow a single performer (or computer) to drive multiple tone generators, audio processors, drum machines, and so forth. Through the use of a **sequencer,** a software application that stores sequences of MIDI data rather than the sounds themselves, a composer may easily change MIDI note, key velocity, tempo, or controller information of a previously encoded performance. When the speed of personal computers greatly increased in the 1990s, digital audio playback, recording, and editing features were also added to sequencers.

The origin of **computer music,** music created with the aid of a computer, may be traced back to the work of Max Mathews at Bell Telephone Laboratories in the late 1950s. By 1962, Mathews had created MUSIC4, the first computer music programming language to be widely adopted by composers. Barry Vercoe's Csound, a digital audio processing and composition environment in wide use today, can trace its origins all the way back to MUSIC4. The first substantial computer music composition was *Illiac Suite* (1957), a string quartet by Lejaren Hiller and Leonard Isaacson that was created with the aid of the University of Illinois at Urbana-Champaign's ILLIAC computer. Known for his **stochastic music,** in which the musical parameters such as pitch, intensity, and duration are determined by the laws of probability theory, Iannis Xenakis was also using the computer in the 1950s and 1960s to aid in the mathematical calculations required by his works for traditional instruments such as *Atrées* (1962) for 10 soloists.

By the 1970s, Stanford University's CCRMA (Center for Computer Research in Music and Acoustics) was on the leading edge of computer music research and composition in America. Chowning's discovery of the FM synthesis technique was but one of its significant contributions to the field. Chowning also created a number of highly original compositions that explored ideas related to his research; for example, he used FM synthesis to experiment with the motion of sounds through space in works such as *Sabelithe* (1966–71) and *Turenas* (1972). Bell Laboratories in Murray Hill, New Jersey, was another important center for research and creative activity. Charles Dodge's *Speech Songs* (1972), on texts by Mark Strand, paved the way for future exploration in the area of digital sampling, analysis, and resynthesis of the human voice. Also influential in this area was Michael McNabb's *Dreamsong* (1978), another work composed at CCRMA that features a wide-ranging palette of digital sounds from FM tones to sampled speech, singing soprano, and crowd noises.

The founding of IRCAM (Institut de Recherche et Coordination Acoustique/Musique) in Paris, France, during the mid 1970s had a profound effect on the expansion of computer music into the realm of real-time interaction. Pierre Boulez's *Répons* (1981), a work for six soloists, 24-member chamber orchestra, and live electronics is one of the most important early works to come out of IRCAM. The live electronics were built around the 4X, a specialized audio processing computer invented at IRCAM. The six soloists, whose sounds are modified by the 4X in real time and projected over six loudspeakers to suggest complex spatial trajectories, are placed around the perimeter of the performance space. The software required to realize works like *Répons* eventually led to the development of personal computer software for real-time interactive composition and performance such as Cycling 74's Max/MSP and Miller Puckette's Pd.

Working at MIT's Media Lab since 1985, Tod Machover coined the term **hyperinstrument** to refer to his use of computers to augment musical expression and creativity. He has composed a series of works for virtuosi performers which includes *Begin Again Again . . .* (1991) for hypercello, a work written for cellist Yo-Yo Ma. The cellist is asked to wear a "data glove" and other sensors that give the performer direct control over the computer-generated musical surface. Machover's *Brain Opera* (1996) is a highly futuristic operatic work based on cognitive scientist Marvin Minsky's book *Society of Mind*. Audience members are invited to participate in its performance through interaction with onsite musical installations such as the Gesture Wall, Rhythm Tree, Melody Easel, Sensor Carpet, and Harmonic Driving system, and real-time interaction over the Internet via a personal computer located at work or home. The *Brain Opera* has since been transformed into the *Future Music Blender* (2000), an installation that permanently resides in Vienna's House of Music.

Like Davidovsky's *Synchronisms*, Paul Lansky's "chatter" series is a landmark in the electro-acoustic musical landscape. Inspired by the rhythms of rap, Lansky wrote three pieces—*Idle Chatter* (1985), *just_more_idle_chatter* (1987), and *Notjustmoreidlechatter* (1988)—that all feature the sampled voice of his wife, Hannah MacKay. Executed on mainframe and mini computers using granular and linear predictive coding synthesis techniques, all three compositions explore the idea of creating percussion music out of incomprehensible speech. Now working on personal computers, Lansky has added two new contributions to the series: *Idle Chatter Junior* (1999), which adds instrumental sounds to the usual textural fabric, and *Chatter of Pins* (2006), a highly original setting of the English folk song "A Paper of Pins." Example 28-9 shows the composer's harmonic reduction of the first 14 measures of *Notjustmoreidlechatter*.

Example 28-9   Lansky, *Notjustmoreidlechatter*, composer's harmonic reduction

The progression is sung by a chorus of computer-generated "background singers" whose incoherent babble is created from thousands of short fragments of words. Notice the simple rock-influenced modal progression that begins with diatonic triads and then progresses to seventh chords and added-tone sonorities. After becoming increasingly chromatic in mm. 9 to 13, the progression works its way back to G minor through a series of chromatic-mediant relationships. The underlying tonal basis of many of Lansky's computer-generated compositions has caused some to describe these complex works as a form of **postminimalism,** a term used to refer to music that seems to have its roots in the minimalist traditions of the 1960s and 1970s.

Self-Test 28-1

(Answers begin on page 642.)

A. Name at least three composers who have made use of expanded instrumental resources through nontraditional use of instrument or voice and briefly describe the techniques they used.

_____

_____

_____

_____

_____

_____

B.
  1. Define the term *aleatory* as it is applied to music.

_____

_____

  2. What is the significance of the composition titled *4'33"* by John Cage?

_____

_____

C. Name at least three American composers who are associated with minimalism:
_____ , _____ , and _____ .

D. Briefly define the following terms associated with electronic and computer music:
  1. sine wave _____
  2. white noise _____
  3. oscillator _____
  4. *musique concrète* _____
  5. MIDI _____
  6. hyperinstrument _____

E.

    1. Name the composer who is usually credited with the discovery of FM synthesis: _____ .

    2. Name at least two composers whose computer-generated compositions have prominently featured the sampling and processing of the human voice: _____ and _____ .

    3. Name at least two important centers for computer music research and composition: _____ and _____ .

Exercise 28-1 See Workbook.

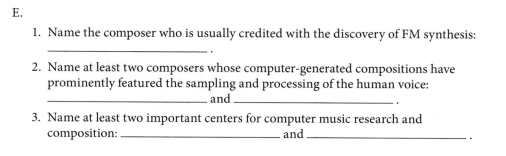

Summary and a Forward Look

Although it is not within the scope of this brief overview to fully cover the myriad developments that have taken place in these areas—expanded textural, timbral, and tuning resources; indeterminacy; minimalism; and electronic and computer music—the foregoing information may serve as a springboard for future exploration of the extraordinary expansion of techniques and materials associated with twentieth-century practice and their implications for the future of music composition and performance.

No one at present can know just how future historians will regard our era and evaluate the primary direction of our musical culture. Surely no component of musical style—pitch, harmony, rhythm, form, texture, timbre, instrumentation—has remained untouched by the stylistic explosion that marked the twentieth century. From the vantage point of the twenty-first century, there seems to be an attempt by many to draw from earlier developments rather than to strike out on totally individual and innovative paths. We can see, in some cases, a fusion of trends that at one time seemed headed in opposite directions. The idea of serialism, for example, which was conceived as a systematic means of escape from the deeply entrenched conventions of tonality, has indeed been pressed into the service of what we hear as very tonal music. Recent efforts in electronic and computer music frequently reflect a consolidation of ideas borrowed from previous movements like serialism and minimalism. Some compositions borrow heavily from the jazz idiom, whereas many contemporary jazz groups perform works that are scarcely distinguishable from today's "serious" concert music. The pace of technological development has wrought profound changes on the music profession itself. However, whatever the direction we seem to be taking, it is indeed a challenging and exciting time in which to be a musician.

Appendix A
Instrumental Ranges and Transpositions

In this appendix we suggest some practical ranges to assist you in composing exercises to be performed in class. These are not extreme ranges, by any means, but the extreme highs and lows of even these ranges should be used cautiously, especially the brasses.

Instrument	Abbreviation	Sounding Range	Written Range
Flute	Fl.		Same
Oboe	Ob.		Same
B♭ Clarinet	Clar. in B♭		Treble clef, M2 higher
Bassoon	Bsn.		Same
E♭ Alto Sax	A. Sax in E♭		Treble clef, M6 higher
B♭ Tenor Sax	T. Sax in B♭		Treble clef, M9 higher
French horn	Hn. in F		P5 higher

Instrument	Abbreviation	Sounding Range	Written Range
B♭ Trumpet	Tpt. in B♭		Treble clef, M2 higher
Trombone	Trb.		Same
Tuba	Tuba		Same
Violin	Vl.		Same
Viola	Vla.		Same
Cello	Vc.		Same; tenor clef also used when convenient
Bass	D.B.		P8 higher

Appendix B
Lead-Sheet Symbols

This appendix is designed to show how lead-sheet symbols can be used to describe basic tertian sonorities and their common extensions and alterations. It also lists common added-tone triads and sus chords. To facilitate comparison, all chords are built on the root C and accidentals apply only to notes they immediately proceed. The interpretation of lead-sheet symbols varies greatly depending on the published source and musical context, and myriad symbols may be used to represent a given chord. A C minor triad, for example, may be indicated by the symbols Cm or C-, and in other ways not listed, such as Cmi, Cmin, and so forth. Furthermore, no single typographical standard for writing symbols exists, so C^{ø7}, Cm7$^{(♭5)}$, and Cm7♭5 are all perfectly acceptable ways of writing the symbol for a half-diminished seventh chord on C.

A staff summarizing the naming conventions for chord members and alteration symbols follows:

Chord Member Names and Alteration Symbols

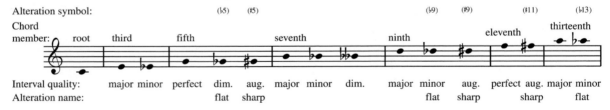

Alteration symbols indicate that a given chord member is to be lowered ("flatted") or raised ("sharped") by a semitone. Note that some alterations, for example ♯5 and ♭13, are enharmonically equivalent. The chord member names and interval qualities are indicated above, along with their associated alteration names (flat-fifth, sharp-fifth, flat-ninth, sharp-ninth, etc.) and symbols (♭5, ♯5, ♭9, ♯9, etc.). To emphasize their function, alteration symbols are enclosed in parentheses.

For triads, seventh chords, and ninth chords, the quality of each chord is indicated below the staff. This system for identifying tertian sonorities is an extension of the system introduced in Chapter 4. It employs the following four quality symbols:

Symbol	Quality
M	Major
m	Minor
d	Diminished
A	Augmented

Triad quality is indicated in bold type. For the seventh and ninth chords, the triad symbol is indicated first, then the quality symbol for the seventh and ninth are added as required. Using C^9 as an example, the quality for its triad is "M", the quality of its seventh is "m", and the quality of its ninth is "M", so its quality symbol is **MmM**.

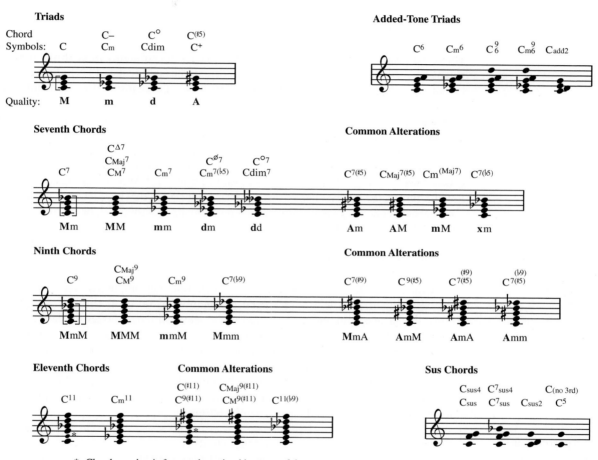

* Chord member is frequently omitted because of the dissonance it creates with another chord member.

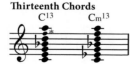

Other types of thirteenth chords may be created by altering members of these basic sonorities. Complete thirteenth chords are rarely encountered. Chord symbols for these sonorities are created in a manner consistent with the principles demonstrated for eleventh chords.

Appendix C
Set Class List

The seven-column table that follows lists all set classes of cardinality three through nine inclusive. The first and fifth columns list the Forte names (abbreviated FN) of set classes in increasing order. The second and sixth columns give the prime forms. The third and seventh columns give the interval vector (abbreviated VECTOR). Some Forte names include a Z, for example, 4-Z29. The Z indicates that there is another set class of the same cardinality that has the same interval vector. Set classes that share the same interval vector, such as 4-Z15 and 4-Z29, are said to be **Z-related.** Inclusion of the Z in the Forte name is optional. The fourth column of the table gives the number of distinct forms (abbreviated DF). Most set classes have 24 distinct forms: 12 under T_n and 12 under T_nI. When nothing appears in the fourth column, the set class has 24 distinct forms. Set classes that have fewer than 24 distinct forms are inversionally symmetrical, transpositionally symmetrical, or both. Intervening spaces have been added to the prime forms and interval vectors to make them easier to read. The intervening spaces should not be used when notating prime forms and interval vectors. In the prime forms, the symbols T and E have been substituted for pc integers 10 and 11, respectively.

The following example should serve to demonstrate the complement relation on which the table is organized. The pc set (C,C♯,D), is a member of 3–1 (012), the first set class listed in the table. The **complement** of a pc set is the set of all pitch classes that are not members of the pc set. For example, the complement of (C,C♯,D) is (D♯,E,F,F♯,G,G♯,A,A♯,B), the other nine pitch classes. This pc set belongs to set class 9–1 (012345678). Notice that the complementary set will always have 12-n members, where n is the number of elements in the pc set. **Complementary set classes** are listed on the same line in the table and have the same number of distinct forms. For hexachordal set classes that are **self-complementary,** nothing appears in fifth, sixth, and seventh columns.

TRICHORDS

FN	PRIME FORM	VECTOR	DF
3-1	(0 1 2)	2 1 0 0 0 0	12
3-2	(0 1 3)	1 1 1 0 0 0	
3-3	(0 1 4)	1 0 1 1 0 0	
3-4	(0 1 5)	1 0 0 1 1 0	
3-5	(0 1 6)	1 0 0 0 1 1	
3-6	(0 2 4)	0 2 0 1 0 0	12
3-7	(0 2 5)	0 1 1 0 1 0	
3-8	(0 2 6)	0 1 0 1 0 1	
3-9	(0 2 7)	0 1 0 0 2 0	12
3-10	(0 3 6)	0 0 2 0 0 1	12
3-11	(0 3 7)	0 0 1 1 1 0	
3-12	(0 4 8)	0 0 0 3 0 0	4

NONACHORDS

FN	PRIME FORM	VECTOR
9-1	(0 1 2 3 4 5 6 7 8)	8 7 6 6 6 3
9-2	(0 1 2 3 4 5 6 7 9)	7 7 7 6 6 3
9-3	(0 1 2 3 4 5 6 8 9)	7 6 7 7 6 3
9-4	(0 1 2 3 4 5 7 8 9)	7 6 6 7 7 3
9-5	(0 1 2 3 4 6 7 8 9)	7 6 6 6 7 4
9-6	(0 1 2 3 4 5 6 8 T)	6 8 6 7 6 3
9-7	(0 1 2 3 4 5 7 8 T)	6 7 7 6 7 3
9-8	(0 1 2 3 4 6 7 8 T)	6 7 6 7 6 4
9-9	(0 1 2 3 5 6 7 8 T)	6 7 6 6 8 3
9-10	(0 1 2 3 4 6 7 9 T)	6 6 8 6 6 4
9-11	(0 1 2 3 5 6 7 9 T)	6 6 7 7 7 3
9-12	(0 1 2 4 5 6 8 9 T)	6 6 6 9 6 3

TETRACHORDS

FN	PRIME FORM	VECTOR	DF
4-1	(0 1 2 3)	3 2 1 0 0 0	12
4-2	(0 1 2 4)	2 2 1 1 0 0	
4-3	(0 1 3 4)	2 1 2 1 0 0	12
4-4	(0 1 2 5)	2 1 1 1 1 0	
4-5	(0 1 2 6)	2 1 0 1 1 1	
4-6	(0 1 2 7)	2 1 0 0 2 1	12
4-7	(0 1 4 5)	2 0 1 2 1 0	12
4-8	(0 1 5 6)	2 0 0 1 2 1	12
4-9	(0 1 6 7)	2 0 0 0 2 2	6
4-10	(0 2 3 5)	1 2 2 0 1 0	12
4-11	(0 1 3 5)	1 2 1 1 1 0	
4-12	(0 2 3 6)	1 1 2 1 0 1	
4-13	(0 1 3 6)	1 1 2 0 1 1	
4-14	(0 2 3 7)	1 1 1 1 2 0	
4-Z15	(0 1 4 6)	1 1 1 1 1 1	
4-16	(0 1 5 7)	1 1 0 1 2 1	
4-17	(0 3 4 7)	1 0 2 2 1 0	12
4-18	(0 1 4 7)	1 0 2 1 1 1	
4-19	(0 1 4 8)	1 0 1 3 1 0	
4-20	(0 1 5 8)	1 0 1 2 2 0	12
4-21	(0 2 4 6)	0 3 0 2 0 1	12
4-22	(0 2 4 7)	0 2 1 1 2 0	
4-23	(0 2 5 7)	0 2 1 0 3 0	12
4-24	(0 2 4 8)	0 2 0 3 0 1	12
4-25	(0 2 6 8)	0 2 0 2 0 2	6
4-26	(0 3 5 8)	0 1 2 1 2 0	12
4-27	(0 2 5 8)	0 1 2 1 1 1	
4-28	(0 3 6 9)	0 0 4 0 0 2	3
4-Z29	(0 1 3 7)	1 1 1 1 1 1	

OCTACHORDS

FN	PRIME FORM	VECTOR
8-1	(0 1 2 3 4 5 6 7)	7 6 5 4 4 2
8-2	(0 1 2 3 4 5 6 8)	6 6 5 5 4 2
8-3	(0 1 2 3 4 5 6 9)	6 5 6 5 4 2
8-4	(0 1 2 3 4 5 7 8)	6 5 5 5 5 2
8-5	(0 1 2 3 4 6 7 8)	6 5 4 5 5 3
8-6	(0 1 2 3 5 6 7 8)	6 5 4 4 6 3
8-7	(0 1 2 3 4 5 8 9)	6 4 5 6 5 2
8-8	(0 1 2 3 4 7 8 9)	6 4 4 5 6 3
8-9	(0 1 2 3 6 7 8 9)	6 4 4 4 6 4
8-10	(0 2 3 4 5 6 7 9)	5 6 6 4 5 2
8-11	(0 1 2 3 4 5 7 9)	5 6 5 5 5 2
8-12	(0 1 3 4 5 6 7 9)	5 5 6 5 4 3
8-13	(0 1 2 3 4 6 7 9)	5 5 6 4 5 3
8-14	(0 1 2 4 5 6 7 9)	5 5 5 5 6 2
8-Z15	(0 1 2 3 4 6 8 9)	5 5 5 5 5 3
8-16	(0 1 2 3 5 7 8 9)	5 5 4 5 6 3
8-17	(0 1 3 4 5 6 8 9)	5 4 6 6 5 2
8-18	(0 1 2 3 5 6 8 9)	5 4 6 5 5 3
8-19	(0 1 2 4 5 6 8 9)	5 4 5 7 5 2
8-20	(0 1 2 4 5 7 8 9)	5 4 5 6 6 2
8-21	(0 1 2 3 4 6 8 T)	4 7 4 6 4 3
8-22	(0 1 2 3 5 6 8 T)	4 6 5 5 6 2
8-23	(0 1 2 3 5 7 8 T)	4 6 5 4 7 2
8-24	(0 1 2 4 5 6 8 T)	4 6 4 7 4 3
8-25	(0 1 2 4 6 7 8 T)	4 6 4 6 4 4
8-26	(0 1 3 4 5 7 8 T)	4 5 6 5 6 2
8-27	(0 1 2 4 5 7 8 T)	4 5 6 5 5 3
8-28	(0 1 3 4 6 7 9 T)	4 4 8 4 4 4
8-Z29	(0 1 2 3 5 6 7 9)	5 5 5 5 5 3

PENTACHORDS

FN	PRIME FORM	VECTOR	DF
5-1	(0 1 2 3 4)	4 3 2 1 0 0	12
5-2	(0 1 2 3 5)	3 3 2 1 1 0	
5-3	(0 1 2 4 5)	3 2 2 2 1 0	
5-4	(0 1 2 3 6)	3 2 2 1 1 1	
5-5	(0 1 2 3 7)	3 2 1 1 2 1	
5-6	(0 1 2 5 6)	3 1 1 2 2 1	
5-7	(0 1 2 6 7)	3 1 0 1 3 2	
5-8	(0 2 3 4 6)	2 3 2 2 0 1	12
5-9	(0 1 2 4 6)	2 3 1 2 1 1	
5-10	(0 1 3 4 6)	2 2 3 1 1 1	
5-11	(0 2 3 4 7)	2 2 2 2 2 0	
5-Z12	(0 1 3 5 6)	2 2 2 1 2 1	12
5-13	(0 1 2 4 8)	2 2 1 3 1 1	
5-14	(0 1 2 5 7)	2 2 1 1 3 1	
5-15	(0 1 2 6 8)	2 2 0 2 2 2	12

SEPTACHORDS

FN	PRIME FORM	VECTOR
7-1	(0 1 2 3 4 5 6)	6 5 4 3 2 1
7-2	(0 1 2 3 4 5 7)	5 5 4 3 3 1
7-3	(0 1 2 3 4 5 8)	5 4 4 4 3 1
7-4	(0 1 2 3 4 6 7)	5 4 4 3 3 2
7-5	(0 1 2 3 5 6 7)	5 4 3 3 4 2
7-6	(0 1 2 3 4 7 8)	5 3 3 4 4 2
7-7	(0 1 2 3 6 7 8)	5 3 2 3 5 3
7-8	(0 2 3 4 5 6 8)	4 5 4 4 2 2
7-9	(0 1 2 3 4 6 8)	4 5 3 4 3 2
7-10	(0 1 2 3 4 6 9)	4 4 5 3 3 2
7-11	(0 1 3 4 5 6 8)	4 4 4 4 4 1
7-Z12	(0 1 2 3 4 7 9)	4 4 4 3 4 2
7-13	(0 1 2 4 5 6 8)	4 4 3 5 3 2
7-14	(0 1 2 3 5 7 8)	4 4 3 3 5 2
7-15	(0 1 2 4 6 7 8)	4 4 2 4 4 3

PENTACHORDS

FN	PRIME FORM	VECTOR	DF
5-16	(0 1 3 4 7)	2 1 3 2 1 1	
5-Z17	(0 1 3 4 8)	2 1 2 3 2 0	12
5-Z18	(0 1 4 5 7)	2 1 2 2 2 1	
5-19	(0 1 3 6 7)	2 1 2 1 2 2	
5-20	(0 1 5 6 8)	2 1 1 2 3 1	
5-21	(0 1 4 5 8)	2 0 2 4 2 0	
5-22	(0 1 4 7 8)	2 0 2 3 2 1	12
5-23	(0 2 3 5 7)	1 3 2 1 3 0	
5-24	(0 1 3 5 7)	1 3 1 2 2 1	
5-25	(0 2 3 5 8)	1 2 3 1 2 1	
5-26	(0 2 4 5 8)	1 2 2 3 1 1	
5-27	(0 1 3 5 8)	1 2 2 2 3 0	
5-28	(0 2 3 6 8)	1 2 2 2 1 2	
5-29	(0 1 3 6 8)	1 2 2 1 3 1	
5-30	(0 1 4 6 8)	1 2 1 3 2 1	
5-31	(0 1 3 6 9)	1 1 4 1 1 2	
5-32	(0 1 4 6 9)	1 1 3 2 2 1	
5-33	(0 2 4 6 8)	0 4 0 4 0 2	12
5-34	(0 2 4 6 9)	0 3 2 2 2 1	12
5-35	(0 2 4 7 9)	0 3 2 1 4 0	12
5-Z36	(0 1 2 4 7)	2 2 2 1 2 1	
5-Z37	(0 3 4 5 8)	2 1 2 3 2 0	12
5-Z38	(0 1 2 5 8)	2 1 2 2 2 1	

SEPTACHORDS

FN	PRIME FORM	VECTOR
7-16	(0 1 2 3 5 6 9)	4 3 5 4 3 2
7-Z17	(0 1 2 4 5 6 9)	4 3 4 5 4 1
7-Z18	(0 1 4 5 6 7 9)	4 3 4 4 4 2
7-19	(0 1 2 3 6 7 9)	4 3 4 3 4 3
7-20	(0 1 2 5 6 7 9)	4 3 3 4 5 2
7-21	(0 1 2 4 5 8 9)	4 2 4 6 4 1
7-22	(0 1 2 5 6 8 9)	4 2 4 5 4 2
7-23	(0 2 3 4 5 7 9)	3 5 4 3 5 1
7-24	(0 1 2 3 5 7 9)	3 5 3 4 4 2
7-25	(0 2 3 4 6 7 9)	3 4 5 3 4 2
7-26	(0 1 3 4 5 7 9)	3 4 4 5 3 2
7-27	(0 1 2 4 5 7 9)	3 4 4 4 5 1
7-28	(0 1 3 5 6 7 9)	3 4 4 4 3 3
7-29	(0 1 2 4 6 7 9)	3 4 4 3 5 2
7-30	(0 1 2 4 6 8 9)	3 4 3 5 4 2
7-31	(0 1 3 4 6 7 9)	3 3 6 3 3 3
7-32	(0 1 3 4 6 8 9)	3 3 5 4 4 2
7-33	(0 1 2 4 6 8 T)	2 6 2 6 2 3
7-34	(0 1 3 4 6 8 T)	2 5 4 4 4 2
7-35	(0 1 3 5 6 8 T)	2 5 4 3 6 1
7-Z36	(0 1 2 3 5 6 8)	4 4 4 3 4 2
7-Z37	(0 1 3 4 5 7 8)	4 3 4 5 4 1
7-Z38	(0 1 2 4 5 7 8)	4 3 4 4 4 2

HEXACHORDS

FN	PRIME FORM	VECTOR	DF	FN	PRIME FORM	VECTOR
6-1	(0 1 2 3 4 5)	5 4 3 2 1 0	12			
6-2	(0 1 2 3 4 6)	4 4 3 2 1 1				
6-Z3	(0 1 2 3 5 6)	4 3 3 2 2 1		6-Z36	(0 1 2 3 4 7)	4 3 3 2 2 1
6-Z4	(0 1 2 4 5 6)	4 3 2 3 2 1	12	6-Z37	(0 1 2 3 4 8)	4 3 2 3 2 1
6-5	(0 1 2 3 6 7)	4 2 2 2 3 2				
6-Z6	(0 1 2 5 6 7)	4 2 1 2 4 2	12	6-Z38	(0 1 2 3 7 8)	4 2 1 2 4 2
6-7	(0 1 2 6 7 8)	4 2 0 2 4 3	6			
6-8	(0 2 3 4 5 7)	3 4 3 2 3 0	12			
6-9	(0 1 2 3 5 7)	3 4 2 2 3 1				
6-Z10	(0 1 3 4 5 7)	3 3 3 3 2 1		6-Z39	(0 2 3 4 5 8)	3 3 3 3 2 1
6-Z11	(0 1 2 4 5 7)	3 3 3 2 3 1		6-Z40	(0 1 2 3 5 8)	3 3 3 2 3 1
6-Z12	(0 1 2 4 6 7)	3 3 2 2 3 2		6-Z41	(0 1 2 3 6 8)	3 3 2 2 3 2
6-Z13	(0 1 3 4 6 7)	3 2 4 2 2 2	12	6-Z42	(0 1 2 3 6 9)	3 2 4 2 2 2
6-14	(0 1 3 4 5 8)	3 2 3 4 3 0				
6-15	(0 1 2 4 5 8)	3 2 3 4 2 1				
6-16	(0 1 4 5 6 8)	3 2 2 4 3 1				
6-Z17	(0 1 2 4 7 8)	3 2 2 3 3 2		6-Z43	(0 1 2 5 6 8)	3 2 2 3 3 2
6-18	(0 1 2 5 7 8)	3 2 2 2 4 2				
6-Z19	(0 1 3 4 7 8)	3 1 3 4 3 1		6-Z44	(0 1 2 5 6 9)	3 1 3 4 3 1
6-20	(0 1 4 5 8 9)	3 0 3 6 3 0	4			
6-21	(0 2 3 4 6 8)	2 4 2 4 1 2				

HEXACHORDS

FN	PRIME FORM	VECTOR	DF	FN	PRIME FORM	VECTOR
6-22	(0 1 2 4 6 8)	2 4 1 4 2 2				
6-Z23	(0 2 3 5 6 8)	2 3 4 2 2 2	12	6-Z45	(0 2 3 4 6 9)	2 3 4 2 2 2
6-Z24	(0 1 3 4 6 8)	2 3 3 3 3 1		6-Z46	(0 1 2 4 6 9)	2 3 3 3 3 1
6-Z25	(0 1 3 5 6 8)	2 3 3 2 4 1		6-Z47	(0 1 2 4 7 9)	2 3 3 2 4 1
6-Z26	(0 1 3 5 7 8)	2 3 2 3 4 1	12	6-Z48	(0 1 2 5 7 9)	2 3 2 3 4 1
6-27	(0 1 3 4 6 9)	2 2 5 2 2 2				
6-Z28	(0 1 3 5 6 9)	2 2 4 3 2 2	12	6-Z49	(0 1 3 4 7 9)	2 2 4 3 2 2
6-Z29	(0 2 3 6 7 9)	2 2 4 2 3 2	12	6-Z50	(0 1 4 6 7 9)	2 2 4 2 3 2
6-30	(0 1 3 6 7 9)	2 2 4 2 2 3	12			
6-31	(0 1 4 5 7 9)	2 2 3 4 3 1				
6-32	(0 2 4 5 7 9)	1 4 3 2 5 0	12			
6-33	(0 2 3 5 7 9)	1 4 3 2 4 1				
6-34	(0 1 3 5 7 9)	1 4 2 4 2 2				
6-35	(0 2 4 6 8 T)	0 6 0 6 0 3	2			

Appendix D
Answers to Self-Tests

The answers given in certain kinds of Self-Test problems must be considered to be suggested solutions because more than one correct answer might be possible. When you have questions, consult your teacher.

Chapter One

SELF-TEST 1-1

Part A, p. 3.

1. C1   2. E2   3. F3   4. B4   5. A5   6. G6   7. D7

Part B, p. 3.

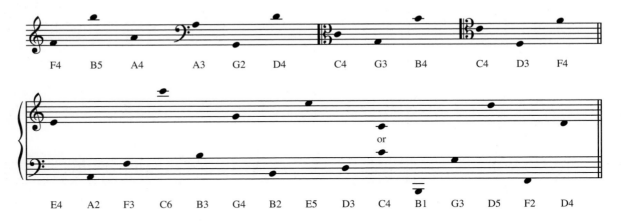

F4   B5   A4   A3   G2   D4   C4   G3   B4   C4   D3   F4

E4   A2   F3   C6   B3   G4   B2   E5   D3   C4   B1   G3   D5   F2   D4

SELF-TEST 1-2

Part A, pp. 8–9.

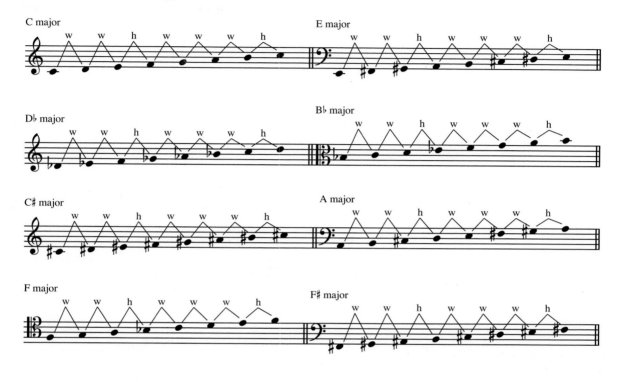

Part B, p. 9.

1. A♭   2. E   3. F   4. E♭   5. G   6. G♭   7. C♯

Part C, p. 9.

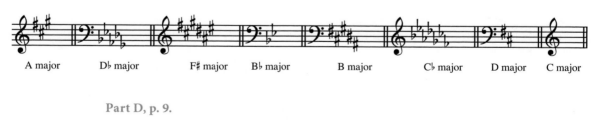

Part D, p. 9.

1. E♭   2. C♯   3. two sharps   4. F   5. four flats
6. five sharps   7. G♭   8. two flats   9. G   10. D♭
11. six sharps   12. seven flats   13. E   14. three sharps

Part E, p. 10.

1. E♭   3♭
2.   5♭   A♭
3.   1♯ $\hat{7}$
4.   5♯   D♯
5.   4♭ $\hat{6}$
6. C♭ $\hat{4}$

SELF-TEST 1-3

Part A, pp. 13–14.

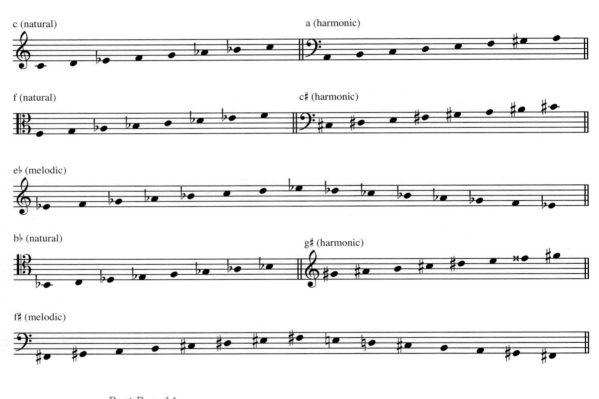

Part B, p. 14.

1. g   2. e   3. c♯   4. f   5. a♭   6. d♯   7. e♭

Part C, p. 14.

Part D, p. 14.

1. one flat   2. e♭   3. c♯   4. three sharps   5. d♯

6. five flats   7. seven sharps   8. g   9. four flats   10. two sharps

11. c   12. seven flats   13. e   14. g♯

SELF-TEST 1-4

p. 17.

1. 2   2. 5   3. 7   4. 1   5. 3

6. 4   7. 8   8. 6   9. 4   10. 2

11. 6   12. 7   13. 8   14. 3   15. 5

SELF-TEST 1-5

Part A, p. 19.

All are "P" except nos. 4 and 7.

Part B, p. 19.

1. M   2. m   3. m   4. M   5. m

6. m   7. m   8. M   9. M   10. m

Part C, p. 19.

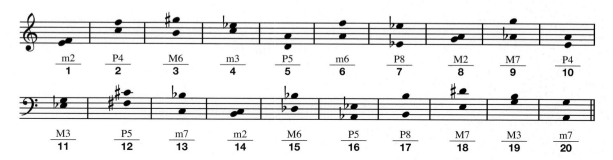

SELF-TEST 1-6

Part A, p. 21.

1. +5   2. °7   3. M3   4. °4   5. +2

6. m7   7. °5   8. °3   9. +6   10. +4

Part B, p. 22.

1. P5   2. m2   3. °7   4. m6   5. +4

6. M7   7. M3   8. °3

Part C, p. 22.

P5	m7	m3	M6	+4	M7	+5	m6	M2	°7
1	**2**	**3**	**4**	**5**	**6**	**7**	**8**	**9**	**10**

Part D, p. 22.

1. m3   2. P1   3. m6   4. P8   5. M3
6. P4   7. m3   8. °5   9. m2   10. +1
11. m2   12. M7

Part E, p. 22.

1. d   2. c   3. c   4. d   5. c   6. d   7. c   8. c   9. d   10. d bass

Chapter Two

SELF-TEST 2-1

Part A, p. 26.

1. 2   2. 4   3. 3   4. 8   5. 4   6. 3
7. 4   8. 7   9. 5   10. 6   11. 2   12. 4
13. 8   14. 4   15. 2   16. 12

Part B, p. 26.

1. triple   2. duple (or quadruple)   3. quadruple (or duple)
4. duple (or quadruple)   5. triple

Part C, p. 26.

1. B♭   2. A♭   3. E   4. D♯   5. E
6. B   7. B♭   8. E♭   9. A♭   10. A
11. G   12. G♯   13. F   14. C♯   15. C♯

SELF-TEST 2-2

p. 27.

1. simple quadruple (or simple duple)
2. compound duple (or compound quadruple)
3. simple triple
4. simple duple (or simple quadruple)
5. compound duple (or compound quadruple)

SELF-TEST 2-3

Part A, p. 29.

1. ♫ ; $\frac{2}{4}$

2. simple triple; ♪ ; ♫

3. simple duple; ♩ ; $\frac{2}{2}$

4. ♪ ; $\frac{4}{8}$

5. ♫ ; $\frac{3}{16}$

Part B, p. 29.

SELF-TEST 2-4

Part A, p. 31.

1. ♫♩ ; $\frac{6}{8}$

2. compound triple; ♩. ; ♩♩♩

3. compound duple; ♩♩♩ ; $\frac{6}{4}$

4. ♪. ; $\frac{12}{16}$

5. compound triple; ♩. ; $\frac{9}{8}$

Part B, p. 32.

SELF-TEST 2-5

Part A, p. 34.

1. simple quadruple; ♩ ; ♫   2. ♫♩ ; ⅜   3. simple duple; ♪ ; ♫

4. ♩. ; 6/4   5. simple triple; ♩ ; 3/2   6. compound quadruple; ♪. ; 12/16

Part B, p. 35.

1. ♫   2. ♫ (or ♪♪)   3. ♪♫ (or ♪♪♪)   4. ♫   5. ♫   6. ♪♪ (or ▬)

Notice that ▬ would not be a good answer for no. 3 because this rest would obscure the beats in the measure (see p. 33).

Part C, p. 35.

1. 9/4   2. 4/4 or 2/2 or c or ¢   3. 3/8   4. 6/16   5. 12/8   6. same as no. 2

Part D, p. 35.

(The syncopation in m. 1 is very common and might well appear as ♩♩♩)

Part E, p. 35.

1.

2.

Part F, p. 36.

1. simple duple (or quadruple); 2 (or 4) over some note value (1, 2, 4, 8, and so on)
2. compound quadruple (or duple); 12 (or 6) over some note value
3. sounds like compound duple or compound single, but notated as simple triple (see pp. 30–31); 3 over some note value
4. simple quadruple (or duple); 4 (or 2) over some note value
5. compound duple (or quadruple); 6 (or 12) over some note value

Part G, p. 36.

1. f	2. G	3. c♯	4. A	5. B♭
6. c	7. D	8. E♭	9. b	10. F
11. g	12. f♯	13. E	14. A♭	

Part H, p. 36.

Part I, p. 36.

Chapter Three

SELF-TEST 3-1

Part A, p. 39.

1. B♭ D♭ F	2. E G♯ B	3. G B♭ D♭	4. F A♭ C♭
5. C E♭ G	6. D F♯ A♯	7. A C♯ E	8. D F A
9. G♭ B♭ D♭	10. B D♯ F♯	11. A♭ C♭ E♭	12. C♯ E G♯

Part B, p. 39.

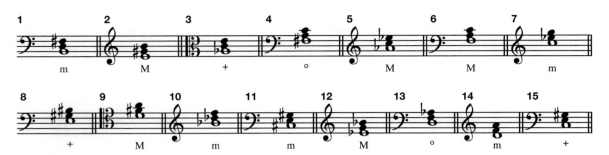

Part C, p. 40.

	1.	2.	3.	4.	5.	6.	7.	8.	9.	10.
Fifth	C♯	B♭	F♯	D♯	G♭	A	E	C♭	G♯	B
Third	A	G♭	D	B	E♭	F♯	C♯	A♭	E	G♯
Root	F	E♭	B	G	C♭	D♯	A	F	C♯	E
Type	+	m	m	+	M	°	M	°	m	M

Part D, p. 40.

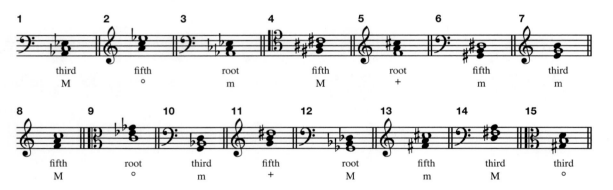

SELF-TEST 3-2

Part A, p. 41.

1. m7   2. M7   3. ⌀7   4. ⌀7   5. M7

6. ⌀7   7. m7   8. Mm7   9. M7   10. Mm7

11. °7   12. °7   13. Mm7   14. °7   15. m7

Part B, p. 42.

1	2	3	4	5	6	7
ø7	Mm7	M7	Mm7	m7	ø7	ø7

8	9	10	11	12	13	14	15
°7	M7	M7	M7	m7	m7	M7	°7

Part C, p. 42.

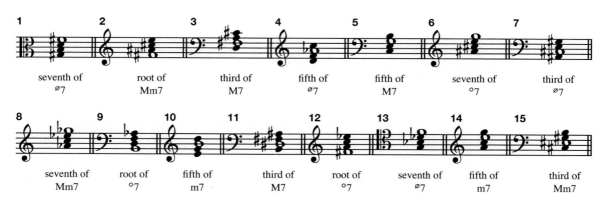

1	2	3	4	5	6	7
seventh of ø7	root of Mm7	third of M7	fifth of ø7	fifth of M7	seventh of °7	third of ø7

8	9	10	11	12	13	14	15
seventh of Mm7	root of °7	fifth of m7	third of M7	root of °7	seventh of ø7	fifth of m7	third of Mm7

SELF-TEST 3-3

Part A, p. 47.

	1	2	3	4	5	6	7	8	9	10	11	12	13	14
Root	E	A	G♯	E	C♯	D	E	G	B	E♭	F♯	G	E	D
Type	m7	M	°7	Mm7	m	ø7	M7	m	ø7	M	°7	m7	°	Mm7
Bps	$\frac{6}{5}$	6	$\frac{4}{3}$	$\frac{4}{3}$	$\frac{6}{4}$	$\frac{4}{2}$	7	6	$\frac{4}{3}$	$\frac{6}{4}$	$\frac{6}{5}$	7	6	$\frac{4}{2}$

Part B, pp. 47–48.

1. G   2. C♯°/E   3. D   4. D♯°/F♯   5. D♯°7/F♯

6. B7/D♯   7. Em   8. F♯7/E   9. Bm   10. E/G♯

11. A/C♯   12. E   13. A

Part C, p. 48.

SELF-TEST 3-4

Part A, p. 50.

1. Fm7   2. A#°7/C#   3. E   4. Fm/C   5. B7/A
6. Gø7/B♭   7. C/E   8. F#/C#   9. D♭7   10. Cø7/B♭   11. F#M7

Part B, pp. 51–52.

1. Fischer.

	1	2	3	4	5	6	7	8	9	10	11	12	13
Root	E	G#	A	F	B	F	G	C	D	B	D	G	C
Type	M	°7	m	M7	ø7	M	Mm7	M	m7	°	m	Mm7	M
Bps	$\frac{4}{3}$	6		7	$\frac{4}{3}$		$\frac{4}{2}$		6	7	6		7	$\frac{6}{4}$

2. Byrd.

	1	2	3	4	5	6	7
Root	F	C	F	E♭	A	B♭	F
Type	m	M	M	M	°	M	M
Bps					6		

3. Schumann.

	1	2	3	4	5	6	7	8	9	10	11	12	13	14	15
Root	A	A	D	D	G	A	G#	A	A	D	D	G	A	D	D
Type	M	Mm7	M	M	M	Mm7	°	Mm7	Mm7	M	M	M	Mm7	M	Mm7
Bps	6	7		6		7	6	$\frac{6}{5}$	$\frac{4}{3}$		6		7		$\frac{6}{5}$

Part C, p. 52.

1. ♩. ; $\frac{6}{16}$ 2. simple duple; ♩ ; ♩ ♩

3. simple quadruple; ♩ ; $\frac{4}{4}$ 4. compound quadruple; ♩♩♩ ; $\frac{12}{8}$

Chapter Four

SELF-TEST 4-1

Part A, p. 58.

1. F♯	2. Em/G	3. B♭m	4. G/B	5. G♯m
V	iv⁶	ii	III⁶	ii
6. G♯°	7. D♭/A♭	8. C°	9. Bm	10. C×°/E♯
vii°	I⁶₄	ii°	iii	vii°⁶
11. G/D	12. D	13. C♯m	14. Gm	15. Cm/G
V⁶₄	IV	i	vi	iv⁶₄

1. F♯ / V 2. Em/G / iv⁶ 3. B♭m / ii 4. G/B / III⁶ 5. G♯m / ii
6. G♯° / vii° 7. D♭/A♭ / I⁶₄ 8. C° / ii° 9. Bm / iii 10. C×°/E♯ / vii°⁶
11. G/D / V⁶₄ 12. D / IV 13. C♯m / i 14. Gm / vi 15. Cm/G / iv⁶₄

Part B, p. 59.

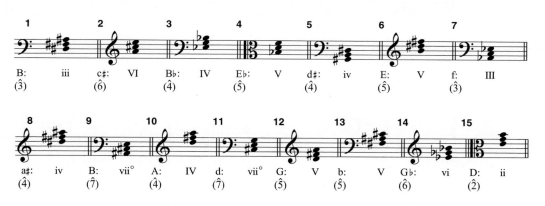

B: iii (3̂)   c♯: VI (6̂)   B♭: IV (4̂)   E♭: V (5̂)   d♯: iv (4̂)   E: V (5̂)   f: III (3̂)

a♯: iv (4̂)   B: vii° (7̂)   A: IV (4̂)   d: vii° (7̂)   G: V (5̂)   b: V (5̂)   G♭: vi (6̂)   D: ii (2̂)

Part C, pp. 59–60.

1. IV	2. V	3. IV⁶	4. V	5. I⁶
6. IV	7. V	8. V	9. I	10. iii
11. IV	12. iii⁶	13. iii	14. IV	15. I
16. I	17. V	18. I	19. IV	20. IV⁶
21. I	22. ii	23. vi	24. vi	25. V
26. V	27. IV	28. vii°⁶	29. I	30. V⁶
31. I	32. I	33. V	34. IV	35. iii⁶
36. vi	37. iii⁶	38. IV	39. I	40. I
41. V	42. ii	43. iii	44. vi	45. iii⁶
46. IV	47. I	48. I		

SELF-TEST 4-2

Part A, p. 63.

1. Cm7
  iv^7
2. EM7/G♯
  I$^{M6}_5$
3. Cm7
  iii^7
4. G^{ø}7/D♭
  ii$^{ø4}_3$
5. CM7
  VI^{M7}

6. DM7/C♯
  IV$^{M4}_2$
7. D^{ø}7
  vii^{o7}
8. F♯m7
  i^7
9. C♯7
  vii^{o7}
10. Em7/G
  vi$^6_5$

11. C7/B♭
  V$^4_2$
12. E7
  V^7
13. C♯^{o}7
  ii^{ø7}
14. F♯m7/C♯
  iii$^4_3$
15. B♭M7
  I^{M7}

Part B, pp. 63–64.

b: i^7 E♭:   V^7 f♯:   iv^7 A: V^7 f: vii^{o7} D: I^{M7} G: vii^{ø7}
($\hat{1}$)   ($\hat{5}$)   ($\hat{4}$)   ($\hat{5}$)   ($\hat{7}$)   ($\hat{1}$)   ($\hat{7}$)

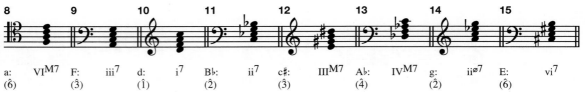

a: VI^{M7} F: iii^7 d: i^7 B♭:   ii^7 c♯:   III^{M7} A♭:   IV^{M7} g: ii^{ø7} E: vi^7
($\hat{6}$)   ($\hat{3}$)   ($\hat{1}$)   ($\hat{2}$)   ($\hat{3}$)   ($\hat{4}$)   ($\hat{2}$)   ($\hat{6}$)

Part C, p. 64.

1. Bach

1. I
2. vi
3. iii
4. IV
5. IV^{M7}

6. V$^4_2$
7. I^6
8. ii$^6_5$
9. V
10. I

2. Schumann

1. I
2. vii^{o6}
3. I^6
4. vii^{o6}
5. I

6. ii$^6_5$
7. V
8. I
9. I
10. I^6

11. IV
12. I^6
13. V$^4_3$
14. I
15. V

Chapter Five

SELF-TEST 5-1

Part A, p. 69.

1.

G: I   V   I   IV   V   I   IV   V   I

a. Resolve $\hat{7}$ to $\hat{1}$.
b. Not in a IV chord.
c. Two leaps should outline a triad.
d. Two focal points.

2.

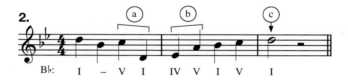

B♭:   I   –   V   I   IV   V   I   V   I

a. Leap of a 7th.
b. Leap of an $^+4$.
c. Two focal points.

3.

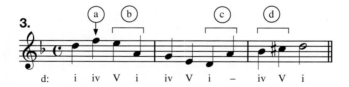

d: i   iv   V   i   iv   V   i   –   iv   V   i

a. Not in a iv chord.
b. Large descending leap should be preceded and followed by ascending motion.
c. Follow large ascending leap with descending motion.
d. Interval of $^+2$.

Part B, p. 69 (sample solutions).

1.

I   V   I   IV I –   vi ii V   I

2.

i   iv i   –   V   – i   iv V i

3.

I   V vi IV   I IV ii V   I

SELF-TEST 5-2

Part A, p. 72.

$$\frac{i}{C} \; / \; \frac{i}{C} \; \frac{V^6}{O} \; \frac{i}{O} \; \frac{iv^6}{C} \; / \; \frac{V}{O} \; \frac{V^4_2}{O} \; / \; \frac{i^6}{O} \; \frac{vii^{o6}}{O} \; \frac{i}{C} \; \frac{ii^{o6}}{C} \; / \; \frac{V}{C}$$

Part B, p. 73.

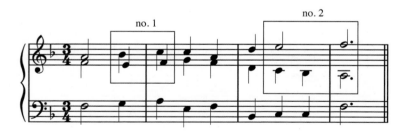

Part C, p. 73 (alternative solutions in parentheses).

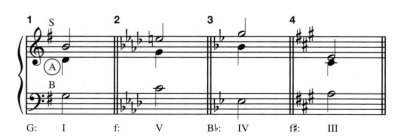

G: I   f: V   Bb: IV   f#:   III

F: vi   e: iv   A: ii   g: VI

SELF-TEST 5-3

Part A, pp. 78–79.

Bᵇm	Gm	Cm/Eᵇ	F

1. o c c   2. c o c   3. o c c
4. st p p   5. o o s   6. o o s

Part B, p. 79.

The progression is G: I / IV I / V / vi V / I /
Parallel 6ths: S/A, m. 1; S/T, mm. 3–4
Parallel 3rds: S/T, mm. 1–3; S/B, m. 3

Part C, p. 79.

Part D, p. 80.

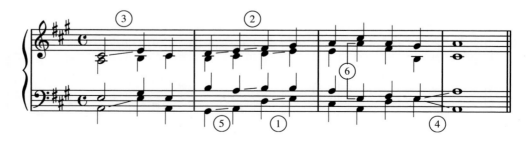

Chapter Six

SELF-TEST 6-1

pp. 82–83 (sample solutions).*

SELF-TEST 6-2

Part A, p. 85.

---

*   Solutions to this and similar exercises throughout the book are sample solutions only. Many other correct solutions are possible.

Part B, p. 85.

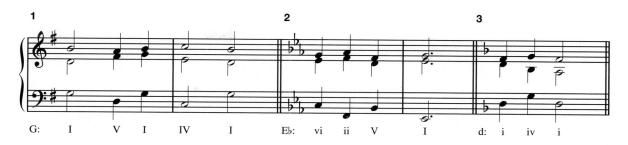

G: I V I IV I   Eb: vi ii V I   d: i iv i

SELF-TEST 6-3

Part A, p. 87.

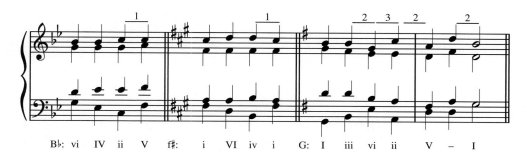

Bb: vi IV ii V   f#: i VI iv i   G: I iii vi ii V – I

Part B, p. 87.

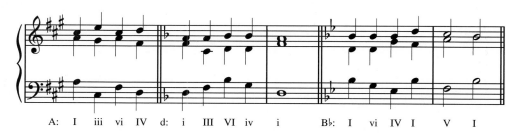

A: I iii vi IV   d: i III VI iv i   Bb: I vi IV I V I

SELF-TEST 6-4

Part A, p. 90.

Part B, p. 90.

E♭: I   vi   V   I   IV   I   IV   V   –   I

b: V   i   VI   iv   V   VI   iv   V   –   i

Part C, pp. 90–91.

a: i   V   i   VI   iv   V   i

2.

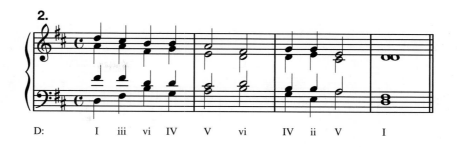

D: I   iii   vi   IV   V   vi   IV   ii   V   I

SELF-TEST 6-5

Part A, pp. 92–93.

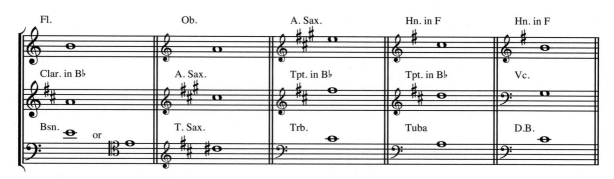

Part B, p. 93.

1.

F: I   vi   ii   V   I

2.

---

*   The melody here made it impossible to follow the usual method for roots a 3rd apart. The solution is correct, however.

Part C, p. 93.
Poulton, "Aura Lee"

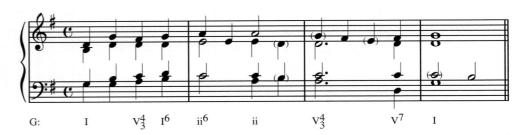

G: I   V$\frac{4}{3}$ I^6 ii^6 ii   V$\frac{4}{3}$ V^7 I

Chapter Seven

SELF-TEST 7-1

Part A, p. 109.

1. iii or V   2. I or ii   3. I or vi
4. iii or vi   5. ii or IV   6. I

Part B, p. 109.

1. ⌐V   ii⌐   2. ⌐VII   I⌐   3. ⌐IV   iii⌐   4. none

Part C, pp. 109–111.

1. G / Em   Bm   C   D7 / Em   D   G
   I   ⌐vi   iii⌐ IV   V   ⌐vi   V⌐ I

2.

g: i   V^6 i   VII^6 III   i^6 iv   ii^{o6} V

i^6 iv   iv^6 V

i   i   iv   V^6 i   iv   V   i

3. e: [iv^7 VII^7 III^{M7} VI^{M7} ii^{ø7} V^7 i]
   m.1   2   3   4   5   6   7

Part D, p. 111.

B♭:   [V   I]   [vi   ii   V]   vi   [V   I]

f♯:   i   [VII   III]   iv   V   VI   iv   [V   i]

Part E, p. 111.

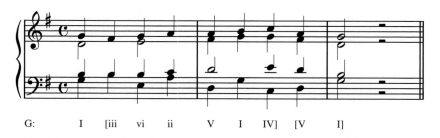

G: I   [iii   vi   ii   V   I   IV]   [V   I]

Part F, p. 112.

1. Three-part chorus (SAB)

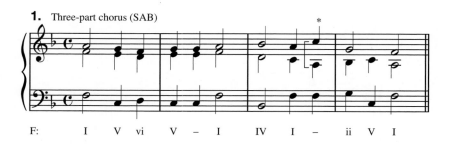

F: I   V   vi   V – I   IV   I – ii   V   I

---

*   The spacing error here is preferable to a leap of a M7 (A to B♭) in the alto between this chord and the next one.

2. Four-part chorus (SATB)

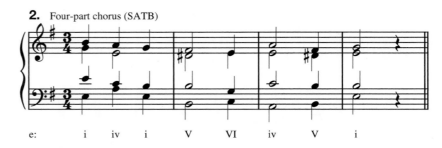

e: i   iv   i   V   VI   iv   V   i

3. Four-part chorus (SATB)

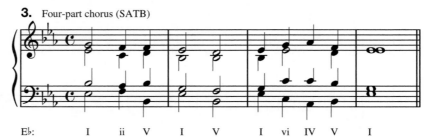

E♭:   I   ii   V   I   V   I   vi   IV   V   I

4. Four-part chorus (SATB)

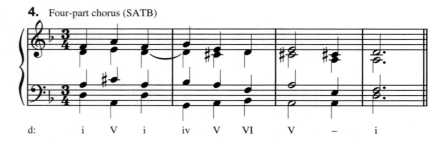

d: i   V   i   iv   V   VI   V   —   i

5. Three-part chorus (SAB)

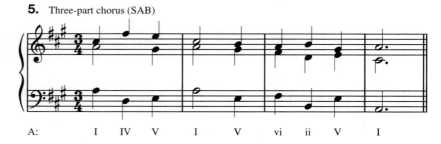

A: I   IV   V   I   V   vi   ii   V   I

Part G, p. 113.

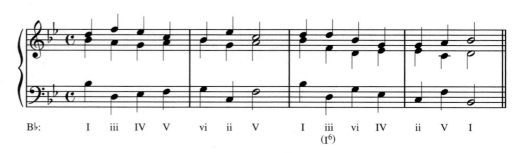

B♭:   I   iii   IV   V   vi   ii   V   I   iii   vi   IV   ii   V   I
                                                                              (I⁶)

Part H, p. 113.

1. V_5^6 2. IV^6 3. iv^7 4. I^{M7} 5. $ii^{\varnothing6}_5$

6. vi^7 7. V_2^4 8. $vii^{\circ6}_5$ 9. ii^6 10. V_3^4

11. iv_2^4 12. I_4^6 13. VI 14. I^{M4}_3 15. V^6

Chapter Eight

SELF-TEST 8-1

Part A, pp. 126–128.

1. The voice-leading features parallel 4ths (arpeggiated in the right hand), as in Example 8–10.

2. I IV^6 iii vi^7 / $vii^{\circ6}$ I^6 V   –   /   I IV^6 V^6 I   / ii^6_5 V   I   /

   Both of the IV^6 chords have the bass and an inner voice doubled, the $vii^{\circ6}$ and the V^6 chords have the soprano and an inner voice doubled, and the I^6 chord has the soprano and bass doubled.

3. /   i   /   / V_5^6 /   /   i   / $vii^{\circ6}$ or V_3^4 /   i6 $ii^{\circ6}{(^{\varnothing6}_5)}$ /   V

   With a little imagination, we can find most of the bass line, both forward and backward, in the melody.

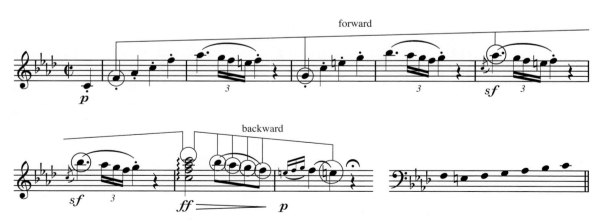

Part B, p. 128.

Mozart, *Eine kleine Nachtmusik,* K. 525, I

The simplification of the outer-voice counterpoint shown below the example makes it easier to see the imitation in the first three measures.

G: V⁷   vi   ii⁶   V⁷   V   I⁶   V   I

Part C, p. 129.

Bb: I   6   V   e: i   V⁶   5/3   i   D: vi   ii⁶   V   vi

Eb: IV   V   I⁶   IV⁶   f#:   i   V⁶   i   iv   d: i⁶   iv⁶   V   i

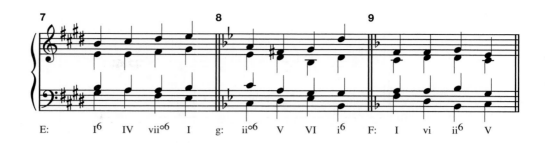

E: I^6 IV vii^{o6} I   g: ii^{o6} V   VI i^6 F: I   vi ii^6 V

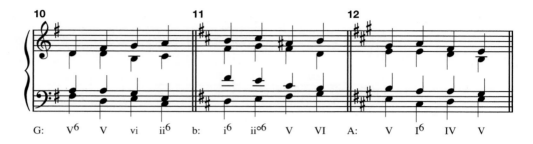

G: V^6 V   vi ii^6 b: i^6 ii^{o6} V   VI   A: V I^6 IV   V

Part D, p. 129.

Bb: I ^{6} V   e: i V^6 $^5_3$ i   D: vi ii^6 V   vi

Eb: IV   V I^6 IV^6 f#:   i V^6 i   iv   d: i^6 iv^6 V   i

Part E, p. 130.

A: I   V⁶   I   ii⁶   V   vi   ii⁶   vii°⁶   I

g: i   V⁶   i   iv⁶   ii°⁶   V   i⁶   vii°⁶   i   V

Part F, p. 130.

Bach, French Suite no. 5, Gavotte
(Compare the first five chords to Example 7-20.)

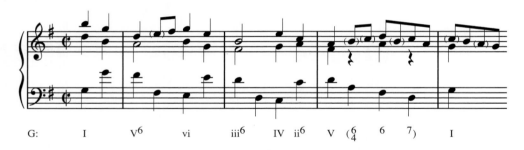

G: I   V⁶   vi   iii⁶   IV   ii⁶   V (6/4   6   7)   I

Part G, pp. 130–131.

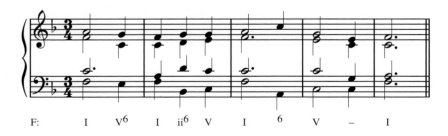

F: I   V⁶   I   ii⁶   V   I   6   V   —   I

b: i vii°⁶ i⁶ ii°⁶ V i⁶ i V⁶ i iv⁶ V i

Parts H and I, p. 131. (Compare to Ex. 7-20 and Ex. 8-7b.)

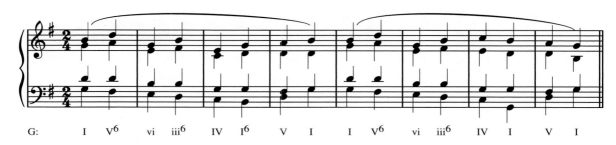

G: I V⁶ vi iii⁶ IV I⁶ V I I V⁶ vi iii⁶ IV I V I

Part J, p. 131

The first five chords of Part F (Bach) are the same in Part H (Beethoven) in mm. 1–3 and 5–7, and the bass lines in those progressions are identical except for the octave arpeggiations in the Bach excerpt. The melody lines are different, but both make use of sequences over the first five chords. As hinted at earlier, both are similar to Example 7-20, but Pachelbel uses the chords in root position. The first 10 bass notes of the Gavotte are also heard at the beginning of the famous "Air" from Bach's Orchestral Suite no. 3, but in a different key and harmonization.

Chapter Nine

SELF-TEST 9-1

Part A, pp. 141–142.

1. g: i / (iv$_4^6$) / – / i / vii°$_5^6$ i⁶ / vii°$_5^6$ i⁶ /

   The iv$_4^6$ is a pedal six-four chord.

2. 1. I⁶ 2. IV 3. I⁶ 4. IV 5. I⁶ 6. IV 7. I⁶ 8. V$_4^6$ 9. I 10. V
   11. I⁶ 12. ii⁶ 13. I⁶ 14. vii$^{ø4}_3$ 15. I⁶ 16. vii$^{ø46}_3$ 17. I 18. I$_4^6$
   19. V⁷ 20. I

   Chord 8 (which might also be analyzed as a vii°⁶ or a V$_3^4$) is a passing six-four, and chord 18 is a cadential six-four. Chords 14–15 suggest another way of analyzing the unusual progression in chords 12–13.

3. G: I V⁶ I / V$_3^4$ ⁶ I / IV⁶ (I$_4^6$) IV I⁶ / vii° I I$_4^6$ V /
                                                                              ⎣___V___⎦

$$I \quad V^6 \quad I \quad / \quad V^4_3 \quad {}^6 \quad I \quad / \quad IV^6 \quad (I^6_4) \quad IV \quad {}^6 \quad / \quad \underbracket{I^6_4 \quad V} \quad / \quad I \quad /$$
$$ V$$

The six-four chords in parentheses are passing six-fours; the others are cadential six-fours.

Part B, p. 143.

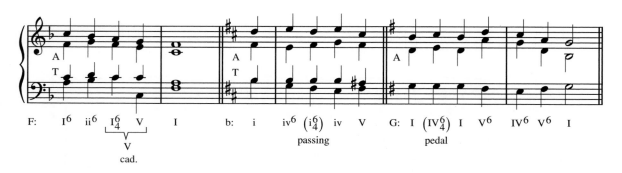

Part C, p. 143.

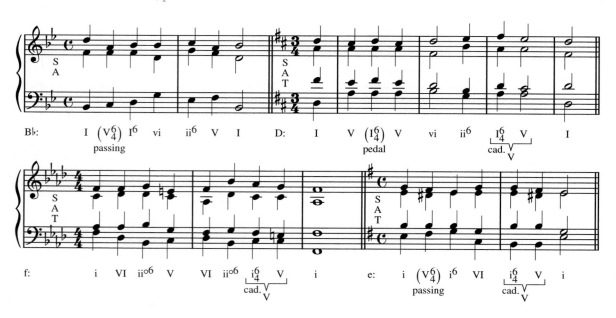

Chapter Ten

SELF-TEST 10-1

Part A, p. 165.

1. Root-position IAC   2. Phrygian HC   3. DC   4. PC
5. Leading-tone IAC   6. Inverted IAC   7. HC   8. PAC

Part B, p. 166.

1. Sentence   2. Parallel period (or contrasting period)   3. Sentence
4. Sentence   5. Parallel period   6. Sentence

Part C, pp. 166–169.

1. This excerpt is a repeated parallel period.

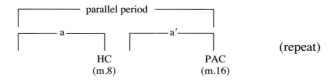

1. I   2. V$_3^4$ 3. I^6 4. I   5. V^6 6. $\frac{5}{3}$ 7. I

2.

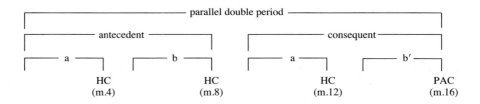

This example resembles Example 10-19 in that two sentences are nested within the larger period form.

Mm. 1–8: Because two cadences are marked in these measures, the excerpt is diagrammed as a two-phrase sentence, with the two phrases and cadences shown.

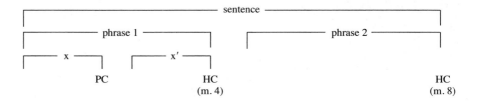

Mm. 9–16:

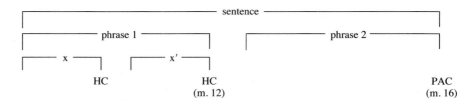

3. Because mm. 1 to 8 constitute a contrasting period, the whole theme can be heard as a contrasting period with a repeated and extended consequent phrase. The difficulty lies in the "cadence" in m. 12. What we expect here is a Cm chord, as in m. 8, but after the space of one quarter note we understand that the harmony is instead a C7—a "secondary" dominant seventh of the iv chord that follows—and the progression drives on toward the cadence in m. 17. Some writers use the term "evaded cadence" for situations like this.

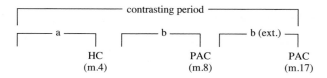

4. This excerpt is a repeated parallel period (not a double period). Octaves by contrary motion occur between melody and bass in mm. 7 to 8 and mm. 15 to 16.

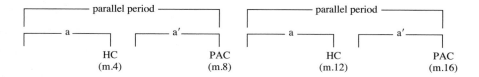

Part D, p. 169.

Chapter Eleven

SELF-TEST 11-1

Part A, pp. 182–183.

1.
Measure	Treble	Bass
1	p	
2	n	p
3	7–6	
5	p	
6	p	p
7	4–3	

2. soprano: p; alto: p, p; tenor: 7–6, p, p

3. The only voice-leading problem seen in the reduction is found in m. 4, where a direct 5th (review p. 77) occurs between the I and IV chords. Bach disguised these through the use of passing tones. The parallel 5ths in m. 2 are not objectionable

because the second 5th is a °5 and because the bass is not involved in the 5ths (review p. 76).

Eb: I   V (7) vi   V6   I   6   V7   I   V6   I   IV6   I   IV   I6   V7   I

Textural reduction

Part B, p. 183.

Part C, p. 184.

Bach, "Herr Christ, der ein'ge Gott's-Sohn"

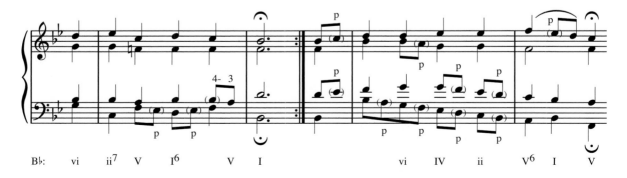

Bb: vi   ii7   V   I6   V   I   vi   IV   ii   V6   I   V

Chapter Twelve

SELF-TEST 12-1

Part A, pp. 194–195.

1. m. 1: p; m. 3: p, p, app; m. 4: app (or 4–3), p

2. m. 24: app, app; m. 25: app, app; m. 26: app, p, p

3. m. 72: n, n; m. 74: 7–6; m. 75: 7–6 (ornamented resolution) app, p; m. 76: p, p; m. 77: (melody) ant, (alto) ant

4. Notice (1) the scalar motion in all voices, inspired, of course, by the melody; (2) the incomplete IV, which contributes to the scalar motion; (3) the root position vii°, appearing here in one of its few typical usages; (4) the $\hat{7}$–$\hat{3}$ movement at the cadence—not unusual for Bach in an inner voice; and (5) the avoidance of parallel motion in the outer-voice counterpoint.

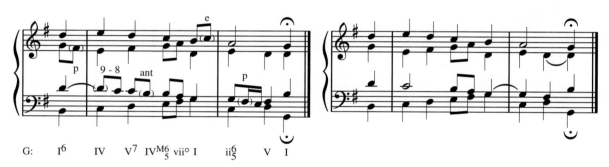

5.

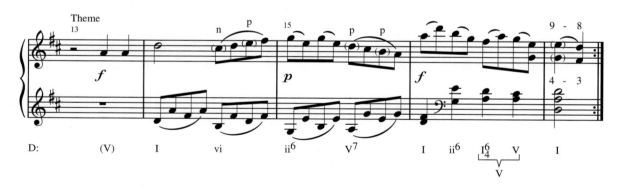

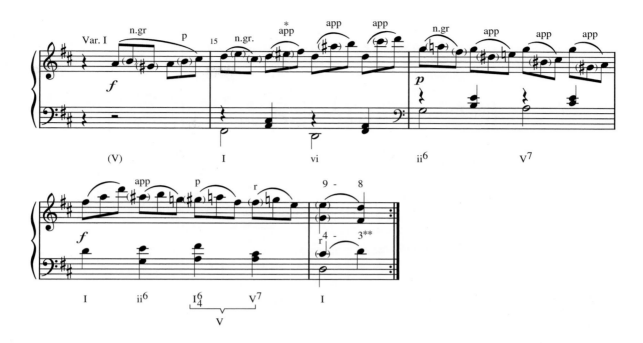

6. Words in italic point out aspects that are uncharacteristic of music of the eighteenth and nineteenth centuries.

m. 2

C is a suspension.

E♭ is an *unaccented* appoggiatura.

D and B♭ are passing tones.

m. 4

F is an *accented* escape tone.

m. 6

F is an upper neighbor.

C is an appoggiatura.

m. 8

The Ds are passing tones.

The B♭ is an *unprepared* anticipation.

Part B, p. 196.

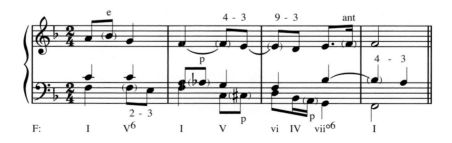

---

*   We label this as an appoggiatura rather than as a passing tone because of the effect of the ⁺2.

**   This could also be labeled as an appoggiatura. The suspension analysis assumes that the G was prepared in the higher octave in the V⁷ chord.

Part C, p. 196.

Mozart, Piano Sonata K. 330, III

Chapter Thirteen

SELF-TEST 13-1

Part A, p. 207.

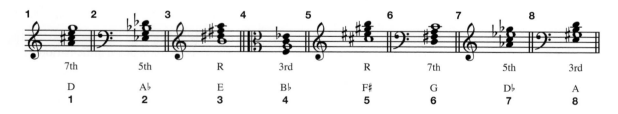

Part B, p. 208.

m. 1 V^7–vi deceptive progression. With $\hat{7}$ in an inner voice and in the major mode, it may move down to $\hat{6}$ instead of up to $\hat{1}$. The 7th resolves normally. All voices move by step.

m. 2 V^7 ornamented by a neighbor and a 4–3 suspension. The V^7 is complete, but the I is incomplete because of the resolution of the leading tone in the alto. The 7th resolves down by step.

m. 5   Another ornamented V^7, but in this case the leading tone is frustrated, leading to a complete I chord. The 7th resolves down by step.

Part C, p. 208.

Part D, p. 208.

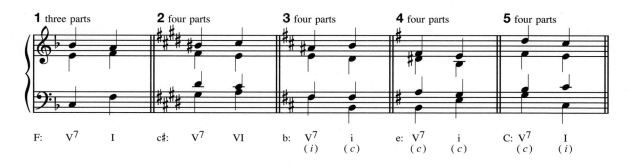

Part E, p. 209.

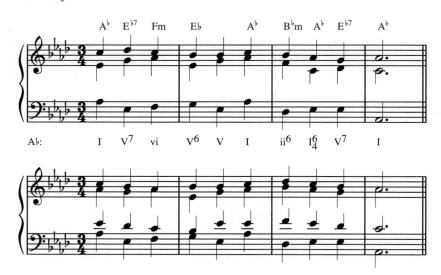

A♭:   I   V^7 vi   V^6 V   I   ii^6 I$^6_4$ V^7 I

Part F, p. 209.

1. Bach, "Kommt her zu mir, spricht Gottes Sohn"

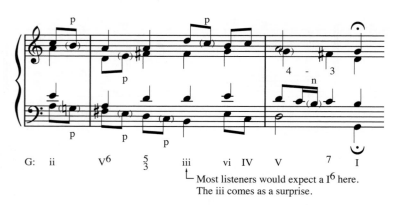

G: ii   V^6 $^5_3$ iii   vi IV   V ^{7} I

Most listeners would expect a I^6 here.
The iii comes as a surprise.

2. Bach, "Jesu, der du meine Seele"

b♭:   i   6   V^7 i   iv^6 ii^{o6} V^7 i

SELF-TEST 13-2

Part A, p. 213.

Chord labels: C: V_5^6 — e: V_3^4 — B♭: V_2^4 — G: V_3^4 — A: V_2^4 — g: V_5^6 — f♯: V_2^4 — A♭: V_5^6

Part B, p. 213.

1. The leading tone (G♯3) resolves up to tonic. The 7th (D3) is approached by a suspension figure and resolves down by step to $\hat{3}$.

2. The leading tone (F♯4) resolves up to $\hat{1}$. The 7th (C5) is approached by a passing tone figure and resolves down by step to $\hat{3}$.

3. There is no leading tone in this chord. The 7th (F4) is approached by an appoggiatura figure and resolves down by step to $\hat{3}$.

Part C, pp. 213–214.

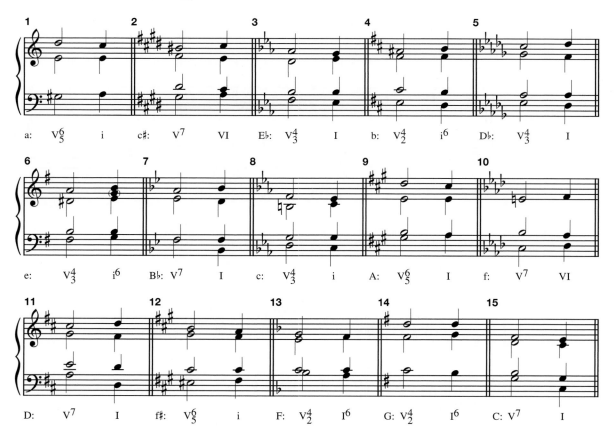

Chord labels:
a: V_5^6 i — c♯: V^7 VI — E♭: V_3^4 I — b: V_2^4 i^6 — D♭: V_3^4 I

e: V_3^4 i^6 — B♭: V^7 I — c: V_3^4 i — A: V_5^6 I — f: V^7 VI

D: V^7 I — f♯: V_5^6 i — F: V_2^4 I^6 — G: V_2^4 I^6 — C: V^7 I

Part D, p. 214.

1. Example 13-10   <u>suspension figure</u>
2. Example 13-11   <u>neighbor tone figure</u>
3. Example 13-20   <u>passing tone figure</u>
4. Example 13-22   <u>ascending passing tone figure</u> (The passing tone figure usually descends, The I–V$_3^4$–I^6 progression being the only common exception.)
5. Examples 13-24   <u>appoggiatura figure</u>

Part E, p. 214.

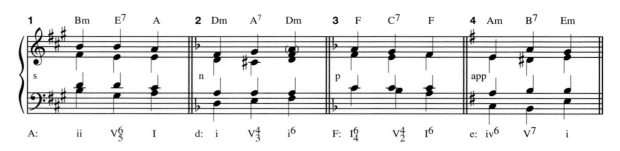

Part F, p. 215.

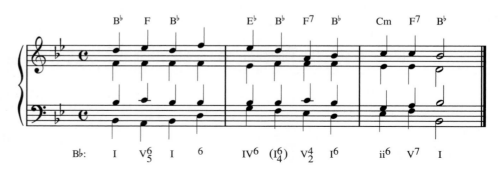

Part G, p. 215.

1. F	2. A	3. E♭	4. G, g	5. E
6. d	7. B♭	8. D	9. E, e	10. A♭
11. D	12. c♯	13. B♭	14. g	15. b

Chapter Fourteen

SELF-TEST 14-1

Part A, p. 226.

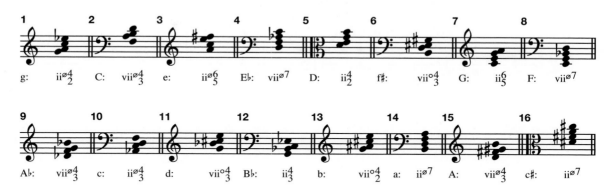

g: ii°$^4_2$ C: vii°$^4_3$ e: ii°$^6_5$ E♭: vii°^{7} D: ii$^4_2$ f♯: vii°$^4_3$ G: ii°$^6_5$ F: vii°^{7}

A♭: vii°$^4_3$ c: ii°$^4_3$ d: vii°$^4_3$ B♭: ii$^4_3$ b: vii°$^4_2$ a: ii°^{7} A: vii°$^4_3$ c♯: ii°^{7}

Part B, p. 226.

1. ii$^6_5$ 2. ii$^4_2$ 3. vii°^{7} 4. ii°$^6_5$ 5. vii°^{7}

6. vii°$^4_3$ 7. ii°^{7} 8. vii°$^4_3$

Part C, pp. 226–228.

1. The ii°$^4_2$ has its 7th approached as a suspension (from the previous chord tone). The large leap in the tenor (C4–F♯3) is necessary because of the motion in the upper voices. The 7th of the vii°^{7} is approached as an appoggiatura (A4 up to C5). The resolution of both tritones leads to a tonic triad with doubled 3rd. In the last complete measure notice (1) the 5–4 suspension, which "works" because of the dissonance with the G4, and (2) the tonic pedal under the final i–iv^7–vii°–i progression.

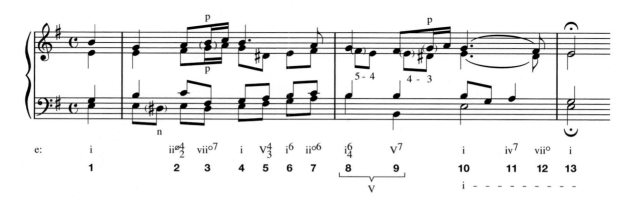

e: i   ii°$^4_2$ vii°^{7} i V$^4_3$ i^6 ii°^{6} i$^6_4$ V^7 i iv^7 vii° i

1   2   3   4   5   6   7   8   9   10   11   12   13

2. The 7th of the vii°7 is approached as an appoggiatura. It is left by arpeggiation, although one could hear it as leading to the B5–A5 in the next measure.

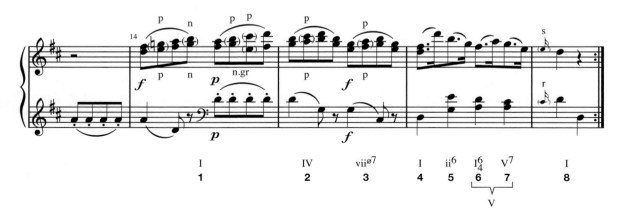

	I	IV	vii°7	I	ii6	I$_4^6$	V7	I
	1	2	3	4	5	6	7	8

V

3. The 7th of the ii$_5^{ø6}$ is approached as a suspension. Resolution from the ii$_3^{ø4}$ is normal, the 7th becoming part of a 4–3 suspension. The main rhythmic motive (♩ ♪ ♪ | ♩) appears three times in the vocal part and three times in the accompaniment, alternating between the two.

4. The 7th of the ii^7 is prepared as a suspension in another voice (the bass in the previous measure). The texture thickens to five parts before the ii^7 resolves normally to the V^7. The asterisks indicate when the damper pedal is to be released. The reduction helps us to appreciate Chopin's imaginative elaboration of a simple progression. Notice that the C5 in m. 15 is analyzed as a passing tone that connects B4 to D5.

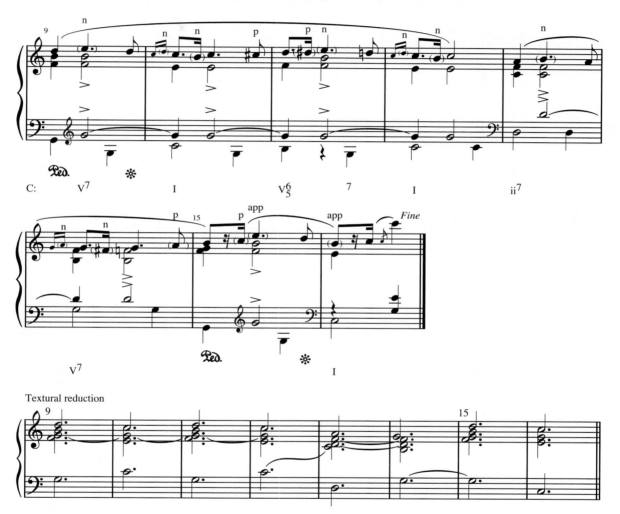

Part D, pp. 228–229.

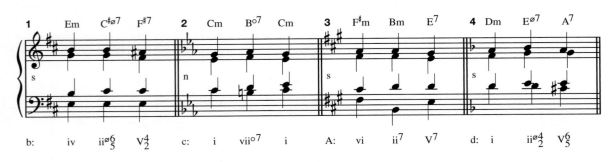

b: iv   ii°$^6_5$ V$^4_2$ c: i   vii°^{7} i   A: vi   ii^7 V^7 d: i   ii°$^4_2$ V$^6_5$

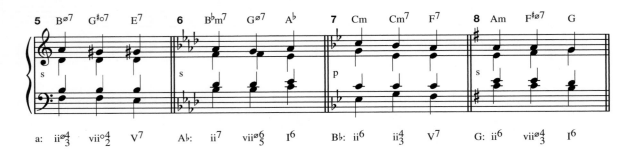

a: ii°$^4_3$ vii°$^4_2$ V^7 A♭:   ii^7 vii°$^6_5$ I^6 B♭:   ii^6 ii$^4_3$ V^7 G: ii^6 vii°$^4_3$ I^6

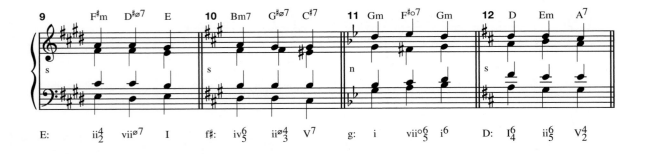

E: ii$^4_2$ vii°^{7} I   f♯:   iv$^6_5$ ii°$^4_3$ V^7 g: i   vii°$^6_5$ i^6 D: I$^6_4$ ii$^6_5$ V$^4_2$

Part E, p. 229.

Corelli, Trio Sonata op. 3, no. 2, II

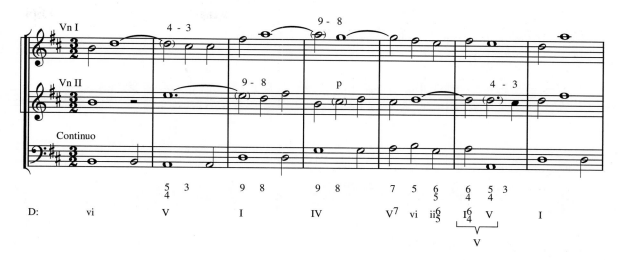

Part F, p. 229.

1. Bach, "Jesu, der du meine Seele"

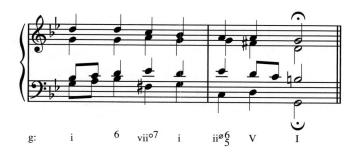

2. Bach, "Wie schön leuchtet der Morgenstern"

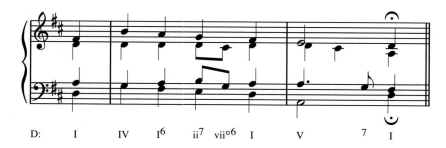

Chapter Fifteen

SELF-TEST 15-1

Part A, p. 240.

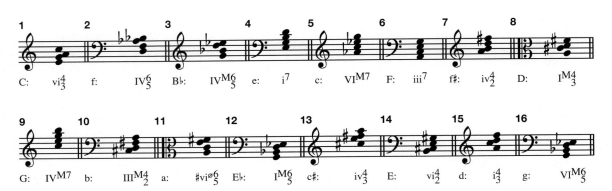

C: vi_3^4 f: IV_5^6 B♭: IV^{M6}_5 e: i^7 c: VI^{M7} F: iii^7 f♯: iv_2^4 D: I^{M4}_3

G: IV^{M7} b: III^{M4}_2 a: $\sharp vi^{\varnothing 6}_5$ E♭: I^{M6}_5 c♯: iv_3^4 E: vi_2^4 d: i_3^4 g: VI^{M6}_5

Part B, p. 240.

1. III^{M6}_5 2. vi_3^4 3. iv^7 4. $\sharp iv^{\varnothing 4}_2$ 5. I^{M4}_2

6. VI^{M4}_3 7. IV^{M6}_5 8. i_2^4

Part C, pp. 240–241.

1. The 7th of the vi^7 is approached as a suspension. The resolution is slightly unusual in that the ii has a doubled 3rd. However, if the tenor had gone to A3, the line would not have been as satisfactory, and parallel 5ths would have been formed with the alto.

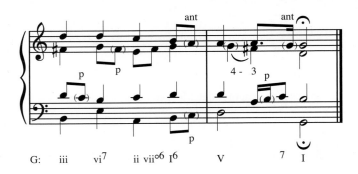

G: iii vi^7 ii vii^{o6} I^6 V ^{7} I

2. Circle of fifths; 5th; it would proceed downward by step, one note per measure: F4–E♭4–D♭4–C4.

   i iv^7 / VII^7 III^{M7} / VI^{M7} $ii^{\varnothing 7}$ / V^7 i

3.

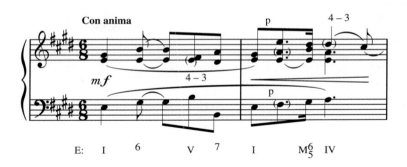

E: I   6   V   7   I   M$^6_5$ IV

4.

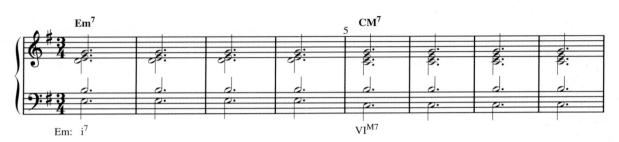

Em: i^7 VI^{M7}

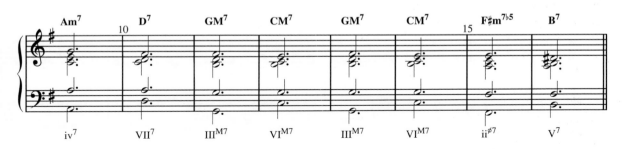

iv^7 VII^7 III^{M7} VI^{M7} III^{M7} VI^{M7} ii^{ø7} V^7

Part D, p. 242.

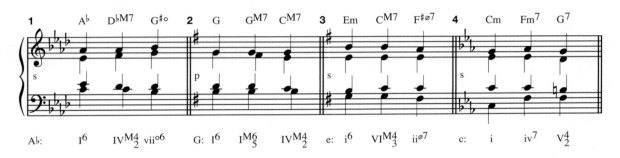

A♭:   I^6 IV$^{M4}_2$ vii^{o6} G: I^6 I$^{M6}_5$ IV$^{M4}_2$ e: i^6 VI$^{M4}_3$ ii^{ø7} c: i   iv^7 V$^4_2$

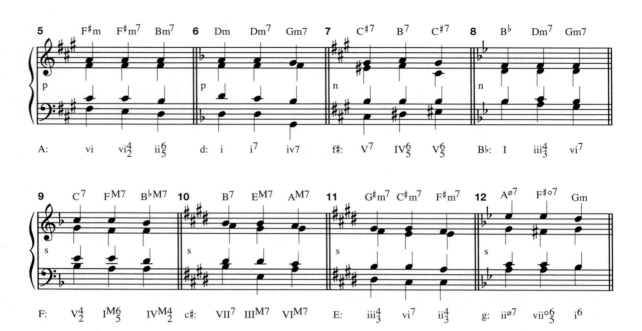

Part E, p. 242.

Notice the similarities between this excerpt and the one in Part C, no. 3.

Bach, French Suite no. 1, Minuet II

Part F, p. 243.

1.

e: i   IV$^6_5$ V$^6_5$ i   i$^4_2$ ii$^{\o4}_3$ V^7 i

2.

F: I   vi^7 ii$^4_3$ V^7 I   V$^4_3$ I^6 IV$^{M4}_2$ ii^7 V   I

Chapter Sixteen

SELF-TEST 16-1

Part A, p. 248.

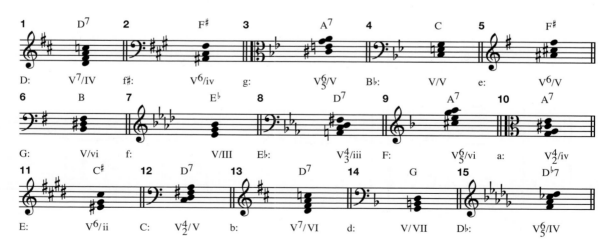

1 D^7 2 F♯   3 A^7 4 C   5 F♯

D: V^7/IV   f♯:   V^6/iv   g: V$^6_5$/V   B♭:   V/V   e: V^6/V

6 B   7 E♭   8 D^7 9 A^7 10 A^7

G: V/vi   f: V/III   E♭:   V$^4_3$/iii   F: V$^6_5$/vi   a: V$^4_2$/iv

11 C♯   12 D^7 13 D^7 14 G   15 D♭^{7}

E: V^6/ii   C: V$^4_2$/V   b: V^7/VI   d: V/VII   D♭:   V$^6_5$/IV

Part B, p. 249.

1. V^6/ii   2. X   3. V^4_2/V   4. X   5. V^4_3/iv

6. V^6_5/vi   7. V^7/III   8. V/V   9. X   10. V^4_2/IV

11. X   12. V^4_3/VI   13. V^6/iii   14. V^7/iv   15. V^4_3/V

SELF-TEST 16-2

Part A, pp. 253–257.

1.

2.

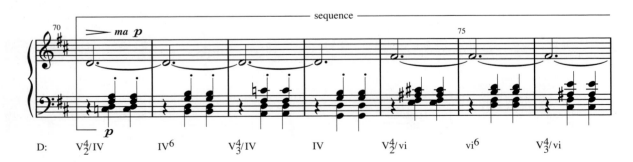

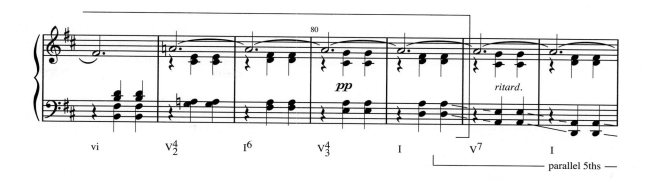

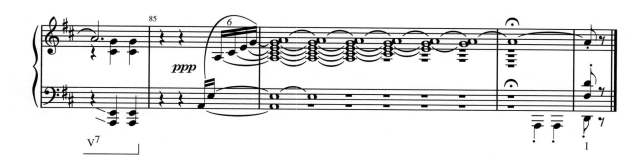

3.

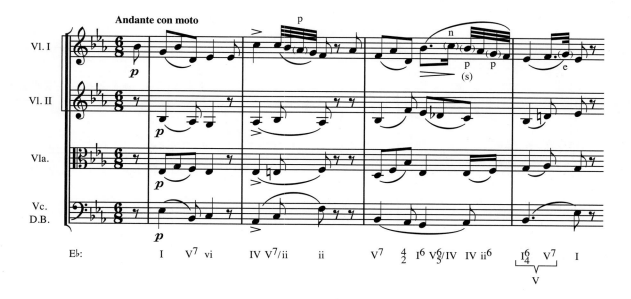

4. Measures 1 to 2 return at a different pitch level in mm. 5 to 6. This is not really a sequence because mm. 3 to 4 intervene. Counting from the bottom, parts 1 and 2 double at the octave. Part 4 doubles 7 (the melody) until the second half of m. 7. Other parallel octaves occur occasionally, as between parts 3 and 6 over the bar line from m. 2 to m. 3.

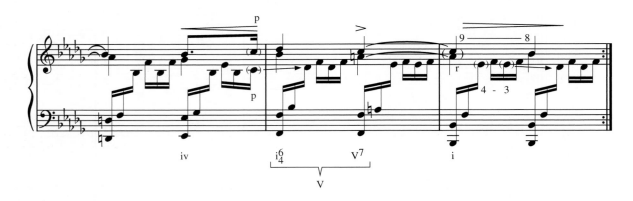

5.

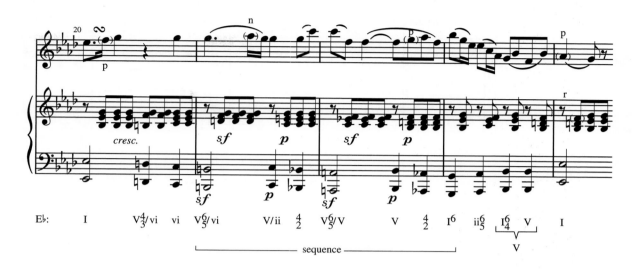

6.

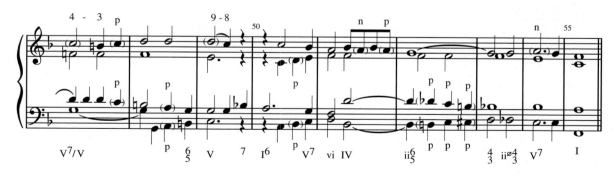

7.

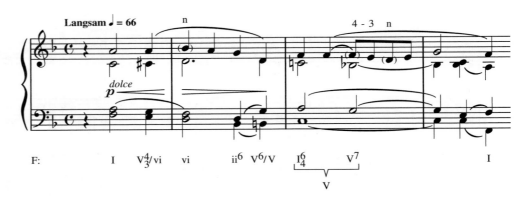

Part B, p. 257.

Part C, p. 258.

1. $V^{(7)}/V$, $V^{(7)}/VII$
2. $V^{(7)}/ii$, $V^{(7)}/V$, V^7/iii
3. $V^{(7)}/V$, V^7/vi
4. V^7/ii, V^7/IV
5. $V^{(7)}/ii$, $V^{(7)}/vi$, V^7/IV
6. $V^{(7)}/iii$, $V^{(7)}/vi$
7. V^7/IV, V^7/V
8. $V^{(7)}/III$, $V^{(7)}/V$
9. $V^{(7)}/III$, $V^{(7)}/VII$
10. $V^{(7)}/iv$, V^7/VII, V^7/V

Part D, p. 258.

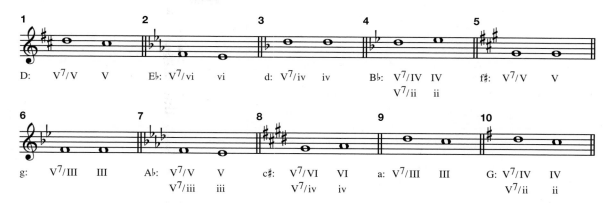

D: V⁷/V   V   Eb: V⁷/vi   vi   d: V⁷/iv   iv   Bb: V⁷/IV IV   f#: V⁷/V   V
                                                         V⁷/ii ii

g: V⁷/III III   Ab: V⁷/V   V   c#: V⁷/VI VI   a: V⁷/III III   G: V⁷/IV   IV
                     V⁷/iii iii   V⁷/iv iv   V⁷/ii   ii

Part E, p. 259.

The hemiola occurs in m. 5, where the cadential six-four chord sounds like the downbeat of a $\frac{2}{4}$ measure.

Part F, pp. 259–260.

1. Bach, "Herzlich thut mich verlangen"   2. Bach, "Christus, der ist mein Leben"

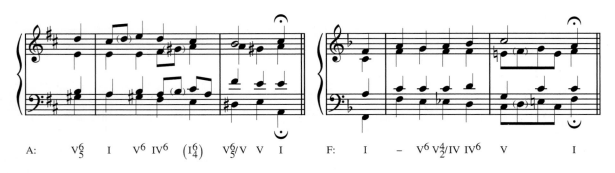

3. Bach, "Ermuntre dich, mein schwacher Geist"   4. Bach, "Christ lag in Todesbanden"

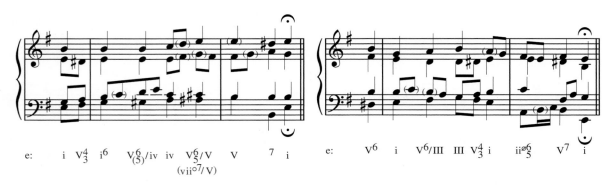

Part G, p. 260.

Chapter Seventeen

SELF-TEST 17-1

Part A, p. 264.

Part B, p. 265.

1. vii°^{7}/vi   2. X   3. vii°^{6}/VI   4. vii°$^6_5$/IV   5. vii°^{7}/VII

6. X   7. vii°^{7}/III   8. X   9. vii°^{7}/ii   10. vii°$^6_5$/V

11. vii$\emptyset$$^4_3$/V   12. X   13. vii°^{6}/iv   14. vii°^{6}/V   15. X

SELF-TEST 17-2

Part A, pp. 280–284.

1.

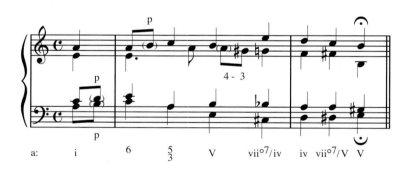

2.

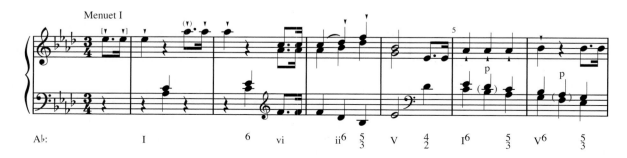

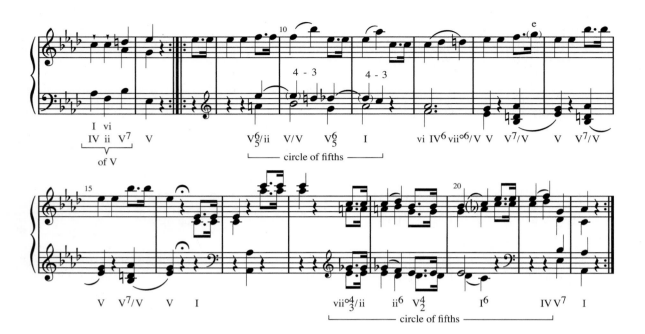

3. A: V^7 | I vi | ii^6 $vii°^7/V$ | I_4^6 (V^7 I_4^6) | V^7 |
                      V

| V^7/IV $vii°_5^6/ii$ | ii^6 $vii°^7/V$ | I_4^6 | V^7 | I |

        or   V

    $vii°_5^6/vi$ vi^6

      of IV

4.

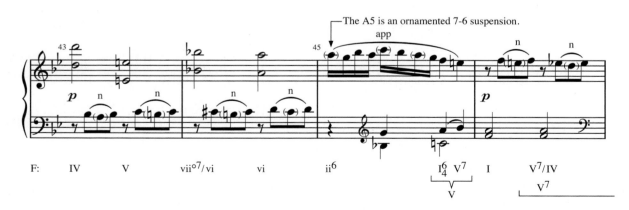

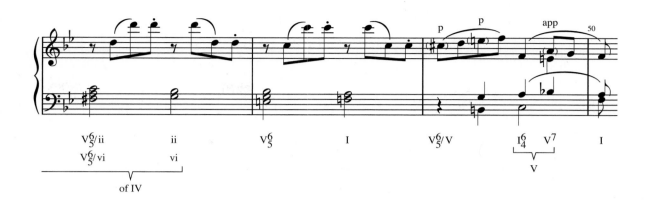

5. The excerpt is not a period because the second cadence is not more conclusive than the first. The first cadence (m. 4) is a PAC, whereas the second (m. 8) is a HC.

   The 5–4 suspension is marked with an exclamation point because it involves a note that is consonant with the bass resolving to one that is dissonant with the bass, exactly the reverse of the commonly accepted definition of a suspension.

6.

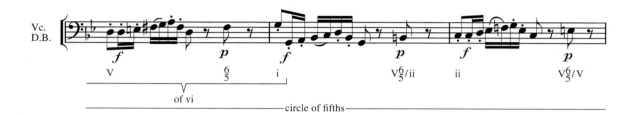

Part B, p. 284.

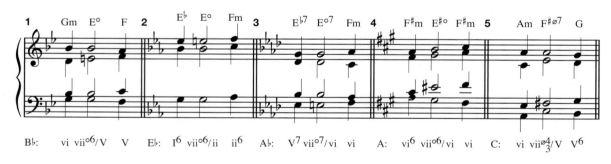

Part C, p. 285.

1. Bach, "Du grosser Schmerzensmann"

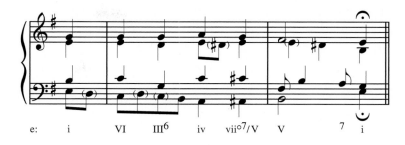

e: i   VI   III⁶   iv   vii°⁷/V V   ⁷ i

2. Bach, "Ach, Gott, wie manches Herzeleid"

Bach has written a very high part for the tenors in this phrase and twice crosses them above the altos. This allows him to pass the ♪♪ ♩ motive among all four parts as well as to enhance the cadence through the power of tenors in their high register.

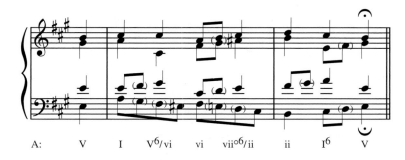

A: V   I   V⁶/vi   vi   vii°⁶/ii   ii   I⁶   V

3. Bach, "Ein' feste Burg ist unser Gott"

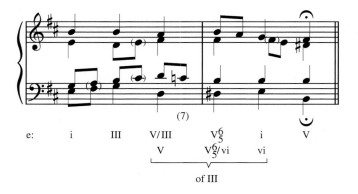

e: i   III   V/III   V⁶₅   i   V
                            V   V⁶₅/vi   vi
                                  of III

Part D, p. 285.

F: I   vii°7/ii   ii   V7   vii°7/vi   vi   ii$^6_5$ V   7   I

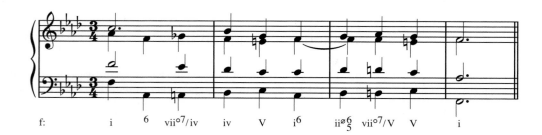

f: i   6   vii°7/iv   iv   V   i6   ii⌀$^6_5$ vii°7/V   V   i

Chapter Eighteen

SELF-TEST 18-1

Part A, p. 290.

1. b	2. D♭	3. A	4. a♭	5. d
6. F♯	7. c♯	8. A♭	9. c	10. B

Part B, p. 291.

1. c, d, E♭, F, g
2. e♭, f, G♭, A♭, b♭
3. E♭, f, g, A♭, B♭
4. C♯, d♯, e♯, F♯, G♯
5. E, f♯, g♯, A, B
6. b, c♯, D, E, f♯

Part C, p. 291.

1. foreign
2. closely related
3. enharmonic
4. closely related
5. relative and closely related
6. closely related
7. parallel
8. foreign
9. relative and closely related
10. foreign

SELF-TEST 18-2

Part A, pp. 296–299.

1.

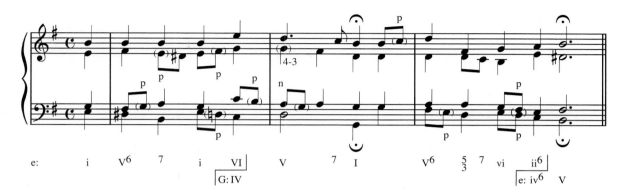

```
e:    i    V6   7   i   VI │   V       7   I       V6   5   7  vi   ii6 │
                                                         3
           │ G: IV                                            │ e: iv6   V
```

2. If the last chord in m. 7 were a ii$^6_5$, the 7th (E♭5) would resolve by step.

```
c:    i    6   vii°6  i   V6  i   V       i      iv6  VI   ii°6   V7   i
                                                              5
```

```
      v6  VI   III6 │  V6    I   V       6   I   IV  V4   I6     I6   V   7  I
                       5                          2          │  4 │
      │ E♭: IV    I6 │                                          V
         ↑        ↑
       either
```

3.

4.

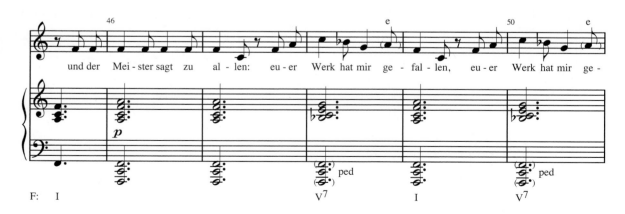

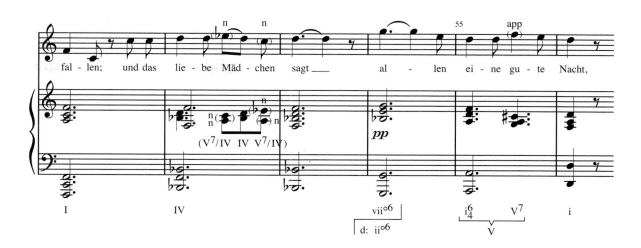

5. The outer voices in the sequence in mm. 9 to 11 could be heard as an elaboration of this pattern.

V$^6_5$ I $\frac{4}{2}$ I^6 V$^4_3$ I V$^4_2$ I^6 V$^4_3$ I   V^7 I

A♭: V

E♭: IV

— sequence —

(The modulation to A♭ is optional and could
be analyzed as a tonicization of IV.)

Part B, p. 299.

1. F   2. A   3. a   4. f♯   5. A♭

Part C, pp. 299–300.

1. First key, A♭:	I	ii	IV	vi	
Triads:	A♭	B♭m	D♭	Fm	
Second key, D♭:	V	vi	I	iii	
2. First key, c:	iv	VI			
Triads:	Fm	A♭			
Second key, f:	i	III			
3. First key, a:	i	III	iv	VI	
Triads:	Am	C	Dm	F	
Second key, F:	iii	V	vi	I	
4. First key, G:	I	iii	V	vi	
Triads:	G	Bm	D	Em	
Second key, D:	IV	vi	I	ii	
5. First key, c♯:	i	ii°	III	iv	VI
Triads:	C♯m	D♯°	E	F♯m	A
Second key, E:	vi	vii°	I	ii	IV
6. First key, D:	I	iii	V	vi	
Triads:	D	F♯m	A	Bm	
Second key, f♯:	VI	i	III	iv	

Part D, p. 300.

Part E, p. 300.

Bach, "Freu' dich sehr, o meine Seele"

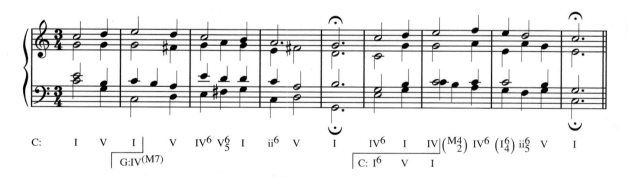

Part F, p. 300.

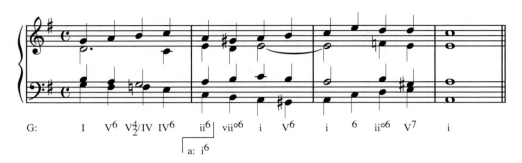

G: I   V⁶ V⁴₂/IV IV⁶   ii⁶│ vii°⁶ i   V⁶   i   ⁶ ii°⁶ V⁷   i

        │a: i⁶

Chapter Nineteen

SELF-TEST 19-1

Part A, pp. 313–316.

1. This modulation might also be analyzed as a phrase modulation.

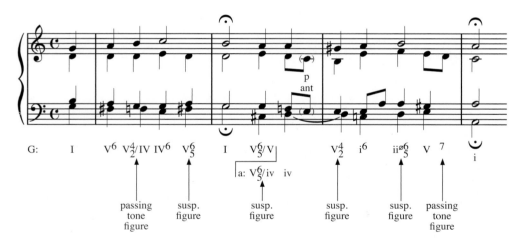

G: I   V⁶ V⁴₂/IV IV⁶ V⁶₅ I V⁶₅/V│   V⁴₂ i⁶ ii°⁶₅ V ⁷   i

                       │a: V⁶₅/iv iv

              passing   susp.   susp.   susp.   susp.   passing
              tone   figure   figure   figure   figure   tone
              figure   figure

2. Yes, D♭ major and A major are in a chromatic mediant relationship, but it is enharmonically spelled (compare C♯–A). The modulation is effected through a common tone, also enharmonically spelled.

3. The modulation from g to f is sequential. The modulation back to g is a direct modulation. The reduction shown below is just one possibility.

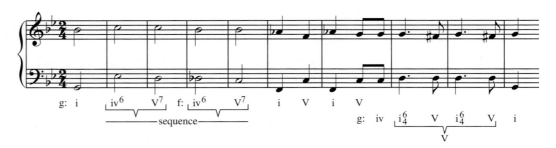

4. The two keys are G major and E♭ major. A monophonic modulation is accomplished in mm. 121 to 123. The relationship between G and E♭ could be described in at least two ways. For one, there is a chromatic mediant relationship between the two keys. Also, E♭ is VI in g minor, the parallel minor of G major.

Part B, p. 316.

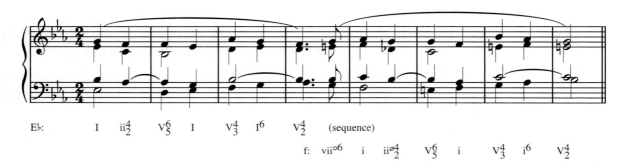

Chapter Twenty

SELF-TEST 20-1

Part A, p. 341.

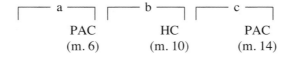

Or b and c could be considered one phrase. Either way, the form is sectional binary, unless you want to use the term *phrase group* (review p. 160).

Part B, pp. 341–342.
Two-reprise continuous rounded binary.

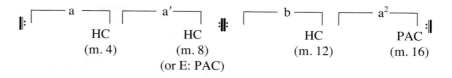

a	a'		b	a²
HC	HC		HC	PAC
(m. 4)	(m. 8)		(m. 12)	(m. 16)
	(or E: PAC)			

1. The first G4 is the 7th of a V⁷/IV. The other is part of a 4–3 suspension.
2. End of m. 6: A: I = E: IV
3. The melodic figures resemble the opening motive (leap up, stepwise down), whereas the bass line is related to the first two bass notes.
4. m. 7, beat 3.
5. m. 7, beat 4 to m. 8, soprano and bass.

Part C, pp. 342–343.
Two-reprise sectional binary.

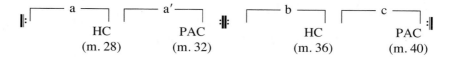

a	a'		b	c
HC	PAC		HC	PAC
(m. 28)	(m. 32)		(m. 36)	(m. 40)

1. The first violins (or the melody) at the octave.
2. Part of a vii°⁶/V.
3. In mm. 28 to 29, perhaps explainable as occurring between phrases.

Part D, pp. 343–344.
Continuous ternary.

a	a¹		b	a²	a³
f#:PAC	A:PAC		c#:PAC	A:PAC	f#:PAC
(or IAC)	(m. 8)		(m. 16)	(m. 20)	(m. 24)
(m. 4)					

1. Schumann moves from i to the relative major (III) to the minor dominant (v) and then back the same way (III, then i). The tonicized pitch classes arpeggiate the tonic triad: F#–A–C#–A–F#.
2. A: vii°⁷/ii / ii / V₃⁴/V V⁷ / I / f#: i V / VI^M7 iv⁷ / i₄⁶ V⁷ / i / /
   $$\underbrace{i_4^6 \ \ V^7}_{V}$$
3. In mm. 21 to 22, V–VI^M7, there are parallel 5ths between the bass and tenor. They are hidden by the anticipation (A3) in the tenor.
4. The double bar after m. 8.

Chapter Twenty-One

SELF-TEST 21-1

Part A, p. 361.

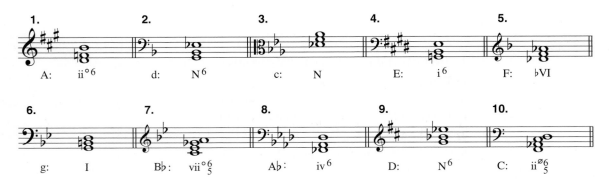

Part B, pp. 361–362.

1. G/B 2. Dm/F 3. G°7/D♭ 4. C♭/E♭ 5. B♭

   N^6 iv^6 $vii^{°4}_3$ N^6 ♭VI

6. E 7. F♯°7/A 8. G 9. G∅7/F 10. C/E

   I $vii^{°6}_5$ ♭III $ii^{∅4}_2$ N^6

Part C, pp. 362–368.

1. It's easy to overlook the E♭ in m. 31.

2. a. c♯: / i (iv$^6_4$) / i / V^7 (i$^6_4$) /

      V^7 (i$^6_4$) V$^4_2$ / i^6 / N^6 / $\underbrace{i^6_4 \ V^7}$ / i /
                                              V

   b. The first three $^6_4$ chords are pedal $^6_4$ chords.

      The fourth one is a cadential $^6_4$.

   c. The form is a period. Most listeners would probably call it a parallel period, even though only the first four notes of the two phrases are similar.

3. Measures 5 and 6 contain diminished seventh chords. Both contain a °5 and a $^+$4, and in both cases the tendency of the °5 to resolve inward and of the $^+$4 to resolve outward is followed. The chords of resolution then have doubled 3rds.

Bb: I^6 / V$^4_2$ / I^6 V / I / vii$^{°7}$/ii ii / (vii$^{°7}$) I / IV V^6/V / V

4. Notice that the excerpt begins with a long circle-of-fifths sequence.

a: i^6 iv / VII^6 III / VI^6 ii° /^{40} V^6 i / N^6|

F: IV^6 V^7 / I / V$^4_3$ I / (IV$^6_4$) I /^{45} V$^6_5$ I /

5. The flutes double the violas in mm. 47 to 51.

A: V / V$^4_2$/ii ii^6 / V$^4_2$ I^6 / IV$^{M4}_2$ ii (bVI^6) / V$^6_5$ I ii^6 V^7 / vi V$^6_5$/V / V^7 / I /
or
vii$^{°6}$

6. The last NCT is an escape tone. The pedal point occurs in m. 194.

F: I / I / I / N / V^7/N / N V$^6_5$ / I vi / ii$^6_5$ V^7 / I /

7. The first modulation is from ab minor to its relative major, Cb, by means of the common chord in m. 5 (ab: i = Cb: vi). A change of mode to cb minor follows in m. 9, notated as b minor. This change of mode simplifies the second modulation, from cb/b to its relative major, Ebb/D, through the common chord in m. 14 (b: iv = D: ii).

Part D, p. 368.

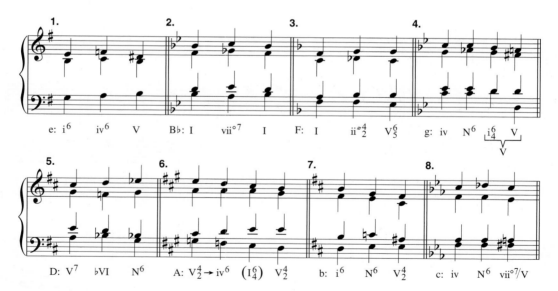

Part E, pp. 368–369.

1.

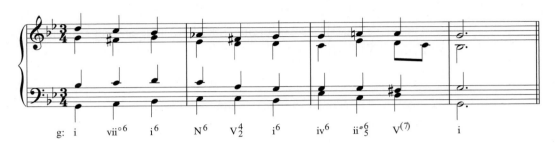

g: i   vii°⁶   i⁶   N⁶   V⁴₂   i⁶   iv⁶   ii°⁶₅   V⁽⁷⁾   i

2.

F: I   vii°⁷/ii   ii   vii°⁷   I   iiø⁶₅   V   I

Part F, p. 369.

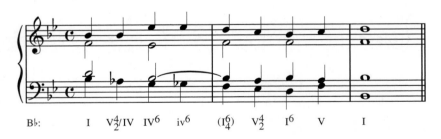

B♭:   I   V⁴₂/IV   IV⁶   iv⁶   (I⁶₄)   V⁴₂   I⁶   V   I

Part G, p. 369.

Chapter Twenty-Two

SELF-TEST 22-1

Part A, p. 383.

1. Ger^{+6} 2. Fr^{+6} 3. vii$^{\circ 6}$/V   4. Ger^{+6} 5. vii$^{\circ 4}_{2}$

6. It^{+6} 7. Fr^{+6} 8. It^{+6} V^6 9. Fr^{+6}/$\hat{1}$ I   10. It^{+6}

Part B, p. 383.

1.   2.   3.   4.   5.

f: Ger^{+6} E: Fr^{+6} c#:   N^6 D♭:   Ger^{+6} F: It^{+6}

6.   7.   8.   9.   10.

a: Fr^{+6} E♭:   V$^6_5$/ii   g: Ger^{+6} D: iv^6 b: It^{+6}

Part C, pp. 384–389.

1. In this key, B♭7–E♭ would be analyzed as V^7/N–N. Here, the context makes it clear that the B♭7 is a Ger^{+6}. Notice the stepwise descent in the bass line.

   d: i / V^6 / V$^4_2$/IV / IV^6 / V$^4_2$/III / III^6 Ger^{+6} V^7 / i /

2. The #$\hat{4}$ and ♭$\hat{6}$ expand to an octave on $\hat{5}$ as expected. Parallel 5ths are avoided by resolving to a i$^6_4$ chord. Notice the unusual unprepared escape tone in m. 4, creating a sharp dissonance with the long-delayed V chord beneath it.

   a: vii$^{\circ 6}_{5}$/V / Ger^{+6} / i$^6_4$ VI i$^6_4$ vii$^{\circ 7}$/V / i$^6_4$ VI ii$^{\varnothing 6}_{5}$ V / i

3. The resolution of the Fr^{+6} is ornamented with a 4–3 suspension in the second violin. The ♭$\hat{6}$ and #$\hat{4}$ expand to an 8ve on $\hat{5}$.

   B: I / ii^6 / V ^{7} / I / V^6

   F#: I^6 V$^6_5$ / I IV^6 Fr^{+6} / V / I /

4.

5. The $\flat\hat{6}$ and $\sharp\hat{4}$ expand to an 8ve on $\hat{5}$. Parallel 5ths are avoided by resolving to a i^6_4 chord. The Ger^{+6} and the V^4_2/N are enharmonically equivalent.

   b: i / i^4_2 / Ger^{+6} i^6_4 / V^4_2/N N^6 /
       V^4_2 i^6 / ii$^{\varnothing 7}$ V^7 / i

6. The chromatic passing tone occurs at the beginning of m. 6 in the first violin. In both Ger^{+6} chords the viola has the 5th above the bass. The parallels are avoided in the first instance by leaping up to $\hat{5}$. In the second Ger^{+6} the parallels are disguised by means of a 6–5 suspension. In the first Ger^{+6} the resolution of $\sharp\hat{4}$ in the second violin is taken by the viola, allowing the violin to leap up to $\hat{2}$ (the 5th of the V chord).

   f: i / (vii$^{\circ 7}$) V^6_5 / i / iv^6 / Ger^{+6} / V vii$^{\circ 7}$/V / V Ger^{+6} / V / /

7. e: N^6 Ger^{+6} / i^6_4 V^7 / I

8. There are other reasonable ways to analyze this excerpt. The +2 occurs in the tenor in m. 3, the °4 in the top voice of m. 6. The form is a parallel period because of the similarity of mm. 1 and 5.

g: I V_5^6 (or vii°7) | i vii°7/V V (7) | VI Ger+6 | V ($_2^4$) |
  i^6 iv V_3^4 | i V^7 VI vii°6/iv | iv (ii°6) $\underline{i_4^6\ \ V^7}$ | i |
   V

Part D, p. 389.

Part E, p. 389.

Part F, p. 390.

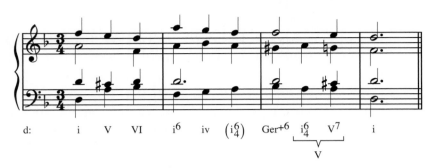

d: i   V   VI i^6 iv (i_4^6) Ger^{+6} i_4^6 V^7 i

V

Chapter Twenty-Three

SELF-TEST 23-1

Part A, p. 400.

D: vii°^{7} = F: vii°$_2^4$ = A♭: vii°$_3^4$ = B: vii°$_5^6$ E♭:   V^7 = D: Ger^{+6}

b: Ger^{+6} = C: V^7 e: V^7/iv   = g♯: Ger^{+6}

Other correct answers in addition to those previously given are possible. For example, the third chord in no. 1 could have been spelled and analyzed as a vii°$_3^4$ in g♯ (or G♯), or as a vii°$_3^4$/V in c♯, and so on.

Part B, p. 401.

1. E: I   /   vii°^{7} /   I   /   V$_3^4$ /   I^6 $_3^5$ /   vii°^{7}|

                |G: vii°$_2^4$ /   V^7 /   I   /   V^7 /   I   /

2. c: i   V$_2^4$ /   i^6 ii$_5^{ø6}$ /   vii°^{7}/V|

         |e: vii°$_5^6$ V$_3^4$ /   i^6 /   ii$_5^{ø6}$ V^7 /   i   /

3. D: I   iii   IV   /   I^6 V$_3^4$ I   V^7/IV|

         |f♯:   Ger^{+6} /   i$_4^6$ V ^{7} /   i   /

                           V

Part C, pp. 401–406.

1. The F–G♭–F figure in m. 65 may be related to the voice line in mm. 58 to 62 (B♭–C♭–B♭) and to the bass in mm. 59 to 63 (F–G♭–F).

G♭: I / V^6_5 / I / V^6_5 / I V^7/IV

            b♭: Ger^{+6} / V ^{6} i ^{6} / V $^6_5$ i ^{6} / V

2. No, this is not an enharmonic modulation. The real key relationships here are D♭ (I) to B♭♭ (♭VI). Anyone would rather read music written in A instead of B♭♭, so the flats are written enharmonically as sharps beginning in m. 39. But the listener is completely unaware of the enharmonicism—the true test of an enharmonic modulation.

3. Notice that a single °7 chord is heard in mm. 45 to 46, and, although the listener is unaware of the shift to sharps at the end of m. 46, the unexpected resolution to a C♯^{7} is clearly audible. We have analyzed the °7 chord in B♭ as a vii$^{°4}_3$/ii because Schubert spelled it that way. However, it has other enharmonic possibilities in B♭—vii$^{°6}_5$/IV, for example—and these are equally valid analyses.

B♭: V^7 (I^6_4) V / (I^6_4) V (I^6_4) V^7 / / vii$^{°4}_3$/ii /

             f♯: vii$^{°7}$ / / V^7 / i /

4. D♭: I V^4_2 I^6 /

    V^7 / I ii^6 V^6_5/V / V / I V^4_2 I^6 / V^7 / vii$^{°7}$/vi

             c:vii$^{°6}_5$/V / i^6_4 V / i
                              V

5. B♭/A♯ is an important pitch class in this passage. It appears melodically as the 7th of the vii$^{°7}$/ii four times in mm. 34 to 41 (the first time accented), and it is used as the enharmonic hinge between the keys of C and E in m. 43.

C: I vii$^{°6}_5$/ii / ii^6 / / V^6_5 / I vii$^{°7}$/ii ii vii$^{ø6}_5$ / I^6 vii$^{°6}_5$/ii ii^6 / ii$^{ø6}_5$ V^4_2 /

I^6 i^6 (V^6_4) vii$^{°7}$/ii / ii V^6_5 / I V^4_2/IV

             E: Ger^{+6} i^6_4 V^7 / I V^6_5 I / V $^4_2$ I^6 V^6_5 / I
                              V

6. C: I / V^4_3 I^6 / ii^6 vii$^{°7}$/V / I^6_4 V^7 /
                                 V

    i / V^4_3 i^6 / ii$^{°6}$ vii$^{°7}$/V / (i^6_4) Ger^{+6} /

             c♯: V^7

    i / V^4_3 i^6 / ii$^{°6}$ vii$^{°7}$/V / I^6_4 V^7 / I
                             V

Chapter Twenty-Four

SELF-TEST 24-1

Part A, p. 424.

Part B, pp. 424–429

1.

E: I / V / V$_2^4$/IV / IV^6 / (I$_4^6$) / vii$^{\circ 7}$/V /

V$_2^4$ / I^6 (V^{+6}/IV) / IV / vii$^{\circ}$/ii ii^6 / V^7 / vi / ii / V^7 / I /

2.

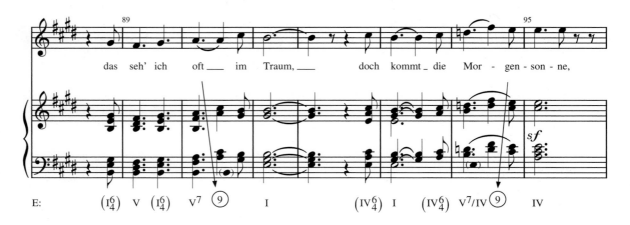

das seh' ich oft __ im Traum, __ doch kommt _ die Mor - gen-son - ne,

E: (I$_4^6$)   V   (I$_4^6$)   V^7 ⑨   I   (IV$_4^6$)   I   (IV$_4^6$)   V^7/IV ⑨   IV

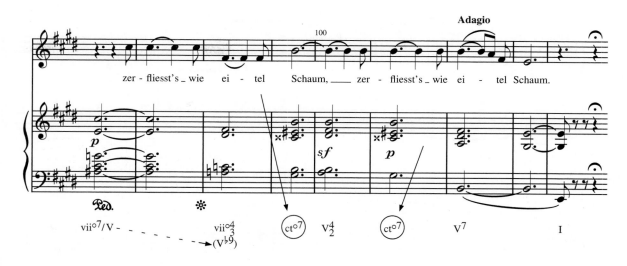

3. F: I $\widehat{ct^{\circ 7}}$ / I V^7/IV / IV / V^7/vi V^7/IV /
    ii^7 $vii^{\circ 7}$/iii / iii^7 vi^7 / ii^7 V^7 I /

    (vi^7/IV)

    The longest circle-of-fifths sequence begins with the $vii^{\circ 7}$/iii and ends with the last chord (the G♯°7 substitutes for an E7 chord). The chromatic mediant relationship involves the A7 and F7 chords.

4. You could also analyze a quick tonicization of F followed by the modulation to C. In either case, the opening C♯°7 is used in three different ways in this excerpt.

    $\widehat{ct^{\circ 7}}$ / V^4_2 $\overset{125}{\widehat{ct^{\circ 7}}}$ / V^4_2 / $vii^{\circ 6}_5$/ii / ii^6 /

    $\underset{\underset{V}{\underbrace{}}}{I^6_4 \ V^7}$ $\overset{130}{}$ / I / $\widehat{ct^{\circ 7}}$ / V^4_2 / $\widehat{ct^{\circ 7}}$ / V^4_2 $\overset{135}{}$ / $\widehat{ct^{\circ 7}}$

    C: $vii^{\circ 4}_2$/IV

    IV ii^6 / $\underset{\underset{V^7}{\underbrace{}}}{I^6_4 \ V^7}$ / I /

5. The form of this piece is continuous ternary.

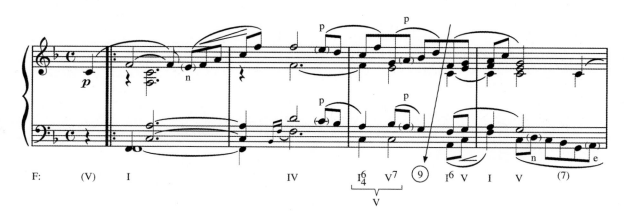

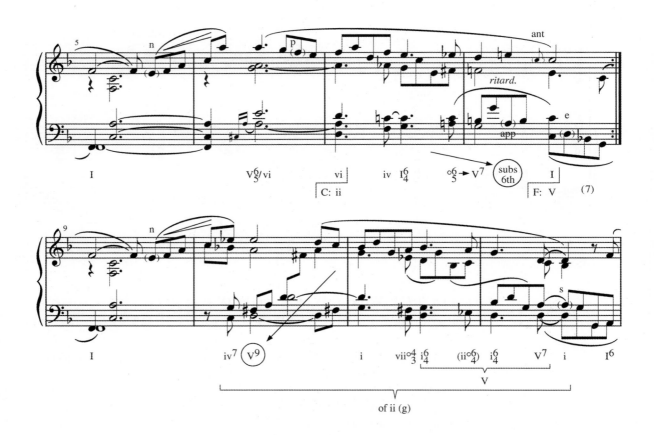

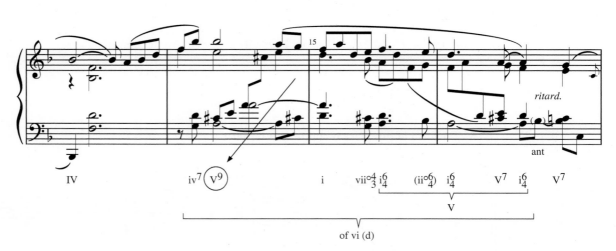

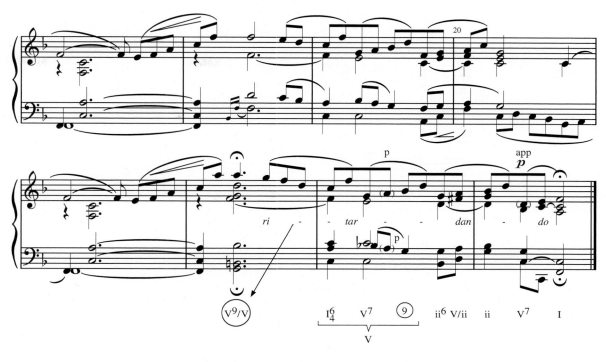

6.

(ct°7)	V⁷	(ct°7)	V⁷	(V⁺⁷)	I	(ct°7)
1	2	3	4	5	6	7

$$\text{I} \quad \text{V}^4_3/\text{vi} \quad \text{vi} \quad \text{V}^6 \quad \underbrace{\text{ii}^{ø6}_5 \quad \text{V}^{(7)} \quad \text{I}}_{\text{of V}}$$

8   9   10   11   12   13   14

Chapter Twenty-Five

SELF-TEST 25-1

Part A, pp. 446–447.

	1	2	3	4	5	
Chord:	E♭m, B♭m⁶	B, G♯m⁶	B, G⁶	Fm, D♭⁶	Fm, D♭m⁶	
Root int:	P5	m3	M3	M3	M3	
Total dist.:	3	2	2	1	2	

	6	7	8	9	10	11
Chord:	A, Fm⁶	F⁷, B$^4_3$	Dm⁷, Em⁷	G^{ø7}, A$^4_2$	C♯⁷, F$^4_2$	D, G
Root int:	M3	+4	M2	M2	M3	P4
Total dist.:	3	2	8	2	4	15

Chromatic mediants: #3, 5, 10

Doubly chromatic mediants: #6

Part B, p. 447.

1.

F   A   A♭   D   D♭

2.

F   a♭   (g♯)   d♭   (c♯)

Note: enharmonic spelling is acceptable.

Part C, pp. 447–449.

1. The key of F♯m.

2. There is an augmented sixth chord in m. 176, beat 4.

3. #1: m. 150, from F♯ to D, common-chord

    #2: m. 167, from D to B♭, common chord

    #3: m. 171, from B♭, to G♭, common-chord

    #4: m. 176, from G♭ to B♭m, enharmonic modulation (Mm^7 to Ger^{+6})

4. There is a complete chain of descending M3-related chromatic mediant progressions (F♯-D-B♭-G♭ (F♯)) and then a return to B♭m using a different modulatory technique (enharmonic reinterpretation).

5. The chord in m. 151, beat 3 is a iv chord, an example of mode mixture.

6. The chord in m. 162, beats 3–4 is a vii$^{\circ 7}$/iv chord above a tonic pedal.

Part D, pp. 449–450.

1. e♭ minor

2. The melody is very angular and contains no leading tone. It does not clearly imply a harmonic background. The phrase concludes on scale degree $\hat{3}$ rather than tonic.

3. VII^7 III^7 / VI^7 II$^{\varnothing 7}$ / V (very traditional!)

4. Measure 8, beat 1: we are led to expect G♭ major because of emphasis on the D♭ dominant seventh chord. Measure 8, end of beat 3: we have been set up for a♭ minor here, especially with G♮ suggesting a leading tone.

5. Measure 9, last two beats feature a Ger^{+6} in E♭.

6. There is no melodic "closure"; that is, the closing phrase is identical to the antecedent phrase that opened the composition. Also, the cadential harmonic motion consists of I$^6_4$ moving directly to I in root position.

Part E, pp. 450–451.

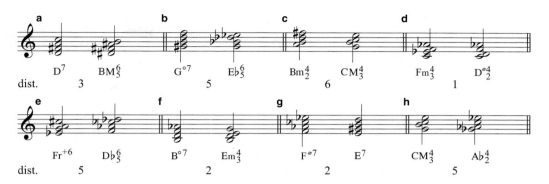

Part F, p. 451.

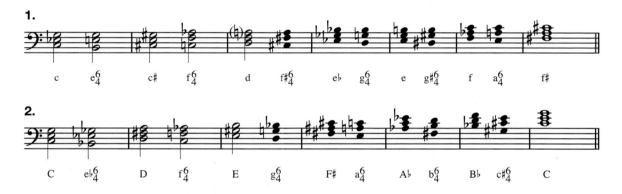

Chapter Twenty-Six

SELF-TEST 26-1

Part A, p. 461.

1. Ionian, Lydian, Mixolydian.
2. Phrygian, Locrian.
3. Whole-Tone and Hexatonic. Both are derived from the augmented triad, in one case superimposed at the interval of a whole step, and in the other, a half step.
4. Lydian-Mixolydian ($\sharp\hat{4}/\flat\hat{7}$).
5. Fully diminished seventh chord, juxtaposed at the interval of a half step or whole step.
6. Diminished, major, minor.
7. Minor 2nd, tritone.

Part B, p. 461.

D-Locrian F-Phrygian

B-Lydian A♭-Mixolydian

G-Dorian B♭-Lydian-Mixolydian (♯$\hat{4}$/♭$\hat{7}$)

Part C, pp. 461–462.

1.

2. The third collection, F♯–G♯–A♯–C♯–D♯

3.

4.

E♭-Mixolydian D-Phrygian

A-Dorian G-Lydian

C-Locrian F♯-Aeolian

Part D, pp. 462–463.

1. Dorian
2. Octatonic
3. Dorian
4. Phrygian
5. Lydian-Mixolydian
6. Aeolian
7. Mixolydian
8. Locrian

SELF-TEST 26-2

Part A, p. 478.

a. E♭/D, polychord
e. Q, quartal chord (inverted)
b. Q, quartal chord
f. A/F, polychord
c. D6, added 6th chord
g. S, secundal chord
d. C9, dominant 9th chord
h. Q, quintal chord

Part B, p. 478.

a. cluster chord
b. cluster chord
c. whole-tone chord
d. split-third chord

Part C, pp. 478–479.

1. major pentatonic.
2. B♭. In m. 6 it changes briefly to D because of the altered bass pattern.
3. Ostinato.
4. Perfect 4th (prominent in the melody and accompaniment as well).

Part D, p. 479.

1.

2.

Part E, pp. 480–481.

Obviously, the sample solution for each of these exercises represents only one of numerous other possibilities. You will observe the following features:

1. Notice how the right-hand melody is designed so as not to reinforce the G major and F major chords that constitute the ostinato pattern. Although the last measure of the phrase may suggest V7 in the key of C, there has been no suggestion of C as tonal center earlier in the piece, leaving us still unaware of any clear tonal center.

2. In addition to featuring secundal harmony, this phrase also seems to wander tonally. The sustained clusters that conclude the phrase do nothing to establish or clarify any sense of key.

3. The right hand clearly emphasizes tonic and dominant in the key of F♯, thereby setting up a sense of bitonality in relation to the "white-key" ostinato found in the left hand.

SELF-TEST 26-3

Part A, p. 490.

The procedures illustrated are the following:

a. asymmetric meter
b. mixed meter
c. added value
d. tempo modulation
e. displaced accent

Part B, p. 490.

a. Not nonretrogradable
b. Nonretrogradable
c. Nonretrogradable
d. Not nonretrogradable

Part C, pp. 491–492.

1. mixed meter
2. tempo modulation
3. alto, m. 469 and m. 471; tenor, m. 469 and m. 470; baritone, m. 470 and m. 471
4. alto, m. 469 and m. 471
5. 72:60 = 6:5
6. m. 5
7. no regular series of pulses, slow tempo, long duration between successive events, and tempo change at m. 13

Chapter Twenty-Seven

SELF-TEST 27-1

Part A, p. 504.

1. 3   5. 1
2. 6   6. 11
3. 10   7. 9
4. 0   8. 5

Part B, p. 504.

1. (9,8,5)   6. (2,3,4)
2. (10,0,5)   7. (1,2,4)
3. (11,2,1)   8. (7,3,4)
4. (0,2,4)   9. (3,2,7)
5. (4,8,0)   10. (3,2,5)

Part C, p. 504.

1. (014)
2. Measure 3, [A,B♭,D♭], half-note chord
   Measures 4–5, [G,G♯,B], chord
   Measures 4–5, [F♯,A,A♯], left hand
   Measure 10, [G♯,A,C], right hand
3. Measures 4–5, [G,G♯,B], chord

Part D, pp. 504–505.

1. a. measure 2, [F,G♭,B], (016), 3–5
   b. measure 3, [A,B♭,D♭], (014), 3–3
   c. measure 10, [E,G♭,A♭], (024), 3–6
   d. measure 11, [F,G,B], (026), 3–8
2. a. measure 9, [C,D,F♯], (026), 3–8
3. [F,G,G♯,A,B], (02346), 5–8
   It is inversionally symmetrical.
4. [F♯,G♯,A,C,D], (02368), 5–28
   It is not inversionally symmetrical.
5. [F♯,A,A♯,B,D], (03458), 5–Z37
   It is inversionally symmetrical.
6.

	B	G♯	G	A	F	E
(016)	x				x	x
(014)	x	x	x			
(024)			x	x	x	
(026)	x			x	x	

SELF-TEST 27-2

Part A, pp. 514–515.

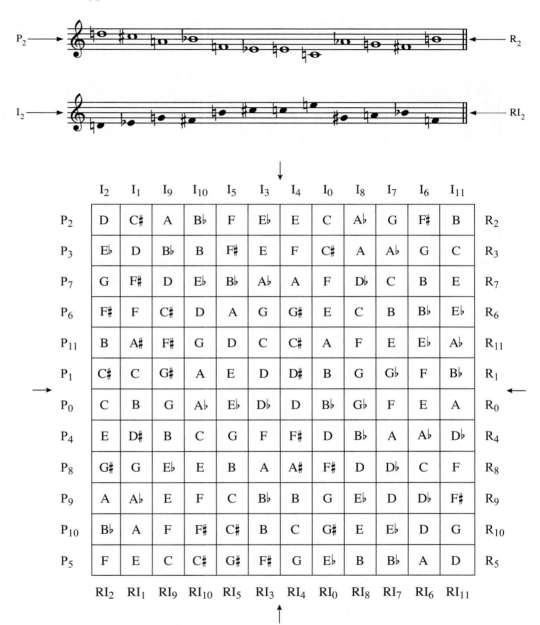

Note: enharmonic spelling is acceptable

Part B, pp. 515–516.

This sample solution might be titled "Seconds and Sevenths." Notice how prominently these dissonant intervals are featured until the third section of the piece, after which we find more consonant sonorities leading to a calmer and more peaceful conclusion.

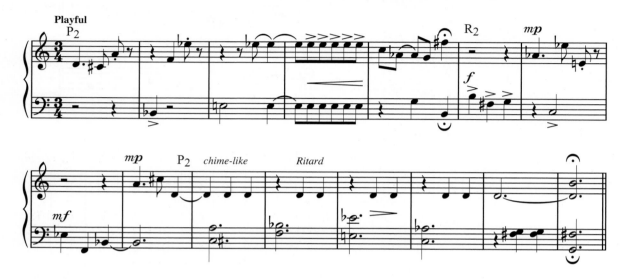

SELF-TEST 27-3

Part A, p. 521.

1. Total serialization is the process whereby nonpitch aspects of a piece are subjected to a predetermined order.
2. Composers such as Boulez and his teacher, Messiaen, were influential in the development of this compositional technique.

Chapter Twenty-Eight

SELF-TEST 28-1

Part A, p. 542.

George Crumb. Amplified piano, pizzicato plucking of strings inside the piano

John Cage. Prepared piano

Henry Cowell. Playing on the strings inside the piano

Edgard Varèse. Use of sirens as part of percussion ensemble

Lou Harrison. Bowing of mallet instruments; use of brake drums

Krzysztof Penderecki. Use of sustained, microtonal clusters; striking various areas of the violin (and other stringed instruments) to create a percussive effect

Arnold Schoenberg. Use of *Sprechstimme*

Part B, p. 542.

1. The term aleatory is used to describe music in which various elements of a composition are, in varying degrees, determined by chance.
2. Because of the way it "frames" or "organizes" silence, *4'33"* heightens the listener's awareness of surrounding sounds or noises, causing what might ordinarily be heard as distractions to become a part of the aesthetic of the listening experience.

Part C, p. 542.

Terry Riley, Steve Reich, Philip Glass

Part D, p. 542.

1. sine wave: a sound without overtones.
2. white noise: nonpitched hissing sound consisting of all audible frequencies at random amplitudes.
3. oscillator: tone generator.
4. *musique concrète*: natural sounds that have been recorded on tape and then subjected to modification by means of altered playback speed, reversal of tape direction, fragmentation, tape loop, and other technical manipulations.
5. MIDI: Musical Instrument Digital Interface, a protocol that allows a computer or synthesizer to drive sound generators, thereby greatly enhancing the capabilities of a single performer.
6. hyperinstrument: a term coined by composer Tod Machover to refer to the use of computers to augment musical expression and creativity.

Part E, p. 543.

1. John Chowning
2. Charles Dodge, Paul Lansky, Michael McNabb
3. CCRMA, IRCAM, MIT Media Lab

Glossary

12-Bar Blues A form type that typically consists of three four-bar phrases in either an aab or abc pattern. A variety of different harmonic patterns are commonly employed in the 12-bar blues.

A

Accidental A symbol that raises or lowers a pitch by a half or whole step.

Added Value A process by which rhythmic irregularity is created through the addition of a note value or rest to a rhythmic figure.

Additive Rhythm A process that has the effect on the listener of unequal groupings of subdivisions being added together.

Aleatory Music in which various elements of a composition are, in varying degrees, determined by chance. Can manifest itself in one of two ways in music: The compositional process itself may be indeterminate in one way or another, or the performer may be given the opportunity to make decisions during the performance of the piece. Also referred to as indeterminacy.

All-Interval Series A series in which all eleven intervals are different.

Altered or Chromatic Chords Chords using notes not found in the scale on which the passage is based.

Ametric Music Music that lacks an aurally perceivable meter.

Amplitude Envelope Gives musical shape to an oscillator's static tone by imparting an attack, decay, sustain, and release phase to the tone's overall loudness profile.

Analog-to-Digital Converter Device that encodes an analog signal as a series of discrete numbers by reading its wave form at precisely spaced intervals of time.

Anticipation A non-chord tone that moves by step or leap to some pitch contained in the anticipated chord that is not also present in the preceding chord.

Appoggiatura An accented non-chord tone that is approached by leap and resolved by step. Typically, though not always, appoggiaturas are accented, approached by ascending leap, and resolved by descending step.

Appoggiatura Figure A melodic figure in which the (chord-tone) 7th of a seventh chord is approached by leap (typically, but not always, from below), then resolves down by step as expected into the next chord.

Asymmetrical Meter Meter that contains an odd number of beats, with the exception of triple meter.

Atonal Music that avoids reference to a tonal center or centers.

Atonal Theory A general term used to describe methods of analyzing atonal music.

Augmented An interval modifier used when a perfect or major interval is made a half step larger without changing its numerical name.

Augmented Dominant Chord that results when the 5th of a V (or V^7) chord is raised a half step (labeled V^+ and V^{+7}). Useful in the major mode, where the raised 5th ($\sharp\hat{2}$) leads to the 3rd of the I chord. Secondary dominants may also be augmented.

Augmented Sixth Chord A category of predominant chords that contain the interval of an augmented sixth that is formed by simultaneously playing the tones a half step above and below the dominant ($\flat\hat{6}$ and $\sharp\hat{4}$).

Augmented Triad ($^+$) A triad featuring a $^+5$ divided into two M3s.

Authentic Cadence A tonic triad preceded by some form of dominant-function harmony (V or vii°) at a cadential point.

B

Balanced Binary A type of binary form in which the two parts are of equal length.

Bar Line A marking that indicates the end of a measure; depicted by a vertical line through the staff.

Bass Informally, the lowest voice in a vocal or instrumental texture.

Bass Arpeggiation A motion of the bass voice in which different pitches belonging to the underlying chord of a given passage are played in succession.

Bass Position An arrangement of the notes of a triad, identified by the chord member that is in the lowest sounding voice.

Bass-Position Symbols Not to be confused with figured bass symbols, these symbols are usually used with a roman numeral as part of a harmonic analysis to indicate what inversion a chord is in.

Bass Suspension A suspension that occurs when the bass voice is suspended, creating a 2nd (or 9th) with an upper voice, resulting in a 2-3 suspension.

Beam Used to connect durations shorter than a quarter note when the durations occur within the same beat.

Beat The basic pulse of a musical passage.

Binary Form A formal design that consists of two approximately equivalent sections, although they may be of unequal length. This term is not used to describe periods and double periods; parallel period is a more informative term for these forms.

Bitonality Two tonal centers heard simultaneously.

Black-Key Pentatonic The pentatonic collection formed by the five black keys on the keyboard.

Borrowed Chords Chords resulting from the use of mode mixture (chords that contain tones from the mode opposite that which is predominantly in use in a given passage).

Cadence The harmonic goal; specifically, a harmonic progression that provides complete or partial resolution of a larger progression.

Cadential Six-Four A tonic six-four that delays the arrival of the root position V chord that follows it. Though the tonic six-four is technically a I chord, it is better to think of it as grouped with the V chord that follows it, as both chords have a dominant function in this context.

Canon A contrapuntal procedure in which the instruments or voices perform identical rhythms and contours, with later-sounding parts being offset by one or more beats.

Cardinality The number of members a pitch class set contains.

Chain of Suspensions The figure resulting when the resolution of one suspension serves as the preparation for another suspension.

Change of Key A shift of tonal center that takes place between movements of a composition.

Change of Mode Takes place when music moves from one key to its parallel key.

Chordal Units The individual chords that are the components of polychords.

Chromatic Mediant Relationship The relationship between two major triads or two minor triads with roots a m3 or M3 apart.

Chromaticism The use of pitches foreign to the key of a given passage.

Circle of Fifths A diagram arranged like the face of a clock that aids in the memorization of key signatures. Moving clockwise around the circle, each new key begins on $\hat{5}$ of the previous key while, moving counterclockwise around the circle, each new key begins on $\hat{4}$ of the previous key.

Circle-of-Fifths Progression A progression consisting of a series of roots related by descending 5ths and/or ascending 4ths. (Most of the 5ths and 4ths will be perfect, but if a diatonic circle-of-fifths sequence goes on long enough in root position, a °5 or +4 will appear.)

Clef Symbol that appears at the beginning of the staff indicating which pitches are to be associated with which lines and spaces.

Close Structure A chord in a four-part texture spanning less than an octave between soprano and tenor.

Closely Related Keys Keys that have a difference of no more than one sharp or flat between their key signatures.

Closing Section The section of a sonata that often ends expositions and recapitulations; it further confirms the prevailing key with simple sequential and cadential gestures.

Coda A special concluding section that can (optionally) be used with many formal types, including binary, ternary, and sonata forms.

Common-Chord Modulation The use of one or more chords that are diatonic in both keys as a kind of hinge or pivot linking the two tonalities (used to make the modulation smoother).

Common-Tone Diminished Seventh Chord   A diminished seventh chord that shares a tone with the root of the chord that it embellishes.

Composite Meter   Meter that is made up of recurring irregular subdivisions.

Compound Beat   A beat that divides into three equal parts.

Compound Intervals   Intervals larger than and including the 8ve.

Compound Single   A piece written in a $\frac{3}{4}$ time signature with a fast tempo that has the aural effect of one beat per measure.

Computer Music   Music created with the aid of a computer.

Conclusive Cadences   Cadences that conclude with a tonic harmony, including authentic and plagal cadences.

Conjunct   Featuring stepwise motion.

Consonant   A quality ascribed to an interval that is pleasing to the ear (including major and minor 3rds and 6ths, perfect 4ths [when they do not occur harmonically above the bass], perfect 5ths, and perfect 8ves). (Triads are also considered consonant when their bass note forms only consonances with the upper notes.)

Continuous   A type of binary or ternary form in which the first section ends with any chord other than the tonic triad in the main key of the form.

Contrary Fifths and Octaves   Occur when two voices forming a perfect 5th or 8ve move in contrary motion into another perfect 5th or 8ve, respectively.

Contrary Motion   A type of motion in which two voices move in opposite directions.

Contrasting Period   A period in which the beginnings of the antecedent and consequent are not similar. (This term can also apply to double periods.)

Counterpoint   The combining of relatively independent musical lines.

Crook   A piece of tubing of a precisely calculated length used with the originally valveless French Horn or other brass instrument that, when inserted, would alter the instrument's fundamental and, correspondingly, its harmonic series (longer crooks would lower the fundamental, while shorter crooks would raise it).

Cross Rhythm   The simultaneous presentation of two or more aurally contrasting rhythmic streams.

Deceptive Cadence (DC)   A cadence that results when the ear expects a V-I authentic cadence but hears V-? instead. The "?" is usually a submediant triad, but there are other possibilities.

Deceptive Progression   The harmonic progression V-vi (or V-VI).

Development   The second main section of a sonata; it may develop motives from the exposition's themes, feature sequential activity, and/or introduce a new theme. The tonal conflict of the sonata is also developed here, and several (usually more distant) keys are touched upon before preparing for the return to the home key.

Diatonic Chords   Chords made up only of notes from the scale on which the passage is based.

Diatonic Modes   The seven scales or modes that can be formed by building a scale using each of the tones of a major scale as a different tone center.

Diatonic Planing   Parallel movement of vertical sonorities whose quality is determined by the prevailing diatonic scale; the numerical value of the intervals will remain constant, but their quality will change as the voices move throughout the diatonic scale.

Diatonic Sequence   A sequence that keeps the pattern within a single key.

Digital-to-Analog Converter   Device that converts numbers into a continuous voltage stream that drives a loudspeaker.

Diminished   An interval modifier used when a perfect or minor interval is made a half step smaller without changing its numerical name.

Diminished Seventh Chord (°7)   Diminished triad with a °7 above the root.

Diminished Triad (°)   A triad with a °5 divided into two m3s.

Direct (Hidden) Fifths and Octaves   Occur when the outer parts move in the same direction into a 5th or 8ve, with a leap in the soprano part. (The bass may move by leap *or* step.)

Direct Modulation   A type of modulation that does not use common chords, common tones, or sequences.

Displaced Accent   A technique that intentionally violates the normal metric accent pattern implied by the meter, shifting the accent to a relatively weak beat.

Dissonant   A quality ascribed to an interval that is not pleasing to the ear (including major and minor 2nds and 7ths, perfect 4ths [when they occur above the bass], tritones, and all augmented and diminished intervals). Triads and other chords are also considered dissonant when at least one dissonance is formed with their bass note.)

Distantly Related Keys   Keys that have a difference of more than one sharp or flat between their key signatures.

Divisions of the Beat   Durations representing the metric organization of a single beat.

Dominant Seventh   Chords which are almost always major-minor sevenths built on $\hat{5}$—that is, when spelled in root position, they contain a major triad plus the pitch a m7 above the root (V^7).

Dominant with a Substituted Sixth   A V or V^7 chord in which the 6th above the root ($\hat{3}$) is used instead of the 5th of the chord ($\hat{2}$).

Dot   A symbol that adds one-half the duration value of the note, rest, or dot that precedes it.

Dotted Bar Line   Symbol used to show how long measures are subdivided into shorter segments.

Double Pedal Point   A pedal point that contains two pitch classes.

Double Period   A multi-phrase unit similar to a period, except that each half of the structure consists of two phrases rather than just one (the second pair typically has a stronger cadence than the first).

Doubled   A note that is duplicated in another octave.

Doubly Chromatic Mediant Relationship   A relationship between chords that have roots a m3 or M3 apart, are of opposite modes, and share no common tones (e.g. C to a♭, c to A).

Duple Meter   Two-beat measure: the typical metric accent pattern is strong-weak.

Duple, Triple, and Quadruple   Refers to the number of beats in each measure.

Electronic Music   Music generated synthetically or manipulated by means of a device such as a synthesizer or a computer.

Electronic Oscillator   An electronic circuit that uses an amplifier and filter to generate a repeating signal.

Elision   A procedure by which the last note of one phrase also serves as the first note of the next phrase.

Enharmonic   Notes that have the same pitch but are spelled differently. Keys can be enharmonic as well.

Enharmonic Modulation   A modulation in which a chord common to both keys is reinterpreted enharmonically to fit into the new key. The chord can be spelled to fit into either key, and it must be able to be heard as a sensible chord in both keys.

Enharmonic Reinterpretation   Technique of treating a chord as if it were spelled in a different key as part of a modulation.

Enharmonic Spelling   Writing a note as its enharmonic equivalent. Technique used by composers to indicate clearly the direction in which a pitch will move, and to make the music easier for the performer to read.

Enharmonically Equivalent Keys   Keys that sound the same but are spelled differently.

Escape Tone   A (typically) unaccented non-chord tone that is approached by step and resolved by leap in the opposite direction.

Essential Chromaticism   The use of tones from outside the key as members of chords (altered chords).

Experimental Music   Music that is composed in such a way as to make its performance unpredictable.

Exposition   The first main section of a sonata; it presents the important themes as well as the tonal conflict between the two most important keys in the movement.

Extended Tertian Sonorities   Ninth, eleventh, and thirteenth chords used as an extension of traditional tertian harmony, both in functional and nonfunctional settings. Also called tall chords.

False Recapitulation   Material that suggests the arrival of the recapitulation but that appears in the wrong tonal location toward the end of the development section.

Fibonacci Sequence   An infinite sequence of numbers in which each number in the sequence is the sum of the previous two numbers, used by many twentieth-century composers to determine a variety of musical information.

Figured Bass (Thoroughbass)   A method of abbreviated notation used in the Baroque era. Consists of a bass line and some symbols indicating the chord to be played above each bass note.

First Inversion   A chord with the 3rd as the lowest tone.

Focal Point   The highest note of a melody.

Foreign Relationships   All key relationships that are not enharmonic, parallel, relative, or closely related.

Form   The way a composition is structured to create a meaningful musical experience.

Forte Name   Method of referring to a set class, developed by theorist Allen Forte. In this system, each prime form is assigned a compact name represented by two numbers; the first denotes its cardinality, while the second denotes its relative position to other prime forms of the same cardinality.

Free Anticipation   A type of anticipation that is both approached and left by leap. In other words, the anticipation and resolution do not feature the same chord tone.

French Augmented Sixth Chord   A chord formed by adding $\hat{1}$ and $\hat{2}$ to the augmented sixth interval ($\flat\hat{6}$–$\hat{1}$–$\hat{2}$–$\sharp\hat{4}$). Symbolized Fr^{+6}.

Fugue   A piece in which each voice states a short theme (the subject) in turn, after which it is tossed about among the voices, fragmented, and developed.

Full Score   A score in which all or most of the parts are notated on their own individual staves.

Fundamental   The lowest tone in a harmonic series.

G

German Augmented Sixth Chord   Formed by adding $\hat{1}$ and $\flat\hat{3}$ to the augmented sixth interval ($\flat\hat{6}$–$\hat{1}$–$\flat\hat{3}$–$\sharp\hat{4}$). Symbolized Ger^{+6}.

Golden Ratio   1.618:1. This proportion is found throughout nature and has been associated with proportional balance in art and architecture.

Grand Staff   A combination of two staves joined by a brace, with the top and bottom staves typically using treble and bass clefs, respectively.

Graphic Notation   A notational style that uses nontraditional symbols to represent musical information.

H

Half Cadence (HC)   A common type of unstable or "progressive" cadence. The HC ends with a V chord, which can be preceded by any other chord.

Half Step   The distance from a key on the piano to the very next key, white or black. This is typically the smallest interval encountered in tonal music.

Half-Diminished Seventh Chord (°7)   Diminished triad with a m7 above the root.

Harmonic Interval   The distance between two pitches that are sounded simultaneously.

Harmonic Minor Scale   A minor scale type, which can be thought of as a natural minor scale with raised $\hat{7}$ or as a major scale with lowered $\hat{3}$ and $\hat{6}$.

Harmonic Progression   In tonal music, goal-directed motion from one chord to the next.

Harmonic Series   The natural frequencies that sound above a given fundamental and are part of any musical tone. The fundamental is the loudest component of a musical tone, but above it, in multiples of the frequency of the fundamental, is a series of other tones, called harmonics, partials, or overtones.

Hemiola   An interaction between rhythm and meter that implies a 3:2 ratio.

Hexatonic Scale   A six-note collection derived from the juxtaposition of two augmented triads at the interval of a half step.

Hirajoshi Scale   Pentatonic collection that can be thought of as being built on $\hat{1}$–$\hat{2}$–$\flat\hat{3}$–$\hat{5}$–$\flat\hat{6}$ of a natural minor scale.

Home Key   The primary (tonic) key of a movement.

Hyperinstrument   An instrument that uses a computer to augment musical expression and creativity.

Hypermeter   A regular grouping of measures that is analogous to meter.

I

Imitation   The repetition of a pattern that occurs between two or more voices.

Imitative Counterpoint   Counterpoint in which similar melodic material is passed from part to part.

Imperfect Authentic Cadence (IAC)   Any authentic cadence that is not a PAC due to the use of vii° instead of V or V^7, the inversion of the dominant or tonic harmony, and/or the arrival on something other than the tonic scale degree over the I chord.

Impressionism   A term originally applied to a style of painting that began in France in the late nineteenth century, the concept was reflected in music by a turning away from more orderly formal procedures of the late eighteenth and early nineteenth centuries and a fascination with color, as expressed through new uses of harmony, instrumentation, and rhythm.

Integral Serialism   The method of ordering musical parameters other than pitch, such as rhythm, dynamics, and articulation.

Interval   The measurement of the distance in pitch between two notes.

Interval Class (ic) The shortest distance (in semi-tones) between two pitch classes.

Interval Inversion A procedure wherein the lower note of an interval is shifted up one or more octaves to a point immediately above the upper note (or vice versa).

Interval Vector Gives a rough approximation of the quality of a sonority by listing the number of occurrences of each interval class in that sonority (can also be referred to as interval-class vector).

Inversion In tonal music, the transfer of the lowest note to any higher octave. In set theory, the compound operation (T_nI): PC inversion followed by transposition (T_n).

Inversion (of a Chord) The transfer of the lowest note of a root-position chord to any higher octave.

Inversion Symbols Numbers used to indicate the bass positions of chords.

Inversionally Symmetrical Sets Sets that map onto themselves under T_nI.

Inverted Pedal Point A pedal point that occurs in a part or parts other than the bass.

Isorhythm In twentieth-century music, refers to a rhythmic technique (associated with Medieval motets and masses) that typically consists of a repeated rhythmic figure called the *talea* (after Medieval theory) in combination with a repeated pitch sequence of a different length called the *color*.

Italian Augmented Sixth Chord Formed by adding $\hat{1}$ to the augmented sixth interval ($\flat\hat{6}$–$\hat{1}$–$\sharp\hat{4}$). Symbolized It^{+6}.

J

Just Intonation A system of tuning in which the intervals are represented using whole-number ratios.

K

Key The scale used in a piece (or some portion of a piece), identified according to its most important pitch—the scale's first degree (e.g. the key of D major).

Key Signature A pattern of sharps or flats corresponding to a key that appears at the beginning of a staff and indicates that certain notes are to be consistently raised or lowered.

Klangfarbenmelodie Translates literally to "sound color melody." Refers to the technique of juxtaposing minute melodic fragments of contrasting timbre

and register, resulting in a melody created by rapidly shifting tone colors.

L

Lead Sheet Symbols Used in jazz and most popular music styles to indicate chords to be played under a given melody.

Ledger Lines Used to extend the staff both above and below the standard five-line format.

Lydian-Mixolydian Scale A seven-note scale with $\sharp\hat{4}$ and $\flat\hat{7}$.

M

Major Interval An interval modifier used only to 2nds, 3rds, 6ths, and 7ths, equivalent to the respective intervals between $\hat{1}$–$\hat{2}$, $\hat{1}$–$\hat{3}$, $\hat{1}$–$\hat{6}$, and $\hat{1}$–$\hat{7}$ from the major scale.

Major Pentatonic Scale Pentatonic collection that can be thought of as being built on $\hat{1}$–$\hat{2}$–$\hat{3}$–$\hat{5}$–$\hat{6}$ of a major scale.

Major Scale A specific pattern of half steps and whole steps (w-w-h-w-w-w-h) encompassing an octave.

Major-Minor Seventh Chord (Mm7) Major triad with a m7 above the root.

Major Seventh Chord (M7) Major triad with a M7 above the root.

Major Triad (M) A triad featuring a P5 divided into a M3 (bottom) and m3 (top).

Measure A grouping of beats (abbreviated m. [singular] or mm. [plural]), the ending of which is indicated with a bar line.

Mechanical Rhythm Rhythm that requires a machine for precise execution.

Melodic Interval The distance between two pitches that are sounded successively.

Melodic Minor Scale A minor scale type with both an ascending and descending form. The ascending form can be thought of as a natural minor scale with raised $\hat{6}$ and $\hat{7}$, or as a major scale with lowered $\hat{3}$. The descending form is the same as the natural minor scale.

Meter The pattern of strong and weak beats that underlies the rhythmic activity of a musical passage.

Metric Accent The pattern of stresses usually found in a meter type

Metronome A device that produces regularly recurring pulses.

Micropolyphony The use of dense chords in which all of the voices move in independent chromatic lines through the sound mass, giving the music a complex, cluster-like surface.

Minimalism Music characterized by the use of restricted pitch materials, static harmony, and rhythmic devices such as repetition, ostinato, polyrhythm, a steady pulse, and phasing.

Minor Interval Formed when a major interval is lowered by one half step without altering its numerical name.

Minor Pentachord The minor scale pattern w-h-w-w.

Minor Pentatonic Scale Pentatonic collection that can be thought of as being built on $\hat{1}$–$\flat\hat{3}$–$\hat{4}$–$\hat{5}$–$\flat\hat{7}$ of a natural minor scale.

Minor Seventh Chord (m7) Minor triad with a m7 above the root.

Minor Triad (m) A triad featuring a P5 divided into a m3 (bottom) and M3 (top).

Mixed Meter The use of rapidly changing meter signatures.

Mixed Planing Parallel voice motion that can be explained neither by consistency of chord type nor by the limitations of a single scale.

Mode Mixture The use of tones from one mode (mode here refers to the major and minor modes) in a passage that is predominantly in the other mode.

Modified Sequence A sequence wherein the repetitions of the pattern are neither tonal nor real.

Modulation A shift of tonal center that takes place within an individual movement.

Modulation by Common Tone Use of a single tone as the hinge between the two keys.

Monophonic Modulation Use of a single unharmonized line to establish the new tonal center.

Motive The smallest identifiable musical idea; it can consist of a pitch pattern, a rhythmic pattern, or both.

MIDI Musical Instrument Digital Interface. Originally developed to allow the keyboard of one synthesizer to drive the tone generator of another and allow a single performer (or computer) to drive multiple tone generators, audio processors, drum machines, and so forth. Through the use of a sequencer (a software application that stores sequences of MIDI data rather than the sounds themselves) a composer can easily change MIDI note, key velocity, tempo, or controller information of a previously encoded performance.

Musical Score A notational tool used by a composer, conductor, or analyst that shows all the parts of an ensemble arranged one above the other.

Musique Concrète A technique wherein natural sounds are recorded and then worked with directly, being subjected to modifications that fall into five broad categories: altered playback speed, reversed tape direction, cutting and splicing of tape, creation of a tape loop, and tape delay (other timbral manipulations are also used).

N

Natural Minor Scale A specific pattern of half steps and whole steps (w-h-w-w-h-w-w) encompassing an octave. The natural minor scale is like a major scale with lowered $\hat{3}$, $\hat{6}$, and $\hat{7}$.

Neapolitan Chord A major triad constructed on lowered $\hat{2}$.

Neapolitan Sixth Chord Another name for the Neapolitan triad due to the fact that it is usually found in first inversion (N^6).

Neighbor Group A pair of non-chord tones used to embellish a single pitch: both an upper and lower neighbor sound in succession in either order before returning to the original pitch. A neighbor group can be thought of as the combination of an escape tone and an appoggiatura in succession.

Neighbor Motion Motion proceeding from a given tone up or down one step followed by a return to the first tone.

Neighbor Tone Figure A melodic figure in which the (chord-tone) 7th of a seventh chord is approached by ascending step, then resolves down by step as expected into the next chord.

Neighboring Tone A non-chord tone that embellishes a single tone; this tone is approached by moving either up or down by step and resolves by step in the opposite direction to the original tone.

New Vocalism Refers to the use of non-traditional or experimental vocal techniques (sometimes used to refer to the techniques based on the talents of a particular performer).

Non-Chord Tone (NCT) A tone, either diatonic or chromatic, that is not a member of the prevailing chord.

Nonessential Chromaticism The use of tones from outside the key as non-chord tones.

Nonfunctional Harmonic Progressions Successions of chords that do not follow traditional or functional patterns or progressions.

Nonretrogradable Rhythms Rhythms that are the same whether played forward or backward.

Normal Order (Normal Form) The most compact arrangement of the members of a pc set, listed from left to right in ascending order within an octave (notated using square brackets with intervening commas).

Objectionable Parallels Occur when two parts that are separated by a perfect 5th or 8ve, or by their octave equivalents, move to new pitch classes that are separated by the same interval.

Oblique Motion A type of two-voice motion in which only one voice moves.

Octatonic Scale An eight-note scale composed of a repeated series of half-whole or whole-half successions.

Octave The interval between any note and the next highest or lowest note of the same letter name and accidental.. This term is used instead of "8th," and can also be written as "8ve."

Octave Register A collection of pitches from one C up to, but not including, the next C (e.g. C4–B4). Each such register is given a numerical label that can be shown after the letter name.

Omnibus A progression used to harmonize a chromatic bass line.

Open Structure A chord in a four-part texture spanning an octave or more between soprano and tenor.

Order Numbers Indicate the relative order position of each pitch class within a particular series form.

Ostinato A musical pattern that is repeated many times in succession.

Pandiatonicism The attempt to equalize the seven tones of the diatonic scale so that no single pitch is heard as a tone center. Some identifying characteristics include use of a key signature, absence of accidentals, free use of the seven (or fewer, in some cases) tones of the major scale associated with that key signature, and the absence of functional harmonic movement.

Parallel Keys Major and minor keys that share the same starting note.

Parallel Motion A type of motion in which two voices move in the same direction by the same interval.

Parallel Period A period in which the antecedent and consequent both begin with similar or identical

material, even if that material is embellished. (This term can also apply to double periods.)

Passing Chord A chord inserted between two more structurally important chords in a harmonic progression that serves to connect or prolong them, typically by means of a prominent melodic passing motion.

Passing Six-Four Chord A six-four chord that harmonizes the middle note of a three-note scalar figure (either ascending or descending) in the bass.

Passing Tone A non-chord tone that is approached and resolved by step in the same direction, filling in the space between two tones, which may belong to the same or different chords.

Passing Tone Figure A melodic figure in which the (chord-tone) 7th of a seventh chord is approached by descending step, then resolves down by step as expected into the next chord.

PC Inversion In atonal theory, subtraction from 12 mod 12.

Pedal Point A stationary pitch that begins as a chord tone, then becomes a non-chord tone as the harmonies around it change, and finally ends up as a chord tone again when the harmony is once more in agreement with it.

Pedal Six-Four Chord A six-four chord that elaborates the root position chord that precedes (and usually follows) it. It is created when the bass note of the root position chord retains the same note while the 3rd and 5th of the triad move up by step (and, if returning to the same root position chord, back down again).

Pentatonic Scale Literally denotes any five-note scale, but typically refers to the major pentatonic: C-D-E-G-A and its transpositions.

Perfect An interval modifier used only in connection with unisons, 4ths, 5ths, 8ves, and their compounds (11ths, and so on).

Perfect Authentic Cadence (PAC) Consists of a V-I (or V^7-I) progression, with both the V and I in root position and $\hat{1}$ in the melody over the I chord.

Period A multi-phrase unit that typically consists of two phrases in an antecedent-consequent (or question-answer) relationship, that relationship being established by means of a stronger cadence at the end of the second phrase.

Phasing Rhythmic process in which two or more voices that have the same material begin in unison, but after a time begin to play at different tempos, moving in and out of alignment with one another, creating different resultant patterns as the different copies of the same pattern create new rhythmic relationships with one another.

Phrase   A relatively independent musical idea terminated by a cadence.

Phrase Group   A multi-phrase unit that consists of several phrases that seem to belong together structurally even though they do not form a period or double period (typically when the final cadence is not the strongest one).

Phrase Modulation   A direct modulation that occurs between phrases.

Phrygian Half Cadence   A special name given to the iv^6-V HC in minor. The name refers to a cadence found in the period of modal polyphony (before 1600) but does not imply that the music is actually in the Phrygian mode.

Picardy Third   A tonic triad that is "borrowed" from the major mode for use in minor.

Pitch   The highness or lowness of a sound.

Pitch Class   Term used to group together all pitches that have an identical sound or that are identical except for the octave or octaves that separate them.

Pitch Class Sets (pc sets)   Term used to describe pitch structures in atonal music; meaningful groups of related pitch classes.

Plagal Cadence (PC)   Typically involves a IV-I progression at a cadential point, often added on as a kind of tag following a PAC.

Plagal Progression   The harmonic progression IV-I.

Planing   The use of chords moving in parallel motion.

Point of Modulation   The first chord that seems to be functioning more naturally in the second key than in the first.

Pointillism   The process of atomizing (separating) the notes of a melodic line.

Polychord   Consists of two or more chords sounded simultaneously.

Polymeter   The simultaneous presentation of two or meters.

Polyrhythm   The simultaneous presentation of two or more aurally contrasting rhythmic streams.

Polytempo   The simultaneous presentation of two or more contrasting tempos.

Polytonality   Two or more tonal centers heard simultaneously.

Postminimalism   Music that seems to have its roots in the minimalist traditions of the 1960s and 1970s, but is not as strict in its application of typical minimalist techniques.

Pre-Dominant   A term that can refer to a chord (typically ii or IV) or a harmonic function; precedes a dominant chord in a harmonic progression.

Preparation   The tone preceding the suspension (it is the same pitch as the suspension).

Prepared Piano   A piano that has had various objects and material placed on or between its strings in order to change the instrument's timbre.

Primary Theme   The theme that, in the exposition, establishes the home key with at least one cadence in that key and that reappears to mark the beginning of the recapitulation. It often sounds more vital, grand, or ceremonial than secondary themes, although lyrical primary themes can also be found.

Prime Form   A way of arranging a pc set so that it begins with 0 and is most packed to the left (notated using parentheses but no intervening commas or spaces).

Process Music   Compositional approach in which an audible musical process structures both the note-to-note details and the overall form of the piece.

Progressive Cadences   Cadences that do not conclude with a tonic harmony, including deceptive and half cadences.

Prolongation   The process by which the domain of a chord is expanded through the use of one or more subsidiary chords.

Proportional Notation   A notational style indicating approximate durations through the spacing of events.

Quadruple Meter   Four-beat measure: the typical metric accent pattern is strong-weak-less strong-weak.

Quartal Harmony   A sonority derived from stacked 4ths.

Quarter Tone   An interval that divides the octave into 24 equal parts.

Quintal Harmony   A sonority derived from stacked 5ths.

Real Imitation   Similar to a real sequence, but with the transposed repetition of the pattern occurring in a different voice than the voice in which the pattern was initially introduced.

Real Planing   Parallel movement of vertical sonorities whose construction remains unchanged; both the numerical value and quality of the intervals will remain constant.

Real Sequence   Transposes the pattern to a new key, which means that the modifiers of the intervals (major, minor, and so on) will not change when the pattern begins on a new pitch class.

Realization   Originally used in performances during the Baroque period, this term refers to the practice of improvising chords based on a given figured bass part.

Recapitulation   The third main section of a sonata; it replays the movement's important themes, usually in the same order, but the modulation to the secondary key is adjusted so that the themes that were originally in the secondary key in the exposition are found in the home key here.

Reduced Score   A score notated at concert pitch, on as few staves as possible.

Relative Keys   Major and minor keys that share the same key signature. The relative major of any minor key starts on $\hat{3}$ of the minor scale, while the relative minor of any major key begins on $\hat{6}$ of the major scale.

Repeated Phrase   Two adjoining phrases that are identical, with the possible exception of embellishing or ornamental differences.

Resolution   The tone following the suspension and lying a 2nd below it.

Retardation   A non-chord tone that functions like a suspension but features an upward stepwise resolution.

Rhythm   A general term used to refer to the time aspect of music, as contrasted with the pitch aspect.

Rondo Form   A type of form in which a refrain theme (which returns several times) alternates with contrasting thematic material. It is often used as the final movement of a sonata, string quartet, or symphony, and sometimes as a slow movement.

Root Position   A chord with the root as the lowest tone.

Round   A canon that is perpetual—there is no notated ending for the ensemble.

Rounded Binary Form   A form type in which the opening A section returns after contrasting material but in an abbreviated form, as in AB½A.

Row   In twelve-tone music, a specific ordering of all twelve pitch classes.

S

Sampler   A device that has the ability to record, store, edit, and play back audio information.

Sawtooth Wave   A jagged nasal tone that contains all harmonics.

Score Order   The typical order in which instruments are listed in a full score; this order is not always the same as order by pitch.

Second Inversion   A chord with the 5th as the lowest tone.

Secondary Function   A chord whose function belongs more closely to a key other than the main key of the passage.

Secondary Key   The key that provides the structurally important tonal contrast with the home key. When the home key is major, the secondary key is often the key of the dominant (V), and when the home key is minor, the secondary key is often the key of the relative major (III), although other options are possible.

Secondary Theme   A theme that sets up the tonal contrast with the primary theme in the exposition by establishing the secondary key and confirming it with a PAC in that key. In the recapitulation, these themes reconfirm the home key. It is often more lyrical or gentle in character than the primary theme, although other possibilities are also common (including being derived from the primary theme).

Sectional   A type of binary or ternary form in which the first section ends on the tonic triad in the main key of the form.

Secundal Harmony   A chordal sonority derived from stacked 2nds.

Segmentation   The process of partitioning a piece of atonal music into pitch class sets based on relationships formed by parameters such as pitch, rhythm, phrasing, register, and timbre.

Sentence   A structural unit characterized by the immediate repetition or variation of a musical idea followed by a motion toward a cadence.

Sequence   A pattern that is repeated immediately in the same voice but that begins on a different pitch class.

Sequencer   A software application that stores sequences of MIDI data and allows a composer to change MIDI note, key velocity, tempo, or controller information of a previously encoded performance.

Sequential Modulation   Occurs when a pattern is immediately restated at another pitch level, establishing a new tonal center.

Series   In twelve-tone music, a specific ordering of all twelve pitch classes.

Set Theory   A general term used to describe methods of analyzing atonal music.

Seventh Chord   Triad with another 3rd added above the 5th of the triad. The added note is a 7th above the root.

Similar Motion   A type of motion in which two voices move in the same direction but by different intervals.

Simple Beat   A beat that divides into two equal parts.

Simple Intervals   Intervals smaller than an 8ve.

Simultaneities   Traditional sonorities that are used in a non-traditional manner. The use of a traditional Roman numeral label is meaningless for such chords, because the resulting tones do not function in the traditional sense.

Sine Wave   A sound devoid of overtones or harmonics that is similar to the sound of a tuning fork or open flute.

Sixth Chord   A triad in first inversion.

Slash Chord   A chord whose bass note is indicated (and the inversion inferred) by the addition of a slash and the letter of the bass after the root note letter.

Sonata Form   A large-scale formal type resembling a greatly expanded two-reprise continuous ternary form and consisting of at least three sections: an exposition with two tonal centers, a tonally unstable development, and a tonic-centered recapitulation that returns the material from the exposition.

Sonata-Rondo   A formal type that combines the Rondo's use of returning refrains with the developmental characteristics and tonal conflict of the sonata.

Split-Third Chord   The sonority that results when both the major and minor triad built on the same root are used simultaneously.

Square Wave   A clarinet-like tone that contains only odd-numbered harmonics.

Staff   An arrangement of five lines and four spaces used to indicate the precise pitch(es) desired; the staff can be extended through the use of ledger lines.

Static   A type of two-voice motion in which neither voice moves.

Stochastic Music   Music in which the pitch, intensity, and duration are determined by mathematical procedures such as the laws of probability theory.

Subject   The short theme that is used as the primary musical material in a fugue.

Subphrase   A distinct portion of a phrase that it is not a phrase either because it is not terminated by a cadence or because it seems too short to be relatively independent.

Suspension   A non-chord tone that occurs when a chord tone is sustained after the other parts have moved on to the next chord, after which it resolves down by step into that next chord. It is preceded by a "preparation" and followed by a "resolution." The term also refers to the "preparation-sequence-resolution" unit in its entirety.

Suspension Figure   A melodic process in which a chord tone is treated as though it were a suspension. A suspension figure often occurs in conjunction with the approach to the 7th of a V^7 chord when that 7th is also a chord tone of the preceding chord and appears in the same voice.

Suspension with Change of Bass   A upper-voice suspension in which the bass moves on to another chord tone at the same time as the suspension resolves.

Symmetrical Meter   Meter based on regularly recurring pulses subdivided into groups of two or three.

Syncopation   Rhythmic figure that stresses a normally weak beat or division of the beat.

Synthesizer   An electronic instrument that allows composers to combine and sequence source signals more efficiently than traditional tape techniques and offers them more control over the parameters of sound.

Synthetic Scale   Any scale that does not bear a clear resemblance to a scale or fragment of a scale associated with the diatonic system.

Tape Loop   A portion of recorded tape that is repeated over and over again.

Tape Music   Music that exists in the medium of magnetic tape.

Telharmonium   A large electronic keyboard instrument developed by Thaddeus Cahill that used telephone network technology to transmit sounds.

Tempo   The rate at which beats occur.

Tempo Canon   Canon in which the individual voices are presented at different tempos.

Tempo Modulation (Metric Modulation)   Method of changing tempo by equating a particular note value to another note value (a proportional note value), usually located in the next bar.

Ternary Form   A three-part form that is structured as statement-contrast-return (ABA). The middle section provides contrast through the use of different melodic material, texture, tonality, or some combination of these and the third section returns all or most of the first. Anything from a short theme to a lengthy movement of a sonata or symphony can be structured as a ternary form.

Tertian   A chord structure built of thirds.

Tetrachord   A four-note scalar pattern spanning a perfect 4th.

Theremin/Ondes Martenot   Examples of early electronic instruments that used electronic oscillators as tone generators.

Third Inversion   A seventh chord with the 7th as the lowest tone.

Third Stream   A movement started after World War II that blends elements of jazz and contemporary music.

Third Substitute   A chord that can be used in place of another chord whose root lies a 3rd away, insofar as they share a common function and two common tones (e.g. iii can substitute for V, as ii can for IV, and vi can for I).

Three-Phrase Period   Consists of three different phrases—two antecedents and a consequent or one antecedent and two consequents (as determined by the cadences).

Tie   A curved line connecting two notes of the same pitch, creating a new duration that is equal to their sum.

Time Signature   A symbol that tells the performer how many beats will occur in each measure, what note value will represent the beat, and whether the beat is simple or compound.

Tonal Sequence   A sequence that keeps the pattern in a single key, which means that modifiers of the intervals (major, minor, and so on) will probably change when the pattern begins on a new pitch class.

Tone Cluster   Any collection of three or more adjacent pitches in secundal relationship (can also be called a cluster chord).

Tonicization   Similar to a modulation, but the shift of tonal center is shorter in duration.

Total Serialization   The method of ordering musical parameters other than pitch, such as rhythm, dynamics, and articulation.

Total Voice-Leading Distance   A measure of the smoothness of the voice-leading motion between one chord and another; it is determined by adding together the total number of half steps that each voice moves from the first chord to the second.

Transition   Generally, a passage that connects different themes or tonal centers. In sonata form, the transition is a passage that appears in both the exposition and recapitulation to destabilize the home key and connects the primary and secondary themes. Transitions may or may not modulate.

Transpose   To write or play music in a key other than the original.

Transposition Index   Indicates the level of transposition in semitones (upward within the octave) from the first pitch class of the series.

Transpositionally Symmetrical Sets   Sets that map onto themselves under T_n (at levels other than T_0).

Triad   A three-note chord consisting of a 5th divided into two superimposed 3rds. The bottom note of the 5th is the root, the top note is the 5th, and the note between them is the 3rd. There are four possible ways to combine major and minor 3rds to produce a tertian triad.

Triple Meter   Three-beat measure: the typical metric accent pattern is strong-weak-weak.

Tritone   The term used for the interval of the +4 or its enharmonic equivalent, the °5.

Tuplet   A rhythmic grouping that is divided in a manner contrary to the prevailing division of the beat, such as the division of an undotted value into some number of equal parts other than two, four, eight, and so on, or the division of a dotted value into some number of equal parts other than three, six, twelve, and so on.

Twelve-Tone Method   Compositional method designed to methodically equalize all twelve pitch classes. Each piece is based on a precompositional series or row, and strictly speaking, none of the tones may be repeated before all twelve have sounded. Each row may be subjected to one of four basic transformations: transposition, inversion, retrograde, or retrograde inversion.

Two-Reprise Form   A movement or theme that consists of two repeated sections.

Unbalanced Binary   A type of binary form in which the two parts are not of equal length.

Unequal Fifths   Occur when a perfect 5th is followed by a °5, or vice versa, in the same two voices. Unequal fifths are considered acceptable unless they involve a °5-P5 between the bass and another voice.

Unison   The interval formed between pitches with the same note name in the same octave register, this term is used instead of "1st."

V

Voice Exchange   Occurs in a harmonic progression when two voices, occupying different members of a chord, each prolong that chord by moving to the chord member the other voice had previously occupied (e.g. $\hat{1}$–$\hat{2}$–$\hat{3}$ and $\hat{3}$–$\hat{2}$–$\hat{1}$ in the bass and soprano voices respectively over the progression I-vii°6-I6).

Voice Leading (Part Writing)   The ways in which chords are produced and connected by the motions of individual musical lines.

Voicing   The distribution or spacing of the notes in a chord.

W

White Noise Generator   A device with an essentially random waveshape that produces a "hissing" sound consisting of frequency components that are equally distributed across the audible frequency spectrum.

Whole Step   The distance between two pitches that are separated by a single key, white or black. This interval is equivalent to the combined distance of two half steps.

Whole-Tone Chords   Vertical sonorities that can be derived from a whole-tone scale.

Whole-Tone Scale   A six-note scale composed entirely of adjacent major 2nds (or their enharmonic equivalents).

Index of Musical Examples

657

Subject Index

A

Accented/unaccented beats, 172
Accidentals, 5–6, 7, 17, 25, 245
Adagio, 25
Added value, 485–486
Added-note chords, 408
Additive rhythm, 483
Aeolian mode, 454–455
Aleatory music, 528–529
Allegro, 25
All-interval series, 512
Alteration symbols, 546–547
Altered chords, 54, 244, 247–248, 302–303
Alto clef, 2, 7
American popular ballad form, 324
Ametric music, 484
Amplitude, 535, 536
Amplitude envelope, 535
Analog-to-digital converters, 540
Anticipation figures, 189
Anticipations, 172, 188–189
Appoggiaturas, 172, 185–186
Appoggiatura figures, 200
Arpeggiation, bass, 115–116, 125, 134
Arrow notation, 249
Ascending orderings, 496–498
Ascending/descending tones, 172
Asymmetrical meter, 482
Atonal, definition of, 494
Atonal theory, 494–504
    equivalence relations, 498–499
    interval vector, 503–504, 548–551
    inversions in, 499–501
    mod 12, 498–499
    normal form (normal order), 496–498
    pitch class sets and notation in, 495–499, 501–503
    prime form, 501–503, 548–551
    segmentation, 495
    set classes, 495–499, 501–503, 548–551
    transposition in, 499–501
    twelve-tone method, 452, 460, 505–516
Audible frequency spectrum, 535
Augmented dominant, 411–414
Augmented intervals, 19–20, 67, 371–372, 381
Augmented sixth, 371–372
Augmented sixth chords, 371–390, 430
    augmented sixth interval, 371–372
    bass positions of, 380–381
    characteristics of, 371
    in circle of fifths, 379
    French, 373–375
    German, 375–378, 445
    Italian, 372–373
    as neighbor chords, 378
    other uses of conventional, 378–379
    resolutions to other scale degrees, 381–382
Augmented triads, 38–39, 54–55, 58
Authentic cadences, 145, 147, 149, 221

B

Balanced binary forms, 321
Ballad form, 324
Bar lines, 25
Baroque period, 44, 125
Basic Atonal Theory (Rahn), 498, 501
Bass, 7
    arpeggiation, 115–116, 125, 134
    bass clef, 2
    contrary to, 87–88
    figured, 44–45, 181–182, 416
    intervals, above the, 44
    as lowest voice, 21
    suspensions, 176
    triad position, 42–43
Bass clef, 2
Bass positions, 42–43, 380–381
Bass-position symbols (bps), 45
Beams, 34
Beats, 24–25, 27, 28, 30, 31, 172; *See also* Rhythm and meter
Binary forms, 318–321, 324–325
Bitonal chords, 467
Bitonal key signature, 471
Bitonality, 467, 471
Black-pentatonic scale, 456–457
Borrowed chords, 174, 346–353; *See also* Mode mixture
Breve, 24
Bridge, 324
Buchla synthesizers, 539

C

C clef, 2
Cadences, 145–149
    authentic, 145, 147, 149, 221
    conclusive, 149
    deceptive, 88–89, 105, 147, 149, 151, 251
    definition of, 145, 150
    example of use of, 152–154
    half, 147–148, 149, 440
    harmonic rhythm and, 149–150
    identifying, 145
    imperfect authentic, 146–147, 151
    perfect authentic, 145, 409
    in phrases, 150–152
    Phrygian half, 148, 233
    plagal, 148, 149, 220, 221, 408
    progressive, 149
    in sentence form, 160, 164–165
    sequential, 96–98
Cadential six-four, 104, 135–137, 138, 267, 376
Cambiata (neighbor groups), 172, 187
Canons, 123, 530–531
Cardinality, 501, 502, 548
Cardinality type, 501
Chain of suspensions, 177–178
Chance procedures, 528
Change of key; *See* Modulations
Change of mode, 287, 289
Changing tones (neighbor groups), 172, 187
Chordal units, 465
Chords; *See also* Common-chord modulations; Forms; Triads; *specific chords*
    added-note, 408
    altered, 54, 244, 247–248, 302–303
    bitonal, 467
    borrowed, 174, 346–353
    chordal units, 465
    chord/scale connections, 467–469
    chromatic, 54
    cluster, 471
    coloristic qualities of, 431
    connecting, 441–442
    diatonic planing, 473
    doubled notes in, 43, 120–121
    eleventh, 414–417, 464
    extended tertian sonorities, 464–465
    half-note, 434
    inversion symbols and figured bass, 44–45
    inversions of, 42–43